Neighbors and Enemies

Neighbors and Enemies provides a new interpretation of the collapse of Germany's first democracy, the Weimar Republic, which ended with the naming of Adolf Hitler as chancellor in January 1933. This study focuses on individual workers in Berlin and their strategies to confront the crises in their daily lives that were introduced by the transformation of society after 1918 and intensified by the Depression. Tensions between the sexes and generations, among neighbors, within families, and between citizens and their political parties led to the emergence of a radical – and at times violent – neighborhood culture that signaled a loss of faith in political institutions. Swett offers an interpretation that marries a history of daily life in Depression-era Berlin with an analysis of the meanings of local politics in workers' communities, shifting our focus for understanding Weimar's collapse and the emergence of the Third Reich from the halls of governmental power to the streets of the urban core.

Pamela E. Swett is Assistant Professor in the Department of History at McMaster University.

Neighbors and Enemies

The Culture of Radicalism in Berlin, 1929–1933

PAMELA E. SWETT

McMaster University

CAMBRIDGE
UNIVERSITY PRESS

PUBLISHED BY THE PRESS SYNDICATE OF THE UNIVERSITY OF CAMBRIDGE
The Pitt Building, Trumpington Street, Cambridge, United Kingdom

CAMBRIDGE UNIVERSITY PRESS
The Edinburgh Building, Cambridge CB2 2RU, UK
40 West 20th Street, New York, NY 10011-4211, USA
477 Williamstown Road, Port Melbourne, VIC 3207, Australia
Ruiz de Alarcón 13, 28014 Madrid, Spain
Dock House, The Waterfront, Cape Town 8001, South Africa

http://www.cambridge.org

First published 2004

Printed in the United States of America

Typeface Sabon 10/12 pt.   *System* LATEX 2ε [TB]

A catalog record for this book is available from the British Library.

Library of Congress Cataloging in Publication Data
Swett, Pamela E., 1970–
Neighbors and enemies : the culture of radicalism in Berlin, 1929–1933 / Pamela E. Swett.
p. cm.
Includes bibliographical references and index.
ISBN 0-521-83461-9 (hb)
1. Berlin (Germany) – Politics and government.   2. Germany – Politics and government –
1918–1933.   3. Radicalism – Germany – Berlin – History – 20th century.   4. Right and left
(Political science) I. Title.
DD880.S84   2004
943'.155085–dc22   2003067584

ISBN 0 521 83461 9 hardback

for my mom and dad

Contents

List of Figures and Plates	*page* ix
List of Abbreviations	xi
Note on Sources	xiii
Acknowledgments	xv
Introduction	1
1 Neighborhoods and Metropolis	24
The Kiez and Community Identity	25
Within the City of Millions	53
2 Rebellion at Home and in the Community	79
Crisis at Home: Gender and Radicalism	80
Crisis at Home: Generational Tension and Radicalism	100
Bloody May	120
3 Republicanism or Radicalism: Appeals to Berlin's Workers	137
Social Democracy and Republicanism	139
Radicalism	160
4 Conflict and Cooperation: Political Independence in Berlin's Neighborhoods	188
Local Initiative	189
Discussion with the Enemy and Membership Fluctuation	207
Disciplining the Neighbors: Denunciation in Berlin	214
5 The Logic of Violence	232
The Anatomy of Street Violence	237
Upholding Order: Street Violence and the Berlin Courts	261
Conclusion	286
The Emergency Decrees	286
The Culture of Radicalism	294
Bibliography	301
Index	319

Figures and Plates

FIGURES

1	Map of Nostizstraße Kiez and immediate Kreuzberg surroundings	*page* xvii
2	Map of Berlin showing administrative districts after 1920	xviii
3	Berlin population density, 1801–1930	46
4	Heights of residential buildings in Berlin by district, 1925	47
5	Youth unemployment in Germany on July 30, 1932	108
6	Reichstag election results for Kreuzberg, 1928–1933	142
7	Reichstag election results for Berlin, 1928–1933	143
8	Assemblies at which police intervened in Berlin, 1931	233

PLATES

1	Women in conversation, photo by Friedrich Seidenstücker, 1929	33
2	"Workers' Hell on Sonnenallee:" Neukölln unemployment office, 1929	89
3	Men's homeless shelter waiting room, 1929	108
4	Generational conflict in the 1933 film *Hitlerjunge Quex*, Hans Steinhoff director	116
5	Politicized children in the Berlin press, *8-Uhr Abendblatt*, 1930	118
6	Police on patrol during May riots, 1929	125
7	The May 1929 riots in the Communist press, *Die Rote Fahne*	128
8	Reichsbanner parade on Unter den Linden for the *Verfassungstag*, August 11, 1929	150
9	RFB members at pub, Breslauer Straße Friedrichshain, 1930	162
10	Swastika and Soviet flag fly together during tenants' strike, November 1932	205
11	SA pub of murdered Stormtrooper Maikowski, photo 1930	241
12	HJ march through Berlin, around 1932	244

All photos, except Plates 4 and 7, are reprinted with the courtesy of the bpk. © Bildarchiv Preussischer Kulturbesitz, 2003

List of Abbreviations

ADGB	Allgemeiner Deutscher Gewerkschaftsbund
AEG	Allgemeine Elektrizitätsgesellschaft
AIZ	*Arbeiter Illustrierte Zeitung*
Antifa	Antifaschistische Junge Garde (Young Antifascist Guard)
AVAVG	Gesetz über Arbeitsvermittlung und Arbeitslosenversicherung
BA	Bundesarchiv
BA-SAPMO	Stiftung Archiv der Arbeiterparteien und Massenorganisationen within the Bundesarchiv Berlin
BDM	Bund deutscher Mädel (League of German Girls)
BL	Bezirksleitung (KPD District Leadership)
BLHA	Brandenburgische Landeshauptarchiv, Potsdam
BT	*Berliner Tageblatt*
BVG	Berliner Verkehrsgesellschaft (Berlin Transport Company)
DDP	Deutsche demokratische Partei (German Democratic Party)
DNVP	Deutschnationale Volkspartei (German National People's Party)
DVP	Deutsche Volkspartei (German People's Party)
EF	Eiserne Front (Iron Front)
EZA	Evangelisches Zentralarchiv Berlin
GStA	Geheimes Staatsarchiv Preussischer Kulturbesitz
HJ	Hitler Jugend (Hitler Youth)
IfZ	Institut für Zeitgeschichte
KbgdF	Kampfbund gegen den Faschismus (Fighting League against Fascism)
KJVD	Kommunistische Jugendverband Deutschlands (Communist Youth League)
KPD	Kommunistische Partei Deutschlands (German Communist Party)
KPO	Kommunistische Partei – Opposition (Communist Party – Opposition)
LAB	Landesarchiv Berlin
NSBO	Nationalsozialistische Betriebszellen Organisation (National Socialist Factory Cell Organization)

NSDAP	Nationalsozialistische Deutsche Arbeiterpartei (National Socialist Party)
OSAF	Oberste SA-Führer/Oberste SA-Führung (SA leadership)
RB	Reichsbanner Schwarz-Rot-Gold
RF	*Die Rote Fahne*
RFB	Roter Frontkämpferbund (Red Front-fighters' League)
RFMB	Roter Frauen- und Mädchenbund (Red League of Women and Girls)
RGO	Revolutionäre Gewerkschafts-Opposition (Revolutionary Trade Union Opposition)
RHD	Rote Hilfe Deutschland (Red Aid Germany)
RJ	Rote Jungfront (Red Youth Front)
RJWG	Reichsjugendwohlfahrtsgesetz (National Youth Welfare Law)
SA	Sturmabteilung (Stormtroops)
SAJ	Sozialistische Arbeiter-Jugend (Social Democratic Youth Organization)
SPD	Sozialdemokratische Partei Deutschlands (Social Democratic Party)
SS	Schutzstaffel (Protection Squads)
UB	Unterbezirk (KPD subdistrict)
UBL	Unterbezirksleitung (KPD local leadership)
USPD	Unabhängige Sozialdemokratische Partei Deutschlands (Independent Social Democratic Party)
VB	*Völkischer Beobachter*
VZ	*Vossische Zeitung*
ZK	Zentralkomitee (KPD Central Committee)

Note on Sources

With regard to the footnotes, there are three points to be made. First, the names of all men and women involved in denunciations, police records, and court trials taken from archival sources have been replaced by individuals' initials, unless the person has already been discussed in other published sources. This step was taken to secure the anonymity of the subjects. Second, all neighborhood street newspaper titles have been italicized as periodicals, though most appeared in very limited numbers and were read by relatively select audiences. Because they were considered by the police and judiciary to be publications as any other, I have treated them as such in the notes. They are not, however, listed alongside those periodicals with mass audiences in the bibliography. Finally, some administrative titles and unpublished document titles have been translated into English, while others have been left in their original German. Decisions on whether or not to translate were made with respect to the ease with which the office or concept has a recognizable English equivalent.

Acknowledgments

Over the years it has taken to complete this project, I have incurred many debts. I will begin with the two people who have had the most influence on me as an historian. My undergraduate mentor at Bryn Mawr College, Jane Caplan, was an inspiring teacher and scholar. I would not have embarked on this career without her to emulate, and I continue to benefit from her guidance. An equal debt of gratitude goes to Volker Berghahn, my graduate supervisor at Brown. It is uncommon to find an historian who is admired as much for his qualities as an individual as for his accomplishments as a scholar. I am proud to have been one of his students.

For the financial support to work in Berlin's archives, I must thank the Deutscher Akademischer Austauschdienst, the Friedrich-Ebert-Stiftung, and the Arts Research Board of McMaster University. I would also like to send my appreciation to all the archivists and librarians who helped me navigate their collections. Gisela Nieguth and Natalie Tadros shared their home with me for almost two years in the Nostiz Kiez. Their generosity is unmatched. Corey Ross and Deborah Smail kept me smiling and well fed in Berlin, and Justin Powell's hospitality always makes visiting the German capital something to look forward to.

Though all shortcomings of this book are mine alone, I would also like to thank those scholars whose advice and criticism over the years helped shape this study, especially Carolyn Dean, Peter Fritzsche, Alf Lüdtke, and Eve Rosenhaft. I also owe much to Jonathan Wiesen and Frank Biess, whose scholarly insight and friendship I continue to depend upon. Maureen Healy and Martin Horn commented on the entire manuscript in its final stages and offered much needed encouragement as well. My editor at Cambridge University Press, Frank Smith, deserves thanks for his interest in the project, for fielding my endless emails, and for choosing three excellent anonymous reviewers whose suggestions for revisions improved the manuscript immensely. A special note of appreciation also goes to Sara Black, Margaret Dornfeld, Jeff Hayton, and Ruth Pincoe for their help in preparing the manuscript for publication; to Heather, Matt, Maggie, and Erika for their assistance in tracking down footnotes and bibliographical information; and to all my colleagues and friends in the McMaster University history department for creating an atmosphere conducive to teaching and writing.

As I turn to those most dear to me, I would like to acknowledge the incredible women at Central Day Care and McMaster University Children's Centre. They too contributed greatly to this effort. My boys, Jack and Nathaniel, have accepted the distractions and travel necessary to complete the project with a joy for life that continues to provide me with much needed perspective. Matt Leighninger has lived with this project as long as I have. Matt has edited the writing and challenged the arguments more than anyone else, and he still seems to find the book worth reading. For all that and much more, I am forever grateful. My greatest debts are owed to my parents, Charlene and Jeremy Swett. They gave me my love of history, and their sacrifices and limitless faith in me have made this book possible. I dedicate it to them.

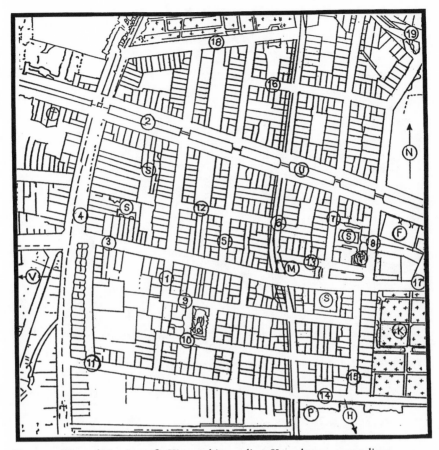

Figure 1. Map of Nostizstraße Kiez and immediate Kreuzberg surroundings.
(1) Nostizstraße, (2) Gneisenaustraße, (3) Bergmannstraße, (4) Belle-Alliance Straße, (5) Solmsstraße, (6) Zossener Straße, (7) Mittenwalder Straße, (8) Schleiermacherstraße, (9) Arndtstraße, (10) Willibald-Alexis Straße, (11) Fidicinstraße, (12) Mariendorfer Straße, (13) Marheinekeplatz, (14) Jüterboger Straße, (15) Heimstraße, (16) Fürbringerstraße, (17) Baerwaldstraße, (18) Baruther Straße, (19) Urbanstraße, (†) church, (M) market hall, (K) cemetery, (S) school, (F) sports field, (U) underground rail station, (V) Victoriapark, (H) Hasenheide, (P) police station.
Source: Drawn by C. V. Swett.

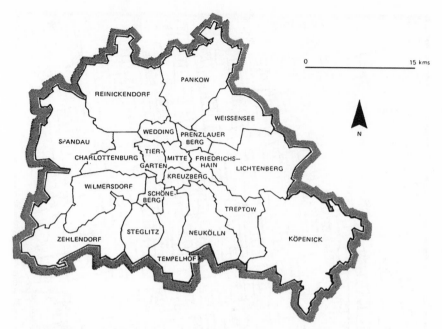

Figure 2. Map of Berlin showing administrative districts after 1920. Source: Richard F. Hamilton, *Who Voted for Hitler?* Copyright © 1982 by Princeton University Press. Reprinted by permission of Princeton University Press.

Neighbors and Enemies

Introduction

Germany's first republic always stood on shaky ground. When Philip Scheidemann, head of the Social Democratic bloc in parliament, announced the dawn of a German republic from a Reichstag balcony on November 9, 1918, his declaration was not universally well received. On the same day, Karl Liebknecht, the leader of the radical Spartacist movement, announced the birth of a socialist republic, and the violence that followed verged on civil war. On August 11, 1919, a constitution was ratified in the city of Weimar, lending the new republic its name and drawing international attention to Germany as arguably the most liberal state in the world. Yet stability did not come to Germany in any sustainable form. The Weimar Republic lurched from crisis to crisis between 1919 and 1923, enduring street violence, a short-lived putsch, political assassinations, and hyperinflation. Even after 1924, questions about economic health, cultural experimentation, and the value of parliamentarism never fully receded from public debate. Nonetheless, no one expected the magnitude of the turmoil that followed. Beginning in earnest in 1929, unmatched levels of economic depression were accompanied by the end of parliamentary rule, violence, and the emergence of a National Socialist Germany by the end of January 1933.

In their attempts to describe the Weimar Republic, and its final years in particular, scholars have frequently turned to the language of natural disasters. "Flames," "deluge," "plague," and "volcano" have all turned up in titles of Weimar studies, as a way to describe the power of the destructive force that swallowed all in its path, including the republican state.[1] Yet such an image of the republic and its collapse is misleading, not in terms of the strength attributed to Nazi evil, but in the sense of helplessness often felt by those who witness a natural disaster. The disintegration of the Weimar Republic did not happen overnight, nor did it happen beyond the reaches of

---

[1] I am referring to the following works: Anton Gill, *A Dance Between Flames: Berlin Between the Wars* (London: J. Murray, 1993); Otto Friedrich, *Before the Deluge: A Portrait of Berlin in the 1920s* (second edition, New York: Harper, 1995); Daniel Guérin, *The Brown Plague: Travels in Late Weimar and Early Nazi Germany*, Robert Schwarzwald, trans. (Durham, NC: Duke University Press, 1994, from the original 1933 Paris edition, *La peste brune a passé par là . . .*); and Thomas Kniesche and Stephen Brockmann, eds., *Dancing on the Volcano: Essays on the Culture of the Weimar Republic* (Columbia, SC: Camden House, 1994).

human intervention. Other scholars have stressed the republic's structural weaknesses, or the detrimental actions of a handful of political and industrial policy makers, but these approaches also downplay citizen involvement in the crisis. This study attempts to fill this void by examining how residents of the capital, especially those living in workers' districts, experienced and participated in the dissolution of the republic. In so doing, I will stress the engagement rather than desperation of radicalized Berliners, who were active in confronting the upheaval of the Weimar period and in the end contributed often in unforeseen ways to the speedy demise of democracy and the legitimization of the Nazi regime.

Though this study is not about the fictional representation of the republic's collapse in Berlin, a few examples from the literary world prove useful as a way to introduce the themes of this book.[2] As if they knew democracy would not be seen again in Germany for some time, novelists and other chroniclers of life in Germany rushed out to capture the moment. Their motivations in writing and their assessments of the situation are as varied as their characters, but two factors remain constant across the late Weimar literary spectrum. First, by looking at novels we are reminded that men and women were coping with the situation in a variety of ways, both acting and reacting to the upheaval. Second, the centrality of Berlin and the transiency of life there, during this period of transition from republic to dictatorship, are notable. Male and female protagonists appearing in German fiction of the late 1920s and early 1930s are constantly running to or escaping from Berlin. They are either drawn to the city, attracted by the hope of economic opportunity or freedom from provincial tradition, or determined to flee it for the emotional safety of life in a provincial town. Even though the capital suffered terribly under the strains of depression, many held out hope that Berlin would offer a solution to crisis. In *Little Man, What Now?*, Fallada's Pinneberg seeks work

---

[2] Among many novels from this period concerned with life in Germany's capital, I mention the following: Rudolf Braune, *Die Geschichte einer Woche* (Berlin: Verlag Neues Leben, 1978; original edition, 1930) and *Das Mädchen an der Orga Privat* (Frankfurt a. M.: Societäts-Verlag, 1930; Munich: Damnitz, 1975); Günther Birkenfeld, *Dritter Hof Links* (Berlin: Bruno Cassirer, 1929); Hans Fallada, *Kleiner Mann – Was Nun?* (Rheinbek bei Hamburg: Rowohlt, 1992; original edition 1932), also *Little Man, What Now?*, Eric Sutton, trans. (Chicago: Academy Chicago Publishers, 1992); Georg Fink, *Mich Hungert!* (Berlin: B. Cassirer, 1930); Erich Kästner, *Fabian: Die Geschichte eines Moralisten* (Zurich: Atrium, 1931), also *Fabian: The Story of a Moralist*, Cyrus Brooks, trans. (Evanston, IL: Northwestern University Press, 1993); Irmgard Keun, *Das kunstseidene Mädchen* (Munich: dtv, 1989; original edition, 1932) and *Gilgi – eine von uns* (1979; original edition, 1931); and Walter Schönstedt, *Kämpfende Jugend* (Berlin: Oberbaum Verlag, 1972; original edition, Berlin: Internationalen-Arbeiter Verlag, 1932). For further analysis of Berlin's role in the literature of the period, see Derek Glass et al., eds., *Berlin: Literary Images of a City* (Berlin: Schmidt, 1989); Hermann Kähler, *Berlin – Asphalt und Licht* (W. Berlin: das europäische Buch, 1986); Erhard Schütz, *Romane der Weimarer Republik* (Munich: W. Fink, 1986); and Peter Wruck, ed., *Literarisches Leben in Berlin 1871–1933* (Berlin: Akademie-Verlag, 1987).

there to support his family, never giving up hope or the dressing table that symbolizes respectability, as he descends the social ladder rung by rung. In *Die Geschichte einer Woche*, Rudolf Braune's Werner arrives in the capital wishing to plant the seeds of revolution by starting a Communist factory cell in the chemical industry. In Braune's *Das Mädchen an der Orga Privat*, Erna leaves her ten siblings behind in the country in search of independence and a typist's wage in Berlin. Also seeking an escape in Berlin is Erich Kästner's title character Fabian. After the disillusioning experience of World War I, Jakob Fabian attempts to make a life for himself in Berlin, hiding behind all the pleasures the modern metropolis offered. After a decade of living as a bachelor ad designer, he loses both his job and his first love. Fabian rejects the capital for the security of his parents' companionship and home. In some ways the city is redeemed, however, because the provincial town brings no solace to Fabian who is confronted with the same nationalist chauvinism he had rejected earlier.

As in *Fabian*, physical mobility and social marginalization caused by the Depression are hallmarks of the era and its fiction. Unemployment is a constant strain on characters throughout all the stories. In the workers' novels, this precariousness was a fact of life, unaltered by the fall of the monarchy in 1918. In fact, working-class life is portrayed as even less stable after the war's end. In Günther Birkenfeld's *Dritter Hof Links*, the young Paul's story ends as it began. He is unemployed and living in Berlin with his widowed mother – only now he is accompanied by his unemployed girlfriend. In the intervening pages, he has bounced from job to job, and lover to lover. His sisters have left the apartment. One was married briefly but is now on her own; the other has become a prostitute. Paul's father had been a skilled mason, but in the postwar period he drank himself to death, unable to deal with his memories of combat.

For the white-collar workers, or *Angestellten*, unemployment brings loss of social status as well as financial crisis. At the conclusion of Fallada's classic *Zeitroman*, middle-class Pinneberg finds himself penniless and living with his wife and child in a garden cabin on the outskirts of the city. At the beginning of Kästner's tale, Fabian's life as a carefree ad executive ends as the novel begins. Soon this PhD-holding young man finds himself opening car doors in front of a department store for spare change. In Irmgard Keun's, *Das kunstseidene Mädchen*, the female protagonist, Doris, gives up her job as a stenotypist in the hopes of becoming a somebody in Berlin by finding a rich male patron to support her expensive tastes. Failing in this goal, Doris lives on the verge of destitution throughout the book. In the last scene she stands prosaically in a Berlin train station contemplating her next move.

Berlin's rail stations play a large role in all of these novels. Symbolic of more than the transiency of life in the German capital, the rail stations also illustrate the modernity of the metropolis. The double-edged nature of urban modernity is of course what draws these fictional characters to the city and

what makes survival such a test. Rail allowed for mobility, not just to and
from the city, but also throughout the sprawling capital – connecting the
once insular communities that made up greater Berlin in the 1920s. Modern
forms of communication and commerce had given the city its cosmopolitan
feel, making it a cultural and economic center in the 1920s as well as the
seat of the national government. The fictional characters of the Berlin novels
discuss the vibrancy and permissiveness of the city's nightlife, read stories
about socialites, and note the popularity of the movie houses. But not everything was new. Just as the hope for prosperity clashed with the reality
of economic instability, the city's growing cosmopolitanism clashed with the
remnants of the German monarchy. The rail terminal itself is a prime example of this dichotomy. Its high-tech machinery, crowds, and noise denoted
the excitement and anonymity of the modern city, while the pomposity of the
nineteenth-century station façade confirmed that Berlin had a conservative,
military, and royal past.

Contemporary chroniclers of daily life in the republic certainly emphasized
the new café culture, the pace of automobile traffic and subways, and the
rationalized workspace. They did not forget, however, the legacy of prewar
and wartime Berlin. Like the façades of the train stations, the layout of the
city and its landmarks were left over from an earlier era. Wealth was still
found in the West and a lack of resources still characterized the East. The
republic's parliament met in a building designed for a monarch's parliament,
greatly restricted in its powers. Though we think of 1920s Berlin as having
a consumer-driven culture – the home of AEG household appliances and
Wertheim department stores – much of Berlin's population was still living in
the crowded tenements erected quickly and with little expenditure toward
the end of the nineteenth century to house the growing numbers of factory
workers entering the industrializing city.

Though the physical remnants of pre-1918 Berlin still shaped life in the
city in the 1920s, so did what was missing. The loss of virtually an entire
generation to the war affected society and politics in ways too numerous
to discuss in this introduction. The novels that appeared at the end of the
1920s, however, do not shy away from confronting the personal and political
devastation wrought by the war. Kästner's protagonist reviles his elders, who
convinced him and his school classmates to enlist and left him with a weak
heart and a debilitating sense of betrayal. In the aptly titled *Mich Hungert!*
(I'm hungry!), the main character Teddy finds himself in a predicament similar to that of young Paul in *Dritter Hof Links*: Teddy's father died in battle,
leaving him to support his siblings and care for a single mother exhausted
by overwork and poverty.

With all of this upheaval and tension between war and peace, prosperity and despair, monarchy and republic, urban modernity and provincial
tradition, it is perhaps surprising that the republic lasted as long as it did.
Without the benefit of knowing the tragic conclusion to Weimar's story,

the era's novelists describe an atmosphere of impending political crisis. In Schönstedt's *Kämpfende Jugend*, the violence between local gangs of Communists and Nazis is growing, and lessons are being learned that the author hopes will serve the young Communists well in the expected showdown between left and right. Likewise, Werner has built his factory cell, which he assumes will grow until the revolution brings the opportunity for the workers to take full control of their company's operations. Keun's "rayon girl," Doris, admits a lack of understanding of the political crises of the day, but she enjoys hearing people debate the issues and even finds herself caught up in one of the ubiquitous demonstrations in Berlin after 1929. Kästner's two protagonists hire a taxi so they can transport two Communist and Nazi paramilitaries who have shot each other to a hospital – even though they find the combatants' political ideologies distasteful. Ironically, the wounded survive but the two liberal Samaritans are unable to find their way in Berlin and die by the end of the book.

It is this process in which political and economic instability culminated in the death of the republic that has interested historians of the era most. Increasing popular support for the far left (communism) and far right (national socialism), coupled with the authoritarian tendencies of officials at the top levels of the republican government, led quite quickly under the pressure of the Depression to the undermining of parliamentary decision making. Simultaneously, in certain parts of the country where far left and far right paramilitaries had grown in number, various forms of street violence became common, challenging the government to take ever more extreme steps to restore civil order. Once the Nazi Party became the largest bloc in the Reichstag, the republic's president, World War I Field Marshal Paul von Hindenburg, and his advisers began seriously to consider involving the young party's leader, Adolf Hitler, in a new cabinet. Hitler turned down what he determined to be compromising posts until he was offered the brass ring, the chancellorship, on January 30, 1933.

The period from 1929, the benchmark for the start of the Depression, to what used to be referred to as the Nazi "seizure" of power is the timeframe for this study. These four years are sometimes labeled the Crisis Period, but Weimar's crises were certainly not limited to this final phase of the republic. As demonstrated here by this brief summary of some of the popular literature of the day, the Weimar Republic was riddled with crises throughout its life. The political turmoil, which captivates us for what it promises to teach about the attractions of fascism and the atmosphere under which Nazism could be successful, must be seen in the context of the legacy of defeat, the costs of losing a generation to war, the challenges of industrial society, and changing gender norms. We must look at individuals and institutions, representation and experience, mentalities and structures.

This is a tall order, and I do not pretend to cast my net nearly so wide. However, this book does offer one perspective that has been missing – a local study that weaves together the multiple levels of the political process, from generational conflict and patriarchal assumption of power in the family, to neighborhood relationships, party camaraderie, and displays of state authority. Surely Berlin is in many ways a unique case.[3] It was the capital city, and the specific ways the crisis unfolded within city limits drew special attention throughout Germany and around the world. One need only read an issue of the *New York Times* from the early 1930s to see that developments within Berlin were followed beyond Germany's borders. Importantly, it was not only the decisions of the Reichstag or the presidential decrees and appointments of chancellors that were deemed newsworthy. The grassroots political crisis and the deepening economic collapse in Berlin were also making headlines.[4]

Yet there are two reasons why the Weimar Republic's demise can be better understood by a focus on the capital. First, though the intensity of unrest among Berlin's workers was perhaps unsurpassed by that of any other city or region, there is no reason to expect that it was qualitatively different elsewhere. Unemployment was a national phenomenon, as were the rise of radical parties and the decline of the political center. Berlin may have had an especially volatile combination of a powerful Communist Party branch and an increasingly well-developed Nazi constituency, but the importance of gender and generational conflict in attracting support for the radical parties seems undisputed by recent studies of other localities.[5]

Second, as a direct result of the special attention focused on Berlin's political climate, the city acted as a barometer for the stability of the whole republic. Therefore, in the quest to understand how the government rationalized the end of parliamentary rule, or to explain why large segments of the population sought radical alternatives to the political crisis, events in Berlin

---

[3] Hamburg and its environs have also served as a case study for a number of important works on the 1920s. For those that correspond most closely to this one, see Eva Büttner, *Hamburg in der staats- und Wirtschaftskrise, 1928–1931* (Hamburg: Christians, 1982); Hermann Hipp, ed., *Wohnstadt Hamburg. Mietshäuser der zwanziger Jahre zwischen Inflation und Weltwirtschaftskrise* (Hamburg: Christians, 1982); Maike Bruhns, Claudia Preuschoft, and Werner Skrentny, eds., *"Hier war doch alles nicht so schlimm"* (Hamburg: VSA-Verlag, 1984); Angelika Voß, Ursula Büttner, and Hermann Weber, *Vom Hamburger Aufstand zur politischen Isolierung. Kommunistischen Politik 1923–33 in Hamburg und im Deutschen Reich* (Hamburg: Landeszentrale für politische Bildung, 1983); and most recently Anthony McElligott, *Contested City: Municipal Politics and the Rise of Nazism in Altona* (Ann Arbor: University of Michigan Press, 1998).

[4] See for example, the *New York Times*, August 12, 1932, "Republic is ignored on Reich Fete Day."

[5] Cf. Klaus-Michael Mallmann, *Kommunisten in der Weimarer Republik: Sozialgeschichte einer revolutionären Bewegung* (Darmstadt: Wissenschaftlicher Buchgesellschaft, 1996); Anthony McElligott, *Contested City: Municipal Politics and the Rise of Nazism in Altona* (Ann Arbor: University of Michigan Press, 1998); and Eric D. Weitz, *Creating German Communism, 1890–1990: From Popular Protests to Socialist State* (Princeton, NJ: Princeton University Press, 1996).

provided answers to contemporaries of the period and should continue to do so today. It is not surprising that Germans or the international community looked to Berlin to judge the extent of the crisis in the early 1930s. If a democratic government could not maintain its credibility among residents of the capital, which benefited from a local prorepublican administration and the visual grandeur available to all capital cities, then what chance did other towns and regions have? As other historians have shown, in various parts of Germany rural particularism, Catholic independence, and distrust of the national government only compounded the problems that were already overwhelming Berlin by the end of the 1920s.[6]

My focus is on the political crisis in the capital, but my analysis is not one that emanates from the corridors of political power, be those governmental bureaus or parties' headquarters. I begin and remain on the streets of Berlin. I seek to understand how citizens, in particular those who lived in the low-rent city center, participated in the collapse of the republic, not in the way they cast their ballots, but in the ways they related to their city, their local leaders, and most importantly each other. At the most basic level, I argue that a deep sense of uncertainty pervaded the city throughout the 1920s. This unease, exacerbated by the social and economic dislocation of a modern society thrust into severe depression, led to a transformation of social and political relationships in the capital. These developments underline the fact that the collapse was not effected solely in a top-down manner, either through governmental directive or party command. Rather with the weakening of the institutions of state and political parties, men and women found authority in themselves and neighborhood activism and ethics. In doing so, some resorted to violence, challenging the state to take increasingly authoritarian steps to rein in radicalism, which ultimately eroded any chance for republicanism and paved the way for a "peaceful" transition to the Third Reich.

The primary goal of the book, then, is to offer an interpretation of the collapse of the republic that emanates from Berlin's neighborhood-based radical culture – a radicalism defined not by membership in or commitment to any political party but by the desire to address actively the problems of daily life. The pervasiveness of radicalism in the capital was not simply a manifestation of economic desperation or a result of conflicting ideologies. Rather the full meaning behind street battles, daily protest, uniforms, and the politicization of once politically neutral spaces should be sought also in the day-to-day relationships between members of these communities and the methods they employed for preserving some degree of familial

---

[6] See Detlef Lehnert and Klaus Megerle, "Problems of Identity and Consensus in a Fragmented Society: The Weimar Republic" in Dirk Berg-Schlosser and Ralf Rytlewski, eds., *Political Culture in Germany* (New York: St. Martin's Press, 1993) and Oded Heilbronner, *Catholicism, Political Culture, and the Countryside: A Social History of the Nazi Party in Southern Germany* (Ann Arbor: University of Michigan Press, 1998).

and neighborhood autonomy in the face of catastrophe. This book will also contribute to our understanding of heightened generational and gender tensions in these years, and the connections between these developments and the growth of radicalism. The debates about female sexuality, consumption, and the "New Woman" and the rhetoric surrounding masculine rebirth, political activism, and the "Lost Generation" signaled the turbulence that surrounded gender relations and existed between the generations. I examine how these issues shaped the opportunities and limitations of male and female workers' political engagement in their neighborhoods and beyond. By analyzing a culture of radicalism, which had less to do with party politics than with individual and community needs, and its impact on the republic's fate more broadly, I endeavor to paint a more complete picture of Berlin during the Depression – one in which men and women were active in the transition from republicanism to dictatorship.

The study of Weimar Germany's collapse is no new undertaking. Clearly the republic's demise at the foot of Nazism leaves us with many questions as to how a modern society could embrace such a party and its brutality, particularly when only fourteen years earlier it had ratified one of the world's most liberal and democratic constitutions.[7] Though most historians would agree that a combination of both long-term and immediate pressures felled the republic, analyses of the political crisis can be separated into three categories. First, there are those who argue that the republic was destroyed by a handful of men at the pinnacles of political and industrial power. Other historians focus on the parties, maintaining that those which supported the republic were challenged and eventually overcome by the radical ideologies and violence of those on the extreme right and left. Finally, there are those who maintain that the middle classes never fully accepted their liberal birthright and were convinced of the republic's shortcomings during the inflation crisis of 1923, which left them without their savings and with little chance for regaining their status in a terminally weak economy. Disenchanted, these citizens failed to support the republic as the decade progressed, jumping ship in ever-greater numbers to the special interest and nationalist parties before the emergence of the NSDAP. This study offers counterpoints to these three approaches. Where others have focused on central power, I have chosen to examine local power, suggesting in fact that the collapse occurred from below. Instead of concentrating on the ways institutions influenced developments in this period, this book emphasizes the challenges posed by politicized men and women to the authority of political parties and state institutions. Finally, I question those analyses that present workers' culture as isolated within the

---

[7] For analysis of the 1919 Constitution and the theorists behind the document, see Peter Caldwell, *Popular Sovereignty and the Crisis of German Constitutional Law: The Theory and Practice of Weimar Constitutionalism* (Durham, NC: Duke University Press, 1997).

republic and middle-class culture as the chief determining factor for political developments in the Weimar era.

To begin with a classic text on the collapse of the republic, Karl-Dietrich Bracher's *Die Auflösung der Weimarer Republik* notes the importance of the economic crisis in pushing the middle classes to the right and many workers to the radical left. However, in this and other texts, Bracher directs most of his attention to the actions taken at the highest levels of government after 1929.[8] It was here that "the combination of political inexperience, lack of familiarity with the workings of parliamentary democracy, and powerful residues of authoritarianism proved fatal."[9] The introduction of rule by emergency decree beginning in 1930 destroyed any chance for a democratic solution, argues Bracher, leaving a political vacuum to be filled by Nazism.

Though the Depression accelerated the downfall of the republic in Bracher's interpretation, what ultimately made the situation after 1929 different from the earlier political and economic crisis faced by the state in 1923 is that those in charge were not willing to find a non-Nazi alternative. Hagen Schulze and Henry Turner have turned even more singularly to the "personal relationships, characteristics, decisions and deficiencies" that intervened in the first weeks of 1933 and led ultimately to the placement of power in Hitler's hands.[10] Though uncovering the significance of personal factors in this process is a thought-provoking exercise, it obscures the broader context in which Hitler could be accepted as chancellor by the majority of the German population. Though the NSDAP failed to gain an electoral majority in 1933, the bulk of the German population willingly accepted the new regime. President von Hindenburg, cabinet members, and party leaders were not only acting according to interpersonal conflicts and personal quests for power but also reacting to specific grassroots political developments and mass discontent.

In contrast to this emphasis on the governmental elite, a second stream of analysis has focused on the actions of the various political parties. As the largest party with the desire to maintain a republican government, the

---

[8] Karl-Dietrich Bracher, *Die Auflösung der Weimarer Republik* (Villingen: Ring Verlag, 1955). Cf. Ian Kershaw, ed., *Weimar: Why Did German Democracy Fail?* (New York: St. Martin's Press, 1990). This collection of essays is particularly helpful for breaking down the so-called Borchardt debate concerning the role of structural economic weaknesses within the republic and Chancellor Brüning's deflationary policies during the Depression in the republic's collapse. For more on these debates, see Knut Borchardt, *Wachstum, Krisen, Handlungsspielräume der Wirtschaftspolitik* (Göttingen: Vandenhoeck & Ruprecht, 1982); the special issue of *Geschichte und Gesellschaft* (Vol. 11, 1985) dedicated to the debate; and the short text by Jürgen von Kruedener, *Economic Crisis and the Political Collapse: The Weimar Republic, 1924–1933* (New York: Berg, 1990).

[9] Karl-Dietrich Bracher, *The German Dictatorship* (New York: Praeger, 1970), p. 169.

[10] Hagen Schulze, "Explaining the Failure of the Weimar Republic," (unpublished manuscript, 1998), p. 3. The focus on the interpersonal relationships of the decision makers surrounding President von Hindenburg is developed most fully in Henry A. Turner, *Hitler's Thirty Days to Power: January 1933* (New York: Addison Wesley, 1996).

inability of the Social Democratic Party to halt the growth of antirepublican forces has received great attention.[11] The SPD's participation in the signing of the hated Versailles treaty, its role as architect of the republic, and the failings of the republic's early SPD-led governments tainted the party as being responsible for every woe faced by the young state. Public opinion further deteriorated once the SPD-sculpted welfare state began to be dismantled by the austerity measures of non-social democrats in the early 1930s. In the 1990s this interpretation was updated, broadening our understanding of the paralysis felt within the party as the evolving social structure and new political strategies of the more radical parties led to internal party discord.[12]

The role of the KPD in the collapse of the republic has also been reevaluated in the last twenty years. Instead of purely institutional histories of the party, which stressed an earlier Stalinization model, Eve Rosenhaft's *Beating the Fascists?* broke new ground in its exploration of political culture.[13] Though she discusses KPD policy quite extensively, Rosenhaft's book also examines the social and cultural roots of radicalism among Berlin's workers and dissects the local violence directed against the growing fascist threat.[14] This important book clearly informs my study in many ways. But

---

[11] For further elucidation of this general position, see the three-volume series on the republic by Heinrich August Winkler, especially volume III, *Der Weg in die Katastrophe. Arbeiter und Arbeiterbewegung in der Weimarer Republik 1930 bis 1933* (Berlin: Dietz, 1987) and also Heinrich August Winkler, ed., *Die Deutsche Staatskrise 1930–1933* (Munich: Oldenbourg, 1992a) and Eberhard Kolb, *Umbrüche deutscher Geschichte*, Dieter Langewiesche and Klaus Schönhoven, eds. (Munich: Oldenbourg, 1993).

[12] See Donna Harsch, *German Social Democracy and the Rise of Nazism* (Chapel Hill: University of North Carolina Press, 1993).

[13] Christian Striefler's *Kampf um die Macht* (Frankfurt a. M.: Propyläen, 1993) revives the claim that the KPD was an insurrectionary party and the main culprit in the downfall of the republic. Local Communist Party documents even in strongholds like Berlin, however, provide no significant evidence that its members held enthusiasm for calls to mass strike – not to mention revolution. His section on anti-Semitism within the KPD is a prime example of how the demonization of the KPD is employed to lessen the guilt of the NSDAP.

[14] Eve Rosenhaft, *Beating the Fascists? The German Communists and Political Violence 1929–1933* (New York: Cambridge University Press, 1983). Rosenhaft and Fischer are somewhat unique in their focus on the KPD. As noted later in this introduction, most research on Weimar violence has targeted developments within the NSDAP. The literature on the SA in particular is quite extensive. Some of the most useful studies remain Richard Bessel, *Political Violence and the Rise of Nazism. The Storm Troopers in Eastern Germany, 1925–1934* (New Haven, CT: Yale University Press, 1984); James Diehl, *Paramilitary Politics in the Weimar Republic* (Bloomington: Indiana University Press, 1977); Conan Fischer, *Stormtroopers: A Social, Economic and Ideological Analysis, 1929–1935* (London: Allen and Unwin, 1983); Michael Kater, *The Nazi Party. A Social Profile of Members and Leaders, 1919–1945* (Oxford: Basil Blackwell, 1983); Peter Longerich, *Die braune Bataillone: Geschichte der SA* (Munich: Beck, 1989); Peter Merkl, *The Making of a Stormtrooper* (Princeton, NJ: Princeton University Press, 1980); Eric Reiche, *The Development of the SA in Nürnberg 1922–1934* (Cambridge: Cambridge University Press, 1986); and Peter Stachura, *Nazi Youth in the Weimar Republic* (Santa Barbara, CA: Clio, 1975). Bruce Campbell's

where she looked at the KPD in isolation, this study situates radical Berlin in the broader context of daily life in the city center. As such for discussion of party policy and for data concerning the social and economic background of Communist street fighters, I refer the reader to Rosenhaft's text.

In an essay that followed the book, Rosenhaft stresses the acceptance of violence in Weimar society and its attraction as a means of self-representation for the individual and for working males as a group. Rosenhaft argues that uniforms, public demonstrations, and acts of "bravery" symbolically reconstituted the male body, which had been weakened by the World War I and the economic crisis. However, the competing visions of the male worker presented by the SA and Communist paramilitaries offered two choices to the working class as a whole. The left-wing paramilitaries saw themselves as representatives of all workers and sought to gain more adherents through their loosely organized marches, which welcomed new converts. The SA offered a different image of the strong worker, symbolized by tightly controlled marching squadrons exhibiting bourgeois self-discipline. The Communists hoped to attract more participants through their public protests, while the SA desired only an audience for its spectacle.[15] Both sets of troops sought to demonstrate their bravery to one another and to their communities. My intention is to show the larger implications their actions had for their neighborhoods, the capital, and even the country.

Following his own work on the SA, in *The German Communists and the Rise of Nazism*, Conan Fischer compares the radical right and left, uncovering similarities in message and strategy among the Nazis and Communists.[16] Some critics, however, have been unwilling to accept Fischer's view that the KPD and NSDAP fought for support within the same social circles and that the parties aroused similar motivations in their members. Detractors claim

contribution to this literature aims at understanding the social profile of the SA's leaders: *The SA Generals and the Rise of Nazism* (Lexington: University of Kentucky Press, 1998). For studies that explain the social make-up and organizational structure of those assigned to control this violence, see the classic work by Hsi-Huey Liang, *The Berlin Police Force in the Weimar Republic* (Berkeley: University of California Press, 1970); Peter Leßmann, *Die Preussische Schutzpolizei in der Weimarer Republik; Streifendienst und Straßenkampf* (Düsseldorf: Droste, 1989); or Alf Lüdtke, ed., *Sicherheit und Wohlfahrt. Polizei, Gesellschaft und Herrschaft im 19. und 20. Jahrhundert* (Frankfurt a. M.: Suhrkamp, 1992), especially the volume's essay by Richard Bessel, "Militarisierung und Modernisierung: Polizeiliches Handeln in der Weimarer Republik." For an overview of modern developments in European policing, see George L. Mosse, ed., *Police Forces in History* (London: Sage, 1975) and Clive Elmsley and Barbara Weinberger, eds., *Policing Western Europe. Politics, Professionalism and Public Order, 1850–1940* (New York: Greenwood Press, 1991).

[15] Eve Rosenhaft, "Links gleich rechts? Militante Straßengewalt um 1930" in Thomas Lindenberger and Alf Lüdtke, eds., *Physische Gewalt* (Frankfurt a. M.: Suhrkamp, 1995), p. 260.

[16] See Conan Fischer, *Stormtroopers. A Social, Economic and Ideological Analysis 1929–1935* (London: Allen and Unwin, 1983) and *The German Communists and the Rise of Nazism* (New York: St. Martin's Press, 1991).

that Fischer paints a picture of apolitical thugs on both ends of the political spectrum, thereby downplaying the particular threat posed by Nazism.[17] Nonetheless, Fischer's study is valuable because it explains how the KPD responded to the support shown by workers to the NSDAP and addresses the connection between the cross-party attractions of radicalism and the social and economic crises.

Fischer also challenges those scholars who depict Communist combatants in a purely defensive position.[18] In *Creating German Communism, 1890–1990*, Eric Weitz agrees that steadily increasing right-wing violence throughout the 1920s does not preclude the possibility of left-wing aggression.[19] Weitz argues that the KPD leadership sought to control violence and use it as part of official party strategy. Though policy changed over time, as did the context for demonstrations, Weitz stresses the continuum of a developing acceptance of violent politics on the far left. This assertion is an important one, and its broader implications are shown in this study as it relates to the relatively smooth transition from republic to Third Reich.

[17] See Fischer's controversial article "Class Enemies or Class Brothers? Communist-Nazi Relations in Germany, 1929–1933" in *European History Quarterly* (Vol. 15, No. 3, 1985), pp. 259–79. A great deal of research has been done on the ways in which the Nazi Party appealed to workers. Though criticized for his broad definition of the working class, see Max Kele's chronological analysis of changes in upper-level NSDAP policy and propaganda toward workers in *Nazis and Workers. National Socialist Appeals to German Labor, 1919–33* (Chapel Hill: University of North Carolina Press, 1972). The first chapter of Francis L. Carsten's *The German Workers and the Nazis* (London: Scolar Press, 1995) gives a short synopsis of the pre-1933 period. Conan Fischer's edited collection, *The Rise of National Socialism and the Working Classes in Weimar Germany* (Providence: Berghahn Books, 1996) is also very helpful in this regard. In particular, see the essay by Günther Mai on the NSBO and Helen Boak's piece on the attractions of Nazism to working-class women. On the subject of Nazi attempts to organize workers on the factory floor, see also Volker Kratzenberg, *Arbeiter auf dem Weg zu Hitler? Die Nationalsozialistische Betriebszellen-Organisation. Ihre Entstehung, ihre Programmatik, ihr Scheitern, 1927–1934* (Frankfurt a. M.: Peter Lang, 1989).

[18] Among others, see Bernd Weisbrod, "Gewalt in der Politik. Zur politischen Kultur in Deutschland zwischen den beiden Weltkriegen" in *Geschichte in Wissenschaft und Unterricht* (Vol. 43, No. 7, 1992), p. 394. Weisbrod's arguments about the effects of political violence on German society are well developed. However, that such violence would have no effect on German workers, except in terms of a defensive reaction, seems to overlook the evidence of local aggression among KPD supporters – aggression that was a problem for KPD leaders, who demanded "revolutionary discipline."

[19] Eric D. Weitz, *Creating German Communism, 1890–1990: From Popular Protests to Socialist State* (Princeton, NJ: Princeton University Press, 1996). Within this long-ranging study, the chapters on street politics and gender are two of the strongest. See also Klaus-Michael Mallmann, *Kommunisten in der Weimarer Republik: Sozialgeschichte einer revolutionären Bewegung* (Darmstadt: Wissenschaftliche Buchgesellschaft, 1996). Though he does not devote much space in the book to the issue of violence, Mallmann stresses the independence of local Communists and their ability to sustain a labor milieu with local Social Democrats despite threats from the NSDAP and the public discord between leaders of the SPD and KPD.

Finally, some recent analyses stress the fragmentation of German society as an explanation for what they see as the failure of democracy to take hold among the middle classes in the 1920s. They argue that the bourgeois parties that supported the republic were never able to forge a sense of national unity. Preexisting regional and religious differences, as well as the isolationist traditions of working-class politics, only deepened as time went on and economic difficulties worsened. This climate of separate "milieus" made the republic vulnerable to the NSDAP, which promised the *Volksgemeinschaft* as a way to unite the nation. Those cultural milieus that remained fairly impenetrable to Nazi propaganda, including Jews and other minority groups and the political left, could then be easily persecuted as enemies to the *Volksgemeinschaft* after 1933. For Karl Rohe and others who look at social integration, the blame for Weimar's collapse rests not with the SPD's paralysis or even with the radical competition. Rather, these historians implicate the middle classes and claim that the roots of instability can be found well before the late 1920s.[20] Recently Peter Fritzsche too has stressed the importance of the inclusive nature of the Nazis' *Volksgemeinschaft* rhetoric in attracting Germans before 1933. By pointing to a series of dramatic events beginning with July 1914 that mobilized large sections of the population, Fritzsche illustrates the force of a nationalist cause.[21]

In order to evaluate whether the republic's collapse was indeed precipitated by conflict between various milieus, however, more case studies from around Germany will need to be conducted.[22] We may find that further regional studies actually demonstrate that the provinces and their milieus were not as dissimilar as once thought. Oded Heilbronner's *Catholicism, Political Culture, and the Countryside*, has begun this trend by demonstrating that Catholics in the South were not as immune to national socialism as previously believed.[23] Even if we continue to believe that particularism remained

---

[20] Cf. Lehnert and Megerle, "Problems of Identity and Consensus in a Fragmented Society" (1993). Although his research interests lie primarily in post-1945 German political culture, Karl Rohe has recently moved away from the concept of "Milieu" to the somewhat more fluid concept of "Lager" (camps) in order to stress "that culture rather than social structure shapes political preferences, i.e. historical experiences and processes which link political ideas and orientations to social structure." Karl Rohe, "Party Cultures and Regional Traditions: The SPD in the Ruhr" in Eva Kolinsky, ed., *The Federal Republic of Germany. The End of an Era* (New York: Berg, 1991), p. 126.

[21] Peter Fritzsche, *Germans into Nazis* (Cambridge, MA: Harvard University Press, 1997).

[22] Historians approaching the success of Italian fascism have greatly benefited from a number of local studies that have illustrated the variety of attractions to fascism. They also show the importance of local priorities, which sometimes led to unexpected political alliances. See Paul Corner, *Fascism in Ferrara, 1915–1925* (New York: Oxford University Press, 1975); Adrian Lyttelton, *The Seizure of Power. Fascism in Italy, 1919–1929* (Princeton, NJ: Princeton University Press, 2nd ed., 1987); and Frank M. Snowden, *The Fascist Revolution in Tuscany, 1919–1922* (Oxford: Oxford University Press, 1989).

[23] Heilbronner, *Catholicism* (1998).

strong in parts of Germany, by 1930 the country's urban centers were characterized by their social and cultural diversity. Tensions still existed between social groups, but the burgeoning service economy and expansion of popular culture had done much to force contact between the classes. If one accepts a lack of social integration, it is still necessary to account for the timing of the republic's demise in the early 1930s.[24]

One weakness of those analyses that depend solely on long-term developments is that they presume a 1930 social structure that was little changed from that of pre-1914 Germany. The evidence offered in this study, however, stresses the uniqueness of the Weimar era and the Depression years in particular. Large numbers of female-led households, industrial rationalization, and a decade of republican government are just a few reasons why Germany's political culture and social fabric in 1929 was very different from that of the prewar era.[25] The Weimar Republic was hobbled by its birth defects throughout its life, but the context in which these problems were debated or given priority had changed dramatically by the end of the 1920s. This assertion in no way questions the existence of an identity crisis among the middle classes or the importance of regional particularism. Rather, it emphasizes the need to address more fully the conditions of the Depression era itself and the new political climate that accompanied it.

The willingness to engage the Weimar Republic on its own terms is one of the greatest strengths of Detlev Peukert's work on the era. Peukert claims that

[24] Bernd Weisbrod also points to the slow growth of discontent among the bourgeoisie. However, for Weisbrod it was not the inability of the middle classes to rally support for the republic that led to its collapse. Instead, traumatic events such as World War I and the inflationary period of the early 1920s undermined any chance for republican allegiance to develop among the middle classes. See Bernd Weisbrod, "Die Krise der bürgerlichen Gesellschaft und die Machtergreifung von 1933" in Hans-Ulrich Wehler, ed., *Scheidewege der deutschen Geschichte* (Munich: Beck, 1995). An English translation, "The Crisis of Bourgeois Society in Interwar Germany," is found in Richard Bessel, ed., *Fascist Italy and Nazi Germany* (Cambridge: Cambridge University Press, 1996). Dirk Schumann's book on political violence in the republic comes to a similar conclusion. He argues that the pervasiveness of right-wing paramilitarism and deep-seated anticommunism in the republic is proof that the vast portion of the bourgeoisie never abandoned its desire to reestablish a more authoritarian political and social structure modeled on the *Kaiserreich*. See Dirk Schumann, *Politische Gewalt in der Weimarer Republik 1918–1933: Kampf um die Strasse und Furcht vor dem Bürgerkrieg* (Essen: Klartext, 2001), pp. 367–8.

[25] Cf. Richard Bessel, *Germany after the First World War* (Oxford: Clarendon, 1993); Hartmut Kaelble, "Soziale Mobilität in Deutschland, 1900–1960" in Kaelble, ed., *Probleme der Modernisierung* (Opladen: Westdeutscher Verlag, 1978); and Ute Daniel, *Arbeiterfrauen in der Kriegsgesellschaft: Beruf, Familie und Politik im Ersten Weltkrieg* (Göttingen: Vandenhoeck und Ruprecht, 1989). Daniel's text has been translated by Margaret Ries as *The War from Within: German Working-Class Women in the First World War* (New York: Berg, 1997). See also Elisabeth Domansky's chapter "Militarization and Reproduction in WWI Germany" in Geoff Eley, ed., *Society, Culture and the State in Germany 1870–1930* (Ann Arbor: University of Michigan Press, 1996).

the Weimar period should be recognized for the experimentation embodied in its constitution and culture, as seen in the rationalization of everyday life through the integration of technology, the institutionalization of class conflict, and the creation of the welfare state. When these experiments failed to deliver social stability and economic prosperity under the particular strain of the Depression, however, other solutions were sought. Among the alternatives, national socialism was victorious, maintains Peukert, not because it rejected modernity, and its many "irritations." Rather national socialism offered a reinterpretation of the Enlightenment project. Rationalization was now the basis for defining racial hierarchies. Racist policy would bring the stability and prosperity unachieved by Weimar democracy. For national socialists, progress could be found in the bureaucratization of killing.

Peukert succeeds in highlighting the dramatic break with the Prussian past made in Germany after World War I and in stressing the severity of the damage wrought by the Depression a decade later. However, because he painted with such sweeping strokes in his provocative text, *The Weimar Republic: The Crisis of Classical Modernity*, his conceptualization of crisis has been rightly criticized as too simplistic. He was correct that men and women living in the Weimar Republic, and nowhere more so than in Berlin, were living with all the contradictions of modern life, but Peukert saw only debilitation coming out of this experience – passivity that opened the door to national socialism.[26]

Though this book does not draw that same conclusion, it does take from Peukert a focus on the rupture caused by World War I and the intensification of crisis after 1929. In particular, this study addresses three interrelated aspects of daily life that witnessed fundamental change after 1918 and increasingly so after 1929: generational and gender relations, the relationship between citizens and political institutions, and the use of violence as a political strategy. The political mobilization of youth has long been recognized as a crucial factor in the study of Weimar's collapse. Germany's young men and women were hit most harshly by the immense unemployment of the

---

[26] Detlev Peukert, *The Weimar Republic: The Crisis of Classical Modernity* (New York: Hill and Wang, 1989). See also, the review essay by David F. Crew, "The Pathologies of Modernity: Detlev Peukert on Germany's Twentieth Century" in *Social History* (Vol. 17, No. 2, May 1992), pp. 319–28. Young-Sun Hong's excellent study of the Weimar welfare state also serves as a correction to Peukert. While Peukert insists that social disciplining and eventually racism were at the foundation of welfare policy before 1933, Hong argues that throughout the Weimar era, even in the last days of republicanism, liberal beliefs about social policy remained intact among many professionals in the field. Cf. Detlev Peukert, *Grenzen der Sozialdisziplinierung: Aufstieg und Krise der deutschen Jugendfürsorge 1878–1932* (Cologne: Bund-Verlag, 1986) and Young-Sun Hong, *Welfare, Modernity, and the Weimar State, 1919–1933* (Princeton, NJ: Princeton University Press, 1998). For a review of a number of Weimar studies from the 1990s, many of which were inspired by Peukert's analyses, see Peter Fritzsche, "Did Weimar Fail?" in *Journal of Modern History* (Vol. 68, No. 3, 1996a), pp. 629–56.

Depression years. Opportunities for vocational training and apprenticeships were drastically cut, and many young people lost or never qualified for welfare benefits in the early 1930s owing to funding cutbacks and bureaucratic red tape. The government and intellectuals alike were greatly concerned about the effects of Weimar's economic weakness on Germany's youth, and historians since have examined closely how youth organizations and the state handled the problems faced by young people.[27] Such studies have contributed greatly to our knowledge of paramilitarism and the disciplinary aspects of work programs and other social welfare policies. However, Germany's youth must also be examined in the context of their families and neighborhoods. This book only begins this difficult task, but even so it becomes clear how tensions between young and old contributed to the republic's demise.

The increasing conflicts between generations, along with the legal equality afforded women by the 1919 constitution, challenged traditional family structure and political institutions. Though supporters of the republic championed this cause initially, the numbers of elected female officials dropped steadily throughout the 1920s at all levels of government. Those who have studied the fate of Germany's female politicos have found that, even in the parties of the left, women lost ground in their struggle for parity with their male colleagues, eventually retreating to traditional "women's issues," namely social work and education, which they could more easily claim as their own.[28]

---

[27] There is quite an extensive body of literature on the family written in the early 1930s by German academics: Alice Solomon and Marie Baum, *Das Familienleben in der Gegenwart* (Berlin: F. A. Herbig, 1930); Günter Krolzig, *Der jugendliche in der Großstadtfamilie* (Berlin: F. A. Herbig, 1930); Annemarie Niemeyer, *Zur Struktur der Familie. Statistischen Materialen* (Berlin: F. A. Herbig, 1931); Ernst Posse, *Die Politischen Kämpferbünde Deutschlands* (Junker und Dünnhaupt, 1930); Bruno Schwan, *Die Wohnungsverhältnisse in der Berliner Altstadt* (Berlin: Deutscher Verein für Wohnungsreform, 1932); Fritz Künkel, *Krisenbriefe. Die Beziehung zwischen Wirtschaftskrise und Charakterkrise* (Schwerin: Bahn, 1933). In addition to Detlev Peukert, *Jugend zwischen Krieg und Krise* (Cologne: Bund-Verlag, 1987b) and Elizabeth Harvey, *Youth and the Welfare State in Weimar Germany* (Oxford: Clarendon, 1993), recent scholarship on youth and the Weimar welfare state includes: Manfred Hermanns, *Jugendarbeitslosigkeit seit der Weimarer Republik* (Opladen: Leske & Budrich, 1990); Wolfgang Krabbe, ed., *Politische Jugend in der Weimarer Republik* (Bochum: Universitäts Verlag, 1993); Peter Stachura, *The Weimar Republic and the Younger Proletariat* (New York: St. Martin's Press, 1989); and Peter Dudek, *Erziehung durch Arbeit. Arbeitslagerbewegung und Freie Arbeitsdienst, 1920–35* (Opladen: Westdeutscher Verlag, 1988).

[28] See, for example, Karen Hagemann, *Frauenalltag und Männerpolitik: Alltagsleben und gesellschaftliches Handeln von Arbeiterfrauen in der Weimarer Republik* (Bonn: Dietz, 1990). Hagemann concludes that women's expectations of their roles in politics had indeed changed during the 1920s, but barriers remained to full participation. As a result, the realities of activism lagged behind expectations. The disenchantment, which grew out of these unfulfilled expectations, led in Hagemann's view to the support shown by some women for national socialism.

Although women's participation in Weimar's political institutions was limited, understanding the relationship between gender and politics remains critical to an analysis of the republic's collapse. The extent to which women's economic, political, and even personal independence increased after World War I remains debatable; however, the contemporary perception was that a "new woman" reflected the modernity, and for many the decadence, of Weimar. Especially during the Depression, employed women were blamed for "stealing" men's jobs. Although there was little statistical evidence to support this attack, the debate illustrated the unease that met women's growing presence in the public sphere, owing in particular to expanding employment, consumption, and leisure opportunities. Simultaneously, some men's worlds were shrinking. Those men threatened by changing times worked to construct a sphere that reaffirmed their power as men. The unemployed experienced this challenge to male identity particularly acutely. Although today a hyper-masculinity, characterized by the glorification of violence, military camaraderie, and discipline, is associated in German history primarily with the NSDAP and Third Reich, it should be remembered that these qualities were also lauded at the end of the Weimar Republic by the German Communist Party and even by some Social Democrats.

Certainly throughout the Weimar Republic the Social Democratic Party continued to mobilize a great many laborers and offered social services and a sense of community. Prewar traditions relating to strikes, demonstrations, and battles with police in urban settings also remained characteristic of the republic.[29] However, by 1930 working-class culture had also undergone some significant changes. The positions of the SPD and trade unions were fundamentally different. By the end of the 1920s, people in many areas throughout the republic had to defend their loyalty to the SPD. The party no longer had the funds or unqualified mass support to compete successfully on a daily basis with the radical parties for control of the politicized public spaces of the city. The trade unions were compromised by massive unemployment, hostile governing coalitions, and association with the SPD. A new generation of workers was coming of age, and these young people had more than one party to choose from – a choice that became a significant one for many workers by the early 1930s. The youngest workers felt they could no longer depend on the cradle-to-grave support of the organizations of the left. They had

---

[29] Cf. Thomas Lindenberger, *Straßenpolitik. Zur Sozialgeschichte der öffentlichen Ordnung in Berlin, 1900–1914* (Bonn: Dietz, 1995). Lindenberger convincingly shows that local politics and a sense of politicized public space were an increasingly central part of the modern urban landscape years before republicanism "democratized" Berlin's political culture. Lindenberger's masterful study provides new insights into the study of political culture by intertwining a close examination of structural changes in the state, housing, transportation, and industrial development with detailed analysis of individual political events in Berlin's working-class neighborhoods.

few memories of the war years and were confronted with changing cultural norms concerning gender and the role of politics.[30] For those a bit older, growing nationalism, the war experience, and the unfulfilled promise of the 1919 revolution had undermined the romanticism of the pre–World War I workers' movement.

In effect, the faith workers placed in their parties and the state was faltering over a decade, the 1920s, in which new opportunities for people to become politically active were opening up. The monarchy was gone, universal suffrage had been introduced, and the press and political organizations were freer than ever before to speak out. People were seeing more of their surroundings and learning more in this emerging age of mass media. I argue that when Berliners took stock of the assets available to them, collaborated to solve neighborhood problems, and manipulated local organizations to make this process of collaborative problem-solving easier, they were creating a culture of radicalism not defined by the political parties or by opposition to the state. The skills and strategies employed by politicized workers in Berlin were not entirely new, but throughout the Weimar period the opportunities to use them grew while the necessity of local action also increased due to the economic crisis and political instability. However, I argue in this book that these strategies, which often included violence, sometimes had an effect opposite of that intended. Rather than helping these families and communities weather the storm, violence and mistrust among neighbors and alienation from political institutions overpowered the possibility of solidarity and invited the state to introduce measures to halt local radicalism.[31]

There are a number of advantages to situating radical activism within the culture of everyday life, rather than as part of a separate political sphere defined solely by political parties. The parties certainly played a large role in the lives of Berlin's workers, but historians have too readily assumed that local activism reflected ideological conviction and obedience to the wills of party leaders.[32] In particular, seeing radicalism as part of everyday life in

---

[30] Dietmar Petzina, ed., *Fahnen, Fäuste, Körper. Symbolik und Kultur der Arbeiterbewegung* (Essen: Klartext, 1986). See especially the article by Gottfried Korff, "Rote Fahnen und geballte Faust. Zur Symbolik der Arbeiterbewegung in der Weimarer Republik," pp. 27–61.

[31] Two books that come to mind when thinking about local organizing and German political culture, albeit in a middle-class context, are Celia Applegate, *A Nation of Provincials. The German Idea of Heimat* (Berkeley: University of California Press, 1990) and Rudy Koshar, *Social Life, Local Politics and Nazism: Marburg, 1880–1935* (Chapel Hill: University of North Carolina Press, 1986). The connections between political culture and *heimat* are at the center of Alon Confino's, *The Nation as a Local Metaphor: Württemberg, Imperial Germany, and National Memory, 1871–1918* (Chapel Hill: University of North Carolina Press, 1997). Confino attempts to combat the *Sonderweg* theory of German development in the nineteenth century by showing how *heimat* was embraced by the members of the bourgeoisie, allowing them to conceptualize the modern state beyond localism.

[32] See the many studies on the KPD by Hermann Weber, including *Die Wandlung des deutschen Kommunismus: Die Stalinisierung der KPD in der Weimarer Republik*, 2 vols. (Frankfurt

late Weimar Berlin can better capture the diversity of activism, especially the significance of localized violence. Our preoccupation with Weimar violence as a precursor to the brutalities of the Third Reich has obscured its meaning before 1933. This is not to deny that the prevalence of political violence in the pre-1933 period foreshadowed the daily acts of terrorism of Hitler's reign. To the contrary, my point is that to understand how a society could accept state-directed violence, we must better comprehend how political violence first gained local legitimacy.

It is increasingly apparent that this legitimacy was not rooted in premodern traditions championed by the right wing exclusively.[33] Why, then, did some citizens, especially after 1929, resort to physical violence? If they were hoping to claim some sense of stability for themselves, their families, and their communities, rather than meeting specific ideological objectives, what exactly did they hope to achieve? Surely since 1914 there had been little sustained peace or prosperity for many Berliners, and as Thomas Lindenberger has shown in his work on prewar Berlin, much the same can be said for the decades leading up to the outbreak of hostilities. I am, therefore, not talking about the restoration of a lost idealized family intimacy or neighborhood harmony. Instead it is more accurate to speak of attempts to lay claim to basic levels of independence. As Detlev Peukert and others have argued, social disciplining had been around for decades, but this erosion of the division between public and private became much more extensive during and after the war. Intrusion was not limited to the investigators and practitioners of modern social welfare policy but also included expanding cultural mediums, such as the press, film, and radio.

While outside forces were moving into the older neighborhoods and tenements, it should be clear that workers, especially the young, were finding

a. M.: Europäische Verlagsanstalt, 1969), or Siegfried Bahne, *Die KPD und das Ende von Weimar* (Frankfurt a. M.: Campus, 1976). See also the selected essays by Eberhard Kolb in Dieter Langewiesche and Klaus Schönhoven, eds., *Umbrüche deutscher Geschichte* (Munich: Oldenbourg, 1993).

[33] One study of the limits of accepted violence in modern German society is the collection of essays edited by Thomas Lindenberger and Alf Lüdtke, *Physische Gewalt: Studien zur Geschichte der Neuzeit* (Frankfurt a. M.: Suhrkamp, 1995). Violence as part of the historical quest for daily nourishment in Germany is discussed in Manfred Gailus and Heinrich Volkmann, eds., *Der Kampf um das tägliche Brot, 1770–1990* (Opladen: Westdeutscher Verlag, 1994). The classic sociological study of these themes is Charles Tilly, Louise Tilly, and Richard Tilly, *The Rebellious Century, 1830–1930* (Cambridge, MA: Harvard University Press, 1975). Donatella Della Porta has followed Charles Tilly's analysis of violence and social movements with a comparison of Italy and Germany in the post-1945 period. Della Porta, *Social Movements, Political Violence and the State. A Comparative Analysis of Italy and Germany* (Cambridge: Cambridge University Press, 1995). Ute Frevert's work on dueling shows quite emphatically that violence was indeed embedded in a modern bourgeois tradition: *Men of Honour: A Social and Cultural History of the Duel* (Cambridge: Polity Press, 1995).

it increasingly easy and attractive, and oftentimes necessary, to leave their neighborhoods for work and pleasure. Similarly, responses to the presence of outsiders should also not be seen as purely defensive or reactionary. My analysis does not point to a retreat to the private sphere, allowing for the success of national socialism. Instead I see a politicization of large numbers of workers in Berlin and an expansion of the intimacy and ownership once associated with the private to public spaces. By the end of the 1920s, workers in Berlin had raised their expectations as to what they could claim as their own – a legacy of the democratic constitution – and they fought to hold on to these spaces, this independent integration, in a variety of ways, some of them violent. This violence, however, should not be viewed in isolation. Its employment, alongside other methods, constituted a complex engagement with modernity among Berlin's workers.[34]

It is a difficult task to understand how power circulated at the grassroots level, but it should be a high priority for the historian of late Weimar. To what extent did German workers agree with, and to what extent did they reject, what they were told by the leadership of the three parties that sought their support? How did Berlin's workers believe they could effect change in their communities, and how did the radical culture that emerged during the last years of Weimar prepare the ground for an acceptance of Nazism? The following outline presents briefly the details of how I plan to answer these and other questions.

The first chapter examines life in the workers' districts as the Depression begins. In particular, Kreuzberg's Nostiz Street *Kiez* is introduced as one useful example. The centrality of pubs, the social and political uses of courtyards and streets, the intimacy of overcrowded tenements, and the changing relationship between the neighborhoods and the city after 1918 created a situation in which neighborhood autonomy and a sense of location within the "city of millions" had developed. The chapter's second section begins by exploring the expansion and restructuring of the capital in the early part of the decade and the place of the workers' districts within the larger entity. I argue that the growing perception of a city divided between an affluent West End and a poor, radical East side affected political organizing and state surveillance and that the tension between East and West

---

[34] This point is reminiscent of an assertion made with regard to deviant youth behavior since 1945 by the ethnographer Jack Katz in his work on "street elites." Katz defines these elites as "adolescent groups that maintain terrifying dominance in urban areas" (p. 116). He claims, however, that street elites do not have to be urban, impoverished adolescents from ethnic-minority groups, as is often presumed in the study of American gangs. What is essential for this phenomenon, argues Katz "is the existence, in the generational background, of a culture humbled at the prospect of entering modern, rationalized society" (p. 163). His choice of the word "humbled" is particularly apropos for Weimar Berlin. Perhaps the historian's obsession with pro- versus antimodern has foreclosed this option. Jack Katz, *Seductions of Crime: Moral and Sensual Attractions in Doing Evil* (New York: Basic Books, 1988).

intensified the self-sufficient political culture in the workers' neighborhoods, or *Kieze*.

The second chapter investigates the process through which this relative stability began to disintegrate by 1929. The chapter presents two main areas in which the Depression undermined the social and political hierarchies of the neighborhood, as discussed in the preceding chapter. First, the experience of long-term unemployment completely altered the way men and women scheduled their days. Gendered boundaries and roles were altered by joblessness, creating fear and resentment among men who felt "feminized" by their new predicament. Second, generational tension also grew as industrial rationalization and layoffs made it nearly impossible for those leaving school to find apprenticeships or the wage-work, which promised a future among the labor elite. As a result, young people rebelled against their elders' social democratic politics and trade union loyalty. The chapter ends with an analysis of the deadly May 1, 1929, riots between workers and police, which demonstrated the growing instability and reintroduced Berliners to the violence that was to define their capital in the early 1930s. The May riots were equally important as an early example of the failure of the state, the SPD, and the KPD to combat the problems of the day. Berlin's workers were left to seek their own solutions, which tested and ignored the boundaries of institutional politics.

The third chapter turns to the appeals made to Berlin's workers by republican and antirepublican organizations. The first section focuses on the challenges faced by the SPD, Reichsbanner, and others who supported the republic and their attempts to offer attractive alternatives to radicalism. The chapter's second section discusses the attractions of radicalism. Throughout, the chapter provides basic information about the Berlin branches of the three parties and examines the demands the parties and their organizations made on their supporters. Specifically, I compare republican, proletarian, and Nazi discipline and demonstrate how the parties attempted to use discipline to generate the daily commitment needed to maintain the republic, fight the revolution, or build the Third Reich.

In the fourth chapter the difficulties encountered by the parties at the grassroots are analyzed. I argue that, contrary to the messages of discipline and authority put out by political institutions, local independence and initiative increased during this period. Financial shortages and rapid membership growth hindered the structural efficiency of the KPD and NSDAP. More importantly, people were using their local party structures to confront neighborhood issues and problems rather than to advance the grand visions outlined in the party programs. The very nature of the radicalism advocated by the parties' leaders stressed individual initiative, and people gladly responded with their own brands of self-help. Conflict arose, however, between the parties and their supporters when neighborhood activism failed to heed the limits of party policies and regulations. Finally, denunciation is explored in depth, as an example of local initiative. Informing political leaders, the police, and the general public of others' political activities or "crimes" against neighbors became a common strategy for regulating behavior. Through denunciation we can learn about the ways people understood the political process, their relationship with their parties, and with their neighbors.

In the last chapter I explore the street violence, which separated these years from Weimar's first decade. In the first section, I present the anatomy of street violence: common causes, sites, and steps from start to finish. Violent activism was not uncontrolled chaos. Nor was it ideologically based compliance with party leaders' commands. Instead, physical confrontation erupted over local moral and economic conflicts and was often an attempt to secure territorial supremacy or demonstrate masculine authority. The chapter's second section focuses on the ways street violence was rationalized by participants and the city's judicial authorities. Grassroots violence was ordered by a highly structured set of rules and expectations, which determined who could participate as well as the limits of aggression. Welfare workers, police, prosecutors, and judges had their own explanations for radicalism, but in many ways they too accepted the discourse that regulated violence on the street.

My primary aim throughout is to investigate the connections between local needs, radicalism, and the end of the first German republic. My analysis has found that at the neighborhood level during the Depression grassroots politics became increasingly localized in setting and aim and personalized in rhetoric and strategy. I argue that it was primarily this development, which in the end pitted neighbors against each other and cut the ties between Berliners and their social and political institutions, undermining the very sense of community needed to confront the mounting economic and social crises. This point is an important intervention because it adds to our understanding of why such a powerful workers' movement – perhaps the strongest in Europe – so easily succumbed to, and in some cases even supported, Hitler's assumption of power in 1933. The prevailing argument is that Hitler stepped into a political vacuum and provided what the public craved, a reinvigorated political sphere. This book offers another interpretation. I show that late Weimar Berlin was in fact a highly politicized society, in which the smallest daily decisions had political implications: where to shop, who to befriend, and what neighborhood to live in. Without functioning political institutions, at either the state or local level, to shape political discourse, some Berliners grew weary of the constant inundation of political decisions, which were much more complicated than simply choosing between "Red" and "Brown." As a result, a regime that promised order through the containment of politics at the executive level, rather than critical engagement at the street level, appeared an attractive alternative.

Such an interpretation of the acceptance of a Nazi state allows for speculation about the new regime. We have to question whether the picture of an enthusiastic populace mobilized behind the swastika represents a politicized people. Perhaps the cause for enthusiasm, at least until the onset of war, had more to do with the deadening of public life, in terms of decision making, debate, and conflict, than with the construction of an energized political culture.[35] The conundrum we are faced with, therefore, in understanding the transition from republic to Nazi dictatorship is not how government leaders could choose such a solution to crisis or whether such a decision was inevitable under the pressures of structural collapse. Instead, we should ask under what conditions a people can accept political anonymity over engagement. The dangers of this transformation became frighteningly apparent as soon as power was invested in Adolf Hitler.

[35] Contrary to previous assumptions, some literature on the Third Reich stresses that the private sphere was in fact a primary site for state intervention, in terms of racist natalist policies. See, for example, Gisela Bock, *Zwangssterilisation im Nationalsozialismus: Studien zur Rassenpolitik und Frauenpolitik* (Opladen: Westdeutscher Verlag, 1986). For a shorter articulation of Bock's position in English, see "Antinatalism, Maternity and Paternity in National Socialist Racism" in Gisela Bock and Pat Thane, eds., *Maternity and Gender Policies: Women and the Rise of the European Welfare States, 1880s–1950s* (London: Routledge, 1991), pp. 233–55.

1

Neighborhoods and Metropolis

In 1932 the American reporter H. R. Knickerbocker toured Berlin to find out why Germany was teetering on the verge of civil war. He described a city divided into opposing camps: rich and poor, Communist and Nazi, decadent and hard working. He spent time in one of the swanky nightclubs in the West End, where champagne continued to flow throughout the deepest months of the Depression, and he spent a night with a homeless man in an abandoned building. He met a Communist couple who remained ardent believers in the party and revolution, and he went to a Nazi rally to hear about the attractions of the promised Third Reich.[1] There is no doubt that Knickerbocker's description of a city torn into pieces is in many ways accurate. It illustrates, in a very real sense, the social inequality made conspicuous by the Depression and the lack of political consensus which made the republic's demise so intense.

Before we can understand the complexities of the republic's collapse, however, there is much more we need to know about its capital.[2] Our historical imagination, like Knickerbocker's portrayal, often only has space for the extremes. Berlin in the Weimar period was a city of culture: expressionist film, avant-garde theater, and modern design. In addition to Knickerbocker, Berlin also captivated Germany's artists: Becher, Döblin, and Ruttmann, to

---

[1] H. R. Knickerbocker, *The German Crisis* (New York: Farrar & Rinehart, 1932a). The German translation appeared as *Deutschland so oder so?* (Berlin: Rowohlt, 1932b). The ironic thing about Knickerbocker's book is that his main motivation was to investigate the security of American investments in the struggling democracy rather than to evaluate the potential for human losses through dictatorship or war. Moreover, this book is a telling example of the overriding anticommunism of many outside observers and their misplaced belief that if Hitler should come to power, the worst likely consequence was that his administration would quickly collapse and a Soviet-style Germany would emerge. For an example, see pages 46–7.

[2] The reunification of Germany, and the rebuilding of Berlin as its capital, has fostered a great interest in Berlin among historians and others. For a recent comprehensive study of the city, see Alexandra Richie, *Faust's Metropolis: A History of Berlin* (New York: Carroll and Graf, 1998). For an analysis of the difficulties of constructing a democratic capital in Berlin, see Michael Z. Wise, *Capital Dilemma: Germany's Search for a New Architecture of Democracy* (New York: Princeton Architectural Press, 1998). Brian Ladd also offers a compelling analysis of how Berlin's landmarks can help us unravel the city's past in *Ghosts of Berlin. Confronting German History in the Urban Landscape* (Chicago: University of Chicago Press, 1997).

name a few. It was a city of consumerism symbolized by the grand department stores Tietz, Wertheim, and KaDeWe. For the early 1930s, our minds also imagine a Berlin of extreme poverty and misery: long unemployment lines, squalid apartments, and political discord.[3] But how do these contrasting images of Berlin fit together? In terms of the city's political culture, and radical politics in particular, we must begin to answer this question by looking in the homes of Berliners and at the street corners. Knickerbocker made certain to get this view of Berlin. The political parties vying for workers' support worked feverishly to bring structure and organization to neighborhood life. The state too attempted to respond locally to the rejection of republicanism and the support for radicalism bubbling up in the urban centers. After January 30, 1933, Hitler tried his hand at extending control to all corners of the city, using information culled from the past government's files on left-wing activists to round up most of Berlin's opposition leaders. This chapter will also focus on the neighborhoods – their physical structure and significance within the "city of millions" – in order to demonstrate what late Weimar contemporaries knew: the collapse of the republic began here.

THE KIEZ AND COMMUNITY IDENTITY

Though most of the buildings in the workers' neighborhoods of central Berlin had been constructed in the third quarter of the nineteenth century, by 1930 much had changed. As explained in one *AIZ* article titled "The Face of the Street": "Who thought decades ago about traffic rules, ... automatic electric traffic lights? No one.... Not only has this outer picture of the city changed from the ground up over the years, but also the speed at which life on the streets runs."[4] The workers' neighborhoods in the city center had become crowded by the infrastructure of modern public transportation, the competition of motorized vehicles, and a vast influx of new residents over the preceding decades. As feared by those who investigated the quality of life in Berlin's tenement communities in the early 1930s, the close quarters and poor conditions of many of the old buildings contributed to a sense of intimacy among neighbors. Such familiarity not only had the potential to foster solidarity, it also bred tension and violence. For better or worse, workers in Berlin knew their neighbors and their neighborhoods quite closely. This process of neighborhood identification had increased significantly in the postwar years, primarily because the turnover rates for residency dropped dramatically. The big wave of migration to Germany's large cities that accompanied

---

[3] In the nineteenth and twentieth centuries, Berlin has had both its defenders and detractors. For an overview of how writers have represented Berlin since the mid-nineteenth century, see Andrew Lees, "Berlin and Modern Urbanity in German Discourse, 1845–1945" in *Journal of Urban History* (Vol. 17, No. 2, 1991), pp. 153–80.

[4] *AIZ*, "Gesichter der Strasse" (Vol. 7, Nr. 4), 1928, p. 4.

industrialization was interrupted by World War I and never regained its intensity.[5] Steve Hochstadt argues in his study of German mobility patterns that the series of peaks in migration rates experienced in the two decades preceding the war was repeated in the postwar period but at "far lower rates." Economic conditions, however, still determined the peaks and valleys. The economic stability of the mid-1920s encouraged more to try their luck in the cities than during the inflationary crisis of the early 1920s, but then the crash of 1929 ushered in another decline. In fact, the statistics presented by Hochstadt help demonstrate the severity of the Depression. The rate of migration took four years to recover from the 30 percent drop suffered in 1929, while in prewar downturns Germans had needed only half that time to get back on the roads.[6]

Overall, therefore, after 1918 – and especially after 1929 – we have fewer newcomers to Berlin, and as residential roots took hold, a sense of neighborhood loyalty also developed. In Kreuzberg, for example, both the most populous and most thickly settled district in 1920, it was clear that the vast influx of new residents had ended with the war. In 1910 there were more than 420,000 inhabitants. To this day, this peak has not been reached again. The census of 1925 counted 377,253 living in Kreuzberg. Though the numbers climbed slowly in the years of Weimar stability, they sank continuously during the Depression, hitting a low of 339,198 in 1933.[7] In some cases, workers chose not to refer to their neighborhoods by the German equivalent, *Nachbarschaft*, but by the more intimate and politically charged term, *Kiez*.[8] The Kiez was not a formal designation on maps of Berlin, and defining it simply as a small neighborhood does not do justice to the fluidity of the concept or its political significance. There were no official boundaries

[5] Berlin had the third largest urban population in Europe by 1800, with 200,000 inhabitants. By the time it became the capital of the united German Reich in 1871, the population reached just over 800,000. However, in the 1870s only 40 percent of the city's dwellers had been born in Berlin. Of those moving into the city, over one-third came from the surrounding Brandenburg province, with those of working age especially well represented among the new arrivals. One generation later, at the turn of the century, Berlin's population had more than doubled to 1.9 million. Thomas Lindenberger, *Straßenpolitik. Zur Sozialgeschichte der öffentlichen Ordnung in Berlin, 1900–1914* (Bonn: Dietz, 1995), p. 36.

[6] Steve Hochstadt, *Mobility and Modernity: Migration in Germany, 1820–1989* (Ann Arbor: University of Michigan Press, 1999), pp. 220–1. The aggregated immigration rates discussed here are compiled from cities with over 50,000 inhabitants. See Fig. 17, p. 220.

[7] Heinrich Kaak, *Geschichte der Berliner Verwaltungsbezirke, Band 2: Kreuzberg* (Berlin: Colloquium Verlag, 1988), pp. 84, 87–8. For full population statistics for all districts, see Hauptamt für Statistik, ed., *Berlin in Zahlen* (Berlin: Berlin Kulturbuchverlag, 1947), pp. 52–3. See also the statistical appendix by Andreas Splanemann in Otto Büsch and Wolfgang Haus, *Berlin als Hauptstadt der Weimarer Republik, 1919–1933* (Berlin: de Gruyter, 1987), pp. 394–8.

[8] In the 1873 Grimm brothers' dictionary, the word "Kiez" is described as "a strange old word from northeastern Germany" meaning "where fishermen lived together." Jacob Grimm and Wilhelm Grimm, *Deutsches Wörterbuch* (Leipzig: S. Hirzel, 1873), pp. 699–700.

to these units, and often both residents and outsiders were likely to hold a number of competing visions of what exactly constituted the Kiez. Where a strong Kiez identity existed, housing, political allegiances, and community landmarks united the inhabitants – though even these basic factors varied from Kiez to Kiez. Nonetheless, there is evidence that a separate sense of community existed at this level, and that these neighborhoods had their own political and social hierarchies, rules of behavior, and sense of communal property or "turf."

In making sense of the social and political power relations of the Kiez, a helpful reference is the work by Alf Lüdtke on industrial culture in the Kaiserreich. Lüdtke has argued that within the factory, worker-constructed power structures and rules of behavior existed alongside the hierarchies and discipline implemented by the employers and trade unions. As one might expect, employees took unauthorized coffee breaks and made other attempts to avoid discipline imposed from above. These worker-generated hierarchies were regulated by physical contact, even violence, and meant that workers did not always cooperate with each other but also created strategies to ensure their own individual survival and success (*Eigensinn*).[9]

To some extent, shop floor hierarchies and codes of conduct were reflected in Kiez power structures. Gender and generational boundaries had been confirmed by decades of labor relations. But rationalized production methods, introduced on a large scale in the mid-1920s, altered relations among workers and changed the rates at which labor steps were performed. As production became simplified, unskilled and female laborers, who received lower wages, became more prevalent in factories. Some skilled workers, once the elite of industry, worried about the stability of their positions even before the Depression hit. Increased expectations about the speed of manufacturing added

---

[9] Alf Lüdtke, "Cash, Coffee-Breaks, Horseplay: *Eigensinn* and Politics among Factory Workers in Germany circa 1900" in Michael Hanagan and Charles Stephenson, eds., *Confrontation, Class Consciousness and the Labor Process. Studies in Proletarian Class Formation* (New York: Westport Press, 1986), pp. 64–95. For further explanation of Alf Lüdtke's use of the concept *Eigensinn*, see also Alf Lüdtke, *Eigen-Sinn. Fabrikalltag, Arbeitererfahrungen und Politik vom Kaiserreich bis in den Faschismus* (Hamburg: Ergebnisse Verlag, 1993) and his edited collection, *The History of Everyday Life: Reconstructing Historical Experiences and Ways of Life*, William Templer, trans. (Princeton, NJ: Princeton University Press, 1995), especially his introduction to the volume. On *Alltagsgeschichte* more generally see also Geoff Eley, "Labor History, Social History, *Alltagsgeschichte*: Experience, Culture, and the Politics of the Everyday – A New Direction for German Social History?" in *Journal of Modern History* (Vol. 61, No. 2, 1989), pp. 297–343. Erich Fromm's 1929 sociological study of the German working class found that 50 percent of those questioned admitted that they refused to lend money or objects to their friends. This example may seem inconsequential, but it lends credence to Lüdtke's findings about shop floor self-interest and forces historians to rethink their understanding of solidarity among Weimar's industrial workers. See Erich Fromm, *The Working Class in Weimar Germany: A Psychological and Sociological Study* (Oxford: Berg, 1984; original edition 1929), pp. 187–92.

stress to workers' lives and removed elements of craftsmanship. Tensions caused by rationalization were inevitably carried home at night, contributing to the sense of upheaval in these communities by the end of the 1920s.[10] For some, it meant that positions of power in the family and neighborhood had to be defended at all costs. For others, the changing industrial situation meant that challenges to hierarchy could be waged elsewhere. In similar ways to those described by Lüdtke with regard to shop floor *Eigensinn*, men and women in Berlin's neighborhoods acted on their own behalf and on what they perceived to be the interests of their Kieze. These interests ranged from securing material necessities and defending community territory to achieving a sense of local autonomy.

In addition to the political activism characteristic of the Kiez, a second common feature was the significance of a street, a square, or a transportation station as focal point for the Kiez. The traffic through these focal points fostered contact between neighbors, and a square or station could serve as a landmark and meeting place. Although Berlin had become a model for metropolitan public transportation by 1929, its neighborhoods, especially the older ones in the city center, functioned on their own. This self-sufficiency was challenged, however, by the modernization of the city. Growing transportation networks meant that neighborhood boundaries were increasingly broached by commuters and pleasure seekers, in that outsiders – including members of the middle classes – passed through Berlin's workers' districts on a regular basis.

As neighborhood borders became increasingly porous and contested, landmarks took on greater significance. In some cases, a centrally located factory still served as the Kiez focal point, employing large numbers of those living in its shadows.[11] The importance of the common workplace was especially significant for workers' enclaves within middle-class districts. It was often the growth of an industrial site that had brought these workers to the district, cramming them into workers' housing. A factory provided much more to its employees than wages; camaraderie and a location for party and trade

---

[10] The connection between the spread of industrial rationalization and the growth of European Communist parties is likely more significant than usually cited. Eric Weitz has argued, for example, that the development of mass Communist parties in Germany, France, and Italy corresponded to the respective periods of industrial rationalization in the three countries. See Eric D. Weitz, *Popular Communism: Political Strategies and Social Histories in the Formation of the German, French and Italian Communist Parties, 1919–1948* (Ithaca, NY: Cornell University Press, 1992).

[11] Two monographs that discuss labor practices in Weimar-era industry as well as the instability and social impact of factory life are Heidrun Homburg's study of Siemens, *Rationalisierung und Industriearbeit. Arbeitsmarkt–Management–Arbeiterschaft im Siemens-Konzern Berlin 1900–1939* (Berlin: Haude and Spener, 1991) and Wolfgang Zollitsch, *Arbeiter zwischen Weltwirtschaftskrise und Nationalsozialismus* (Göttingen: Vandenhoeck & Ruprecht, 1990). See also Dagmar Reese, ed. *Rationale Beziehungen? Geschlechterverhältnisse im Rationalisierungsprozess* (Frankfurt a. M.: Suhrkamp, 1993).

union activities were equally important. The landmarks or borders of the Kiez were not always as dramatic as a towering industrial complex around which apartment buildings, pubs, and shops took root. Borders could be as simple as the railway line that physically separated one neighborhood from its surroundings; and landmarks could have specific local meaning to the inhabitants: a market place, parade ground, historical monument, or pub.

Throughout this study, the Kiez around Kreuzberg's Nostizstraße will serve as the chief example of this basic social and political unit and illustrate how the culture of radicalism within Berlin's workers' neighborhoods was central to the republic's demise. The Nostizstraße Kiez, located in the western half of the most populous and most thickly settled district in the city, was a Berlin stronghold for communism in the 1920s and early 1930s (Figures 1 and 2). Not everyone who lived in the neighborhood voted for the KPD, but a large enough percentage of residents were Communist to have their own KPD youth groups, paramilitary units, and street cells.[12] There were also a handful of explicitly Communist pubs in the area, which were monitored closely by the police because of the alleged traitorous intentions of the patrons. The Nostizstraße Kiez was also the location of a number of incidents of political violence in the final years of the republic. Nostiz and the surrounding residential streets, therefore, developed a reputation as one of the "Reddest" neighborhoods in Berlin. The neighborhood's reputation as a self-contained political and social unit was even well known enough to provide the setting for the 1932 novel *Kämpfende Jugend* by Walter Schönstedt.[13] Though the popularity of the novel further solidified the image of the Kiez, some have criticized the singularity of Schönstedt's depiction of Nostiz as the Communist *Hochburg*, or fortress. Nonetheless, his fictional account is useful for its descriptions of the neighborhood through the eyes of members of the Communist milieu.

In the example of Kreuzberg's Nostiz-area Kiez, a number of physical elements served to punctuate public life and the semiprivate existence of its

---

[12] The number of actual party members is quite small. The KPD counted about two thousand Kreuzberg residents on its rolls, and about sixty-five hundred carried SPD party membership. In the November 1932 Reichstag election, the KPD in Kreuzberg as a whole received 34.5 percent of the vote, followed next by the Social Democrats with 24.2 percent. The NSDAP came in third with 23.7 percent, down from the peak of 26.6 percent in July. For party membership information, see Jörg Klitscher, "Die KPD in Berlin-Kreuzberg Während der Weimarer Republik" (unpublished manuscript, 1995), p. 24. For voting statistics, see Figures 6 and 7 in this volume.

[13] Walter Schönstedt, *Kämpfende Jugend* (Berlin: Oberbaumverlag, 1972; original edition, Berlin: Internationalen-Arbeiter Verlag, 1932). Schönstedt grew up in the Nostiz neighborhood and was active as a young man in some of the Communist organizations he wrote about. The novel was originally published as part of the series "Der Rote 1-Mark Roman." For information on this series, see Hanno Möbius, "Der Rote Eine-Mark-Roman" in *Archiv für Sozialgeschichte* (Vol. 14, 1974), pp. 157–71.

inhabitants.[14] The Nostizstraße was and is still today situated in the western, more affluent end of Kreuzberg. Before World War I, this area of the city was home to civil servants, former military officers, other members of the middle classes, and even its share of intellectuals including Theodore Fontane.[15] Amid this prosperous section, the streets around Nostiz were inhabited primarily by workers. One resident remembered that by 1900 the neighborhood already had a reputation as a tough area. In part, this reputation came from the "*Frauenkneipe . . .* a pub with *lady-waitstaff,* prostitutes, like on Friedrichstraße, but only the crummiest of the bunch."[16] The number of workers in the western half of the district increased dramatically after 1918, but these few blocks remained western Kreuzberg's poorest. Its most politically active segment ran from Gneisenau in the north to Arndt in the south, even though the street was a bit longer, with Belle-Alliance and Zossener roughly providing the eastern and western boundaries.

At the center of this area was the Nostizstraße itself, a narrow commercial and residential street named in 1865 on the fiftieth anniversary of the Battle of Waterloo after the General Graf August von Nostitz (1777–1866). By 1930 it had become crowded by five-story apartment buildings erected largely between 1864 and 1878, with small shops and pubs competing with apartments at the ground floor and basement level. Passing from the street through an archway of a typical building, a person reached successive courtyards surrounded by more apartments, workshops, and commercial space. As in the rest of the city, the rent and size of the apartments generally decreased as one proceeded further back from the street and further up from the ground floor, though the disparity in the size and quality diminished through the Depression. During these years many of the large, four-room apartments in the street-facing section of the large houses stood empty until owners split them into two smaller dwellings to appeal to the decreasing incomes of the tenants.[17] Even in the 1930s, the residents above the courtyards faced the potential annoyance of living above cow stalls. On Nostiz Street alone, there

---

[14] Michael Haben describes the intimacy of the neigborhood as a "half-open, half-closed public" in " 'Die waren so unter sich': Über Kneipen, Vereine und Politik in Berlin Kreuzberg" in Karl-Heinz Fiebig et al., eds., *Kreuzberger Mischung: Die innerstädtische Verflechtung von Architektur, Kultur und Gewerbe* (Berlin: Äesthetik und Kommunikation, 1984), p. 242.

[15] Gerhard König, *Berlin – Kreuzberg und seine Nostizstraße* (Berlin: Druckerei der pbw, no date), p. 8.

[16] Lothar Uebel, "Verkehrslokale und andere Budiken" in Geschichtskreis Kreuzberg, ed., *Nostitzritze. Ein Straße in Kreuzberg* (Berlin: Gericke, 1992), p. 44.

[17] Between 1925 and 1944, only 186 new apartments were built in Kreuzberg. The remaining of the close to 10,000 new dwellings that appear in this period came from cutting up preexisting large apartments. Splitting the larger apartments was done usually by building a dividing wall through the long *Berliner Zimmer.* With this change, the once-grand parlor became a small kitchen and a windowless room. Kaak, *Geschichte* (1988), p. 93. See also Cornelia Ganz, "Wohnen hinter Stuckfassaden" in Geschichtskreis Kreuzberg, ed., *Nostitzritze. Ein Straße in Kreuzberg* (Berlin: Gericke, 1992), p. 9.

were three courtyard dairies that provided milk, cheese, and butter to the neighbors. Living amongst livestock, naturally, meant the sound and smell of the animals was a constant presence – not to mention the hygienic concerns.[18] To today's reader, however, this option may sound better than living at number sixteen Nostiz, the address of the local horse butcher. The business had prospered within this poorer community since 1891. By the end of the Weimar Republic, a man named Muthow was proprietor. His *Pferdebouletten*, "warm from the pan, ten cents a piece," were a popular snack among young people in the neighborhood, even though munching on the unseemly black horseburgers left one vulnerable to the jokes of friends. The odor was also quite memorable, and even made its way into the Schönstedt novel. When the character Emil returns to the neighborhood after time away he remarks: "Everything was as before, so old and gray, the same smell hung in the air, it even still smelled like Pferdebouletten."[19]

What made this street the heart of the Kiez, however, was its strong KPD representation. Walter Lorenz owned the most notorious Communist bar in the Kiez also at 16 Nostizstraße. It was one of seven pubs along this barely 500-meter-long street, but as the official hangout for the local Communist groups and the site of a number of brawls and police searches, this bar was essential to the culture of the Kiez.[20] Lorenz, or Othello, as he was known to his radical regulars, shows up by name in Schönstedt's novel as a supportive yet disciplining father figure for the young Communists. Much more will be said about the political importance of pubs, including this one, throughout this study, but here it is important to remark briefly on the social function of these neighborhood institutions. There were three types of drinking establishments all with different roles to play, not counting other entertainment spots, such as dance halls or full-service restaurants. First, we have the larger taverns, which clung to the corners of main thoroughfares, like Gneisenau, because they counted on heavy traffic to fill their tables. The side streets were

---

[18] Lothar Uebel, "Milch vom Hinterhof" in Geschichtskreis Kreuzberg, ed., *Nostitzritze. Ein Straße in Kreuzberg* (Berlin: Gericke, 1992), pp. 24–30. In 1939 there was an outbreak of foot and mouth disease in Berlin, which led to the closing of at least two Kreuzberg dairies.

[19] Fritz Schilde and Lothar Uebel, "Fleisch vom Ross" in Geschichtskreis Kreuzberg, ed., *Nostitzritze. Ein Straße in Kreuzberg*, (Berlin: Gericke, 1992), pp. 34–6. In 1930 there were still ninety members of the Berlin horse butchers' association. See further, Schönstedt, *Kämpfende Jugend* (1972), p. 29.

[20] Toward the end of 1931, after a routine check on the status of the bar, the police reported that Lorenz had a falling out with the local Communists and no longer planned to associate his bar with the party. At first the police were suspicious that the close ties between Lorenz and the KPD had been broken, but on finding the bust of Lenin and red decorations removed from the interior, they were convinced. The unwanted KPD supporters quickly found a home at Lipinski's pub at 63 Nostizstraße. There was even a rumor that Lorenz subsequently allowed the growing SA to hold its functions at his pub, but the owner denied the accusation. See BLHA, Rep. 30, Berlin C, Title 95, Sektion 9, Nr. 164, Report from 112th police station Berlin, August 4, 1931.

home to the *Familienkneipen* (family pubs) and catered to a regular clientele of neighborhood residents. These pubs often had rooms for the private meetings of clubs. Finally, the political pubs were known also for their local customer base, but the majority of the regulars, like those who considered Walter Lorenz as "their" barkeep, were connected to a political association or party that used the pub as its main meeting site. This drinking culture was not new to German workers, of course, but the sort of intimate climate that persisted and intensified in the family and party pubs is important for our understanding of the neighborhood and radicalism in this era. As Thomas Haben concludes from his oral interviews with Kreuzberg residents during this era: "The public space of the pub [*Kneipenöffentlichkeit*] was closed to the outside and at the same time open for members of the neighborhood. Under these conditions, a type of communication and discussion developed, which could integrate the entire spectrum of guests and attract the attention of all. Experiences, exciting events, news, and practical jokes could be told, without offense being taken, even if outsiders were present."[21]

Nostizstraße itself, however, was only one important landmark. Three blocks to the east was a small square, Marheinekeplatz, which included a market hall dating from the 1880s.[22] The inhabitants of the immediate area shopped there for food and other household items numerous times during the week. The square also served as a meeting place, and the market hall included a pub. The pub was unusual in that for a while it served no alcohol, and as such was a gathering place for health-conscious workers, including those in the Fichte sports club that met here regularly. Inside the market hall, news circulated among neighbors, especially women, and political brochures of all types (legal and illegal) passed from hand to hand [Plate 1]. To the southwest, Viktoriapark served as a recreational area for the workers of the neighborhood, especially in the summer, and here too one could enjoy a beer in the park's *Biergarten*. One of the most popular of the park's offerings, especially among young adults, was the *Rummel* (Fortuna amusement park).

---

[21] Haben, "'Die waren so unter sich'" (1984), p. 246. In his study of tavern violence in New York City at the beginning of the nineteenth century, Michael Kaplan goes so far as to single out pubs as "the communal institutions... in which young native-born and immigrant working-class men constructed their social identities." See Michael Kaplan, "New York City Tavern Violence and the Creation of a Working-Class Male Identity" in *Journal of the Early Republic* (Vol. 15, Winter 1995), p. 601.

[22] The market at Marheinekeplatz was built in the 1880s as a part of a city-wide plan to construct fourteen small market halls to replace the weekly outdoor markets that supplied fresh food to the urban population. See Manfred Stürzbecher, "Stadthygiene" in J. Boberg, T. Fichter, and E. Gillen, eds., *Exerzierfeld der Moderne* (Munich: C. H. Beck, 1984), pp. 168–9. In 1929, Mayor Gustav Böß reported that the city's central and auxiliary market system had become overburdened and needed continued expansion. See Böß, *Berlin von Heute* (Berlin: Gsellius, 1929), pp. 97–101. This Kreuzberg market still serves today both as a landmark for the Kiez, which is now heavily populated by Turkish families, and as one of the last remaining nineteenth-century indoor markets in the city.

Plate 1. Two women share some news outside a market. Photo by Friedrich Seidenstücker, 1929. Source: © Bildarchiv Preussischer Kulturbesitz, 2003.

Unlike the theaters, the *Rummel* had no entrance fee. So it was the perfect place for watching people and meeting friends even once the Depression struck. We can see the importance of this amusement park in its inclusion in Schönstedt's novel and Kästner's *Fabian*. It had all of the typical amusement park offerings, but the frequency at which locals attended meant that, as one former patron explained later in an interview: "one recognized the faces of most of the visitors." He remembered that his friends all spoke regularly with the performers and knew the difficulties faced by these "global sensations." Clearly the young people of the area were at home here, and for them "as a meeting place the *Rummel* was irreplaceable."[23] A sure sign that the *Rummel* was a beloved hangout for local young people was the series of unsuccessful attempts made by the city's family welfare administrators to have it shut down on account of its "corrupting" influence.[24]

On the edge of the park, the Schultheiss brewery employed many of the local workers.[25] Though unemployment was high in this neighborhood during the Depression, the tradition of common employment at the brewery helped to build a sense of unity. Finally, the main thoroughfare through the Kiez, Gneisenau Street, was serviced by an electric tram and by underground trains beginning in 1924, the stations of which served as meeting points and landmarks. Gneisenau was also significant in the life of the Kiez because it was a boundary to the north, separating the Nostiz-area Communists from the growing Nazi contingent only a few blocks away around Urban Street.

These physical landmarks were also frequently the sites of conflict in Berlin's political struggle because they served as the public heart of the Kiez. Residents were humiliated if "their" market, pub, street, or square was overtaken in some manner by members of a rival neighborhood; this kind of defeat demonstrated a lack of political discipline and Kiez solidarity. When the SA marched across Gneisenau, for example, they were consistently met by an angry crowd of inhabitants from the Nostizstraße area.[26] Forays like this one into a neighboring, antagonistic Kiez demonstrated bravery and commitment but could also be very dangerous. When successful, however, invading a rival Kiez allowed for public posturing by the aggressors. For example, even though crowds of inhabitants were prepared to meet a large marching

[23] König, *Berlin* (no date), pp. 22–3.

[24] Excerpts from Alwin Jabs's oral interview are from Werner Tammen and Lothar Uebel, "Freizeit im Kiez" in Kunstamt Kreuzberg, ed., *Kreuzberg 1933. Ein Bezirk erinnert sich* (Berlin: Dürschlag, 1983), p. 71.

[25] Beer consumption decreased during the Depression and eventually the brewery's restaurant and beer garden were closed. See Hasso Spode, "Die Schultheiss-Brauerei auf dem Kreuzberg" in Helmut Engel, Stefi Jersch-Wenzel, and Wilhelm Treue, eds., *Geschichtslandschaft Berlin. Orte und Ereignisse, Band 5: Kreuzberg* (Berlin: Nicolai, 1994), pp. 399–413.

[26] About sixty SA men were turned back from entering Nostiz by Kiez residents in October 1932: "SA-Sturm auf die rote Nostizstraße misglückt," in *RF*, October 27, 1932.

contingent of Hitler Youth in Neukölln in December 1930, the NSDAP was quick to emphasize the inability of the neighborhood to repel their advance. A newspaper article following the demonstration taunted the "poor KPD."[27] Sometimes less dramatic methods were employed to challenge the authority of Kiez turf: a midnight plan to tear down the election posters of an opposing political group in favor of one's own, only to have this propaganda covered over the following day, was a frequent strategy in the ongoing struggle to appear strongest in the larger community.[28] Once residents stepped outside their individual dwellings, therefore, they were immersed in the life of the Kiez. What outsiders would count as public space, from tenement courtyards to sidewalks, market halls, transportation stations, and parks, had been turned into "commons areas," belonging to all residents.[29] What became critical during the Depression, however, was that while workers recognized the need to rely on neighborhood culture to weather the crisis, many felt this way of life was under threat.

Though oral histories of those who lived in the Nostiz area offer support for the assertion that a community spirit reigned, to the middle-class observer the intimacy of the Kiez signaled chaos and misery. Many nonresidents feared the spread of dangerous Red politics, which they believed was inextricably linked to the living conditions of the Kieze. However, these neighborhoods were not isolated communities. There were numerous outsiders who had daily business in the Kieze, from factory managers to welfare workers and passengers on public transportation. In fact, the presence of nonresidents was increasing. Among all outsiders, the uniformed police remained the most visible representatives of state, that is, non-Kiez, authority. As the most identifiable group, the growing police presence in these neighborhoods throughout the 1920s and into the 1930s further provoked Kiez independence and radicalism. Even a man affiliated with no political party, like Fallada's Pinneberg, might see the representatives of the state as an intrusive and privileged group: "Pinneberg had nothing against the police, . . . but he could not help feeling that they looked irritatingly well-fed and clothed, and

---

[27] *VB*, "Hitler-Jugend erobert das rote Neukölln," Nr. 288, December 4, 1930.

[28] For visual illustrations and analysis of the extent of the propaganda war that was waged in Berlin toward the end of the republic, see Gerhard Paul, "Krieg der Symbole. Formen und Inhalte des symbolpublizistischen Bürgerkriegs 1932" in Diethart Kerbs and Henrich Stahr, eds., *Berlin 1932. Das letzte Jahr der Weimarer Republik* (Berlin: Hentrich, 1992) and Gerhard Paul, *Aufstand der Bilder: Die NS-Propaganda vor 1933* (Bonn: Dietz, 1990).

[29] Though the subject of his case study, African-American alley communities in Washington DC, is very different from the one presented here, James Borchert makes claims similar to mine with regard to the sense of community and level of satisfaction among impoverished and racially oppressed residents of the American capital. See James Borchert, *Alley Life in Washington: Family, Community, Religion, and Folklife in the City, 1850–1970* (Urbana: University of Illinois, 1980), p. 131.

behaved, too, in rather a provocative way. They walked among the public like teachers among school-children during the play interval: – Behave properly, or – !"[30]

The Berlin *Schutzpolizei* also played the most direct role in the day-to-day efforts to control radicalism and, for their efforts, received harsh criticism from all sides. The mandate given to the Berlin *Schutzpolizei*, however, was not an easy one. Although workers were right to criticize the force for its often brutal and unfair treatment of the left, the police did face twenty-four-hour shifts and great resistance at times from activists. Even those not directly involved in battles with police would often come to the aid of their activist neighbors by assisting in their getaways, pelting police with debris from their apartment windows, or simply refusing to cooperate with criminal investigations. Most historians who have studied the Prussian *Schutzpolizei* have stressed the steps taken during the Weimar Republic to modernize the internal bureaucratic structure and technological capabilities of the force.[31] Berlin's department too touted its new weapons in the fight against crime, while the radical workers' press took critical aim at what they viewed as costly expenditures that did not protect but instead prepared the state for the "second civil war" against the "domestic enemy," the working class.[32] We should not, however, exaggerate the efficiency of the Berlin police. In fact, their often-inadequate response to neighborhood radicalism frustrated Berliners precisely because the capital was thought to possess such a modern and effective force. Even in the police district Alexanderplatz, site of *Schutzpolizei* headquarters and base for the protection of city hall and other political hotspots, their ability to react quickly was often lacking. During crises police telephone systems were constantly overloaded, leading to misinformation and delayed response.[33] On the outskirts of town, conditions were dismal. Small police stations were sometimes a mile or two from the local assembly hall where political brawls would break out. If backup support was needed during the evening to aid the men covering the assembly, it could take an hour to retrieve others, who often had to walk to the scene.

[30] Hans Fallada, *Little Man, What Now?* Eric Sutton, trans. (Chicago: Academy Chicago Publishers, 1992), p. 367.
[31] While Richard Bessel questions the accuracy of the claim made during Weimar that the police force had been democratized, he emphasizes the modern "professional" quality of the Weimar police's goals and methods. See Richard Bessel, "Policing, Professionalisation and Politics in Weimar Germany" in Clive Elmsley and Barbara Weinberger, eds., *Policing Western Europe. Politics, Professionalism, and Public Order, 1850–1940* (New York: Greenwood Press, 1991b). Peter Leßmann's *Die Preußische Schutzpolizei in der Weimarer Republik: Streifendienst und Straßenkampf* (Düsseldorf: Droste, 1989) does much to dispel the image of a democratized police force in Weimar Prussia.
[32] Among many examples, see the *AIZ*, "Das II. Burgerkriegsheer," Nr. 16, 1929, pp. 4–5.
[33] BLHA, Rep. 30, Berlin C, Title 90, Nr. 7547, Polizei-Inspektion Wedding, Report Abt. I, Tgb. Nr. 1180/29, May 7, 1929.

More important than these technical shortcomings, police were often demoralized by the treatment they received by politicized residents on their beats. Even in very public settings, police were frequently harassed for breaking up demonstrations. After being taunted during the removal of rowdy KPD Reichstag members from the parliamentary assembly room in December 1929, a *Schutzpolizei* commander wrote to the chief of police declaring that protection for his men was "immediately needed . . . against insults while carrying out this especially difficult service." The commander added that his men often complained to him that they "felt powerless against the offensive attacks by the public, since no one stands behind them, while behind the public stand newspapers of all colors, which eagerly snatched up such cases to sensationalize at the officers' expense."[34]

It is not surprising that Communists would see the police as oppressors, but the *Schutzpolizei* were also not immune from criticism by Kiez residents who felt threatened or bothered by the radicalism in their neighborhoods. Handwritten notes sent to all levels of police administration often charged the police with not doing enough to ensure that order was maintained on their streets. One such letter began: "We would be thankful to you, if you would keep a much closer eye on the Communist activities in our area, so that we can safely sleep and walk to our apartments. When we come home in the dark, this riffraff comes out of the neighboring homes . . . bothers us in the crudest ways and shoves us." After listing the names of men and women in the neighborhood suspected of this behavior, the author ended the letter anonymously because if identified "we tenants and business people will be threatened with death."[35] Another letter asked facetiously: "The inhabitants of Mulak Street would like to ask whether the 7th Police Station has any policemen? Since during the entire night neither postings nor police patrols can be seen." The author, who also remained anonymous out of fear for personal safety, complained that a police presence was needed in the neighborhood because at one bar there was noise and disruption into the morning hours and "suspicious cars and bikes" were seen on the street.[36] These complaints were taken seriously by the police and often resulted in investigations of the problem areas. Nevertheless, it must have added to the sense of frustration, and even failure, felt by police to be told in such a demeaning way that they were not doing their jobs.

As some of the preceding examples demonstrate, the intimacy of the Kiez led to tension as well as cooperation. All Kieze had strong connections

[34] BLHA, Rep. 30, Berlin C, Title 90, Nr. 7485, memo from the Schutzpolizei command to the chief of police, December 28, 1929, p. 172 backside.

[35] BLHA, Rep. 30, Berlin C, Title 95, Sektion 9, Nr. 164, anonymous letter to Reich Minister Bracht, August 22, 1932, p. 39.

[36] BLHA, Rep. 30, Berlin C, Title 95, Sektion 9, Nr. 164, anonymous letter to the Berlin chief of police, July 12, 1931, p. 311.

to the working-class movement in Berlin, but not all residents appreciated these ties. Furthermore, it must be remembered that not all Kieze were located in the Red districts of the city's East and North Ends. For example, the neighborhood at Karl-Friedrich-Platz provides an interesting contrast to the area around Nostiz because of the cultural diversity of its inhabitants and strong Kiez identity despite being situated in the heart of bourgeois Charlottenburg.[37] In 1862 some of the land near the Charlottenburg palace had been sold to private developers. The land was attractive to speculators because it was connected to Berlin by the state railroad in 1877 and by the city rail in 1882. By 1881 the manufacturer Schering had moved into the cleared land, soon to be followed by Siemens in 1883. Between 1871 and 1910 Charlottenburg's population grew from 20,000 to 306,000. In order to house a good number of the workers employed at these large industrial sites, five-story apartment buildings were constructed on adjoining land. The resulting area, which was less than one square kilometer in size, held 27,000 inhabitants during the Weimar period and was at times the most thickly settled neighborhood in the city.[38] Part of the neighborhood's strong Kiez identity came from the fact that these workers felt isolated in bourgeois Charlottenburg, yet united in their close living quarters and common employment.

We should not presume, however, that there was political consensus or cultural unanimity among the inhabitants. There was a significant minority of Polish immigrants in the Karl-Friedrich-Platz Kiez, making up about 20 percent of the population. The language barrier divided them from their neighbors as formidably as their Catholic faith and church activities. It is not likely that active Catholics here voted for the Communist party during the Weimar Republic, which was waging a very vocal campaign against the Catholic Church's social conservatism and religious influence in education. However, the non-Catholic majority, which had shown strong support for the SPD before 1918, developed into a loyal KPD contingent during the 1920s. Both groups used public symbols to advertise their presence in the Kiez, and they competed against each other for preeminence. The Communist

---

[37] Karl-Friedrich-Platz was renamed Klausener Platz in 1952 to honor Erich Klausener, a Catholic cleric who was murdered in the Röhm Putsch of 1934.

[38] Eva Brücker, "Soziale Fragmentierung und kollektives Gedächtnis. Nachbarschaftsbeziehungen in einem Berliner Arbeiterviertel 1920–1980" in Wolfgang Hofmann and Gerd Kuhn, eds., *Wohnungspolitik und Städtebau, 1900–1930* (Berlin: Technische Universität, 1993), pp. 290–2. The Karl-Friedrich-Platz neighborhood consists of nine average-size city blocks and three smaller plots cut by rail lines. The area received little damage during World War II. Now known as Klausener Platz, the square lies in Charlottenburg along Spandauer Damm at the northern end of the Kiez. Schloßstraße lies to the west and the railroad to the east. In the south, Knobelsdorffstraße forms the edge of the neighborhood. In this article, Brücker explores how the sense of neighborhood is constructed and given meaning. She traces how memories and perceptions of this Charlottenburg Kiez altered over time, as its inhabitants changed.

inhabitants had an annual bike race, which was sponsored on alternating years by two sport clubs, which had their own neighborhood pubs. There was competition between the two clubs, but the race was primarily a way for the politically radical residents to host a spectacle that brought everyone together and received citywide press coverage. By the 1920s, the Karl-Friedrich-Platz race, which began in the nineteenth century, had become an important date on the city's racing schedule and a symbol of Communist enthusiasm in Berlin.

The St. Kamillus Catholic parish made itself visible through its annual procession through the Kiez to celebrate the feast of Corpus Christi. Its march was not as old as the bicycle race, beginning only in 1925, but by 1932 the parish had enough local and financial support to build a new religious complex, housing the church, a home for the elderly, a cloister, and a kindergarten. Importantly, this addition to the neighborhood was constructed at the Kiez focal point itself, Karl-Friedrich Square. The Corpus Christi procession around the open green space of the square was more contained than the race, which traversed the roads throughout the neighborhood, but in both cases attention was drawn to the event by the security provided by the police and the halting of all traffic through the area. On the Catholic feast day, there were other such processions in the city, though they were certainly not pervasive in the largely Protestant capital. The participation of St. Kamillus parish in this public event, however, affected the identity of the Kiez. In the memories of inhabitants interviewed by historian Eva Brücker, it remained a workers' Kiez, with competing political worldviews. The competition between Communists and Catholics in the neighborhood did not erode the sense of unity because both events connected the inhabitants as participants or spectators and reaffirmed the separateness of the Kiez from its surroundings.[39]

The case of the Karl-Friedrich-Platz Kiez was unique because of its Catholic and Communist population. Though all Kieze were inhabited by social democratic and Communist workers, radical Kieze – under surveillance by others – were aligned with the more radical KPD. In some cases social democratic workers, being in general more highly skilled and more employable, chose to move out of the poorest neighborhoods, either to other urban workers' neighborhoods with better apartments or to outlying areas where the city was constructing modern, yet more expensive housing. It is also likely that by 1929 or 1930 the reputation of some Kieze scared off workers who were uncomfortable living in these radical and sometimes rowdy neighborhoods. Though most Berliners who moved in these years stayed within the same city district, some were able to escape Kiez radicalism merely by moving a few blocks away.

It is worth stressing, however, that Social Democrats and others did remain in the Communist Kieze throughout the Weimar period. One former

---

[39] Ibid., pp. 300–1.

resident of the Nostiz Kiez has noted that Bergmann, Gneisenau, and to some extent Zossener and Solms Streets, all either crossing or within two parallel blocks from Nostiz, were home to higher concentrations of Social Democrats than Communists.[40] The SPD still had enough support in most workers' neighborhoods for its members to feel comfortable. Even when they were in the minority, they remained because of employment or to hold on to their affordable, perhaps street-facing apartments. SPD workers were the backbone of the republic and, in general, felt comfortable throughout the workers' North and East and in mixed districts like Schöneberg. Moreover, social democratic political culture never emphasized the need to live in close contact with other party members. Even in the early 1930s, party strategy did not focus on residential solidarity because the SPD still controlled the city's industrial trade unions and had a strong voice in the Berlin and Prussian governments. Although there was tension and competition among supporters of the KPD and SPD in the workers' districts, it is apparent, especially before 1929 but also into the early 1930s, that KPD and SPD neighbors and their neighborhood political organizations tolerated each other.[41] Even while party officials traded insults and blamed each other for the failure of a united workers' front during the last years of the Weimar Republic, there is evidence that some sense of solidarity or at least mutual acceptance in the social democratic and Communist neighborhoods existed. Both parties kept a watchful eye on the other's activities, but there was little sabotage or violence.

Central to the social and political life of any neighborhood is the housing available to residents. Berlin had a mixed reputation in terms of housing its workers. From 1900 into the mid-1920s, no major European city had housing conditions worse than those in Berlin.[42] Yet the Weimar legacy in

---

[40] König, *Berlin* (no date), p. 10.

[41] The extent of solidarity between members of the SPD and KPD remains debatable. Traditionally, historians have assumed that the antagonism exhibited by the parties' leaders was reflected in animosity at the grassroots level. More recent research has shown that this position is not completely accurate. In his monograph on the KPD in the Saar region of Germany, Klaus-Michael Mallmann argues that during the 1920s a leftist worker's milieu existed. Including members of both parties, this milieu was based on common social interests and cultural associations. While some of this social mixing decreased under the strain of the Depression in Berlin (not chiefly as a result of conflict among the parties' leaderships), the traditions discussed by Mallmann continued to support some level of grassroots social cooperation and empathy. See Klaus-Michael Mallmann, *Kommunisten in der Weimarer Republik: Sozialgeschichte einer revolutionären Bewegung* (Darmstadt: Wissenschaftliche Buchgesellschaft, 1996), especially pp. 166–81 and 261–83.

[42] For a long-term look at city planning in Berlin, including a critical view of housing in the city, see Werner Hegemann, *Das Steinerne Berlin. Geschichte der grössten Mietskasernenstadt der Welt* (Berlin: Gustav Kiepenheuer, 1930). For more recent analyses of Berlin's housing history, see the three-volume series by Johann Friedrich Geist and Klaus Kürvers, *Das Berliner Mietshaus* (Munich: Prestel, 1980) and Gert Kähler, ed., *Geschichte des Wohnens, Vol. 4: 1918–1945: Reform, Reaktion, Zerstörung* (Stuttgart: Deutsche Verlagsanstalt, 1996).

housing was the SPD-led reform of architectural standards and building programs for Berlin's poor. The designs of numerous well-known architects, among them Bruno Taut and Hans Poelzig to name just two, should not be overlooked, but neither should the squalid conditions that remained the fate of most, until the reconstruction efforts that followed World War II. In fact, it was in part the public attention given to the construction of new apartment complexes on the outskirts of the city in the 1920s that highlighted the lack of adequate housing in the city center and amplified the calls for change.

The model for the urban development of Berlin in the mid-nineteenth century was Haussmann's Paris. Broad avenues and streets were constructed and lined with ornately decorated apartment buildings. The changes were expensive, forcing developers to rely on high-density dwellings to pay for rising land prices. As a result, the gardens that had traditionally existed behind residential buildings were eliminated in order to make space for more apartments. In addition, existing housing codes did little to regulate apartment size, amount of sunlight, or amenities, so that landowners in the *Kaiserreich* were free to pack as many tiny bare units onto a city block as possible. The lack of legal safeguards and the desire to build quickly at the highest possible profit margin led to the emergence of the *Mietskasernen*. These hulking tenements presented themselves grandly to the facing street but hid successive wings of drab, cramped apartments behind the ornate facades. By 1914 the average building in Berlin housed seventy-six people, twice the occupancy rate in Paris.[43]

One young man, who lived in the Nostiz Kiez as a teenager, remembered his family's life in one of these apartments in the following way: "My father was [employed] at the Schultheiss brewery, earning 37 marks per week. We were four people, living in one room and kitchen, toilet in the hallway.... I did not have a corner for my personal things, also no closet, only a bed and nightstand. Everything else was for general use, for example a table in the middle. I kept books on the nightstand; one didn't have much, only a few books [from the library on Baruther Street]." The family of another young man, who lived on Marheinekeplatz in these years, shared a one and a half room apartment. The large room served as living space and the sleeping space for the parents. Four children were crowded into the small half room. When the mother took work outside the home, they brought in a *Stubenmädchen*, who slept with the girls in the small room, leaving the sons to share the kitchen at night."[44]

[43] Ronald Wiedenhoeft, *Berlin's Housing Revolution. German Reform in the 1920s* (Ann Arbor: University of Michigan Research Press, 1985), pp. 2–3.

[44] Oral history interviews collected by Lothar Uebel for "Lieber draußen als zu Hause" in Kunstamt Kreuzberg, ed., *Kreuzberg 1933. Ein Bezirk erinnert sich* (Berlin: Dürschlag, 1933), p. 17.

Living conditions in Berlin's tenements turn up frequently as the targets of criticism for fiction writers and policy makers throughout the Weimar era.[45] Though fictional, Justus Erhardt's *Straßen ohne Ende* from 1931 provides us with a stark portrayal of the crowded conditions in Berlin's apartment blocks and the extent to which proximity meant neighbors knew each other's concerns and tragedies:

> Evenings at home.
>
> The house is dark.
>
> It has ten entrances. One goes through the main gate to the courtyard, houses to the left, houses to the right, on to a second courtyard, houses, houses, hundreds of windows.
>
> Thousands of sorrows.
>
> Little worries, great worries.
>
> Workers. Clerks. Master craftsmen.
>
> There lives one who is drunk practically every evening. He then beats his wife. One can hear her screams three courtyards away.
>
> There live two girls. They always have visits from men. The boys and girls take notice, when one comes. They *know* what happens behind the door. . . .
>
> Hans lives off of the second courtyard. Fourth floor.
>
> Frau Rust lives on the first floor. Her husband is putting in three and a half years at the penitentiary for a repeated burglary offence.
>
> . . .
>
> One floor higher Herr Senf. He threw his wife out eight days ago, because she received visits from men and other things, while her husband was at work. The whole house had known for two years. Herr Senf found out first eight days ago. Now he hasn't left the apartment in eight days.
>
> And so it continues.[46]

Even a more optimistic chronicler of life in Berlin's tenements like Walter Schönstedt opened his novel with a description of the unending noise of the Kiez tenements. After an argument between two female residents, ending with the slamming of apartment doors and name calling, the narrator continues: "One experienced such events daily in the Nostizstraße. There was always a racket. People insulted each other senselessly. Sad accordion players returned endlessly, always playing the same songs. Rag-and-bone men hollered, and every morning an old man came by, who wanted to exchange firewood for potato peelings."[47]

Concern about moral collapse, which takes center stage in *Straßen ohne Ende,* and the political radicalism that Schönstedt championed seemed to

---

[45] See Anthony McElligott's collection of documents on urbanism for a varied look at the way Berlin and other German cities have been imagined, analyzed, and criticized. *The German Urban Experience, 1900–1945* (London: Routledge, 2001).

[46] Justus Erhardt, *Straßen ohne Ende* (Berlin: Agis, 1931), pp. 42–3. The translation provided here is my own.

[47] Schönstedt, *Kämpfende Jugend* (1972), pp. 3–4.

many contemporaries inextricably linked to the low-grade housing available in the city center. Fears about both consequences led to a number of reform-minded investigations during the Depression.[48] In 1932, Bruno Schwan, as representative of the German Society for Housing Reform, published some of his findings of a three-year study titled "The Housing Crisis and Housing Poverty in Germany." He advocated immediate reform because a current drop in the rate of population growth offered an opportunity to implement change while the pressure to house people was in relative decline. It is quite clear from the earliest pages of his study that Schwan saw nothing more than chaos and danger in these neighborhoods and presumed that by improving housing he would also be "creating order in the heart of the city." As leader of this expeditionary force, Schwan praised the courage of his team: "From street to street, from building to building, from apartment to apartment we wandered and have not shied away from dirt and odor, from danger of infection and bodily threat, in order to understand why, three steps from the bustle of the metropolis, [this area] has sunk over time into a slum."[49] In one part of Schwan's study, he focused on a small section of south-central Berlin. He surveyed 3,635 apartments and found that 3.55 percent were vacant and 10.7 percent were also used for some sort of income-generating activity.[50] Out of 3,506 apartments in the same area, Schwan calculated 16.5 percent to be overcrowded (occupied by more than two people per room). However, in one neighborhood, this figure reached as high as 21.52 percent.[51] The

---

[48] Though ending a decade earlier, one of the best collections of photographs of the housing situation in Berlin's poorest neighborhoods was commissioned by the health insurance company AOK between 1901 and 1920 to accompany their own survey of living conditions. The firm hoped to shed light on the housing problems that contributed to the ailments suffered by their customers. Their annual findings were edited by Albert Kohn and released as *Die Wohnungs-Enquêten* (Jg. 1902–1922). Each volume was published one year after the survey was completed, as such the photographs were taken beginning in 1901. For some analysis of the studies and a substantial collection of the photographs taken, see Gesine Asmus, ed., *Hinterhof, Keller, und Mansarde: Einblicke in Berliner Wohnungselend, 1901–1920* (Reinbek: Rowohlt, 1982). Some of the rooms photographed look deceptively inviting. Asmus explains, however, that most of the images were taken with the use of flash photography, since even during the day these apartments received little, if any, sunlight. Poor living conditions play a pivotal role in Ruth Weiland's study of the effects of the Depression on children: Ruth Weiland, *Die Kinder der Arbeitslosen* (Berlin: E. & C. Müller, 1933).

[49] Bruno Schwan, *Die Wohnungsverhältnisse der Berliner Altstadt* (Berlin: Deutscher Verein für Wohnungsreform, 1932), p. 3. The decline in Berlin's birthrate was not simply a result of the devastating economic crisis of the early 1930s. Even during the relative calm that pervaded society in the mid 1920s, Berlin's birth rate did not compete well with the rest of Germany. In 1928 Berlin finished last among all German states and regions with only 10.2 births per thousand inhabitants. The average figure for the republic as a whole was 18.6.

[50] Ibid., pp. 8–9.

[51] The researchers were surprised by the small number of children living in the overfilled tenements, concluding that the most crowded dwellings were inhabited mainly by retirees or older childless workers. Ibid., p. 12.

rest of the study was devoted to Schwan's description of the living conditions of those he surveyed. Schwan stressed the absence of sunlight in these tiny, airshaft-facing apartments, and reserved intense criticism for the lack of adequate indoor plumbing in the old tenements. The best tenements only had communal toilets on each or every other floor. It was not uncommon, however, for a building's only available toilets to be located in the courtyard. One street newspaper ridiculed a house in Neukölln as "the tenants' paradise" for having only six courtyard toilets for about one hundred people in thirty-two families. "Each must answer the call of nature in buckets and pots," the article continued, "which are then emptied in a sand pit in the courtyard."[52] Without romanticizing the situation, it is fair to say that sharing toilets with neighbors certainly meant a more intimate knowledge of others' behaviors than we can easily imagine. One author of a Nostiz Kiez memoir even recalled accompanying a younger sister to and from the courtyard toilets around the time of World War I, because the facilities were available to the male patrons of the building's ground floor pub and because the courtyard's horse stalls attracted rats.[53] In all situations, the provisions were inadequate, and the plumbing was often in disrepair, creating unpleasant and unsanitary conditions.

In another study of living standards published in 1931 by the German Academy for Social and Pedagogical Women's Work, Annemarie Niemeyer reported findings similar to those of Schwan. With data taken from the census of 1925, she illustrated the extent to which the housing crisis affected Berlin more than other German cities. She claimed that 69 percent of Berlin's dwellings were considered small, with three or fewer rooms, whereas the average percentage of small apartments in the rest of the republic's urban areas was only 49 percent. Just over 78 percent of the dwellings in Berlin were rental units, a figure similar to that for other large German cities.[54] A comparison of the information about overcrowding in Berlin provided by the two studies demonstrates the great extent to which the overcrowding was limited to the workers' districts. Niemeyer and Schwan both defined overcrowded as more than two people per room, with two children counting as one person. Using this formula, Niemeyer concluded that 5.6 percent of all households in Berlin were to be considered overcrowded.[55] In Schwan's study of the workers' neighborhoods of south-central Berlin, he found between 16 percent and 21.5 percent of all dwellings to be overcrowded. Niemeyer confirmed Schwan's findings by looking at the percentage of overcrowded apartments that were also considered small. She found that 82 percent of

[52] BA-SAPMO, RY1/I3/1-2/55, "Die Mieter Paradies" (no date, likely 1930).
[53] König, *Berlin* (no date), p. 16.
[54] Annemarie Niemeyer, *Zur Struktur der Familie. Statistischen Materialen* (Berlin: F. A. Herbig, 1931), pp. 125–32.
[55] Ibid., p. 135.

those apartments she determined to be overcrowded consisted of three or fewer rooms, and over half of the cases existed in dwellings of only one to two rooms.[56]

In Figure 3 the density of the city interior becomes clear. The original six districts of Berlin were inhabited by over ten thousand people per square kilometer by 1910. The most densely settled area extended beyond the borders of the city at that time, covering parts of Wilmersdorf, Schöneberg, and even Steglitz in the west and Neukölln in the east. By 1930, only small pockets of rural land were left on the perimeter, where only two generations earlier the city center had seemed worlds away.[57] Even more astounding is Figure 4, which shows the distribution of five-story tenement-type apartment buildings by district versus lower buildings and homes. In five out of the six original city districts, less than 5 percent of the homes were one- or two-story buildings; more than 50 percent of the apartment houses had five stories, and in three districts (including the Nostiz area's district of Kreuzberg) the percentage was over 80 percent.[58]

These statistics become important as we begin to look at how Berlin politics became increasingly localized after 1929. One direct example was the frequency of tenants' strikes, which sprung up around the city in the early 1930s. Faced with the inability to pay monthly rents, which seemed excessively high for the poor quality of the dwellings, impoverished workers staged KPD-supported strikes under the slogan "Erst Essen, dann Miete" (First Food, then Rent). These demonstrations were significant not only because they did succeed at times in forcing better maintenance and forestalling rate hikes. In addition, rental strikes showed the ability of residents to band together without much outside assistance and effect change in their daily living conditions. Unlike many of the examples that will be covered in this book, in which men sought to assert local power, women were centrally involved in the *Mieterstreiks*. Female residents often took the lead because they were forced to make ends meet with the meager financial resources available to them and were most familiar with the problems in their apartments and the extended semiprivate space of the tenement.[59] These same gender divisions, however, meant that women's daily political activism was limited

---

[56] Ibid., p. 135.

[57] Friedrich Leyden, *Groß-Berlin. Geographie der Weltstadt* (Berlin: Gebr. Mann Verlag, 1933; reprinted 1995), p. 90.

[58] Ibid., p. 112. The data for this graph comes from the 1925 census. Leyden also notes that by 1925 in Mitte and Tiergarten the percentage of one-story buildings was significantly less than 1 percent.

[59] There has been little research done on *Mieterstreike* in Berlin. For some basic information, see Rainer Nitsche, ed., *Häuserkämpfe, 1872, 1920, 1945, 1982* (Berlin: Transit, 1981) and Henrik Stahr, "'Erst Essen – dann Miete!' Mieterkrawalle, Mieterstreiks und ihre bildliche Repräsentation" in Diethart Kerbs and Henrik Stahr, eds., *Berlin 1932. Das letzte Jahr der Weimarer Republik* (Berlin: Hentrich, 1992), pp. 90–114.

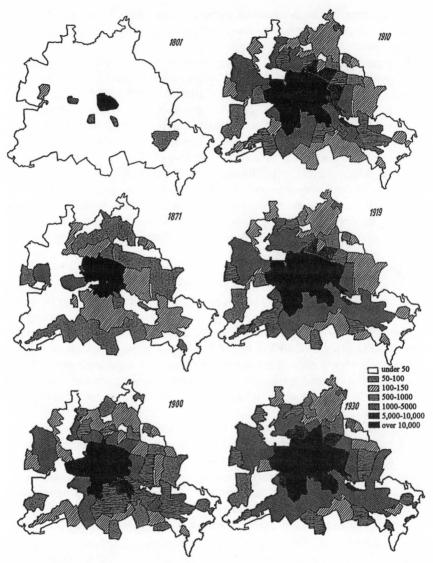

Figure 3. Berlin population density in residents per square kilometer, 1801–1930.
Source: Friedrich Leyden, *Groß-Berlin. Geographie der Weltstadt.* Copyright © 1995
Gebr. Mann Verlag. Reprinted by permission of Gebr. Mann Verlag.

beyond this sphere. Though the KPD tried to control these protests through
advice and financial support, most of the organizing was done by residents
themselves, who sometimes represented a range of political backgrounds and
resented the intrusion by party functionaries.

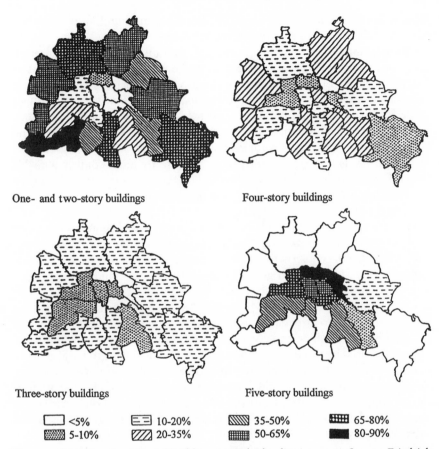

One- and two-story buildings   Four-story buildings

Three-story buildings   Five-story buildings

☐ <5%	⊟ 10-20%	▨ 35-50%	▦ 65-80%
▨ 5-10%	▨ 20-35%	▥ 50-65%	■ 80-90%

Figure 4. Heights of residential buildings in Berlin by district, 1925. Source: Friedrich Leyden, *Groß-Berlin. Geographie der Weltstadt.* Copyright © 1995 Gebr. Mann Verlag. Reprinted by permission of Gebr. Mann Verlag.

The architects of the Weimar Constitution had made efforts to address the housing crisis. Articles 153 and 155 of the Weimar Constitution provided for greater governmental control of land.[60] For the first time, the German government was taking the lead in housing construction. At the height of the building boom, during the short window of opportunity between the economic stabilization of 1924 and the onset of the Depression five years later, public funds were used in the completion of more than 70 percent of

[60] Article 153 permitted land expropriation in cases that served the common good. Article 155 reinforced the state's role in seeing that land was not misused. In particular, it called for the state to take an active role in providing all Germans with a proper dwelling. Finally, it placed a legal duty on property owners to make use of their property in ways that benefited the community. See *Die neue Reichsverfassung* (Berlin: C. Heymann, 1919).

all new housing units in the capital.[61] The resulting building projects are counted today as major republican accomplishments.

The most important figure in the attempts to transform Berlin's reputation for poor housing was Martin Wagner. This Social Democrat served first as *Stadtbaurat*, City Building Commissioner, in Schöneberg in 1918. In the early 1920s he worked as the leader of the *Verband sozialer Baubetriebe* and was made *Stadtbaurat* for Berlin in 1927. He held this position until his removal in March 1933.[62] Throughout his tenure in the capital, Wagner's controlling leadership style and sympathy for the KPD created tension with his colleagues at the top levels of city administration. Despite frequent conflict with his co-workers, including Mayor Gustav Böß, Wagner was instrumental in the construction of fourteen thousand new residential units in Berlin between 1924 and 1933.

In order to address the lack of sunshine and garden plots and provide more living space, architects and social critics in the immediate postwar period demanded the construction of small communities of row houses outside the city center, replete with green spaces, larger rooms, and some modern amenities, in particular electricity and indoor toilets. This row-house strategy was applauded by both the political left and right. For the left, the new housing promised to provide modern, healthful living to the city's poor, while the right hoped sunshine and greenery would combat the moral delinquency allegedly caused by urban living. There was a practical need to build quickly in order to relieve the shortage, which had become dire by 1918, but it was believed that innovation would not have to be sacrificed if cheaper, prefabricated supplies were used. Until the mid 1920s, this row-house settlement model served as the goal for urban planners like Wagner and architects like Taut. Wagner's Lindenhof development, built between 1919 and 1920 for the still independent community of Schöneberg, was typical of this phase. The site was chosen in order to highlight two ponds and a grove of linden trees, which would help the tenants reconnect to their natural surroundings. The plan of the settlement was so successful in achieving its goal of low-density living that urban planners in the 1950s added buildings to the site in order to counteract what they saw as "excessively" low occupancy.[63]

Before long, however, Wagner and others recognized that these low-density row-house settlements were not a practical solution to Berlin's housing needs.

[61] Barbara Miller Lane, *Architecture and Politics in Germany, 1918–1945* (Cambridge, MA: Harvard University Press, 1968, 1985), p. 88.

[62] On Martin Wagner, see Wiedenhoeft, *Berlin's Housing Revolution* (1985) and Ludovica Scarpa, *Martin Wagner und Berlin. Architektur und Städtebau in der Weimarer Republik* (Braunschweig: F. Viewig & Sohn, 1986). On the SPD's policies toward social and administrative reform in Berlin, see Böß, *Berlin von Heute* (1929) and Emma Woytinsky, *Sozialdemokratie und Kommunalpolitik. Gemeindearbeit in Berlin* (Berlin: E. Laubsche, 1929).

[63] Wiedenhoeft, *Berlin's Housing Revolution* (1985), pp. 59–65.

The dwellings remained too costly to construct because a minimal number of units were placed on the maximum amount of space. During the last six years of the republic, a new model was implemented with the financial assistance of building cooperatives, especially the *Gemeinnützige Heimstätten-Aktiengesellschaft,* or *Gehag.* The *Gehag* was only one of the large building cooperatives in Berlin, but it was extremely productive because it received most of its funds from the socialist trade unions and had the support of social democratic leaders in Berlin, including Wagner. The housing projects constructed in Berlin in this final phase were much more ambitious in size and innovative in design than the earlier developments. They were located on the outskirts of town, where large tracts of land could still be found. Many of the goals of the projects remained the same: sunshine, fresh air, modern kitchens, heating, and plumbing. Standard, modestly sized floor plans and economical building methods were again used to keep the prices of construction down. Although some of the earlier favor shown toward a green suburban setting was retained, the sheer massiveness of these projects, some of which included over one thousand units, reinforced their urban feel. Nonetheless, the modern style of the buildings, with their flat roofs and clean geometric designs, was intended to reflect both the rationalized efficiency of the architectural plan and the "well-ordered" lifestyles of the inhabitants.[64] The *Gehag* sponsored the construction of two such large developments. First came the *Hufeisen Siedlung,* so called for the horseshoe-shaped building found at the center of the plan. Wagner and Taut began construction on this mammoth complex in 1925 on farmland in the most southern section of Neukölln known as Britz. The following year, Taut began another project, the *Waldsiedlung* or "forest development," in the southwestern district of Zehlendorf.

The city government alone planned the erection of 2,080 new units in 1929, among other large projects that sprouted up along Berlin's borders. This number was achieved through the construction of two large developments. One, *Gross-Siedlung Reinickendorf,* was located on the northern edge of the city, and the other was part of the famous *Siemensstadt.* Some of Germany's best architects, including Walter Gropius and Hans Scharoun, worked on the latter project in Charlottenburg. The site was conveniently located near a large park, *Jungfernheide,* and the Siemens factory, to which over fifty thousand workers commuted each day. The city's S-Bahn rail service

---

[64] It is important to remember that while many leftist intellectuals criticized the rationalization of the workplace, which had the potential to increase the monotony of industrial labor and replace workers with machines, there was some acceptance in these same circles that rationalized daily habits and modern living quarters would improve the lives of workers. See Mary Nolan, *Visions of Modernity: American Business and the Modernization of Germany* (New York: Oxford University Press, 1994); Carola Sachse, *Industrial Housewives: Women's Social Work in the Factories of Nazi Germany* (New York: The Haworth Press, 1987); and Anson Rabinbach, *The Human Motor. Energy, Fatigue, and the Origins of Modernity* (Berkeley: University of California Press, 1992).

had been recently extended to reach this northwestern end of Charlotten-burg, providing quick transportation to the rest of the city. Yet, in some ways, *Siemensstadt*'s low-income housing was a retreat from the postwar goals of radical architecture. It was 1929, and the economic crisis was be-ginning to be felt by the investors involved in the project. There were no single-family row houses in the plan and no spaces for individual gardens, and the buildings reached five stories, even higher than the new building code normally allowed. The first priority remained the urgent need to lessen overcrowding in the city center. The goal of providing workers with plots for gardens had to be abandoned as a luxury. There was still plenty of land-scaped greenery between buildings, and efforts were taken to alleviate the anonymous industrial look of the housing blocks.[65] At *Siemensstadt* and the other large developments, some communal buildings were incorporated into the plans, ranging from stores, restaurants and meeting rooms to common washing facilities, but communal living was never an integral part of these developments.

Though these housing developments continue to serve Berlin today, and have received praise over the decades for their architectural innovation, at the time they were hotly debated. Much of the controversy surrounded the rents for the apartments in new buildings. Even with the standardization of building materials and methods, these apartments came with higher rents than the crowded tenements in the heart of the city. The plans for building large apartments on city land met with especially harsh criticism from the KPD and left wing of the SPD, but even the small apartments intended for low-income families were attacked by the political left for being out of the financial reach of most of Berlin's needy. There were also concerns on both ends of the political spectrum that cutting corners and packing large numbers into these massive complexes made the projects little better than the rental barracks closer to town.[66] Mayor Böß responded to left-wing criticism in the city assembly, contending that because middle-class, lower middle-class, or elite working-class families occupied the new apartments, their previ-ous apartments would become free for the city's poorest. This trickle-down

---

[65] Wiedenhoeft, *Berlin's Housing Revolution* (1985), pp. 123, 132–5. There seems to be some disagreement as to the sponsors of the *Siemensstadt* project. Barbara Miller Lane argues that it was the work of the Siemens building cooperative, while Ronald Wiedenhoeft maintains that the initiative came from the municipal authorities.

[66] In 1935 Bruno Schwan criticized the large-scale developments as having only "little [to] distinguish themselves from the older buildings." He complained further that in "the many-story terrace-buildings the inhabitant is only a figure among the [great] number of his fellow inhabitants." He, therefore, congratulated the new national socialist government for encour-aging a return to prioritizing ownership over renting, and "homestead"-style dwellings over multistory apartment buildings. See Bruno Schwan, ed., *Städtebau und Wohnungswesen der Welt – Town Planning and Housing throughout the World – L'Urbanisme et L'Habitation dans tous les Pays* (Berlin: Verlag Ernst Wasmuth, 1935), p. 133.

theory of housing was never accepted by the Communists, and the housing projects, despite their good intentions, deepened the gulf between the two workers' parties.

The KPD made great propaganda use of one housing development in particular. Between 1929 and 1931, a large settlement was built in the heart of the workers' district Wedding, with sections designed by Taut and the team Mebes & Emmerich. In honor of the first republican president (SPD) who had died in 1925, the development was named *Groß-Siedlung Friedrich Ebert*. His name was printed on the side of one of the buildings, commemorating the social democratic reform efforts of his administration. However, because the rents were restrictively high for many workers in Wedding, especially by 1931 when the project was completed, the Friedrich Ebert settlement was used by the KPD to support its claim that the SPD failed to represent the interests of workers. Although the Social Democrats living in the development (totaling 1,600) did make up the largest and most active section of the SPD within Wedding, it should be noted that a number of Communist Party functionaries, journalists, and other KPD supporters who could afford the high rents also chose to live in these modern apartments.[67]

Because the government was heavily involved in the financing of new dwellings in the mid- and late 1920s, ground breaking for new apartment buildings practically came to a halt when the economic crisis hit. Large cities were affected the most by the failure of national unemployment insurance to supply long-term relief to citizens. The unemployed, who quickly ran through their unemployment insurance or whose work never qualified them for this form of aid, soon depended on their communities for assistance. According to the 1927 national welfare legislation, after the first twenty-six weeks of joblessness, during which the communities only paid a small portion of welfare assistance, local governments were responsible for the entire cost of assistance. Therefore, by the early 1930s, it was no longer possible for the city to spend public funds on new construction while the welfare coffers were running dry. As a result, the number of housing starts in Berlin fell dramatically by the end of 1930. During the second half of 1930, building permits numbering 21,227 were registered in Berlin, and in the same six months during 1931 only 2,606 such applications were processed.[68]

[67] Communists and Social Democrats were not the only politicized groups living in the Friedrich Ebert housing development. There was also a large enough Nazi population to support its own residential newspaper, *Das Hakenkreuz über die Wohnsiedlung Friedrich Ebert*. See LAB, Rep. 58, Nr. 1716, Film 752. Documents like this one provide further evidence of the political diversity of workers' neighborhoods in late Weimar Berlin.

[68] Tilman Harlander, Katrin Hater, and Franz Meiers, eds., *Siedeln in der Not. Umbruch von Wohnungspolitik und Siedlungsbau am Ende der Weimarer Republik* (Hamburg: Christians, 1988), p. 40. Other large cities, such as Hamburg and Cologne, reported similar declines in the numbers of new dwellings.

As a result of the drastic slowdown in construction, the impact of new building on the long-standing apartment shortage was minor. In fact, as the Depression worsened even the lower middle classes had trouble paying the high rents and taxes associated with the new developments. Soon some of the modern apartments stood empty, while families crowded into the tenements.[69] The search for housing became a typical story of the era. The *AIZ* presented a couple in 1929 who wrote firsthand about their own search. They began at the housing bureau before the marriage but were turned away until legally wed. After the marriage, they were able to fill out the proper forms but were informed that the two- or three-room apartment they sought might be theirs as they "celebrated their silver wedding anniversary" because as long as they were a two-person family or three people with a child under fifteen, they only had a chance for a one-room apartment. Attempting to go through a private agency, they stood speechless in front of the window which "extolled countless wonderful apartments as . . . 'modern and inexpensive.'" Their hopes were dashed, however, when they were told they needed a 1,000 mark advance payment.[70] In Hans Fallada's *Little Man, What Now?* the reader follows the Pinneberg family on their social descent, which is reflected in the declining quality of their living conditions. Thousands in the city experienced the same process. There were those who lost their factory-owned housing when their jobs disappeared or were unable even to keep up with the rents demanded for Berlin's worst housing due to long-term unemployment. One young man remembers his family's brush with homelessness in 1931 when they were evicted from a dwelling on Solms Street in the Nostiz Kiez: "My parents were three months behind in the rent and so their lease was canceled by the landlord and [they] had to get out immediately. By chance my father found a basement apartment in the Gneisenaustraße, otherwise we would have ended up in a homeless shelter. For that unemployment was to blame, which was a fact of the time, because otherwise my father had always had work and had always paid his rent on time."[71] Those families who were not as lucky did find themselves homeless, putting yet another burden on the city government to fund shelters. The majority of workers struggled as long as possible to hold on to the apartments they had or sought less expensive dwellings, most often in the same neighborhood or close by. If all else failed, like Fallada's protagonists, a growing number resorted to living in the *Laubenkolonie*, makeshift dwellings erected in garden allotments surrounding the city. As Fallada explains, these huts were especially difficult to bear during Berlin's winter months: "Of these three thousand little plots

---

[69] In 1935 Bruno Schwan reported that newer buildings, with larger apartments, still stood empty due to the "impoverishment of the people" and that smaller dwellings were "as much in demand as ever." Schwan, *Städtebau und Wohnungswesen* (1935), p. 133.

[70] *AIZ*, "Wir suchen eine Wohnung," Nr. 5, 1929, p. 6.

[71] Oral history interviews collected by Uebel, "Lieber draußen als zu Hause" (1933), p. 19.

of land hardly fifty persons were left this winter; anyone who could raise the money for a room, or get himself taken in by relatives, had fled to the city to escape the cold and dirt and solitude."[72] This too was the fate of the "reporters" for the *AIZ*, who in the end turned to one of these colonies to build their "own villa out of some roofing felt and a few planks nailed together."[73]

WITHIN THE CITY OF MILLIONS

The borders of Red Berlin, the industrial working-class section of the city, are subject to interpretation (Figure 2). In the conservative Weimar press, everything east and north of Tiergarten park was considered under the grip of the "Sozis and Kozis." In Richard Hamilton's study of Nazi voting patterns, he divides the city districts into three categories: middle-class, workers', and mixed districts, the last of which included the outlying communities of Treptow, Pankow, Reinickendorf, and Cöpenick. Omitting these four and the seven he identifies as middle-class districts, we are left with eight workers' districts: the pre-1920 Berlin core minus Tiergarten, plus Lichtenberg, Weissensee, and Neukölln. It is unwise, however, to assume that these socioeconomic categories necessarily corresponded directly to political affiliation. Indeed, the area known as Red Berlin was not always politically, economically, or socially homogeneous. For example, in some instances, similarities can even be found when compiling voting statistics from Hamilton's workers' districts and middle-class districts. In the May 1928 Reichstag elections, the workers' district Spandau only returned 17.23 percent of the vote for the KPD, while bourgeois Tiergarten cast 20.32 percent for the Communists, and "mixed" Reinickendorf cast close to 28 percent of its vote for the KPD.[74] Because the workers' districts are the main focus of this study, it is important to describe some of the significant characteristics and differences among the sections of Red Berlin.

In the center lay Mitte, the oldest part of the city, which was home to some of Berlin's recent immigrant groups. Mitte was also known for its

[72] Fallada, *Little Man, What Now?* (1992), p. 346.
[73] *AIZ*, "Wir suchen eine Wohnung," Nr. 5, 1929, p. 6.
[74] Spandau had a unique political tradition. Though inhabited mostly by industrial workers, Spandau was isolated from the rest of working-class Berlin in the far northwest corner of the city. The Nazi Party attracted support here early on, which increased throughout the Crisis Period. In terms of voting, Spandau's support for the NSDAP led all figures from workers' districts. Reinickendorf, though on the outskirts of town and in the still rural north, also shared a border with Wedding and inherited some of its radicalism. Tiergarten was home to many wealthy Berliners but also contained the working-class area known as Moabit close to the city center. For Hamilton's analysis of these statistics, see Richard Hamilton, *Who Voted for Hitler?* (Princeton, NJ: Princeton University Press, 1982), pp. 64–100, especially the table on p. 78.

criminal elements, as described so memorably by Alfred Döblin in *Berlin Alexanderplatz*.[75] Politically, Mitte was important because of the location of City Hall, seat of the city assembly, which drew protesters of the financial cuts to unemployment insurance and other programs during the Depression. Mitte was also home to the Karl Liebknecht House Communist Party headquarters situated on Bülowplatz. The area around Communist headquarters was also identified by the police as a trouble spot because of its proximity to the *Scheunenviertel*, where authorities housed impoverished Jews from Eastern Europe. These immigrants were looked upon with great suspicion by the rest of the population. Even the leftist *AIZ* described the foreign quality of this neighborhood – comparing it to the Jewish quarters of Poland – and presented it as a haven for swindlers and prostitutes. Yet the weekly newspaper also remarked sympathetically that its residents were being pushed out as tenements were toppled to make way for new high-priced dwellings in this centrally located area.[76]

To the west of Mitte, the subdistrict of Moabit, which remained part of wealthy Tiergarten, had developed quickly in the mid nineteenth century as an industrial neighborhood. It housed Borsig's large machine works, which manufactured locomotives and other products for the transportation industry. Moabit also played an important role in Berlin's violent political culture because the city's criminal court and the system's holding jail were located here. Bordering Mitte to the east was Friedrichshain. Friedrichshain had a reputation as the slum of the capital and home to criminals and rabble-rousers. Many residents were employed at the cattle market and slaughterhouses that lay in this district on the Spree River. Politically, Friedrichshain boasted the *Volkspark*, an historically popular spot for a Sunday afternoon walk and for large-scale working-class orations and assemblies. Sizable meetings could also be held indoors at the *Saalbau Friedrichshain*, a regular venue for socialist and Communist functions.

To the south and southeast of Berlin's center lay Kreuzberg and Neukölln. Running north/south through Kreuzberg was Friedrichstraße, a busy commercial street and the heart of Berlin's theater and cabaret district. A few blocks away, Anhalter train station served Dresden, Leipzig, and Munich, among other desirable destinations. As already explained, Kreuzberg was known for its mix of prosperous and poor neighborhoods and radical politics. Tempelhof airport was also located here and was a public as well as commercial attraction throughout the Weimar period and the site from

---

[75] Alfred Döblin, *Berlin Alexanderplatz. Die Geschichte Von Franz Biberkopf* (Berlin: Fischer 1929). For the English translation, see *Berlin Alexanderplatz: The Story of Franz Biberkopf*, Eugene Jolas, trans. (New York: F. Ungar, 1983).

[76] *AIZ*, "Im Berliner Scheunen-Viertel," Nr. 23, 1929, p. 7. This short article offered a number of pictures of the *Scheunenviertel*, including those of street salesmen, a pickpocket, and a "typical character in the Jewish quarter."

time to time of the Sarrasani Circus. Neukölln was known for its radical neighborhoods too, and for the riots, which placed parts of the district under martial law in May of 1929. The new housing developments in the southern end, called Britz, was still rural, but large new housing developments were drawing families away from the city center. Like Kreuzberg, Neukölln had both significant Communist support and an active Nazi contingent throughout the period of this study. The large numbers of supporters of both political extremes made these workers' districts two of the most violent in the years after 1929.

North of the city center were the most industrial districts, Prenzlauer Berg and Wedding. As the nineteenth century came to a close, large manufacturing concerns began to seek cheap land beyond the city core. As factories sprang up in Wedding, Prenzlauer Berg and even into Reinickendorf, the workers followed. The biggest factories in these areas, such as AEG electrical, employed tens of thousands of workers each, until the Depression led to massive layoffs at the end of the 1920s and into the 1930s. Some of the most dismal *Mietskasernen* were quickly constructed here in the late nineteenth century in order to house arriving factory employees. One of the more infamous tenements in Wedding, Meyers-Hof, was a "city within the city," including six courtyards back-to-back, numerous stores and workshops, and twelve hundred people who called it home.[77] Meyers-Hof was not demolished until damage incurred in World War II made it a necessity, though some new "progressive" housing did go up in these districts in the second half of the 1920s. Politically these two districts were consistently loyal to the parties of the left, although Depression-era unemployment aided the growth of the KPD versus the SPD. The KPD received more votes in Wedding than any other party in Reichstag elections as early as 1928, and Communist support at the polls continued through 1932.

There were also significant pockets of workers in the middle-class districts. Foremost were the Borsig and Siemens factory workers living in Tiergarten's Moabit. However, as more room was needed, both Borsig and Siemens built on undeveloped land in northwestern Charlottenburg at the end of the nineteenth century. Siemens would continue to expand production space and living quarters from the 1880s through the 1920s, and the *Siemensstadt* residential development was built to house its workers withinin this swanky district, which had once been home to royalty.

In accordance with this residential mapping of the city, the favored political venues also helped define the identity of various districts. The vast majority of political protests and assemblies were small and will be discussed in greater

---

77 For photos of Meyers-Hof, see "Meyershof – eine Stadt in der Stadt" in *AIZ*, Jg. 8, Nr. 19, 1929, p. 5. This report was the first of many on the massive building. One Munich illustrated publication claimed 2,500 residents called 132 Ackerstraße home (Geist and Kürvers, *Das Berliner Mietshaus* [1980], p. 413).

detail later. For large-scale demonstrations, however, the three parties that sought the support of Berlin's workers (SPD, KPD, and NSDAP) all had preferred sites. Unter den Linden and the government quarter were attractive locations for any sort of political demonstration, but both were off limits to unauthorized political assemblies. The Tiergarten park, though centrally located, did not play a big role, because high tree density made it hard for large groups to gather, hold banners, see speakers, or march. The Lustgarten, on the other hand, was a large flat clearing in the city center, which made an excellent spot for the massive outdoor assemblies that had long been central to German workers' political culture.

In the 1920s, as the gulf between the SPD and young KPD deepened, the two parties shared fewer and fewer physical spaces for demonstration. After 1929, the SPD continued to celebrate May Day primarily in the Lustgarten, for example, while the KPD staged protest marches in the less central workers' districts of Wedding and Neukölln to evoke memories of police brutality in those neighborhoods beginning on May 1, 1929. In most cases, Communist assemblies took place in Bülowplatz so the Karl Liebknecht House could be draped with political banners and offer a powerful backdrop for photographers.[78] The SPD also chose to stage many of its rallies near its party headquarters on Lindenstraße.

The Nazi Party and its affiliated organizations consistently held major events at the Berlin Sports "Palace." It was the biggest venue in town, necessary for the large, loud, impressive spectacles the party desired. Outdoors, Nazi supporters were the most frequent demonstrators in front of the Reichstag building, whereas the KPD preferred to picket smaller state institutions like welfare offices or city hall. The SPD and Reichsbanner rarely organized protests at governmental buildings because of their allegiance to the republic. Though all three parties organized major political events on holidays and at election time, political organizing in Berlin remained to a large extent local. Especially as the economic and political crises worsened after 1929, the *Kleinarbeit* – the daily grind of local activism – became the true hallmark of politics in Berlin. These local protests and activities intensified the sense of neighborhood identities and conflict as well as the division between a workers' East and a bourgeois West.

What united the workers' neighborhoods during the Weimar Republic was not simply the political beliefs of their inhabitants – for these neighborhoods were increasingly politically diverse and the workers' movement was deeply divided between SPD and KPD – but their distinct contrast to the West. Much of this contrast had to do with the physical look of the workers'

---

[78] For a roadmap to the favorite sites of working-class organizing in Berlin, see Heinz Habedank, *Geschichte der revolutionären Berliner Arbeiterbewegung*, II, *1917–1945* (E. Berlin: Dietz, 1987), pp. 342–3. The map provided lists sixteen demonstration sites, nineteen assembly halls, and eleven office headquarters used by both the SPD and KPD.

neighborhoods: the "rental barracks," gray facades, treeless sidewalks, and factory landmarks. Berliners in the North and East Ends recognized that their half of the city symbolized the industrial powerhouse that Berlin had become, and that their cityscape better reflected Berlin's rapid growth over the preceding fifty years than the middle-class homes of the West or the farms of the borderlands. In a 1931 book written in Wedding to celebrate the changes witnessed in the area since the 1920 *Groß-Berlin-Gesetz*, the district was described in the following way:

With its overwhelming worker population Wedding is in every way the most outspoken contrast to Berlin-West. The streets and the houses and also the people make this known: everything built in the last century, the entire city district from Oranienburg Gate to See Street . . . carries the characteristics of the industrial age. . . . A lack of housing and the rapid changes from crisis and boom in the last ten years has resulted in the majority of Berlin's workers living far from their places of work. Wedding is richly blessed with industry, factories are built in the middle of the most populated residential quarters. But the workers of Wedding travel in all directions and to all city districts in Berlin, and in turn workers come from Moabit and Neukölln . . . from wherever workers are closely packed for a daily invasion of Wedding.[79]

From descriptions like this one, we see how residents of Red Berlin saw their half of the city: as multiple districts united by their commuting workers and their industrial architecture, as an area critical to the success of the city. Though the book does not mention the politics of Wedding explicitly, it recognized the western and eastern halves of Berlin as two opposing worlds.

This sense of geopolitical division within the capital was encouraged openly by the middle-class and workers' presses. Every major political position was represented by a daily in Berlin, sometimes more than one by the late 1920s, and people were judged by which newspapers they read. Even though the population had felt betrayed by the inaccurate news coverage during World War I, the new constitution reassured Germans that they could count on the information contained in newspapers. Scholars agree that Germans believed what they read and considered the printed word the most valuable tool in understanding the political issues of the day – even more valuable than the spoken word. Most newspaper editors reasoned that in 1918 German citizens had been given political power without having the knowledge necessary to decipher the issues of the day. The role of the journalist, therefore, was to digest the events and opinions of politicians and

79 Fritz Rück, *Der Wedding in Wort und Bild* (Berlin: E. Laubsche, 1931), pp. 7–8. This book was meant as a positive portrayal of the district in the throes of the Depression. The pictures throughout are of new, modern buildings, including updated façades and newly erected hospitals and housing.

present an interpretation, not an "objective" account of the news.[80] This mediating role was accepted by readers and added to their confidence that news articles contained necessary and useful analysis. As a result, a wide spectrum of opinion was represented by the German press, and newspapers enjoyed the staunch loyalty of their readers.

Berlin, and Kreuzberg in particular, was "the indisputable heart of publishing in Germany."[81] At the center of the *Zeitungsstadt* stood two important liberal papers: the *Berliner Tageblatt (BT)* and the *Vossische Zeitung (VZ)*.[82] These dailies never disguised their support for the Democratic Party and its successor, the *Staatspartei*, but they did reserve the right to hold opinions independent of party policies. The respect afforded to these two papers was substantial. Modris Eksteins has noted that many who voted for the Center Party, the SPD, and even the DNVP and NSDAP during this period read these papers for their "truthful" accounts of events and issues. While most workers were loyal to their own party presses, chiefly the SPD *Vorwärts* or the KPD *Rote Fahne (RF)*, the parties of the left did find some balanced, if not entirely positive, treatment of their politics within the pages of the *BT* and *VZ*. On some occasions *Rote Fahne* even published excerpts from these newspapers as respected analyses, if their coverage was not explicitly critical of KPD policy. At the other end of the political spectrum were right-wing papers, many of which belonged to Alfred Hugenberg's printing conglomerate. Some of the largest conservative publications in Berlin were *Der Tag, Berliner Lokal-Anzeiger,* and *Berliner Börsen-Zeitung*. Finally, there was the Nazi press, which got a relatively late start in Berlin. The *Völkischer Beobachter (VB)* remained the chief

---

[80] Modris Eksteins, *The Limits of Reason. The German Democratic Press and the Collapse of Weimar Democracy* (London: Oxford University Press, 1975), pp. 70–3. Eksteins reports that: "By 1932 the total number of papers in Germany had increased to 4,703 – including dailies, weeklies, and local editions of parent papers; their total daily printing was in the vicinity of 14 million copies" (p. 74). For an analysis of how newspapers "fashioned the nature of metropolitan experience" in turn-of-the-century Berlin, see Peter Fritzsche, *Reading Berlin 1900* (Cambridge, MA: Harvard University Press, 1996b). For information on the workers' AIZ see Heinz Willmann, *Geschichte der Arbeiter-Illustrierten Zeitung, 1921–1938* (Berlin: Dietz, 1975).

[81] Eksteins, *The Limits of Reason* (1975), p. 74.

[82] The *Berliner Tageblatt* belonged to the Mosse concern along with numerous other newspapers in the capital. The *Vossische Zeitung* was the respected, but financially unsuccessful, publication of the large Ullstein concern. Ullstein had far more luck with the profitable *Berliner Illustrierte Zeitung*. Since many of the owners and editors of these two large publishing houses were Jewish, held liberal political beliefs, and had connections to republican officials, they were frequently the objects of anti-Semitic criticism of the "Jewish press." For a brief overview of the Mosse, Ullstein, and Scherl publishing houses, see Agnes Lanwer, "Das Berliner Zeitungsviertel" in Helmut Engel, Stefi Jersch-Wenzel, and Wilhelm Treue, eds., *Geschichtslandschaft Berlin: Orte und Ereignisse. Band 5: Kreuzberg* (Berlin: Nicolai, 1994), pp. 183–203.

party organ, but its circulation in the capital reached only 41,000 in 1931.[83] In Berlin, Nazi sympathizers could also read Joseph Goebbels's weekly, *Der Angriff*, the primary purpose of which – even more so than the *VB* – was to incite anger at opponents and drum up enthusiasm for the party among its readers.

By the late 1920s, the *BT* and *VZ* were considered important weapons in the fight against radicalism. Reports of demonstrations, riots, and trials of political criminals became daily fare for their readers. Many articles in liberal and conservative newspapers alike claimed or implied that the danger was spreading from the poor and radical East (i.e., Red Berlin) to the pristine avenues and middle-class neighborhoods of the West. Moreover, bourgeois newspapers alleged that Berlin's East side was connected directly to a city further east, Moscow. The insinuation was that revolutionary conspirators had been sent from Moscow to eastern Berlin, where they worked undercover in preparation for further advances westward. The continual portrayal of radicalism by the bourgeois newspapers as a criminal conspiracy emanating from the East had unintended effects. First, for those who did not witness the events, the extensive coverage of political upheaval in the capital illustrated just how desperate the situation had become in the East End, fostering greater fear and division within the city. Second, in addition to depicting the conspiratorial intentions of looters, protesters, and street brawlers, newspapers were always explicit about the numbers of physical injuries or deaths in each case of violence and the indecision that weakened the state's response. Coupling the consequences of violent outbreaks with the shortcomings of police actions led many bourgeois readers to question the ability of the republican government to address the disorder. Some of this criticism was probably intended to motivate the police and other policy makers, but readers developed an image of the capital as chaotic and came to see city authorities as lacking the legitimacy needed to govern. Overall the middle-class readers of the liberal press began to doubt the republic's ability to weather the crisis. Naturally, the papers further to the left and right were more inflammatory in their critiques of the state's response, but the implications of the articles appearing in the *BT* and *VZ* were more detrimental because people expected accurate appraisals of events and objective yet genuine support for the republic from these two newspapers.

In their coverage of political violence, newspapers frequently depended on rumors and stereotypes as evidence of the growing threat from Red Berlin. In 1929, two months before the Communist paramilitary group the Roter Frontkämpferbund (RFB) was banned, a young Stahlhelm member was murdered in the still somewhat rural northern district of Pankow. In a report printed in the *Deutsche Tageszeitung*, it was assumed that the

[83] Ibid., p. 185.

perpetrator was a member of the RFB from Neukölln, the southeastern district known for its political disturbances. Though no one was apprehended at the scene, suspicion of a Neukölln connection prevailed because on the previous Friday night, the Neukölln RFB had met – and from there it was alleged that troops were sent to Pankow. The article supported its claims by explaining that the RFB's new method was to send "shock troops" on bicycles to far-removed districts, so witnesses could not recognize the perpetrators of the crimes.[84] Basing a story on such thin evidence may seem to be poor journalism, but it was common to presume the threat of violence emanated from the "trouble-spots" in the East, and that this danger was "unrecognizable." Three days later a suspect had been arrested. He was a former member of the Communist Rote Jungsturm from Pankow, not Neukölln.[85]

The KPD was not the only party represented as having learned their revolutionary ways from Moscow. The NSDAP borrowed some of its tactics from the KPD, and the liberal press was quick to pick up on this connection. In 1930 the *VZ* ran the article "National Socialist Cells Designed on Communist Model." In case readers were unaware of the origins of that model, they were reminded that the "heritage" of street and factory cells was among revolutionaries in "czarist Russia." The article described in great detail how Nazi officials had been instructed to set up street and housing-block cells in a tightly organized plan that would encompass all Berlin. The author was less interested in describing the policies advocated by the NSDAP than he was in demonstrating the loss of privacy that would accompany the Nazi invasion of Berlin's neighborhoods. Nazis would fill mailboxes with handouts and keep tabs on the political loyalties of the inhabitants. The "more conscientious the party official is," reported the *VZ*, "the more comprehensive the material sent to the party leadership."[86] These illegitimate political tactics, he argued, were not German in origin but came from the revolutionary (Russian) East.

When the conservative press had its turn to raise the specter of fear over foreign influence and conspiracy from within Red Berlin, it linked the prorepublican SPD to the KPD. In the summer of 1932, the *Berliner Börsen-Zeitung* reported that the "Berlin Bolshevists" had issued a "fighting deployment" under the slogan: "March to the fascist West!" On the same day, the article continued, the central newspaper of the Berlin SPD declared: "We are marching to the West!" For good measure the author added that in the coming evening a "March of the Iron Front [SPD] to the West" was also scheduled, proving that the SPD and KPD were not only in ideological agreement, but

---

[84] *Deutsche Tageszeitung*, "Kommunistischer Meuchelmord. Ein Jungstahlhelm von Rotfront-Radfahren hinterrücks niedergeschossen," Nr. 93, February 23, 1929.

[85] *Vorwärts*, "Pankower Bluttat aufgeklärt," Nr. 95, February 26, 1929.

[86] *VZ*, Nr. 280, April 16, 1930.

also that they *"march* together in all places."[87] The danger of this imminent physical invasion was clear, and there was no sense that anything would be done to stop it. In fact, the article added that the keynote speaker for the evening demonstration of leftist might was to be "comrade" and Prussian Interior Minister Carl Severing.

Also common in the bourgeois press (both liberal and conservative) were articles that covered a number of incidents of political violence in the city in such a way as to lead the reader to believe that the events were connected or at least had some common denominator. In one example from the *Kreuz-Zeitung*, the stories of three people who were severely injured on the same day in various sections of Red Berlin were presented. The way the article was structured, however, the reader was likely to conclude that these incidents were all part of a pattern of attack and revenge among political adversaries. In fact, all three cases were unrelated, and the bulk of the article pertained to a pub altercation that developed between two Nazis. In that incident, patrons of the pub called the police to quiet things down. When a passing patrolman tried to arrest the Nazi troublemaker, who happened to be a doctor, he resisted, and the officer was forced to fire a warning shot. There are few other details of the situation, but we do know that the disagreement was between two men of the same party who had been drinking and arguing over nonpolitical issues. The title of the article, "Police officer shoots in self-defense. Again severe conflict in Berlin – a doctor is injured,"[88] however, makes it sound like a clear-cut case of political street brawling and police intervention. Examples like this one are not meant to point out simple inconsistencies in reporting; newspaper coverage was often highly detailed and accurate. The point here is that Berlin's newspapers, even when accurate, added to their middle-class readership's sense that the threat came from the East and that the situation was beyond the control of authorities.

By 1932, many reports on the political crisis in the bourgeois press, which focused on the division between East and West, warned of the imminence of a Bolshevik-style revolution. This fear turned attention away from Nazi aggression in Berlin, which was gaining in frequency and audacity. For example, in the strike of the Berliner Verkehrsgesellschaft (BVG, Berlin Transport Company) of November 1932, the right-wing press claimed that "strike-terrorists" were

not concerned with carrying the strike through, but with instigating unrest to distract the police, and according to the plans of the men pulling the strings of this action, creating the opportunity to take control of relatively weakly guarded official buildings

---

[87] *Berliner Börsen-Zeitung,* "Lindenstraße und Bülowplatz," Nr. 326, July 14, 1932. The emphasis is present in the original.

[88] *Kreuz-Zeitung,* "Polizeioffizier schiesst in Notwehr," Nr. 359, December 25, 1932.

and life-sustaining industries. The impression becomes ever clearer, that behind the strike far-reaching revolutionary political goals are hidden.[89]

It was true that the KPD had more than theoretical blueprints for the coming revolution. The party had indeed drawn up diagrams of the "belt" they would tighten around Berlin when the revolt began. These diagrams vividly brought to life bourgeois fears of a Communist offensive, which would originate in the slums of Berlin and then extend outward to paralyze the entire capital by targeting utilities and transportation. Articles like this one about the BVG strike, however, were not based on any actual Communist maneuvers. They were designed to scare readers, taint the entire political left, and implicitly lend support to the right. As a result, the focus on the KPD as the largest threat to public order prepared the middle classes to accept the right-wing authoritarian solution to the crisis, which came three months later.

The radical newspapers, however, also joined in these territorial scare tactics. The Communist *RF* used the differences between East and West Berlin to its advantage whenever possible. Editors believed workers would be enraged by the disparities and emboldened by the idea of invasion from the East. In early 1930, the KPD published an article titled, "*Bannmeile* crossed, Police fled." It described an "enormous demonstration march" which took place in the "holy *Bannmeile*," the section around the main governmental offices, which had been closed to political demonstrations since the revolutionary period after World War I. The article claimed that the workers held their ground and that the intimidated police returned to their vehicles and disappeared.[90] By successfully crossing into the heart of the government district, the KPD proclaimed its strength and its intention not to be isolated in the neighborhoods of the North and East.

When demonstrations geared toward penetrating the borders of the tranquil West End failed to intimidate, or when they led to violence, the Communist press could take the moral high ground, as it did in December 1932. On Christmas Eve, the KPD organized a "Hunger-march" through the main shopping district of West Berlin. This holiday protest had become an annual event, and it always drew ire from the bourgeois press. The conservative *Deutsche Zeitung* complained that the most terrible aspect of the march was that the "Communists were allowed unhindered... to 'demonstrate' against the German Christmas-fest." The "foreign" marchers came from "Neukölln and the East side of Berlin" and were called together by their "string-pullers."[91] During the 1932 march, the police fired warning shots out of fear that the demonstration would incite looting or

---

[89] *Berliner Börsen-Zeitung*, "Voller Einsatz der Polizei," Nr. 521, November 6, 1932.

[90] *RF*, "Die Bannmeile durchbrochen, Schupo flüchtet," February 21, 1930. For further explanation of the purpose and significance of the *Bannmeile*, see Chapter 3.

[91] *Deutsche Zeitung*, "Straßenkrawall am heiligen Abend," December 25, 1929.

physical attacks on wealthy holiday shoppers. In typical *Rote Fahne* prose, the paper responded by portraying the marchers as "shivering from hunger and cold, with tattered clothing and shoes falling apart, but with fists clenched with hate for those responsible for their obvious misery." Their protest chants, cheered the Communist daily, "stopped the contented with luxury-limousines overfilled with Christmas packages."[92] This portrayal of physically downtrodden unemployed Berliners was probably accurate, though both the *Rote Fahne* and the conservative newspapers refused to see such demonstrators as physically incapable of sustained revolt. The *RF* had to add that after the dispersal, marchers remained defiant and ready for action, whereas the conservative *Berliner Börsen-Zeitung* dramatized the aborted march as a "systematic KPD disruption of Berlin's Christmas peace."[93]

The Nazis also made their presence felt on Berlin's West End shopping avenues. There were a number of incidents, especially in late Weimar, in which groups of SA men accosted or attacked "Jewish-looking" pedestrians or threw rocks at the windows of Jewish-owned businesses, especially the high-profile banks and large department stores such as Wertheim. Even within the liberal press there was relatively little coverage of these incidents. In 1930, fifty-three Nazi men were arrested because they had smashed shop windows around the city after a party rally was broken up in front of the Reichstag, but the case only received a few lines from the semiofficial republican Wolff news wire.[94] The short description of the damage did not even mention the anti-Semitism behind the vandalism. The following year the liberal *Berliner Tageblatt* did report that a "horde" of Nazis had attacked pedestrians in the late evening on the main shopping avenue in the West, Kurfürstendamm. One attacker had a gun, and fights broke out on the "Kudamm" and surrounding streets. The incident began with Nazi cries of "Jews out of Berlin!" but the police only apprehended a few of the men.[95]

Both radical parties, therefore, made attempts to infiltrate public spaces and sites of social and political power in the West End. They wanted to demonstrate their political strength and discipline, and the bourgeois press responded. Even in their criticism, the bourgeois press took the two parties seriously and depicted them as organized and cunning. However, it was

[92] *RF*, "Polizei schiesst am Weinachtsabend," Nr. 225, December 25, 1932. For the Christmas Eve march in 1929, the *RF* ran the article, "Hunger-march through the Bourgeois-District," which satirized the "protection" provided by the mounted police to the holiday shoppers at the department store KaDeWe. *RF*, Nr. 265, December 25, 1929.

[93] *Berliner Börsen-Zeitung*, "Planmässige KPD-Störung des Berliner Weinachtsfriedens," Nr. 605, December 25, 1932.

[94] *Wolff's Telegraphische Büro*, "Der Polizeibericht die Ausschreitungen in Berlin," Nr. 2070, October 16, 1930.

[95] *BT*, "Hakenkreuzler-Pöbeleien am Kurfürstendamm," Nr. 259, June 4, 1931.

clearly the Communist danger alone that was represented as a criminal threat to public order, republicanism, German culture, and basic decency. This threat was surely at home in the districts of Red Berlin, but the East side was certainly less isolated every day, as new laws and an expanding mass culture challenged the divisions between East and West, creating new concerns for Berliners who feared the "other" and new problems for a government trying to unite the whole.

The question of unity was not a new one to city officials in Berlin.[96] The city had been in transition since the fall of the monarchy on November 9, 1918. The USPD, SPD, and DDP, who were determined to shape the new nation, applauded the end of imperialist grandeur and militaristic pomp in Berlin, and supported the creation of a new capital, which would reflect the democratic spirit of Weimar. The structural make-up of the city itself was the first target for significant change. Republican leaders favored the annexation by Berlin of a number of the surrounding communities. During the first two decades of the twentieth century, the municipalities surrounding Berlin had grown in size and in their interdependence with the city. Yet they all held on tightly to their administrative independence. Local pride and competition among communities sometimes had unfortunate consequences. For example, the towns of Tegel and Reinickendorf, northwest of the city, dumped their wastewater into Tegel Lake, from which Berlin took its drinking water. In nine communities, Berlin's gas pipes ran under the streets alongside the pipes of the other towns. In the greater Berlin area there were seventeen water works, forty-three gas works, and fifteen electricity works, all of which used separate rate scales and had individual governing bodies.[97] The inefficiency caused by this overlap had enormous costs for all municipalities.

[96] From its earliest days, Berlin was an amalgamation of independent municipalities. Berlin and Cölln joined together in the early fifteenth century on land fed by two rivers, the Havel in the west and the Spree in the east. At the beginning of the eighteenth century, three small surrounding communities were annexed. This process continued into the twentieth century, but the districts always retained some level of individual administration. Celia Applegate has argued in the larger context that the tradition of German particularism was inherent also in the Weimar Republic's new constitution. Applegate argues against the position that localism ultimately must lead to the failure of democracy by prohibiting national integration. Instead she argues that it also can reflect a democratic will through the desire for self-governance. See Celia Applegate, "Democracy or Reaction? The Political Implications of Localist Ideas in Wilhelmine and Weimar Germany" in Larry Eugene Jones and James Retallack, eds., *Elections, Mass Politics, and Social Change in Modern Germany* (Washington, DC: German Historical Institute and Cambridge University Press, 1992) and Celia Applegate, *A Nation of Provincials. The German Idea of Heimat* (Berkeley: University of California Press, 1990). Andrew Lees also discusses German provincialism in comparison to French and English thought concerning the advantages and disadvantages of urban life in *Cities Perceived* (New York: Columbia University Press, 1985).

[97] Hans J. Reichhard, "Stadterweiterung," in Jochen Boberg, Tilman Fichter, and Eckhart Gillen, eds., *Exerzierfeld der Moderne. Industriekultur in Berlin im 19. Jahrhundert* (Munich: Beck, 1984), p. 96.

Beginning in 1919, the parties of the left, the USPD, SPD, and the DDP advocated for an expansion of city boundaries and the restructuring of Berlin's administration. The parties on the right, the DVP and DNVP, were against any such changes. Conservatives in the communities targeted for amalgamation were particularly repulsed by the idea of forfeiting their independence to become part of the city of millions, with its crime, anonymity and alleged lack of morality. After close to a year of debate in the Prussian *Land*-parliament, however, a law to enlarge Berlin was passed. The *Groß-Berlin-Gesetz* was accepted by the Prussian parliament on April 27, 1920. The German capital now sprawled over 878 square kilometers of land, making it the largest city in Europe, and counted 3.85 million inhabitants. The main point of contention, which had kept the bill from passing for so many months, was that of power sharing between the communities. The new western and southern districts added in 1920 were more suburban, wealthy, and green than the original six. Schöneberg, Wilmersdorf, Charlottenburg, and Steglitz boasted chic shopping districts, outdoor cafés, and theaters, as well as some of the nicest urban residential neighborhoods in Berlin. These communities, in particular, had maintained a united front against relinquishing authority to a new city government.[98] In addition to the old city center and these new suburban communities, within city limits the farming districts of Zehlendorf, Weißensee, and Treptow had remained largely self-sufficient communities but now needed to be incorporated into the city's governing structure. In the end, a compromise solution was reached in which a central administration would cooperate with twenty individual district governments. The original city center, which had been governed previously as one unit, was also affected by the law. The governing body of "Old-Berlin" was replaced by six individual district administrations for Mitte, Tiergarten, Kreuzberg, Friedrichshain, Wedding, and Prenzlauer Berg, as in the rest of the city. The first of three stages in constructing this new entity of *Groß-Berlin* was to be completed by October 1920. By then, elections for city and district assembly members and town councilors were to have been conducted. It would take longer for other steps to be completed, such as the building of bureaucratic offices for some newly created districts, like Steglitz, which was itself an amalgamation of small communities.

During the summer of 1920, the first elections for the new city assembly were held. The left achieved a solid victory, paving the way for further democratic changes in the capital. The greatest number of votes went to the USPD, which took 38.4 percent of all ballots cast. When combined with the 17.2 percent garnered by the SPD, the two parties controlled a majority of

---

[98] Andreas Splanemann, "Bewährung und Begrenzung der Berliner Demokratie. Die erste Magistratsbildung der neuen Stadtgemeinde Berlin 1920" in Otto Büsch, ed., *Beiträge zur Geschichte der Berliner Demokratie, 1919–1933/1945–1985* (Berlin: Colloquium Verlag, 1988), p. 3.

over 56 percent of the seats in the city assembly. In September the conservative DNVP faction in the Prussian parliament tried again to defeat the *Groß-Berlin* law before its full implementation, in order to keep the nation's capital out of the undisputed control of the left. They almost succeeded in getting the support of the DDP, but in the end, the democrats stood in favor of continuing the process of integration and restructuring. In September and October, voting within the assembly for salaried positions went ahead, even though conservatives excused themselves in protest of the majority rule by the left. The SPD and USPD responded by voting with some members of the DDP as a majority assembly. Through this process the USPD and SPD were able to fill all salaried town councilor positions and the majority of non-salaried positions with their own members.[99]

The SPD/USPD coalition was not entirely successful however. Their candidate for school superintendent, Dr. Kurt Löwenstein (USPD), faced loud criticism. He was thirty-five years old, and many within the Center Party, DVP, and DNVP contended that he lacked the experience needed for the job. Behind these doubts, others voiced caution about his atheism and his plans for educational reform. Since Löwenstein was a Jew, some members of the city assembly resorted to anti-Semitic language in their fight against his candidacy. In the end, Löwenstein was elected, but the president of the Prussian parliament refused to confirm his appointment.[100] Löwenstein was the only official chosen for the new government not allowed to take office. The mayor-elect Adolf Wermuth, who aligned himself with no particular party, was acceptable to the left and to moderate liberals for his support of the revolution and past service as mayor of "Old-Berlin." The following year Wermuth was replaced by Gustav Böß, who was without party affiliation but would later join the DDP. Böß would remain the mayor of Berlin until 1930. Working closely with the parties of the left, Böß did much to transform the city from the relatively small monarchical seat into a vast capital center.[101]

Berlin was becoming a modern metropolis. Crucial in this development of a metropolitan identity, which included all of the territory added in 1920, was the creation of a city transportation system. Berlin's rail era had begun as early as 1838 with the opening of Potsdamer station, followed by other major terminals, including Anhalter, Lehrter, and Görlitzer. Local transport was introduced with the building of the ring line in the years between 1871 and 1877 and the construction of an interior East–West connection in 1882. Although the number of rail passengers rose quickly, the system's initial purpose was to serve military and commercial needs in the

---

[99] For the results of the elections of September and October 1920, see ibid., pp. 30–1.
[100] Ibid., pp. 26–9.
[101] For a view of Berlin through the mayor's eyes, see Böß, *Berlin von Heute* (1929).

years surrounding the unification of the country in 1871, and the terminals built to service these lines reflected the confidence and grandeur of the monarchy.

For a while there was no great need to update the public transportation system. The horse-drawn buses and carriages, which had been in service since the middle of the nineteenth century, could easily handle the traffic. Most people lived, worked, and shopped within the same neighborhood. By the end of the century, this pattern began to change. The expansion of large industrial complexes into the open lands further to the north and west, including Siemens' 1898 construction in Spandau, meant that by 1900 large numbers of people began for the first time to commute long distances to the workplace, made affordable by the 1891 introduction of commuting rates on the rail system for workers. Germany also led the way among European nations in electrifying its urban tramlines, introducing the world's very first electric streetcar in 1881 and virtually completing the task of electrification in Berlin by the close of 1902.[102] The increased use of public transportation in the capital between 1870 and 1918 was astounding. An average of 13 trips on public transportation per person in 1871 grew to 374 rides per person by 1917.[103] About half of these trips were taken on the electric street trams. In the years preceding World War I, the city was forced to expand some tram stations, which had already become overcrowded during commuting hours. The case of Beussel Street in Wedding was not uncommon: between 6:30 and 6:45 A.M., 3,900 passengers entered the station, but one hour later, in the same fifteen minute span only 184 people boarded the trams at this location.[104] These statistics for the total number of rides taken per person in Berlin are even more significant when we consider the fact that before 1918 the new elevated and underground lines, which were in the hands of private companies, serviced mainly the wealthy southwestern neighborhoods and suburbs and were also too expensive for most workers to use on a regular basis.[105] This discrepancy, however, would fade in the 1920s.

---

[102] Ibid., p. 73.

[103] See the graph representing Berlin's growing use of public transportation in Lindenberger, *Straßenpolitik* (1995), p. 41.

[104] Ibid., pp. 40–9.

[105] Brian Ladd, *Urban Planning and Civic Order in Germany, 1860–1914* (Cambridge, MA: Harvard University Press, 1990), p. 208. The elevated tracks may have encountered initial resistance from city dwellers, but the idea of an underground transportation network, first advocated in the 1890s by the pioneering electrical engineers at Allgemeine Elektrizitäts-Gesellschaft, faced outright rejection. The men at AEG were not dissuaded by the naysayers, and set out to prove that it was indeed possible to construct rail tunnels in the damp ground of Berlin. Once they succeeded in finding the engineering solutions, city planners began to warm up to the idea. See Peer Hauschild, "Bahnhöfe in Berlin" in Wolfgang Gottschalk, ed., *Bahnhöfe in Berlin: Photografen von Max Missmann* (Berlin: Argon, 1991), p. 10. That the first U-Bahn cars (1902) were designed for the wealthy patrons who lived around their

After World War I, Berlin's transportation system grew along with the population's pride in and dependence on the vast network of trams, trains, and buses. Though building was limited in the early part of the decade owing to the financial crisis that accompanied defeat, the lengthening of existing lines and construction of new lines took off again after the stabilization of the economy in 1924. In 1927, Berlin's public transportation network provided 4.3 million daily rides; 2.3 million of those were taken on electric streetcars, 400,000 on buses, 600,000 on the S- and U-Bahn lines, and close to one million on the city, ring, and regional train lines.[106] By the end of the 1920s all of the city's railway lines, including the most recently constructed suburban lines, were electric, and the BVG, uniting the tram, bus, elevated and underground train companies, was the largest community transit firm in the world.[107] Electrification meant cleaner air and quieter travel compared to steam, and shortened the travel time by one-third.[108] The *AIZ* concluded in 1929: "Each year the population of Berlin grows by about 100,000. And with it, the stream of masses to means of transportation swells year to year at an astounding rate."[109]

By the beginning of the new decade, the city's transit system encompassed 248 stations, 65 of which were either overhead or underground stations. Each year 1.5 billion passengers, roughly equal to the world's population in the early 1930s, traveled on public transportation in the German capital.[110] Potsdamer Platz was not the busiest square on the continent, but it and several other Berlin transportation nodes, including the stations at the Zoo and Auguste-Viktoria-Platz in the West and Leipziger- and Alexanderplatz in the East, were central meeting points for friends, commercial hotspots, and congregation points for the homeless and criminals.[111]

The noise created by motorization was a shock to visitors and transplants in Berlin. For many, who had pulled together their "small savings and one day with pounding heart boarded the slow train, fourth class and rocked toward the tempting destination," a Berlin rail station was the first introduction to

---

lines is demonstrated by the mahogany interiors and red leather upholstery on the seats. Even though ticket prices were significantly higher on the new underground rail than other public transportation services, close to thirty million rides were taken on the limited U-Bahn in its first full year of service. See Goerd Peschken, "Die Hochbahn," pp. 132–3, and Heinz Jung and Wolfgang Kramer, "Die U-Bahn," pp. 138–9 in Boberg et al., eds., *Exerzierfeld der Moderne* (1984).

[106] Remy, "Bahnhofsumbauten in Berlin" (1929), excerpt found in Alfred Gottwaldt, *Berliner Fernbahnhöfe: Erinnerungen an ihre Große Zeit* (Düsseldorf: Alba, 1983), p. 73.

[107] Richie, *Faust's Metropolis* (1998), p. 331.

[108] Peter Bley, "Eisenbahnknotenpunkt Berlin" in Boberg et al., eds., *Exerzierfeld der Moderne* (1984), p. 122.

[109] *AIZ*, "27,000 im Dienste des Berliner Verkehrs," Nr. 43, 1929, p. 4.

[110] Thomas Friedrich, *Berlin Between the Wars* (New York: Vendome Press, 1991), p. 159.

[111] Ibid., pp. 158–60.

the city itself and to urban living in general.[112] Erich Kästner captured the fear and bewilderment of new arrivals in his 1930 poem "Besuch vom Lande." His visitors stand paralyzed on Potsdamer Platz listening to the "rattle" of the rails, the "screams" of automobiles, and "prefer to be back at home" away from the "wild" metropolis.[113]

The grand stations remained etched in the memories of those who passed through them and hold a special place in the fiction of the late Weimar era. In some novels, the rail stations are the quintessential symbol of the urban landscape and play a role as important as any character in the book. In Kästner's satirical look at life among the educated but impoverished middle class, urban transport characterizes the modern metropolis and eventually provides an escape from the difficulties of life in Berlin. In despair over his future and the suicide of his best friend, Fabian wanders to Anhalter Bahnhof. Though he had once sought the hustle and bustle of the city of millions, he now finds no comfort in its presence or the traffic outside. As Kästner imagined: "He leaned against the wall, not far from a group of porters, and closed his eyes. But now the noise tormented him. It was as though the trams and omnibuses were driving right through his body."[114]

In Irmgard Keun's *Gilgi – eine von uns*, the train stations of Berlin have a different meaning. They serve as gateways to possibility. Early in the story, Gilgi's friend Olga, single and independent, plans to take the train from Cologne to Berlin to work as a painter, attract American patronage, and perhaps use it as a jumping off point for other adventures. At the end of the story, single and pregnant, Gilgi decides her only chance for survival is likewise to leave depressed and conservative Cologne to join her friend in Berlin, where she presumes all are welcome and work is waiting.[115] These two novels and many more testify to the impact of Berlin's transit system on the ways people imagined the German capital and experienced it on a daily basis.

Though this vast transportation network was a hallmark of the city's importance, all along the ideological spectrum Berliners eyed the system with

---

[112] *AIZ*, "Ankunft in Berlin," Nr. 24, 1930, p. 464. This article was pessimistic about the chances new arrivals from the countryside had for happiness in the big city, mockingly referring to them as "Hans and Grete."

[113] Erich Kästner, "Besuch vom Lande" in *Ein Mann gibt Auskunft* (Zürich: Atrium Verlag, 1930; second edition, Munich: DTV, 1988), pp. 66–7. In fact, the paralysis is so intense that the visitors are eventually run over by the speeding traffic. The visual image of Berlin as the bustling metropolis is best captured by the 1927 film *Berlin, Sinfonie der Großstadt* by Walter Ruttmann. The viewer is shown a complete day in the fragmented, fast-paced and loud city, which begins with the sunrise and the start of the workday.

[114] Erich Kästner, *Fabian: The Story of a Moralist* (Evanston, IL: Northwestern University Press, 1993), p. 118.

[115] Irmgard Keun, *Gilgi – eine von uns* (Düsseldorf: Claassen, 1979; original edition, 1931), pp. 23, 252–8.

political interest. Those on the far left believed that when the proletarian revolution came, securing the capital city's transportation system would be an immediate priority for achieving their goal of overthrowing the republic. This strategy had indeed been used successfully in 1920 by supporters of the republic, who in declaring a general strike brought the city's traffic to a halt and the right-wing Kapp Putsch to a speedy end. Many moderates viewed the network at times as the Achilles heel of the capital. In November 1932, for a short time it appeared that perhaps the worst would be realized when both Communist and Nazi BVG workers united in a strike action. The amount of press coverage and general public attention the strike received was due in part to this fear that a disruption of the transportation system could bring down the government. During the upheaval, one female art student was arrested for passing out a prostrike pamphlet in Friedrichshain. Though she claimed it was simply Communist campaign material, the police and judiciary saw the literature as much more threatening. The authorities claimed that the KPD did not see the BVG strike as "an economic weapon, rather used it for political aims," which were "to turn this isolated strike into a general or mass strike, in order to lead the way to a revolutionary crisis...in order to overthrow the current government and in its place set up a dictatorship...on the Russian model."[116]

When evaluating the impact of urban development on Berlin's inner-city districts, which tended to be workers' neighborhoods, our initial impulse is to presume that the building of the transportation network – primarily city rail, S- and U-Bahn lines – weakened the sense of community at the local level. After all, we know that the construction of the lines disrupted the built environment of many Berlin neighborhoods. Indeed, whole blocks of homes were sometimes leveled to make way for elevated and underground tracks and stations. Once imposed upon the landscape, rail lines divided communities, cutting off friends and neighbors from one another. Access to transportation also meant residents could leave their familiar surroundings for work or pleasure. After glimpsing new opportunities, some young people in particular chose not to return to the streets where they had grown up, diluting neighborhood continuity and loyalty. By connecting the various city districts, public transportation also made it increasingly easy for outsiders to enter these neighborhoods. Some were simply passing through, but others were among the growing number of representatives from various governmental departments coming to investigate life in Berlin's "slums" – or, in the case of police patrols of public transportation nodes and lines, to control these newly created public spaces.

Though these four factors certainly posed a challenge to neighborhood identities in Berlin, in the end the growth of the city's transportation network,

---

[116] LAB, Rep. 58, Nr. 1478, Film 740, Concluding report concerning "Kampf gegen Lohnraub und faschistische Diktatur," November 4, 1932.

with particular regard to the local rail, S- and U-Bahn stations and lines, effectively supported and even amplified the sense of community at the grassroots level in Berlin by the late 1920s and early 1930s. Evidence for this assertion can be found in the social and commercial uses of transit stations. More importantly for this era of German history, this claim is supported by the ways these stations and even the rail cars themselves became sites of contention in the increasingly violent, radical culture that developed.

One reason why the importance of transportation hubs to neighborhood life is often overlooked is that the unique qualities of the small stations have been overshadowed by the drama of the grand, yet impersonal, terminals. It is true, as Wolfgang Schivelbusch and others have argued, that the large railway stations built in the mid- and late nineteenth century were initially seen as "alien appendages" that tore up the landscape, often dwarfing the surrounding buildings and stigmatizing the industrial districts in which they were located, because they attracted prostitutes and vagabonds.[117] But the later, much smaller, local S- and U-Bahn lines and their stations were more easily integrated into the fabric of the existing community. Moreover, since many of the S-Bahn stations had open sheds (or no sheds in the case of many tram stations), one never left the landscape of the surrounding area. Even those *Hochbahn* stations in Berlin with closed halls were designed with light iron skeletons and thin walls, with plenty of windows and light, retaining the visual connection to the surroundings.[118] A visit to one of the monumental stations offered a much different experience. Once behind the imposing façades, these stations offered a concourse hall as a transitional space between the city and the machinery of the tracks and cars located in the shed.[119] Amid the throngs of unfamiliar faces in the concourse hall, or unable to speak over the sounds of the approaching and departing locomotives in the shed, Berliners at the grand terminals had clearly entered a separate world. At the local station, standing in the open air watching the neighborhood hustle and bustle, or crowded among recognizable faces during commuting hours, Berliners maintained contact with their communities.

When Berlin's first viaduct-style rail architecture was introduced in 1882 after over six years of construction, it was greeted as a great achievement, a suitable heir to the Roman aqueducts from which it hailed stylistically.[120] For the neighborhoods in which these stations were built, however, it was more important that the space under the elevated tracks would soon house

---

117 Wolfgang Schivelbusch, *The Railway Journey* (New York: Berg, 1986), p. 171.

118 Peschken, "Die Hochbahn" (1984), 133.

119 Anthony Raynsford, "Swarm of the Metropolis: Passenger Circulation at Grand Central Terminal and the Ideology of the Crowd Aesthetic" *Journal of Architectural Education* (Vol. 50, No. 1, 1996), p. 4.

120 *Nationalzeitung*, February 7, 1882, cited in Lothar Binger, "Stadtbahnbögen" in Boberg et al., eds., *Exerzierfeld der Moderne* (1984), p. 106.

pubs, craftsmen's studios, and market stalls. These stations clearly provided more to the local residents than simply the means for travel out of the neighborhood. The viaduct design of the elevated system brought commerce to the neighborhood, helping to maintain these communities as self-sufficient entities and drawing more residents to the station on a regular basis. On a less dramatic scale, the presence of newspaper and snack stands in the underground stations also helped to foster ties. The above-ground entrances of the U-Bahn and tram stations also attracted pubs and restaurants, making these stations important meeting spots for friends. The rail lines themselves also played a role in the maintenance of local identity, by forming the border separating one neighborhood from another. This separation could be seen as isolating. However, it also gave the residents of the enclave, such as the Karl-Friedrich-Platz neighborhood, a sense of location within the city of millions.[121] Because these workers were physically separated from the surrounding area by rail lines on one side and a commercial thoroughfare on the other, those living there – who were not homogeneous in terms of political loyalties or ethnicity – felt united and at home during the turbulent 1920s.

Beyond creating social cohesion and economic vitality for the neighborhoods in which they were situated, local stations and rail lines also had significant political functions in the city's neighborhoods. Because of the heavy traffic at these transportation nodes, political parties distributed party literature, hung political posters, and stationed their newspaper salesmen here. Train stations were also frequent sites for political confrontation. Representatives of one party would cross the path of their opponents en route to the countryside for campaigning or military exercises. Brawls on train platforms were also common when speakers arrived from other cities, to be greeted by supporters and detractors. Police tried to stay informed of those political groups entering and leaving the city via train in order to keep the peace between passengers, and in the waning days of the republic the police lobbied to have all political literature banned from city transport stations in order to cut down on the disruptions at these sites.

The trains and buses that coursed along, below, and above Berlin's streets were also used to reach entertainment and sites of relaxation. Inner-city dwellers traveled outward to reach the countryside of the Brandenburg province. Berliners also sought time away from the bustle of downtown at their small garden allotments, which seemed to cover all open spaces within city limits. These small gardens were used to grow flowers and fruit trees and, in hard times, became an important source of fresh food, especially vegetables. By 1932, there were over one hundred thousand such garden plots in Berlin, most of which also contained a small cabin used for weekend and summer vacation living. Though many of these were owned by the middle classes, workers were not left out of the popular small-garden movement.

[121] Brücker, "Soziale Fragmentierung und Kollektives Gedächtnis" (1993), pp. 290–2.

Nor were these colonies oases from the political crisis of the early 1930s. The allotments were often organized into small clublike communities with a central governing body, and in some cases the members took a joint political stand. This process became increasingly common as the unemployed moved into these garden communities year-round to save money on rent. By 1932, eighty makeshift tent cities had also been erected around Berlin, housing thirty thousand of the city's poor and homeless in the warm months.[122] When residents chose politically charged names for their settlements instead of the pastoral sounding *"Ruhleben"* (Quiet Life), confrontations with police or nearby political opponents often followed. The Communist sports association Fichte played a large role in a number of settlements, providing inhabitants with leisure activities and organizing antifascist campaigns.

When Berliners wanted to escape life in the metropolis without leaving downtown, they were likely to go to one of almost four hundred movie houses in the city. This entertainment medium was truly an option for all classes. In 1931, about half of all movie theaters were located in the six small, but densely populated, poorer districts of the city center. Although the economic crisis hurt attendance, which dropped from more than fifty-five million visits in 1931 to just under fifty-two million the following year, these numbers remain staggering for a city with a total population of around four million.[123] While much has been written about the artistic innovations of Weimar cinema, which was centered in Berlin, it is important to remember that film was also central to daily life in the republic for its ability to unite different social groups in a common cultural experience.[124] Movies

[122] The garden communities were not solely a republican era phenomenon. The housing shortage that resulted from the war of 1870 had first ushered in the movement, which grew substantially after World War I. By 1925, there were already more than one hundred thousand people living on their garden plots in the capital. For more on the garden communities and their potential as sites of Nazi resistance, see Rita Klage, "Proletarische Fluchtburgen oder letzte Widerstandsorte? Zeltstädte und Laubenkolonien in Berlin" in Berliner Geschichtswerkstatt, ed., *Projekt: Spurensicherung. Alltag und Widerstand im Berlin der 30er Jahre* (Berlin: Elefanten, 1983), pp. 117–36.

[123] *Statistisches Jahrbuch Berlin*, 8. Jahrgang (Berlin, 1932), pp. 166–7. In addition to the opera and other musical offerings, in the depths of the Depression the city also supported thirty-six theaters and six cabarets.

[124] For a concise overview of the arts in Weimar, see Detlev Peukert, *The Weimar Republic: The Crisis of Classical Modernity* (New York: Hill and Wang, 1989), pp. 164–77; Jost Hermand and Frank Trommler, *Kultur der Weimarer Republik* (Munich: Nymphenburger Verlagshandlung, 1978); Peter Gay, *Weimar Culture. The Outsider as Insider* (New York: Harper & Row, 1968); and John Willett, *Art and Politics in the Weimar Period: The New Sobriety* (New York: Pantheon, 1980). Robert Taylor's monograph on Berlin culture provides an extensive history of literary and artistic developments in the city: *Berlin and its Culture* (New Haven, CT: Yale University Press, 1997). Alexandra Richie also devotes a chapter to Berlin's avant-garde in *Faust's Berlin* (1998). Among the many studies on Weimar cinema, see in particular, Andreas Huyssen, *After the Great Divide. Modernism, Mass Culture and Postmodernism* (Bloomington: Indiana University Press, 1986); Patrice Petro,

and newsreels both stressed the possibilities of modern life. Berliners saw themselves pictured on the road toward an American-style consumer society, which promised technological advancement from household appliances to the airplane that Charles Lindbergh flew across the Atlantic.[125] While Berlin was not as "advanced" as New York or Chicago, its affinity to urban America was strengthened by the newsreel spots that showed how "distant" the cultures of Asia, Africa, *and* rural Europe were from the lifestyles of Berlin's inhabitants. In forty-eight newsreels shown in Berlin between 1929 and 1933, sixty-four reports on the United States appeared, which averages to more than one American story per film (each film contained seven or eight segments).[126] Among other highly popular subjects were non-American entertainment topics, which were represented ninety-six times, and reports that highlighted technological advancements from outside the United States. The entertainment category included sporting events, especially the 1932 Olympics, and the travels and accomplishments of artists and writers. The technological stories, included seventy-three times in the forty-eight newsreels viewed, focused primarily on the speed of planes, Zeppelins, motorbikes, and automobiles and on modern production methods. Politics ranked very low indeed, with no stories devoted to the domestic political crisis and very few that focused on European politics, other than the marriages of European royalty.[127] Asia, Africa, and the Middle East were represented in thirty-three reports, which emphasized the contrast between European and non-Western cultures. Besides coverage of the Sino-Japanese war, stories

---

Joyless Streets. Women and Melodromatic Representation in Weimar Germany (Princeton, NJ: Princeton University Press, 1989); Anton Kaes, Wolfgang Jacobsen, and Hans Helmut Prinzler, *Geschichte des deutschen Films* (Stuttgart: Metzler, 1993); Thomas J. Saunders, *Hollywood in Berlin: American Cinema and Weimar Germany* (Berkeley: University of California Press, 1994) and also the classic Siegfried Kracauer, *From Caligari to Hitler: A Psychological History of German Film* (Princeton, NJ: Princeton University Press, 1947).

[125] Much has been written in recent years about the relationship between Germany and America, from the Weimar period through the Third Reich to the divided Germanies. For more on this unique relationship, see Mary Nolan, *Visions of Modernity: American Business and the Modernization of Germany* (New York: Oxford University Press, 1994); Philipp Gassert, *Amerika im Dritten Reich. Ideologie, Propaganda und Volksmeinung, 1933–1945* (Stuttgart: Franz Steiner, 1997); and Michael Ermath, ed., *America and the Shaping of German Society* (Providence: Berg, 1993).

[126] One of the weekly newsreels was produced by Fox and the rest by Emelka, Deulig, and Ufa. The newsreels were silent films until the fall of 1930. Most of the reports not covered by these statistics involved weather conditions and disasters throughout the world. Only fourteen stories focused specifically on women. These ranged from new fashion ideas and beauty contests to stories of female athletes. Two clips from an Opel-Deulig-Ufa film on scenes from the 1920s showed Claerenore Stinnes, daughter of industrialist Hugo Stinnes, as she defied convention by racing her convertible and dressing in men's fashions. See BA-Außenstelle-Filmarchiv, Wochenschau, Nr. 1294.

[127] Coverage of the proceedings at the Lausanne disarmament conference in 1932 provides a notable exception to the absence of political news.

focused, for example, on Muslim festivals and other seemingly "exotic" traditions. Life in rural Germany and other rural regions of Europe were the subject of twenty-three newsreel reports. This coverage was similar to the film accounts of life in Asia and the Middle East. The people featured wore traditional costumes and participated in village festivals or performed customary dances. Berliners would have certainly recognized more from their own lives in the films on the United States than they would have in the depictions of rural Europeans.

The newsreels were clearly designed to appeal to an urban audience of young people who wanted to escape the difficulties of the times. There was no mention of unemployment statistics or job curtailment, and the films always ended on an upbeat note, with a comical clip, soccer highlight, or the like. As becomes clear from the preceding figures, the overall focus of the films was entertainment, modern life, and America. Rapid travel, independence and the release from urban monotony were the dreams of many Berliners, especially the young. Both working men and working women were captivated by the symbols of freedom projected on the screen. Many young working women were new to the city and/or from working-class backgrounds. The sense of personal autonomy that came with a paycheck from a white-collar job as a salesperson or office clerk was thought to be the first step to financial and sexual independence. Many soon learned, however, that their careers were tainted by sexual harassment, low pay, and insecurity. Out from behind their desks, young women also found Berlin's public spaces unwelcoming. The city's streets never belonged to the "new woman," where she confused and angered men of all social classes unable to make sense of women in public who were neither mothers nor prostitutes.[128]

Young men too dreamed of independence from family obligations, monotonous jobs, or the feelings of failure that came with unemployment. The cinema was a place to escape parental criticism, and the newsreels, which showed the possibilities of life, successful love affairs, and the achievements of masculine heroes and their machines, were a hopeful contrast to their own situations. In a survey carried out in 1928 in an unnamed large industrial city in Germany, researchers questioned 500 young unskilled workers and 500 young apprentices. They found that among the 14 and 15 year olds, 41 percent were regular cinema visitors, meaning they went to the movies each time a new show was playing. Among the 16 year olds, 53 percent of

---

[128] Katharina von Ankum, "Gendered Urban Spaces in Irmgard Keun's *Das kunstseidene Mädchen*" in Katharina von Ankum, ed., *Women in the Metropolis* (Berkeley: University of California Press, 1997), pp. 162–85. Von Ankum argues that, "while a man could experience flanerie as an extension of his private sphere, the flaneuse was limited to the role of the prostitute." The protagonist in Keun's novel, therefore, is thwarted in her attempts to emancipate herself by the gendered nature of public space in Berlin. She eventually accepts the role of wife after rejecting the sexual advances of her boss and strangers on the street. See in particular von Ankum, pp. 162–8.

the apprentices and 69 percent of the unskilled workers were regular theater attendees. The figure reached as high as 82 percent for unskilled 17 year olds, while it dropped to 29 percent for apprentices of the same age. The young people were asked why they attended the movies so often. The most common responses were to alleviate boredom, to escape family problems, and to meet the opposite sex, as well as because the price of admission was low and the themes of the films were exciting and uplifting.[129]

While some moviegoers may have hoped Berlin was charting the same path set by Chicago and New York, the passage of the *Groß-Berlin* law in 1920 and the early restructuring that followed had not brought an end to the debate about city structure or identity. Throughout the 1920s, conservatives complained about the forfeiture of power in the districts to central authorities and argued that the law had done little to improve municipal efficiency. At the end of the decade, some reporters were still asking the question: "What is Berlin?" Others tried to make Berlin, still relatively new in structure and character, more tangible to their readers. Journalists and political leaders believed that citizens around the country would develop a better sense of their capital if they were given details such as the numbers of vehicles operating in the city (100,000) or the kilograms of beef consumed per day (70,000).[130]

It is not surprising that Germans who lived far from Berlin knew little about the city in 1930, but even within Berlin, politicians and the public were still mulling over the effects of modernization and the 1920 restructuring. As the extent of the Depression began to emerge, leaders at both ends of the political spectrum began to criticize the city's bloated bureaucracy and demand further "rationalization." The right returned to its argument of the previous decade by insisting that only decentralization could save "the too-big-Berlin."[131] Those on the left supported a rationalization of the "over-bureaucracy" which would entail the dissolution of all district boundaries to be replaced by one Berlin administration.[132] Though the proposed reforms

---

[129] H. Muer, "Kino und Jugend" in *Jugendführung* (Nr. 15, 1928), pp. 246–9. The authors of the study concluded that attendance dropped off for apprentices, because, in contrast to the unskilled workers, as they matured they found more valuable ways to occupy their time. The study's findings, which were used to argue that movie theaters were leading to the delinquency of Germany's urban youth are also found in Jens Flemming et al., eds., *Familienleben im Schatten der Krise. Dokumente und Analyse zur Sozialgeschichte der Weimarer Republik* (Düsseldorf: Droste, 1988), pp. 238–42.

[130] *Osnabrücker Zeitung*, "Was ist Berlin?" November 19, 1928. Statistical estimates come from the article. For additional views of the capital from around the republic, see LAB–Außenstelle, Rep. 01-02, Nr. 653.

[131] *Berliner Börsen-Zeitung*, "Das zu große Berlin," morning edition, February 5, 1930.

[132] VZ, "Berliner Überburokratie. Keiner darf entscheiden," morning edition, February 19, 1930. For other liberal interpretations of the controversy, see *Berliner Morgenpost*, "Keine Zerstückelung von Berlin!" January 26, 1930, and *BT*, "Die Grosse Reform," February 1, 1930.

varied, all agreed that even the most mundane policy decisions were subject to input from a number of governmental offices, and that city authorities were largely unresponsive to citizens' needs.

The debate over Berlin's size and governing structure continued even after the passage of additional administrative reforms on March 5, 1930. Such discussion highlights the general dissatisfaction with Berlin and lack of certainty about Berlin's future. Even though Berlin would be close to 700 years old in 1930, city councilors sensed an increasing urgency in this period of crisis to combat any mistrust or sense of alienation from the larger urban entity. One strategy involved a series of radio shows hosted by prominent members of city government. Civic themes were selected for the programs, which first aired in April of 1929, by their ability to dispel apprehension and foster municipal pride. "The aim of the Communal Hour, which takes place about every four weeks," wrote the representative of the broadcaster to city administrators, "is to teach Berlin radio listeners about the activities and goals of the municipal administration and agencies in an objective way without polemics and party politics."[133] The series opened with a presentation by Mayor Gustav Böß on "Self-government and the Metropolitan Population." Other shows dealt with the central government in Berlin and city and district elections. One quizzed listeners on the peculiarities of their capital. The announcer probed mysteriously: "which of you, ladies and gentlemen, know where in Berlin pile-supported dwellings still exist? . . . Who knows the immortal city councilor, the ladies without backs, the Buddhist village . . . ? In light of these curiosities it is with certainty that we assume, that our capital will now lose its reputation as an uninteresting city."[134]

Through measures such as this one and the Constitution Day discussed in Chapter 3, republican leaders tried to create a sense of belonging and reassure their constituents that in the past decade progress had been made in creating a new stable Berlin. However, as the continued debate over the April 1920 law illustrates, there was no status quo in Berlin on which to base an identity for the city; fundamental aspects of life in the capital were constantly in flux, under construction. The unending state of transition only intensified in the early 1930s under the strain of the Depression, making it entirely conceivable to the population that republicanism too was just a temporary phase.

The physical structure of the neighborhoods and the metropolis played a key role in the formation of Berliners' political convictions and forms of activism. In what follows, we will see how the built city and the tension between

---

[133] LAB-Außenstelle, Rep. 01-02, Nr. 2386, letter from the Berliner Funkstunde AG to Stadtrat Dr. Richter, August 27, 1929.

[134] Ibid. Text of a speech to be read during the "Kommunale Stunde," 1929. Author is likely Dr. Franz Lederer.

neighborhood and city identities and structures influenced the development of radicalism in the capital. For example, the housing crisis did not lead simply to the recognition of social inequality and the formation of ideological solidarity among workers; it also led to grassroots initiatives directed at specific daily life issues and increased the potential for conflict between family members and neighbors. The division between East and West affected how those living in the West End perceived the apparent disorder across town and influenced the way law enforcement authorities and the republican government responded to political unrest. Finally, the growing transportation network increased the traffic in and out of the city's neighborhoods testing the strength of local identity and challenging some to defend local landmarks.

2

Rebellion at Home and in the Community

Though Berliners were feeling increasingly settled in their neigborhoods by the end of the 1920s, the Depression that followed intensified the need to identify with others locally and accelerated a certain process, which to many living at the time threatened to undo the sense of stability so desired at home and in the community. This chapter focuses on the ways the economic crisis challenged the integrity of these neighborhoods first from the inside – through the escalation of gender and generational crisis – and then from the outside – in terms of police surveillance and state intervention. For example, the industrial rationalization of the mid 1920s followed by the long-term unemployment associated with the economic collapse more abruptly challenged traditional family roles and relationships between men and women than the gradual increased employment of women outside the home had over the previous fifty years. These pressures also created strain between the generations inside families and throughout society. Those coming of age at the end of the 1920s believed (perhaps mistakenly) that their parents and grandparents had enjoyed a degree of economic and political stability that was no longer available to them. In this new climate, some within the younger generation rebelled against the politics of their parents as inapplicable to the times. Throughout this chapter, it will also become clear how the Depression undercut support for city and state authorities. Republicanism was naturally implicated in this rejection of outside authorities, but the favoring of local power was more central to radicalism than any party-driven alternatives to the status quo.

The last section focuses on the Berlin riots of May Day 1929. This tragedy illustrates the increasing mistrust between East and West, between citizens and the republic, and between workers and their political parties. The chapter concludes with the *Blutmai* violence, because it had both symbolic and tangible consequences for Berlin's culture of radicalism. It provides important clues regarding the political implications of gender and generational conflict in Berlin, and how political and social stability unraveled first at the neighborhood level. The 1929 riots served as the beginning of the end of the republic by sanctioning the use of political violence, by further undermining trust in local authorities, by amplifying the discord between the

Social Democratic and Communist Parties, and by teaching workers that their political leaders could not lead.

CRISIS AT HOME: GENDER AND RADICALISM

Changes to family life among workers in late Weimar Berlin did not appear overnight in 1929. Long-term developments in the economy, such as relatively high unemployment, industrial rationalization, and increased use of female labor, had begun before 1914. The growth of the service sector of the economy created new, socially acceptable, white-collar positions for women. This economic freedom, combined with the personal independence experienced during World War I and the political rights won in 1919, meant new opportunities for some women, especially in urban centers like Berlin.[1] In the postwar period, the call from socialist women's organizations and some members of the bourgeois women's movement for sexual freedom also grew louder. Workers' organizations were especially vocal in their demands for information about contraceptives and for a repeal of the legal code that criminalized abortion procedures. But though these changes were dramatic, they did not signal a wholesale reversal of the roles traditionally assigned to women. Middle-class women who were able to move into the service sector had short career paths, which rarely promised advancement and almost always ended with marriage. Daughters and wives of working-class families might labor their whole lives to make ends meet, but if they did so they were still expected to care for their children and homes. Despite the rhetoric of the parties of the left, skilled male laborers earning good wages in a secure

---

[1] The Weimar Republic has attracted substantial interest by historians of women and gender: Lynn Abrams and Elizabeth Harvey, eds., *Gender Relations and German History* (Durham, NC: Duke University Press, 1997); Helen Boak, "Women in Weimar Germany: The *Frauenfrage* and the Female Vote" in R. Bessel and E. J. Feuchtwanger, eds., *Social Change and Political Development in Weimar Germany* (London: Croom Helm, 1981); Renate Bridenthal, Atina Grossmann, and Marion Kaplan, eds., *When Biology Became Destiny* (New York: Monthly Review Press, 1984); Ute Frevert, *Women in German History* (Oxford: Berg, 1989); Ute Frevert, "Traditionale Weiblichkeit und moderne Interessenorganisation: Frauen im Angestelltenberuf 1918–1933" in *Geschichte und Gesellschaft* (Vol. 3/4, 1981), p. 507–33; Atina Grossmann, "*Girlkultur* or Thoroughly Rationalized Female: A New Woman in Weimar Germany?" in Judith Friedlander et al., eds., *Women in Culture and Politics* (Bloomington: Indiana University Press, 1986); Atina Grossmann, *Reforming Sex: The German Movement for Birth Control and Abortion Reform, 1920–1950* (New York: Oxford University Press, 1995); Karen Hagemann, *Frauenalltag und Männerpolitik* (Düsseldorf: Dietz, 1990); Karin Hausen and Heide Wunder, eds., *Frauengeschichte – Geschlechtergeschichte* (Frankfurt a. M.: Campus, 1992); Kate Lacey, *Feminine Frequencies: Gender, German Radio and the Public Sphere, 1923–1945* (Ann Arbor: University of Michigan Press, 1998); Tim Mason, "Women in Germany, 1925–1940: Family, Welfare and Work" in Jane Caplan, ed., *Fascism and the Working Class* (Cambridge: Cambridge University Press, 1995); and Cornelia Usborne, *The Politics of the Body in Weimar Germany: Women's Reproductive Rights and Duties* (London: Macmillan, 1992).

field strove to keep their wives at home in emulation of bourgeois ideals. Domestic violence, often ignited by alcohol abuse, remained a significant, rarely questioned, aspect of neighborhood life.[2]

The very strength of these traditional assumptions about relations between the sexes and the woman's role in the family was bound to collide with the realities of a changing twentieth-century society. This confrontation intensified at the end of World War I, when traumatized soldiers returned defeated to a Berlin that seemed alien to them. The republic's birth had been announced before the armistice was even signed, and long before most men returned from home. Women had successfully maintained nontraditional jobs and sustained their families during the previous four years, and hundreds of thousands of war widows would continue to do so throughout the coming decade.[3] Politicized by the war experience and now armed with the vote, women's enthusiasm for shaping a new Berlin and Germany caused many on the right to brand women as traitors to the war cause and the defeated nation. By the mid 1920s, however, measures taken by the state and by employers had assisted demobilized soldiers in regaining their jobs, while women returned to historically female occupations and the growing bureaucratic ranks.[4] Jobs such as sales clerk, office assistant, and welfare worker all seemed to comply with the caring feminine ideal and had little advancement potential, forcing women to remain focused on the more "natural" goals of marriage and family life. Female blue-collar workers were increasingly shunted into low-paying, unskilled positions as the rationalization of the workplace made the steps of manufacturing simpler. Though the political situation for women in 1919 had held great promise, especially for female supporters of the political left (SPD, USPD, and later KPD), in this realm too the number of women serving as party officials and running for election at all, steadily dropped throughout the 1920s. Party officials had been initially enthusiastic about drawing female members and voters to their parties, but they soon grew wary of male members' negative reactions to politicized women and of what party leaders categorized as inherent female conservatism at the voting station.

The results of Erich Fromm's 1929 survey, which was focused primarily on workers in urban areas around the Weimar Republic, lend credence to the

---

[2] See Martin Soder, *Hausarbeit und Stammtischsozialismus. Arbeiterfamilie und Alltag im Deutschen Kaiserreich* (Giessen: Focus Verlag, 1980), pp. 53–61.

[3] Karin Hausen estimates that there were six hundred thousand war widows in Germany at the end of World War I, one-third of whom were able to remarry by 1924. Karin Hausen, "The Nation's Obligations to the Heroes' Widows of World War One" in Margaret R. Higgonet, ed., *Behind the Lines. Gender and the Two World Wars* (New Haven, CT: Yale University Press, 1987), p. 128.

[4] Richard Bessel refers to the reemployment of World War I veterans as "the great success story of the economic demobilization." Richard Bessel, *Germany after the First World War* (Oxford: Clarendon, 1993), p. 127.

assertion that despite the challenges posed to traditional relations between the sexes, conservative views about women's sexual and economic roles still dominated within the working class at the end of the decade. When asked, over 80 percent of Social Democrats and Communists rejected the use of powder, perfume and lipstick by women as "unnatural, immoral or bourgeois." Women reacted even more negatively to the idea of make-up than their male counterparts. About 75 percent of these same SPD and KPD respondents declared themselves in favor of women's right to work. When the question was changed to specify married women, however, only 25 percent of Social Democrats and 45 percent of Communists still supported this right, and many found it acceptable only under certain circumstances.[5]

The "semblance of normality" that characterized the German political and economic situation in the mid 1920s, therefore, was due in part to a perceived sense of growing normalcy between the sexes. Surely, gender relations had not reverted to those of the nineteenth century, but the dramatic transformation that had begun during the war years had at least slowed by the second half of the 1920s, as the country tried to "right" itself after the trauma of war. The bourgeois parties had a very limited conception of what women could offer their organizations, and even the two workers' parties were unable to integrate women and feminist issues into their platforms. Their hesitancy derived not only from the Marxist tenet that gender equality would come as a matter of course once the socialist revolution had been won, but also from the inability of male and some female leaders in both the SPD and KPD to view women as political actors beyond their motherly interests in pacifism and social welfare. Anxiety about the changing power dynamic between the sexes, however, erupted again during the Depression. It did not always manifest itself in demonstrations explicitly championing the values of a patriarchal society, but these desires were just below the surface, and subsequently fed into the discontent, violence, and militarism of the final years of the republic.

The Depression had two main effects on gender relations. First, through mass unemployment, many men were forced to relinquish their roles as the primary breadwinners for their families. Long-term joblessness, which for many men lasted over one year, also meant boredom and the loss of the camaraderie of the masculine work sphere. The researchers in the Marienthal, Austria study found, even more dramatically, that with long-term unemployment men even lost their identities as workers. When asked to state

---

[5] Erich Fromm, *The Working Class in Weimar Germany: A Psychological and Sociological Study* (Oxford: Berg, 1984; original edition, 1929). For the statistics about the use of make-up and female employment, see in particular, pp. 158–70. Results did vary according to age and whether the respondent was single or married. The category "Left Socialists" in some cases responded with higher rates of affirmative answers than their social democratic or Communist counterparts.

their occupation, over half of the male respondents wrote simply "unemployed" and another 23 percent stated the occupation but qualified it by
noting their unemployed status.[6] Second, these unoccupied men were forced
to share the cramped home space with women and children. Though women
still had numerous chores to perform in this space, men often felt superfluous. In some cases, women were more employable than their husbands
because of the low pay they received for their work, leading to a further
feminization of men, in what amounted to a reversal of the traditional division of labor. The pressures of this new daily routine had great consequences for the political culture in Berlin's industrial core. Politics became
more focused on the local questions raised by the Depression, concerning
male power in their families and neighborhoods. Many of those radicalized
by the Depression were not acting irrationally or out of ideological conviction, but were seeking immediate solutions to what they perceived as a crisis
at home.

One popular campaign to defend the sanctity of the patriarchal household in late Weimar Berlin was the effort to restrict the earning potential
of *Doppelverdiener* (double earners), married working women whose husbands still had jobs.[7] The political right, and the Nazi Party in particular,
attacked this issue as a symbol of the "unnatural" Weimar system. They
argued that it was simply wrong that men should be unemployed, while
married women continued to earn a paycheck. In fact, for the Nazi Party,
the entire "women's question," or *Frauenfrage,* was much more a "men's
question." As one Nazi Party member explained in language that went far
beyond the issue of *Doppelverdiener*: "Because man has forgotten in the
course of the last one hundred years to act as his *natural duty* would have it,
woman has found it necessary to 'emancipate' herself.... The further man
has gone from his natural duties, the more [he] becomes feminized [and] the

---

[6] Marie Jahoda, Paul F. Lazarsfeld, and Hans Zeisel, *Marienthal. The Sociography of an Unemployed Community* (Chicago: Aldine, 1971), p. 83 [first edition, *Die Arbeitslosen von
Marienthal,* 1933]. The authors found that young men, close to their apprenticeship experiences, and men over 50 tended to hold on to their occupational identities longest. Those who
fell between these two age groups were most likely to describe themselves as a part of a new
class of unemployed.

[7] There was a long history, which went back to the early days of industrialization, of gaining supplemental family income through wives' and children's work. Household manufacturing such
as cigar rolling, caring for lodgers, and mending or laundering clothes were common tasks
performed in the home by family members. What politicized the issue of female employment
during and after World War I was the fact that more married and single women found work
outside the home in the male-dominated economic sphere. For more on the history of women's
work and supplemental income in nineteenth-century Berlin, see Rosemary Orthmann, *Out
of Necessity. Women Working in Berlin at the Height of Industrialization, 1874–1913* (New
York: Garland Publishing, 1991), and Barbara Franzoi, *At the Very Least She Pays the
Rent. Women and German Industrialization, 1871–1914* (Westport, CT: Greenwood Press,
1985).

more woman becomes masculinized."[8] These conditions, in which women served as both housewife and co-breadwinner, created "in the long run an unbearable situation for the affected family as well as for the entire Volk."[9]

The campaign against the *Doppelverdiener* targeted directly only the small numbers of middle-class working wives. However, it had larger social implications than the size of the population in question would suggest, and the workers' parties did participate in the public debate. While the KPD and SPD officially recognized a woman's right and financial need to retain employment, the parties' rank-and-file generally retained their traditional assumptions about women's natural roles. A Communist-sympathizing women's newspaper from Berlin-Hohenschönhausen entitled *Distress and Struggle* reported in the spring of 1931: "The working woman toils for nine or more hours at the work site not for her own enjoyment, only to still care for the household afterward; rather she toils in order to lessen the suffering of the family because the husband's wage does not suffice."[10] Women's jobs needed to be protected, therefore, only because the economic system, and the Depression in particular, had upset the ideal division of labor in which a man could independently provide for his family.

While the NSDAP decried the "immoral shame" of the married working woman, and the KPD lamented the unfortunate necessity of the *Doppelverdiener*, the liberal minority also voiced its opinion against wage-earning wives. An editorial in the liberal *Berliner Morgenpost* was quite explicit about its lack of support for the *Doppelverdiener*. The article began by noting the great outpouring of letters from readers, presenting "not unfounded" arguments against the *Doppelverdiener*. Concessions were made for "individual cases" in which the wife is forced to bring in wages, but the author insisted that these "do not in any way make up the majority of the cases." In conclusion, the newspaper explained that its endorsement of the campaign against working wives was grounded in an effort to bolster unemployed men's self-worth. The author admitted quite clearly that "unemployment...cannot be brushed aside or even significantly lessened through the fight against the *Doppelverdiener*. For that their number [among the middle classes] is much too small. However, the man, who must be on the dole day after day, the man whose soul is worn down through the endless wait for any work, finds it doubly difficult, when he must see that in other [families] two earn."[11]

[8] *VB*, "Die Stellung der Frau im Nationalsozialismus," Nr. 114, December 3, 1930.

[9] *VB*, "Der Berufstätige Frau wählt Adolf Hitler," March 13–14, 1932.

[10] BA-SAPMO, RY1/I4/15/3, *Not und Kampf, Zeitung der werktätigen Frauen der Siedlung DIKIFA*, Hohenschönhausen, Nr. 1, March 1931.

[11] BA, Rep. 8034 II, Nr. 5467, *Berliner Morgenpost*, "Gegen die Doppelverdiener," Nr. 10, January 11, 1931. There were many proposals for ways to remove *Doppelverdiener* from their jobs. In most suggested plans, some sort of financial compensation, called "family assistance," would be given to women who volunteered to leave paid employment. Again, it is clear in the public discussion of these potential solutions that the goal of returning

Across the political spectrum, therefore, there was public acknowledgment of the need to combat what was perceived as an "unnatural" development in the relationship between the sexes.

Although the *Doppelverdiener* campaign focused primarily on middle-class wives, the "soul" of the male worker was also "worn down" by the loss of his job. Without employment men were forced to share the cramped living quarters of the small workers' apartment with women and children, a constant reminder of their failure to provide. As one author reasoned in the *AIZ* in 1931: "if one takes eight hours for the normal workday, then in Germany a mass of five million people asks daily the question, what it should do with the forty million hours that involuntarily must be spent."[12] For unemployed men, the options for answering this question and escaping the uncomfortable domestic sphere were limited. In the winter, libraries, museums, and pubs were the only choices, unless one wanted to visit the shelters set up by the religious charities and state welfare offices. During the summer, the choices were better. Parks and street corners provided hours of respite from the demands of family members and the fruitless job search. However, this kind of activity was only an escape, and it did nothing to reestablish what had been a very male-focused culture. As the authors of the seminal sociological study of the effects of the Depression in Marienthal, Austria explained: "The term 'unemployed' applies in the strict sense only to the men, for the women are merely unpaid, not really unemployed. They have the household to run, which fully occupies their day. Their work has a definite purpose, with fixed tasks, functions, and duties that make for regularity."[13] They cooked and cleaned – chores that became more complex and time-consuming as resources ran low. They mended clothes and minded the budget so that the family's meager income or public assistance lasted until the next installment.[14] They bartered and shared goods or services such as childcare with neighbors in order to leave the home for paid employment. The Marienthal researchers found that most men failed to accept much of this burden. Light household duties, if any, were taken on, and these seem to have been the more pleasurable ones. Instead of scrubbing floors, for example, some men helped out with shopping. Instead of cooking the family meals, a husband might take the children for a walk.[15] Basically, men were

women solely to the role of housewife was just as important as opening up a few positions for male workers. See for example, *Berliner Volkszeitung*, "Wer ist 'Doppelverdiener'?" Nr. 152, March 31, 1931.

[12] *AIZ*, "Der Tag ohne Arbeit," Nr. 8, 1931, p. 146.

[13] Jahoda et al., *Marienthal* (1971), p. 74.

[14] The best source for a glimpse into the daily schedule of a female German worker is Alf Lüdtke, ed., *"Mein Arbeitstag–Mein Wochenende." Arbeiterinnen berichten von ihrem Alltag 1928.* (Hamburg: Ergebnisse Verlag, 1991).

[15] Jahoda et al., *Marienthal* (1971), pp. 66–77. The researchers also noted that men slept an average of 90 minutes longer per day than their female partners (p. 74).

witnesses to the hectic schedules of their wives. The directionless way men spent their days compared to women came through in one specific test in the Austrian study. From a concealed position along the town's main street, one hundred pedestrians were viewed. The male subjects were found to stop much more frequently than the women, and when moving the men did so at a slower pace.[16]

Working-class Berlin did not become a female-dominated culture in the Depression years, but in accordance with their greater responsibilities, some measure of authority within families and communities transferred from men to women. In her 1933 study of German families affected by unemployment, Ruth Weiland explained: "in many unemployed families the authority of the father sank.... The children experience daily how the mother must struggle in order to make ends meet with the meager aid. The mother receives all of the incoming money, the father holds at best a bit of pocket change. The child is dependent on the mother for every wish, not from the father. Respect sinks and develops into aversion and contempt if the father . . . tries to maintain or win back his position of authority in the family through brutality."[17]

In response to this changing climate, Erich Fromm concluded that "the powerlessness of the individual [male] in society . . . meant that the obedience of wife and child had an important compensatory function which would not be given up easily."[18] Even in politicized communities of workers that espoused pacifism on the world stage, the acceptance of a husband's prerogative to exercise power over his wife and children – or, perhaps better put, to wield force in compensation for a dwindling sense of power – was simply part of daily life. In the scanty research that has been compiled on domestic violence among Berlin's workers, we can see why the incident rates of abuse may have risen during the Depression. Even before the period under study here, abused women feared "*Prügelfreitag*" (beating Friday). Since Friday was payday, some husbands with change in their pockets would visit the pub and return home drunk, angry, and violent. During the Depression, concerns about money and instability provided more reason to drink and assail "loved ones." In families where the wife was the sole breadwinner, an increasingly common situation during the economic crisis, payday aroused jealousies or feelings of inadequacy among unemployed husbands that were manifested in the *Prügelfreitag*.[19] Domestic violence provides a useful corrective for

---

[16] Ibid., pp. 66–7.

[17] Ruth Weiland, *Die Kinder der Arbeitslosen* (Berlin: E. & C. Müller, 1933), pp. 44–5. Weiland adds that schoolteachers reported their teenage female students had developed a greater respect for women's work and ability than previous cohorts.

[18] Fromm, *Working Class* (1984), p. 163.

[19] Eva Brücker, "'Und ich bin heil da 'rausgekommen': Gewalt und Sexualität in einer Berliner Arbeiternachbarschaft zwischen 1916/17 und 1958" in Thomas Lindenberger and Alf Lüdtke, eds., *Physische Gewalt* (Frankfurt a. M.: Suhrkamp, 1995), pp. 337–65. For other sources on domestic violence, see also Linda Gordon, *Heroes of Their Own Lives: The*

any romanticization of the "solidarity" felt within workers' neighborhoods. Those Berlin women interviewed by Eva Brücker consistently stressed their isolation in the face of this widely accepted abuse. Neighbors did not come to one another's aid during the incident, even though the cries of victims could be heard, as fictionally described in the excerpt from *Straßen ohne Ende*. Women checked in on each other afterward and complained together, but there was no recourse to be taken.

Some men clearly felt that their right to victimize women and children extended to those outside their immediate families and that their area of control ranged at least as far as the entire semiprivate space of the tenement's community facilities. Women reported that there were a number of places they did not feel safe, in particular the communal toilets and the roof tops, where women went to dry laundry and could be cornered by unwanted visitors hiding among the hanging linens. What is most telling here is that, when excluding those incidents of violence within the confines of the married couple's apartment, most women feared other residents of the neighborhood.[20] That many perpetrators were not strangers illustrates that men felt a sense of ownership throughout the tenements and into the surrounding courtyards and streets.

Stability was further threatened by increasing state intervention into family matters. The frequent appearance of welfare workers at the homes of the poor and the constant need to visit the offices of welfare authorities, unemployment agencies, and food distribution centers eroded families' sense of independence. The need to discuss personal finances and shortcomings with members of an impersonal bureaucracy led to feelings of shame and humiliation for the hundreds of thousands of Berliners receiving the various forms of public aid in the early 1930s. The Weimar welfare system was the legacy of military defeat and the early strength of social democracy. Financial crises in the early 1920s meant slow implementation of new legislation, so that the full thrust of the welfare state was not felt until the latter half of the decade. Moreover, we know from recent studies of the Weimar system that as funds became increasingly tight during the Depression, case workers found it necessary to be ever more intrusive into the lives of their clients to uncover the "undeserving" and the "troublemakers." Apartment cleanliness was inspected, as was the potential for alcohol abuse, tendencies toward

Politics of Family Violence, Boston 1880–1960 (Urbana: University of Illinois, 2002); Anna Clark, *The Struggle for the Breeches: Gender and the Making of the British Working Class* (Berkeley: University of California Press, 1995), pp. 72–7, and her earlier book *Women's Silence, Men's Violence: Sexual Assault in England, 1770–1845* (London: Pandora, 1987); and Jan Lambertz and Pat Ayers, "Eheliche Beziehungen, Geld und Gewalt in Liverpool, 1919–1939" in Jutta Dahlhoff, Uschi Frey, and Ingrid Schöll, eds., *Frauenmacht in der Geschichte* (Düsseldorf: Schwann, 1986), pp. 253–64.
20 Brücker, "'Und ich bin heil da 'rausgekommen'" (1995), pp. 349–54.

"work-shyness," or other "moral" deficiencies.[21] In Berlin, the bureaucracy was unprepared to deal with the financial and logistical nightmare presented by the more than 675,000 registered unemployed at the height of the Depression.[22] In Kreuzberg alone more than 64,000 men and women, or 34 percent of the working population, were unemployed.[23] As a result, terrible conditions were faced by all connected to the welfare system. Aid recipients were forced in some cases to walk miles to their assigned unemployment office. Once there, lines often snaked outside the building even during the coldest months of winter [Plate 2]. Tempers ran high for the clients and caseworkers. Welfare workers could be physically abused by citizens enraged at hearing their assistance had been reduced or cut off.[24] As the traditional breadwinners and protectors of the home, men were most humiliated by welfare regulations they found degrading and by their inability to shield their families from this intrusion. One aid recipient from Kreuzberg could still recall years later the humiliation he and others faced in this process and their attempts to stand up for themselves:

Our welfare office was in the Rathaus on Yorckstraße. And there was also a sort of annex, where we got the bath tickets in the Kreuzbergstraße. We went up there, and there was such a crazy guy who gave the things out. For him the most important thing came first: 'all caps off, otherwise you get nothing!' We called out [to the others] to keep the caps on, in order to anger him. [The attendant warned]: 'You really want to take the caps off!' At first we made a big show, but then we gave in and only then did he give us the bath tickets.[25]

In a similar sense, working-class Berliners felt they were losing the battle for neighborhood autonomy to outside authorities. There were more unwelcome outsiders, including welfare caseworkers, bank officials, and policemen, on the streets of Red Berlin during the Depression than ever before. All families dwelling in the tenements knew the welfare authorities, and a visit to one family meant inspection of the entire building and interviews

---

[21] See among other recent studies of the Weimar welfare system, David F. Crew, *Germans on Welfare: From Weimar to Hitler* (New York: Oxford University Press, 1998) and Young-Sun Hong, *Welfare, Modernity, and the Weimar State, 1919–1933* (Princeton, NJ: Princeton University Press, 1998).

[22] Andreas Splanemann, "Berliner Wahl- und Sozialstatistik, 1919–1933" in Otto Büsch and Wolfgang Haus, *Berlin als Hauptstadt der Weimarer Demokratie, 1919–1933* (Berlin: de Gruyter, 1987), p. 319. The data are from June 1933.

[23] Almost twice as many men as women were unemployed in 1933. Ibid., p. 395.

[24] For examples of violence in Hamburg's welfare offices, see Crew, *Germans on Welfare* (1998), pp. 157–65.

[25] Oral history interviews collected by Lothar Uebel for "Lieber draußen als zu Hause" in Kunstamt Kreuzberg, ed., *Kreuzberg 1933. Ein Bezirk erinnert sich* (Berlin: Dürschlag, 1933), p. 31.

Plate 2. A sea of men outside the Neukölln employment office on Sonnenallee in 1929. Though this office was known as the "Workers' Hell" for its long lines, many middle-class hats can be seen among the laborers' caps. Source: © Bildarchiv Preussischer Kulturbesitz, 2003.

with neighbors about the family's reputation and living conditions.[26] More hated than the representatives of the welfare system were the bank and court authorities who came to evict a family or hold an auction of their belongings on the sidewalk, encouraging neighbors and other Berliners to bargain for their possessions. In a Prenzlauer Berg street newspaper article, "Court Marshal as Sadist," the story of an unemployed male worker's inability to protect his wife and family from an official with power is retold: a family has fallen severely behind in its rent, and the landlord wins a court order to repossess their belongings in order to collect the money owed to him. The report explains that the husband had been out of work for some time, and his wife, who had been supporting the family on her own, had fallen ill and could no longer work to make ends meet. With the marshal on her doorstep, however, she was able to make an arrangement with her landlord for one more week's time, and the officer of the court was forced to leave the apartment.[27]

However, the marshal did not return to his office. Instead, the report alleged, he waited in the hallway of a neighboring building until "the husband went to have his unemployment card stamped." Then he returned and made sexual advances toward the wife and her elderly mother. When the two women refused to accommodate his demands, he beat them and locked them in one room while he stole some of the family's furniture. Not only did stories like this erode any faith workers had in the state and its representatives, but it also reinforced men's feelings of inadequacy. If the husband had not been unemployed, the family would not have been in these financial straits. If he had not been forced to go to the welfare office, his wife would never have had to negotiate with the marshal or been vulnerable to his assault. The sexual element of the attack and the loss of material possessions further confirmed the husband's lack of control over "his" territory. The article ended with a direct appeal to its male readers: "How long do you want to put up with such unspeakable scandalous deeds? Should your wives and children be left at the mercy of such brutes of the Third Reich?"[28]

The police presence in the workers' districts also increased dramatically during the Depression. The Berlin force expanded the number of men it had on city streets throughout this period, and the leadership kept a list of trouble spots that were guarded closely in the years after 1929. Police surveillance in the workers' districts was not new. Spies in pubs and patrolmen stationed on street corners and at political rallies had been common since the nineteenth

---

[26] See Chapter 5 for more on the relationship between welfare workers and the families they served. David F. Crew (*Germans on Welfare* [1988], pp. 63–6) provides clear statements by welfare workers indicating that their clients viewed them as unwelcome intruders.

[27] LAB, Rep. 58, Nr. 1370, Film 737, *Der Rote Hammer. Organ der Werktätigen der Schliemannstraße*, Nr. 15, September 1932.

[28] Ibid.

century, especially under the auspices of the Anti-Socialist Laws from 1878 to 1890. However, the police became much more numerous and aggressive in late Weimar. Because of the fear of a Soviet-style revolution, which would purportedly originate in the dark slums of the eastern or northern districts, police regularly searched apartment buildings, political meeting sites, shops, and pubs looking for weapon stores, revolutionary writings, and the conspirators themselves. As the Berlin force became more mobile with the aid of motorcycles, troop transport vehicles and increasingly sophisticated armored vehicles, it was more difficult to set up barricades to keep the police out of the neighborhoods. This extensive surveillance left the inhabitants of Wedding, Neukölln, Kreuzberg, Friedrichshain, and other troubled districts feeling under siege and struggling to retain any sense of privacy. Even many men and women uninvolved in radical politics viewed the scrutiny as unwarranted, while others wished for more patrols. Differing opinions led to conflict between neighbors, especially when police solicited denunciations or asked for tips about suspicious behavior. The police presence, whether viewed as unjust or inadequate, led to the same conclusion: that the republic did not respond to local needs.

It was through radical politics that many men sought to halt the dissolution of male authority in the home and neighborhood. The first step in creating a political realm responsive to men's new needs was to make sure women felt unwelcome. Weimar politics had never been completely open to women, but, as described earlier, women did make inroads into this area at the beginning of the 1920s. However, by the early 1930s women's roles in the leadership, activism, and propaganda within the republic's political parties had been severely limited. Day-to-day party activities were being conducted in a way that not only restricted female involvement but also emphasized masculine camaraderie and confirmed men's authority as fathers and as neighborhood patriarchs.[29] These two steps worked together, resulting in a radical culture in Berlin that was neighborhood-based in strategy and wholly masculine in its rules and expectations.

While the Social Democrats and Communists certainly had reservations about incorporating women into their activities, it was, in fact, male workers – not party leaders – who put up the greatest roadblocks to their wives, sisters, and daughters. As the Berlin SPD and KPD continued to call for more female candidates and popular participation, male party members

---

[29] Jack Katz notes with regard to his subjects: "Whatever the realities of private relations between the sexes, the public life of the street elite expresses male dominance in an overt manner that further elaborates the group's claims to a privileged status." Jack Katz, *Seductions of Crime: Moral and Sensual Attractions in Doing Evil* (New York: Basic Books, 1988), p. 126. His comments are reiterated throughout the literature on gangs. The all female gangs that exist tend to be small, enjoy less stable organizational structures, and remain dependent on the fortunes of the male gangs in their areas. See, for example, Anne Campbell, *The Girls in the Gang* (Oxford: Basil Blackwell, 1984).

consistently sought to thwart these efforts.[30] The Nazi Party never made an effort to encourage female involvement, except as voters and in other very limited capacities, such as volunteers in food drives or as students and teachers in national socialist childrearing classes. The official separation of the sexes and their political roles was one basic reason why support for the NSDAP grew rapidly after 1929, first with the middle classes in Berlin but later to some extent among workers as well.

Long-standing doubts that women were conservative or too emotional to handle the difficult political issues of the day persisted among male workers, making it difficult, even impossible, for women in the parties of the left to be treated as equals by their male comrades. These lingering doubts were only exacerbated at the end of the 1920s, when the Depression led local-level Communists and Social Democrats in Berlin to call for extreme measures in the time of crisis. Among Communists, the prevailing attitude was that revolution, like all wars, was a man's business no matter what the party program claimed. As late as September 1932, KPD publications were still citing Lenin's slogan that "a class struggle without women is half a class struggle and half a class struggle is no class struggle." Yet when the party canvassed its constituents to determine whether women should be allowed in the newly formed mass organization *Roter Massenselbstschutz* (Red Mass Self Defense), the members responded with a resounding no. The only compromise the party leaders could fashion was to create separate female units with separate tasks.[31] For Berlin Social Democrats, reform not revolution was the primary goal. But this aim too, under Depression-era conditions, demanded the sort of military discipline that many believed the party had lacked in recent years. In the midst of economic collapse and a changing political climate, male Social Democrats believed it was time to get serious, and women and *their* issues were not serious.

Attempts to dampen female enthusiasm for politics, while encouraging men to recognize their duty to take up the fight, can be uncovered in the local street newspapers of the Berlin KPD as well as the more widely circulated Communist Party propaganda. For example, it was not uncommon to find stories about female suicide in the party newspapers or neighborhood-based circulars.[32] Reports of suicides vary only slightly and infrequently refer to

---

[30] At the end of 1929 the KPD decided to set a quota for female candidates on some electoral party lists to combat resistance from male members and to live up to the ideological claims of equality between the sexes. The new rules, which promised that one-third of party list candidates would be female, applied only to local elections. The SPD responded by stating that they too would see to it that more room was made on their electoral lists for female candidates. BA-SAPMO, SgY2/V/DF/VIII/62, "Mitteilungen für die Funktionäre der SPD," Bezirksverband Berlin, Nr. 1, January 1930.

[31] BA-SAPMO, RY1/I4/9/4, progress report by the Reichseinheitsausschuss der Antifaschistischen Aktion, "Kampferfahrung VIII, Massenselbstschutz," September 1932.

[32] Suicides in Berlin did increase dramatically during the Depression. In 1925, there were 1,587 incidents of suicide reported, with male suicides occurring at a rate twice that for

male victims, even though men took their own lives at a rate considerably higher than that of women. In one typical article, a young female allegedly reports firsthand about the terrible conditions she experienced in a youth welfare institution. Her father was lost during the war, and her mother was unable to support her on the meager widow's pension she received from the state. The young woman had been in the home for one year and was treated poorly because of her Communist political beliefs. She adds: "My comrade [in the institution] is to the point where she wants to end her life. We have already tried it four times. The situation is simply unbearable.... Can't you help us?"[33] The fact that the young girl was alone and without a father, an innocent victim of the war and Depression, reflects the common themes in reports of female suicide.

In another account published in the *RF*, the suicide of a twenty-nine-year-old female employee at the Wedding AEG plant is reported. Her husband had died two years earlier of tuberculosis, and she had fallen into debt while paying for his funeral arrangements. The article's message was clear: "Female workers must realize that [suicide] is no solution. We should not die, capitalism should."[34] While this editorial comment presented the gender-inclusive party line to readers, it reinforced the belief that women were lacking the proper consciousness and bravery needed in the political struggle. In fact, these stories showed in a most literal sense that women could not survive on their own. Gender relations were considered critical in an *AIZ* report of a failed joint suicide attempt in Berlin by five twenty-somethings – two women and three men – who were saved by a neighbor who smelled the leaking stove gas in the apartment of one victim. The three unemployed men were all described as having been born out of wedlock and the two female victims were both pregnant at the time of the incident, while there is no mention of revolution providing the solution.[35]

females. By 1930, the total had risen to 1,831, and the following year it reached 1,903. In the early 1930s, the rate of female suicides also increased, although the gap between the sexes remained significant. Since male suicides were not reported in the left-wing press to the same extent as the less common female tragedies, we can speculate that incidents of female suicide were a greater affront to social norms. For suicide statistics, see *Statistisches Jahrbuch der Stadt Berlin*, Jg. 2 (1926), Jg. 8 (1932), Jg. 9 (1933).

33 BA, R15.01 (St. 10), Nr. 127, *Die Junge Garde*, "Selbstmordversuche im Erziehungsheim," April 14, 1930. For a grassroots account of female suicide, see LAB, Rep. 58, Nr. 1164, Film 729, *Klassenkampf. Wochenblatt für die Einwohner der Waldenserstraße und der umliegenden Straßen*, Nr. 35, February 2, 1932. This Kiez newspaper described the terrible working conditions suffered by a young woman in a neighborhood bakery, which eventually drove her to take her own life. Her desperation was blamed on the "Satan" who ran the bakery and on her social circumstances. As an unmarried woman, the article claimed, she had been forced into such employment.

34 *RF*, "Die todbringenden Lohntüten der AEG. Wieder ein Selbstmord einer AEG-Metallarbeiterin, weil die AEG-Löhne nicht zum leben ausreichen..." Nr. 187, October 22, 1931.

35 *AIZ*, "Eine alltägliche Geschichte," Nr. 1, 1928, p. 13. While working-class women's suicides seemed to garner the most interest in their neighborhoods, the deaths of middle-class

In another *AIZ* article, which presented the shocking story of a mother's murder of her seven-year-old daughter in a Berlin tenement, the mother is not held responsible for her actions. "What drove Frau Jahn to her act?" asks the reporter: "The house residents all offer the best references for the thirty-two-year-old Martha Jahn. They speak differently about the husband, the thirty-six-year-old carpenter Alfred Jahn. He is a 'Christian' worker, who has mistreated his wife continuously for years, a drinker, who blows his money on girls that he picks up on the street and even takes into his own house."[36] In both the national Communist weekly and in neighborhood newspapers, therefore, it was made clear that men were needed in these families as husbands and fathers. Male workers should join the political struggle, not necessarily to create the Soviet state, an intangible ideal, but to end the conditions that made men superfluous and made women helpless victims.

This crusade to uphold male dominance in the home and neighborhood consequently shaped the ways men participated in Berlin politics. The violence which became pervasive on the streets of the capital by 1930 will be discussed primarily in Chapter 5, but through other political words and deeds, Berlin's activists competed to prove that their party represented true masculinity.[37] First, charges of deviant sexual behavior, including homosexuality, were commonly used to discredit opponents. A Friedrichshain neighborhood newspaper alleged in 1932 that Nazi rhetoric about "German morality" was hypocritical, since the local SA men were known to drink and be sexually involved with two girls, aged thirteen and fourteen, who lived above their cellar pub. The "fascist" parents of the two girls were also attacked for doing

---

male youngsters fostered great fear in Berlin's West End. One such tragedy, which received widespread attention in the bourgeois press, was the 1927 case in which eighteen-year-old student Paul Krantz was charged with planning the murder of the apprentice Hans Stephan with his school friend Günther Scheller. Krantz and Scheller were supposed to take their lives after Stephan was dead, though only Scheller died of a self-inflicted gunshot wound. Krantz, who later became a successful novelist under the name Ernst Erich Noth, was born illegitimately and had come into the social circle of the Scheller siblings Günther and Hildegard by attending gymnasium as a gifted scholarship holder. In the court proceedings and newspaper coverage that followed the shootings, much of the blame for the downfall of these well-educated young men was placed on the "hyper-modern" Scheller parents and the flirtatious ways of Hilde Scheller. For more on this case, see Joachim Schiller, *Schulerselbstmorde in Preussen: Spiegelungen des Schulsystems* (Frankfurt a. M.: Peter Lang, 1992).

[36] *AIZ*, "Eine Mutter hat ihr Kind getötet," Nr. 9, 1928, p. 4.

[37] Naturally, all paramilitary organizations were male-only structures. For a discussion of the rhetoric of masculinity among paramilitary units in the pre-1929 period, see Dirk Schumann, *Politische Gewalt in der Weimarer Republik: Kampf um die Straße und Furcht vor dem Bürgerkrieg* (Essen: Klartext, 2001), pp. 255–61. The cliques may have rejected the militarism connected with the parties' organizations, but they too recapitulated traditional masculine privileges. In general, only the girlfriend of the clique "bull" was allowed to travel with the group. The rest of the members were to abstain from sexual involvement unless young women known as "clique cows" were brought in for everyone's enjoyment. Gertrud Staewen-Ordemann, *Menschen der Unordnung* (Berlin: Furche Verlag, 1933), pp. 130–2.

nothing to end the liaisons.[38] In another state-run home for youngsters in Berlin, the KPD alleged the teacher was a Nazi who "conducted homosexual orgies." The male inhabitants of the home were routinely "forced into the NSDAP." The article also claimed the boys "must wear the swastika" or receive punishment.[39] No proof was presented that the young men participated or were forced to perform sex acts, but the predatory implications were clear.

In 1931, a self-described opposition group from within the NSDAP printed a series of newsletters in Berlin. Addressed to members of the SA, the letters lampooned the "feminine" weaknesses of the party's leadership. In addition to criticism of SA Chief of Staff Ernst Röhm's homosexuality, there were similar accusations about Hitler himself.[40] One of the letters concludes: "Are such people – they can hardly be called men – renewers of the Reich? Are they the revivers of our youth?"[41] Six months later, another edition provided a psychological profile of the party leader: "Hitler is an outspoken female spirit: his understanding, his ambition, his will are not at all masculine. He is a weak person, who hides behind the mask of brutality, in order to cover his lack of energy, his astounding weaknesses, his moral egoism, his unfounded pride."[42]

Communists and Nazis alike also claimed that their enemies were cowardly in physical combat. An article in a Prenzlauer Berg street newspaper printed by the area's section of the Communist *Kampfbund gegen den Faschismus* recounted a story allegedly received from an SA man himself, in which a group of SA members in Prenzlauer Berg avoided a rally brawl by escaping through the meeting site's bathroom window.[43] In another neighborhood newspaper, SA men were derided for feigning injuries from nonexistent

---

[38] LAB, Rep. 58, Nr. 1479, Film 740, "Mieterstreik in Gollnowstraße 32," November 1932. This circular was printed for the occasion of the tenants' strike on Gollnow Street. The demands of the strike were listed along with other neighborhood concerns such as the "scandal in the SA basement."

[39] BA, R15.01 (St. 10), Nr. 127, *Die Junge Garde*, "Im 'Erziehungsheim' Waldhof prügeln Nazi Erzieher und feiern homosexuelle Orgien," Nr. 55, July 12, 1931.

[40] On homosexuality and the NSDAP, especially the case of Ernst Röhm, see Burkhard Jellonnek, *Homosexuelle unter dem Hakenkreuz: Die Verfolgung von Homosexuellen im Dritten Reich* (Padeborn: F. Schöningh, 1990), pp. 51–79.

[41] BA, NS26/322, SA-Gau Berlin, Letter to SA-members, July 25, 1931. The party claimed that this propaganda was written by members of the KPD, not dissenters within their own ranks. Such pamphlets were in some cases the work of local Communists. This series, however, may have been written by former SA men. The letters did not encourage readers to switch to the KPD or its organizations, and some spoke highly of the local Nazi Party leader, Joseph Goebbels. For more on these *Zersetzungsschriften*, see the work of Timothy Brown, "Beefsteak Nazis and Brown Bolshevists: Boundaries and Identity in the Rise of National Socialism" (unpublished manuscript, 2002).

[42] BA, NS26/322 SA-Gau Berlin, Letter to SA-members, January 4, 1932.

[43] BA, R15.01 (St. 10), Nr. 153, Band 2, *Der Rote Angriff auf dem Prenzlauer Berg*, Nr. 2, likely 1931.

political battles. The author claimed that if a member of the SA "had a headache, he received an enormous bandage for his head" in order to look like a wounded hero.[44] The KPD was also ridiculed as lacking courage by both the SPD and NSDAP for having women and children in the front lines of many of their marches. The other parties argued that Communist men hid behind these marchers even when they knew the protest carried the potential for violence. Therefore, the Communist men were doubly at fault. They were not manly enough to fight, shirking their duty by placing women and children at the head of their parades. In addition, they were morally suspect for putting their own family members at risk.

Any female participation in activities that did not concern issues deemed specifically feminine – such as health, education, child welfare, or food prices – was viewed across the political spectrum with disdain. Nonetheless, women were drawn into the political mêlée by the responsibilities placed on them to secure food, clothing, and other necessities for their families. As a result, from time to time women in Berlin were involved in riots and other forms of political violence. When compared to the overall statistics for violent political behavior in this period, the number of incidents that involved women was quite small. However, despite its infrequency, the press coverage of female participation in political violence was extensive. Articles that described women's participation – as aggressors or victims – signaled that the disorder had reached new heights. In fact, one of the reasons why the Berlin May Day violence of 1929 took on such significance was that a number of women were among the dead, including two housewives shot on their balconies as they innocently watched the commotion below.

Any incident in which women were injured led to especially harsh criticism of the political party deemed responsible. The social democratic *Vorwärts* took the side of the KPD after Nazis attacked a Communist bar, in part because two women were seriously injured. The article noted the women's names, addresses, and injuries so as to personalize the victims.[45] However, the same summer *Vorwärts* also turned its criticism on Communist demonstrators who rioted when the police tried to break up a KPD protest march. The violence escalated, and a nearby pub was pelted with stones. "This completely senseless act by some fanatical adolescents injured the female employee whose head was hit by a thrown rock." The article further described the riot as "the same tactic and same maneuver that was used by the Nazis on the day before."[46]

---

[44] LAB, Rep. 58, Nr. 1534, Film 745, *Die Rote Laterne. Organ der Werktätigen Adlershof,* December 1931.

[45] *Vorwärts,* "Blutnacht in Berlin. Das Nazimotorkorps mordet/Systematische Feuerüberfälle auf KPD-Lokale," July 3, 1932. July 1932 was an especially bloody month in Berlin; see Chapter 5 for more analysis of the summer's violence.

[46] *Vorwärts,* "Tumulte am Potsdamer Platz. Kommunisten zertrümmern Fensterscheiben," Nr. 255, June 2, 1932.

It was also common for newspapers to take special note of the numbers of female demonstrators present at any political rally. A reporter from the *Vossische Zeitung* was careful to explain that when the police detained 244 Communists, who were allegedly gathering at Helmholz Platz in order to break up a Nazi rally at a nearby Friedrichshain assembly hall, thirty women were among those held by the police. Their presence was even more shocking when a search of the surrounding area turned up "twelve revolvers, eight clubs, six knives, five pipes, four nightsticks, numerous brass-knuckles, and sixty ammunition casings."[47] The VZ also published an article in 1929 after the Communist Party faction in the City Assembly was forced to leave the meeting hall because of disorderly conduct. When the police came to escort them out, many of the representatives resisted. The reporter was sure to point out that the "manliest resistance against the police was shown by some of the female demonstrators."[48] This disturbance was also covered by *Vorwärts*, which was eager to show the unbecoming tactics of the KPD representatives. The SPD paper argued that the Communist members of the City Assembly "made specific use of the women [demonstrators]." They instructed the women to show the "first and greatest resistance" to the attempts by police to identify Assembly members so that they could be removed. When the police began to clear the women from the room, the article claimed that KPD men charged the police with assaulting defenseless women."[49] While at first these reports appear solely to be criticizing women who act politically in the public sphere, they also show distaste for the party's strategies and imply that male members were unable to fight their own battles. Public criticism of female participation made it increasingly difficult for the KPD to mobilize women in their political campaigns and made it impossible to convince male workers that their wives and sisters should become involved.

To disassociate themselves from any hints of feminization, radicalized men sought out political spaces that discouraged female involvement and encouraged masculine camaraderie and a sense of purpose. The main site for political involvement in Berlin's neighborhoods was the pub. The local bar had played a central role in workers' politics since the nineteenth century, especially for the SPD during Bismarck's antisocialist campaign.[50] Its main advantage for political mobilization was that it was a semiprivate space.

---

47 VZ, "244 Kommunisten Sistiert. Polizeiaktionen im Norden Berlins," Nr. 18, January 11, 1930.
48 VZ, morning edition, Nr. 587, December 13, 1929.
49 *Vorwärts*, "Die Kommunisten Parole," morning edition, Nr. 583, December 13, 1929.
50 The Anti-Socialist Laws were instituted in 1878, criminalizing the SPD and giving much greater powers of surveillance and censorship to the police. Even though the Laws were lifted in 1890, spying on political organizations remained a central activity of police forces in urban centers with large SPD and later KPD populations. Richard Evans has written on the thousands of reports filed during the Wilhelmine era by Hamburg's undercover political policemen, who sat in workers' pubs and listened to patrons' conversations. See Richard

Though open to the public, regular patrons knew each other well and out-siders were easy to identify. This semiprivate status allowed for intimacy. For a number of reasons, Berlin's pubs took on a special significance during the last years of the republic.[51] First, increased police presence meant that public spaces free of surveillance were few and far between. Second, mass unemployment and employers' suspicion of radicalism limited the use of the factory site as a political venue. Third, alcohol and tobacco consumption had always been male prerogatives. Therefore, the pub was *the* quintessen-tial male worker's oasis.

Women were allowed at SPD and KPD party meetings in pubs, as long as the assembly was not concerned with (male) paramilitary issues. However, the conditions under which members met often discouraged women from attending. It is clear from reading minutes of political meetings, especially ones held in the closed quarters of pubs, that the excessive smoking and drinking made some female attendees uncomfortable. Others may have felt unwelcome by the fact that women's washroom facilities were inadequate. One 1930 report by a building inspector of a pub in the Nostiz Kiez noted that the pub and its indoor facilities were in good order and added: "For women, who are hardly allowed to frequent the pub, a courtyard toilet is available."[52] Women's complaints hurt their standing as serious participants and were dismissed as petty bourgeois moralizing. In *Kämpfende Jugend*, one of the few young female comrades in the Nostiz Kiez asks her com-rades to extinguish their cigarettes and pipes as a meeting gets under way and faces immediate resistance. Though in this fictional account the group's leader eventually seconds her request, such support was not likely found in most cells.[53] For example, in one report from a local KPD instructor in

---

J. Evans, *Kneipengespräche im Kaiserreich: Die Stimmungsberichte der Hamburger politis-chen Polizei, 1892–1914* (Reinbek bei Hamburg: Rowohlt, 1989).

[51] Studies of late Weimar have always stressed the centrality of the politically affiliated bars in the radicalism and violence that ravaged the city. Yet, it is often forgotten that there was much turnover in the relationships between bar owners and their politicized patrons. The police tried to keep track of which bars were official sites for which parties, and these lists constantly had to be amended. The disruption caused by some political rowdies and the poverty of others sometimes made their patronage no longer feasible for proprietors. In some cases, it seems that the owners simply changed political coats and decided to support other organizations. In late 1931, the Berlin police department made over one hundred changes to their records of KPD and NSDAP politically affiliated pubs. See BLHA, Rep. 30, Berlin C, Title 95, Sektion 9, Nr. 164, police department internal memo, "Verkehrslokale der KPD und NSDAP," December 29, 1931.

[52] Report by the building inspector found in Lothar Uebel, "Verkehrslokale und andere Budiken" in Geschichtskreis Kreuzberg, ed., *Nostitzritze. Ein Straße in Kreuzberg* (Berlin: Gericke, 1992), p. 46.

[53] Walter Schönstedt, *Kämpfende Jugend* (Berlin: Oberbaumverlag, 1972), p. 39. Though Elly receives support for her smoke-free zone, discussion of the matter is followed by a contri-bution from Trude. She is interrupted rudely by a number of others around the room, after which she finds it impossible to reenter the conversation.

Schöneberg, a case was presented of a man named Hans. He began attending the cell meetings at his neighborhood pub to the dismay of his wife, who was displeased that he drank on each occasion. When the cell meetings failed to meet his expectations, he decided participation was not worth the grief he got at home. His story was relayed in the brochure, "How do we get our cells moving?" The lesson for street cell organizers was not to cut back drinking practices or to make a greater effort to involve wives. Rather, local leaders were instructed to keep cell meetings exciting and focused on the big political questions of the day so that husbands would choose politics over domestic harmony.[54]

Of the three parties that courted workers in Berlin, the KPD relied most heavily on the pub during the Depression era. The KPD was never outlawed during the republic nor were its activities restricted in Berlin until 1929. But throughout the 1920s and increasingly after 1929, the KPD remained under close supervision by the police, much more so than Berlin's Nazi organizations. There was no safer place than the Kiez pub to show allegiance to the KPD or dissatisfaction with the current situation.[55] To do so at the workplace could lead to unemployment, and in mixed workers' neighborhoods, Communists were sometimes looked down upon as rabble or even criminal and lazy. Within the confines of KPD territory, however, at the center of which was often the party pub, the bravado of young radicals flourished. The pubs provided a sanctuary for supporters where everyone knew each other. And when there was a threat of surveillance, there was always a meeting room closed off from the rest of the patrons.[56]

Social Democrats and national socialists also made wide use of the pub as a social space, local campaign headquarters, and meeting site. "Acquiring"

---

[54] BA-SAPMO, RY1/I3/1-2/83, "Wie aktivisieren wir unsere Zellen?" October 1932. It is not clear from the document whether Hans was an actual Berlin Communist or whether his story was fabricated for didactic purposes.

[55] This is not to say that the pub was always a safe place for clandestine political activities. Neighbors, fearful of Communist conspiracy or simply angered by late-night noise, often shared with the police their suspicions about pub regulars. Some claimed to have witnessed the publication of illegal pamphlets and even the movement of weapons in and out of pubs. See BLHA, Rep. 30, Berlin C, Title 95, Sektion 9, Nr. 164. This file contains a number of letters to the police denouncing alleged activities in Berlin's KPD bars. Most of these claims were followed up by the police, though the information rarely resulted in charges being brought against pub owners or patrons. There are two likely reasons why these investigations turned up little. First, many denunciations were based on neighborhood conflicts that had little to do with political crimes. Second, those who were involved in the underground RFB worked diligently to hide printing materials and other incriminating evidence.

[56] After June 1, 1931, it was illegal to place any decorations that announced the political affiliation of a pub on the building's façade. Failure to comply brought warnings and fines to the proprietor. The public decorations were thought to incite violence between political opponents and were therefore deemed a threat to public order. See, BLHA, Rep. 30, Berlin C, Title 95, Sektion 9, Nr. 164, letter from police headquarters (Abt. I) to the female pub owner E. D., October 20, 1931.

pubs in workers' neighborhoods was a major aspect of Goebbels's "struggle for Berlin." It was a highly successful plan because residents who harbored respect for the SA had their interest validated by the local presence of a Nazi outpost, making the radical right a more attractive option. It was also a crippling strategy for workers' neighborhoods. The emergence of each new Nazi-aligned bar was seen by members of the SPD and KPD as a major blow to the autonomy of the workers' neighborhood because its presence weakened the common political bonds between neighbors and meant there was one less site for left-wing socializing. As workers' districts became increasingly crowded by pubs of all political stripes, these single-sex neighborhood institutions played a central role in the violence that plagued the city in these years. Political violence was largely organized behind the closed doors of pubs or took place in and around these establishments. When a Communist bar opened on one street corner, the SA tried to set up a rival space a few buildings away. Antagonism escalated as both sides used propaganda displays and physical aggression in their efforts to exhibit masculine dominance and rule supreme in the neighborhood.

CRISIS AT HOME: GENERATIONAL TENSION AND RADICALISM

In addition to gender turmoil, the Depression caused a widening of the gap between the generations, especially among men. This conflict too affected political discourse and radicalism at the neighborhood level. Intergenerational conflict is always difficult to analyze because the generations themselves belie simple definition. Scholars still debate what constitutes a generation. Sociologists, in general, have focused on the phases of the life cycle as constituting generations. As the individual ages, he or she moves from one generation to another defined by new responsibilities. Rebelliousness and conflict develop between the young and old because of differences in their social positions. Historians have generally explained generations differently. They place the focus on discontinuity. The individual does not leave one generation for another depending on his or her position in the life cycle. Rather, certain defining experiences separate one group of historical cohorts from another. In many cases, these cohorts are conscious of their commonly formed identity and see themselves as a generation apart from others.[57] Certainly those in Weimar Berlin sensed that young people were being shaped by a new set

---

[57] For a concise explanation of the various approaches to studying generations throughout German history, see Mark Roseman's introduction in Roseman, ed., *Generations in Conflict. Youth Revolt and Generation Formation in Germany, 1770–1968* (Cambridge: Cambridge University Press, 1995), pp. 1–46. The concept of historical cohorts has been taken largely from the work of Karl Mannheim, who himself was inspired to study the issue after witnessing the emergence of generational conflict in the 1920s. See Karl Mannheim, "Das Problem der Generationen" in *Kölner Vierteljahrshefte für Soziologie* (Vol. 7, 1928), pp. 157–85,

of experiences. A new generation was coming of age in a very different political, economic, and cultural landscape than the one that had welcomed their parents. Nonetheless, it remains impossible to tie strict limits of age or experience to the generations under discussion.

In order to make the terms somewhat more manageable, I will refer to the younger generation as those born in 1900 and after.[58] For the purpose of this study, I will focus on the subgeneration of Berliners born between 1900 and 1910. They would have only childhood memories of a peaceful *Kaiserreich* and only a few would have seen war service. The youngest members of this historical cohort were not likely to have much memory of fathers who fell on the battlefield. All would have significant recollections of wartime, but most would have come of age during the November revolution or the early 1920s. For those living in the Nostiz Kiez, the battles at the *Vorwärts* building on Lindenstraße, home to the SPD daily and only a few hundred meters away, hit especially close to home. One memoir recounts how the defeated spartacist fighters were led by foot, for all to see, through the Kiez to the police barracks on its southern end at Friesenstraße.[59]

Of course, there is some overlap between the generations, and those individuals born around the turn of the century would feel closer to one group or the other depending on their experiences. For example, the writer Ernst Glaeser clearly felt he was living in a society shaped by generational identities. Born into a prosperous family in 1902, this member of the "younger generation" bemoaned that position and wrote in his classic generational tale, *Class of 1902*: "we regretted our youth, for it kept us from being heroes."[60] Nonetheless, for ease of discussion, the older generation will refer to those born between 1880 and 1900. The phrase "front generation" can be useful to the historian as a way to characterize this group's common bond. About 85 percent of all German men eligible to serve did participate in the war effort at some stage. Of these, about two million never returned to careers or families. Those in this cohort too young to serve were old enough to follow the campaigns, be conscious of the fortunes and misfortunes of war, and desire a more active role. However, not all soldiers shared an identical war experience or postwar mentality. In fact, during the Weimar Republic the

---

309–30. In English, see Karl Mannheim, "The Problem of Generations" in *Essays on the Sociology of Knowledge* (New York: Oxford University Press, 1952), pp. 276–320.

[58] For the most part, I will refer to the conflict between generations of men. This is not to say that women did not belong to these generations or that there was no conflict between younger and older women. My focus on the men stems from my interest in how generational tension led to radicalism and violence in Berlin, phenomena from which women were largely excluded.

[59] Gerhard König, *Berlin – Kreuzberg und seine Nostitzstraße* (Berlin: Druckerei der pbw, no date), p. 24.

[60] Ernst Glaeser, *Class of 1902*, Willa and Edwin Muir, trans. (New York: Viking, 1929; original German edition, 1928), p. 269.

phrase "front generation" "represented an attempt to cover over divisions rather than to assert real unity of experience or perspective."[61] Among those who did survive, their earliest memories would be of a peaceful, industrializing empire and an increasingly powerful workers' movement, including the Social Democratic Party and its trade unions. From its start, many had particularly strong feelings either for or against the republic because they had known another system and witnessed the defeat of war. Included within this cohort were some surviving fathers of the post-1900 generation.

There are a number of reasons why generational issues should be central to the study of Weimar. First, the devastation of World War I led contemporaries and later scholars to wonder how those remaining would adapt, and how the loss of so many would affect postwar society.[62] The front generation may have been a construction of the postwar period rather than an accurate reflection of a new rank of men forged in the trenches, but the very existence and acceptance of the term illustrates how significant the war was in bringing generational identification and conflict to the center of Weimar politics. Second, the radical parties, the NSDAP and KPD, both presented themselves to voters as parties of young people. Party propaganda stressed the need for youthful energy and idealism, and members of the younger generation flocked to these parties as the heralds of a new era that they could call

---

[61] Richard Bessel, "The 'Front Generation' and the Politics of Weimar Germany" in Mark Roseman, ed., *Generations in Conflict* (Cambridge: Cambridge University Press, 1995), p. 126. For a comparative look at how World War I led to the growth of the SA in Germany and the fascist *squadrismo* in Italy, see Sven Reichardt, "Gesellschaften im Übergang. Überlegungen zum Vergleich faschistischer Kampfbünde in Italien und Deutschland" in Armin Triebel, ed., *Die Pragmatik des Gesellschaftsvergleichs* (Leizpig: Leipziger Universitätsverlag, 1997), pp. 139–54.

[62] There are numerous books about the war generation and readaptation to peacetime society. For a Europe-wide view on how the war affected intellectuals and culture, see Modris Eksteins, *Rites of Spring* (New York: Doubleday, 1989); Edward T. Tannenbaum, *1900: The Generation before the Great War* (New York: Anchor Press, 1976); and Robert Wohl, *The Generation of 1914* (Cambridge, MA: Harvard University Press, 1979). For Germany, see George L. Mosse, *Fallen Soldiers: Reshaping the Memory of the World Wars* (New York: Oxford University Press, 1990); Klaus Theweleit, *Male Fantasies, Vol 1: Women, Floods, Bodies, History* (Cambridge: Polity, 1987); Deborah Cohen, *The War Come Home: Disabled Veterans in Britain and Germany, 1914–1939* (Berkeley: University of California Press, 2001); Eric Leed, *No Man's Land* (New York: Oxford University Press, 1979); and Robert Whalen, *Bitter Wounds: German Victims of the Great War, 1914–1939* (Ithaca, NY: Cornell University Press, 1984). For a generational interpretation of political radicalism and violence that focuses on those who experienced the war as children and not soldiers, see the work of Peter Loewenberg. He has argued that the psychological traumas of death and deprivation on Germany's children during World War I and the immediate postwar period led this younger generation to support national socialism in adulthood. Peter Loewenberg, "The Psychohistorical Origins of the Nazi Youth Cohort" in *The American Historical Review* (Vol. 76, No. 5, December 1971), pp. 1457–502. See also Michael Kater, "Generationskonflikt als Entwicklungsfaktor in der NS – Bewegung vor 1933" in *Geschichte und Gesellschaft* (Vol. 11, No. 2, 1985), pp. 217–43.

their own. Third, the Depression had specific consequences for Germany's youth.[63] In Berlin, unemployment hit those in the eighteen to twenty-four age group the hardest, and many entered the job market without hope of gaining steady work. Fourth, the political violence that so marked Berlin between 1929 and 1933 was largely an activity of males in their twenties.[64] Fifth, the generational divide also kept some members of the older generation, especially those in the SPD, from adequately recognizing and responding to youth discontent.[65]

As with gender conflict, the divide that grew between the generations did not develop overnight. However, the transformation of German society after 1918 in particular led to an escalation of tension between generations by the end of the 1920s. The long tradition of strong organized youth movements was one way in which generational conflict seemed almost built into Weimar society, even before the Depression struck. Like much in German society, the youth movement was split between the bourgeois *Wandervogel* youth clubs and their socialist counterparts. Beginning in the nineteenth century, these clubs engaged children and teenagers in camping, hiking, and other outdoor activities. By 1926, the *Reichsausschuss der deutschen Jugendverbände*, the national umbrella group that oversaw seventy-six youth organizations, represented over 4.3 million members between the ages of fourteen and twenty-one.[66] Naturally, in the organized setting of regular meetings and uniformed camaraderie, it was easier to recognize and voice common complaints and challenge the status quo. The size of Berlin and mobility within

---

[63] A number of books on Germany's youth, the Depression, and radicalism have been written. Among others see Detlev Peukert, *Jugend zwischen Krieg und Krise* (Cologne: Bund-Verlag, 1987b); Peter Stachura, *The Weimar Republic and the Younger Proletariat* (New York: St. Martin's Press, 1989); and Eve Rosenhaft, *Beating the Fascists? The German Communists and Political Violence, 1929–1933*, (Cambridge: Cambridge University Press, 1983).

[64] That most of the men involved in street fighting were young adults in their twenties is confirmed by Dirk Schumann's study of Sachsen, *Politische Gewalt in der Weimarer Republik 1918–1933. Kampf um die Straße und Furcht vor dem Bürgerkrieg* (Essen: Klartext, 2001), pp. 329–30. Two-thirds of his sample of 106 street fighters from the Left and Right were born between 1900 and 1910.

[65] As shown in Chapter 3, the criticism that the SPD was becoming ossified by outdated ideals and strategies was made frequently by young party members in Berlin. For more on how the SPD leadership dealt with this attack, see Donna Harsch, *German Social Democracy and the Rise of Nazism* (Chapel Hill: University of North Carolina Press, 1993). Although the SPD sometimes had trouble after 1929 holding onto younger supporters born into the social democratic tradition, Weimar's liberal parties often had trouble attracting any young members. See Larry Eugene Jones, "German Liberalism and the Alienation of the Younger Generation in the Weimar Republic" in Konrad H. Jarausch and Larry Eugene Jones, eds., *In Search of a Liberal Germany: Studies in the History of German Liberalism from 1789 to the Present* (Oxford: Berg, 1990), pp. 287–321.

[66] There was a total of nine million Germans within this age range. For a breakdown of the popularity of certain types of clubs, see Detlev Peukert, *The Weimar Republic: The Crisis of Classical Modernity* (New York: Hill and Wang, 1989), p. 90.

the city certainly made it easier for young people in the 1920s to assert their independence, but the organized youth culture also helped set young men and women apart from their parents and united them in their interests and desires.

The war dramatically altered family structure. Millions of fathers never came home at all, but even the sons and daughters of those who did spent a large part of their childhoods without fathers. In fact, while mothers worked in Berlin's wartime economy, the city's tenements "belonged to the children," who were often supervised only by older siblings or neighbors.[67] Youngsters were often given essential tasks, such as standing in line for food and coal.[68] Many sons and daughters found it difficult to readapt to the authority of a father in the home after the war. For hundreds of thousands born after 1900, single-parent homes or the incorporation of a stepfather were the consequences of war. Alternatively, some war widows chose to live unmarried with their companions and children. Though considered morally improper by some, this solution was popular because marriage meant the loss of the widow's pension. In the Nostiz Kiez, the saying went: the pension was a sure thing, partners often were not. And the children born into such relationships were referred to as "*Josephskinder*" because they were the product of a union which appeared to outsiders as "chaste as that of the biblical Joseph and Mary."[69] Regardless of these other options, in a society that so valued the presence of a male head, the large numbers of new single-mother households signaled a crisis for the young republic and its children, who were considered at risk for immoral behavior and political radicalism.[70]

In many cases, stepfathers created particular difficulties. Desperate mothers, struggling to make ends meet, sometimes married men who brought more harm than good to their families. Youngsters caught in the Berlin welfare system frequently recounted stories of stepfathers who shipped them off to abusive apprenticeships or treated them poorly at home. Novels from the period also highlight the difficulties faced by young people in female-led households or under the oppressive hand of a new stepfather. In *Dritter Hof*

---

[67] Ernst Erich Noth, *Die Mietskaserne* (Frankfurt a. M.: Societätsverlag, 1931). This Depression-era novel begins during World War I. Noth adds that many women also worked night shifts in factories, while children slept unattended in their apartments. Noth's fictional account is confirmed by Belinda Davis, *Home Fires Burning: Food, Politics, and Everyday Life in World War I Berlin* (Chapel Hill: University of North Carolina Press, 2000), p. 186.

[68] Police reported that women pushed their children to protest food shortages and encouraged them to vandalize stores. Ibid., pp. 41–2.

[69] König, *Berlin – Kreuzberg* (no date), p. 12.

[70] In 1923, the republic's Labor Ministry estimated there to be 1,192,000 war-orphans in Germany. Richard Bessel, "Die Erblast des verlorenen Krieges" in Frank Bajohr et al., eds., *Zivilisation und Barbarei: Die widersprüchliche Potentiale der Moderne* (Hamburg: Christians, 1991a), p. 100, and Whalen, *Bitter Wounds* (1984), p. 95.

Links, a woman struggles to keep her family of three children together by cleaning wealthy Berliners' homes. Her husband never recovered from the trauma of war and drank himself to death. A series of other men bring nothing to the situation except additional mouths to feed. The older children turn to prostitution and boxing to earn money. Finally, a case of incest between siblings signals the complete degeneration of the family.[71] In another story of poverty in Berlin, *Mich hungert!*, the protagonist Teddy's father dies during the war, and his mother eventually dies as well from overwork. The oldest of three children, Teddy tries to support the family on his own, but his sister too becomes a prostitute and his brother ends up in jail.[72] Among others, these two novels from authors on the political left portray long-term family problems caused by World War I and stress the early sexual maturation and independence of Berlin's children as a warning about the fate of families without "proper" fathers.

For those two-parent households that remained intact through the war and the early instability of the republic, the Depression brought new stresses. While male unemployment weakened the man's position vis-à-vis his wife, the same was true of his relationship with his children. In her study of proletarian fathers in Weimar, Heidi Rosenbaum found more diversity in paternal roles than the stereotype of the detached, strict father. From oral interviews, she created three types of working-class fathers: "traditional, Social Democratic, and petty bourgeois." While she painted individual pictures for each category, Rosenbaum stressed, not surprisingly, that one characteristic that applied to all fathers was his role as breadwinner.[73] When unemployment changed this expectation, youngsters were forced to take on the responsibility of wage earning themselves and began to question the authority of their fathers in the home. In one Berlin newspaper cartoon from 1930, a welfare worker knocks on a client's apartment door. When a four-year-old boy answers, the caseworker asks to speak to his father. The twelve-year-old brother approaches and responds: "Here, I am the father. Our fathers are long since dead." The story goes on to explain that after his father's death in the war, the older boys' mother had married again. The second husband died of tuberculosis, after fathering the younger brother and infecting the boys' mother. His mother's illness and the absence of a paternal figure forced the older son to assume this role and work as an errand boy for a cheese shop.[74]

---

[71] Günther Birkenfeld, *Dritter Hof Links* (Berlin: Bruno Cassirer, 1929).

[72] Georg Fink, *Mich hungert!* (Berlin: Bruno Cassirer, 1930).

[73] Heidi Rosenbaum, *Proletarische Familien. Arbeiterfamilie und Arbeiterväter im frühen 20. Jahrhundert zwischen traditioneller, sozialdemokratischer und kleinbürgerlicher Orientierung* (Frankfurt a. M.: Suhrkamp, 1992). See in particular pp. 240–76.

[74] BA, Rep. 15.01 (St. 10), Nr. 118, Vol. 1, *Die Trommel*, Nr. 11/12, December 1930. *Die Trommel* was a KPD-produced newspaper written for and distributed at schools. This story is likely a fictional account, but the paper's editors must have presumed some of their readers would identify with this family's hardships.

These examples, though melodramatic, illustrate how Depression-era un-employment, death, or temporary absence due to the war, challenged the norm of the patriarchal household and resulted in boys and girls who saw themselves as adults. This early maturation process had the potential to lead to early politicization – much to the pleasure of the radical parties and the dismay of the state authorities and some parents.

Another factor that exacerbated generational conflict was the number of welfare and labor codes that either failed to protect youth or actually discriminated against them. In 1922, the *Reichsjugendwohlfahrtsgesetz* (National Youth Welfare Law) was passed by the Reichstag, incorporating youth protection into the emerging Weimar *Sozialstaat*.[75] The RJWG, hailed as a prime example of SPD-led reform in the early republic, set up a comprehensive set of public youth welfare offices, *Jugendämter*, throughout the country to spearhead reform in education and combat youth-related diseases such as rickets and measles. To mollify the Catholic and Protestant leaders, religious youth welfare agencies were left intact and were reassured by the young Reich government that they still had an important role to play. The KPD and some leaders of the SPD criticized the religious influence still present under the new arrangement, and others worried that such an unwieldy system would lead to bureaucratic inefficiency.[76] The law did have its shortcomings. For example, it never covered illegitimate children, who amounted to 123 out of every 1,000 German births in 1927.[77] Nor did the law provide much assistance to

---

[75] The debate about the Weimar welfare state continues today. A number of studies that have appeared in the last fifteen years take different positions as to the intentions and results of the republic's welfare system. Some historians, such as Peter Stachura, argue that the system, even as it affected the lives of youth, was intended to achieve social equality and support humanitarianism in an increasingly complex world. Others, foremost Detlev Peukert, have taken a much more pessimistic view, implying that in exchange for a fairly incomplete social net to catch those falling into poverty, individuals had to give up much of their privacy to an increasingly invasive and disciplining welfare bureaucracy. This position is taken further by Paul Weindling's study on health and German politics. Weindling asserts that the Weimar welfare system was part of a trend beginning in the nineteenth century, in which the state took a growing interest in the social body. As one step in a long process, therefore, the categorizing and disciplining of welfare recipients during the Weimar Republic led quite directly to the racist eugenics of the Third Reich. Most recently, Young-Sun Hong has taken aim at the criticism of the Weimar welfare system, especially at Peukert's thesis. She argues that Weimar's Progressives and confessional welfare reformers never abandoned the humanistic principles on which their efforts were based. Stachura, *The Weimar Republic and the Younger Proletariat* (1989); Detlev Peukert, *Grenzen der Sozialdisziplinierung: Aufstieg und Krise der deutschen Jugendfürsorge 1878–1932* (Cologne: Bund-Verlag, 1986); Paul Weindling, *Health, Race and German Politics between National Unification and Nazism, 1870–1945* (Cambridge: Cambridge University Press, 1989); and Young-Sun Hong, *Welfare, Modernity, and the Weimar State, 1919–1933* (Princeton, NJ: Princeton University Press, 1998).

[76] Stachura, *The Weimar Republic and the Younger Proletariat* (1989), pp. 76–82.

[77] Annemarie Niemeyer, *Zur Struktur der Familie. Statistischen Materialien* (Berlin: F. A. Herbig, 1931), p. 68.

vagrant youth, whose numbers had reached 200,000 by 1924.[78] The passage of the legislation did, however, clear the way for the creation of the juvenile court system the following year. Youth welfare offices would henceforth deal with offenders under the age of fourteen. The cases of criminals between the ages of fourteen and eighteen would be handled by the new juvenile courts. The sentences handed out in the new system stressed educational programs and probation; hard labor, life imprisonment, and capital punishment were prohibited.[79]

From the beginning, the lack of political consensus at the Reich and state levels, and concerns about the ability to fund the ambitious youth welfare and criminal justice systems, threatened to keep the new system from ever being implemented. In fact, the new legislation was largely put on hold during the inflation crisis of 1923 and came into effect only after the currency stabilization of 1924. Throughout the decade, debate persisted between Reich and state administrators over how the operation should be managed and funded. However, as the years passed and the growing conservatism of the republic grew less and less amenable to social democratic ideals, opposition to the *Jugendämter's* authority weakened the efficacy of the entire system. As a result, the system itself and the youngsters who were to have benefited from its policies since 1922 were unprepared to cope with the financial and personal crises of the Depression.

In terms of the labor market, the generational cohort of those aged twenty-five and under at the time of the 1925 census had reached 28.5 million males and females. About half of this total were at least fourteen and therefore of working age. Of these fourteen million young people, more females than ever were seeking employment in the 1920s, creating what was the largest-ever pool of young job seekers in Germany.[80] The instability of the Weimar economy throughout the 1920s meant that great numbers of these competing young workers would have already faced unemployment before the Depression even began. Young workers faced uncertainty as a fluctuating economy and the rationalization of the workplace made their unskilled and semiskilled positions the most vulnerable [Plate 3]. Once the Depression began, unskilled workers and new hires in urban centers like Berlin were hit the hardest, and young people leaving school often found it impossible to attain jobs. As is clear in Figure 5, the chances of gaining and retaining stable employment went down for those between fourteen and twenty-five as they got older.[81] This combination of factors resulted in a new social phenomenon

---

[78] Stachura, *The Weimar Republic and the Younger Proletariat* (1989), pp. 92–3.

[79] Ibid., pp. 82–3.

[80] Ibid., p. 95.

[81] Detlev Peukert, "Die Erwerbslosigkeit junger Arbeiter in der Weltwirtschaftskrise in Deutschland, 1929–1933" in *Vierteljahrschrift für Sozial- und Wirtschaftsgeschichte* (Vol. 72, No. 3, 1985), p. 313.

Plate 3. The crowded waiting room in a Berlin men's homeless shelter, 1929. Source: © Bildarchiv Preussischer Kulturbesitz, 2003.

Age Group (years)	Males	Percentage	Females	Percentage	Total
14	10,953	1.1	9,913	2.3	20,866
15 to 18	68,370	6.6	60,838	14.5	129,208
18 to 21	339,837	32.8	142,313	33.9	482,150
under 21	419,160	40.5	213,064	40.7	632,224
21 to 25	617,536	59.5	207,094	49.3	824,630
Total	1,036,696	100	420,158	100	1,456,854

Figure 5. Youth unemployment in Germany on July 30, 1932. Source: Data taken from Kurt Richter, "Maßnahmen zur Betreuung der erwerbslosen Jugend" in Kurt Richter, ed., *Handbuch der Jugendpflege* (Vol. 14, Berlin, 1933), p. 18. These are the figures for those officially registered as unemployed. The actual numbers of jobless were undoubtedly higher. Those who had never worked were often missed in the counting, and unemployed females were less likely to register with the local authorities.

after 1929: a large population of long-term out-of-work youth, many of whom had never known full-time employment.

The republic's unemployment assistance program (*Gesetz über Arbeitsvermittlung und Arbeitslosenversicherung, AVAVG*) had been restructured in 1927. Debates about the new law focused on how to assist the "deserving" and deter the "work-shy" from abusing the system. "Where the young were concerned," Elizabeth Harvey has argued, "the need to deter the work-shy was seen as being particularly acute, an assumption which influenced legislation and administrative practice with regard to the young unemployed throughout the Weimar period."[82] Under the 1927 law, all employees contributing to the mandatory sickness insurance who had worked for at least 26 weeks in the year they became unemployed received unemployment benefits for 26 weeks. After this allotted period, those still in need of assistance along with those who had worked at least 13 weeks could apply for "crisis relief." Once this source was exhausted, the needy were left to pass a means test in order to receive the remaining municipal welfare funds.

Those young adults who sought welfare assistance found that the laws frequently discriminated against them and, as the financial crisis wore on, imposed increasingly stringent criteria for aid. Apprentices, for example, did not make contributions until the last six months of their training, a provision included in the law so employers could keep their costs down. Therefore, if the contract was terminated before schedule, an apprentice might not receive benefits. Moreover, even before the Depression began to empty the assistance coffers, young people were more likely than older applicants to be forced to attend retraining courses or to accept work assignments in order to receive their payments. Once the Depression began, young recipients were the frequent targets of cost-cutting schemes. Under the Social Democratic Chancellor Hermann Müller, those under twenty-one years of age were denied crisis relief – the last source of public aid for those who no longer qualified elsewhere. After 1930, for those under seventeen, the income of relatives was also considered in means testing even at the first level of unemployment assistance. With the signing of the emergency decree of June 5, 1931, all those under twenty-one were included in this cutback. The decree had a significant impact on young people and parents alike. As one Kreuzberg man remembered his youth: "At first I received assistance, 5 RM per week and afterward [June 5, 1931] – after a half a year – I got nothing, because

[82] Elizabeth Harvey, *Youth and the Welfare State in Weimar Germany* (Oxford: Clarendon Press, 1993), p. 113. At the same time, the 1927 AVAVG was an improvement for young people over the previous system because there was no longer a minimum age in order to qualify for assistance. See further the study by Marcus Gräser, *Das blockierte Wohlfahrtsstaat: Unterschichtjugend und Jugendfürsorge in der Weimarer Republik* (Göttingen: Vandenhoeck & Ruprecht, 1995).

my father worked."[83] Since families were therefore responsible for caring for those under twenty-one, many young men and women were forced to relinquish their own apartments and return home.[84] Another unemployed young Kreuzberg cabinet maker who already lived with his parents in June 1931 tried to fake a separate residence so as not to lose his 7.20 RM per week assistance, but this meant: "One always had to be on the ball" – available to welfare examiners at the phony address and not present at the parents' home when the authorities came by. In the end, he was discovered at his family residence and lost his weekly support.[85] Some parents resented this forced guardianship of their adult children, and young people were angered by their loss of independence.

The effects of long-term unemployment on youth were dramatic. After spending varying amounts of time searching for work, many unemployed lose hope in securing work, and the search fades. Without this goal to shape the day, boredom sets in. In Depression-era Berlin, as described previously, those without jobs were seen in parks, pubs, welfare offices, and the publicly or privately operated centers for the jobless, which consisted of game rooms, libraries, and cafeterias offering free or discounted meals. For the young man, unemployment often came at the same time he had hoped to marry and settle down. Without financial independence, plans to start a family and set up a home away from the parents were put on hold indefinitely, adding to his sense of personal failure. Though it was believed by welfare administrators and psychologists alike that unemployed females faced a less traumatic experience because they could be occupied with household chores, they too had to cope with delayed dreams of financial independence or marriage.[86] The assumption that women were content helping out at home resulted in lower benefits for female unemployed and fewer opportunities to participate in work programs and retraining. Younger siblings who witnessed the dilemma of their older brothers and sisters often lost interest in schooling and job training. It seemed useless when the only likely job prospect was thought to be "going on the dole."[87] Some of the unemployed withdrew completely from their families and society. For others conflict with parents intensified

---

[83] Oral history interviews collected by Lothar Uebel in "Jugend auf der Straße" in Kunstamt Kreuzberg, ed., *Kreuzberg 1933. Ein Bezirk erinnert sich* (Berlin: Dürschlag, 1983), p. 60.

[84] Harvey, *Youth and the Welfare State* (1993), pp. 116–19.

[85] Oral history interviews collected by Lothar Uebel in "Jugend auf der Straße" (1983), p. 61.

[86] In chapter 8 of *Menschen der Unordnung*, Gertrud Staewen-Ordemann presents a number of examples of common Depression-era problems that led to generational discord. She also argues that the smaller number of young women who became active in political organizations were also seeking a sense of companionship that was missing at home. Staewen-Ordemann, *Menschen der Unordnung* (1933), pp. 139–54. See also Josepha Fischer, *Die Mädchen in den deutschen Jugendverbänden* (Leipzig: R. Voigtländer, 1933) and Alice Rühle-Gerstel, *Das Frauenproblem der Gegenwart* (Leipzig: S. Hirzel, 1932).

[87] Peukert, *Jugend zwischen Krieg und Krise* (1987b), p. 180.

after the search for work was abandoned. Sleeping late and "wasting the day" playing cards or sitting in a pub spending precious family resources led to frustration and anger.

While it is difficult to generalize about the consequences of unemployment, especially the links between joblessness and radicalization, it is clear that state officials and other contemporaries saw the two phenomena as directly connected. The sense of personal failure and parental conflict that accompanied youth unemployment was assumed to lead to criminal behavior, including political radicalization. As Reich Interior Minister Joseph Wirth insisted, political radicalization was "the most pressing danger" brought by unemployment. "The unemployed admit frequently," he added, "that they lose belief in the state and society, that their family life is destroyed by the mental burden [of unemployment], and that in time they lose the ability to adapt to any type of order."[88] It is worth emphasizing that many of Berlin's young workers had expected their lives to be largely predetermined by family tradition. One study has shown that chances for upward mobility did increase slightly in the early twentieth century, but the great majority of workers' sons in Berlin after 1918 still planned on becoming workers themselves, often in the same trade as their fathers.[89] Termination of schooling by the midteens, they expected, would lead to an apprenticeship or training period on the factory floor. Learning a skill also meant an introduction to the political and social organizations of the social democratic or Catholic trade unions. This transition, from school pupil to worker, was such an important political step that the KPD planned recruitment parties at the time of school dismissals, in the hopes of winning over young people before they entered a working world dominated by the SPD.[90]

The possibility of following this plan was dashed for many young Berliners by the Depression. Unemployment and the subsequent loss of contact with the trade union and factory floor organizing did more, for example, than the Communist attempts at recruitment to interrupt this political continuity across generations. Lost to the political traditions and organizations of their fathers, the opportunity for Berlin's unemployed or unskilled young men to seek new associations to replace the older ones was more present than ever.

---

[88] BA, Rep. 43 I, Nr. 785, Reich Interior Minister Wirth to the Reich Chancellery, January 23, 1931.

[89] See Hartmut Kaelble, "Soziale Mobilität in Deutschland, 1900–1960" in Hartmut Kaelble, ed., *Probleme der Modernisierung* (Opladen: Westdeutscher Verlag, 1978).

[90] BA-SAPMO, RY1/I4/1/58, "Material für Schulentlassungsfeiern und Einführungsabende, Zentralkomittee des KJVD," Abteilung Agitprop, 1930–1. The instructions suggested that the evening's program should be "lively, exciting" not "petty-bourgeois stiff," in the hope of differentiating from the "older" traditions of the SPD. Simultaneously, the Berlin Reichsbanner, led by Social Democrats and liberals, was recommending to its city chapters that they should limit dancing at meetings to appear politically serious and less like a workers' social club. See, BA, Rep. 43 I, Nr. 2701, Berlin-Brandenburg Reichsbanner memo, Nr. 5, 1930.

The Social Democrats in Berlin were conscious of this danger, and there was much discussion in SPD circles as to how to counter it, as in this newsletter for leaders of social democratic youth programs:

Let's recognize one thing: the strong ties of the mature comrades come from tradition; they have fought for the progress from *Kaiserreich* to republic. For them the socialist tradition is the spiritual and political homeland, without which they cannot rightly imagine their lives. They stand unwavering in this connection to the party and trade unions, and falter neither from the traitorous screams of the Communists and the National Socialists nor from the burden of the economic emergency. This does not hold the youth. Their loyalty to the party must first be developed, experienced and guarded.[91]

In addition to the effects of unemployment and deskilling, young workers were less willing to develop ties to the older working-class traditions for the simple reason that they were associated with the status quo. While the KPD and NSDAP promised their young supporters a new era, which would be characterized by their ideals, the SPD and Reichsbanner consistently stressed the "duty" of youngsters to follow in their fathers' footsteps.[92] The older generation had begun the creation of the socialist state, in the form of the republic, and now, the SPD declared, it was the younger generation's turn to protect this accomplishment and oversee its further development. The Social Democrats did not adequately recognize the difficulties of mobilizing two generations under the same banner.[93] For the Reichsbanner, members were described simply as "veterans and veterans' sons."[94] For many young workers in Berlin, being defined solely in terms of their fathers' accomplishments was not a sufficiently compelling political identity. In the end, it was not surprising that among those young people from the Nostiz area Kiez who joined Communist organizations toward the end of the republic, one who himself fell into this category remembered that "the vast majority . . . came from Social Democratic households."[95] The internal family conflict that could result is apparent in a number of late Weimar novels. In *Kämpfende Jugend* a social democratic father argues with his son who has secretly joined the KPD. The

[91] BA, Rep. 15.01, Nr. 13118, *Der Führer, Monatsschrift für Führer und Hilfer der Arbeiter-jugendbewegung,* "Politische Erziehung in der Krise," Nr. 7, July 1931.

[92] For further analysis of the duty of young republicans and the Reichsbanner's use of generational politics, see BLHA, Berlin Rep. 30, Berlin C, Title 95, Sektion 10, Nr. 26, *Burschen Heraus (Zeitschrift zur Reichsbanner Werbung),* June 1930.

[93] Cf. Hans Mommsen, "Generationskonflikt und Jugendrevolte in der Weimarer Republik" in Thomas Koebner, Rolf-Peter Janz, and Frank Trommler, eds., *"Mit uns zieht die neue Zeit": Der Mythos Jugend* (Frankfurt a. M.: Suhrkamp, 1985), pp. 50–67. Mommsen also stresses the difficulty the SPD had with generational conflict and the belief that leaders were out of touch.

[94] BA, Rep. 15.01, Nr. 25966, *Das Reichsbanner,* "Einig, wachsam, kampfbereit!" Nr. 44, October 31, 1931.

[95] König, *Berlin-Kreuzberg* (no date), p. 30.

son's comrades have vandalized the family's home to punish his father who was considered a traitor by his neighbors for working as a doorman at the local unemployment office.[96] In Fallada's *Little Man*, the female protagonist's father and brother turn to insults aimed at each other when they first meet her petty bourgeois fiancé. The young radical weighs in: "'Sooner an honest bourgeois any day than you Social Fascists.' 'Social Fascists,' raged the old man. 'Who's a fascist, you little Soviet toady!' 'Who!' says Karl. 'You damned old jingo.'"[97]

It might seem contradictory to argue that generational conflict led to radicalization among the younger generation, when, as we have seen, some middle-aged family men also sought radical politics as a way to protect neighborhood and familial power structures. Though those arrested for political violence in these years were mostly young men in their twenties at least informally associated with the paramilitary wings of both the KPD and NSDAP, the two parties did draw significant numbers of the older cohort. Members of the two generations, however, were joining for somewhat different reasons. Young men were attracted to these groups primarily for the material assistance, the sense of belonging and order, the action-first mentality of radicalism and the accompanying glorification of the male body, and the fact that these parties were new and emphasized the role of youth in fashioning Germany's future. The official goal of the Hitler Jugend in 1930, for example, was to demand "economic and social protection and justice for German young workers and apprentices, so that a strong empowered youth can raise a new state out of the ruined system of the older generation."[98] Men in their thirties and forties could also be attracted to the male space created by these organizations' camaraderie and discipline, and they too were drawn by the hope of creating change in their neighborhoods and families. However, while teenagers and twenty-somethings called attention to the failure of their fathers to act as arbiters of social order and saw themselves as the rightful heirs of this power, men in their forties saw themselves as competent heads of family and community.

The reconstructed "family" provided by the local chapters of the radical parties appealed to some members of both age groups. With single-parent families on the rise and familial problems escalating, leaving young men feeling alienated from their fathers and middle-aged men facing the inability to carry out their traditional roles, radical politics provided ersatz father/son relationships. Both paramilitary organizations, the Nazi SA and the Communist RFB, mimicked traditional family and shop-floor structures by creating rites of passage and official training corps. One Nostiz Kiez Communist

---

[96] Schönstedt, *Kämpfende Jugend*, pp. 5–6.

[97] Hans Fallada, *Little Man, What Now?*, Eric Sutton, trans. (Chicago: Academy Chicago Publishers, 1992), p. 20.

[98] *Der Nationalsozialist*, "Was will der Hitler-Jugend?," Nr. 55, April 27, 1930.

youth remembered that the job of the young people in the neighborhood was to perform "*Lehrlingsarbeit*," or apprentice's work, such as toting the buckets of paint on a graffiti campaign.[99] The transition from youth organizations into adult membership was marked by pomp and circumstance. New initiates were then restricted to the training corps, where they were instructed by the more mature members until they were deemed capable of taking on greater responsibility.[100] Both organizations also made use of family rhetoric in their recruitment propaganda. In Goebbels's Berlin newspaper, *Der Angriff*, he reported that each national socialist should be "proud and joyful" about the progress of the Hitler Jugend. These emotions, he exclaimed: "must be compared to the joy of the father over the growth of his son."[101] In the memos of the RFB, the leadership constantly reminded its men: "We are *one* family. Each stands for the other."[102] The Communist youth group, the KJVD, even conducted "Three-Generation Events" as a way to reunite families and pass on party traditions.[103]

These events were sorely needed by the parties. While generational tensions seemed to cause more discord in the SPD, Communist functionaries also worried about the rifts between older and younger comrades. In one evaluation of two cells in the East End, the KPD functionary complained:

Looking at both cells, it is immediately apparent that in the street cell we have two groups. One consists of the old comrades, who... are not well-situated to carry through on campaigns with the necessary élan [or] able to train the younger comrades to work and a group of younger party members who came into the party full of fire, full of élan..., but who are not happy with the attitude of these older comrades, so that soon the danger arises, that they run away from the party and turn to an organization that satisfies them.

In the factory cell we discover the fact that we are only dealing with old comrades, who have absolutely no desire to take on younger comrades.[104]

Where the ties between generations had broken down, the radical organizations were ready to pick up the slack. Berlin's Communist-dominated Fichte sports club used working parents' sense of failure at raising their children to gain new members. The organization's literature explained: "the capitalist

99 Lothar Uebel, "Ein heisses Pflaster" in Geschichtskreis Kreuzberg, ed., *Nostitzritze. Ein Straße in Kreuzberg* (Berlin: Gericke, 1992), p. 56.
100 On the RFB's *Lehrzüge*, see BA-SAPMO, RY1/I4/2/13, Richtlinien über den Aufbau der Lehrzüge, no date, likely 1930 or 1931.
101 *Der Angriff*, "Unsere Hitler-Jugend," Nr. 22, March 16, 1930.
102 BA-SAPMO, RY1/I4/2/13, "Roter Frontkämpferbund – Rundschreiben zur militärpolitischer Arbeit," no date, likely 1931.
103 BA-SAPMO, RY1/I4/1/82, "Material zur Schulentlassungskampagne" addressed to all BL of KPD youth organizations, February 4, 1931.
104 BA-SAPMO, RY1/3/1-2/24, investigation of the party work in Cell 1719 and Gas Cell in the UB East, no date.

system of exploitation does not permit the father to earn enough money to provide for his family. Therefore the mother must also work. As a result, both have no time to engage sufficiently with the children."[105] Fichte promised to take on this responsibility, ensuring that the children would be "properly" educated about politics and adulthood. In the fictional account of radicalism in the Nostiz Kiez by Schönstedt, one of the most ardent young Communists is the son of a fallen spartacist fighter. In his absence, the young Karl has taken over his father's struggle. Despite his mother's concerns about the busy schedule he keeps, it is the party scene and the bookshelves overflowing with Marxist literature that nourish him more than the cabbage his mother can offer.[106]

In the well-known Nazi film, *Hitlerjunge Quex* (1933), a young worker's son is harangued into joining the Communist youth organization by his overbearing father. On the first recreational outing with his new companions, the boy is repulsed by the rowdy behavior, drinking, and flirtation of the co-ed group. He wanders off in the woods only to come upon the disciplined, male-only campground of the local HJ unit. Captivated by the light of the bonfire and the solemn unity of the boys, he rebels against his father's wishes and tries to befriend the young Nazis. After many tests, through which he proves his loyalty to his new mates, and the suicide death of his impoverished mother (a fate he narrowly escapes when his mother intentionally leaves the gas stove on while he sleeps nearby), the boy chooses to leave his father's home and move into the local HJ home [Plate 4]. The local leader and older members of the HJ thereafter take over the direction of his moral and political upbringing in a "family," which more closely resembles "a unit of combatants."[107]

Despite the cozy familial rhetoric employed by their leaders, radical youths elicited the greatest public fear in Berlin. Because of their political immaturity, economic instability, and youthful exuberance, defenders of the republic and radical party leaders alike recognized these new actors on the political stage as the biggest threat to the status quo. Since large numbers of middle-class youngsters were attracted to radicalism, especially Nazism, the politicization

---

[105] BLHA, Rep. 30, Berlin C, Title 95, Sektion 9, Nr. 10, "Festschrift zum 14. Kreisfest Fichte," Berlin, June 1929, p. 22.

[106] Schönstedt, *Kämpfende Jugend* (1972), p. 50.

[107] This phrase comes from Elisabeth Domansky's argument about the dissolution of the patriarchal family during World War I and its replacement in the Weimar era by state intervention and ersatz militarized family units. See further, Elisabeth Domansky, "Militarization and Reproduction in WWI Germany," in Geoff Eley, ed., *Society, Culture and the State in Germany, 1870–1930* (Ann Arbor: University of Michigan Press, 1996), p. 462. As in the movie, the HJ leaders recognized the potential in Berlin of attracting young still "untouched" (*unbelekten*) sons from workers' families. In 1929 leaders reported that up to 80 percent of members in some HJ groups in the capital had "marxist parents." BA – NS28/81 HJ – Reich leadership report to all local leaders, February 1929.

Plate 4. Generational tension on film: for the young protagonist, leaving his father's politics behind also means leaving his father's home for the Hitler Youth home
in Hans Steinhoff's 1933 film *Hitlerjunge Quex*. Source: © Bildarchiv Preussischer
Kulturbesitz, 2003.

of the younger generation – from the affluent West End to the poor East side –
became a preoccupation of the bourgeois press.

The Communist Party's children's groups never succeeded in drawing large
numbers of members. Only the children of the most passionate Communists
tended to join. Yet all party activities connected to the young, especially agitation in Berlin's schools, met harsh criticism in the bourgeois press. School
strikes were tried throughout the North and East in this period, often erupt-
ing over the firing of a popular teacher or deplorable building conditions.
Individual strikes, when motivated by local concerns, did in some cases draw
significant support. In late 1929, a strike broke out at the 223 Community
School on Putbusserstraße in Wedding. The main concern of the parents,
though the *AIZ* stressed the danger the curriculum posed to "proletarian
ideology," was the fact that three students had recently died of diphthe-
ria and ten others were ill with what appeared to be the same disease. Of

the seven hundred who attended the school, on average only ninety continued to attend classes, while the others waited until they were satisfied that hygienic standards were acceptable.[108] In the spring of 1930, the KPD sponsored a citywide school strike to protest financial cuts in education, inadequate school conditions, nationalist and religious curricula, and the use of corporal punishment. The strikes, tied to less tangible party issues, were hardly successful, drawing interest in only a handful of schools. However, the amount of press coverage devoted to these strikes was extensive, with dozens of articles appearing during the five days of the strike. Headlines against the strikes such as "School Bolshevism," "The Child in the Class Struggle," and "School Anarchy in Neukölln" were among many which decried this tactic of the radical left.[109] The press made it clear that the political involvement of children and youth was unacceptable.

An ironic school-strike cartoon, which reflects the sense of disorder linked to the strikes, appeared in one of the city's popular dailies, the republic-friendly *8-Uhr Abendblatt*. The cartoon shows a small schoolboy being led to class by two large policemen, one with nightstick in hand. Other striking schoolboys try to convince their classmate to turn around. The message does not explicitly target the KPD; there is in fact no reference to the party's involvement in the strikes, nor is it specifically critical of the police. The ironic juxtaposition of the baton-wielding police and sweet-looking children, however, illustrates to the reader that something was wrong in Berlin. The caption is telling: "Berlin hasn't seen that yet..."[110] [Plate 5]. Organizers of the strikes told supporters to keep their children at home, and the picket lines were formed primarily by adults. The implication of the cartoon, however, was that politics, as it should be conducted, had deteriorated in the capital to the extent that such a scene was potentially on the horizon.

While reports of politicized young people in the poorer districts were symbolic of the larger threat from Berlin's East side, the radicalization of middle-class youth was a problem that hit bourgeois readers much closer to home. When the middle-class press covered incidents in which radical youth activism disrupted what was considered the legitimate political sphere, reports offered one interpretation almost exclusively. It was assumed that the young men in their late teens and twenties were not legitimate political actors but instead were being "misused" by party leaders. For example, in April 1930 (the same month as the KPD-organized school strikes), a Democratic Party assembly in Schöneberg was overrun by rowdy young Nazis, who heckled the host and drowned out his speech with chants. They made a couple of rushes

---

[108] *AIZ*, "Schulstreik im Berliner Wedding," Nr. 46, 1929, p. 6.
[109] These three headlines ran respectively in the following newspapers: *Berliner Börsen-Zeitung*, Nr. 161, April 5, 1930; *Deutsche Tageszeitung*, Nr. 174, April 13, 1930; *Deutsche Zeitung*, Nr. 78b, April 2, 1930.
[110] *8-Uhr Abendblatt*, "Schulstreik in Neukölln bricht zusammen," Nr. 79, April 3, 1930.

Das hat Berlin noch nicht gesehen . . .

Plate 5. The liberal press responds negatively to the idea of politicized children. The caption reads: "Berlin hasn't seen that yet..." Source: *8-Uhr Abendblatt*, Nr. 79, April 3, 1930.

toward the speaker's podium. Though one DDP member was knocked down on the stage, no serious injuries were reported. In comparison to some of the political assemblies of the period, this disturbance was fairly uneventful. Nonetheless, the democratic *Berliner Volkszeitung* railed at the conduct of the "half-grown audience members," whose "unrestrained, undisciplined and mindless [behavior]...was the most shameful evidence of [their] poor political upbringing."[111] On the same day, the *VZ* offered a similar analysis of the DDP assembly. Its article also took aim at the NSDAP by describing the "bad impression [created at the assembly] of nationalist-style upbringing." Moreover, the *VZ* article described the conduct of the young Nazis in a way that would be repeated by newspapers, government officials, and criminal justice experts. The reporter claimed that the Nazis "misused youth."[112] This charge was also leveled against the KPD by its critics. The charge of

[111] *Berliner Volkszeitung*, "Nazis sprengen eine demokratische Versammlung," Nr. 170, April 11, 1930.
[112] VZ, "Goebbels will nicht diskutieren. Gewalt statt Aussprache," Nr. 173, April 11, 1930.

"misuse" had less to do with radical politics per se than it did with youth involvement because the term was only employed in reference to *young* NSDAP and KPD party members and sympathizers. Supporters of republican politics clearly did not approve of, and in fact feared, the prospect of new social groups, such as women and young people, moving into the political arena.

By treating youth involvement in radical politics as misuse, the liberal press downplayed the attractions these parties held for young men and underestimated the discontent of large numbers of middle-class and working-class youth. In early 1932, a sixteen-year-old Hitler Jugend member, Herbert Norkus, was stabbed to death while he and other HJ members distributed invitations door-to-door. The particularly young age of the victim shocked the city and made powerful propaganda for the NSDAP, which used the "martyrdom" of Norkus as a stock tale of the party's rise to power throughout the Third Reich. At the time of the incident, the HJ had been circulating their flyers in a workers' neighborhood in Moabit, and the police were quick to carry out searches of the houses in the neighborhood where Norkus was attacked. Within two days, six inhabitants of the area had been arrested. The KPD responded with criticism of the police surveillance of the neighborhood, and its newspapers portrayed the incident as a two-way conflict between the Nazi and Communist youngsters in the area rather than as an unprovoked attack.[113] The Nazi press took the opposite tack, publishing articles such as "Hitler-youngster Herbert Norkus attacked and stabbed to death by 40 Muscovites,"[114] which exaggerated the KPD strength and Russian influence in the neighborhood.

The liberal press, of course, had a third view of the events. In the *BT*'s first account of the incident, its reporter wrote: "According to the latest evidence the Communists hold the blame this time for the murder, in which a sixteen-year old fell as victim, and the results of which show in all clarity the political instigation and politicization of youth by the radicals who themselves send school children onto the streets."[115] The author used the misuse argument against both radical parties in this case, shifting the responsibility for violent action away from those involved and placing it on anonymous string-pulling "radicals." This case also garnered attention because of the time and place of the murder. It was a "bright Sunday morning."[116] As the *BT* saw it, families and their children should have been dressing for church services or gathered

---

113 *RF*, "Sechs Moabiter Arbeiter verhaftet," Nr. 21, January 27, 1932.

114 *VB*, "Hitlerjunge Herbert Norkus von 40 Moskauern überfallen und zusammengestochen," Nr. 27, January 27, 1932.

115 *BT*, "Politische Bluttat in Moabit. Nationalsozialistischer Schüler auf der Strasse erstochen," Nr. 41, January 25, 1932.

116 *Berliner Montagspost*, "16 Jähriger erstochen. Straßenkampf zwischen Radikalen," Nr. 4, January 25, 1932. The *Berliner Montagspost* was a product of the liberal Ullstein publishing house.

around the breakfast table, rather than circulating propaganda or fighting political enemies. Instead the young boy's body was found in the doorway of an apartment house. No one realized that Norkus had been gravely injured until he was found unconscious after the brawl ended. It was shocking that such an act could happen so close to home. The scene of the crime was not a pub or political assembly; Berlin's political crisis had landed literally at the front door. This intrusion of politics, and especially political violence, into the semiprivate space of the residential courtyard and front stoop did more than cast moral doubt on the workers who lived in this neighborhood and the parents of the HJ unit. The liberal readers of the *BT* were given the impression that in the capital there no longer existed a public space for rational political debate among men or a private sphere safe from political radicalism.

BLOODY MAY

The chain of events that began on May 1, 1929, led to the deaths of thirty-three citizens, the injuries and arrests of over one thousand mainly in Wedding and Neukölln and shaped city politics and neighborhood radicalism for the remaining years of the republic.[117] The May riots also hardened the differences between the two workers' parties, the SPD and KPD, and led to the banning of the major Communist paramilitary organizations. It served as a lasting illustration that the autonomy of workers' neighborhoods was under threat, leaving inhabitants ever more mistrustful of the republic and its institutions. During the *Kaiserreich,* this sense of threat would have strengthened support for political organizations that represented workers' interests. The complicity of the social democratic city authorities in the crackdown and the irresponsibility of the KPD in its handling of the situation, however, left many workers in Berlin doubting whether either political party was willing

---

[117] Klaus Neukrantz soon wrote the novel *Barrikaden am Wedding* about the events surrounding May 1, 1929. It caused a great deal of debate in the city because of its sympathetic view of the workers involved. Neukrantz's novel is a prime example of the literary representation of Berlin's Communist milieu. The poverty of Wedding's inhabitants is stressed, as is their class, but not necessarily party, solidarity. In other words, neighbors assist each other in their struggles because of their common living conditions and sense of powerlessness, but the book says little about the KPD as the solution to oppression. The novel also describes in great detail the importance of street possession to both the police and the residents. See Klaus Neukrantz, *Barrikaden am Wedding* (Berlin: Oberbaumverlag, 1931). An English translation followed: *Barricades in Wedding* (Chicago: Banner Press, 1933). Historians' accounts include Eve Rosenhaft, "Working-class Life and Working-class Politics: Communists, Nazis, and the State in the Battle for the Streets, Berlin 1928–1933" in Richard Bessel and E. J. Feuchtwanger, *Social Change and Political Development in the Weimar Republic* (London: Croom Helm, 1981), pp. 207–40, and Chris Bowlby, "Blutmai 1929: Police, Parties and Proletarians in a Berlin Confrontation" in *The Historical Journal* (Vol. 29, No. 1, 1986), pp. 137–58.

or able to solve the local crises they were facing. Finally, to some extent political violence was validated as a political strategy by the May tragedy, making it possible for some Berliners to choose violence as a way to deal with these problems.

Though the economic crisis and its consequences were not felt on a large scale in Berlin until later in 1929, instability had already arrived in the capital by spring. Paramilitary organizations were growing. The RFB was paramount, but the Berlin SA was beginning to make its presence felt. In November and December 1928, at least two right-wing activists were killed in Berlin by political opponents. The conservative press took aim at the police for "allowing" left-wing violence, criticism which had larger implications because the Social Democrat Hermann Müller had recently been named prime minister.[118] Prussian Interior Minister Albert Grzesinski already supported the prohibition of the RFB, but Reich Interior Minister Carl Severing argued that the level of danger to state security posed by the RFB did not yet warrant legal action. With no action taken, workers and the KPD began to plan for the annual May 1 demonstrations and celebrations. Simultaneously, Grzesinski, with the cooperation of Police President Karl Zörgiebel in Berlin, issued a ban on demonstrations for Prussia. In the weeks preceding May 1, the ban was lifted for the occasion in other Prussian cities but remained in force in Berlin.[119] The police ban covered all outdoor demonstrations that threatened to disrupt public order and any indoor assemblies of an "unpeaceful character." These limits on political activism were published alongside a warning from Grzesinski, in which he pleaded for an end to the disruptive political behavior, "so that differences of political opinion can again be expressed in rational forms." If this "last chance" to reject radicalism was ignored, Grzesinski promised to protect the "peace-loving" population by banning any political organizations that disregarded the May Day prohibition on demonstrations.[120]

Social democratic organizations in Berlin were not directly affected by the ban because their activities were not seen as a threat to public safety. No matter what Berlin SPD members thought of the ruling, their press and leadership kept quiet, since the party was implicated in the decisions made by the Social Democrats Grzesinski and Zörgiebel. The KPD reacted angrily, declaring that this policy was evidence that the SPD was in fact a "social fascist" party and an enemy of the city's workers. In the days leading up

---

[118] *Deutsche Tageszeitung*, "Kommunistischer Meuchelmord," Nr. 93, February 23, 1929. The same death of an eighteen-year-old Stahlhelm member led to criticism in a number of other newspapers as well. See also *Berliner Börsen-Zeitung*, "Wie lange noch dürfen die RF-Mörder ihr Unwesen treiben?," Nr. 93, February 24, 1929.

[119] The ban had actually been issued for Berlin alone in December 1928, and it was not until March that the ban was widened to encompass all of Prussia.

[120] The ban on demonstrations and declaration by Grzesinski can be found in many newspapers. For example, see *BT*, "Eine letzte Warnung," Nr. 158, March 24, 1929.

to the first of May, the Communist press urged Berlin's workers to attend the traditional rallies and marches. Though the Berlin KPD wanted it to appear that the ban was irrelevant and that everything would go forward as planned, precautionary measures were circulated through confidential memos. Members of the RFB were warned not to carry weapons at the demonstrations, wear their uniforms in public, or march in columns on May 1. Local leaders were even instructed to stay away from their homes, in case there was any sort of widespread round-up of party functionaries by police.[121]

On the morning of May 1, 1929, citizens filled the streets as usual throughout the workers' districts. The SPD held its large demonstration in the Lustgarten, as it had done for years, and smaller, more loosely organized KPD marches formed in a number of districts, including Wedding, Neukölln, Mitte, Friedrichshain, and Kreuzberg. In expectation of resistance to the ban, special police orders for May 1 were issued during the last week of April. The entire *Schutzpolizei* was put on alarm status beginning at 7 A.M. No officer was to go out on patrol alone, and posts were strengthened by shifting men away from those areas of the city not expected to experience disturbances. In an aggressive preemptive strike against gatherings, patrols were sent to the regular KPD and RFB demonstration sites before protesters arrived. Members of the *Schutzpolizei* were warned that KPD marches might be led by women and children, implying that force would likely be needed to break up the unlawful demonstrations. Finally, extra troops and transport vehicles were sent as reinforcements to the police stations expected to face the greatest resistance, including Alexanderplatz and stations in Wedding and Neukölln.[122]

As commanded, the police attempted to break up the street gatherings and protests as they formed. The Nostiz area was on the list of possible sites of disruption, and police were in position to disperse the morning march here, which they succeeded in doing by the time the procession reached Hallesches Tor north of the Kiez.[123] In other neighborhoods, however, violence erupted when the police moved in. Shortly after ten in the morning the first shots were fired on Wedding's Kösliner Street, and before noon the first two deaths were reported at the square Hakescher Markt in Mitte. In a number of hotspots, particularly in Friedrichshain, Wedding, and Neukölln – areas

---

[121] BA, R15.01, Nr. 1031. A copy of this internal KPD memo was dated April 25, 1929, and sent from Berlin's police chief to the Prussian minister of the interior, p. 242.

[122] BLHA, Rep. 30, Berlin C, Title 90, Nr. 7547, "Instructions from the Kommando der Schutzpolizei concerning May 1, 1929," April 28, 1929. In the following days further commands were issued. Patrolmen away from the city on training missions were recalled to Berlin. Further, red flags were not to be unfurled in public, and banners that hung over streets were also prohibited. See BLHA, Rep. 30, Berlin C, Title 90, Nr. 7547, police chief memo: "Addendum concerning May 1, 1929."

[123] König, *Berlin – Kreuzberg* (no date), pp. 27–8.

that police had clearly targeted in their pre-May planning – barricades started to go up as police arrived. In the Nostiz Kiez too, radicals barricaded Gneisenau with materials taken from a U-Bahn construction site to keep the police at bay while they held an afternoon assembly.[124] Throughout the day, police informed their superiors of the disturbances they encountered. These short accounts filed by members of the *Schutzpolizei* were quite different from the stories of barricaded resistance publicized after the fact by the police department and the KPD. During the summer months that followed, police officials rationalized their aggression by describing an uprising of potentially revolutionary character. Similarly, the KPD supported tales of brave protesters who, in demonstration of their revolutionary preparedness risked their lives in confrontation with an unjust police force. Despite the drama of the official accounts emanating from both camps after the fact, most of the reports turned in during the rioting by police on the street described unrest led by groups of unarmed young people (often of both sexes), whose tactics were mainly to taunt the police with calls such as "Blood hound" and "Down with the Zörgiebel guard." Patrolmen did not often comment on any clear party affiliation among the demonstrators, remarking most frequently on their youth and their "stupid sayings."[125] When the police instructed those gathering on the streets to go home, the unwillingness of some to do so, coupled with continued jeering, was considered by the police sufficient provocation to make use of their rubber truncheons. Though the *Schutzpolizei* turned to their firearms in many cases, almost all the police reports submitted during the fighting describe demonstrators throwing only cobblestones, bricks, coal, flower pots, bottles, and glasses.[126]

Throughout the day and into the evening, the police worked to clear the streets. Only in the areas around Wedding's Kösliner Street and Neukölln's Prinz Handjery Street had there been major battles. In these locations, armored vehicles and water cannons had been used to remove barricades, and the streets were closed off and guarded. In the mid-afternoon on May 2, *Schutzpolizei* reinforcements responded to a call that those stationed on Kösliner Street were again under attack. In a report issued by the political police, section IA, the patrolmen were being pelted by rocks, and one officer had been cut on the hand. Eight shots were fired to clear the street, which the

---

[124] Ibid.
[125] BLHA, Rep. 30, Berlin C, Title 95, Sektion 2, Nr. 173, political police IA report, May 2, 1929. In reports like this one, the youngsters had made no violent moves toward the police, but the use of the club was still deemed "necessary and correct."
[126] In fact, days after the violence began, internal police reports stressed the ease with which barricades were dismantled by the authorities. One report was so blunt as to say that the Communist opposition "still had a lot to learn, if they wanted to become dangerous to the Schutzpolizei in battle." BLHA, Rep. 30, Berlin C, Title 90, Nr. 7547, Polizei-Inspektion Wedding report, May 7, 1929.

reporting officer admits further angered the residents. Later that afternoon "an inhabitant called the police station at nearby Pank Street pleading in the name of tenants from a number of houses along the street not to shoot there any more that night, since the residents were already greatly infuriated by the events of the preceding evening."[127] Around midnight, barricades were set up on nearby Wiesen Street, and shots were exchanged between police and protesters. The same scenario took place north of Kösliner on Reinickendorfer Street, and it was 3 A.M. before the police had cleared the barricades and taken away about two dozen prisoners.

On May 2, violence had also erupted again in Neukölln, and sporadic disturbances were registered in other districts. The entire length of Nostizstraße was closed off to traffic. As during the previous evening, police allegedly fired shots again, which were answered by debris being hurled from the windows above.[128] The KPD hoped to gain immediate public support by focusing on the civilian deaths and by staging large indoor assemblies to protest the "murder of workers" by the police. The largest such rally was a private affair held for five thousand to six thousand party functionaries in the Sophiensäle in Mitte. Two other assemblies in Moabit and Wedding were open to the public and drew about fifteen hundred people. Party functionaries and eyewitnesses to the violence spoke, and the message stressed the brutality and "sadistic and perverse inclinations" of the *Schutzpolizei*.[129]

On May 3, the violence intensified in Neukölln around Hermann Street. While Severing, Grzesinski, and Prussian Minister-President Otto Braun met to discuss the dissolution of the RFB, armored vehicles fought protesters, leading to four additional civilian deaths by early afternoon. By midafternoon, new measures were announced to quiet the "remaining trouble spots." Sections of both Wedding and Neukölln were deemed "endangered districts," and new restrictions were put into effect. Gathering in groups of more than two people, standing in courtyards or driveways, coming and going on the street, opening windows, and bicycle riding were prohibited [Plate 6]. All vehicular traffic was halted between 9 A.M. and 4 P.M., except for medical personnel, and no windows facing the street were to be lit.[130] Those who did venture out were questioned and searched by special patrols. These conditions remained in force until May 5, when the alarm was

---

[127] BLHA, Rep. 30, Berlin C, Title 95, Teil 2, Nr. 173, Berlin political police IA, "Report about the events of May 2, 1929."
[128] König, *Berlin – Kreuzberg* (no date), pp. 27–8.
[129] BLHA, Rep. 30, Berlin C, Title 95, Teil 2, Nr. 173, Berlin political police IA, "Report about the events of May 2, 1929."
[130] BLHA, Rep. 30, Berlin C, Title 90, Nr. 7547, *Schutzpolizei* directive, "Special conditions for fighting the remaining trouble spots from May 1," May 3, 1929. The areas faced with these restrictions were the Wedding section between Wiesen, Pank, Nettelbeck, and Reinickendorfer Streets and the Neukölln neighborhood between Boddin, Weise, Leyke, Steinmetz, and Berliner Streets.

Plate 6. A show of force in the "remaining trouble spots": armed *Schutzpolizei* questioning pedestrians in the days after the May 1929 riots. Source: © Bildarchiv Preussischer Kulturbesitz, 2003.

downgraded and police began limiting searches to "suspicious people."[131] On May 6, the decision made three days earlier to ban the RFB in Prussia was made public.

In the weeks following the May tragedy, the public, the KPD, and the police all struggled to understand why the situation had become so deadly. By May 4, thirty-one people had been killed, seven of whom were women.[132] No members of the Berlin police force died in the fighting. The ages of the deceased ranged from sixteen to seventy-nine, with twelve falling between the ages of twenty and thirty. Except for a journalist caught in one of the last gun battles of the May violence, all of the people who lost their lives died within their own neighborhoods. These were not protesters who traveled to Wedding or Neukölln just to be part of the confrontation with police. One man died after being hit by a police truck. Another received his fatal injuries in police custody. The remaining twenty-nine died of gunshot wounds.[133]

---

[131] BLHA, Rep. 30, Berlin C, Title 90, Nr. 7547, Polizei-Inspektion North Abt. I, May 5, 1929.

[132] Bowlby cites data from F. Timpe's *Weltbühne* article that thirty-eight had died by December due to injuries incurred in the May violence. Bowlby, "Blutmai 1929" (1986), p. 149.

[133] Leon Schirmann, *Blutmai Berlin 1929* (Berlin: Dietz, 1991), pp. 335–9.

The *Schutzpolizei* reported on May 25 that their troops had suffered fifty-one injuries. Only one policeman was shot – through the hand. Most of their injuries were bone fractures and concussions from hurled debris. In addition to the deaths, there were about two hundred injuries among protesters and over twelve hundred arrests in the three days of fighting. A large number of these were charged with ignoring the ban on demonstrations, while others were accused of resisting the authorities and disturbing the peace.[134]

The police and all noncommunist newspapers blamed the KPD and its paramilitary wing, the RFB, for orchestrating the violent events, even though according to police records only 119 of the 1,200 arrested, or 10 percent, were members of Communist organizations.[135] As was often the case in Berlin, the political police sought Soviet architects behind the tragedy. Though they could produce no evidence of a conspiracy, some newspapers joined in the rumors that agitators had been sent to Moscow with the purpose of planning the rebellion.[136] Even without the proof they sought, from their earliest public statements the police maintained their position that the KPD, as a manipulative and criminal institution, was at fault and that all police actions were justified and necessary. "In the cases in which Communists went from passive resistance to attacks on police officers," declared the Berlin police department during the unrest, "the police were forced to make use of their firearms. However, firearms were used only at the most troublesome locations in the moments of greatest danger."[137] By the fourth of May, the frustration among the *Schutzpolizei* on the streets was evident in their own reports. The branch office in Wedding reported back to its superiors: "the mood among the men was at first good, most officers fulfilled their orders with great dutifulness." Over the three days, however, the mood had turned "bad." They had tired from the constant emergency status and the difficult task of dealing with a hostile public.[138]

---

[134] BLHA, Rep. 30, Berlin C, Title 90, Nr. 7547, *Schutzpolizei* directive, "Vorgänge in den ersten Mai-Tagen," May 25, 1929.

[135] Bowlby, "Blutmai 1929" (1986), p. 150.

[136] For police suspicions about the involvement of Russian emissaries in the May violence, see BLHA, Rep. 30, Berlin C, Title 95, Teil 2, Nr. 174, Police IA reports from May 8 and June 10, 1929. In the first, the author reluctantly admits that no Soviets had been arrested in the violence, only a Dutchman, an Italian, and a Pole. See also *Neue Zeit: Das illustrierte Morgenblatt*, May 4, 1929, which ran the article "Gestern acht Todesopfer in Neukölln – von Russen organisiert," before the unrest had been squelched. In addition, see GStA, Rep. 84a, 2.5.1, Nr. 10569, for a letter from the district attorney for the Landgericht II to the Prussian Minister of Justice, May 11, 1929 which discusses the difficulties of arresting any leaders for the unrest between May 1 and 3.

[137] GStA, HA I, Rep. 77, Title 4043, Nr. 211, *Amtlicher Preussischer Pressedienst*, "Das Berliner Polizeipräsidium zu den Vorgängen am 1. Mai," May 2, 1929.

[138] BLHA, Rep. 30, Berlin C, Title 90, Nr. 7547, report from Polizei-Inspektion Wedding to the Polizei-Gruppe North, May 4, 1929.

KPD leaders were perhaps the most surprised by the outcome of their call to defy the ban.[139] Not only was the armed conflict not orchestrated from above, the party leadership discouraged this use of violence and refused to issue weapons to those on the streets. Members of the RFB in particular may have been urged to take to the streets on May 1, but the RFB leadership in Berlin was not expecting a deadly three-day battle. Only a few pistols were recovered by the police in their extensive searches of the apartment buildings in the troubled neighborhoods, many of which were souvenirs of World War I combat. Those residents who took part in the violence did so mainly to resist the police incursion into their neighborhoods.

Although the KPD never expected such extensive street actions on May 1, the party tried to make the most of the events. What was termed *Blutmai* (Bloody May) by party leaders would be employed, for the rest of the republic's existence, as the most potent symbol of the Berlin SPD's betrayal of the radical left. Though the *Rote Fahne* was banned for three weeks beginning during the unrest, the *AIZ* and other newspapers presented the party's portrayal of the events. In the first *AIZ* edition to be released after the violence, the cover photo captured a worker being led away by two uniformed policemen and one well-dressed gentleman, above the caption: "Like this one, thousands more were arrested and beaten." This dramatic photo served as the lead-in for a pictorial spread depicting police brutality and workers fleeing from mounted patrols.[140] Only a small portion of the spread was devoted to photos of demonstrators marching despite the prohibition. A week later, an article titled "The Dead Cry Out in Condemnation!" highlighted those victims of police bullets who best proved that this police aggression was unwarranted. The pictures showed a balcony where two women were shot, the spot where another onlooker was severely wounded by a bullet-shattered window, and a former male civil servant and invalid who was also shot on his balcony.[141] Immediately after the ban on the *RF* was

---

[139] The lack of control exerted by the KPD over its supporters is highlighted in Thomas Kurz's analysis of the May violence as a way to defend the party against those who blame it for the failure of SPD/KPD cooperation. Kurz maintains that the tensions between skilled and unskilled workers, which predated the 1929 bloodshed, were exacerbated by the oncoming Depression and led to a bifurcation of the working class, leaving only Berlin's rabble for KPD membership. Therefore, according to Kurz, the Communist Party was unable to carry on serious party work but was still held responsible for the irrational behavior of its supporters in conflicts such as the May riots. While it is important to note the conflict between party leaders and local Communist activists, such an argument takes the easy way out by holding unemployed Berliners to blame, without examining how these neighborhoods operated, why violence erupted, or what the relationship between SPD and KPD members was really like. See further Thomas Kurz, *Blutmai* (Berlin: Dietz, 1988). For a contrasting analysis of the KPD's response to the events of *Blutmai*, see Rosenhaft, *Beating the Fascists?* (1983), pp. 33–5.

[140] *AIZ*, Nr. 20, 1929, p. 1. Photo spread follows on pages 2 and 3.

[141] *AIZ*, "Die Toten klagen an!," Nr. 21, 1929, p. 3.

Die Wahrheit ist „verboten!"

SPD. als „Staatseinrichtung" unter Schutz der Klassenjustiz

Plate 7. "The truth is forbidden." The *RF* blames the Berlin police for the violence of May 1929 and the justice system for condoning it. Source: *Die Rote Fahne*, May 24, 1929.

lifted, a scathing cartoon appeared in the newspaper; the cartoon claimed the truth about the tragedy was being covered up by a judicial decision to ban a KPD pamphlet describing the events of *Blutmai*. Berlin Police Chief Zörgiebel (SPD) is shown trying to wash the blood of demonstrators from his hands, while a judge calmly shows him that the Communist interpretation of the violence has been censored[142] [Plate 7]. In addition to the criticism the KPD leveled at the republican government, and the SPD in particular, the

---

[142] *RF*, "Die Wahrheit ist 'verboten'!," Nr. 103, May 1, 1929. It should be noted as well that the SPD used the opportunity of the May tragedy to show the KPD in a poor light. Articles appearing in *Vorwärts* during and after the unrest described the aggression of Communist troops as following orders from Moscow and the actions of police as being purely defensive. For example, see *Vorwärts*, "Die Namen der neun Opfer. Die traurigen Nachklänge der kommunistischen Krawalle," May 3, 1929.

party called for a mass strike on May 2.[143] The results of the strike, during which twenty-five thousand workers in Berlin and another fifty thousand in other parts of the country stayed home from work, were not as impressive as hoped, but the strikes could not be considered a total failure either. Those who died between May 1 and May 3 were viewed collectively as martyrs, and all those who participated in the upheaval were hailed by Communist Party leaders as proof of the revolutionary consciousness of Berlin's workers.[144]

Though the police searched for ringleaders of the May unrest among Berlin's activists, they were never able to find any such persons. As a result, the criminal cases dealt only with minor offenders. In trials that continued into November 1931, thirty-eight defendants received prison sentences. For twenty-eight of these cases, the time in prison amounted to a total of almost twelve years, with the other ten cases receiving shorter sentences adding up to just over one year. The harshest jail sentence handed down to a *Blutmai* demonstrator was nine months, given to one man for his participation in barricade building in Wedding on the night of May 2.[145] The defenses presented ranged from mistaken identity to the more defiant position that the ban on public demonstrations was itself illegal.[146] Neither tactic worked when confronted with numerous police witnesses who swore to the identity of the defendant and circumstances of the arrest. In addition, Berlin's prosecutors and judges, who were convinced of the revolutionary potential of KPD activism, had little sympathy for politically engaged residents of Red neighborhoods.

Citizens, however, did seek justice for what they viewed as excessive police brutality and in some cases murder. Suits filed against the Berlin police department were very hard to win because the police often argued that in the mêlée it was impossible to prove which gun had fired the fatal shots. While forensics might have shown in which cases police bullets were the causes of death, families of victims were often unable to gain access to this information.[147] In other investigations of the May deaths, the police simply dragged

---

[143] For the ZK call to strike, see *Internationale Presse-Korrespondenz*, Nr. 38, May 3, 1929. This article provides a prime example of the blame placed by the ZK on the Berlin SPD and the *Schutzpolizei* for the May Day violence.

[144] BA-SAPMO, RY1/I3/1-2/20, BL for Berlin, "Resolution über die Lehren der Maikämpfe und über die nächsten Aufgaben," May 1929. The city's KPD leadership made specific reference to three victories of the May unrest: the masses took to the streets and fought, resistance to the police marked the arrival of a higher stage in the class struggle, and the strikes that followed showed solidarity in the city and throughout the republic.

[145] Schirmann, *Blutmai* (1991), pp. 344–55. This handy summary of the penalties received by Berliners for the May 1929 violence can be retraced through the individual trials available in GStA, Rep. 84a, 2.5.1. and the LAB, Rep. 58.

[146] For examples of these cases and their failed defense strategies, see GStA, Rep. 84a, 2.5.1.

[147] GStA, Rep. 84a, 2.5.1., Nr. 10570, letter from attorneys Fritz Löwenthal and Eduard Alexander to the Berlin district courts, February 26, 1930. Löwenthal and Alexander were representing the husband of one of two older women shot on May 3, 1929, while standing

their feet. After seventeen months, one frustrated Berliner wrote directly to the Prussian justice minister asking him to pressure those at the district court level who had halted the investigation of the police role in his son's May 1929 death.[148] Public hearings into the May violence were held in Berlin at the beginning of June to quiet the public outcry against a perceived police cover-up of the situation. The "Committee for the public investigation of the May events" met at the *Grosse Schauspielhaus* concert hall in the city center to listen to witnesses of police brutality. The committee was organized by a small group of prominent city leftists and intellectuals, including the KPD Reichstag deputy Ottomar Geschke, Professor Alfons Goldschmidt (chair), and the writer Karl von Ossietzky. Hearings continued for one month, meeting in districts throughout the city to attract new audience members. At the first meeting, the committee heard from a small number of the two hundred witnesses they had previously interviewed. These included a worker, a mail carrier, and a hairdresser, and all swore they were telling the truth in describing police injustices. The *Berliner Tageblatt*'s coverage of the meeting also noted that a "KPD doctor" reported that all the corpses he examined after the riots were shot from the back or side and none from above, where Communist radicals rather than police might have been operating from apartment windows.[149]

Though the Prussian government never found a Communist conspiracy behind the May Day disturbances, they still felt the violence presented the opportunity to crack down on left-wing radicalism, a step that had been under consideration for some months. The position taken by the Prussian interior ministry focused on the *Rote Fahne*'s encouragement of its readership to disobey the ban and the RFB's instructions to its members that marchers should not wear any RFB uniforms or insignia. As the dissolution order explained: "From this [evidence] it is clear, that the RFB consciously

---

on a balcony overlooking the street violence below. Their deaths became symbolic of the arbitrary nature of police actions during the riots. In this letter, the attorneys representing the widower are trying to overturn the court's decision to suspend the investigation into their client's complaint.

[148] GStA, Rep. 84a, 2.5.1., Nr. 10570, letter from August Engel to the Prussian minister of justice, October 22, 1930.

[149] *BT*, "Die Maivorgänge. Volksversammlung im Grossen Schauspielhaus," Nr. 264, June 7, 1929. At the hearings, a film of the violence was shown. The film was perhaps *Kampfmai 1929*, which the KPD used as evidence that many innocent workers were harassed and brutalized by overly aggressive police during the May riots. Mounted police are shown time and again in the film clearing the streets, while local residents (without demonstration posters or the like) run from the horses. There is little dialogue in this eyewitness-style documentary, except for a few partisan statements such as, "The police not only struck demonstrators, but also uninvolved pedestrians." Others are shown being searched and arrested. The film does capture some of the barricades, but these appear very rudimentary. See BA-Außenstelle Filmarchiv, SP14208/1, *Kampfmai 1929*.

and systematically tried with all of its means to break the prohibition on demonstrations issued by the Police President and other responsible authorities in Berlin." When no uniformed RFB men were spotted in the mêlée, the government concluded that all party instructions were followed. Therefore, the violence too must have been the result of a well-executed plan orchestrated from above. At the end of the decree dissolving the RFB, the interior ministry betrayed its chief motivation in making this decision. "For years Communist Party politicians and RFB leaders have viewed and referred to the RFB as the elite troops for the coming revolution."[150] The government and much of the Berlin population had been convinced of this portrayal of the RFB; and the May violence, though presenting no real manifestation of revolutionary potential among these "elite troops," presented the long sought after opportunity to ban the organization. This application of the Law for the Protection of the Republic, or *Gesetz zum Schutz der Republik*, initially affected only Prussia, but within weeks the rest of the *Länder* joined in the prohibition of the RFB and its youth organization, Rote Jungfront, and small marine corps.

The Law for the Protection of the Republic first went into effect in July 1922, after the murder of Foreign Minister Walther Rathenau by right-wing extremists. Its aim was to provide greater means to combat conspirators against the republic, especially those planning assassinations. It made outlawing subversive political organizations possible and gave the courts the right to place temporary bans on newspapers that incited political violence. Though it was scheduled to expire after five years, its life was extended in 1927 and again in 1929. During the battle over the law's renewal in 1929, Reich Interior Minister Carl Severing delivered an impassioned speech criticizing the initial failure of the Reichstag to support the law's extension. The title of the speech, which was published in *Vorwärts*, was "Constraint and Freedom." In the article, Severing recalled the reasons the law was enacted in the early part of the decade and admitted that "in the course of the years through their decisions some courts have communicated the opposite of the motives behind the Law for the Protection of the Republic, and also the administrative bodies may have caused a blunder here and there in a newspaper ban or in the dissolution of a political organization." Nevertheless, argued Severing, the law was needed to protect not only the republic's leaders but also the republic itself.[151] Regardless of his plea, the law had many opponents. Conservatives in the Reichstag believed that the law placed unnecessary constraints on political freedom. They fought against the extension of the law, to obtain what Severing referred to in his speech as the "absolute

[150] BA, Rep. 15.07, Nr. 1091ii, Prussian minister of the interior, "Dissolution of the RFB, Roter Jungfront and Roter Marine," May 3, 1929.
[151] *Vorwärts*, Carl Severing, "Zwang und Freiheit," Nr. 373, August 11, 1929.

freedom to insult." The radical left was against its extension primarily because they saw it as an anticommunist law, which never seemed to slow right-wing aggression despite the promises of politicians like Severing.

There was great confusion in the days and weeks following the prohibition of the RFB. While RFB leaders discussed how to carry on underground, local members tried to hold on to their cells, often still meeting in the same pubs as before, under new, "harmless" sounding names. While the ban immediately scared off large numbers of members and sympathizers, in mid June 1929 police infiltrators reported with surprise that the Berlin RFB was still collecting two-thirds of its monthly membership dues, almost twice the average for the rest of the Reich.[152] The accuracy of these figures is hard to judge, but such reports made city authorities believe that the underground RFB continued to pose a serious threat to Berlin and Germany.

Though this fear remained, the dissolution of the RFB and its affiliated youth organization changed the political landscape in Berlin. The ban was never reversed nor was a similar ban placed on the paramilitary Nazi SA, outside of the ineffective three-month halt to the SA's activities in 1932. The *Blutmai* events were used by both KPD and SPD leaders in the ever-widening war of words between these two parties on the left. For the Social Democrats, the Communist role in the violence was evidence of the party's revolutionary aspirations and reckless behavior. For the KPD leaders, the involvement of social democratic leaders in the decisions to ban public demonstrations and criminalize the RFB, and the party's connections to police actions through the leadership of Social Democrat Zörgiebel, made the SPD "the greatest enemy" to the workers' cause.

The substantial number of deaths and injuries affected how Berliners viewed the police. Some were in favor of the force exercised by the police, and only questioned why it had taken so long for the state to act against these radical insurgents. Others felt betrayed by a democratic government founded on the goal of economic and social justice for workers. Even among those who wanted to show support for the *Schutzpolizei*, from May 1929 on it became increasingly difficult to maintain that Berlin's police were effective in the prevention of violence and restoration of order. The republican press continued to stand by the police, claiming in articles pertaining to political chaos in the capital that "[the *Schutzpolizei*] remained everywhere master of the situation."[153] Through the use of the phrase "master of the situation," the liberal press attempted to convince its readers that the police did indeed keep the peace and regulate the limits of political action, fulfilling the basic parameters of their assignment.

---

[152] BA, Rep. 15.07, Nr. 1091ii, unsigned police spy report on the Berlin RFB, June 18, 1929.

[153] Among others, see *Berliner Montagspost*, "Ein Nationalsozialist durch Kopfschuß getötet," Nr. 7, March 7, 1932, and *VZ*, "120 Sistierungen in Berlin. Zahlreiche nächtliche Zusammenstöße – Die Polizei überall Herr der Lage," Nr. 301, June 24, 1932.

The problem with this representation of police capabilities was that the praise often came toward the end of a long article in which the very opposite was demonstrated. Following the frustration and mixed responses to their actions in May 1929, top police administrators and men on the beat increasingly felt the strain of containing radicalism in the capital. The *Schutzpolizei* knew that their forces were rarely the "masters of the situation," and instead were routinely outnumbered by political demonstrators. From 1929 on there were constant attempts to strengthen security around the governmental quarter and other sites of political tension.[154] These efforts were made not only to defend against possible coup attempts by the radical right or revolution from the left but also to counter the daily unrest that made the police look incapable of carrying out their mandate.

In addition to the banning of the RFB, the further intensification of SPD/KPD mistrust, and the damage done to the image of the police, the unrest of May 1929 was symbolic of a more fundamental shift taking place in the city's political culture. This transition began at the grassroots level and set the stage for the sort of violence seen in May 1929 and for years afterward. Chapter 1 illustrated the division of the city into two opposing sides. It is not unusual for an urban center to have wealthy and poor districts, nor is it uncommon for the poor section to be regarded as dangerous and criminal. By the end of 1929, however, this mistrust of the eastern and northern parts of Berlin had taken on an additional political characteristic.[155] Now the poorer districts were seen not only as rowdy but also as conspiratorial, a foreign body (in terms of presumed Soviet infiltration) at the heart of the nation's capital. H. R. Knickerbocker, writing from an American perspective, linked poverty, the May violence, and communism quite explicitly: "if Wedding is the reddest district in Berlin, the Koesliner Strasse is the reddest street in Wedding. It was on the Koesliner Strasse that the barricades went up on the night of May 1, 1929. And it was to the Koesliner Strasse that I went, in the rags of a homeless tramp, to explore the

---

154 There were many changes in security measures around the city. The *Schutzpolizei* heightened readiness, strengthened the number of men in certain locations, increased the weaponry and number of vehicles stationed at trouble spots, and improved communication between posts. For the specifics of such changes, see the numerous files in BLHA, Rep. 30, Berlin C, Title 90.

155 Thomas Lindenberger's *Straßenpolitik* rightly points out that the East–West dichotomy existed in pre-1914 Berlin. However, the mistrust and fear he describes is somewhat different than that found in the later period. In Lindenberger's cases he points to a bourgeois disdain for disorder, in terms of social and economic unrest such as strike actions. While this same discomfort with disorder continued to play a role throughout Weimar, in the earlier period there was not the same belief that these poor workers had the political intention or the military potential to overthrow the government in favor of a Soviet-style Germany. See Lindenberger, *Straßenpolitik. Zur Sozialgeschichte der öffentliche Ordnung in Berlin 1900–1914* (Bonn: Dietz, 1995).

question: 'How great is Germany's poverty?' "[156] This political anxiety about the East side of Berlin had led to the ban on demonstrations in the first place. The ban was an attempt to contain the "revolutionary" workers, to keep them in their homes or at least in private indoor assemblies, which could be more easily supervised. This fear also preconditioned the police to look for unrest in these neighborhoods. They expected and provoked violence through constant surveillance and the concentration of troops and weapons in these areas before conflict even arose.

Chapter 1 also discussed how, throughout the 1920s, neighborhoods within workers' districts claimed social and political autonomy. Challenges to the rules and hierarchies of these Kieze, in the form of intrusion by state agencies or oppositional political forces, threatened the local order that had existed in these areas. The May violence serves as an early and dramatic example, but not a unique one, of the determination of some Kieze inhabitants to combat what they perceived as an attack on their territory. In the years that followed, the pressures of the Depression, related gender and generational tensions, and political rivalries within neighborhoods would continue to wreak havoc on these communities. Unfortunately, residents' attempts to fight the dissolution of local power, manifested here in resistance to the police, only led to more disorder: legal battles, physical violence, and further questioning of existing social and familial hierarchies.

For example, we know from police reports of the May demonstrations that the majority of those who were active were young people. Not only were these young participants challenging police authority to control the streets, some were also challenging their parents, whose political views and/or sense of civic responsibility kept them inside on May 1. These were some of the same young men who were attracted to radical organizations, as will be shown in the next chapter, and who continued to participate in the political violence discussed in Chapter 5. The May violence not only drew attention to the streets of the workers' neighborhoods as the setting for political expression and violence during the remaining four years of the Weimar Republic, it also set a precedent for who could participate. The speed at which the morning demonstrations turned violent, with the first deaths being reported around midday, was evidence for what many people throughout the city already believed: political actions were no place for women. There was more public outrage that two middle-aged women had been killed while overlooking the chaos than that thirty-three people in all died in the fighting. The KPD was criticized as cowardly for "allowing" women to be on the streets that day. Henceforth, male workers would do more to ensure that "their" women were protected and did not embarrass their male cohorts by participating.

---

[156] H. R. Knickerbocker, *The German Crisis* (New York: Farrar & Rinehart, 1932a), p. 8.

The bourgeois press and other political parties were not the only ones to blame the KPD for the disaster. In fact, many within the Communist rank-and-file found fault with the party's lack of decisive leadership in avoiding bloodshed, and with the ZK's attempts to put a positive "spin" on a tragedy that left so many dead. In a resolution by the Prenzlauer Berg KPD assembly, the district representatives openly criticized the ZK's representation of the May events. They complained that the overly general and revolutionary language used by the party leadership did not "correspond to the reality of the May fighting." The resolution also noted the lack of an appropriate strategy to create "proletarian self-defense organizations" in the weeks following the violence. Finally, the Prenzlauer Berg Communists denounced "the poor implementation of the mass strike," which in contrast to press releases by the ZK "did nothing to increase confidence in the party."[157] One editor of the *Rote Fahne* wrote to the district leadership to announce his withdrawal from the party and accused the party of playing "games with workers' lives." He added: "One does not throw membership to a party, in which one has belonged for 11 and $\frac{1}{2}$ years, away like an old dress. I have spoken with many comrades in the last few days, who in their criticism of the party line (which leads to an abyss) were much harsher than I."[158] As statements like these illustrate, the May violence was significant not only because it undermined the last vestiges of faith many workers had in the republic, but also because it greatly reduced the image of the KPD as a political institution in the eyes of Berlin's most radical workers. The KPD would continue to increase its vote tallies in the years to come, but in the demonstrations and street fighting of 1929 we can already see how little power the KPD had in regulating the actions of those who supported the party. This independence would grow in the period that followed.

Finally, the May tragedy in Berlin stands out as a precursor to the violence of the 1930s. Berlin had certainly seen political violence before. The fighting during the November Revolution and the roving bands of Free Corps and political assassinations of the early 1920s had all to some extent prepared Berliners to accept violence as a political strategy.[159] We should not lose sight, however, of the separate characteristics of these two violent periods. In the early 1920s, much of the political violence was directly associated with the crisis of defeat in World War I and the collapse of the monarchy. The fighting at the end of the decade had its own causes and, for the most part, involved a new generation of participants. The roots of the May violence

---

[157] BA-SAPMO, RY 1/I3/1-2/33, UBL for Prenzlauer Berg, resolution on the May struggle, 1929.

[158] BA-SAPMO, RY 1/I3/1-2/26, letter from Fritz Köhler to the Communist BL in Berlin, May 5, 1929.

[159] For example, see Bernd Weisbrod, "Gewalt in der Politik. Zur politischen Kultur in Deutschland zwischen den beiden Weltkriegen" in *Geschichte in Wissenschaft und Unterricht* (Vol. 43, No. 7, 1992), pp. 391–404.

and the street battles that continued until the demise of the republic in 1933 were much more localized than the examples from the early 1920s. The earlier violence was about national identity, whereas the later violence was about neighborhood identity. In the rest of this book, I will examine how neighborhood radicalism sought to combat but in fact exacerbated the local crises it targeted.

3

Republicanism or Radicalism
Appeals to Berlin's Workers

As kids we always collected the different election posters of the various parties at election time. I had a cigar box half full of cardboard swastikas, and one time someone yelled: "Flags are being handed out on Nostiz!" We all headed to the KPD-pub and there stood someone who was giving out red paper flags. Everyone wanted to have such a flag and jumped in to grab one. During this [frenzy] someone pushed against my cigar box, which fell and nothing but cardboard swastikas lay in front of the KPD-bar! As a kid, one didn't think much about such things. In any case I got a terrible thrashing, and a red flag was thrust into my hand and it was explained to me that it was the right one. I then ran home crying with the flag of the Communist Party, red with hammer and sickle. And as I got there, my father tore it out of my hand and threw it in the fire, because namely he was in the Reichsbanner. Then I got another round of beatings and I was left with nothing.[1]

Even in the Berlin neighborhoods that had a Red reputation like Nostiz, workers had choices to make, and by the end of the 1920s these were more intense than ever before. At the voting box and beyond, workers, including the throngs of the unemployed, were called on to participate in defending or disavowing the republic.[2] Though the republic faced many challenges in its

---

[1] This oral memory by H. B., a metalworker who was born in 1925 and lived in the Nostiz Kiez on Solms Street, is reproduced in Lothar Uebel, *Viel Vergnügen. Die Geschichte der Vergnügungsstätten rund um den Kreuzberg und die Hasenheide* (Berlin: Nishen, 1985).

[2] The republic had been created as a compromise between moderate Social Democrats and conservative elites on the understanding that those allowed to take power after the Kaiser's abdication would rein in the revolutionaries who sought a more radical solution. The establishment of a legitimate government, acceptance of a constitution, and recruitment of antisocialist paramilitary forces, known as the *Freikorps*, effectively brought an end to the revolution in 1920. The fresh memories of military defeat in World War I and the trauma of civil war left a shadow over the young republic. The compromise embedded in the republic and its constitution, which came into effect on August 11, 1919, left those on the right and left highly dissatisfied. It was a defeat to those on the right because the republic symbolized the alleged betrayal of the home front in the last days of the war. To them, the republic was the work of unpatriotic elements who had proceeded to prostrate themselves before the enemy by signing the humiliating Versailles Peace that branded Germany as the aggressor. Those on the left wing of the Social Democratic Party and those who left the SPD for the Independent Social Democratic and Communist Parties believed the ideals of the proletarian revolution had been betrayed by the acceptance of capitalism, liberalism, and the brutal destruction of

first decade, mass radical sentiment had not manifested itself until the end of the decade when a sense of great impending change swept through the population. There were many reasons for this perception that a transformation was under way in Berlin. Key republican figures had died in recent years, in particular Gustav Stresemann, whose passing in 1929 was mourned respectfully even by the KPD as the party's most worthy enemy.[3] Though many had hoped that the 1924 currency stabilization would usher in a period of economic prosperity, German industry needed five more years to reach the levels of production attained in 1913, and unemployment had already reached the 2 million mark in 1926.[4] By 1929 it was clear that mass unemployment was taking hold. At its high point in early 1932, the known unemployed in Germany numbered 6,128,000. If the "invisible" unemployed are included, as many as 7,619,000 are estimated to have been out of work.[5] At the two welfare offices that covered Kreuzberg's unemployed, there were 15,087 receiving unemployment or crisis aid in 1928. By 1930, the number had risen to 57,859. Though many of these individuals would no longer be collecting state aid by 1932, there were still 81,917 receiving one of the two forms of assistance in January of that year.[6] In Berlin, the May violence of 1929 betrayed authorities' fears of the possible political consequences of the economic collapse, confirming the weakness of republican rule and the willingness to use violence by some representatives of the state and certain segments of the population.

---

the radical Spartacus League. They too condemned the acceptance of Versailles because it promised the payment of reparations to the victors, money that would come from the blood and sweat of workers.

[3] The *AIZ* coverage of Stresemann's death referred to him as the "smartest and most able leader of the German bourgeoisie." *AIZ*, Nr. 42, 1929, p. 2.

[4] Heinrich August Winkler, *Der Schein der Normalität. Arbeiter und Arbeiterbewegung in der Weimarer Republik 1924 bis 1930* (Berlin: Dietz, 1988). Winkler's data for industrial production in the period 1924–29 come from Rolf Wagenführ, "Die Industriewirtschaft: Entwicklungstendenzen der deutschen und internationalen Industrieproduktion 1860 bis 1932" in *Vierteljahreshefte zur Konjunkturforschung* (Berlin: Sonderheft 31, 1933), pp. 29 ff. For further discussion of the social ramifications of unemployment, see Richard J. Evans and Dick Geary, eds., *The German Unemployed* (New York: St. Martin's Press, 1987) and Peter Stachura, ed., *Unemployment and the Great Depression in Weimar Germany* (New York: St. Martin's Press, 1986).

[5] There are even higher estimates of the number of unrecorded unemployed. See Heinrich August Winkler, *Der Weg in die Katastrophe. Arbeiter und Arbeiterbewegung in der Weimarer Republik 1930 bis 1933* (Berlin: Dietz, 1987), pp. 23–4.

[6] Those living in the North End of Kreuzberg fell under the auspices of the Arbeitsamt Mitte, which also took in unemployed from Mitte, parts of Prenzlauer Berg, and Tiergarten, an area comprising about 500,000 residents. Those living in the southern half of Kreuzberg reported to the Arbeitsamt Südost, which also cared for those in Tempelhof, an area covering about 270,000 residents. Statistics are from Axel Reibe, "Zwischen Arbeitsamt und Volksküche" in Kunstamt Kreuzberg, ed., *Kreuzberg 1933. Ein Bezirk erinnert sich* (Berlin: Dürchschlag, 1983), p. 13.

Though times were uncertain, the summer of 1929 marked the tenth anniversary of the republic. This milestone provoked reflection on the achievements of German democracy, criticism of its shortcomings, and calls for its abolition. However, many of those who continued to support the republic through the traditional pillar of working-class politics, German Social Democracy, also began to demand an escalation of activism and a role in the struggles against economic collapse, political radicalism, and the breakdown of the *Rechtsstaat*, or rule of law. This chapter begins with an analysis of the attempts by the SPD and Reichsbanner in Berlin to keep workers in the fold by defining an activist republican discipline. It will then turn to the annual *Verfassungstag* or Constitution Day holiday on August 11. Supported by key Social Democrats and other republicans, this initiative was envisioned as a proactive "positive" measure – in stark contrast to the reactive and repressive May Day violence – to counter radicalism by offering a dynamic image of republicanism.[7]

The two main radical parties, the KPD and NSDAP, and the attractions of radicalism to Berliners during these last years of republican rule will be the focus of the second section. What made the Communists and Nazis radical was both their insisting that fundamental change was necessary and imminent and their stressing that the rank-and-file must play a major role in bringing about that change. Participation, therefore, meant more than election-day duties; it meant regular activism in political organizations and demonstrations. It meant distrust of existing political institutions and the willingness to challenge their authority in speech, print, and action. Radicalism also manifested itself in the politicization of aspects of daily life once considered outside the political realm. Increasingly it also meant violent behavior: brawls at political meetings, battles with police, and impromptu attacks on political opponents. In exchange for the various forms of assistance they provided during the economic crisis, the two radical parties hoped to build disciplined mass movements. The chapter concludes, consequently, with a focus on the two competing visions of party discipline. What would set the ideal Nazi or proletarian apart from all others in this increasingly chaotic time, claimed their leaders, was discipline – knowing the proper bounds of radicalism.

SOCIAL DEMOCRACY AND REPUBLICANISM

For all the accusations leveled at the SPD as a corrupt tool of Jewish Marxists or as an ossified bureaucracy that had betrayed the proletariat in favor of

---

[7] Cf. Gotthard Jasper, *Der Schutz der Republik. Studien zur staatlichen Sicherung der Demokratie in der Weimarer Republik, 1922–1930* (Tübingen: J. C. B. Mohr, 1963; original edition, 1930). Jasper's text also differentiates among measures taken to protect the republic in this way. Besides the *Verfassungstag*, other "positive" measures Jasper discusses include the republican flag, the creation of the "Fund for the Protection of the Republic," and republican school curricula.

capital, it was still the main workers' party and the mainstay of republican-ism throughout the Weimar era.[8] In the 1928 Reichstag elections, the SPD regained the Reich chancellorship for the first time since 1922. In Berlin's Kreuzberg, the strategic center of the Nostiz-area Social Democrats was the pub Heidelberger Krug at Arndt Street 15. The local Reichsbanner troops met regularly at a cafe at number 15 Willibald-Alexis-Street, and its band played regularly to enthusiastic crowds on the Chamissoplatz, between Willibald-Alexis and Arndtstraße. The local SPD youth group (SAJ) was given the official designation "Hallesches Tor," but its members went by the name "Future." One former Communist resident remembered the importance of coeducation in the SAJ, and the large numbers of young women who partic-ipated. The local KPD youth ridiculed the SAJ in turn as a "marriage club" but commended its members for their theoretical training and their belief that "knowledge is power."[9] Social Democrats continued to play a major governmental role at the local and state levels, including the positions of mayor and Prussian minister president. Otto Braun had assumed this latter position in 1921 and remained a highly respected, staunch advocate of the party and the republic. He did not leave office until July 1932, when a pres-idential decree dissolved the Prussian government and set a Reich overseer in its place. Braun was even considered a candidate for chancellor in 1928, but he had insisted on retaining his ministerial post in Prussia at the same time. Eventually, Hermann Müller, a competent politician who had served as cochair of the SPD since 1919, and had knowledge and experience in international affairs, was chosen to take the post at the head of a coalition government.[10]

The SPD, therefore, clearly enjoyed what Donna Harsch refers to as an "Indian Summer" at the end of the 1920s. But the party was about to suffer a number of political blows that would erode grassroots loyalty and lead to criticism from the Reichsbanner. In the first of two controversies in the Reichstag, the cabinet had agreed, without much hesitation, to fund the construction of the Panzerkreuzer A battleship. Müller and the Minister of the Interior Carl Severing (SPD) had made this decision out of fear that refusal

---

[8] For more on the SPD in the Crisis Period, see Donna Harsch, *German Social Democracy and the Rise of Nazism* (Chapel Hill: University of North Carolina Press, 1993). For an overview of German social democracy during Weimar, see Richard Breitman, *German Socialism and Weimar Democracy* (Chapel Hill: University of North Carolina Press, 1981); W. L. Guttsmann, *The German Social Democratic Party, 1875–1933* (London: Allen and Unwin, 1981); and Richard Hunt, *German Social Democracy, 1918–1933* (New Haven, CT: Yale University Press, 1964).

[9] Gerhard König, *Berlin–Kreuzberg und seine Nostizstraße* (Berlin: Druckerei der pbw, no date), pp. 34–5.

[10] The cabinet included men from the SPD, BVP, Center Party, DDP, and the DVP, but there was so little common ground among the parties represented that this cabinet was thought of as a "cabinet of personalities" rather than a Great Coalition of allied political parties.

might lead to an early collapse of their government. Most other SPD leaders and rank-and-file members disagreed with their support of naval expansion, and division arose as Social Democrats, first in the Reichsrat and then the Reichstag, attempted to scuttle the plan. At the local level, the controversy drew large numbers to party meetings in Berlin, and when the issue was finally raised in the Reichstag months later, the cabinet was forced to confirm the party's antimilitary stance and withdraw the earlier approval of the plan. In the end, the SPD motion against the Panzerkreuzer was defeated, but the party had looked foolish and its leaders weak.[11]

By the end of 1928 labor problems also had erupted in the Ruhr. One of the great achievements of the republic had been the 1923 institutionalization of state arbitration to mediate labor disputes. Enjoying a much more advantageous position vis-à-vis the trade unions in 1928 than in 1923, the conservative antiunion steel managers in the Ruhr simply refused to accept an arbitrated decision on a wage dispute. To force their point, they organized a lockout of steel and ironworkers, which encompassed about 220,000 employees. Eventually a compromise was reached by Interior Minister Severing, but this event signaled industry's willingness and ability to challenge the social democratic-inspired *Sozialpolitik* of the Weimar Republic.[12] The trade unions never fully recovered, which in turn further undermined the faith of workers in the SPD and republicanism.

In 1929, the SPD's image was further tarnished by the police brutality, which accompanied the May Day riots in Berlin. And before 1929 was over, another controversy led directly to the downfall of the SPD-led coalition. Already weakened by the disappointing compromise in the Ruhr, the ADGB was further frightened by rumors that the financially strapped government would be forced to cut unemployment benefits. After close consideration of Catholic Center Party cabinet member Heinrich Brüning's proposed solution to fund the ailing unemployment system, the SPD chose not to accept the plan, knowing full well it would bring down the Müller cabinet. A combination of factors led to the decision, not the least of which were the anticoalitionist sentiment among trade unionists and the negative backlash the party suffered over the Panzerkreuzer Affair. Unfortunately for the SPD's political future, its leaders did not recognize the significance of growing political radicalism or the difficulties they would face working outside the coalition.[13] This SPD-led cabinet, which bowed out in March 1930, would

---

[11] Harsch, *German Social Democracy* (1993), pp. 46–51.

[12] Severing's autobiography offers his view of the major difficulties facing the republic. Carl Severing, *Mein Lebensweg, Band II* (Cologne: Greven Verlag, 1950). For more on the situation faced by the trade unions, see Maria Hüber-Koller, *Gewerkschaften und Arbeitslose: Erfahrungen der Massenerwerbslosigkeit und Aspekte freigewerkschaftlicher Arbeitslosenpolitik in der Endphase der Weimarer Republik. 2 vol. (Pfaffenweiler: Centaurus, 1992).

[13] Harsch, *German Social Democracy* (1993), pp. 51–9.

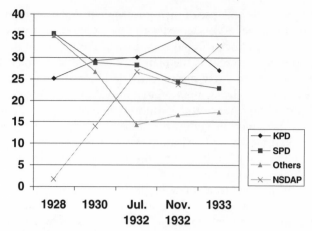

Figure 6. Reichstag election results for Kreuzberg (in percentages), 1928–33. Source: Andreas Splanemann, "Wahl- und Sozialstatistik des demokratischen Berlins 1919–1933" in Otto Büsch and Wolfgang Haus, *Berlin als Hauptstadt der Weimarer Republik 1919–1933* (Berlin: de Gruyter, 1987), p. 396. Splanemann's data are taken from the *Statistische Jahrbücher der Stadt Berlin, 1928–1933*.

be the last such cabinet of the Weimar Republic. For the next three years, the party witnessed consistently disappointing results in its election tallies (see Figures 6 and 7).

Through the SPD's ups and downs of the 1920s, the Reichsbanner Schwarz-Rot-Gold (RB), the only prorepublican paramilitary organization, had been a steadfast ally.[14] Founded in 1924 to defend the young state against political enemies, the RB was a multiparty organization, which welcomed all men who believed in the republic. Its headquarters were in Magdeburg, but it drew large numbers wherever the SPD, Center, and the small liberal parties had a following. The SPD and Center Party dominated but were not always equally represented in the local columns of the three-million-strong RB. In Berlin-Brandenburg it was estimated that 80 percent were active in the SPD and only 10–15 percent were supporters of the Center Party.[15] With its own uniforms, membership oath, mass rallies, and grassroots functions, the RB was a successful propaganda tool at state-sponsored events and in the election campaigns of its member parties' candidates.

By the end of the 1920s, however, the RB's multiparty status was leading to great tension. Many connected to the Center Party complained that their political interests were represented less and less in the organization's policies, while in Berlin members hoped to make the RB a purely socialist

[14] The definitive monograph on the Reichsbanner remains Karl Rohe, *Das Reichsbanner Schwarz-Rot-Gold* (Düsseldorf: Droste, 1966).
[15] Ibid., p. 266, fn. 3.

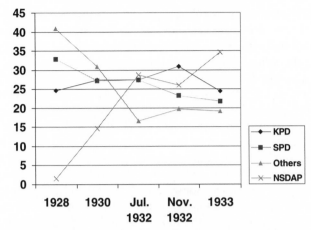

Figure 7. Reichstag election results for Berlin (in percentages), 1928–33. Source: Alexander Wilde, "Republikfeindschaft in der Berliner Bevölkerung und der Wandel der kommunalen Selbstverwaltung um 1931" in Otto Büsch, ed., *Beiträge zur Geschichte der Berliner Demokratie, 1917–1933/1945–1985* (Berlin: Colloquium Verlag, 1988), pp. 112–13. Wilde's data are taken from the *Statistische Jahrbücher der Stadt Berlin, 1928–1933*.

organization. In the spring of 1930, the conflict between the two parties came to a head because of Brüning's cuts to social programs. There was talk of disbanding the group altogether, or simply restructuring it as an SPD-only *Kampfbund*.[16] Eventually the RB executive council decided that the organization would retain its multiparty status. This solution did not satisfy anyone. The Center Party continued to criticize the favor shown by the RB to SPD rallies and causes, and in Berlin many SPD members felt that the RB's ties to the Brüning government left them unable to compete with the antifascist troops of the Communist organizations and the Nazi SA as a legitimate voice for change.

In the fall of 1930, the RB reorganized its troops into a two-tier structure to satisfy those frustrated by the group's "soft" image. The top level consisted of the defense formations (*Schutzformationen* or *Schufo*), young active men who received military and technical training. The lower level consisted of reserve troops (*Stammformationen*, *Stafo*), older men and others who were unable or chose not to commit to regular involvement or military preparedness. By the spring, 250,000 new members had been recruited, seemingly reviving the stagnant Reichsbanner.[17] The main responsibility of the new

[16] The conflict between the SPD and Center Party carried on for a number of weeks and received much attention in the press. For examples of how the debate was covered, see *Deutsche Zeitung*, Nr. 81a, April 5, 1930; and *BT*, Nr. 252, May 30, 1930.

[17] Rohe, *Das Reichsbanner* (1966), p. 374. The Reichsbanner claimed 400,000 new members, but the lower estimate is more accurate.

Schufo was to defend the republic against a possible Nazi putsch or Communist revolution. Until that day, however, their duties were to provide more effective *Saalschutz* (the protection of assembly speakers) during campaigns and a more disciplined visual symbol of republican loyalty.

The SA and the KPD reacted furiously to what they viewed as greater collusion between the RB and the state. The *RF* alleged that Berlin police and the RB together formed the "civil war troops of Social Democracy," which would take up arms against workers in the event of revolution.[18] The Nazi *Der Angriff* also described the *Schufo* as a way for the SPD to prepare for civil war, but its article was more sarcastic when it suggested that these "strong men" were nothing more than tools of the SPD party bosses who could not face the recent election results.[19] Perceptively, Goebbels's editors focused on the unclear relationship between the state and this new militarized Reichsbanner. Rumors abounded in the daily press that the RB was training regularly with police, and some even claimed that *Schufo* members were already assisting police in their daily duties. Prussian Interior Minister Carl Severing was adamant that such cooperation should be prohibited, declaring in April 1932: "The protection of the state and the protection of state installations is the work of state organs. Prussia will not divert from this stance.... No auxiliary forces are needed to supplement the police, neither from the Reichsbanner nor from any other organization."[20] Despite official sanctions, in cities like Berlin where police were often also members of the new republican guard, there was likely some truth to the rumors of cooperation.

Even with the reorganization of the RB, however, the fact remained that the Reichsbanner had never been a radical organization like those with which it wished to compete. For one thing, the RB's basic desire to preserve the status quo lessened its ability to convince the public that the Reichsbanner or SPD could create change. It might have been possible to do so had the state ever been explicit about its willingness to accept Reichsbanner help in the event of a coup or revolution, thereby providing the troops with an official mandate. As obvious forces of the opposition, Communist and Nazi paramilitaries did not need this legitimacy, but the RB's position was weakened without it: at once linked to the state, but without real power. The second problem was that the Reichsbanner had never been much of a military organization. In fact, in its earlier years, the RB program included a pacifist clause that was only discarded after much internal debate. Consequently, despite all the concerted efforts after the September 1930 elections to "militarize" the RB by demanding stricter discipline, snappier uniforms and better training, its

---

[18] BA, Rep. 15.01, Nr. 25965, *RF*, Nr. 22, January 27, 1931.
[19] BA, Rep. 15.01, Nr. 25965, *Der Angriff*, Nr. 35, February 21, 1931.
[20] BA, Rep. 15.01, Nr. 13117, letter from Prussian Interior Minister Severing to Reich Minister of the Interior Groener, April 26, 1932, p. 73.

members, who were often settled, employed family men, were never all that willing to fight or look and act the part.[21] In other words, the problems that caused frustration in the Berlin SPD by the end of the 1920s – that the other paramilitary organizations were more successful bringing in new members and protecting their supporters – were still present after the restructuring.

In July 1931, the leftist *Die Welt am Abend* likened the supposedly reinvigorated Reichsbanner to Sleeping Beauty, charging: "If one looks at the history of the Reichsbanner from its establishment until today, one comes to the conclusion, that never before in Germany's history has a political movement experienced such a great boom and perhaps also never before has a fighting organization so quickly fallen asleep."[22] By December, SPD leaders were discussing new ways to infuse the party rank-and-file with some hope and fervor, and by the middle of the month the creation of the Eiserne Front (EF) had been announced.[23] Although the EF welcomed all who wanted to protect the republic, unlike the RB it discouraged the participation of non-workers. Nonetheless party leaders had competing views as to its role. There were those who wanted to see the EF respond aggressively in the battle for Berlin's streets. Others simply wanted fresh legs for SPD propaganda duties, and still others saw the EF as an additional military unit in case of outright civil war. The lack of a coherent policy concerning the EF persisted, leaving local units to design their own mandates. In Berlin, the EF served as a propaganda agent for the SPD, but it also took on a more active role in the physical fight against Nazi expansion than other groups connected to the SPD. More than any other SPD-sponsored organization in the capital, the Berlin EF joined forces on occasion with the KPD, but this cooperation did not lead to further understanding between the leaders of the two parties.

The EF was most active in the election campaigns of 1932, which the league conducted under the new slogan: "The state is ours – the power is ours! We are on the attack!"[24] With such language, the EF showed a willingness to compete with the aggressive tone of the Communist and Nazi parties. And the new methods did generate renewed interest and excitement in the party. After witnessing how swastikas on Heidelberg's streets had been vandalized by a slashing stroke of paint, Sergei Chakhotin transformed the slash into a downward arrow.[25] He finalized the symbol, which soon appeared over swastikas, on flags, buttons and posters, by using three identical arrows

---

[21] Rohe, *Das Reichsbanner* (1966), pp. 374–5.

[22] *Die Welt am Abend*, "Dornröschen schläft. Das Reichsbanner muß wieder marschieren lernen," Nr. 30, July 27, 1930.

[23] For more on the Iron Front, see Harsch, *German Social Democracy* (1993), pp. 169–202.

[24] At the end of 1931, the RB commanded the state to "act quickly." *BT*, "Jetzt ist es genug, Staat greif zu! Riesenkundgebung des RB," Nr. 564, November 30, 1931. Two months later, the EF no longer wanted to leave it up to the state to act.

[25] Harsch, *German Social Democracy* (1993), pp. 177–9.

to stand for "unity, activity, discipline" and also the three pillars of the movement – SPD, RB, and trade unions. Party leaders were not altogether happy with the *Drei Pfeile* (three arrows) graffiti campaign that sprung up on streets in Berlin and elsewhere because they feared the abstract symbolism distanced them from the rational and coherent political style that the SPD had always supported. However, the three arrows, daily marches, door-to-door campaigning, and vibrant rallies – all of which the EF had copied to a great extent from the more radical parties – were welcomed by Berlin's Social Democrats.

While the SPD was addressing these problems with the mass movements, the party was growing increasingly worried that its female supporters might be attracted to the NSDAP's promises to eliminate the double burden and "allow" women to concentrate their efforts on the home.[26] Instead of responding with straightforward support of the right of all women to work outside the home, party literature stressed the necessity of work for the close to five million unmarried women and pointed out the "lies or stupidity" of the Nazi claim to provide a man for each single woman in the Third Reich.[27] Social democratic propaganda aimed at women implied – with varying degrees of subtlety – that women's inferior status under Nazi rule would include sexual as well as legal subordination. The visually explicit flyer titled "Women, this is how it will be for you in the Third Reich!" contained three pictures of female service. The first showed a woman tying the boot of a uniformed SS officer. In the third, a caricature of Goebbels is presented spitting at a woman wearing judicial robes. The middle image portrayed two SA men and a man in a suit whipping a young woman in a tattered dress. The caption read: "In the courtyard after the Hitler Putsch she is laid across a wagon shaft [where the horse or ox would be yoked] and worked over with the driver's whip until there was not one white spot left on her behind."[28]

---

[26] See Karen Hagemann, *Frauenalltag und Männerpolitik* (Düsseldorf: Dietz, 1990) for analysis of the mixed message given by the SPD to female Social Democrats in Hamburg. On one hand, the SPD was steadfast in upholding the tradition of advocating for women's political and economic rights. Because they fought for and won legislative changes in these respects, some party leaders of both sexes expected greater political contributions from women in the 1920s. But despite the legislative victories, the opportunities for women to take on more significant roles in the SPD and in governmental offices remained limited because of continued prejudice among male workers and the strength of traditional roles for women. This situation led to disappointment and retreat by feminists, who sought ground on which they could more easily succeed, resulting in the relegation of female SPD activists to the realm of social welfare. On attempts by all parties in the Weimar Republic to attract female voters, see Julia Sneeringer, *Winning Women's Votes: Propaganda and Politics in Weimar Germany* (Chapel Hill: University of North Carolina Press, 2002).

[27] BA-SAPMO, SgY2/V/DF/VIII/62, "Frauen wehrt euch!" SPD flier warning working-class women against Nazi rhetoric. This undated flier was printed no earlier than 1931.

[28] BA-SAPMO, SgY2/V/DF/VIII/62, "Frauen so geht's euch im 3. Reich!" (Berlin: Vorwärts, no date).

Though the SPD rightly warned women of the potential for Nazi oppression, the party's own message during the Depression also increasingly stressed the role of women as housewives and mothers. Few of the posters and flyers designed for women represented the political and economic equality advocated by the SPD. Women were not encouraged to vote for the SPD in the tradition of 1848 or the founding of the republic. Disciplined women were expected to stay loyal to the SPD as the only party outside the KPD that recognized the demands on modern women and blamed the Brüning government, not women themselves, for despairing husbands and disorganized homes.[29] Many women, even those who still enjoyed a family income during the Depression, were embittered by their overcrowded homes and unstable job prospects. SPD propaganda recognized these demands but reminded their disciplined readers to be patient and ask at present for no more than the necessities: sun and light for the children, baths and washrooms, free time, and sunny homes for the elderly.[30] At the same time, however, Social Democratic rhetoric did not dissuade female supporters from holding on to the fantasy of the middle-class domestic ideal. One party leaflet captured domestic bliss in the following manner: "One looks around the cozy living room, where the husband and a group of happy, healthy children sit around a set table and the housewife carries over the aromatic roast. In the kitchen everything shines and the cabinets and pantry are full of provisions. And also the bedrooms – separate rooms for the parents and children, as it should be – each with his own freshly-laid white bed." The female reader was reminded, however that "there has never been such a home for proletarian families."[31] This bourgeois feminine private sphere and nuclear family remained the ideal held out to the disciplined social democratic woman, but she would have to be patient, for its realization still lay in the distant future.

The refashioning of the RB and the creation of the EF were attempts to make republican support more attractive in this activist political culture. A decade after this parliamentary democracy had been founded, state authorities agreed that they too must take a more active role in shoring up the republic because the population had not yet been won over to republicanism and was easily swayed. Ministerial adviser Karl Spiecker (Center Party and RB member) confessed: "We all carry in us still a bit of thinking of the prewar era....The understanding that we are the state today, that we are its girder and foundation ... this consciousness is not very widespread in Germany and is not at all deeply ingrained in the soul of the people." With the proper education, however, the masses could be enlightened still to the

---

[29] Sneeringer, *Winning Women's Votes* (2002), pp. 204–5.
[30] BA-SAPMO, SgY2/V/DF/VIII/62, "Wie lange noch Kindernot?" (Berlin: Vorwärts, early 1933).
[31] BA-SAPMO, SgY2/V/DF/VIII/62, "Wer teuert Dir das Leben?" (1931).

tenets of republicanism, argued Spiecker: "[W]e must know that political education, democratic learning, is not a present that falls from heaven; that we must invest much more strength and will, in order for our people to grow into a true democratic and free nation."[32]

With this goal of educating the masses in mind, discussions were held in 1929 between the Deutsches Lichtspiel-Syndikat AG and the Reich Interior Minister about the inclusion of a speech by a government representative in weekly "consciously democratic" newsreels. The consortium explained to the interior ministry that such lectures were needed, because "it is a sad fact that the overwhelming majority of the population is not educated or used to considering the current political questions." The company assured the government that these films were a better propaganda tool than any newspaper article, "which in most cases is neither read nor properly understood." Film, however, could be used "to support and influence an entire election campaign" or to enlighten the public about a certain political issue.[33] The Reich interior minister responded positively to the suggestion, declaring to one of his colleagues that contributing to the newsreels "would provide the opportunity to present an objective explanation of the work of the government to the population."[34]

In order to build consensus about the republic's guiding principles and instill pride in the population, republicans in the capital had also long sought a national holiday with the same level of popularity as France's Bastille Day or America's July Fourth.[35] Since the early 1920s, the *Verfassungstag* [Constitution Day] had been a quiet, even cautious, affair. During the relatively stable middle part of the decade, republicans tried slowly to extend the scope of the holiday. The success of the SPD in 1928, however, led some to begin planning for mass participation in the tenth anniversary celebration. The plans reflected a conscious attempt by republican leaders to

---

[32] BA, Rep. 15.01, Nr. 13123/2, undated speech by Ministerial Director Spiecker entitled "Radikalismus, die grosse Gefahr unserer Zeit" (Radicalism, the Great Danger of our Time).

[33] BA, Rep. 15.01, Nr. 25634, letter from the Deutsches Lichtspiel-Syndikat AG on April 4, 1929, to Berlin Police Chief Zörgiebel.

[34] BA, Rep. 15.01, Nr. 25634, Reich minister of the interior to the Reichszentrale für Heimatdienst, June 6, 1929, p. 5. A meeting followed in which representatives of the interior ministry and Heimatdienst discussed the project. There was general agreement to proceed, but the project was put off because of financial constraints. These would only worsen in the years to come, limiting the government in its ability to counter effectively the flood of propaganda that came from the KPD and NSDAP.

[35] As Alon Confino explains in his work on *Heimat*, "Every society sets up imagined pasts. But to make a difference in a society, it is not enough for a certain past to be selected. It must steer emotions, motivate people to act, be received; in short, it must become a sociocultural mode of action." Alon Confino, *The Nation as a Local Metaphor. Württemberg, Imperial Germany, and National Memory, 1871–1918* (Chapel Hill: University of North Carolina Press, 1997), p. 11.

compete aggressively with idealized Nazi and Communist visions of unity and harmony.[36]

From 1922 on, the basic structure of the official celebration of the constitution in the capital had remained the same.[37] The day began with a morning ceremony in the Reichstag, which was closed to all but members of the government and their guests. Afterward there was a small military parade outside the Reichstag. Later political élites met again at the State Opera for an evening of musical recitals and speeches by dignitaries. Early organizers of the *Verfassungstag* realized they needed to address two shortcomings of this schedule, if the holiday was ever to achieve the political significance they hoped for. First, they needed to transform the celebration from an official bureaucratic event for members of the government into one that welcomed citizen participation. Even more daunting was the second task: to develop an explicitly pro*republican* celebration, which would present a unified positive image of Germany's recent past, present, and future to those at home and abroad.

These problems were addressed in numerous ways between 1923 and 1929. In 1928, for example, the Reichszentrale für Heimatdienst issued poems, music, and other writings on the constitution in order to teach citizens and aid local officials in planning their own celebrations to honor the constitution and republic. The successful *Verfassungstag*, as promoted in these publications, combined state direction with local initiative to encourage prorepublican reflection.[38] The violence of May cast a pall over

---

[36] With respect to the problem of holidays and the divisiveness of Weimar's sociopolitical milieus, see Detlef Lehnert and Klaus Megerle, eds., *Politische Identität und nationale Gedenktage. Zur politischen Kultur in der Weimarer Republik* (Opladen: Westdeutscher Verlag, 1989). Although state holidays and memorials continue to be of interest to historians, little work has been done on Weimar's political holidays. For a more complete description of the debates surrounding these holidays, see Fritz Schellack, *Nationalfeiertage in Deutschland von 1871–1945* (Frankfurt a. M.: Peter Lang, 1990). For a short analysis of the potential of each of the possible political holidays, see Dietmar Schirmer, *Mythos–Heilshoffnung–Modernität. Politisch-kulturelle Deutungscodes in der Weimarer Republik* (Opladen: Westdeutscher Verlag, 1992), pp. 108–12. For the parliamentary debates that failed to make the *Verfassungstag* a national holiday, see Jasper, *Der Schutz der Republik* (1963), pp. 229–39.

[37] Schellack, *Nationalfeiertage* (1990), pp. 182–93. In the end, Chancellor Wirth was left to give the speech. Reichskunstwart Edwin Redslob's account of the festivities highlights the tension between republicans and conservatives. He remarks that it was "unbearable" for those still mourning the passing of the monarchy to see the black-red-gold republican decorations in the opera house and notes that many guests refused to stand as Chancellor Wirth entered the theater. Edwin Redslob, *Bekenntnis zu Berlin. Reden und Aufsätze* (Berlin: Stapp, 1964), p. 12.

[38] Schellack, *Nationalfeiertage* (1990), pp. 217–18. These pamphlets should also be seen as early evidence of the state's belief that a republican style of ritual could be created and that this style could win over the minds and hearts of German citizens. See, for example, Reichszentrale für Heimatdienst, ed., *Zum Verfassungstag: Eine Materialsammlung* (Berlin: Reichszentrale für Heimatdienst, 1928).

Plate 8. Under the banner "Unity, Freedom, Fatherland," the Reichsbanner cele-brates the tenth anniversary of the republic with a march down Unter den Linden on *Verfassungstag*, August 11, 1929. Source: © Bildarchiv Preussischer Kulturbesitz, 2003.

the summer months of 1929, turning the anticipation of the tenth anniver-sary celebrations into anxiety.[39] Nonetheless, the special preparations for the 1929 *Verfassungstag*, beyond the annual morning ceremony in the Reichstag and evening celebration for state dignitaries at the State Opera, continued in the capital. Commemorative stamps, postcards, and a special edition of the constitution itself were printed and made available to the public. The day's festivities also received widespread radio coverage[40] [Plate 8]. The bronze and iron medals previously given to winning athletes in the sporting

---

[39] A secondary goal for the celebrations, especially from 1929 on, was to make a good impres-sion for the foreign press. Positive reports in European and American newspapers would pacify worried statesmen and investors alike. Because there were no major disturbances surrounding the festivities, Germany's international image slowly recovered from the 1929 May Day violence. The *New York Times* covered the events in a front page story on August 12, 1929, "Germans Reaffirm Faith in Republic." The article stressed the desire of the gov-ernment to integrate workers into the republic and continue Germany's peaceful role on the world stage.

[40] Schellack, *Nationalfeiertage* (1990), p. 221.

competitions were upgraded to ones made of silver and bronze.[41] The most significant change was the addition of an afternoon celebration in the Berlin Stadium, representing the first officially organized *Verfassungstag* jubilee for the masses.

Most of the planning for the highly choreographed event was carried out by the office of the Reichskunstwart, Edwin Redslob.[42] The thousands of participants included children, students, workers' choral groups, gymnasts, soldiers, and members of the Reichsbanner. Included among the thirty thousand expected were Reich President von Hindenburg and other members of the government.[43] The theme for the show was unity. After official greetings and two musical selections, hundreds of "craftsmen" entered the stadium with gold rods and worked to connect them. Next the chorus spoke the following lines, which were repeated in an echo fashion:

> Brother on another shore listen,
> We are one people, we are creating a work – the living Reich,
> Ancient inheritance from ancestors and fathers handed down to us,
> In the errors of life, in the confusion of our ways, continued hope.
> Steadfast goal.
> Come to us
> The bridges are broken
> The staves are splintered
> The work is in vain.[44]

With their initial efforts to bind the rods together a failure, they called on the "purity" and "triumphant strength" of youth to bring the work to completion. This time young men entered the stadium, half of them carrying the colors of the federal states and the other half the Reich colors. All declared in unison: "We want to build a golden bridge." Those carrying the black, red, and gold colors of the republic responded by moving about the stadium in formation as a "living flag." After more singing and the raising of the actual

---

[41] BA, R32, Nr. 422, letter from Prussian Interior Minister Severing to the Deutschen Reichsausschuss für Leibesübungen, May 6, 1929, p. 85. The same memo was sent to the Zentralkommission für Arbeitersport und Körperpflege, where it was added "that only with the participation of the broadest sections of the population can the *Verfassungstag* achieve the character of a real people's festival." May 6, 1929, p. 85.

[42] For information on Edwin Redslob or the office of the Reichskunstwart, see Annegret Heffen, *Der Reichskunstwart, Kunstpolitik in den Jahren 1920–1933: Zu den Bemühungen um eine offizielle Reichskunstpolitik in der Weimarer Republik* (Essen: Die Blaue Eule, 1986). The Office of the Reichskunstwart was set up within the interior ministry in 1919 to determine how best to represent the state artistically.

[43] The SPD daily newspaper claimed fifty thousand filled the stadium in Berlin-Grünewald for the show. *Vorwärts*, "Das Volksfest im Stadion," second special edition on August 12, 1929.

[44] BA, R32, Nr. 430, the Reichskunstwart's description of the Berlin Stadium celebration on August 11, 1929, pp. 84–6.

flag of the republic, the spectacle was brought to a close with all present singing the national anthem, "Deutschland über Alles."[45]

The desire to create symbolically a united front against regionalism and antirepublicanism was the obvious intent of the show, and the emphasis on youth as the savior of the dream demonstrated the willingness of republicans to compete with the NSDAP and KPD for the political energy of the younger generation. What makes this state-organized spectacle fascinating, however, is its explicit dramatization of the negative. Although the climax of the show represented the future achievement of republican unity, the spectacle began with an admission of failure. As a description by the organizers of the celebration explained: "the working people of the Reich are at the task of reconnecting the broken bridge to a *Volksgemeinschaft.*"[46] After ten years of republicanism, this was not a positive assessment of the social and political climate of the nation. As a visual affirmation of republicanism, it was counterproductive. It is hard to imagine an official American July Fourth celebration featuring a show highlighting racial or socioeconomic inequality. Yet, instead of emphasizing the decade's accomplishments – the victory of republicanism over the monarchy or the initial codification of social justice ideals within the constitution – the stadium show emphasized the "errors" of the recent past, the present "confusion," and the work that still needed to be done.[47]

It has been argued that Redslob's desire to create a feeling of community through his stadium shows was an attempt to reconstitute an earlier festival

---

[45] Ibid.

[46] Ibid., p. 93. The following year, the Berlin, Prussian, and Reich governments argued over how to cut the *Verfassungstag* budget, which had ballooned to 102,000 RM for the 1929 capital festivities. There were thoughts of eliminating the "popular" afternoon stadium show, but because the recent evacuation of the Rhineland by French troops provided the organizers with a theme suitable to unite all political interests, the official evening gala at the opera was eliminated instead. *VT*, morning edition, July 1, 1930. In 1932, the evening festivities were again eliminated and all other expenditures were cut to 40,000 RM.

[47] Redslob and others argued that theatrical displays, such as the one described here, could be used in a democratic state to embody a "mass expression." Public spectacle had the potential to appeal to the individual experience while inspiring a sense of belonging to the community. "The *social* play," explained one *Verfassungstag* stadium show planner, "meets the necessary requirements of our times; a play, that as a general expression of the common experience of problems, characterizes the individual, independent of national or religious ties, as a member of the whole." This collective sentiment was to be embodied not only in the actions of the participants, but also in the totalizing artwork that was the stadium show. "Poets, architects, directors and musicians" all made contributions to the effort. The final element was the audience. They were not to sit idly by as in traditional theater. Rather, "this theatrical form knows no separation between audience and actor, it knows no presentation of the individual will, only the order of all factors into the expression of the totalized will (*Gesamtausdruckswillen*). See further BA, R32, Nr. 273, "Versuch einer Festspiel-Theorie (Anläßlich des Befreiungsfestspiels 'Deutschlands Strom' von Edwin Redslob)," Dr. C. B. Kniffler and A. J. Wenk, undated, pp. 65–7.

culture that had been supplanted by the imperial style of the *Kaiserreich*.[48] While some of the rituals and visual imagery used in the *Verfassungstag* pageant were taken from earlier religious and *volkstümlicher* symbolic culture, the desire to invent a new republican theatrical form that would represent the emotional connection between the nation and its sovereign people should not be underestimated. The somber self-criticism of the show in 1929 was a product of the Redslob administration's desire to develop a rational political sphere through theater. The new art form, as imagined by Redslob, would strip public occasions of the pomp that had alienated the population from their leaders during the Wilhelmine period. Instead audience members would be invited to see themselves in the goals of the nation.

The organizers of the Berlin festivities faced many problems in preparation for the holiday in 1929. In addition to the financial difficulties that had worsened considerably by the summer and the tension that remained after May 1, Redslob and his supporters had to maneuver among those opposing interests they hoped to win over with the celebration.[49] It was also feared that any show of republican confidence would be countered on Berlin's streets with riotous behavior by Communist and Nazi forces. A fourth problem, however, was more critical in determining the success or failure of the holiday. Though organizers were satisfied with showing the republic as a work in progress, the vision of what this republic would eventually represent needed to be coherent and powerful. They had to create a message that would sell the republic to a largely unconvinced – if not outright hostile – population. In the end, though the tenth anniversary was seen as a milestone, it failed to provide any new, more convincing, images of republicanism. The mass spectacle of the stadium celebration presented a new venue and form through which to represent the German nation, but the creation of "the living flag" left few lasting impressions on the population as to the sort of society it stood for.[50]

The annual *Verfassungsrede* [Constitution speech] of 1929 was delivered to parliament by one of the republic's staunchest supporters, Reich Interior

---

[48] Schellack, *Nationalfeiertage* (1990), pp. 226–7. Schellack agrees on page 252 that in the 1930s there was a concerted effort to create a new republican cultural form.

[49] At the administrative level, prorepublican forces risked provoking more conservative state governments, which might in turn refuse to observe the holiday in their regions. Observance of the *Verfassungstag* holiday had never passed into federal law.

[50] The symbolic value of the flag was debated throughout the Weimar era. The republican defense organization, Das Reichsbanner Schwarz-Rot-Gold, took its colors into its name, but those on the left wanted the red flag of revolution. Those on the right never honored it and ridiculed it as "black, red and yellow" (instead of gold). As Sabine Behrenbeck rightly points out, the republican flag was an especially poor symbol for use at state celebrations and commemorations because it was at the root of the divisive political conflicts that such events were trying to overcome: Sabine Behrenbeck, "The Nation Honours the Dead: Remembrance Days for the Fallen in the Weimar Republic and Third Reich" in Karin Friedrich, ed., *Festival Culture in Germany and Europe* (Lampeter: Mellen, 2000), p. 310.

Minister Carl Severing (SPD). The speech was a mixed bag of cautious optimism, reverence for the past, and nationalist melodrama. He began by comparing the crisis faced by Germany in 1929 to that of the inflation disaster of 1923 and expressed his hopes that the international group of leaders meeting in The Hague to restructure Germany's schedule of reparations payments would find a solution to "finally wind up the war." He complained: "it is not at all easy for the republic to celebrate holidays. On her scales stands no splendor, no golden abundance, rather the most bitter need, the hardest privation."[51] Severing described Weimar democracy as part of a longer tradition, which was manifested not only in the work of the 1848 Frankfurt Assembly but also in the political achievements (expansion of suffrage, among other rights) of the Wilhelmine period. He stressed that republican accomplishments were not limited to "saving the country from the fall into bolshevism" but included the continued unity of the Reich and the belief among workers "that the new state is their state." He concluded that the republic had always been threatened by external and internal enemies, but that the fight would continue for a state based on "the solidarity of all social ranks."[52]

While the public image portrayed by Severing and others in the capital was hopeful, a great deal was being done behind the scenes to ensure that things ran smoothly in Berlin during the festivities. As early as June 13, 1929, Redslob requested police support and protection against "malicious disruptions" at the practice sessions of the nine thousand singing and dancing children, which were to take place at sports fields around the city during the two weeks leading up to the Constitution Day.[53] In a separate document, the *Schutzpolizei* were reminded of the importance of positive press reports and photographic coverage of the festivities. Officers were told to assist reporters where possible and make certain that the festivities were "under no circumstances" marred in any way.[54] The police were also called on to protect the estimated one hundred thousand Reichsbanner men arriving in the capital from around the country. Extra trains were scheduled, and the police insisted on knowing each regional group's arrival time so as to station protective forces at the city's terminals.[55]

---

[51] *Vorwärts*, "Severings Festrede," Nr. 374, August 12, 1929. Much appreciation goes to Sebastian Simsch for locating a copy of this speech for me on short notice. For the texts of the preceding years' speeches, see *10 Jahre Weimarer Verfassung. Die Verfassungsreden bei den Verfassungsfeiern der Reichsregierung* (Berlin: Reichszentrale für Heimatdienst, 1929).

[52] "Severings Festrede," *Vorwärts*, Nr. 374, August 12, 1929.

[53] BLHA, Rep. 30, Berlin C, Title 90, Nr. 7531, Reichskunstwart Edwin Redslob, June 13, 1929, p. 156.

[54] BLHA, Rep. 30, Berlin C, Title 90, Nr. 7531, *Schutzpolizei* memo, July 1929, p. 172.

[55] BLHA, Rep. 30, Berlin C, Title 90, Nr. 7531, correspondence between the Reichsbanner Berlin-Brandenburg and the Polizeipräsident Abteilung II at the beginning of August 1929, pp. 297, 318.

The Reichsbanner was the most enthusiastic participant in the annual *Verfassungstag* celebrations. It was their day to show off their numerical strength, patriotic loyalty, and close relationship with state authorities. For the 1929 festivities, the Reichsbanner planned two days of events. On August 10, the Reichsbanner's national leaders were greeted upon arrival in Berlin with music and a triumphal accompaniment to their hotel, and in the evening they rubbed shoulders with state ministers, including Severing, Wirth, and Berlin Mayor Gustav Böß, in the State Opera House. The first day came to an end with a concert on the Square of the Republic and a "Demonstration for State Unity" in front of the Reichstag. On the following day, the various Reichsbanner troops, who were housed by their Berlin comrades, marched from all corners of the city to the Lustgarten Park where they listened to the words of their commander, Otto Hörsing. This speech was followed by a march down Unter den Linden and dispersal. The men then returned to the neighborhoods for "people's festivals."[56] The intention of the Reichsbanner's plan was clearly to take over the streets of Berlin, in a way that mimicked the tactics of antirepublican forces, while also showing their welcome and comfort in the governmental quarter.[57]

The Reichsbanner's presence in the capital's administrative center was a special privilege. The *Bannmeile*, which prohibited unofficial political demonstrations within a proscribed area surrounding governmental buildings, was not a result of the heightened radicalism at the end of the 1920s. This law protecting the area around the Reichstag dated from 1920 and was changed little until its lifting in 1934.[58] The *Bannmeile* was taken quite seriously throughout the Weimar era, and permission to traverse its boundaries in closed formation required approval from a number of high-ranking officials, including the offices of Prussian interior minister, Reich interior minister, and Reich chancellor. Although the Reichsbanner was not the only organization that was given such permission for the Constitution Day celebrations in 1929, it was by far the largest and most visible. Permission was granted on a case-by-case basis, and in theory the permittee had to convince the authorities that the proposed parade was "private" or "apolitical." Security may have been the official rationale for the strict control of the *Bannmeile*, but it is clear that those who determined access also used their powers selectively to create an image of a

---

[56] BLHA, Rep. 30, Berlin C, Title 90, Nr. 7531, Reichsbanner program for the Constitution Celebration, 1929, p. 277.

[57] Cf. Thomas Lindenberger, *Straßenpolitik. Zur Sozialgeschichte der öffentlichen Ordnung in Berlin, 1900–1914* (Bonn: Dietz, 1995). Lindenberger analyzes the political significance afforded to public spaces and the increasing competition between the population, political organizations, and state authorities for control of these politically charged spaces.

[58] The official name of the law was "Das Gesetz über die Befriedung der Gebäude des Reichstags und der Landtage." It went into effect on May 8, 1920, and was lifted on March 23, 1934.

stable republic.[59] Thanks to this secondary consideration, the paramilitary Reichsbanner was given permission to march on August 11, 1929. The political right took great offense to the decision, declaring it "an example of state corruption of legal rights." Reichsbanner access, charged the same conservative Berlin newspaper, amounted to preferential treatment that belied the constitution's foundation of "equal rights for all." This injustice, added the reporter, was a "provocation to all citizens," and an example of "how a state is not to be governed."[60]

The uniqueness of this opportunity to make an impression of popularity, strength, and discipline was not lost on the Reichsbanner leadership. In preparation for the 1929 festivities, a brochure was issued to Reichsbanner

[59] In one case, the police requested the denial of permission for a *Verfassungstag* parade by a national society that promoted horse breeding. There may have been concern that this organization did not fulfill the goal of portraying a modern industrial state. The Prussian interior minister suggested to the Reich interior minister that the organization might be persuaded to hold their parade in the highly populated, but less serious, shopping district. See BA, R15.01, Nr. 25681/2, pp. 110–11.

[60] *Der Tag*, "Reichsbanner und Bannmeile," Nr. 145, June 19, 1929. Also in BA, R15.01, Nr. 25681/2, p. 109. During the early 1930s there were many breaches of the *Bannmeile*, as the increased use of motor vehicles made it easier to make a quick entrance and exit. A truck with hidden flags and banners could pass fairly easily into the governmental quarter, stage a miniparade on Unter den Linden or near the Reichstag building, and quickly drive back over the border. Those with less courage found convenient sites for demonstration just beyond the *Bannmeile*. In May 1930, the Reich minister of labor pleaded with the interior minister to extend the monitored area to include his offices, which were being barraged by daily demonstrations of the unemployed. He feared the possibility of their "cutting off the ministry's communication with the Reichstag and other governmental offices." BA, R15.01, Nr. 25681/1, letter from the Reich minister of labor to the Reich minister of the interior, May 8, 1930, p. 2. His request was denied by the interior minister, who believed there would be public outcry against expanding the law, which had been intended to protect the parliament only. His request to include the labor ministry within the *Bannmeile* was also rejected due to the impractical layout of the proposal. See also R15.01, Nr. 25681/1, Letter from the Prussian interior minister to the Reich interior minister, June 26, 1930, p. 14; Reich minister of the interior to the Reich labor minister, June 30, 1930, p. 16. The defense used by protesting trespassers, when caught, was that the borders were unclear. In 1930, officials considered placing signs along the streets that bordered the prohibited area so that trespassers would no longer have this convenient excuse. For an explanation of the need for clearer borders to the prohibited area, see *BT*, "Der Bannkreis. Neue Schilder, damit man die Grenzen besser erkennt," February 28, 1930. Though this change was not made, the law remained in force until 1934. By then, with all opposition fragmented and terrorized, there was no more need for a buffer zone. In March, Hitler drew attention to his lifting of the *Bannmeile* as a way to remind Germans of the defunct republic's failure to build consensus. The explanation for the lifting of the *Bannmeile*, which "since early 1933 had no longer been needed," appeared in *Wolff's Telegraphisches Büro*, Nr. 640, March 24, 1934. Nonetheless, the government still relied on the protection afforded by the restricted area, prompting a number of newspapers to print articles in May, emphasizing the need to respect the *Bannmeile* and reminding readers that all organizers of parades and demonstrations needed to apply for permission at least one week ahead of the scheduled event. See *Berliner Lokal-Anzeiger*, "Strengste Beachtung der Bannkreis-Bestimmungen," Nr. 224, May 13, 1933.

men from around the country to make their visit to Berlin more pleasant and more controlled. The tips, maps, and regulations included a list of "ten commands for RB-men in Berlin." The suggestion to see the tourist attractions of the city was followed by the more earnest command to "practice discipline" so as to make an orderly impression on the "critical Berliners" and other tourists in the city. The visitors were also warned of the possibility of provocation from their opponents: "Don't discuss politics with the misled. . . . However do not put up with insults of the republic, your emblems or leaders." Finally, the Reichsbanner leadership insisted that their men abstain from overindulgence in alcohol, refrain from complaining within the listening range of others, and steer clear from "nightly adventures," all of which "damaged the image of the Reichsbanner."[61]

Throughout the 1920s, the KPD and NSDAP had made little concerted effort to organize any large-scale resistance to the August 11 holiday. Both parties took a public stance against the celebration, but perhaps because they knew most people would want to enjoy the festive atmosphere of a summer holiday, little was done to dissuade them. Berlin's Communists did try to mount a campaign against the day's observance in Berlin's schools. The party tried to convince parents to protest nationalist as well as religious teachings in schools under the banner "proletarian school fight against the nationalist constitution-bustle." They urged parents to hold their children back from school-sponsored parades and festivities.[62] Police detachments were posted at targeted schools, and patrolmen accompanied children on their parades to ward off any meddling by KPD activists.[63] In 1929, there were small counterparades and concerts sponsored by the KPD around the city on August 10, but the party's request to stage a larger protest on the eleventh at their favorite gathering place – Bülowplatz, site of KPD headquarters in the Karl Liebknecht House – was denied because the Reichsbanner had already cunningly registered the "reddest" square in Berlin with the police as one of the many stepping off points for its large Lustgarten assembly.[64]

The extent of the police surveillance of the KPD leading up to the holiday demonstrates that there was a much greater concern that the KPD, and not the NSDAP, would orchestrate attempts to disrupt the proceedings. Police spies reported on plans for Communist parliamentary and City Assembly members to attend the Reichsbanner assembly in the Lustgarten and through one-on-one conversation convince them to join the more radical party. Another police spy suspected that members of the Communist youth

[61] BA-SAPMO, SgY2/V/DF/VII/58, "Orientierungsplan für die Reichsbannerkameraden zur Bundesverfassungsfeier des Reichsbanner Schwarz-Rot-Gold am 11. August 1929 in Berlin," p. 9.
[62] *RF*, morning edition, Nr. 143, August 6, 1929.
[63] BLHA, Rep. 30, Berlin C, Title 90, Nr. 7531, *Schutzpolizei* memo, August 8, 1929, p. 273.
[64] BLHA, Rep. 30, Berlin C, Title 90, Nr. 7531, letter from the police chief (IA) to the KPD Berlin-Brandenburg, August 7, 1929, p. 391.

groups, the KJVD and the banned Rote Jugend, were organizing at the rail stations to "greet warmly" the arriving Reichsbanner men. The following day, the young men were to receive postings along the Reichsbanner parade routes and at the Lustgarten assembly to pelt marchers with stones and steal their flags. Perhaps sensing continued solidarity between some SPD and KPD rank-and-file, or understanding the desire among Communists for a day off from confrontations with police, the spy conceded: "it remains questionable, whether these commands will be followed."[65] Berlin police station diary entries provide a thumbnail sketch of the problems that did arise on the weekend of the anniversary celebration. There were at least fifty-seven fights and attacks that were ruled political; none led to serious injury or death, but many arrests were made. There were three incidents deemed "acts of sabotage" by the KPD, which in reality were nothing more than anti-*Verfassungstag* propaganda activities.[66] In the end, the day's events ran quite smoothly, and the Chief of Police Albert Grzesinski (SPD) was so pleased that he granted two days vacation to all those who had served under his command.[67]

Two years later, Grzesinski's mood was far less cheerful. When he addressed his men on August 11, 1931, the police chief admitted: "under these circumstances there is no celebratory feeling [on this Constitution Day] and many of our fellow Germans ask themselves, how long can these conditions last?"[68] He referred to the *Verfassungstag* of 1923 and insisted that, now as then, panic was the worst possible reaction to the crisis. Rather "public discipline, patience, steady will and clear volition" were needed. Grzesinski must not have believed that these virtues were entirely enough because he also insisted on the necessity of a strong state to right Germany's path: "The state cannot act, carry out the laws and decrees which reach deep into the life of the nation without a strong, united executive, which sets forth with

---

[65] BLHA, Rep. 30, Berlin C, Title 90, Nr. 7531, memo from political police IA to the *Schutzpolizei*, August 9, 1929, p. 392 and Police-Inspektion Neukölln spy report of a KPD meeting on August 9, 1929, p. 395.

[66] BLHA, Rep. 30, Berlin C, Title 90, Nr. 7531. These tallies were gathered from the notes taken down by police for internal records of police activities. These numbers should not be seen as completely accurate totals, but they do provide a measure of what the police believed to be a smooth weekend in Berlin. During the 1930 and 1931 celebrations, drunkenness was the main public nuisance noted by the police. Though incidents of violence had increased dramatically by 1931, especially during the hot summer months, grave problems never developed on the *Verfassungstag*. The lack of unrest is explained by the heightened police patrols, the unwillingness by republican opponents to confront the great influx of Reichsbanner visitors, and the desire by all to enjoy the summer day of rest. By 1931, however, the increasingly negative atmosphere surrounding the holiday may also have played an important role. There was really very little to protest.

[67] BLHA, Rep. 30, Berlin C, Title 90, Nr. 7531, *Schutzpolizei* memo, August 13, 1929, p. 411.

[68] BLHA, Rep. 30, Berlin C, Title 90, Nr. 7532, speech by Albert Grzesinski to the Berlin police force, August 11, 1931, p. 338.

life and limb for the strength and security of the state."[69] He then thanked his men for their contributions in these efforts and closed with a moment of silence for the members of the force who had fallen in service.

Leaders of the Reichsbanner similarly called for change.[70] In August 1931, the organization's official newspaper carried an article that illustrated the move the RB had taken toward the left, as the SPD rank-and-file lost patience with their party's policies of tolerance toward the Brüning government, and Center Party members' standing declined within the organization. Speaking for his comrades, the author declared that support for the republic was still strong, but that they "desired a purer, clearer and more decisive" republic and constitution. He called for an end to the "rival governments" within the republic and pointed specifically to the power wielded by industrial interests. Indeed, the author doubted whether the republic had any future at all, arguing that "freedom will first be secured, when the terrible conflict between capital and labor has been fought to an end."[71]

The reorganized Reichsbanner was left in a tough spot between its republican ideals of a transparent government and educated polity and the reality of an increasingly radical political culture. Republican discipline was based on the defense of state and constitution. Yet the organization's very existence gave weight to the argument that neither was functioning properly. The government was operating by presidential decree, and the citizens were perceived as lacking the necessary political consciousness. Moreover,

---

[69] Ibid., p. 339.

[70] The discontent within the Reichsbanner went all the way to the top. Its leader Otto Hörsing had fundamental disagreements with the SPD over economic policy and on July 2, 1932, resigned his post in the RB and left the party to form the *Sozialrepublikanische Partei Deutschland*. See Rohe, *Das Reichsbanner* (1966), pp. 379–91.

[71] BA, R15.01, Nr. 25966, see *Das Reichsbanner*, August 8, 1931, Nr. 32, "'Nun erst recht – es lebe die Republik!' Ein Ansprache zur Verfassungsfeier" by Theodor Haubach. By 1932, even the Reichsbanner was prohibited from holding its annual march through the restricted area; a July decree banning all public political assemblies and parades forced them to celebrate inside. Because of the prohibitions on political speeches, uniforms, certain decorations, and political assemblies, the holiday took on a mostly apolitical character in 1932. Instead of boycotting the curtailment of political activities, the Reichsbanner announced that it would go along with these new conditions because many area branches of the organization had already invested local funds for their own small-scale parties. What had once been envisioned as a unifying day to celebrate democracy had effectively turned into a seasonal holiday, devoid of any political or national significance. *Vorwärts* joined other newspapers in announcing the "Summer festivals instead of Constitutional celebration." *Vorwärts*, Nr. 377, August 12, 1932, "'Sommerfeste' statt Verfassungsfeiern." The *New York Times*, however, was most perceptive in its description of the atmosphere at the morning Reichstag ceremony as "a funeral rather than birthday party." The American newspaper reported that Interior Minister Wilhelm von Gayl's *Verfassungsrede* described the constitution as "woefully inadequate. It cramps everybody, and worse. Instead of making a happy family it 'severs mind from mind,' and it must be rebuilt." Recognizing what was de facto the case, the speeches by von Gayl and Chancellor von Papen that followed did not include one utterance of the word "republic." The *New York Times*, August 12, 1932, "Republic is ignored on Reich Fete Day."

the Reichsbanner and other supporters of democracy felt partly to blame. As the social democratic Prussian minister of culture explained: "We have left everything to the institutions of the state, to the justice system, police and army for much too long believing that these institutions would see to it that the lion-sized courage of politicized braggarts would not cause any mischief. But finally it is clear, that the state and its institutions are not separate from us, and that they are only as much as we make of them."[72]

Without a viable republican state to represent, the RB tried to invoke the ghost of democracy past. In an article aimed at potential young recruits, the RB looked back to the youth who had fought in the revolutionary *Vormärz* period (1840–8). The article praised the ideals for which they had fought, even if "these real patriots were seen as enemies to the state." The article then jumped to the experiences of World War I. Using the nationalist language of the time without romanticizing the Wilhelmine period, the author did homage to the fallen young of the war: "We bend our knee in honor of the spirit of sacrifice of the dead at Langemarck, and we know today: their death was a tragic error! Thousands went to their deaths, not for the fatherland, but for an outwardly powerful and internally empty state system."[73] This criticism extended to the present day, through the author's wholesale discrediting of Weimar and call for "creating a new state system." The goal for this new generation of German youth was to "make a state out of the republic, which is the beloved home for all its inhabitants, to fill the republic with the spirit of political unity and social justice: is there a more wonderful message for a youth who believes in the future and marches under its banner?"[74] The republican discipline called for by the Reichsbanner was a difficult request, especially for prospective young members. They were commanded to honor the unrealized democracy of their great-grandfathers, encouraged to reject the one existing example of republican rule, and enlisted to work faithfully for an undetermined future. This message was especially confusing when compared to the less complicated messages they were receiving from the KPD and NSDAP.

RADICALISM

The economic collapse, political instability, and missteps of the SPD provided a great opportunity for the Communist Party, and its leaders hoped to make the most of it. In some ways, the KPD should have had it the easiest of all major parties in these years. Party chairman Ernst Thälmann declared

---

[72] *VT,* "Das Reichsbanner im Sportpalast," weekend edition, Nr. 88, February 21, 1931. Includes the speech by Prussian Minister of Culture Grimme (SPD) to those in attendance.
[73] BLHA, Rep. 30, Berlin C, Title 95, Sektion 10, Nr. 26, *Burschen Heraus (Zeitschrift zur Reichsbanner Werbung),* June 1930.
[74] Ibid.

that the KPD was the sole true representative of a politicized industrial proletariat. The KPD *Reichsleitung* claimed that the "Social-Fascist" SPD had
clearly betrayed the cause of workers in its complicity in the republic.[75] For
over a decade, argued the KPD Central Committee (ZK), the SPD had been a
political powerhouse owing to its large percentage of seats in the Reichstag,
and yet capitalism continued to rule the day. Workers still struggled to find
decent housing and secure work, tasks that were becoming increasingly difficult during the Depression. The KPD leaders did not stop here in their
accusations. They charged the Social Democrats with building a corrupt and
brutal state, in which officials lived like "fat cats" and police were instructed
to crack down violently on worker-led activism.[76] To make their point that
behind the worker-friendly façade top Social Democrats were capitalists living the good life, the party press frequently reprinted photographs of evening
events at which tuxedoed Social Democrats such as Albert Grzesinski or Carl
Severing were "caught" sipping champagne and smoking cigars.

As per Leninist theory, the RFB was the advance guard of the Communist
movement. After the revolution, the RFB was to form the core of the people's
army, but until then it was a paramilitary organization that mobilized thousands of young men throughout the republic to prepare for revolution.[77]
The RFB was founded in 1924 in the central German city of Halle. Like all
paramilitary organizations in Weimar, the RFB claimed at its inception that
the organization aimed to bring together those who had fought in World
War I, and to keep alive the memories of those who never returned. This
nationalist-sounding rhetoric was tempered by the RFB's stated hope that
such memories could be used to hinder imperialist aggression in the future.[78]
Nonetheless, an alliance with veterans' interests never really fit with the KPD,
and such language was soon dropped.

In 1927, the RFB leadership admitted that the parameters of its mandate
had not been altogether clear at first, but that the organization's founding
was a "sign of the reawakened fighting spirit of the proletariat" resurrected in

---

[75] This KPD critique of the SPD known as social fascism, in which the SPD was decried as
being the handmaiden or even an equal to the fascist threat on the Right, has received much
attention by historians of the KPD, especially those interested in analyzing the reasons for the
split in the Left. For further explanation of this KPD policy, see Ben Fowkes, *Communism in
Germany under the Weimar Republic* (New York: St. Martin's Press, 1984), pp. 153–66; and
Hermann Weber, *Hauptfeind Sozialdemokratie, Strategie und Taktik der KPD 1929–1933*
(Düsseldorf: Droste, 1981).

[76] The most infamous case of corruption surrounded the illegal business dealings of the Sklarek
brothers, two of whom were in the SPD, and the "hush money" received by a number of low-
level SPD city officials. For more on this case, see Donna Harsch, *German Social Democracy*
(1993), pp. 69–71.

[77] For a history of the RFB, see Kurt G. P. Schuster, *Der Rote Frontkämpferbund, 1924–1929*
(Düsseldorf: Droste, 1975). Cf. Helga Gotschlich, *Zwischen Kampf und Kapitulation* (East
Berlin: Dietz, 1987).

[78] BA-SAPMO, RY1/I4/2/7, "Satzungen des RFB," 1924, p. 91.

Plate 9. At this RFB pub in Friedrichshain, visitors to the *Rote Pfingsttreffen* are assigned lodging at the homes of local comrades. In a Communist twist of the Pentecostal message, the wall mural reads: "Lenin is dead. His spirit lives." Source: © Bildarchiv Preussischer Kulturbesitz, 2003.

response to the failure of the 1918–19 revolution and the growth of "fascist" paramilitarism, which in the years before the emergence of a strong Nazi SA meant the nationalist Stahlhelm, Jungdeutsche Orden, and Wehrwolf. Their disciplined presence on city streets was to have two messages for passersby: "Friends are excited that the idea of proletarian military readiness is alive and well. Enemies are scared and jealous when they see the grave, disciplined, class-conscious marchers."[79] In the mid 1920s RFB activities emphasized this aspect of consciousness raising. Members dressed in Russian blouses over military trousers and participated in mass rallies, sporting competitions, and election campaigns. The cap and armband depicted the RFB's clenched-fist emblem and, when purchased along with the rest of the uniform and boots in the late 1920s, cost workers in Berlin over 34 RM[80] [Plate 9].

It is difficult to discern how many members belonged to the RFB in the last months before the organization was banned along with its youth branch, Rote Jungfront (RJ), in May 1929. The national estimates range from 65,000 to 200,000. If one includes those who participated but never paid dues,

[79] BA-SAPMO, RY1/I4/2/7, "Was will der Rote Frontkämpferbund?" May 1927, p. 32.
[80] It appears that the RFB uniform could only be purchased through the store Gebagos located in Essen and Berlin. For their price list, see BA-SAPMO, RY1/I4/2/7, pp. 68–75.

the total probably came fairly close to 100,000.[81] With 11,000 members in Berlin before its prohibition, it is clear that the RFB was a significant political force in the capital before May 1929.[82] Only men were allowed to join, but membership was not restricted to those already in the KPD. Rather all male workers were invited to join. After the May violence, the RFB continued to organize secretly, but its illegal status hindered it from ever regaining the public presence or mass following of the earlier period. Police and government officials were never sure how many men were organizing in spite of the ban, and debates continued in these circles as to whether the crackdown had helped at all to stem the tide of radicalism. There was one official successor to the banned RFB and Rote Jungfront, the Antifaschistische Junge Garde. From its inception, this new association was wrought with internal discord, the threat of illegality, and what appears to have been rowdy and even criminal elements among its membership.[83] As a result, the organization never really got off the ground and was disbanded by the KPD itself within months. Though unfounded, official fears of vast networks of terrorist cells continued, while the RFB – fighting illegality and dwindling resources – shrank in the early 1930s to at best a couple hundred members in Berlin.

Though the banning of the RFB and RJ in 1929 did not lead to the total destruction of the RFB, it did affect the way Berlin radicalism developed in the following three years. The ban resulted in the creation of a smaller, more localized, and secretive RFB. This process of decentralization also made it more difficult for the police to track RFB activities. This dilemma contributed to the paranoia exhibited in police estimates of the size and revolutionary readiness of the group. It also undermined the ability of the KPD, as an institution, to control many of its most active supporters or pose a serious threat to the republic. Many shied away from the illegal activities of the RFB after May 1929, or simply lost contact in the growing confusion, continued to participate in radical street politics by joining one of the *Außerpartei-* or *Nebenorganisationen* (extra-party organizations), the Kampfbund gegen den Faschismus (KbgdF) or the Roter Massenselbstschutz, which organized residentially, at unemployment offices, and in factories.[84] Party members

---

[81] Schuster, *Der Rote Frontkämpferbund* (1975), pp. 239–41.

[82] Eva Brücker, "Wohnen und Leben in SO 36, zum Beispiel in der Wiener Straße 10–12" in Helmut Engel, Stefi Jersch-Wenzel, and Wilhelm Treue, eds., *Geschichtslandschaft Berlin: Orte und Ereignisse, Band 5 Kreuzberg* (Berlin: Nicolai, 1994), p. 369.

[83] BA-SAPMO, RY1/I4/9/3, Bericht der Reichsleitung des KbgdF, February 1931, pp. 39–40. The Antifaschistische Junge Garde, also known simply as Antifa, should not be confused with the later electoral slogan Antifaschistische Aktion (Antifa Aktion), used by the KPD to advocate unity among all voters against fascism.

[84] More detrimental in the eyes of party leaders were the actions of some members who instead of joining other KPD-sponsored organizations simply formed their own independent cliques. See BA-SAPMO, RY1/I4/2/20, "Richtlinien über Aufbau und Arbeit der Roten Jungfront," August/September 1929, pp. 8–9.

still had their street and factory cells, and youth were still trained in the KJVD. There were also innumerable social and cultural organizations that served the recreational needs of workers and, in some cases, took on increasingly active political agendas, such as the Fichte sports association. As many as ten thousand children and adults were members in Berlin, and some listed this sports club as their only political affiliation when questioned by police for illegal political activities.

Although the party officially supported women's involvement in all aspects of the class struggle, women and men were sometimes organized separately, especially in the newly forming antifascist associations. Small units existed at the base of each organization, the size of which depended on the level of secrecy in the respective organizations.[85] As to be expected, the KPD also made every effort to establish local chapters of all its organizations in Berlin's factories. However, because the economic situation was so dismal, the KbgdF and other party organizations had more luck recruiting supporters at unemployment offices and in residential areas than at industrial sites. Groups of RFB columns, street cells, and KbgdF units sent representatives to a neighborhood functionary board. This body contributed to the *Unterbezirksleitung* (UBL). Finally, the eight UBL which made up Berlin's KPD contributed representatives to the city leadership, or *Bezirksleitung* (BL). Although there was cooperation among the different organizations, there was also competition for the best administrators and most enthusiastic members, as well as for the financial support and interest of the city's party leaders. At the lowest level, most functionaries were elected, the position of political leader being the most important, but confirmation from higher levels was often required.

Although some of the organizations connected to the Communist movement were direct reflections of the changing political climate (the KbgdF is the prime example), the general make-up of the movement had changed little since the founding of the KPD in 1919. In fact, one could argue that the German Communist Party, as an institution, was exceedingly conservative in the early 1930s. The ZK refused to recognize fully that the factory floor was no longer a profitable site for organizing in Berlin. Although propaganda consistently proclaimed the necessity to mobilize those "on the street, at home and at the welfare offices," citywide evaluations and instructions from above continued to invest valuable resources and "proletarian self-criticism" into factory politics. As explained in 1929 by the ZK:

Despite illegality, now as before [the ban] the RFB must retain its character as a mass organization outside of the party. However, while earlier it appeared in public mostly in the form of independent marches and events, now the emphasis must lie

---

[85] Each organization had its own complex set of regulations. See, for example, Kurt Schuster's *Der Rote Frontkämpferbund* (1975) for a published example of the RFB codes or BA-SAPMO, RY1/I4/9/3, pp. 15–18 for those issued in 1930 concerning the KbgdF.

in the participation in a broad proletarian self-defense based in the factory.... The organization of the proletarian self-defense must be carried out at the factory, because the factory must be the starting point of the revolutionary mass-offensives by the proletariat.[86]

Part of their refusal to abandon the party's efforts on the shop floor lay in the KPD's political program. Since workers' chief political weapon was their labor, the first step in revolution could be taken only by the mass strike. Consequently, the insistence on factory organizing was also rooted in the party's ideal of a disciplined Communist. The ideal images portrayed by party propaganda were the politicized industrial male worker and his rural cousin, the class-conscious peasant.[87] Even though fewer and fewer of their supporters in Berlin reflected this image of a larger-than-life, ideologically informed, disciplined male worker, the ZK was unwilling to alter its ideals. In fact, the masculine strength and bravery idolized by the KPD was only exaggerated by the sense that the revolution was near.

Party images did try to incorporate women into this ideal some of the time, but the masculinized female fighter with her broad shoulders and chiseled facial features had little resonance with working women. The rest of the time, the proletarian woman and mother was represented as tired and passive, an object of pity and outrage but not inspiration.[88] The party's women's organization, the Roter Frauen- und Mädchenbund (RFMB), was never very successful in mobilizing large numbers of Berlin's female workers. The few most activist-minded women wanted to join the RFB,[89] but this show of equality was never permitted. The rest found the mimicking of the RFB's militarism unappealing. The "new woman" of Weimar – young, active, independent and often employed in white-collar work – did not serve as a suitable model for the KPD heroine because it was assumed that she was interested in pleasure not politics. Even if many Berlin steno-girls had working-class backgrounds, their lipstick, modern attire, and vulnerability to male superiors' sexual advances led some on the left to criticize these women as the mistresses of capitalism.[90] The message was clear: both

---

[86] BA-SAPMO, RY1/I4/2/8, resolution concerning the work of the RFB, 1929, p. 21.

[87] Eric D. Weitz, *Creating German Communism, 1890–1990* (Princeton, NJ: Princeton University Press, 1996), pp. 188–231.

[88] See Patrice Petro's work on female images in the *AIZ* in *Joyless Streets: Women and Melodramatic Representation in Weimar Germany* (Princeton, NJ: Princeton University Press, 1989), pp. 127–39.

[89] Weitz, *Creating German Communism* (1996), p. 223. At the end of 1930, the political police (IA) noted the dissolution of the RFMB. The KbgdF was taking over its responsibilities for organizing women, a turn of events that was met with jubilation according to the police. BLHA, Rep. 30, Berlin C, Title 95, Teil 2, Nr. 117, Bd. 2, memo from the chief of police IA, December 17, 1930.

[90] Cf. Rudolf Braune, *Das Mädchen an der Orga Privat* (Munich: Damnitz, 1975). The first edition of this Berlin workers' novel appeared in 1929–30. This story focuses on the efforts

working men and women were enslaved by capitalism, but only men had the power to emancipate both sexes from their bondage.[91] The art work of Käthe Kollwitz and others selected to appear on party posters and brochures depicted the misery and strength of poor women in this period. Their strength was in their steadfast commitment to their families and their willingness to sacrifice. It was not a strength, however, that reached beyond the private sphere.

In 1928–9 the Berlin NSDAP was not in as strong a position as their Communist rivals to take advantage of the crisis that was beginning to grip the nation. Throughout the 1920s, the party had been slow to gain supporters in the capital. Berlin was, of course, both a cosmopolitan city and a stronghold of the workers' movement. The Nazis had no roots in Berlin and no legends yet to build on like the murders of Rosa Luxemburg and Karl Liebknecht, which the KPD used to rally workers to their cause. There was much in Berlin that the NSDAP felt needed changing, but they recognized this was all still a long way off. The strength of the political left and the liberal press, the large well-integrated Jewish community, and the modern urban lifestyle enjoyed by many of its inhabitants made the capital a special target of Nazi disdain, as described in this 1926 report by Berlin's Nazi propaganda chief:

Berlin! What wishes and hopes, curses and threats are released at the sound of this name! Berlin – the magical destination which pulls in all those seeking adventure, the international meeting place of all the races and peoples of the earth, the breeding place for the worst kind of piracy.... And in the casemate of this red fortress are people [Nazis] who swim against the current and because of it receive the filthy hate of an over powerful press. They are spit upon...and if they fall in the hands of the masses [they are] beaten, kicked, murdered.... In plain German: Berlin is red and Jewish at the same time. Each political occasion, each election proves it again.[92]

Practically speaking, the party's effectiveness in Berlin during the mid 1920s was also hampered by a lack of strong leadership. Top party strategists had not wanted to waste their best talent on an unresponsive city, but by 1926 it was obvious the capital warranted more attention. As a result, in November Joseph Goebbels was sent to turn around the Berlin Gau. The difficulties faced by the NSDAP in Berlin served as a strong motivator for party organizers, especially for Goebbels. As illustrated earlier, in Berlin more than in other parts of the republic, Nazis fancied themselves missionaries and martyrs in Gomorrah. They were fond of retelling in later years the story of their first humble headquarters in Berlin, the arrival of Goebbels, and their

led by one young typist to organize a strike in her office after a single colleague is fired due to a pregnancy from which she later dies. The least willing strikers are portrayed as only interested in finding rich husbands to provide them with clothes and spending money.

[91] Weitz, *Creating German Communism* (1996), pp. 205–8.
[92] BA, NS 26/133 situation report from the NSDAP propaganda cell in Neukölln, June 1926.

arduous fight to be heard amid their enemies.[93] They railed against the SPD as the bureaucrats who were too passive to effect real change. The leaders of the republic had sold out to "Jewish" influences and were handmaidens to the victor nations of World War I.

While the supporters of republicanism were "Jewish capitalists" and "philistines" who had no vision of a great and powerful Volk, the Communists were "*Pöbel*" or low-life. Communism was the biggest threat to Germany's future, proclaimed the Nazis, and only they could stop it. On the one side, the Nazis were the activists, who would not back down to reparation-demanding foreign powers or "internal enemies." On the other side, they presented themselves as the keepers of order. Only they could make the calls for "*Brot, Arbeit, und Freiheit*" (bread, work, and freedom) a reality.[94] The NSDAP has been rightly characterized as a *Sammelbewegung*, drawing its supporters from all walks of life.[95] Nationally the party was most popular among the middle classes and rural Protestants, but in an industrial city like Berlin the party was forced to present itself as an attractive option to those who had voted in the past for the parties of the left.[96] A 1932 memorandum from the party's propaganda bureau suggested strategies to appeal to a variety of constituencies in the upcoming Reichstag elections:

For the [Catholic] Center Party we are the warning to upright Christians, who want to turn away the danger to religion conjured up by this [Center] Party and whose duty it is to protect the Church from it.... All steps taken by Center politicians are to be marked as fundamentally un-Christian.

For the Social Democrats we are the far-sighted Socialists, who always knew that the party line was wrong, because it could do nothing other than create an enormous opposition, instead of exciting people for socialism.

---

[93] For a grassroots example of how the party enjoyed reliving its expansion from humble beginnings, see the history of the Ortsgruppe Luitpold in Berlin, written on the occasion of its tenth anniversary, December 1941 in BLHA, Rep. 61, Gau Berlin, Nr. 14.11.1. For a more extensive description of the alleged "Jewish persecution" of the fledgling Nazi movement in Berlin, see the account by Joseph Goebbels, *Kampf um Berlin* (Munich: Zentralverlag der NSDAP, 1939).

[94] The slogan "bread, work, and freedom" had been a long-standing rallying cry of the workers' movement in Germany but was used frequently by both the KPD and NSDAP during the Depression.

[95] Much has been written on the reasons for middle-class rejection of republicanism. For a concise analysis, see Bernd Weisbrod, "The Crisis of Bourgeois Society in Interwar Germany" in Richard Bessel, ed., *Fascist Italy and Nazi Germany. Comparisons and Contrasts* (Cambridge: Cambridge University Press, 1996), pp. 23–39.

[96] For the most complete look at the NSDAP's membership, see Michael Kater's large-scale study, *The Nazi Party: A Social Profile of Members and Leaders, 1919–1945* (Oxford: Basil Blackwell, 1983). See William Brustein, *The Logic of Evil: The Social Origins of the Nazi Party 1925–1933* (New Haven, CT: Yale University Press, 1996). See also Michael Kater's review of Brustein's study in *Central European History* (Vol. 30, No. 2, 1997), pp. 339–40.

For the Communists we are the old revolutionaries, who always warned against getting worn down against the main enemy, before the working class could be united.[97]

With propaganda aimed at workers in this way, the party's Stormtroops, or SA, hoped to make their presence felt in the traditionally Red neighborhoods of Berlin. In 1928, the SA still only counted eight hundred members in the city; however, by July 1931 the police estimated that the Berlin SA comprised eighty-five thousand to ninety thousand men, which reflected the great increase seen throughout the republic.[98] Goebbels's "struggle for Berlin" paid dividends in Kreuzberg as well. The Nazis preferred to set up party pubs on corners, where they could be more easily defended (especially in hostile territories) and more noticeable to passers-by. The SA–Sturm 24 had its meetings at "Zur Hochburg" on the corner of Gneisenau and Solms, only one block from Nostizstraße. This SA tavern was situated between the Lorenz pub on Nostiz and the other RFB *Lokal* in the Kiez, Tante Emma, located at Nr. 20 Schleiermacher on the corner of Gneisenau. SA Sturm 24 lost two men in battles with these two KPD bars. On September 9, 1931, its leader Herman Thielsch, along with three others was shot in front of Zur Hochburg by Communists associated with the Nostiz bar. In June of the following year, Helmut Köster was shot in a tumult with those from Tante Emma.[99] Further east, Kreuzberg Sturm 27 met at the restaurant Wiener Garten. The large size of the establishment meant that the Wiener Garten was used also for leadership training courses, HJ and national socialist student assemblies, and after January 1933 interrogation and imprisonment.[100]

Like the KPD's paramilitary organizations (the RFB, RJ, and to a lesser extent the KbgdF), the SA attracted many young unemployed men. Unlike the looser regulations of the RFB, all SA members were required to first join the NSDAP, but such rigorous standards were not always met in the chaotic days before January 30, 1933. In general, however, the NSDAP had much stricter rules for mass participation than the KPD. Linking the mass

[97] BA, NS22/2, Reich Propaganda Leadership memo to all Gaue concerning the July 1932 Reichstag election.

[98] BA, NS23/470, "Mitteilungen aus den Landeskriminalpolizeiamts (IA) Berlin," Nr. 14, July 15, 1931, p. 102740. Hitler claimed the SA had four hundred thousand members nationwide by 1932. The Berlin membership figure comes from Brücker, "Wohnen und Leben in SO 36" (1994), p. 369.

[99] For a fascinating description of all sites in the capital associated with the Nazi "Kampf um Berlin," see the party's own travel guide: Julius Engelbrechten and Hans Volz, *Wir wandern durch das nationalsozialistische Berlin: Ein Führer durch die Gedenkstätten des Kampfes um die Reichshauptstadt* (Munich: Zentralverlag der NSDAP, 1937).

[100] Brücker, "Wohnen und Leben in SO 36" (1994), pp. 370-1. Engelbrechten and Volz, the authors of *Wir wandern durch das nationalsozialistische Berlin* (1937), note that the old bowling alley, which was used to hold prisoners after the *Machtergreifung*, was renovated but only as a "meeting room" (p. 168).

organizations more closely to the party made it easier for the party leadership to keep an eye on the ambitions of the lower-level functionaries who ran the secondary organizations: Hitler Youth, Women's Corps, SA, and others. On a more ideological level, the prerequisite of party membership also helped to ensure that all new recruits were first introduced to the Nazi worldview before joining other national socialist organizations; whereas the KPD tried to mobilize people according to class with the goal of eventually educating them in communism. Therefore, only male Nazis could rightfully join the SA, but all male workers could join the RFB.

The SA was not just a propaganda tool but also the private army of the national socialist movement. Accordingly, one of its missions was to "protect" supporters of the party, including speakers at rallies and demonstrators. The nationalist element in SA propaganda continued to present a romanticized World War I front experience. Only in the last years of the republic, however, was the organization able to convince many veterans to reject the traditional right-wing nationalist veterans' association, the Stahlhelm. The emphasis on militarism and the founding myth of the organization, which was centered around the violent 1923 Munich Beer Hall Putsch, has led Martin Broszat to argue that "the *bündische* soldierly demeanor of the Free Corps movement was in fact more typical of many SA leaders (most of whom were former front line officers of World War I) than party loyalty."[101] This belligerent tradition was compelling to some of the young unemployed in Berlin, whose "nothing to lose" attitude and stronger connections to the socialist ideals of the workers' movement led to heated internal conflict between the party leadership in Munich and the SA and HJ in Berlin.

The conflict between the party and SA in Berlin culminated in an official break between the head of the Berlin SA, Walter Stennes, and the NSDAP in 1930.[102] Stennes and his men had been angered in the early summer months by Hitler's declaration that the party would only come to power by legal means, and by his purchase of a lavish villa in Munich (known as the Brown House) for party headquarters. These incidents were viewed as a betrayal of the revolutionary roots of the SA and as an affront to the hardships many SA men were suffering. By the end of August, SA units in Berlin were refusing to take their posts as guards at Nazi election rallies – a significant breach of duty – until more independence for the SA within the movement was granted. Although the climate improved temporarily when Hitler himself made peace with Stennes by assenting to some of his wishes, the fact remained that the

[101] Martin Broszat, *Hitler and the Collapse of Weimar Germany* (New York: Berg, 1987), p. 20.

[102] Stennes was perhaps too well suited for the job as commander of the Berlin and East German SA, having served valiantly in World War I and then continuing his military engagement in the Free Corps after the war's end and as an officer in the early republican Berlin police force (from which he was suspended). His military credentials and his revolutionary beliefs made him popular with his men but also led to the conflict with Hitler's policies.

Berlin SA believed that the party had distanced itself from its revolutionary goals. The following spring, Stennes was finally expelled from the party, but he did manage to take a number of Berlin SA men with him.[103] The party leadership, as well as the Berlin KPD, kept close watch on the fallout of what became known as the Stennes Revolt. In May 1931, the Berlin KPD leadership sent guidelines to its cells urging them to hold discussions with SA columns to measure the support for Stennes and to see if there was any hope for a full break between the SA and Hitler. Party literature suggested key phrases to sway borderline SA members on issues such as "Race struggle vs. Class struggle" and "Nationalism vs. Internationalism." Berlin's Communists were told to emphasize that, in contrast to the NSDAP, KPD members voted for their leaders.[104] The main branch of the Berlin SA, however, was quick to rebound from this mutiny. Whereas the RFB had once shown great strength on the streets of the capital, the SA was making significant strides in recruitment by the end of 1930.

The fact that all members of national socialist organizations were required to join the party helped the NSDAP avoid some of the bureaucratic confusion that burdened the KPD. The only exception to this rule was the National Socialist Factory Cell Organization (NSBO). The NSBO was a latecomer to the field of proliferating political organizations and was also unique within the Nazi movement for its grassroots origins.[105] The party leadership had never wanted to get into trade unionism, but when blue- and white-collar workers who supported the NSDAP found that they had no structures to compete with the Free Trade Unions of the SPD or even the struggling RGO of the KPD, they began to organize on their own. Wanting to keep track of the activities of these party supporters, Hitler was finally forced to create an organization to fit both their needs and his. The NSBO was never

---

[103] The NSDAP was quick to purge the SA of all who supported Stennes. Much has been written about the Stennes Revolt: see Broszat, *Hitler and the Collapse of Weimar Germany* (1987), pp. 20–2; and Richard Bessel, *Political Violence and the Rise of Nazism. The Storm Troopers in Eastern Germany, 1925–1934* (New Haven, CT: Yale University Press, 1984), pp. 62–5. For a contemporary account of the conflict written by an assistant to Stennes as a defense of his superior's actions, and edited by Stennes himself, see Stennes, ed., "Wie es zur Stennes-Aktion Kam!" in IfZ, Fa88/Fasz.83. In this account we also find evidence for the rivalry that had developed between the SA and SS.

[104] BA-SAPMO, RY1/I3/1-2/99b, "Rechtsinformation," Nr. 3, May 1931, pp. 580–1. Also BA, Rep. 15.01, Nr. 13123/4, "KPD Rechts-Inform," May 3, 1931. This document is a report summarizing the effects of the Stennes Revolt on most SA sections throughout the city. The report outlines the disruption and reorganization experienced after the break between the SA and Stennes and demonstrates both the interest the KPD had in the SA's affairs and the knowledge the Communists possessed about the SA's internal workings.

[105] For information on the NSBO, see Volker Kratzenberg, *Arbeiter auf dem Weg zu Hitler? Die Nationalsozialistische Betriebszellen-Organisation. Ihre Entstehung, ihre Programmatik, ihr Scheitern 1927–1934* (Frankfurt a. M.: Peter Lang, 1989) and Gunther Mai, "Die NSBO. Zum Verhältnis von Arbeiterschaft und Nationalsozialismus," *Vierteljahrshefte für Zeitgeschichte* (Vol. 31, No. 4, 1983), pp. 573–613.

allowed to call itself a union, however, because of Hitler's true disdain for the working-class movement and socialism. "The more we break through the Marxist factory front," reasoned the NSBO organizational leader in Berlin, "the easier it will be on other fronts, to destroy our main opposition – which remains Marxism."[106] By 1929, local leaders within the Berlin NSBO reported significant growth in the financial sector and transportation and metal industries but complained that the organization "hung in the air" because it lacked political leadership from the party, and because the individual cells had little contact with one another. "Total disorganization" was even said to characterize the situation, and it was feared that the party line would not be adequately represented at the workplace.[107] This fear persisted partly because the NSBO remained the one organization in which nonparty members could participate, as long as they were willing to be educated and "represent the ideas of National Socialism in the factory."[108]

Similar to the Communist hierarchy, Nazi Party members were organized into residential cells at the base of the party. These units were collectively organized into a *Sektion*, which with others formed an *Ortsgruppe* (local group). The Berlin Gau was comprised of these *Ortsgruppen*. Next to the SA, the HJ was considered by far the most important mass organization, since its members graduated to the SA and party membership at age eighteen. Because of the strong competition among youth organizations, led by the Wandervogel movement and socialist clubs since the late nineteenth century, the HJ grew slowly. At the end of 1929, all the national socialist youth organizations together counted fewer than thirteen thousand members throughout the republic. By January 1932, the number had grown to 37,304, and on the eve of Hitler's Chancellorship there were 55,365 young Germans participating in NSDAP-sponsored organizations.[109] There were over one thousand members of the HJ alone in Berlin by the start of 1932.[110]

Both radical parties were fighting for the support of German youth, but their respective attempts to involve women in their political struggles cannot be compared. The KPD may have had a muddled relationship with female workers, but the NSDAP was explicit in its policy of limiting women's

---

[106] BA, NS18/5025, Reinhold Muchow, Organisationsleiter der NSBO, "Nationalsozialistische Betriebszellen. Das Vernichtungsinstrument gegen den Betriebesmarxismus," no date, p. 2.
[107] BA, NS22/1049, "Bericht über die Betriebszellen-Organisation des Gaues Gross-Berlin," July 30, 1929.
[108] BA, NS18/5025, Reinhold Muchow, Organisationsleiter der NSBO, "Nationalsozialistische Betriebszellen. Das Vernichtungsinstrument gegen den Betriebesmarxismus," no date, p. 5.
[109] Statistics provided by Günter Kaufmann, *Das kommende Deutschland: Die Erziehung der Jugend in Reich Adolf Hitlers* (Berlin: Junker und Dünnhaupt, 1940), p. 39. The same table is found in Peter Stachura, *Nazi Youth in the Weimar Republic* (Santa Barbara, CA: Clio, 1975), p. 269.
[110] Stachura, *Nazi Youth* (1975), p. 267. Stachura reports that the 631 HJ members in Berlin in 1931 had grown to 1,080 in one year.

participation. The chief women's organization, Frauenschaft, and the girls' Bund deutscher Mädel (BDM) were not comparable to any male associations, and their activities consisted of little more than performing charity works, studying home economics, singing folk songs, and learning the importance of maintaining "racial purity."[111] The BDM was not an independent association, nor was it the junior section of the Frauenschaft. It was thought that the Frauenschaft was concerned "purely [with] charity work" and that the girls also needed training in "ethical-cultural" matters.[112] As a result, the BDM was a subordinate section of the HJ.

Presumably large numbers of women in the party were satisfied with what they believed to be the party's respect for femininity and motherhood, but not all Nazi women were pleased with the limitations on their political participation.[113] In September 1932, a high-ranking female leader in Berlin wrote directly to Hitler with the following complaint:

The entire leadership of the Berlin BDM and that is over 120 women have directed me to ask you to review and correct the part of the new service instructions which deal with the women's corps. What stands is not acceptable for real women, the kind of women our country needs and the kind we want our girls to become. If these commands remain as they are, the women's corps will no longer attract thinking women with pride and self-worth. It will only bring together modest women, whose horizons do not go past [charitable] collections and potato peeling. And I feel sorry for the movement and the men who are dependent on such women.[114]

Her complaint most certainly fell on deaf ears, for the Nazi and KPD organizations alike both prioritized the goals and needs of the men in their movements. Much of the cachet of the SA came from its connection to Hitler and the ideal of the upstanding man of action. Although the closeness between the SS and Hitler eventually overshadowed that of the SA, in these early years the Stormtroopers were viewed as Hitler's comrades, the successors of those who fought with him in the 1923 Munich Beer Hall Putsch. The air of respectability surrounding the SA was aided by their uniforms and the more lenient treatment they received from the press and courts. For many reasons, the SA was a difficult target for republican officials who might have favored outlawing the organization. Since the SA was an official arm of the NSDAP, a ban on the SA could be construed as a ban on a political party,

---

[111] For information on the NS-Frauenschaft during the Third Reich, see Claudia Koonz, *Mothers in the Fatherland: Women, the Family and Nazi Politics* (New York: St. Martin's Press, 1987) and Jill Stephenson, *The Nazi Organisation of Women* (London: Croom Helm, 1981).

[112] BA, NS22/420, *HJ Zeitung*, 1931, "Wir lehnen den politischen Amazonentyp in jeder Form und Gestalt ab."

[113] For more on why working women might have been attracted to the NSDAP during Weimar, see Helen Boak, "National Socialism and Working-Class Women Before 1933" in Conan Fischer, ed., *The Rise of National Socialism and the Working Classes in Weimar Germany* (Providence: Berghahn Books, 1996).

[114] BA, NS22/1049, letter of September 7, 1932.

and that did not seem to correspond to the political freedom outlined in the constitution. By safeguarding the openness of party politics in this manner, the SA was endowed with a political legitimacy never enjoyed by the RFB or other mass organizations tied to the KPD. Among the SA rank-and-file, this legitimacy translated into a not unfounded confidence that their political behavior, even when violent, would be tolerated.

Unlike the image of the SA, the KPD had the allure of the forbidden. Its large paramilitary organization had been banned, issues of the *RF* were confiscated on a regular basis, and everyone knew that the police were most suspicious of those wearing the red star of the Soviet Union. Like "hanging around with the wrong crowd" in school, even among other workers, Communists were looked down upon as rabble-rousers and heavy drinkers. The wealthier western half of the city may have had no respect for the KPD, believing its supporters to be little more than unemployed hoodlums, but they did fear it. For many men embittered by the drudgery of industrialized work, the monotony of rationalization, or – especially during the Depression – the boredom of unemployment, the thrill of generating fear helped mitigate their own feelings of persecution.

A second attraction of the Communist and Nazi Parties was their radical visions of the future. It is difficult to quantify how many KPD supporters seriously believed in revolution. Privately, party functionaries in Berlin were certainly not convinced that their followers were ready to take up arms or even risk unemployment in order to lead a political strike. Nonetheless, the party skillfully made use of propaganda which made a "Soviet Germany" seem like a pleasant reality. The workers' weekly, the *Arbeiter-Illustrierte-Zeitung*, and other party publications were resplendent with pictures of young, happy, healthy Soviet workers, athletes, and mothers. The image created by pro-Soviet propaganda was strong enough to entice a few Germans, not just intellectuals, into moving to the USSR for a period to see the workers' paradise in operation. This experience was sometimes a shocking disappointment. The Soviet ideal was powerful enough, however, for the NSDAP to make a concerted effort to disabuse Berlin's workers of the notion that the Soviets had achieved all the KPD claimed. Those disenchanted with the USSR were welcomed at Nazi rallies in the capital to tell horror stories of starvation and a failed Soviet economy. In one such case at an assembly in the city district of Friedrichshain, one man even passed around Soviet bread so audience members could inspect and taste its poor quality.[115]

The Nazi vision of the future was less coherent than that of the KPD, and it is impossible to assess the appeal of each aspect of party rhetoric. Within the SA there was disagreement as to whether the NSDAP ought to be working toward revolution or not. But members did agree that, once in power, the

---

[115] *Vorwärts*, "Neumann-Goebbels-Theater. Grosse Vorstellung am Friedrichshain – Heinz Neumann zweiter Sieger," Nr. 107, October 29, 1930.

party would provide order. The merry-go-round of Weimar's governing cabinets and coalitions, the influence of Marxism, and the obligations imposed on Germany by the Allies would all be ended. Order also meant financial security and a reestablishment of conservative bourgeois values at home. To those ends, women's roles in the public sphere would be limited to the benefit of men, and at the national level the Führer appeared as a father figure who would lead Germany into the promised land. By citing "Jewish influence" at every turn as the cause of Germany's increasing woes, it was also clear that in the Third Reich measures would be taken at the very least to isolate Jewish interests and curtail assimilation.

A third feature that attracted supporters to the radical organizations was the opportunity for activism. Male paramilitary members who had lost their jobs had also lost the camaraderie and structured order of the workplace. In 1932, a female Nazi Party member described how men and their families reacted to unemployment in the NSDAP Gau-Berlin bulletin, *Die Berliner Front*:

With the loss of work the needed earnings are not all that is taken from the man, his sense of life is also taken. The unemployed man sees the ground beneath his feet disappear and with it his position and rank are gone. Through the work place, the worker had his place within the community of human society. By losing work, he loses his justification to be, and not only in the community of the Volk, but also in his small family circle.[116]

In addition to the uniform and identity card that came with membership in most political organizations, participation meant a circle of friends, a pub to pass the time in, a cause to support, and activities to fill the otherwise long, empty day. In *Kämpfende Jugend*, Walter Schönstedt describes the activities of a handful of Communist youth in the Nostizstraße Kiez. One of the strengths of this fictional account of Communist street politics is that it shows more accurately than most of the workers' literature from this period the boredom, frustration, and hunger faced by these young men.[117] The characters, however, do have each other, and they fill the day by circulating propaganda, holding meetings about the lack of factory organizing, and drinking a beer or two when they can afford it. This daily agenda differed little from that of the far right. Beyond traditional forms of political activism, organizations at both ends of the spectrum kept their supporters busy with sports and weekend trips, and both the NSDAP and KPD worked diligently

---

[116] IfZ, Db203.07, Irma Fiebig, "Die Gefährtin des Arbeitslosen," in *Die Berliner Front*, October 29, 1932.

[117] Compare, for example, Walter Schönstedt's, *Kämpfende Jugend* (Berlin: Oberbaumverlag, 1972; original edition, Berlin: Internationalen-Arbeiter Verlag, 1932) to Willi Bredel's *Maschinenfabrik N. & K. Ein Roman aus dem proletarischen Alltag* (Berlin: Aufbau Verlag, 1982; original edition, Vienna: Internationaler Arbeiter-Verlag, 1930).

to finance summer excursions and stays outside of Berlin for youngsters, even during the Depression.

For the unemployed male worker, the only other option might be to stay home in what was considered the feminine sphere. Besides the fact that doing household chores or minding children was considered demeaning to most men, workers' apartments were exceedingly small and cramped. The 1932 article in *Die Berliner Front* describes the problems created by this alternative:

Through the continued presence of the man at home, the normal rhythm of family life is destroyed. Even more so in the smaller apartments, the tightness of shared space and the unequal work distribution – the woman is mostly overburdened by the difficult upkeep of the home – leads to unwished and often unintentional friction.

The man feels expendable, he becomes helpless, cramped and nervous. More and more he loses his self-confidence, the necessary foundation for successful productivity, which has been buried by the humiliation of the welfare system, the useless job applications, the sitting in waiting rooms, and the "sympathy of good friends."[118]

It is easy to see why a wife or mother would not want to share the little space in which she had to work, especially with a man who was of little use to her. Likewise, it made sense for men to seek out any escape from this process of emasculation, and an escape that allowed them to combat their feelings of powerlessness with bravado, physical challenge, and militarism would be especially attractive.

Keeping party members and sympathizers busy, however, exacted a heavy toll on the radical organizations. The vast numbers of party posters, brochures, and newsletters printed during election campaigns were expensive. In addition to the regular costs of running a large political organization, supporters hoped for, and even expected, a fourth feature of radical activism: material compensation for their hard work. The KPD had the most trouble fulfilling the needs and demands of its members. In part this was the result of mismanagement, but mostly it was caused by the low level of contributions from the Communist rank-and-file. Feared and despised by all the moneyed sectors of society, the Berlin KPD could never compete with the financial expenditures of the NSDAP or SPD. The ZK was still able to fund the mass demonstrations, party congresses, and bureaucratic network necessary to keep the movement afloat, but financial instability hurt the KPD on the streets. In contrast, the perception of the NSDAP was that it had money to burn. For the most part, the NSDAP image benefited from financial solvency, but when the party seemed to spend extravagantly so that a few top leaders could live in luxury, the party's perceived wealth bred feelings of jealousy and betrayal at the local level.

---

[118] IfZ, Db203.07, Irma Fiebig, "Die Gefährtin des Arbeitslosen" in *Die Berliner Front*, October 29, 1932.

The most common type of aid was food and clothing collections, made especially during the winter months. The SA had success, for example, in Kreuzberg offering "free" boots to new recruits.[119] Another expanding mode of assistance was the *Heime* for unemployed single male party members. These barracks were used extensively by the paramilitary SA. The KPD would have had trouble financing such a network of barracks in Berlin, even if the illegal status of its paramilitary wing had not made it impossible. The men received not only shelter and food but also the camaraderie, familial structure, and hierarchy many were seeking. The NSDAP was well aware of the emotional support these homes provided. SA Chief of Staff Ernst Röhm sent instructions down the chain of command in the summer of 1931 outlining the need for increased local assistance to SA men. He reasoned that, since the presidential decree of March 1931 had drastically curtailed legal demonstrations, the opportunities for his men to gain comfort from activism had been limited.[120] In exchange for the camaraderie offered by the *Heime*, the SA was able through the barrack system to gather twenty or so men in one location; this made these buildings the launching points for offensives, as well as the objects of attack. The KPD was largely limited to the cheaper option of providing meals and other types of assistance from central points, but it was common knowledge in the capital that the NSDAP had a better response to the basic "*Magenfrage*" (stomach question, in the words of Gregor Strasser).[121] As the political climate grew more violent in the early 1930s, both the KPD and NSDAP found ways to support financially those injured or killed in the line of duty and to help those who had been arrested for political crimes by providing legal assistance and even birthday and Christmas packages in prison.[122]

Employment opportunities were also expected by party members and sympathizers. The parties did not want to bankroll their supporters, but there was a rivalry between the two parties to provide the best services, and their leaders knew that if members felt slighted by a lack of party support in return for their loyalty they might try their luck with the competition. While many jobs were strictly voluntary, it was not uncommon for supporters in Berlin to attempt to get paid positions within these political organizations. When the

---

[119] One former Kreuzberg resident remembered the popularity of the *Stiefelschlacht*, or boot-offensive. See Bernd Busch, "'Nur politisch ... denn hast doch keene Freizeit mehr'" in Kunstamt Kreuzberg, ed., *Kreuzberg 1933. Ein Bezirk erinnert sich* (Berlin: Dürchschlag, 1983), p. 93.

[120] BA, NS26/306, OSAF command, June 26, 1931.

[121] BA, NS22/428, NSDAP Chief of Administration Gregor Strasser to the Gaue leaderships, August 26, 1932. The attraction of free meals is discussed further in Alf Lüdtke, "Hunger in der Großen Depression: Hungererfahrung und Hungerpolitik am Ende der Weimarer Republik," in *Archiv für Sozialgeschichte* (Vol. 27, 1987), pp. 145–76.

[122] BA, NS22/428, NSDAP Chief of Administration Gregor Strasser to the Gaue leaderships, November 21, 1932.

Berlin KPD received a visit in early 1932 from a Kreuzberg man claiming to be an ardent supporter requesting an active, paying job within the party structure, his plea was turned down, even though he claimed to be well known by the Communists who frequented the Nostiz Kiez party pub, Tante Emma. This "committed Communist" had made the mistake of admitting that he had first offered his services to the NSDAP, but had been "shown the door" by Joseph Goebbels.[123] Especially at election time, the Depression's effects could be seen in the letters sent to the NSDAP-*Reichspropagandaleitung* suggesting campaign slogans, designs for election posters, and other gimmicks such as Nazi calendars. Although these ideas were unsolicited, their authors often requested financial compensation in exchange for the use of the suggestion. And as in the previous example, when their ideas were rejected, or they were refused jobs in other capacities, some moved on to offer the same marketing strategies to other parties.[124] One man wrote to Hitler directly, offering to make monthly oral presentations on German poetry and culture for a small fee "to help me and also my family."[125] Another who worked at Berlin's Tempelhof airport floated to Gau headquarters the idea of painting "Vote NSDAP" on the underside of a plane. He even calculated that the plane could be flown over the city before the upcoming Reichstag elections at the cost of 150 RM per hour.[126]

If republican discipline was a complex tribute to democratic idealism, then Nazi discipline was a visible manifestation of order. While the ideal Reichsbanner man was like a sentry guarding the eternal flame for a republic missing in action, his counterpart in the SA sought to demonstrate the power of the movement in the present day. The orders sent down from the national SA leadership (OSAF) made clear that SA discipline was to be reflected in all aspects of Stormtrooper operations. Pages and pages of instructions about uniform detailing, flag colors, and the correct sizes and proportions of the emblems to be used on banners were issued on a regular basis to regional and local SA leaders. In addition to "protecting the movement from outside terror . . . carrying out propaganda and the training of young male [party] members," the chief aim of the SA, as explained by party headquarters, was the "disciplining of the masses."[127] This is not to say that such orders were

---

[123] BA-SAPMO, RY1/I3/1-2/93, report on E. K., March 3, 1932, p. 222. Somehow the cell also got hold of a letter E. K. had written to Goebbels, which included a sample of this Kreuzberg author's writing: "Wach endlich auf deutscher Proletarier." See BA-SAPMO, RY1/I3/1-2/93, letter from E. K. to Joseph Goebbels, February 4, 1932, p. 224.

[124] BA, NS18/1512. The printing company promised not to offer the calendar idea to any other parties in the upcoming 1930 elections but could only promise this exclusivity if the NSDAP acted quickly on their bid.

[125] Ibid., September 1930.

[126] Ibid., July 1930.

[127] BA, NS26/304, September 1929, "OSAF Richtlinien für die Neuaufstellung von SA-Gruppen."

always followed. In 1932, SA Chief of Staff Ernst Röhm complained about the lack of uniformity in recent public appearances by his men. Although he understood that the economic crisis had made it difficult to purchase all required clothing and gear, he insisted that some visual uniformity be preserved:

Whoever does not own a complete service suit must march in a white or at least a light shirt with brown suspenders, breeches, high boots, or puttee and suitable shoes. Also short leather pants with white stockings and black or brown shoes is permissible. With this outfit a hat is to be worn, no work caps, and all mixes of civil and service uniforms are prohibited. What does belong in this outfit is the party badge on the suspender and the arm band on the left upper arm. . . . Forbidden is the wearing of long pants and the carrying of items in the hand or under the arm (leather cases, coats etc.). Also children and dogs have no place in the marching column.[128]

The conservative newspaper *Der Berliner Lokal-Anzeiger* criticized the Reichsbanner's lack of military discipline to demonstrate that the reorganization of the Reichsbanner at the end of 1930 had done nothing to transform the organization into an effective force. The newspaper argued that the failure of the RB men to impress those who watched the massive rally, which had been designed specifically to exhibit the RB's new fighting spirit, was evidence of poor training and indifference among the troops: "With backpacks and without, with coats and without, the troops stood before their leader, and while he spoke some Schufos put their hands in their pockets, shifted from one foot to the other in the cold, and spoke undisturbed among themselves."[129] Reichsbanner military training was deemed inadequate, but the attack on their level of ideological discipline, represented by the men's disinterest toward their leader's speech, was a much harsher condemnation.

In contrast to this image of the Reichsbanner, the orderly uniforms and marches of the NSDAP were to reflect the members' commitment to the movement, to "the idea" of national socialism, and to the leadership of Adolf Hitler.[130] The Nazi Party attempted to generate strict discipline in many ways other than public marches. First, as described previously, membership in the party was taken very seriously. Only those too young to join were permitted to participate in the party's organizations without NSDAP membership. While the SPD and KPD tried to expand their ranks through inclusion, the NSDAP was more successful by emphasizing the exclusivity of

---

[128] BA, NS23/2, "OSAF: SA-Aufmärsche," July 7, 1932.

[129] *Der Berliner Lokal-Anzeiger*, Nr. 91, February 23, 1931.

[130] On the development of Hitler's image, from the simple "drummer up" of the early movement to the heroic "Führer" by 1933, see Ian Kershaw, *The 'Hitler Myth': Image and Reality in the Third Reich* (New York: Oxford University Press, 1987).

the party.[131] The perception of the party as a club whose fringe benefits now, and in the future, could only be enjoyed by members was an attractive incentive to get on board. Second, by becoming a member, one pledged loyalty to Hitler. It was assumed even by local Berlin functionaries that such leadership would overcome "the danger that the great [ideological] line could be blurred by the assimilation [of new members]."[132] This loyalty to Hitler and his ideas, however, would not be sustained by blind faith alone or even by soup kitchens and election posters. Rather, daily activism was necessary in order to demonstrate as well as foster discipline, so that the movement would grow not only in size but in strength, becoming "able to follow the smallest hand gesture of the Führer."[133] Education was also taken seriously within the party. Once again, it was not the inclusive education of the public as sought by republicans. Instead the focus was on the creation of a cadre of leaders who would then train those they led. Leadership training classes were set up around the nation to cover all aspects of the Nazi *Weltanschauung*, including culture, geopolitical forces, and racism. This curriculum proved to be a heavy load for students, so that preparatory schools also were set up to teach the basic tenets of discipline: physical fitness, command and reporting techniques, and front maneuvers. The role of this preparatory education was to make the future leaders more ready and able to process the national socialist worldview.[134]

The goal of these measures to instill discipline was also to control the politicization process and the instruments of supporters' participation. Just as the interior ministry sought ways to influence the news received by filmgoers, the NSDAP tried to regulate the ways in which its supporters viewed the political climate. The homes for SA men were a great means for keeping these men together, *away* from those who might convince them to give up their newly found political engagement, and *with* those who would support and even lead them. In addition to the leadership schools, starting in 1932 the SA printed educational pamphlets to discipline the mind. The first in the series began: "We SA men are no military, we are also not political speech makers. We want to be the political soldiers of the Nazi movement of Adolf Hitler. Therefore, it must be our job – next to the care given to physical fitness in the military sport sense – to be politically schooled, so that we are in the condition, at any moment and in any spot, to represent our national socialist ideas in action."[135] Each volume in the series presented articles on

---

[131] This strategy was employed in the years immediately following 1933. By constantly threatening to limit and even end new memberships in the party, Nazi leaders always succeeded in increasing enrollment.

[132] BA, NS18/5004, letter from a local Berlin propaganda functionary to Heinrich Himmler, January 7, 1929.

[133] Ibid.

[134] BA, NS26/306, OSAF command, October 29, 1931.

[135] BA, NS26/311, *Der Politische Soldat*, Nr. 1, September 15, 1932.

current policies or thematic interests of the party, followed by a short quiz to test comprehension.

The concept of Nazi discipline for women, however, was different than that for men. Whereas men were to become disciplined through their participation in the larger body of men, becoming one with the movement, the party emphasized the importance of "self-discipline" for its female members. Members of the women's corps were also "fighters for the German idea," but their contribution was in presenting an image of disciplined femininity. The main avenue allowed them for political expression was in their role as childrearers. "Through the personal example that we set [for our children] in our self-discipline and steadfastness, they will be raised to develop personalities which will once again bring honor to the nation and enrich community life."[136] The difference was just as pronounced between the regulations concerning the young men's association, the Hitler Jugend, and the Bund deutscher Mädel. As Claudia Koonz has argued: "Boys heard the command to act; girls to be."[137] For example, the party leadership did not allow the BDM to march, because "[i]f the BDM was to make the impression during parades of a girl-battalion, it would destroy the image of our work to educate female youth. We reject every masculinization [of the girls]. We must require what fits girls. We know that such a style will develop, when nothing foreign disturbs it – marching is foreign! To move in file and discipline, girls must be prevailed upon to do that!"[138] Hitler himself ordered that even during the party's mass rallies no women or girls were to march by him. Instead he took the time to pass by them approvingly.[139]

The KPD hoped to defend its ideological authority and hierarchical party structure, while distancing itself from the control exhibited by the NSDAP over its supporters. As a result there was an attempt to differentiate between bourgeois and proletarian discipline. As one observer explained in 1930: "Proletarian discipline seeks order not subordination. It calls for understanding which benefits the whole, individual thinking and shared responsibility."[140] Nonetheless, like the SA-man who was a "political soldier" of the Nazi movement, the RFB-man was a "political soldier of the Red class-front." Self-control was the first duty of this military ideal: "He must always carry himself so that the image of the Red class-front is not injured or weakened in any way. He doesn't gamble or drink, he trains his body,

---

[136] BA, NS22/452, "Grundsätze der NS – Frauenschaft," September 26, 1932.

[137] Koonz, *Mothers in the Fatherland* (1987), p. 196.

[138] BA, NS26/345, "Richtlinien für den Bund deutscher Mädel," not dated.

[139] Ibid. See also, BA, NS22/420, *HJ Zeitung*, 1931, "Wir lehnen den politischen Amazonentyp in jeder Form und Gestalt ab."

[140] Paul Franken, *Vom Werden einer neuen Kultur: Aufgaben der Arbeiter-Kultur-und-Sportorganisationen* (Berlin: e. Laubsche, 1930), quoted by Adelheid von Saldern, "Arbeiterkulturbewegung in Deutschland in der Zwischenkriegszeit" in Friedhelm Boll, ed., *Arbeiterkulturen zwischen Alltag und Politik* (Vienna: Europa-Verlag, 1986), p. 42.

is disciplined. He is always a helpful friend to workers and the oppressed and an unrelenting enemy to the oppressor and class-opponent."[141] There are a number of reasons why this focus on social mores was common in KPD writings. Alcohol abuse was prevalent in workers' communities, and alcohol dependence reduced the effectiveness of activism and led at times to unwanted violence. Drunkenness and rowdy behavior added to the negative image many Berliners had of Communists. Although the KPD pretended not to care about public opinion – its goal after all was revolution, not a majority in the Reichstag – it did take itself seriously as a player in the German political scene and wanted others to do so as well. While the party did not make any dramatic effort to bring drinking among workers under control, it did often make official statements against alcohol.

Though the KPD was conscious of the need to keep nonmember sympathizers active without forcing them to join the party itself, the Berlin KPD leadership never wavered from its belief that the most disciplined units within the party should be "the factory cells . . . comprised of proletarians, who are to be regarded as the real avant-garde of workers."[142] Beyond factory party cells, all KPD members were expected to exhibit exemplary discipline in their capacity as part of the party faction within the RFB, or any other Communist organization such as the RGO, Fichte sport clubs, or KbgdF. The "faction-discipline" of members entailed superior enthusiasm and commitment to the organization, since they acted as the link between the mass organizations and the party. It was also hoped that these men, as the most dependable, would defend the organization against any attempts at infiltration by spies. The Communist members were also to be the salesmen of the party. They were expected to win over to membership the sympathizers within the RFB and other organizations by exhibiting unwavering support of the KPD and its policies. To these ends it was stressed that Communists were never to show signs of discord among themselves. One description of the faction's duties within the RFB noted that the paramilitary organization was "no debate club" and that its KPD members, above all, were to display "strict discipline and internal cohesion."[143]

In contrast to the NSDAP's popular faith in Hitler or even in Joseph Goebbels in Berlin before 1933, the members of the KPD never held the same type of admiration for any of their party's leaders. The KPD did have ideological patriarchs in Marx, and more so in Lenin, and its ideals for activism came from the martyred efforts of Karl Liebknecht and Rosa Luxemburg. But all these figures were dead, and Comrade Stalin was too distant to foster

---

[141] BA-SAPMO, RY1/I4/2/7, RFB Membership book, not dated.
[142] BLHA, Rep. 30, Berlin C, Title 95, Sektion 9, Teil II, Nr. 88, Bd. 2, "Sekretariat des BL Berlin an alle UB-, Ortsgruppen-, Betriebs-, und Strassenzellenleitungen," July 3, 1930.
[143] BA-SAPMO, RY1/I4/2/7, "Richtlinien über Aufgabe der Fraktionen im RFB," October 1926.

any sense of loyalty or even personal interest among Berlin's rank-and-file Communists.[144] Ernst Thälmann, chairman of the KPD and presidential candidate in 1925 and 1932, was a skilled politician who, with Stalin's help, saved his career from numerous scandals and infighting through the years, but he too never enjoyed a popular following among the party's members. Rather the party relied on its idols of the past to attract new members and represent proletarian discipline. The annual memorial demonstration on the anniversary of Liebknecht's and Luxemburg's murders in the capital was a highlight on the KPD calendar. The city's Communists participated in well-attended marches from the Eden Hotel, where the two leaders were ambushed in 1919, to the cemetery where they were buried. There were also a number of skilled speakers in the party who were able to draw large crowds in these final years, but the party did nothing to promote them as personalities.

Like their competitors, the KPD's main strategy for instilling discipline was through education. There are hints of condescension in many party directives, which complain about the lack of understanding of communism by Berlin's party members. The KPD produced massive amounts of party literature. Topics ranged from the "ABC's of Building Street Cells" to novels and booklets describing tactics for street fighting. Every organization connected to the party had its own national newspaper, and many local weekly bulletins were also published. The party organized the production of school newspapers, radio enthusiast magazines, and literature about life in the Soviet Union. These brochures and newspapers were sold door-to-door, through subscription, and at party rallies and demonstrations. H. R. Knickerbocker, the American researcher who visited German cities during 1932, commented that the average Communist spent 15 percent of his monthly wages on party literature and dues.[145] This estimate for literature expenditure is certainly too high for the average KPD sympathizer, and many party members also likely received printed material secondhand, but the drive to educate through the written word was successful enough that the party's opponents tried to emulate the KPD's publishing strategies. In the summer of 1931, the Nazi Reich propaganda leadership announced the appearance of a new NSDAP-monthly series *Der Flammenwerfer* (The Flame-thrower) as "a necessity to compete with the flood of cheap Marxist agitational publications."[146] Months later

---

[144] Pictures of Marx, Lenin, Lassalle, Bebel, Luxemburg, Liebknecht, and even Friedrich Ebert hung in the homes of Berlin's workers, demonstrating loyalty and admiration for these past leaders of socialism. However, current leaders Ernst Thälmann and Joseph Stalin were not revered in this way. Erich Fromm, *The Working Class in Weimar Germany: A Psychological and Sociological Study*, (Oxford: Berg, 1984; original edition, 1929), p. 131. Survey originally carried out in 1929.

[145] H. R. Knickerbocker, *Deutschland so oder so?* (Berlin: Rowohlt, 1932b), p. 14.

[146] BA, NS26/285, "Monatsbericht der Reichpropagandaleitung," Nr. 6, December 1931.

they lauded the steps taken to increase the production of party literature, but admitted that the KPD still well outpaced them in the circulation of party reading materials.[147]

In early Weimar, the KPD was so focused on political recruitment and building financial stability – and so intent on disassociating themselves from the outing clubs, women's teas, and cultural associations of social democracy, which were condemned as bourgeois – that it did little to develop the social side of party life.[148] At first it did not seem problematic that most KPD members, as former SPD or USPD members, simply maintained their connections to the workers' social clubs. Tension existed mostly between those who were politically active and those who were not. One former Fichte member in Kreuzberg recounted: "We had our meetings every four weeks. We would discuss sports, association news, and beyond that politics. That's when there were differences: 'Oh, here it goes again with politics,' [some members would say and then] stand up and leave.... And the others, who were interested in politics, stayed. These were the Social Democratic and Communist leaning [members]."[149] But as the 1920s came to an end and tension between the two parties grew, discord between SPD and KPD members developed in the mixed social organizations. In Berlin this strain often led to a split in the group, and some members would go off and form their own separate organization. Where once there had been a Workers' Small Caliber Shooting Club, for example, there was now also a Revolutionary Workers' Small Caliber Shooting Club.

Even then the body that organized these new clubs, the Fighting Association for Red Sport Unity (Kampfgemeinschaft für Rote Sporteinheit), admitted that "a large section of the working class still follow[ed] those masquerading as socialists[;] however," they added with hope, "the strength of this political betrayal was breaking more and more under the influence of the Opposition."[150] Sportsmen in Neukölln agreed that, with a little education, the KPD clubs would surely be able to win over those workers still socializing with and voting for the SPD and other parties because "it was mostly out of ignorance, that workers joined these types [SPD and bourgeois] of sports

---

[147] BA, NS26/284, "Monatsbericht der Reichpropagandaleitung," Abteilung Nachrichtendienst, November 1931, Nr. 5.

[148] For a text about workers' culture in the pre-1914 period, see Vernon Lidtke, *The Alternative Culture* (Oxford: Oxford University Press, 1985).

[149] Oral interview of Erwin E. collected by Heide Kortwich, "Kulturelle Sozialisation im Arbeiter- und Handwerkeralltag von 1900–1933; eine Fallstudie als Beitrag zur Stadt- und Alltagsgeschichtlichen Kulturarbeit" (unpublished Diplomarbeit, Freie Universität Berlin, 1989), p. 166.

[150] BA-SAPMO, RY1/I4/10/2, Kampfgemeinschaft für Rote Sporteinheit membership book, February 1932.

club."[151] The Kampfgemeinschaft had two goals concerning discipline. The first was to recondition the "bodies and spirits" of workers, which had been worn down more than ever before by the increasingly "refined methods of [shop floor] rationalization."[152] The second goal was the popularization of "defense-sports," which were to be practiced by the "masses" and not just "elite troops." The activities within this category included track and field, marksmanship, and martial arts.[153] The combination of physical training and political education was thought essential to develop the sort of discipline needed for the revolution.

Surprisingly perhaps, sport was also used as a way to attract women to the party. The propaganda aimed at Communist women, though, was less about physical discipline or preparedness for the coming revolution and more about constructing a beautiful body. One women's sporting magazine, *Frau und Sport*, was replete with photographs of beautiful Soviet female athletes, often trim swimmers in form-enhancing suits. Photographs of smiling, toned "revolutionary" women provided stark contrast to adjoining articles about Nazi plans for implementing "work-service" for women or the efforts of a bourgeois women's organization to prepare for war against the Soviet Union by practicing the use of gas masks. The reader is left wondering whether the most serious crime is targeting the USSR or donning the aesthetically displeasing gas masks.[154]

Communist women were also special targets for disciplining education because of their role as mothers. Although the party professed equality, party propaganda did not question that women still performed the bulk of the household work and childrearing. Therefore, it was essential that these women be educated. Otherwise, even with the best intentions, it was assumed that most would raise their children in an "unproletarian" manner. In 1931, the party sought their attention and votes by printing the first issue of the women's magazine *Der Weg der Frau*. While the magazine promised to include essays on "science, medicine, politics and economics," it was duly noted that space would also be devoted to "clothing, proletarian house-keeping...and a children's section. This magazine is at first glance incomparably more interesting than bourgeois housewives' journals and above all cheaper."[155] Election propaganda aimed at women was based on separate,

[151] BA-SAPMO, SgY2/V/DF/VIII/38ü, *Neuköllner Kraftfahrer*, Nr. 1, likely 1931. This first bulletin of the Neukölln district motorcycle club was trying to explain its need for a monthly publication.

[152] BA-SAPMO, RY1/I4/10/2, Kampfgemeinschaft für Rote Sporteinheit membership book, February 1932.

[153] BA-SAPMO, RY1/I4/10/2, *Die Spartakiade*, Nr. 1, February 1931.

[154] BA-SAPMO, RY1/I4/10/2, *Frau und Sport. Zeitung für alle werktätige Sportlerinnen*, Nr. 1, July 1932.

[155] BA-SAPMO, RY1/I4/15/3, *Die Frauendelegierte*, Nr. 2, March 1931.

lower expectations of female Communists' understanding of "revolutionary discipline." As late as March 1932, the KPD's National Committee for Working Women suggested to the party's women's groups in Berlin the following oversimplified and inaccurate information to be used in the upcoming presidential election:

Who is Hindenburg? Hindenburg is a Field Marshal General and made the comment: 'I take a war like a spa bath!' . . . Behind Hindenburg stand capitalists, generals, dukes and barons. . . . Who is Hitler? Hitler was until recently a governmental administrator in Braunschweig. He is leader of the Nazis. The party, which under the instructions of capitalists, beats up workers [sic]. The Nazis treat working women as inferior and want them to be the slave, servant and maid to the man. . . . Who is Ernst Thälmann? Ernst Thälmann is a transportation worker and the leader of the KPD. He represents the interests of working women and works hard for their demands. Ernst Thälmann is the candidate for peace.[156]

Clearly the party did not expect women to be disciplined in a military sense, since their own candidate, Thälmann, is presented to women as a candidate for peace and order, not revolution.

This chapter has provided a sketch of some of the chief political options available to workers in Berlin. The weakening of the traditional dominance of the SPD among Berlin's laboring citizens led the SPD and RB to call for greater republican discipline, which would close the ranks against the aggressive competition from the right and the left. Though praising the republic was the goal, the section on the *Verfassungstag* holiday illustrates the difficulty republican supporters faced in finding an acceptable vernacular for celebrating the republic.

Competing visions of political discipline have also been examined. The discipline demanded by the Reichsbanner should not be seen, however, as a simple reaction to the radicalism of national socialism. Nor should the claim of revolutionary readiness by the KPD be interpreted solely as desperation caused by unemployment, or the uniformed militarism of national socialism be viewed alone as a manifestation of the will to power. Instead, in combination with these factors, the three parties were playing off each other – borrowing one another's strategies. They were also responding to their own traditions and to Germany's past: the growth of liberalism in the mid-nineteenth century, World War I, the settlement and revolution at war's end, and the modernization of society and politics during Weimar. Most importantly, the three parties and state were reacting to the needs and demands of their constituencies. All were attempting to create structures and strategies that responded to many people's desire for greater engagement in solving the problems of the day. Appeals to unemployed young men were especially

---

[156] BA-SAPMO, RY1/I4/15/4, Instructions from the Reichskomitee werktätiger Frauen on the upcoming presidential election, March 3, 1932.

successful because they implied that restructuring the political order would signal a reinvigoration of masculinity and vice versa.

These institutions faced the increasingly difficult task, however, of trying to contain and control this activism so as to make it usable in achieving their ultimate goals of a strong republic, proletarian revolution, or national socialist Reich. In each case, an array of policies were introduced; these policies stressed ideological education, visual propaganda, entertainment, political tradition, social amelioration, and strong leadership to foster discipline in their ranks. For the SPD and Reichsbanner, and their advocates in the government, creating republican discipline was increasingly difficult once the taint of Depression-era austerity left little to recommend it. Problems also dogged the Communist and Nazi Parties. As membership rolls and bureaucracies grew in Berlin, it became harder still to foster any sort of discipline among supporters who were less well trained and more diverse. Leaders of both parties were wary of newcomers, especially in the crowded metropolis, who might not have the organizations' best interests at heart. They warned members to be suspicious of strangers who claimed to be friends and instructed them to watch for unusual behavior. "An SA group is never totally safe from spies," declared one SA instructional manual:

One can make [the spy's] infiltration more difficult, by checking in particular the political stance and dependability of each new recruit, especially in the city. In the case of unclear information, it is better not to take him in! . . . Also under other masks they will try to draw you out [for information]: at the beer table sits a friendly, welcoming, fat man, who shakes your hand excitedly with tears in his eyes saying, 'You are the men of the future! Come let us have a drink together.' The SA man is too proud to accept drinks or gifts.[157]

The KPD circulated similar instructions on how not to be fooled by "liars, spies, swindlers, and embezzlers."[158]

By reminding their members to check the backgrounds of all who claimed adherence and to stay sober during political discussions, the parties hoped to limit the effectiveness of police informants, spies, and ideological renegades. Through such instructions, leaders also sought to instill a sense of mission – the belief that the movement was encircled by enemies and in need of complete commitment and sacrifice. We should not presume, however, that local supporters shared the political goals of their leaders. Workers in

---

[157] BA, Rep. 15.01, Nr. 13123/5, OSAF manual, September 2, 1931.
[158] The KPD also had a set of contingency plans ready to go into effect if the party was declared illegal. These plans did not come into use during Weimar, but the system did survive during the Third Reich, even with the imprisonment and murder of many KPD leaders. For examples of how the cells would function entirely underground, see Bundesarchiv, R 15.01, Nr. 26162/1 or Detlev Peukert, *Die KPD im Widerstand: Verfolgung und Untergrundarbeit an Rhein und Ruhr 1933 bis 1945* (Wuppertal: Hammer, 1980).

Berlin prioritized the present not the future, and this basic difference made the three parties' individual aims of molding a disciplined rank-and-file ready for political battle largely unattainable. As a result, much to the dismay of party leaders, politicized Berliners in the early 1930s relied increasingly on the rules and regulations of a neighborhood-based radical culture to set their priorities and define their actions.

4

Conflict and Cooperation

Political Independence in Berlin's Neighborhoods

The efforts to discipline Weimar's workers through propaganda, uniformed militancy, and the rhetoric of revolution and victimization had far-reaching effects. Many were swayed by the anti-Semitic hate professed by the NSDAP to huge crowds at the Berlin Stadium and to small groups in the backrooms of pubs. Many others found the revolutionary predictions of KPD leaders convincing, and a few even made trips to the Soviet Union to learn how to build a similar society in Germany. And there were also those who never lost faith in the republic, heeding the calls of the SPD for steadfast commitment to social justice through parliamentary reform. Regardless of their motivations for joining, ideological or otherwise, during the Depression increasing numbers of supporters of all three parties came to believe that simply following party leaders would not allow them to achieve their personal political goals. Radicalized Berliners began to take matters into their own hands, seeking self-sufficiency for themselves and their communities. Their strategies varied, but their self-styled activism was consistently met with consternation from party officials who sought disciplined compliance to carefully constructed ideals.

This independence tells us as much about Berlin's culture of radicalism as the ideological conviction that stands at the center of much of the historical literature. It also tells us about gender relations, class antagonism, levels of political participation, and the ways people regulated activism at the end of the Weimar Republic. The first half of this chapter examines examples of local initiative. Despite the restrictions placed on formal democratic structures by the presidential decrees and the increasingly top-heavy SPD, KPD, and NSDAP, for better and for worse many Berliners believed they had more of a personal stake in the political sphere than ever before. Indeed, it is because a growing number believed their needs were not being met by traditional political means, including party and trade union membership, that they set out to find their own strategies to face the mounting political, economic, and social crises. At times, party officials attempted to channel this initiative so as to benefit the larger organizations; on other occasions they tried to squash what they saw as breaches of discipline or even acts of betrayal. In both instances, conflict arose at the grassroots level between parties and their supporters and among "comrades" themselves. A tug-of-war ensued between radical players and their parties over the shape and content of the daily struggle. This manifested itself in a rhetorical battle over concepts such as discipline, class, activism, and enlightenment. The pervasiveness of radicalism in Berlin was not simply a manifestation of economic desperation or a result of conflicting ideologies. Rather, the meaning behind street battles, daily protest, uniforms, and the politicization of once politically neutral spaces should be sought in the day-to-day relationships between members of these communities and the methods they employed for preserving familial and neighborhood autonomy. In the final section of the chapter, the practice of denunciation within workers' neighborhoods serves as a detailed case study of local neighborhood initiative. Denunciation tells us much about social relationships and how politics existed above and beyond a formal political sphere.

LOCAL INITIATIVE

It is natural that workers with long-term connections to the Social Democratic Party and its trade unions would feel a strong sense of loyalty and commitment to both the party leadership and its policies. Unemployment and the fear and anger that accompanied it affected fewer skilled workers and hence fewer Social Democrats, eliminating one of the main motivations toward radicalism. The SPD had not wavered from its long-term strategy of legislating reform, which privileged the ballot box as the chief site of citizen involvement. Election results show a steady decrease of support for the SPD after 1928, but this decline reflected the loss of nonmember voters and a failure to attract new members. There is, however, evidence that rank-and-file Social Democrats in the capital were also losing patience with the party's lack of aggression and its official toleration of Brüning's government and his deflationary economic plan. Complaints to this effect were recorded by Communist moles who attended SPD meetings throughout the city. Even if internal party discord was exaggerated by Communists who wanted to show the SPD in disarray, there is enough tangible evidence to conclude that a sense of frustration had spread among some party members. Even members "who otherwise always follow the party line" criticized Brüning for cutting social services and wages and for his refusal to curtail the violence of the SA. Others believed that the SPD had lost its edge and identity as a party of activists. Although the KPD reporters admittedly found little to suggest that revolution was on the minds of Berlin's Social Democrats, they did note that local activists felt unprepared to face the challenges posed by the NSDAP and the KPD. One SPD man allegedly reported, "at a union meeting [he had] hardly noticed the presence of comrades, because no one dared show any signs of enthusiastic agreement." He accused further: "the party shows too little energy. The SPD is no longer a pure workers' party, there are a large number of academics in it."[1] Another added that the opposition was better trained and more engaged. Generational tension also appeared when it was suggested that young Social Democrats were unable to discuss politics on the same level as their Communist cohorts, and therefore failed to win them over.[2] Reichsbanner men were frustrated with their inability to compete on the increasingly physical political field. At a RB meeting in Kreuzberg, one member declared that he was no longer willing to take part in the Sunday afternoon practice marches outside the city center unless they were told ahead of time where the march was to take place. Although this secrecy was intended to protect the Reichsbanner men from ambush, the RB critic explained that they were still harassed and threatened by opponents who always managed to discover their destination. He feared that he could be injured in the ensuing violence, without his wife even knowing his whereabouts.[3] Criticism was also voiced here against Brüning, but less for his disastrous economic policies than for his refusal to halt Nazi aggression.

Lending some credibility to the accuracy of the reports submitted by Communist spies, the KPD is discussed with mixed emotions at the SPD and Reichsbanner meetings. Some speakers suggested the need for closer ties with local Communists, while others argued that cooperation with the KPD remained "impossible, because [the Communists] are enemies equal to the Nazis."[4] A Reichsbanner man in Berlin-Mitte exclaimed, to the applause of his comrades, that when a Communist came to his door with propaganda he had thrown him out on his ear. This story prompted another to raise the stakes, claiming that he always kept a piece of thick cable nearby so that when KPD propaganda men came soliciting party materials, he could pack an extra powerful punch.[5] In general, however, by the summer of 1931, reports show signs of weariness and even embarrassment within the SPD. There was recognition that "in ever greater numbers the masses are losing their trust in the party." Yet few solutions to the stagnation were put forward. General agreement that the leadership should be moved to end its toleration of Brüning was tempered by the fear that any armed conflict would result in victory for the NSDAP. Eventually, leaders sought to combat the dissatisfaction within their ranks with the creation of the Eiserne Front and reorganization of the Reichsbanner.[6] Both steps should be understood in this

[1] BA-SAPMO, RY1/I2/705/23, KPD spy report of the SPD Zahlabend on February 25, 1931, pp. 289–90.

[2] Ibid., p. 291.

[3] BA-SAPMO, RY1/I2/705/23, KPD spy report from the Reichsbanner-Zugversammlung Kreuzberg, March 4, 1931, pp. 152–3.

[4] Ibid., p. 152.

[5] BA-SAPMO, RY1/I2/705/23, KPD spy report from the shooting practice of the Reichsbanner Third Kameradschaft in Mitte, on November 9, 1931, p. 185.

[6] Cf. Donna Harsch, *German Social Democracy and the Rise of Nazism* (Chapel Hill: University of North Carolina Press, 1993), pp. 127–45.

context of discontent. These moves were well calculated by the SPD, not just as a way to keep up with their rivals, but as a strategy of internal control to quiet the voices calling for change, before the fundamental principles of the party were challenged.

The KPD too struggled in its goals of maintaining physical and ideological discipline among its supporters. The financial shortfall caused by a largely unemployed constituency is the most commonly cited problem the party was facing. Administrative confusion also made for a daily reality that contrasted starkly to the *Kampfbereit* or battle-ready image presented in party directives. Both were key factors in the KPD's own grassroots discontent. For example, members were frustrated by administrative miscues that obstructed channels of communication between leaders and the Kieze. Similarly, financial cutbacks made control visits by middle-ranking functionaries less common, leaving local cells largely on their own to criticize and improvise. Even in the Communist novel, *Kämpfende Jugend*, party instructors are regularly absent. When one functionary fails repeatedly to attend regularly scheduled events, the cell leader, Theo, encourages his comrades: "I believe we are strong enough to conduct our meeting without advisers."[7]

The most well-documented breaches of party discipline are those stemming from ideological conflict. At the end of the 1920s, there were three large-scale purges of the KPD, which emptied the party of leaders who had "strayed" to the right or the left of party line.[8] The first and most significant crisis for the party in Berlin came in the battle to isolate the "leftists," who demanded a return to Leninism and rejected Stalin's policy of socialism in one country. Ruth Fischer and Arkadi Maslow were among those expelled from the party during this wave in 1926. The second purge took place at the end of 1928 and may have affected as many as six thousand Communists across Germany, though the "Conciliators" attracted less support in the capital.[9] Their leaders, including Heinrich Brandler and August Thalheimer, questioned the efficacy of revolution and recommended some steps toward reconciliation with the SPD and, after expulsion, went on to set up their own party – the Communist Party of Germany, Opposition (KPO). Finally in 1932 one of the young and rising orators of the KPD, Heinz Neumann, who had served, ironically, at the forefront of the 1928 dismissal, was removed from his leadership position. Neumann had fallen out of favor for arguing that the KPD needed to turn its efforts solely toward defeat of the

---

[7] Walter Schönstedt, *Kämpfende Jugend* (Berlin: Oberbaumverlag, 1972), p. 38.

[8] Ben Fowkes, *Communism in Germany under the Weimar Republic* (New York: St. Martin's Press, 1984), gives a detailed description of the internal conflicts that led to each purge.

[9] Ibid., p. 152. This estimate of six thousand Communists purged from the KPD is taken by Fowkes from K. H. Tjaden, *Struktur und Funktion der 'KPD-Opposition' (KPO)* (Meisenheim am Glan: A. Hain, 1964), p. 100.

NSDAP, thereby rejecting the party's official prioritization of the struggle against the SPD's "social-fascist" policies.

These incidents illustrate the culture of conflict within the party, but a concentration on ideological purges dramatizes upper-level infighting and overshadows local discord, which had very different roots and followed separate patterns. In fact, most complaints about local activism noted a total lack of ideological understanding among rank-and-file members. In one report sent by a low-level functionary about the KJVD group at a Siemens plant in Berlin, the author commented that there was no set agenda for the meetings, which often consisted of the young men "telling jokes about Nazi co-workers." Worse than the lack of seriousness among the KJVD members were the limitations of their ideological training. One of the Siemens workers reportedly asked the visiting functionary for an explanation of the term "class conflict" because a Nazi co-worker was always asking him why the KPD "wants class struggle instead of the *Volksgemeinschaft*." The young Communist had never known how to respond beyond: "I don't like your kind. The Nazis don't want anything good for the workers."[10] This evidence of discussion among Communists and Nazis is interesting in itself, but the man's lack of understanding certainly was not what the party hoped for, nor was this an isolated case. Party leaders would have found this incident most discouraging, since the assumption prevailed that factory-organized Communists, as opposed to those mobilized in street cells, were better-schooled and possessed a more disciplined commitment to the movement.

Complaints about the lack of political knowledge led to a great deal of condescension toward local activism. After May 1929, RFB leaders predicted correctly that illegality would lead to the loss of many who were not ideologically committed. However, the organization contributed to this numerical decline by consciously dropping additional "not so politically schooled" men from their ranks. Ideological training was equated with trustworthiness – an essential quality when working underground.[11] While the plan was to create a lean and reliable RFB, some smaller branches of the group dissolved entirely, limiting the RFB's overall effectiveness. Though the importance placed

---

[10] BA-SAPMO, RY1/I4/1/72, report about the work of the KJVD within Berlin's Siemens plant, February 18, 1932, p. 362.

[11] BA-SAPMO, RY1/I4/2/22, report by the Reichsfraktionsleitung in the RFB, February 23, 1930, pp. 88–9. The lack of Marxist–Leninist understanding was even a problem for those attending the RJ-leadership training school in 1926. This evaluation reported that a portion of the participants, many in their early twenties, "did not have the slightest preparatory training and only a small number had a certain amount of basic political knowledge." Thirty-seven delegates enrolled. Considered poor attendance, the low enrollment figure was blamed on the 100 RM fee per student. Ten students were twenty years old or younger. Twenty-five were unemployed. Complaints of this sort demonstrate that the problem was not just a result of the influx of new party members during the Crisis Period. See BA-SAPMO, RY1/I4/2/21, evaluation of the first national RJ-leadership training school, 1926, p. 70.

on education became even greater after 1929, it appears functionaries had a difficult time trying to convince cell members to take an interest in ideological training. One functionary sent to Friedrichshain to evaluate Communist sympathizers reported that they believed themselves to be underschooled. Yet when the local Communists organized a course on such matters in order to allay the sympathizers' doubts and prepare them for membership, only eight of the twenty who had signed up for the course attended. Even if all twenty had appeared, the class would have represented only one-eighth of the 160 workers at the factory who read the *AIZ* and were therefore likely to be KPD sympathizers. The functionary concluded that the "materials appear to be too difficult."[12] This disjuncture comes as little surprise when one considers that the BL in Berlin never wavered from issuing directives that failed to prioritize political issues with daily relevance, such as unemployment, housing, and neighborhood conflict. Instead, local functionaries were asked to cover questions and themes like the following, which were recommended for the 1932 presidential election in which Thälmann, Hitler, and Hindenburg were the candidates:

1) What are the connections between the world economic crisis and the imperialist raid of China? 2) Which positions do the SPD and Nazis have in relation to this imperialist war? 3) What are the tasks for the working class in capitalist countries? 4) What is the task for the Communist Party in China? 5) What are the signs for the full realization of socialism in the USSR?[13]

There were divisions within the NSDAP as well. The best known were the revolt by Walter Stennes, detailed earlier, and that of Otto Strasser, who was expelled from the party in 1930. After the incident, Strasser claimed that his break with the NSDAP was explained by his allegiance to socialism and the causes of workers, which Hitler had betrayed. The extent to which the dispute was indeed ideological and not disciplinary is debatable, and it is likely that Strasser exaggerated his socialist leanings in later years in order to exonerate himself of his connections to Hitler.[14]

Questions of ideological discipline and loyalty to Hitler were important factors in these two significant purges in the NSDAP before 1933. At the grassroots level, however, shortcomings in organizational rather than ideological discipline were the usual criticisms levied at local activists. Party leaders were fast to react when the intricate structure of the party and its organizations was ignored or violated. For example, when it became known that

---

[12] BA-SAPMO, RY1/I3/1–2/34, Friedrichshain commission on party fluctuation, June 17, 1931, p. 76.
[13] BA-SAPMO, RY1/I3/1–2/100, "Der revolutionäre Propagandist, Material für die Propagandisten zur Präsidentenschaftswahlkampagne," BL Berlin-Brandenburg, ed., February 15, 1932.
[14] See Max Kele, *Nazis and Workers. National Socialist Appeals to German Labor, 1919–33* (Chapel Hill: University of North Carolina Press, 1972), pp. 156–60.

members of the BDM had not chosen to join the women's NS-Frauenschaft at age eighteen because they believed it ignored their age-specific interests, and instead had been forming what they had called the NS-Mädchenschaft or Girls' Corps, the *Reichsorganisationsleiter* Robert Ley nipped this grass-roots development in the bud.[15] The SA inspector's quarterly report at the end of 1931 similarly reprimanded the creation of new units within the Berlin SA without first ascertaining the proper sanctions from the national leadership.[16]

Though the NSDAP and KPD advocated activism in the form of day-to-day *Kleinarbeit*, which when multiplied by millions of people would lead to proletarian revolution or national socialist victory, the leaders of both parties mistakenly believed that they could design and control the strategies and goals of the activists. Grassroots methods, however, were more influenced by the codes of behavior which ordered life in the overcrowded neighborhoods of the city than by the programmatic commands of their leaders. Likewise, the priorities of local activists were to create immediate change in order to defend threatened familial and neighborhood hierarchies and achieve economic stability. The radical parties provided a structure for the advancement of these local goals, but where the structures proved a hindrance, Berlin's radical workers presumed that the call for *Kleinarbeit* gave them free reign.

These reports of discontent within the parties – from the top down and from the bottom up – provide some sense of the climate in which local initiative took place. Berlin's neighborhoods were the site of both planned and spontaneous independent mobilization by citizens with varying levels of commitment to party structures and beliefs. Party leaders were never fully able to control their constituents for several reasons. The desire for economic gain led some to act on their own. Others interpreted the call for radicalism differently than their leaders had intended. Finally, an already existing sense of neighborhood autonomy made it difficult for parties and organizations to keep track of their supporters.

The importance of economic necessity should not be underestimated as a motivating factor for homespun activism. The food and other aid that could be gained from association with the radical parties was obviously an enticement to don the insignia of the SA or the RFB. The connections made through these organizations could also be used to secure further assistance. In other words, under the guise of "official" collections in name of the *Volk* or the working class, or in roving bands that had little in common with the disciplined images of the parties, members and sympathizers created strategies for gathering food and funds beyond the mandates given to them by party officials. Throughout this entire period, but with increasing frequency

[15] BA, NS22/452, Nazi Chief of Administration Robert Ley to all Gaue leaderships, November 21, 1932.
[16] BA, NS26/306, OSAF Quarterly Report, December 1931.

as the economic crisis worsened into 1932, the looting of grocery stores was a common occurrence in Berlin, including the stalls at the Marheineke market in the Nostiz Kiez.[17] This phenomenon is recreated in *Kämpfende Jugend*, when the young men, hungry and frustrated with their lack of options, decide to satisfy their stomachs and prove that they are willing to fight. Schönstedt is clear that his protagonists are not merely being selfish. One of the men, Peikbeen, throws an armful of stolen meats to working-class women in the street with the cry: "To my people! Now gobble it up!" The novelist is also careful not to connect the KPD to the actions of these young Communists. In the novel, there are no orders from above which lead the Nostiz Communists to target the store, and Schönstedt even describes them as "wolves" attacking the store like a vulnerable "herd of sheep."[18]

In depicting the men as independent actors in this scene, Schönstedt was following the party line. Store looting was one local strategy that the party did not try to claim as its own, since simple vandalism and theft did not elicit much public sympathy. One police memo noted sixty-two plundering cases in the capital from August to October 1931.[19] At the December meeting between the Berlin chief of police and the grocers' association, one storeowner counted thirty-six incidents in one week in which "beggars" entered his store.[20] If nothing was "given," he explained to police, the beggars would just take what they wanted. Moreover, a shop owner's refusal often provoked a return visit by a larger band of young men or boys, usually unarmed, who would plunder at will. Threatening letters sent to butchers and grocers demanding donations of food to the neighborhood's unemployed were also common and were followed by threats of looting if the demands were ignored.[21] Most incidents took place in poorer neighborhoods, and the theft usually took place without violence. Since the sales clerks were often women (especially at the larger chain stores), and telephones were rarely available for quick notification of the police, the young thieves were rarely caught.

Police tried extra patrols, and soldiers were stationed at the store branches most frequently hit. Police spies were also told to listen for clues about where

---

[17] Agnes Lanwer, "Marheineke-Markthalle" in Helmut Engel, Stefi Jersch-Wenzel, and Wilhelm Treue, eds., *Geschichtslandschaft Berlin. Orte und Ereignisse. Band 5: Kreuzberg* (Berlin: Nicolai, 1994), p. 482. For more on the politics of hunger in the 1920s, see Alf Lüdtke, "Hunger in der großen Depression: Hungererfahrung und Hungerpolitik am Ende der Weimarer Republik," in *Archiv für Sozialgeschichte* (Vol. 27, 1987), pp. 145–76.

[18] Schönstedt, *Kämpfende Jugend* (1932), p. 34.

[19] BLHA, Rep. 30, Berlin C, Title 90, Nr. 7538, memo from chief of police (Abt. I), October 31, 1931, p. 164.

[20] BLHA, Rep. 30, Berlin C, Title 90, Nr. 7538, meeting between the Einzelhandelgemeinschaft Gross-Berlin e.V. and the Berlin police chief, December 15, 1931, p. 185.

[21] BLHA, Rep. 30, Berlin C, Title 90, Nr. 7538, threatening letter presented as evidence to the Schutzpolizei in Mitte, August 9, 1931, p. 75.

and when attacks were planned. None of these measures had much effect, however, and through the end of 1932 looting was still a growing cause for alarm. Though most of the financial losses to stores usually came from broken windows, the details of these crimes received an inordinate amount of attention in the press. The KPD was summarily blamed for organizing a massive plot to rob the stores. In the bourgeois press, the violence of the incidents was often exaggerated, as was the role of the Communist "men behind the scenes" who followed the "methods of Russian agitators" in planning the highly orchestrated attacks. In a case of Berlin police fairness toward the KPD, internal memos show that the police disagreed that there was such a conspiracy. To the contrary, they believed "no [party] political motivation comes into question. It has much more to do with acts of self-subsistence of hungry unemployed."[22] Even police administrators went on the record to "stress emphatically that there have not been any signs that the KPD or any other large organization is behind the plundering."[23] This left the KPD in a somewhat sticky position. The looting gave them the opportunity to point out how the republic had driven workers to law-breaking, yet the extensive press coverage described its members as ruffians and depicted its leaders as string-pullers who swindled good citizens into breaking the law. Furthermore, the party was averse to condone grassroots activism that it could not control. In the summer of 1931, the police relaxed their guard for a week because they had information that the KPD was investigating the members of the unemployed committees.[24] The police rightly assumed that the street-organized, loosely bound committees of unemployed would scale back their unsanctioned operations while the functionaries were in town and then return to their own strategies after the investigation had ended.

The Nazi leadership also looked down on such activism because it damaged the party's carefully crafted image as an order-respecting organization. The Gauleiter sanctioned the Berlin SA and additional party members in the fall of 1932 for conducting their own locally organized looting campaigns. These "wild collections" of money and food were even more threatening to party reputation than those conducted by KPD members and sympathizers because they were conducted by men wearing the party uniform. However, instead of focusing on neighborhood shops, the Nazis chose to descend on

---

[22] BLHA, Rep. 30, Berlin C, Title 90, Nr. 7538, local police report of looting on Brückenstraße, August 1931, p. 96.

[23] BLHA, Rep. 30, Berlin C, Title 90, Nr. 7538, minutes from the meeting between the chief of police and advisers on December 20, 1932, p. 229. There was extreme concern that the situation would escalate further in the days leading up to the Christmas holiday, leading to this meeting of high-ranking officials. There were some present at this meeting who believed the disturbances to be politically motivated.

[24] BLHA, Rep. 30, Berlin C, Title 90, Nr. 7538, memo from the political police IA, June 6, 1931, p. 3.

small villages just beyond the city boundaries.[25] The abundance of the Brandenburg farmers' crops was probably noticed by the Berlin SA during their frequent trips to the nearby countryside for marching practice and other military exercises.

In the early 1930s, it became popular among unemployed SA men to travel as a way to escape the economic and personal crises at home. Some went so far as to reach Italy on foot. Along the way they enjoyed the clean beds and free meals provided by the party's many hostels and SA barracks, and in Italy they begged and relied on the hospitality of their political cousins, Mussolini's Black Shirts. In February 1932, OSAF sent out a directive that had come down from the party's *Reichsorganisationsleiter* declaring that "[i]n spite of repeated prohibition, the wandering of Brown Shirts out of the country, especially in Italy, continues to grow. For a movement which in the foreseeable future will hold power in its hands, it is unbearable to be represented in foreign lands by begging party members." The letter also included regulations that threatened dismissal from the party for those caught outside of Germany without permission from the party leadership.[26] Eight months later a memo was issued relaying complaints from Italy that they were "flooded" with penniless Nazis in uniform. In response, OSAF demanded once again that Stormtroopers who desired to travel seek advance permission, which would be given only after the planned length of stay and resources for the trip were confirmed. In addition, it was stressed that the uniform was not to be worn outside of the country, where the party could have little control over the actions of the wearer.[27] Even within Germany, changes were made to limit the length of hostel stays so as to remind men these were not to be permanent homes.[28]

One aspect of the NSDAP's appeal through the 1930s was Hitler's ability to make party members feel a personal connection to him and his party. This personal relationship was already evident before 1933, and it is one reason why people thought they could act on their own. As a result, letters from party members, often without an official position in the party, to high-ranking leaders such as Himmler and Hitler himself were common. "During years of *Kleinarbeit*," began one friendly letter sent at the beginning of 1929 from Berlin-Mitte, "I have had a number of experiences in the political struggle, which I would like to offer to you as Propaganda chief of the party [Himmler]. You are likely familiar with the majority of the suggestions, but perhaps you can make practical use of some of these small points." In his suggestions about assemblies he stressed that the presenter should speak in

---

[25] BA, NS22/435, letter of complaint from the Gauleiter for Brandenburg, September 9, 1932.

[26] BA, NS26/307, OSAF I, Nr. 358/32, February 3, 1932.

[27] BA, NS26/307, OSAF II, Nr. 2949/32, October 20, 1932.

[28] BA, Rep. 15.01, Nr. 13123/5, Cologne SA memo, July 28, 1931. The SA in Cologne issued a directive limiting the stay in its hostels to one night, except in emergency cases.

"popular German, [be] lively, never professional." He also added that those circulating pamphlets should be "young, well-disciplined party members in street clothes, who will make a good impression through their friendly appearance."[29] Confident in their own abilities, some Nazis believed that they, like the author of this letter, had approval from above to design their own activist strategies. KPD rhetoric also encouraged independence by stressing the innate connection between workers and a workers' political program, as represented by the KPD. Party leaders assumed that, with training, supporters would naturally develop the proper consciousness and fall in line behind the revolutionary leadership. But because KPD literature stressed the natural connection between workers' needs and the party program, members presumed their needs and actions as workers represented de facto the party line without requesting clearance for their methods. Therefore, along with economic necessity, the very definitions of party radicalism used by the KPD and NSDAP created a second reason for increased independence at the local level.

The two radical parties preferred, when possible, to harness the methods developed at the street level for their own purposes. This response was much easier and more productive than trying to alter the behavior of the recalcitrant local cells and units. For example, at the end of 1930, the KPD decided to create a new mass organization, the Kampfbund gegen den Faschismus (KbgdF) as a way to provide structures for impromptu local organizing. Local functionaries, such as the author of the following party memorandum from Wedding, were enthusiastic about the new strategy and encouraged their followers to retain the grassroots characteristics of the organization:

The experiences gained through market demonstrations must be made use of further. It must be recognized that one agitation group at the market is not enough, numerous groups must appear simultaneously. Comrades must move around and learn to limit their speaking, so as not to sound like 'instructors from above'. . . . Create set speaking troops, which can be sent out for apartment house and courtyard [propaganda] and to our demonstrations. Use short speeches, but always stay current![30]

Organizers of the KbgdF "speaking troops" recognized that their constituents were interested in the current events that affected their lives. Workers were concerned about food prices, the lack of jobs, and the disappearance of welfare benefits, as opposed to Japanese aggression in China or Stalin's latest speech. Ready-made audiences could be found at the market or in the courtyard and might also appreciate the entertainment provided by these propaganda troops. Women were less likely to feel welcome at official meetings,

---

[29] BA, NS18/5004, letter from Herr G. to Heinrich Himmler, January 7, 1929.
[30] BA-SAPMO, RY1/I3/1-2/57, UB North directive: "Turn to new agitation-propaganda methods," January 1931, p. 160.

but the market was their territory.[31] If the topics focused on issues they felt close to, they were more likely to listen.

To sanction agitation "at the markets and in the courtyards" was a way to rein in those who already passed out party materials, staged short allegorical plays, or sang revolutionary songs in the neighborhoods. It was not just an alternative to the failed factory organizing; it was also a response to the ways workers understood politics, responded to political messages, and organized themselves. Certainly the party hoped also to broaden the party's membership and rebuild a mass organization after the prohibition of the RFB. The KbgdF, however, was not a replica of the RFB; it was not even an organization in a very formal sense – and this too reflected the independence of Berlin's workers.

Even with a very loose structure in place to connect the small groups based in apartment houses, factories, streets, and unemployment offices, the KbgdF's national leadership found it more difficult than expected to unite and control the local activism that already existed in Berlin and other cities. Their frustration began to show a few months later:

in the Reich there were already numerous proletarian revolutionary defense organizations, about which the party had either no knowledge or only slight knowledge. These "Worker Resistance," "Proletarian Self-protection," "Proletarian Protection Associations," or whatever else they call themselves, were to a small degree legal ex-RFB groups, but the largest number were spontaneously generated local defense organizations without centralized connections, without political leadership, for the most part self-directed.[32]

The report went on to describe disappointedly the "resistance" to the new umbrella organization mounted by these neighborhood associations and the "local egoism," which kept them from joining the party proper. The KPD was shocked that workers would see something as loosely structured as the KbgdF as an intrusion into their neighborhood space. The semiprivate sphere of their communities – their courtyards, markets and front stoops – were living spaces treasured more dearly than their cramped apartments. Like the pubs, these too were spaces in which neighbors felt the privacy and sense of community needed to discuss political issues, and activists were increasingly less willing to share this space with outsiders, even Communist ones.

---

[31] KPD officials in Berlin were constantly reporting difficulties trying to integrate women into party meetings and assemblies. Male members made it clear that they did not want women present, and this opinion was undoubtedly made known to the women. In late 1930, one KPD bulletin sent out to low-level party officials in Mitte, referred to women's involvement as the "step-child" of the movement. The author pleaded with the men to "have patience" and cease making complaints such as: "with the women it is terrible, you can't get anywhere with them." BA-SAPMO, RY1/I3/1-2/53, *Unsere revolutionäre Massenarbeit, Funktionärsorgan des UB Zentrum*, Nr. 2, Nov./Dec. 1930, p. 61.

[32] BA-SAPMO, RY1/I4/9/3, "Report of the KbgdF national leadership concerning the development of the organization," February 1, 1931, p. 39.

The "wild cliques" of Berlin and other large cities provide a second example of independent radicalism outside the institutional hierarchy offered by the three parties.[33] It has been estimated that, in the early 1930s, six hundred cliques existed in Berlin. In the Nostiz neighborhood, at least one clique, "Südpol," existed. It had between fifteen and twenty members and was led by a "bull" with the unoriginal name of "Tarzan."[34] Although historians often emphasize the criminal influence among some of these bands of young people, their political motivations, albeit less clear than party organizations, should not be ignored. Like those who joined the paramilitary organizations of the political parties, these young males (and the females often attached to the groups) were seeking the affirming camaraderie that came from belonging to a group that exerted local authority. The cliques had their own rules, territories, hierarchies, and even simple uniforms or flags. Some cliques had roots in the more formal youth movement. Like other youth organizations, their popularity highlights the discontent among young adults in the capital. Detlev Peukert has argued that though clique joiners tended to be from the workers' milieu, they were not generally workers in terms of training and employment status. Instead, these were the rebels par excellence. Having shunned apprenticeships and school when available, the clique member was surprisingly "self-assured" and considered himself a "real man," for leaving behind the dependence these roles required.[35] There were cliques on the political right and left, and competition among groups and with the larger paramilitary organizations often became heated.[36]

Both the NSDAP and KPD tried, not always with success, to integrate sympathetic cliques into their institutional structures as a way to gain more supporters and limit the influence these independent gangs had over their own young members. One of the central plot lines in Schönstedt's pro-KPD novel about the Nostiz Kiez is the process by which members of the clique, Edelsau, eventually come to realize that their desire for change can only be met through the Communist youth organization. When Edelsau's leader begins to question his clique's ability to alter the class-biased justice system that sentenced his hungry, food-stealing friend to four months in prison,

---

[33] Gertrud Staewen-Ordemann, *Menschen der Unordnung* (Berlin: Furche Verlag, 1933), pp. 124–37. Staewen-Ordemann estimates that only 10 percent of Berlin's cliques were primarily criminal organizations. For a report of life in a clique during the Depression, see Ernst Haffner, *Jugend auf der Landstraße Berlin* (Berlin: Bruno Cassirer, 1932).

[34] Gerhard König, *Berlin – Kreuzberg und seine Nostitzstraße* (Berlin: Druckerei der pbw, no date), p. 33.

[35] Detlev Peukert, "Die 'Wilden Cliquen' in den zwanziger Jahren" in Wilfried Breyvogel, ed., *Autonomie und Widerstand. Zur Theorie und Geschichte des Jugendprotestes* (Essen: Rigodon, 1983), p. 69.

[36] Eve Rosenhaft cites an observer's report that 21 percent of Berlin's cliques had sympathies with the KPD and 7 percent aligned themselves with right-wing parties and organizations. See Rosenhaft, *Beating the Fascists? The German Communists and Political Violence, 1929–33* (Cambridge: Cambridge University Press, 1983), pp. 131–8.

he is not yet ready to articulate his doubt and shame. Schönstedt, however, does it for him by including the clique leader's "unspoken" words: "Actually something ought to be done against it [this system].... Last year the Nazis shot to death our friend Walter Neumann. The murderers were acquitted. One must fight against it. Our clique is a piece of filth. I don't want to have anything more to do with it."[37]

One man who belonged to the "Gesundbrunner" clique in Wedding before eventually joining the SA has described all of his clique mates as unemployed and some without any regular public assistance. The clique was well aware of the different political affiliations available to them and the relationships between left and right. They had a small marching band that was often asked to perform at nationalist public events. From the start, they had success playing for the crowds who came to watch Nazi marches: "We first thought the crowd had gone crazy. We didn't want to believe our eyes.... 'Bravo, bravo' they cried out to us. A new spirit had taken hold." Other nationalist audiences, described as philistines, did not react so well to their energetic music, "whispering among themselves about quieter, more demure times." Thereafter, the clique decided to perform only for the dynamic SA.[38] One member of a left-leaning clique from Moabit reported years later:

Each who had something [money or food] shared it with the others.... Through this practice an incredible solidarity developed. Within the clique the strictest justice was upheld. If for example someone committed an offense, which affected the clique, for instance theft among comrades or if something happened with a girl, then that was cleaned up and he got a terrible thrashing, he was jabbed up to his head for two hours, all the others sat around and heaped it on him. He was also prohibited from traveling with the clique. But after he was given his punishment, everything was again in order.[39]

This former clique member noted that a number of Berlin cliques were co-opted by the NSDAP because the party offered to pay for their trips and uniforms. Although he claimed to sympathize with the Communist Party, he was not comfortable with the idea of joining the KPD because of the demands of party rules and regulations. "In the clique discipline was good, but they did not want to let themselves be commanded. [It was] very simple. There was the clique leader, he was like the king, the controller, and what he did, that was good enough."[40] Sometimes his clique worked with the KPD

---

[37] Schönstedt, *Kämpfende Jugend* (1932), p. 82.

[38] BA, NS26/514, "Remembrances of the *Kampfzeit*," 1936. It is hard to know if this man's essays were commissioned by the party. There were party branches in other parts of the country that involved larger numbers of their members in writing down their memories of the "struggle," but only a few individual essays survive from the Berlin NSDAP.

[39] Hans Benenowski, *Nicht nur für die Vergangenheit. Streitbare Jugend in Berlin um 1930* (Berlin: Verlag in Kreuzberg, 1983), p. 12.

[40] Ibid., p. 15.

and its organizations, and other times it even cooperated with those who had left the SA with Stennes.[41]

Along with economic need and local interpretations of party calls for radicalism, a third factor in the gulf that grew between parties and their rank-and-file members was that parties found it increasingly difficult to keep track of their supporters' whereabouts and activities. Though fewer people were moving to urban centers during the Depression, people were on the move within Berlin – from the second floor to the fifth floor in search of a cheaper apartment, in the commute from Mitte to Neukölln for a new job, or home to the parents' flat because of public assistance cuts.[42] For most Berliners, mobility in the early 1930s was a matter of necessity not choice. During times of economic crisis, neighborhood networks were crucial because family members and friends could help out with loans, childcare, and the search for work. Other case studies confirm that there was a draw to remain in familiar settings among trusted neighbors, even when the surroundings themselves were in dire need of improvement.[43] Despite the desire to maintain this sense of community, many residents believed their way of life was under threat owing to the conditions of the times, leading them to activism beyond the reaches of party officials.

[41] Ibid., p. 20. The severity of some of the young men's poverty is illustrated by their willingness to prostitute themselves to men for money or accommodations (see p. 17).

[42] The large, often progressively designed, housing developments were going up on the outskirts of the metropolitan area, and most of these new dwellings exceeded the financial limitations of those living in older apartments in the city center. Cf., Stephan Bleek, "Das Stadtviertel als Sozialraum. Innerstädtische Mobilität in München 1890 bis 1933" in Klaus Tenfelde, ed., *Soziale Räume in der Urbanisierung: Studien zur Geschichte Münchens im Vergleich 1850 bis 1933* (Munich: Oldenbourg, 1990), pp. 217–34. Although the study focuses on Munich, its analysis of the importance of residential location to city dwellers is useful. The increased frequency of moving and the reality of the trauma that could be associated with finding a suitable new apartment are common themes in the novels of the period. The most famous example is Hans Fallada, *Little Man, What Now?* (Chicago: Academy Chicago Publishers, 1992). See also Irmgard Keun, *Gilgi – eine von uns* (Düsseldorf: Claassen, 1979; original edition, 1931) and Rudolf Braune, *Das Mädchen an der Orga Privat* (Frankfurt a. M.: Societäts-Verlag, 1930; Munich: Damnitz, 1975) for the difficult experiences faced by two single women.

[43] Though James Borchert's study of alley life in Washington, D.C., has significant racial implications not at issue among Berlin's workers, the sense of community in the alley neighborhoods studied by Borchert has many similarities to that in the German capital. The fact that many of Washington's alley dwellers desired to remain in their homes even when maintenance was fully lacking is evidence, argues Borchert, that the neighborhood had a powerful social role to play in their lives – a role that they feared would not be fulfilled elsewhere. Borchert also provides data from families who move from address to address within the same neighborhood and those who return after trying life elsewhere. For further discussion of "satisfaction" in these "slums," see James Borchert, *Alley Life in Washington: Family, Community, Religion, and Folklife in the City, 1850–1970* (Urbana: University of Illinois Press, 1980).

With politicized workers acting increasingly beyond the gaze of institutional politics, the scope of neighborhood activism expanded to challenge any who still believed that private space and certain public spaces should be beyond the taint of politics. The growth of localized politics had some unintended benefits for female participation.[44] Female workers did not stop expressing their political views after 1929, but for the most part the radical culture stressed the virtues of masculinity and referred to opponents as weak and feminine, affecting even the SPD by the end of the 1920s. As a result, politicized women were often forced to act on their own in smaller groups. Women felt most welcome in demonstrations that were locally organized and focused on issues that affected their daily worries: prices, housing, education, and unemployment. Since such issues were taking precedence in the 1930s and unemployment had effected a power shift in some families, women were able to take to the streets. In December 1932, for example, a group of female Berliners from Neukölln sent written demands to the City Assembly. They called for a "sufficient supply of cake, food stuffs, and *warm* winter clothing. We request *all* [party] factions of the city assembly to intercede for our … demands."[45] These modest protests received little coverage from the press, unless a government official hoped to gain publicity by meeting with the women, or a scuffle broke out between the protesters and police. Whenever violence was linked to women's political participation, all parties tried to gain from the shock value of the incident. The right-wing press jumped on the occasion as a way to illustrate the breakdown of "civility" and the

---

44 Women had learned the impact their demands could have on the political process from their wartime involvement in demonstrations for food and against the continuation of hostilities. For analysis of the connections between women's political roles and daily economic issues during World War I, see Ute Daniel, *Arbeiterfrauen in der Kriegsgesellschaft: Beruf, Familie und Politik im Ersten Weltkrieg* (Göttingen: Vandenhoeck & Ruprecht, 1989) and Belinda Davis, "Food Scarcity and the Empowerment of the Female Consumer in World War One Berlin" in Victoria de Grazia, ed., *The Sex of Things. Gender and Consumption in Historical Perspective* (Berkeley: University of California Press, 1996). The KPD was also at the forefront of the campaign against §218 of the criminal code, which had criminalized abortion. Although the leaders of this campaign were often medical professionals and feminist organizers, the popular mobilization against the statute included many female and male workers. See Atina Grossmann, *Reforming Sex: The German Movement for Birth Control and Abortion Reform, 1920–1950* (New York: Oxford University Press, 1995) and Cornelia Usborne, *The Politics of the Body in Weimar Germany: Women's Reproductive Rights and Duties* (Basingstoke: Macmillan, 1992; Ann Arbor: University of Michigan Press, 1992).

45 LAB-Außenstelle, Rep. 01-02, Nr. 2031, letter from a delegation of women from Neukölln to the Berlin City Assembly, dated December 15, 1932. On December 17, this group of twenty-five to thirty women took their demand for potatoes directly to "the city fathers" in the City Assembly, after they had been treated poorly by the SPD faction's representative. See also in this file, the report by Neukölln welfare workers about one of the women and the police interview of the group's leader and her husband, who had nothing to add to his wife's description of the event. Both statements were taken on December 17, 1932. The group wrote again to the City Assembly two weeks later to see what had become of their demands.

"Amazonian" masculinization of leftist women, while the Communist press used these incidents to show women as victims of an oppressive regime.[46]

However, female workers also became active in the tenants' movement, which gained momentum and resulted in a number of apartment house strikes in the early 1930s against increasing rents and poor conditions. Tenants' issues were a safe space for women's activism because of their traditional and growing authority in matters of the home. Other neighborhood protests included resistance to evictions. Neighborhood residents would be notified of a planned eviction through local flyers and street newspapers. As the eviction got under way, neighbors would physically return furniture to the apartment and harass those who had come to bid on the family's belongings. Although the KPD claimed the responsibility for organizing these actions, most participants in such events were Kiez residents who were politicized more by witnessing the plight of their neighbors than by KPD rhetoric. In fact, when the KPD organized a district tenants' congress for Tiergarten-Moabit in 1932, of the 213 representatives who showed up, only forty-one claimed KPD membership, and one admitted being a Social Democrat. The remaining 182 who responded to the survey checked off "partyless."[47] The financial restrictions, lack of trained functionaries, and resistance by residents generally made it difficult for the KPD to intervene behind the scenes to the extent the party claimed. When the party was successful in connecting one of its slogans to these largely local movements, as with "First food, then rent,"[48] which became the catch phrase for many tenement strikes, it was because they had found a saying that reflected the daily needs of the workers [Plate 10]. In one KPD report from a party section in Friedrichshain, a low-ranking functionary noted that there had been a number of "independent" actions in his area recently, which included a demonstration after the arrest of some militant workers, a protest for bread and work at the employment office, instances of eviction resistance, and looting. His initial excitement about these developments turned to frustration, however, because "large numbers of the workers resist organizing themselves formally."[49] Nevertheless, because KPD leaders insisted that they were the masterminds of neighborhood mobilization, the Berlin press and police treated these demonstrations with great suspicion as part of the grand KPD conspiracy.

---

[46] Of course by presenting women as fragile victims, the party could not easily turn around and claim that women would be able to fight in the "coming revolution" with strength equal to men.

[47] BA-SAPMO, RY1/I3/1-2/31, report on the Bezirksmieterkongress Tiergarten-Moabit on July 25, 1932.

[48] Cf. Henrick Stahr, "'Erst Essen – dann Miete!' Mieterkrawalle, Mieterstreiks und ihre bildliche Repräsentation" in Diethart Kerbs and Henrick Stahr, eds., Berlin 1932. Das letzte Jahr der Weimarer Republik (Berlin: Hentrich, 1992), pp. 90–114.

[49] BA-SAPMO, RY1/I3/1-2/54, UB East report, p. 22. The document is not dated, but it was probably written in 1931.

Plate 10. "First food – then rent!" Residents fly the hammer and sickle or the swastika during a tenants' strike on Köpenicker Straße, November 11, 1932. Source: © Bildarchiv Preussischer Kulturbesitz, 2003.

One last consequence of grassroots independence was that, without the sort of oversight desired but never achieved by the party, some politicized workers transgressed the barriers that kept politics within sanctioned spaces. While the pub had always been a site for political meetings, by the early

1930s, many pubs had to be closed down temporarily because of the violence that so frequently spilled out onto the streets around them. Streets and courtyards were also taken over by graffiti, flags, and posters, so much so that apartment landlords started instituting lease clauses to limit political expression in their buildings.[50] The expansion of political imagery in these ways helped retain a sense of belonging among like-minded neighbors and served as a challenge to others.

Politics also invaded areas that had been previously considered beyond the reach of politics. For example, to many Berliners' dismay, politics infiltrated the city's schoolyards and classrooms. Besides the official attempts made by the KPD and NSDAP to organize school-age children, even teachers and principals expressed frustration in trying to keep classrooms free of the political radicalism and conflict that had begun to overrun the streets. At a conference for teachers and administrators to address the issue of politics in the schoolroom, all agreed with the sentiments of one Neukölln principal's speech, which was then sent to the superintendent: "It can be asserted," exclaimed the principal, "that up until now the parents and teachers did not have the wish to bring the school into the political fight." However, the climate had changed, and the teachers needed to address the new situation:

The teachers of the 41st and 42nd schools have, with practically no exceptions, children in front of them who come from working-class families, in whose homes more is spoken about the political issues of the day than in the houses of the propertied classes, for reasons that are generally known by all. The discussions of the parents about contemporary political questions awaken questions in the children, which in an objective way are to be handled and answered by the teachers of a workers' district, as it is in Neukölln. It is not the job of a school to practice party politics, because as experience has shown, this can lead to serious dangers for the life of a school. But the school may and must attend to the factual discussion of current political happenings.[51]

Schools were not the only sites which experienced a controversial influx of political debate. In the same city district, there was also a scandal surrounding the politicization of a Neukölln hospital. The District Assembly sent an investigative committee to the hospital in 1932 to examine rumors that the "relationship between doctors and nurses and also between the other staff members was explicitly tense under the daily political disputes."

---

[50] Rathaus Neukölln, File Nr. 407. The standard lease used for city-owned rental units by the district of Neukölln included a regulation banning political posters on rented property. Although this order was typed in at the bottom of the printed form in 1932, by 1937 it had become formulaic and given priority as rule four.

[51] LAB, Rep. 214/A525, Nr. 31 and 32, letter to the Schulrat des Bezirks Neukölln-Ost, May 15, 1930. The investigative committee was made up of five SPD representatives, four from the KPD, one from the middle parties bloc, and one from the DNVP. For more charges see, Rathaus Neukölln, File Nr. 1890.55, district assembly minutes, Nr. 3, May 4, 1932.

These suspicions were confirmed, and the committee reported that patients were also involved in the intense debates. Small flags and posters for numerous parties hung on patients' beds, and political newsletters circulated within the wards.[52] Although the vote to fire the district health secretary over the scandal failed to pass, he was directed by the District Assembly to bring an immediate end to the political agitation that had turned the hospital into a "political playground." Disciplinary measures were also taken against some staff members within the institution.[53] Clearly, some citizens felt it acceptable to broaden the playing field of political participation, while state authorities and party leaders of the center and right felt the expansion of the political sphere beyond sanctioned spaces was a threatening development.

DISCUSSION WITH THE ENEMY AND MEMBERSHIP FLUCTUATION

Surely, it must have seemed as if everyone was taking sides. The Communist and Nazi camps took aim at each other in the press, in political speeches, and on the streets. Where one shopped or drank beer was a significant political statement, as was the newspaper one chose to read. The radical parties themselves portrayed political participation as an either/or decision. Polarized rhetoric was used by both sides in order to draw distinction between the two parties: victim versus perpetrator, savior versus demon. This sort of conscious self-representation and the violence that lent tangible proof to the fears that Berlin was sliding into a chaotic civil war have overshadowed a significant aspect of this radical culture: the relationships that often existed at the local level among activists. Familiarity is not uncommon in civil conflict; the stories of Protestant and Catholic neighbors in Northern Ireland who lived together peacefully for years before growing to despise each other are well known. In the case of Germany, because differences in the overall make-up of each party's membership have been stressed, the contact that existed between Communists and Nazis has been largely overlooked.[54] In fact, this familiarity often led to political discussions among Berlin's rank-and-file Nazis and Communists.[55]

---

[52] *Neuköllner Tageblatt*, Nr. 224, September 23, 1932.

[53] *Neuköllner Tageblatt*, Nr. 254, October 28, 1932. The vote to remove the official failed though it received support from the parties of the "middle" and German Nationalists.

[54] In addition to Jürgen Falter, who has shown statistically that the Nazi electorate was more socially diverse than once assumed, Conan Fischer has argued that the KPD and NSDAP were often courting the same voters. See Conan Fischer, *The German Communists and the Rise of Nazism* (New York: St. Martin's Press, 1991).

[55] One exception is the work of Timothy S. Brown, "Beefsteak Nazis and Brown Bolshevists: Boundaries and Identity in the Rise of National Socialism" (unpublished manuscript, 2002).

The KPD advocated discussion between its members and those of the SPD and Reichsbanner. The social-fascism thesis of the Stalin-influenced KPD stressed the betrayal of SPD leaders and their policies but maintained that SPD members were mostly duped proletarians who could still be won over for the sole defender of the revolution, the KPD. While the leaders of these parties never heeded their own calls for unity, rank-and-file SPD and KPD members were encouraged to talk to each other by the official pronouncements to build Red Unity (SPD) or the Antifascist United Front (KPD). Ideological divisions certainly existed. Moreover, SPD members were seen by their KPD cousins as the proletarian elite, workers who had grown too comfortable to struggle for change, whereas Communists were viewed by Social Democrats as unskilled rabble-rousers. However, workers of both parties still shared a common history within the German labor movement; even though some of the cultural isolation of the nineteenth century had diminished in the face of a developing consumer society, workers and middle-class Berliners were still quite segregated.[56] Trying to capitalize on this daily contact, the parties printed discussion topics to be used when speaking with members of the opposition. In one typical instructional memo, for example, KPD members were told to stress the role of the "SPD and reform-minded unions as the bulwark to capitalist control."[57]

The KPD-issued newsletter *Die Rote Einheitsfront*, which was designed as informational material for SPD workers, frequently criticized the policies of the SPD-led Berlin police. In January 1931, for example, the newsletter claimed that the police chose to side with the SA, even after the murder of Reichsbanner men.[58] It is doubtful that these pamphlets engendered much more than scorn for the taunting KPD. However, there were examples of Reichsbanner men who worked with Communist sympathizers in the fight for Berlin's streets, and the lack of substantial violence between socialists and Communists in Berlin is likely the best proof that some level of toler-ance – if not camaraderie – remained between the two parties' supporters. Neighborly contact and the common enemy to the right were the real reasons for collaboration, not the provocative propaganda issued by both parties to build "unity."

---

[56] Cf. Klaus-Michael Mallmann, "Milieu, Radikalismus und lokale Gesellschaft" in *Geschichte und Gesellschaft* (Vol. 21, No. 1, 1995), pp. 5–31.

[57] BA-SAPMO, RY1/I3/1-2/28, KPD instruction memo to all factory and street cells, August 26, 1931.

[58] BA-SAPMO, RY1/I3/1-2/99a, *Die Rote Einheitsfront. Informationsmaterial für sozial-demokratische Arbeiter*, January 1931. In the same file, see also the KPD publication *Der Kommunistische Agitator*, Nr. 9, August 1930, which gave tips on how to talk to Nazis. The KPD clearly recognized that the NSDAP was having some success attracting workers because the pamphlet urged members to stress the KPD policies on strikes and unemployment and the NSDAP's support of a mandatory work service program.

The most infamous example of KPD-NSDAP cooperation was the parties' combined efforts in the Berlin transportation strike (BVG) of November 1932.[59] One Nostiz KPD-sympathizer even recalled having visited the SA pub in the Kiez, zur Hochburg, and the local SA men returned the favor at Lorenz's pub during this short-lived "cease fire."[60] Cooperation was more damaging for the KPD than for the NSDAP. The strike did not last long enough to hurt the NSDAP's relationship with industrial interests, and the Nazi claim to be a worker-friendly party was made more credible. For the KPD, the failure of the strike only showed the weakness of their shop floor support and organizational skills, and their cooperation with the NSDAP made the Communists look desperate and confused. At the street level, the men involved in the strike reportedly had little trouble working together. A full two years before the strike, a meeting of BVG employees organized by Nazis drew an equal number of Communists. A police spy reported that the words "we belong together" were heard frequently, and that both sides greeted each other on entering the room. Although such public cooperation was not repeated in other examples of Berlin labor politics, the police reporter captured the threat this togetherness represented to the republic. By way of an oxymoronic coupling of terms of solidarity and conflict, he described the atmosphere at the 1930 meeting: "The two enemy brothers were of one heart and one soul."[61] Two years later the fear remained for a conservative Berlin newspaper. Though the strike only lasted a few days, a reporter for the *Berliner Börsen-Zeitung* exclaimed during the November events that it was becoming increasingly clear "that behind the strike lie far-reaching revolutionary political goals."[62] Descriptions such as these have been used as proof that these two movements were also "brothers" in their revolutionary opposition to the SPD and the republic. Although this similarity did exist, the two parties should not be equated. As expected, when their combined efforts in the strike began to fail, the NSDAP newspaper, *Der Angriff*, was quick to stress the NSBO's ability to carry on alone. The Goebbels-edited paper explained coolly that "we are men enough to fight for our due rights and need no partnership with any party or group."[63] The cooperation among party leaders in this instance was permitted primarily because of each party's need to show radical support for workers, a

---

[59] Cf. Klaus Rainer Röhl, *Nähe zum Gegner. Kommunisten und Nationalsozialisten im Berliner BVG-Streik von 1932* (Frankfurt a. M.: Campus Verlag, 1992).

[60] Oral interview with H. D. in Lothar Uebel, "Ein heisses Pflaster" in Geschichtskreis Kreuzberg, ed., *Nostitzritze. Ein Straße in Kreuzberg* (Berlin: Gericke, 1992), p. 60.

[61] BA, Rep. 15.01, Nr. 26133, from the report of a Nazi meeting in the Wiener Garten, dated September 23, 1930, p. 33.

[62] *Berliner Börsen-Zeitung*, Nr. 521, November 6, 1932. Also found in BA, Rep. 15.01, Nr. 26178.

[63] *Der Angriff*, Nr. 288, November 4, 1932.

willingness to act, and the ability to create change. The experiment was not repeated.

Grassroots discussions between the two opposing forces, however, were much more common in Berlin throughout this period. Local units of both parties regularly invited members of the other party to their meetings, and the presence of both NSDAP and KPD supporters in a meeting hall did not always lead to violence. When violence did occur it was usually at the large rallies. At these assemblies, a representative of the hosting organization would typically hold the floor for an extended period of time. This speaker was followed by a representative of the opposing party, who was given fifteen minutes of "speaking freedom." His address was followed by closing arguments from both sides. It is true that this orderly structure was not always followed, and that in many cases the provocative words of highly skilled speakers assigned to travel from assembly to assembly led to brawls that disrupted the proceedings. On one hand, a NSDAP *Reichspropagandaleitung* memo warned party sections that KPD speakers were sent to the large rallies specifically to cause unrest. On the other hand, when KPD sympathizers were invited to NSDAP educational courses, the memo continued, "[the opponents] then spoke in the discussion and the evening turned out especially interesting."[64]

Discussions at local meetings seem to have run smoothly quite often, and both parties believed that this strategy helped clarify their positions and win over supporters. At one point, Nazi officials banned the SA in Friedrichshain from holding discussions with KPD members, but it appears that many of the SA men ignored the command when KPD men took the lead by initiating discussions on SA territory by entering Nazi bars. The conversations lasted on average twenty to sixty minutes. One evening when they were all asked to leave the bar, probably by the Nazi owner who was displeased by their mingling, one of the SA men responded: "we aren't discussing, we're simply talking."[65] Even after the crowd left the pub, the conversation continued for an hour on the street. Whether complex political issues were debated at these meetings is difficult to know, but the fact that they existed casts doubt on the argument that this was a completely polarized political culture in which adversaries met only in the Saturday night brawl.

The goal of these discussions, as far as party officials were concerned, was to convince a member of the opposition to break ranks and join his former enemies. This phenomenon was termed fluctuation by the parties

---

[64] BA, NS26/284, monthly report of the Reich Propaganda Leadership, Nr. 5, November 1931.

[65] BA-SAPMO, RY1/I3/1-2/34, report about discussions with Nazis in the UB Friedrichshain, September 1932, pp. 81–2. These were not isolated instances. In Southwest Berlin, for example, the local KPD reported that four cells had met with NSDAP counterparts and three cells had been involved with the SPD in the area: BA-SAPMO, RY1/I3/1-2/56, report for the Southwest UB Parteitag, summer 1931, p. 14.

involved, all of which kept close account of the numbers lost and gained through this process. Historians have tried to track the impact of membership fluctuation on voting patterns at the end of Weimar. Jürgen Falter has argued that fluctuation did not have a very important influence on voting, and that the peaks and valleys in the total votes garnered by the NSDAP came mostly from the mobilization of new voters and the deterioration of the liberal parties.[66] His evidence is convincing, but it should not dissuade us from analyzing how fluctuation may have played a more significant role at the neighborhood level, a role not reflected in national voting statistics. Timothy Brown has rightly argued that oppositional infiltration and party switching could only take place within a common rhetorical realm that allowed for conversation and debate between both Nazis and Communists.[67] Sharing the language of revolution, class solidarity, and concerns about their own status at home and in their communities meant that in the last years of the republic Nazi and Communist identities remained fluid.

In 1931, the Reichsbanner circulated a cartoon in Berlin expressing their dismay over fluctuation between the KPD and NSDAP. The leaflet pictured a man in the uniform of the SA and another in the Soviet-style uniform of the illegal RFB. The SA man says to his adversary: "Hey, I know you. You were in the SA when I was in the Red Front."[68] The cartoon provides further evidence that there was daily contact and familiarity between members of the two organizations. Its importance, however, is greater. The artist was surely poking fun at the two radical camps, characterizing them as similar gangs rather than serious political movements. But he chose this subject, over the violence or provocative propaganda favored by the two parties, because it demonstrated the breakdown of the republican system the Reichsbanner still revered, in which party traditions and ideological consistency meant something. Put differently, their criticism was directed toward fluctuation in order to unmask the feigned bravado and false loyalty represented by the two turncoats.

Many KPD members left the party simply because they could not pay the dues. All parties and their associated organizations charged monthly dues, and members were supposed to support the cause further through the additional purchase of party publications, uniforms, and other materials. Sometimes this became too much, and people just dropped from the membership rolls. On one hand, the KPD was very concerned with this attrition and feared that their losses could become others' gains. On the other

[66] See Jürgen Falter, "Die Jungmitglieder der NSDAP zwischen 1925 und 1933" in Wolfgang Krabbe, ed., *Politische Jugend in der Weimarer Republik* (Bochum: Universitätsverlag, 1993) and Jürgen Falter et al., *Wahlen und Abstimmungen in der Weimarer Republik: Materialien zum Wahlverhalten, 1919–1933* (Munich: Beck, 1986).

[67] Brown, "Beefsteak Nazis and Brown Bolshevists" (unpublished manuscript, 2002).

[68] LAB, Flugblättersammlung, SPD/9, 1931.

hand, functionaries reasoned that poverty was not the most worrisome cause for inactivity. After all, those who could not afford to participate in the KPD could not likely afford membership elsewhere, especially considering the other parties usually kept closer track of dues. They cited instead the possibility of cell dissatisfaction or boredom. If the party failed to offer its members the sort of "spirit and effective power" they were searching for, explained a local functionary: "they will walk away from the [KPD] and turn to an organization that does."[69] In Wedding, UBL officials set up a "fluctuation committee" to track down its wayward members in an area that covered seventy-seven apartment houses. They knew that, in the Reichstag election of 1930, the KPD had received the highest number of votes in this community, followed by the NSDAP and then the SPD. They described the population as 75 percent purely proletarian and 25 percent lower middle class. The street cells were active enough to agitate in nearby factories and had succeeded in sponsoring "oppositional [KPD]" ballots for union council elections at all the major work sites in the vicinity. Yet the KPD cell records only had twenty-nine names registered, seven of which were women. When the investigators tried to speak with these comrades, only fourteen could be located. Among the others, a number had moved; three were no longer familiar with the cell structure; and seven refused to speak with the functionary. Of the fourteen he did speak with, all were unemployed, and ten had been in the party for less than two years.[70] There were obviously hundreds more who voted for the KPD in this block. The situation was not always this dismal, but the party certainly had a terrible time keeping track of its supporters.

With such a weak party structure, it is not hard to imagine that some members might be wooed away by the radical slogans of the NSDAP. Although the numbers are impossible to estimate, party leaders admitted in internal documents that they were losing members directly to the NSDAP, and the SA in particular. One police officer reported the complaints of a speaker at a party meeting in northeast Berlin, who blamed the ZK's policies for leading to violence and an inability to build the party's "ideological influence among the masses," making it "no surprise when masses of previous supporters of the party and even members of the KbgdF [switched] to the NSDAP."[71] Some former Communists even admitted that the NSDAP had offered more for their services. For example, one Neukölln rowdy known

[69] BA-SAPMO, RY1/I3/1-2/24, addendum to the evaluation of party work in Berlin cell 1719 and the Gas Cell in UB East, no date.

[70] BA-SAPMO, RY1/I3/1-2/24, report of the Fluctuation Commission North, no date.

[71] BLHA, Rep. 30, Berlin C, Title 95, Sektion 9, Nr. 191, police report from party membership meetings on May 3 and 4, 1932, in UB Northeast. Complaints such as this one, which directly targeted ZK policy, were not uncommon and illustrate the diversity of opinion among Berlin's Communists.

throughout the community as "Lude" made it clear that he had left for the NSDAP after the KPD failed to support him adequately during a civil court case.[72]

The NSDAP also had to deal with members who could no longer pay their monthly dues. The real concern for party officials, however, was the possibility of defection to the KPD. Propaganda from the SPD and KPD attempted to sway Nazis to abandon the SA in particular, since the other two parties believed that many Stormtroopers were disaffected workers who could more easily be convinced that their interests and revolutionary zeal would only be truly represented by the left. Fearing that this propaganda was a cause of recent disappointing election results, the SA announced in December 1932 that in order to counteract the influx of propaganda materials aimed at its members, from the "Stahlhelm to the Red Front," the command structure would gather and publicize more aggressively the stories of those who had switched to the NSDAP, as well as any further information on internal conflicts within the opposition.[73] Although the NSDAP gained more supporters than they lost to their adversaries in these years, they were on the losing end of the most publicized case of uniform switching. The army officer Lieutenant Richard Scheringer, who was serving time in prison in 1931 for his activities in the NSDAP, publicly denounced his association with Hitler and proclaimed a proletarian revolution as the only salvation and the KPD as its herald. Naturally, an ex-army officer was not the sort of member who easily fit into the KPD's carefully constructed ideal of the male proletarian, but the party certainly did not want to turn him away. Indeed Scheringer was accepted with open arms, and his criticism of the Nazi "false-revolution" was used in many party pamphlets and brochures.[74] The NSDAP also used former Communists as propaganda tools; the converts commonly appeared on stage at Nazi rallies (preferably wearing the uniform from their earlier KPD days) to tell the audience of their conversions.[75] Naturally, there was always suspicion that new members, especially those who had prior connections to the "enemy," had been sent to the other side with orders to bring back information to their comrades. All political organizations were anxious about this possibility, and as conflict rose in Berlin so did the denunciation of political "crimes."

---

[72] BA-SAPMO, RY1/I3/1-2/89, denunciation from July 1, 1930.

[73] BA, NS23/3, OSAF command, December 20, 1932.

[74] See Richard Scheringer, *Erwachendes Volk. Briefe an Leutnant a. D. Scheringer* (Berlin: Agis Verlag, 1931). In this pamphlet, Scheringer responds to letters he claims to have received since his pronouncement that communism not national socialism is the solution for Germany. His answers detail the faults of the Nazi Party and stress the need in nationalist language for a revolution.

[75] BLHA, Rep. 61, Gau Berlin, Nr. 14.11.1, history of the NSDAP Ortsgruppe Luitpold, written on the tenth anniversary of its founding, December 1941.

DISCIPLINING THE NEIGHBORS:
DENUNCIATION IN BERLIN

Denunciation provides an excellent test for a number of the points that have been made in this chapter. By looking at these very personal political relationships among neighbors in the early 1930s, we can see the extent to which daily life in these neighborhoods was politicized and how politics invaded what was previously considered nonpolitical space. The conflicts between parties and their supporters, and the ways in which local initiative and independence flourished, also become evident. These examples demonstrate further that local issues, rather than ideological conflict, were more often the motivating factors behind the political struggle. The denunciations presented here also give credence to the argument that these neighborhoods were indeed both socially and politically diverse, and that contact between political groups and across classes was common. In addition, we see the ways in which gender and sexuality played a central role in this radical culture. Finally, in our goal of understanding the collapse of the Weimar Republic, denunciation is a useful example of how the strategies employed at the neighborhood level to confront the mounting crises may have been intended to protect the autonomy of these areas, but in fact served to undermine the social fabric of the community.[76]

It is difficult to determine the frequency of denunciation cases in this period, but we do know that the police were successful in obtaining denunciations that led to arrests in political crimes. Money played a crucial role in attracting informants to the police. In major cases, the police published offers of financial reward, which were undoubtedly a large incentive to impoverished citizens. It was general knowledge that the police would also pay for tips on less important cases. Denunciations of small-time informants were common, as in the following report on a Kreuzberg RFB member and alleged police snitch:

K. G. is suspected as a police spy by a number of residents of the houses at 13 and 48 Cuvry St. Comrades Willi F. and Max S., both of 13 Cuvry, share the following: From a tip by Frau N., also a resident there (and sympathizer with the party) the hairdresser B. (SPD member and former welfare administrator) told her in the salon that he had the opportunity to take a look at police files and there to his surprise

---

[76] This relationship between radical politics and neighborhood stability is apparent in analyses of gang life. Gangs and their communities strike up a working relationship, which lasts as long as the gang performs necessary services and the community in return supports the gang members in exercising control over their turf. If either side breaks the code, the relationship disintegrates, often spelling the demise of the gang. Denunciation within the community and providing information to the police or other gangs are all signs that this relationship is breaking down. Attempts by the gang to retain neighborhood control often involve violence. See further Martin Sanchez Jankowski, *Islands in the Street: Gangs and American Urban Society* (Berkeley: University of California Press, 1991), pp. 179–211.

he discovered official statements about residents of Cuvry St. 13, mostly members of the KPD and also RFB which carried K. G.'s signature. B. was enraged and said: "You have such scoundrels and elements in the ranks, such traitors and snitches are my sworn enemies, I fight against this type no matter what party they belong to."[77]

These informants, or *Achtgroschenjungen*, were at the bottom of the activist hierarchy. The police were universally looked upon with suspicion, so to turn one's comrades or even neighbors in to the police was considered an act of betrayal. In the attempts to protect neighborhood autonomy, most residents believed it was always better to avoid involving outsiders, like the police or other state representatives, in addressing local concerns.

Those in custody sometimes denounced their neighbors in return for leniency from the police. The police were quick to expand their questioning on one matter to include the individual's political activities. On November 7, 1932, a seventeen-year-old worker from Wedding gave the following statement to the police:

I was taken into custody on November 6, 1932 for breaking into a store and have sat in the Berlin jail since that time. Freely I have offered to provide the police with information regarding the production and sale of writings for the [Communist] infiltration of the police. On Thursday November 3, 1932 I stopped around 11:30 P.M. at a pub near the gas station on the Straße am Nordhafen. Supporters of the KPD meet there, without it really being considered a party pub. I myself am known there as a Communist. [But he is not a KPD member and claims elsewhere to have applied to the Stahlhelm for membership. – PS] From the bar I could see through an open basement door, how four unfamiliar people were busy with the reproduction of flyers on a mimeograph machine. The content of the flyer was aimed at police officers and said to the effect that they should also be in favor of the strike. . . . I must still have one or more copies in my apartment, either in or on the counter in the kitchen. I would not like to say, who brought them to me. . . . I did see how the copying machine was at the end packed in the cabinet of a loud speaker and remained in the basement. The owner of the pub must be in on it and may know the name of the production manager.[78]

The most valuable information he provided was the hidden location of the mimeograph machine. This central weapon in the propaganda wars required a large investment, and low-level radicals did everything possible to keep the machines out of the hands of the police. Often numerous street cells would contribute to its purchase, and the machine would be frequently moved from one hiding spot to another to avoid detection during the unannounced

---

77 BA-SAPMO, RY1/I3/1-2/89, denunciation concerning K. G. October 14, 1930. For more on the Cuvry Street KPD cell, see Michael Haben, "'Die waren so unter sich': Über Kneipen, Vereine und Politik in Berlin Kreuzberg" in Karl-Heinz Fiebig et al., eds., *Kreuzberger Mischung. Die innerstädtische Verflechtung von Architektur, Kultur und Gewerbe* (Berlin: Ästhetik und Kommunikation, 1984), pp. 257–9.

78 BLHA, Rep. 30, Berlin C, Title 95, Sektion 9, Nr. 164, statement by K. Z. to the police IA, November 7, 1932.

police searches. The Berlin political police were astonishingly diligent in their investigation of such tidbits of information, even though the stories sometimes turned out, as did this one, to be fabrications. After finding no flyers in his apartment and discovering that the pub's cellar was not visible from the bar as he had described, the investigators concluded: "that the information provided by Z. appears purely invented in order to put himself in a good light with the police."[79]

Denunciations were also frequently sent directly to the police from neighbors disgruntled by what they saw as a breakdown of order in their surroundings. The theme of disorder plays a paradoxical role in this section on denunciation. I have argued that one of the main reasons for the popularity of radical political behavior in this period was the desire to uphold a sense of order – order in the home and in the neighborhood. Yet this desire to assert power only further exacerbated the sense of disorder. Letters of complaint to the police illustrate the dissatisfaction with disorder. Typical of this type of denunciation was the following letter, sent in May 1930 to the local police station's political department by an anonymous inhabitant of Ebers Street in Schöneberg:

As a citizen of the state I take it as my duty with regard to today's unrest to inform you that the ringleader is Herr E. S. who lives at Ebers St. 42 (in the house with Mayer bakery). As helpers, his wife (the blond woman) and his minor son (perhaps 16 years old), who lives in the same house with E. S., are those in question. As recently as yesterday, S. had his son call on local Communists by way of a note carried to a pub. Today, S. walked around with a stick all afternoon yelling threats, he then had his wife (the blond woman) telephone from a pub (probably in the Sedan Street), again to round up Communists who then this afternoon and evening gathered and led the riot, shooting and beating. . . . [The letter was signed] "an inhabitant [of Ebers Street] who wants some quiet.[80]

With the deepening mistrust of the police after the May 1929 violence, however, workers turned away from this delegitimized force and depended increasingly on their own neighborhood forms of justice. They preferred to deal with "unproletarian behavior," sexual improprieties, and breakdowns in organizational discipline, by handling them inside the community. The parties welcomed denunciations by their members and sympathizers as a way of instilling the discipline they demanded. Both the NSDAP and KPD developed formal methods for dealing with problems within their own ranks. Committees decided each case of internal party malfeasance, and systems for appeal existed in some instances. Every section of the RFB, for example, had

---

[79] BLHA, Rep. 30, Berlin C, Title 95, Sektion 9, Nr. 164, report of the police IA, after their search of K. Z.'s apartment, November 8, 1932.

[80] LAB, Rep. 58, Film 366, Nr. 143. Although it is unclear whether this author was a man or a woman, many of these kinds of denunciations came from women who felt threatened by the violence that seemed to dominate some of Berlin's streets.

its own commission of three members to rule on all "crimes, infractions, or other cases of conflict of either an organizational or personal nature among comrades."[81] Members were elected to the committee, and the decisions were made public in the party press after both sides in the dispute undersigned them. A party court system was in operation in the NSDAP as well. It is likely, however, that many conflicts were settled outside of these formal channels. In 1929, for example, the VZ reported that a Nazi who had been embezzling from party coffers had been "arrested" by another Nazi impersonating a policeman and held overnight for questioning by armed party members. The article reported that the eighteen-year-old man was released the next morning after signing a statement in which he swore not to divulge what had happened while in custody.[82]

Two types of denunciation came into play on the streets of late Weimar Berlin. There was the denunciation of the "enemy." The targets of these denunciations were residents of working-class neighborhoods, who had acted as "enemies of the proletariat." These denunciations were announced publicly to others living in the neighborhood through street newspapers and flyers. There were also denunciations by KPD or NSDAP party members of others within their own ranks. Although we know that this type of denunciation existed in the Nazi Party and SA before 1933, and stories of denunciation within the Third Reich are familiar to all, there is only a scant record of denunciations *within* the NSDAP before 1933.[83] Nevertheless, the examples given here of internal Communist Party denunciations still allow for more general conclusions about the use and purpose of denunciation within this culture of radicalism.

One of the difficulties dealing with these internal party documents is that we do not in most cases have first-person accounts reading: "I saw X doing Y."[84] In addition, informants' names were rarely provided and functionaries always used code names.[85] That said, there are hundreds of short and longer second-hand typed versions of oral denunciations put to paper by the local

---

[81] BA-SAPMO, RY1/I4/2/7, "Richtlinien des RFB," 1928.

[82] BA, Rep. 15.01, Nr. 25789, VZ, Nr. 30, January 18, 1929, "Selbstjustiz bei den National-sozialisten." The conservative newspaper *Deutsche Zeitung* (Nr. 15a, November 18, 1929) defended but did not deny the events recorded in the preceding article.

[83] Robert Gellately has argued convincingly that citizen denunciations were key to the control and fear maintained by the Gestapo. See Robert Gellately, *The Gestapo and German Society: Enforcing Racial Policy, 1933–1945* (New York: Oxford University Press, 1990) and *Backing Hitler: Consent and Coercion in Nazi Germany* (New York: Oxford University Press, 2001).

[84] Although state authorities tried to stay well informed about all developments within the KPD (much more so than the NSDAP), they did not take much interest in local espionage unless it involved the state itself. As a result, the documentation remains fairly free from state intervention, except in the case of public denunciations appearing in posters and newspapers, which could potentially break libel laws and require police investigation.

[85] Although many of the upper-level KPD *Decknamen* have been decoded by archivists, this work has not been done for the UB level.

Gegner-Obmann to be sent along to the UBL and the BL in Berlin.[86] There were also some letters within the files written by KPD members in defense of their actions. In almost all cases, the address of the Communist under suspicion is recorded, so we have some idea where these conflicts arose.[87] Finally, in a number of cases, we see contact between the KPD in numerous cities, as members move in search of work or to flee from accusations, and the party attempts to track down their wayward members.

To return to the denunciations found in the neighborhood newspapers, the growth of street cells and their newspapers toward the end of the republic would have been encouraging to the KPD leadership had it not made the failure of their shop floor political campaign all the more evident. Originally, these "reserve troops" of housewives and the unemployed were to assist in the event of a local strike by protecting against strikebreakers and catering to the needs of those affected by the strike. But by 1930 the party had to

---

[86] The KPD intelligence branch had existed since the founding of the party in 1919 and survived as the espionage and counterespionage branch of the party for years into the Third Reich. In late 1931, the Regierungspräsident in Düsseldorf wrote to the chief of police in Berlin about the proliferation of KPD intelligence activities in his area. He described the formation of what was termed a military-political apparatus. Every city district was to form a team of eight reliable men who would coordinate the efforts for their region, acting as middle men between the local party cells and the national leadership within the increasingly complicated KPD hierarchy. Officials in Berlin assured their colleagues in Düsseldorf that the political police were tracking the developments of the KPD's intelligence service. See BLHA, Rep. 30, Berlin C, Title 95, Sektion 9, Teil II, Nr. 81, letter from the chief of police (IA) in Berlin, December 11, 1931, p. 324. Not long after these first inquiries from smaller cities to the west, the chief of police in Berlin circulated a copy of the KPD's directives on local espionage. The KPD memo explained that: "The head of the counterforces is one of the most important functionaries and together with the Political Leader is responsible for creating a goal-conscious and well-planned initiative toward the opposition for the entire party." The first task listed in the memo was the regular surveillance of adversarial organizations and the filing of reports on their activities. The opposition included all other political parties and military organizations, with emphasis on the NSDAP, SA, and Reichsbanner as well as the police and armed forces, and the surveillance was done mostly through spies. Second, the head of local counterforces also had the duty of coordinating address lists of neighbors who belonged to non-KPD organizations, but who might be won over to the Communist Party through personal contact and written propaganda. This functionary was also responsible for keeping the KPD cells "clear" of all spies and provocateurs and "cleansing" the local groups when necessary. The party regulations went on to add that the qualities needed to fill such a position included the ability to keep activities secret, even from family members, and to remain "strictly objective and faithful to the truth." See BLHA, Rep. 30, Berlin C, Title 95, Sektion 9, Teil II, Nr. 81, chief of police to the Prussian minister of the interior, March 9, 1932, p. 333–5. For more on the KPD's security branch, see Bernd Kaufmann, ed., *Der Nachrichtendienst der KPD, 1919–1937* (Berlin: Dietz, 1993). For discussion of the position of the Reichswehr in the political upheaval of the early 1930s, see Francis L. Carsten, *The Reichswehr and Politics, 1918 to 1933* (Berkeley: University of California Press, 1973) and Thilo Vogelsang, *Die Reichswehr und die Politik, 1918–1934* (Hannover: Niedersächsischen Landeszentrale für Heimatdienst, 1959).

[87] The anonymity of all persons mentioned in the files will be preserved by the use of initials.

swallow the bitter pill that these street cells were in fact the most active section of the party, and were in many cases responsible for agitating in the factories themselves to try to raise awareness and support for the KPD. While I have found denunciations in factory newsletters, the street cell versions were more effective and less risky because they could be printed and circulated with less threat of sanctions.

The party had little control over what went on at the street cell level, including what was printed in the newspapers. This is not to say they did not try. In the 1930s, the KPD leadership even began producing a monthly magazine of its own, *Der kommunistische Agitator*, which gave suggestions on how these papers should be put together. Every issue included a story on some aspect of the KPD program, and it was suggested that these themes be covered by articles in the local newspapers.[88] In addition to policy statements on housing, education, and other issues, they also wanted articles to present Communist critiques on aspects of oppositional party programs, such as the Nazi economic vision. Although some ideological articles made it into the newspapers, they were in the minority. And compared to the topics of the other articles, it is doubtful that these received much attention from readers. The fact that the local party members who wrote and edited these newspapers ignored most of the directions provided by their leaders often resulted in pointed criticism from the *Bezirksleitung*. Party leaders in Mitte circulated the following negative review of their local newspapers:

Many mistakes arise [in the newspapers] mostly due to the speed and individual work that is required from many editors. In the individual newspapers these mistakes are not very visible, but when we look at all of the papers together, they present a somewhat distorted picture of our party-line. The increasing fascist terror and the resulting increasing importance of our newspapers, must lead us all to present clearer political content and more effective workmanship. This critique can serve as stimulation toward these ends.[89]

The programmatic statements favored by the party were crowded out by references to neighborhood problems and events, association and election news, and even more frequently denunciations.

One common type of *Straßenzeitung* denunciation targeted apartment house owners. Typical accusations were that the owner did not take proper care of the building, harassed his tenants for rent, and evicted those who fell on hard times. These landlords were not only denounced as enemies to all workers but were also often accused of being Nazis. In addition to the complaints of managerial incompetence and ill treatment, there were also numerous veiled charges of sexual harassment, and even rape, of female

---

[88] For copies of *Der kommunistische Agitator*, see BA-SAPMO, RY1/I3/1-2/99a.

[89] BA-SAPMO, RY1/I3/1-2/99b, circular on agitation and party literature by the BL Berlin, likely 1932, p. 592.

tenants. In the summer of 1932, such claims were leveled against the "Nazi house-pasha" at 49 Paul-Singer Street in the *Rote Andreasplatz*. The newspaper alleged that although a worker did not have his August rent ready on the first, he was ready to pay in full by the fifteenth. When he tried to deliver his payment: "The house-pasha claimed not to be at home, in order to avoid collection of the rent money! Because this Nazi pig prefers to 'work out' the back rent personally with the women. This scoundrel did not succeed in his goal! Now he wants to steal the tidy inherited furniture of the young couple."[90] It would be clear to the readers that the woman had rejected the landlord's advances, prompting his attempts to confiscate their property in retaliation.

Another recurring type of landlord denunciation was brought on by the harassment and eviction of politically active tenants. A neighborhood flyer entitled "To the Pillory" made it public that the cigar salesman C. had evicted a barber and cobbler who were serving on the house tenants' council. The authors warned: "The Surveillance-Council of the North will see to it from now on that all antiworker shop owners like C. are sent to the pillory! Antiworker shop owners will no longer be supported by the business of the proletariat."[91] Attempts by workers to wield economic power through boycotts were common. This strategy illustrates the socially mixed nature of these neighborhoods and the recognition of interdependence between groups. As the Depression deepened and the buying power of workers declined, the conflict and denunciation across class lines in these neighborhoods increased.

Others who incurred the wrath of neighbors were police informants and shop owners who "overcharged" their customers. The accused were characterized again as Nazis, but only in some cases was specific evidence presented connecting the accused to the NSDAP. In a flyer addressed to the inhabitants of the neighborhood around Hansa Street, the author claimed that since the beginning of the year the basement at Hansa Street 4 had served as a "*Nazikaserne,*" "a foothold of the brown murder-terror, a new home base for the cowardly, insidious, bloody acts of the Swastika Band." The flyer went further in charging that Z., the owner of the house, "only employed SA men in his bakery and what's more paid them below the wage rates." The reader was then addressed directly: "Did you know that 25–30 [SA] men sleep there every night? Did you know that you are no longer safe

---

90 LAB, Rep. 58, Nr. 1303, Film 734, *Der Rote Andreasplatz*, Nr. 9, August 1932.

91 LAB, Rep. 58, Nr. 1739, Film 735. The cigar salesman filed a complaint with the police. Both the barber and cobbler were brought in for questioning. Neither belonged to a political party or admitted any connection to the flier's appearance. There were no other leads, and the investigation was ended in the summer of 1932. It should also be noted that the name "Surveillance Council of the North" was not to my knowledge a KPD-sanctioned name, which means that this was likely a neighborhood organization with tentative ties to the KPD.

when returning home in the evenings? Incidents of harassment by Nazis have already occurred."[92]

It is easy to imagine that stories like these, with subtle sexual imagery or a threatening tone, would captivate readers. Raising awareness and fear was a powerful way to increase support for the local self-defense organization, which was described at the bottom of the flyer. These accusations were also effective in isolating the denounced within the neighborhood. Long denunciation stories almost always had some element of sexual impropriety, secret political activism, or violence. They were neighborhood-based and, as in the preceding two examples, were quick to name names and addresses.

But such eye-catching stories were not the only avenue for denunciation in the street newspapers. Lesser offenders found their names and addresses included in the "blacklist" of people to be boycotted by the community. In an issue of the *Simeon Bogen* from February 1932, the last page included a call for members of all parties and the politically indifferent to band together to keep the neighborhood free of Nazis. This appeal was followed by a list of addresses for twelve Nazi barracks in the traditionally Red Southeast.[93] As in the example of the cigar shop owner, it was made explicit that the shops listed were to be boycotted. The names of teachers who beat their pupils, forced the singing of patriotic songs, or were not up to date on the benefits of sport were also listed in the school newspapers. Police who took the side of Nazis in street brawls, or cracked down harshly on workers' demonstrations, could also find themselves described as *"Nazilumpen"* in the pages of the *Straßenzeitungen* and among those blacklisted.[94] The threats did carry some weight, since members of the *Schutzpolizei* often walked the beat near their own homes. One police lieutenant, who was aware he was being targeted, complained at his station that the local *Straßenzeitung* "agitated against me in the strongest, most detrimental way, undoubtedly with the goal of

---

[92] LAB, Rep. 58, Nr. 1696, Film 751, early 1932. A twenty-six-year-old single man was arrested for handing out the flier. He admitted to the crime of circulating nonregistered political materials but asked for a mild sentence because "the publication contained no important political content" (judicial statement by the accused, Jan. 20, 1932). There is no record of a court decision in the file. The last comment is from the district attorney's office to police headquarters on March 11, 1932, calling attention to a precedent case from the year before that sheds doubt as to whether handing out fliers among neighbors should be seen as public circulation.

[93] LAB, Rep. 58, Nr. 1723, Film 752, *Simeon Bogen*, Nr. 4, February 1932.

[94] LAB, Rep. 58, Nr. 1303, Film 734, *Der Rote Andreasplatz*, July 1932. The NSDAP was able to recruit some members of the force, acquiring as many as two hundred to three hundred supporters within the *Schutzpolizei* before 1933. These numbers remain small, however, in relation to the overall size of the force, which during the 1920s averaged about fifteen thousand, including five hundred officers. Hsi-Huey Liang, *The Berlin Police Force in the Weimar Republic* (Berkeley: University of California Press, 1970), p. 92. See pp. 81–94 for more on attempts at subversion in the Berlin police force by both ends of the political spectrum.

rendering me ineffectual."[95] When the blacklist followed a story on how Nazi violence was treated lightly in the courts while Communists were given harsh sentences, it is easy to imagine how the boundary between economic and physical revenge began to disappear.[96]

In addition to local police, others denounced as "workers' enemies" also received copies of the street newspapers. Many of the accused were quick to bring charges against those who wrote and circulated the information. However, the police could do little to stem the circulation of publications that were often deposited anonymously in mailboxes. Most street cells knew either to forego listing the editor's name or use a false name. Even though people selling the newspapers could be arrested, the law was written so that the person circulating the newspaper had to be aware of its content in order to be held responsible. From the judicial records, it is clear that the vast majority knew they would be freed if they claimed they had no knowledge of what they were distributing or selling. It is possible that many actually were unaware of the content of the circulars, since during the Depression, the selling of political news was one occupation that was expanding. Those questioned on charges relating to selling illegal political publications were not typically professional political activists. Rather, they were simply unemployed workers, often women (for the KPD), who were known by name in their neighborhoods and had only tenuous ties to the political organizations they represented.

One difference between the denunciations found in the street newspapers and the internal KPD party documents is, of course, that the latter were not for public consumption. But it was likely, especially if disciplinary action such as expulsion from the party was the result, that friends and neighbors would eventually hear rumors. A certain level of secrecy, however, encouraged those with information to come forward and feel safe in their accusations. The other main difference between the two groups of sources is that the second deals almost exclusively with suspected enemies within the politicized proletariat. However, we should be careful not to define these people solely in terms of socioeconomic class. As will be demonstrated here, one's status as friend or enemy was determined much more by one's actions, and there was no sense that class adherence was somehow hereditary, as has been found in Soviet denunciation files from the 1930s.[97]

To be denounced for "unproletarian behavior" could mean many things. Least often it meant that one was suspected of harboring ideological beliefs

---

[95] LAB, Rep. 58, Nr. 1303, Film 734, internal police memorandum, August 5, 1932.

[96] For example see, "Sondergericht," LAB, Rep. 58, Nr. 1308, Film 734, September 1932.

[97] Cf. Sheila Fitzpatrick, "Signals from Below: Soviet Letters of Denunciation of the 1930s" in *Journal of Modern History* (Vol. 68, No. 4, 1996b), pp. 831–66. The volume also appeared as, Sheila Fitzpatrick and Robert Gellately, eds., *Accusatory Practices: Denunciation in Modern European History, 1789–1989* (Chicago: University of Chicago Press, 1996a).

that strayed from the party line. When this was the case, the denunciations tended to be about participation in SPD-sponsored activities or preparing too arduously for terroristic or revolutionary offensives. For the most part, however, it seems that even those who strayed often lived in harmony within the KPD cells. If they were denounced, expulsion could follow, but this was not usually the case.[98] In one case, a man had been relieved of his cell duties by his local comrades because it was found out that he was simultaneously a member of the SPD. The Berlin leadership, however, was not willing to lose this low-level functionary, declaring that this "was a typical case... of what happens when a comrade with a good proletarian will to fight" is hindered by a cell that has more "good talkers" than "practical, working comrades." Party superiors clearly thought it was worthwhile to overlook his fraternization with the "social-fascist enemy" and were convinced it would be easy to set this good comrade back on the correct – KPD – path.[99]

Acting on ideological denunciations could lead to challenges of local or city leadership authority. In one such case, the political leader of the Eighteenth Street Cell in Neukölln was removed from his duties (but not kicked out of the party) because someone accused him of spending his evenings with members of the *"Rechten"* (the oppositional Communist faction). A meeting of the cell was called; at this time a representative from the UBL was present to turn over the command of the group to another man. When the charges were read, the members of the cell refused to accept the transfer of power. At first the accused claimed he was not a member of the faction but had only visited their meetings to educate himself. He defended his reasoning: "It can not be held against me that I visited these meetings, since the party also sends us to the meetings of the Nazis."[100] He finally admitted that up until two months prior he had been a dues-paying member of the KPO. Even this evidence did not dissuade his supporters, who claimed his assurance that he was no longer an active member of the opposition was "good enough" for them. The frustrated visiting functionary was forced to close the meeting having failed to implement his orders.[101]

Accusations about a member's social behavior were more common than allegations of ideological inconsistencies. In most cases, this suspicion was not tied to specific charges of spying or betraying the party in any way. Even the vaguest of accusations passed on to the right sources, however, could lead to questioning, house searches, or other modes of surveillance. A number of Berlin's Communists came under suspicion when it was discovered

---

[98] Cf. BA-SAPMO, RY1/I3/1-2/89, p. 325. This file contains a discussion of the request of a man to rejoin the KPD.

[99] BA-SAPMO, RY1/I3/1-2/91, March 8, 1932, pp. 123–4.

[100] BA-SAPMO, RY1/I3/1-2/89, p. 400, minutes of the November 26, 1930, meeting of the Eighteenth Street Cell in Neukölln.

[101] Ibid. We can be fairly sure that this minor rebellion was not fabricated since the minutes were kept by the man who was himself supposed to replace the denounced political leader.

that they had ties to foreign countries, including holding foreign passports or having knowledge of a foreign language, especially if this knowledge was gained through formal education. It is easy to see why KPD members might hide a middle-class background in order to pass as a member of the proletariat. In some cases, revelations about a person's background could lead to accusations of spying; in others, it resulted in charges of "salon-Communist"[102] or "fair-weather Communist."[103]

Another behavior that upset local members, but was usually overlooked by party officials, was heavy drinking. Drunkenness too often led to bragging and aggression that resulted in unwise offensives and needless injuries. Local Communists complained further that frequently intoxicated members and functionaries reinforced the negative image of the party. Only when drunkenness was connected to repeated party criticism or "loose lips" about party plans, however, did the KPD leadership take steps to confiscate the party membership book of the offender.[104] Sometimes difficult decisions had to be made. Thus, the intelligence liaison man in a Charlottenburg *Häuserschutzstaffel* (house defense squadron) sent in a report in the spring of 1932 complaining of the disturbances caused by one functionary who was too drunk to remember meetings, instigated reckless battles with other political organizations, and made unfounded claims about his comrades.[105] He had already faced the party tribunal for his drinking and fighting with other party members in 1931, but because he was a good organizer, his superiors appointed him leader of the squadron. The Berlin leadership was finally forced to terminate his membership, after the second denunciation of behavior "known to police, bureaucrats and the opposition."[106]

Perhaps not surprisingly, "unproletarian behavior" was frequently blamed on the poor influence of wives or other women. A hard-working man who had stolen party funds in order to pay medical bills to treat his tuberculosis was shown leniency. When he did it again, the blame was placed on his wife. Even though she was a party member, her accusers referred to her as a "backward type, without a hint of class consciousness." The couple's Charlottenburg party cell included some more prosperous members, and

---

[102] BA-SAPMO, RY1/I3/1-2/89, p. 375. In this case the woman involved attracted suspicion because she spoke High German.

[103] BA-SAPMO, RY1/I3/1-2/91, p. 271. This member was overheard speaking Spanish with another comrade.

[104] BA-SAPMO, RY1/I3/1-2/93, p. 70. In one such incident, the man chose to read the socialist *Die Welt am Abend* instead of the *RF* for his political news, but his real crime was that he was a "hopeless drunk and totally falling apart."

[105] BA-SAPMO, RY1/I3/1-2/91, p. 188.

[106] Ibid., p. 185. He also still owed money to a number of political organizations. In contrast to the conventional picture of the KPD in the early 1930s, it should be noted that not everyone who wanted to enter the party was accepted. Information of past criminal connections in most cases hindered one's application for membership. The party was conscious of its public image. For examples, see BA-SAPMO RY1/I3/1-2/89, pp. 74, 225–8.

party officials reasoned that the wife wanted comforts her husband could not afford.[107] When another female KPD member denounced her husband as a police informant, she herself came under suspicion for spending time with an ex-RFB man who had been expelled from the party and was now assumed to support the NSDAP.[108] One man, who had recently joined the KPD, quickly came under suspicion when he claimed that he was being sent by superiors to fraternize with "Nazi girls." This statement proved to be untrue, and the fact that he had been recently evicted for "going after" the fourteen-year-old daughter of his landlord led others to conclude that he fit the character profile of a spy.[109] These files point to a strict moral code that censored greed and sexual improprieties more than ideological independence. The man was not likely a spy so much as a sexual predator, but by using the politicized language of the day, this community could safeguard itself from his threatening behavior.

Party members who moved from house to house, living off the goodwill of other comrades, also drew attention as engaging in suspicious behavior. A great deal of time was spent at all levels of the party apparatus trying to trace the whereabouts of people who had disappeared, or the backgrounds of new arrivals who claimed to have been very active KPD members in other cities. If these questions could not be answered satisfactorily, the warning would be sent out that the person in question was not to be trusted. While the party was most interested in uncovering spies planted by the police or NSDAP, vagabonds often turned out to be nothing more than common thieves, supporting themselves by accepting room and board from other party members and then skipping town with any items of value from the apartment of the generous host.[110]

The following example of a warning from an UBL in Göttingen written to colleagues in Berlin illustrates how petty crimes were used as evidence to implicate party members for more serious political infractions.

Valued Comrades! We have already twice sent you information about L. L. who was in Göttingen from 1929 to 1930, joined the party in 1930, was also member of the Kampfbund, Rote Hilfe.... L. was even a member of the UBL. He suddenly disappeared from Göttingen. He had betrayed and stolen from many comrades, embezzled party funds, and took the luggage of one comrade with him. He owed

---

[107] BA-SAPMO, RY1/I3/1-2/90, May 15, 1931, p. 308.

[108] BA-SAPMO, RY1/I3/1-2/94, January 14, 1932, p. 274. Female Communists were not infrequent subjects of denunciation. Most commonly, they were charged with embezzling, which is not surprising since female Communists frequently served as treasurers of their local party cells.

[109] BA-SAPMO, RY1/I3/1-2/90, October 2, 1931, p. 456.

[110] See also BA-SAPMO, RY1/I3/1-2/91, p. 145. As in many cases, this man turned up in a KPD bar claiming to have been a member in Nuremberg, although he had no party identification. After spending two weeks on a female Communist's apartment floor he disappeared, leaving numerous debts in town but taking his host's jewelry with him.

four months rent to another comrade, and had debts with another. In Braunschweig he stole a comrade's bicycle.[111]

After a quick description of his background, which highlighted his time spent in the Reichswehr and NSDAP, they concluded: "Our comrades in Berlin should have taught him a lesson, because he is certainly a spy. It was also often noticed, that he always had large sums of money, even though he was unemployed."[112] We see in this example the difficulty the party had in ousting those who were threats. As this functionary explains, the Berlin branch of the party had been warned twice, but nothing appears to have been done.

As in this last example, a variety of infractions could lead to suspicions of spying for either an opposing party or the police. Although the party was always encouraging its members to become more active in the political fight, it was dangerous to appear too anxious to take on more responsibility. In one report, a young man was too interested in party literature, especially illegal *militärpolitische Schriften*. His cell reported this anomaly and added "that K's physiognomy is that of a typical spy."[113] In Berlin-Mitte, one Communist was characterized as "either a careerist or a Nazi spy. Proof: he is trying with all means to get a position within the cell or party structure." His refusal to read the KPD's daily, *Die Rote Fahne*, was also widely known.[114] In another such case, the evidence was strengthened when neighbors heard the man's mother say in the stairwell, "You only joined the KPD to spy on them."[115]

The mother's exclamation on the stairs certainly hurt his reputation, but so did the fact that his father was a "strict SPD-man and Reichsbanner leader." In fact, in a large percentage of cases, information about relatives or friends of the person in question played an important role in the denunciation. Anxiety about the intentions of one female KPD member arose solely out of her relationship with a man in the conservative DNVP. The party even searched her house to see if any evidence of her true political leanings could be ascertained. They found Church literature and even more damning: "the room was rather nationally decorated, that means sofa pillows with the iron cross, patriotic pictures [on the wall] and more.... In a notebook we found the lyrics of a number of nationalist songs."[116] Two days later she was fired

---

[111] BA-SAPMO, RY1/I3/1-2/93, p. 189.

[112] Ibid.

[113] Ibid., p. 272.

[114] BA-SAPMO, RY1/I3/1-2/90, report about Herr J., October 5, 1932, p. 4.

[115] BA-SAPMO, RY1/I3/1-2/93, p. 259. These files also contained letters written by accused spies in defense of their actions. There was an appeal process, and the KPD claimed not to publish anyone's name on the official "warning list," which was circulated throughout the country, until they had gathered irrefutable evidence. See further, BA-SAPMO, RY1/I3/1-2/91, February 16, 1932, p. 305.

[116] BA-SAPMO, RY1/I3/1-2/91, pp. 308–9.

from her long-time job as a typist for the *Handelsvertretung*, which had connections to the KPD and the Soviet Communist Party.

House searches like this one were conducted frequently to investigate the information provided in the denunciations. In order to check up on one man, two KPD "friends" went to his apartment building and asked the porter for information first. As they left they saw the family in question on its way to a birthday celebration. The intelligence officer reported: "They were all well-dressed, H.'s son was without a hat and made a fascist impression."[117] In a second attempt to test their political loyalties, a KPD representative attempted to sell the family party literature at their home. The daughter welcomed them in, and the wife bought two brochures. The investigation did not end here; six weeks later the opportunity arose to speak with the suspicious son, who was sixteen or seventeen years old. The KPD man introduced himself as an NSDAP functionary and explained that the young man had been recommended as an NSDAP sympathizer. He then personally invited the teenager to an upcoming HJ meeting. In the words of the KPD spy: "the son of H. regretted very much not to be able to attend, since his parents have forbidden him to take part in such events."[118] The third and final report on the family seemed more confident that its members were committed to the KPD, but some suspicion still lingered, for it had been recently discovered that the man's sister-in-law hung small swastikas in her windows.[119]

In many ways, these examples bring the book's arguments full circle. First, they remind us how important living conditions in the neighborhoods were to this culture of radicalism. From these sources, we can learn much about how these neighborhoods functioned in this period. Without the cramped housing blocks, there simply could not have been so many overheard conversations, which in this climate often led to denunciations. It is astounding, in comparison to the lives most of us lead today, the amount of knowledge neighbors had about each other's daily schedules, personal problems, income levels, and social circles. There are stories in which neighbors tell the police that a man must be a KPD activist because there is constant traffic of party members in and out of his apartment. There was also a man who arrived in another city claiming that he had been forced to leave the capital because he was wanted by the police for his illegal party activities. This city was informed in turn by Berlin that the new arrival was not an active rowdy. Instead, the functionary explained, it was common knowledge the braggart was only trying to escape a bad marriage.

Second, these sources illustrate the economic and political diversity of even these most traditionally Red workers' neighborhoods. There is a strong sense of interdependence as well as tension between shop owners and customers,

[117] BA-SAPMO, RY1/I3/1-2/93, p. 249.
[118] Ibid., p. 250.
[119] Ibid., p. 251.

pub owners and their regulars, and even patrolmen and the public. One "conscientious police officer," who was not a Communist, was still praised in a spy's report for his "great intelligence" and "unquestionable personal courage."[120] We must recognize that the economic realities of the day were as significant as ideological differences, if we want to understand the increasing antagonism between neighborhood groups. For example, in one case a pub owner took on a Nazi clientele instead of his previous KPD customers simply because he was not able to stay open with the business the Communists assured. Likewise the SA was kicked out of its share of bars because they caused too much property damage. The political diversity in these neighborhoods also provides a crucial ingredient to the mix. Only in recent years has there been a growing acceptance among historians that there was some support, or perhaps even significant support, for the NSDAP among workers in the early 1930s. Such claims are very difficult to quantify with my sources, but it is evident that the vision of a polarized situation in which political rivals had little or no contact is a misconception. The denunciation files show that Communists had friends and even relatives who supported other parties. Brothers in the SA and RFB were not unheard of. One former Nostiz Kiez resident remembered one family from Mittenwalder Street with two KJVD sons and a third son in the SA, who contributed to his movement by collecting funds for wounded comrades at Yorck Street rail station wearing a conspicuous head bandage allegedly received in the line of duty against the "Communist terror."[121] There is also ample evidence that people at this level did switch sides from left to right and sometimes (when the parties allowed it or simply did not notice) back again. In 1930, the BL Berlin-Brandenburg overrode a decision by the UBL South to disband the Neukölln Antifa (named Red Storm). The band of men had accumulated debt and had connections to the SA. The city leadership attempted to whip them into shape, but eventually they were forced to recognize what those below had tried to tell them: "The connections with Nazis date from earlier times, since many members of the SA today were organized in the Communist Youth. The relationship of the Antifa today is such, that the members are somewhat friendly with the members of the SA."[122]

Third, these sources tell us much about the KPD and the way the party was organized and operated at the local level. Although we often hear of the structural hierarchy and complex bureaucracy of the KPD, the picture that emerges from these files is one of disorganization. Party books were out

---

[120] BA-SAPMO, RY1/I3/1-2/96, p. 24. He had been suspected as spying on KPD activities, but the investigation concluded that he was not a spy, just a friendly policeman. This case was not typical, but nonetheless shows that such relationships were possible.

[121] König, *Berlin-Kreuzberg* (no date), pp. 30–1. König also recalls the occasional changing of political affiliations within the Kiez.

[122] BA-SAPMO, RY1/I3/1-2/94, final report on the liquidation of the Antifa Neukölln, September 28, 1930, pp. 238–9.

of date, lost, mistakenly confiscated, and sometimes issued to current Nazis. People joined the party, were expelled for various infractions of party rules or because they simply stopped participating, and then rejoined years later. Members sometimes refused to participate in the vital street organizing for fear of retribution by employers or neighbors, and many demanded compensation for the loss of work and wages that often came with radicalism. The chain of command constantly broke down because the local cells would not (or could not) respond to requests by their superiors for further investigation or confirmation of denunciations. Finally, as I have argued throughout this chapter, there was a strong sense of independence at the local level. On many occasions, street cells simply ignored instructions from above, and most of the party's attempts to control its members were in vain.

This brings me to my fourth point, that these files also shed light on how people defined politics and their individual roles within the party and beyond. For example, the party tried to rein in one man who was known throughout his neighborhood as a KPD fighter, in the literal sense. He had been arrested numerous times for his physical aggression, and his actions were damaging the reputation of the party. It turned out that, although he fought the battles of the proletariat on Berlin's streets, he had never bothered to actually join the KPD. Party functionaries visited him at home and tried to make it clear that he needed to take his place within a street cell and become "politically educated."[123] He responded angrily: "I stress emphatically: formally speaking, until official membership in the party, the party has no power of command over me!" After listing a retinue of service to the cause over the years, he continued: "My struggle has made a reputation for me as a good fighter. If I now became a member of the party..., I have no intention to lose my qualification as a fighter. And my fighting-power will be taken away from me, if I must fight... under the aforementioned conditions."[124] When he was brought in front of the party arbitration court two months later, he complained that his case should be decided by "active fighters" instead of "membership book holders." "It is my proletarian right, to answer to fighters and not any old unschooled comrades!"[125]

This man's self-constructed identity is typical of the street brawler whose masculinity or "fighting-power" is based on his actions in his community and not membership in an organization. In fact, he feels threatened by even this most radical political institution. Though this KPD fighter is not typical of all those present in these documents, his defense helps us understand why denunciations were central to this radical culture. Whether the denunciation was based on immoral behavior or ideological conflict, about possible spies or those who sold information to the police, there are three similarities.

[123] BA-SAPMO, RY1/I3/1-2/90, letter of October 30, 1931, p. 17.
[124] BA-SAPMO, RY1/I3/1-2/90, letter of October 29, 1931, p. 19.
[125] BA-SAPMO, RY1/I3/1-2/90, letter of November 22, 1931, to the UBL North, p. 32.

The sources emphasize the necessity of local action, and both denouncers and the denounced stress the importance of personal and also community reputation. Taken together, therefore, these sources also provide evidence for the existence of a separate, neighborhood-regulated political sphere that transcended the institutional structures offered by the parties and republic.

If denunciations reflected many characteristics of Berlin's radical culture in crisis, what purpose did they serve in these workers' communities? On the one hand, it should be clear that I do not believe denunciations were common simply because the KPD told its members to root out the enemy. The KPD did indeed advocate such a policy, and the party tried to use the information received to control its supporters and protect the "revolutionary potential" of its organizations. However, the party had little success in attaining either goal. On the other hand, this assertion does not mean that I believe denunciations arose solely out of apolitical motivations such as personal revenge, paranoid suspicion, or monetary gain. Rather, in this period of crisis, the social relationships that made these communities function were increasingly difficult to maintain, and the denunciations were a form of internal discipline. Everyone knew that providing information to the police or political opponents was a way to make money, and in these overcrowded housing blocks everyone had information. But if members of the community knew that doing so would lead to a public denunciation, they would be less likely to sell or share their stories. As a result, denunciations could limit the influence of outsiders and help maintain neighborhood autonomy under threat.

This self-disciplining did not develop out of fear of party retribution or commitment to ideological ideals. I am arguing instead that workers, regardless of what the KPD or NSDAP advocated, knew that in these difficult times certain behaviors, such as stealing, spying, excessive drunkenness, bragging, and other social infractions, hurt the ability of all to weather the storm. I am not necessarily describing class solidarity, nor did neighborhood discipline demand political homogeneity. As I have demonstrated, there was a great deal of accepted political and social diversity in these neighborhoods. It was a delicate balance, and when the actions of outsiders or accepted individuals weakened the social relationships that benefited all, denunciation was the best way to isolate the offender and warn others. We can imagine that there were other manifestations of this visual surveillance, but even when limited to denunciation, we should recognize in this behavior attempts to establish "defensible space" through "an intricate and effective intelligence and communication system."[126] This is clearly a paradoxical situation. For

---

[126] Borchert, *Alley Life in Washington* (1980), pp. 129–31. The phrase "defensible space" is used by Borchert but comes originally from Oscar Newman, *Defensible Space: Crime Prevention through Urban Design* (New York: Macmillan, 1973). Jankowski also refers to a similar concept. He says that interviewees in gang-controlled neighborhoods argue that

communities in which political institutions had lost legitimacy, denunciation was an attempt by people to maintain order in their own lives. However, over the long term, the suspicion fundamental to all denunciation practices could only serve to undermine the very community they were hoping to safeguard.

these neighborhood authorities do a better job defending the neighborhood than the police because they are more evenly distributed through the territory and know "who belongs and who doesn't." See Jankowski, *Islands in the Street* (1991), p. 184.

5

The Logic of Violence

On December 2, 1930, the following report was issued by the political police (IA) on the Communist pub at number 16 Nostiz:

Not too long ago a bar opened at Nostiz Street 16, and this bar became a regular meeting-pub for the KPD. Owner is a certain Lorenz. From this bar KPD attacks are organized and carried out on political opponents almost daily. The perpetrators of the individual assaults are assisted in the organization of the attacks by certain people, among whom are women and girls, who unceasingly crisscross the area, inform their accomplices about the current stationing of individual officers and patrols, and shortly before the attack is carried out, open apartment building doors and attend to hiding places and lodging for the perpetrators. In particular these attacks are carried out on Gneisenau and its cross-streets, Schleiermacher, Mittenwalder, Zossener, Solms, Nostiz, Belle-Alliance, Baruther, Fürbringer etc. . . .

In the above noted streets the political hooliganism has gotten so out of hand in recent times, that police officers, who must carry out their duty in these streets, are daily under attack. In individual cases, officers have been hit with heavy objects (stones, flower pots) that have been thrown out of the apartment houses.[1]

This officer's report shows that a real sense of politicized territory had been created in the Nostiz Kiez, space over which there was competition for control. He does not mention outside party authorities, and he recognizes the input of women, even if he is shocked by their involvement. Like denunciation, Berlin's political violence was regulated by codes of behavior that participants were expected to follow. This chapter will examine how such patterns and rules could lend violent behavior a sense of logic in the Nostiz Kiez and beyond, thereby legitimating brutality as a political strategy. But as with denunciation, grassroots political violence only worsened the social instability of these neighborhoods, leading to greater incursions from the outside, more citywide fear of Red Berlin, and responses by the state, which ultimately brought the republic to an end. The unrest of May 1929 has been described here as a turning point in the development of radicalism, and yet the violence that followed it was quite different. The Berlin riots surrounded a particular controversy: the police ban on public May Day demonstrations. Therefore, the riots had easily identifiable sides and boundaries. Although

[1] LAB, Rep. 58, Nr. 161, Film 372, police IA report, December 2, 1930.

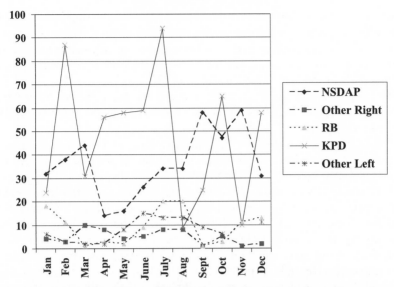

Figure 8. Political assemblies at which police intervened in Berlin, per month 1931. Source: GStA, Rep. 77, Title 4043, Nr. 121. These statistics were collected by the Berlin police force and presented to the Prussian interior ministry at the beginning of 1932 for the Prussian police annual report, "Wegweiser durch die Polizei."

the extent of the bloodshed was unexpected, once the upheaval quieted there was no chance for a recurrence of violence around this issue. In fact, the May Day celebrations of 1930 to 1932 ran quite smoothly. The violence that did become quite common in the early 1930s was more pervasive, more bloody, and certainly more of a threat to political stability. In Kreuzberg alone, there were twenty-five significant violent political incidents and at least six deaths between 1929 and the end of 1932.[2] Police in the capital came to expect brawls at most campaign rallies and marches. For example, see the numbers of assemblies requiring police intervention in the city during 1931 in Figure 8.[3] But in general, the violent outbreaks that characterized this period,

[2] By "significant" I mean incidents of violence that the police recognized and investigated. There were certainly many more small-scale scuffles that did not register with the police. For a timeline of these twenty-five, see Axel Reibe, "Mit den Sturmabteilungen der NSDAP fängt es an" in Kunstamt Kreuzberg, ed., *Kreuzberg 1933. Ein Bezirk erinnert sich* (Berlin: Dürchschlag, 1983), p. 49.

[3] Statistics from GStA, Rep. 77, Title 4043, Nr. 121. These statistics were collected by the Berlin police force and presented to the Prussian interior ministry at the beginning of 1932 for the Prussian police annual report, "Wegweiser durch die Polizei." These figures illustrate the tense political atmosphere in Berlin when compared to the data for the entire Prussian state. In 1931, there were 1,290 cases of police intervention at political assemblies in Berlin alone. In Prussia, there was a total of 2,904 such incidents in that year. Therefore 44 percent of all cases of police action at political assemblies in Prussia during 1931 took place in Berlin.

and that became so difficult to control, were the incidents that involved only a handful of people on a street corner or in a courtyard. These confrontations took place regardless of day or hour and were impossible to prevent. This sort of daily turbulence was more frustrating for the police than large-scale mêlées at election rallies or the riots of 1929 because they could not always identify a clear perpetrator or cause for the violence. It was also more unsettling for Berliners who could see no end to the chain of attacks and counterattacks.

The extent of the violence in Weimar Germany, and Berlin in particular, is difficult to quantify. For the early part of the 1920s, we only have the totals of deaths compiled by the political parties themselves. They tended to keep track only of those who died in battles with the opposition, which excluded the police and minor political organizations. The national socialists and Stahlhelm claimed to have lost only thirty and twenty-six members, respectively, to left-wing radicals across the entire country between 1924 and 1929. From 1923 until the beginning of 1930, the KPD lost ninety-two supporters throughout the Reich to "fascists," while the Reichsbanner counted thirteen dead between 1924 and 1928.[4] As the violence increased at the end of the 1920s, state officials also began to keep records of the number of deaths and injuries caused by the unrest.

These governmental statistics show a dramatic rise in the early 1930s. Reich officials reported that 143 Nazis died and 18,515 were injured in political violence between 1930 and 1932. One hundred seventy-one Communists died in political battles, and over eighteen thousand were injured, between 1930 and the middle of 1932. In the last four years of republicanism, the Reichsbanner lost close to forty men, or roughly three times as many as had died in the previous four years. Even so, the definition of political violence used to compute these statistics by the interior ministry neglected a great deal of the small-scale violence so common in this period. Only those violent outbursts that had extensive public impact were counted. This impact was measured by the number of participants, the form of the attack, the weapons used, and the level of physical harm that resulted. Officials were explicit that they had ignored those attacks "between man and man."[5] As will be shown in this chapter, however, these small skirmishes between individuals often led to significant injuries themselves or caused a chain reaction of additional, and sometimes greater, confrontations. We can only assume, therefore, that many injuries and even deaths attributable to the political crisis are not included in these numbers.

[4] Eve Rosenhaft, *Beating the Fascists? The German Communists and Political Violence, 1929–1933* (Cambridge: Cambridge University Press, 1983), p. 6.
[5] GStA, Rep. 77, Title 4043, Nr. 126, letter from the commander of the Landeskriminalpolizeiamt I to the Prussian interior minister, October 12, 1932.

The available data for injuries and deaths attributable to the political crisis in Berlin are also quite fragmentary. City authorities counted seventeen deaths and over four hundred injuries during 1931. In the first half of 1932 alone there were fourteen deaths and over six hundred registered injuries.[6] From July 21 until the end of August there were three more deaths and roughly fifty additional injuries in the capital.[7] The Berlin *Schutzpolizei* counted 147 injuries among their own men between January 1929 and the end of 1932. In the summer of 1931 alone four officers were killed in the line of duty; all four deaths were attributed to the KPD. Of the 147 injuries to police from 1929 to 1932, only thirty-five were blamed on noncommunist radicals, or were considered unsolved.[8] Even without statistics for 1930 and the end of 1932 and knowing that the recording methods of the police overlooked large numbers of violent incidents, it is clear that the bloodshed was mounting.[9]

This chapter will focus mostly on these small-scale disturbances, describing only briefly the larger, campaign-related conflicts. The local outbreaks of violent behavior fit well into my description of Berlin's neighborhood culture. Though not always initially apparent, these disruptions often had common causes. Some fights originated in arguments about money, others in personal jealousies. Revenge for earlier physical and nonphysical acts of aggression was a similarly prevalent motivation. The desire for territorial control was perhaps the most common source of neighborhood violence. The locations for these incidents also conformed to certain patterns, which reflect the local significance of the violence. Besides the large campaign rally sites and meeting halls, the landmarks of the Kieze ranked high as trouble spots. Transportation nodes, neighborhood pubs, and central squares all exhibited their social and political importance by their centrality in the turmoil. As shown in the last chapter, political conflict also began to touch new spheres in this period. Schools and welfare offices, for example, were not immune to the violence. Furthermore, by looking at specific cases it becomes clear that the violence

---

[6] GStA, Rep. 77, Title 4043, Nr. 121. Both the NSDAP and KPD calculated higher death and injury tolls. A Berlin proletarian women's group sent the police what they viewed to be a more accurate account of the figures for murdered workers than those offered by the police. Their total for 1931 was twelve workers killed by right wing organizations and police. The *Schutzpolizei* was also asked by the Prussian interior ministry to verify a list printed in *Der Angriff* and *VB* in April 1932, which made it appear that the Berlin NSDAP was the sole victim of the capital's street violence.

[7] GStA, Rep. 77, Title 4043, Nr. 126, interior ministry report dated November 23, 1932.

[8] GStA, Rep. 77, Title 4043, Nr. 122, "Nachweisung über die seit dem 1.1.28 durch Angehörige politischer Organisationen getöteten oder verletzten Schutzpolizeibeamten," which covers the period from January 1928 until October 10, 1932. For the statistics from October until the end of 1932, see the memo from the chief of police (Abt. I) to the Prussian interior minister dated February 3, 1933 in the same file.

[9] For the official statistics compiled by the Berlin *Schutzpolizei* and Prussian interior ministry, see GStA, Rep. 77, Title 4043, Nr. 121 and 126.

itself followed a common set of rules and behaviors. These standards were not sanctioned by any official body, but they too demonstrate that the disorder served a purpose in these people's lives. Acts of violence were structured around ritualized displays of bravery and were based on commonly held assumptions about the defense of turf and comrades. Participants even expected that rules of "fair play" would be followed and censured those who did not stay within these bounds. This assertion may seem far-fetched, but those studying American gang violence, a phenomenon that has certainly led to more deaths than the incidents examined here, make similar claims. Martin Sanchez Jankowski argues "that while gang violence is often vicious and brutal, it is not unrestrained." Instead "restraining mechanisms" that include "internal organizational codes" and a "code of conduct" both condone the violence and regulate it.[10] What we have here are struggles for local power. Radicals believed that the demonstrations, flood of propaganda in circulation, denunciations, and, for a minority, even violence would play an immediate role in effecting change in their lives, by affirming their status in the community as arbiters of right and wrong.

In this chapter's second section, I turn to the court system, within which many street fighters found themselves entangled, often at a very young age. The focus of this section will be to analyze the rationalization of violence that gripped this society. There were three sets of actors who had a say in making sense of the turmoil. First, there were the defendants themselves. Through their police statements and courtroom defenses, we see how they conceptualized their actions. Naturally, these records should be used with caution, for the men likely responded in ways they hoped would help their position in the eyes of the law. Nonetheless, even responses tailor-made for the police and courts tell us a great deal about social standards for behavior. Second, in many cases the opinions of youth welfare administrators, who often had long histories with these adolescents and young men or their families, were crucial in determining punishment. Through their assessments of the defendants and their crimes, we learn what welfare officials understood the causes of radicalism in Berlin to be. The comments and rulings of the third set of actors, the prosecutors, judges, and *Schöffen* (judicial lay assessors), further clarify the limits of this form of criminality and also the legitimacy afforded to political violence in this society.[11]

---

[10] Martin Sanchez Jankowski, *Islands in the Street: Gangs and American Urban Society* (Berkeley: University of California Press, 1991), p. 139.

[11] The best known studies that document injustices in the Weimar justice system are: Heinrich Hannover and Elisabeth Hannover-Drück, *Politische Justiz, 1918–1933* (Frankfurt a. M.: Fischer, 1966); Gotthard Jasper, "Justiz und Politik in der Weimarer Republik" in *Vierteljahrshefte für Zeitgeschichte* (Vol. 30, No. 2, 1982); and Manfred Krohn, *Die deutsche Justiz im Urteil der Nationalsozialisten, 1920–1933* (Frankfurt a. M.: Peter Lang, 1991). For contemporary diatribes, see Eike von Repkow (pseud. Robert M. W. Kempner), *Justiz-Dämmerung. Auftakt zum Dritten Reich* (Berlin: Volksfunk Verlag, 1932; second edition,

The goals of this chapter, therefore, are numerous. At the most basic level, my intentions are to unravel the processes by which violent actions were carried out on Berlin's streets and shed light on the participants and their motivations. In doing so, it becomes clear that these actions cannot be separated from the radical neighborhood-based culture in which they flourished. Alongside daily demonstrations, street newspapers, and boycotts, acts of violence served as literal manifestations of a larger fight against disorder, a fight in which party affiliation was only a detail. The analysis of this unrest, and its representation and rationalization in the Berlin judicial system, contributes to our greater understanding of how the stability of the entire city, and even the republic as a whole, could be undermined by small-scale, at times even personal, localized conflicts.

THE ANATOMY OF STREET VIOLENCE

In the study of violence during Weimar's final years, much attention has been focused on the Communist and Nazi Parties and their policies of instigating and organizing violent behavior among their supporters. There is no denying that the local and national leaderships of the KPD and NSDAP supported violent behavior through their militaristic rhetoric and organizational structure, through combat-like exercises and physical training, and through the aggressive tone of their propaganda, which targeted enemies and outlined historical struggles.[12] On the other hand, the extent to which the parties' local

1963) and Ernst Fraenkel, *Zur Soziologie der Klassenjustiz und Aufsätze zur Verfassungskrise, 1931–1932* (Berlin: E. Verlagsbuchhandlung, 1927; second edition, Darmstadt: Wissenschaftliche Buchgesellschaft, 1968). On the political motivations of lawmakers and justice department officials in reestablishing the use of the death penalty during the early 1930s, see also Richard J. Evans, "Die Todesstrafe in der Weimarer Republik" in Frank Bajohr, Werner Johe, and Uwe Lohalm, eds., *Zivilisation und Barberei. Die widersprüchlichen Potentiale der Moderne* (Hamburg: Christians, 1991) and Evans, *Rituals of Retribution. Capital Punishment in Germany, 1600–1987* (New York: Oxford University Press, 1996). To help navigate through the terminology of the Weimar justice system, see Fritz Stier-Somlo, Alexander Elster, Erich Volkmar, and Günther Küchenhoff, eds., *Handwörterbuch der Rechtswissenschaft, Bände I–VI* (Berlin: Walter de Gruyter, 1926). Though Peter Caldwell's recent book discusses the competing visions of popular sovereignty held by the republic's leading constitutional theorists, it is an important contribution to the literature on the contradictions of Weimar's "constitutional culture." See further Peter Caldwell, *Popular Sovereignty and the Crisis of German Constitutional Law: The Theory and Practice of Weimar Constitutionalism* (Durham, NC: Duke University Press, 1997).

[12] The KPD issued a confidential monthly newsletter informing those involved in illegal demonstrations how to conduct themselves in marches that were expected to turn violent. One issue of *Oktober* told its readers to wait in the side streets before the demonstration began, so as not to attract attention, to leave any site of confrontation as soon as it was over, to stick together in self-defense, to keep track of the leader, and to take advantage of any opportunity to disarm police officers. This issue of *Oktober* specifically targeted ways to circumvent the March 21, 1931, presidential decree, which banned all outdoor political assemblies. See,

leaders played a direct role in organizing street violence is difficult to trace. It was certainly common for local party units to orchestrate violent outbursts at opponents' rallies. Yet there were also many confrontations that developed in an impromptu manner or were planned only by the participants themselves.

Communist violence in Berlin has often been characterized as self-defense from Nazi aggression.[13] However, this assessment is not entirely accurate. Communists had a tradition of physical confrontation with the Stahlhelm and social democratic organizations, especially the Reichsbanner, throughout the 1920s. These groups and the *Schutzpolizei* – the "tools" of the Social Democrats – were seen as the traditional enemies of Berlin's revolutionary proletariat, as witnessed by the May 1929 violence. In the early part of the decade, Berlin's Communists did not judge the NSDAP to be a serious competitor. This relationship only changed as the SA began to make its presence felt in the city's escalating turmoil. Nazi-led attacks on Jews and supporters of the left were encouraged by Goebbels and his underlings as part of the "Struggle for Berlin" aimed at workers' neighborhoods and in line with the party's anti-Semitic policies.[14] By the end of the summer of 1929, Horst

---

GStA, Rep. 77, Title 4043, Nr. 1, "Mitteilungen aus den Landeskriminalpolizeiamt," Nr. 23, December 1, 1931. One way the NSDAP encouraged violence was by financially supporting the consequences of violence. Pub owners were paid for the damage their establishments incurred through the use of rowdy party members. The families of young people involved in the HJ or NSS could receive party funds if their sons had been injured in party-related activities. In rare cases, the party even made efforts to get new school assignments for members. See, BA, NS 26/278 and NS 26/347.

[13] Some historians have stressed the aggression of a middle-class NSDAP, which was met by "resistance" from the politicized working class in what amounted to class warfare. For example, see Anthony McElligott " ' . . . und so kam es zu einer schweren Schlägerei': Strassenschlachten in Altona und Hamburg am Ende der Weimarer Republik" in Maike Bruhns, Claudia Preuschoft, and Werner Skrentny, eds., "*Hier war doch alles nicht so schlimm*" (Hamburg: VSA-Verlag, 1984), p. 60. Conan Fischer's work offers a different perspective. Concerning the NSDAP, Conan Fischer makes the point that "the Nazis' physical struggle was, almost unequivocally, offensive in nature." For the KPD, he separates the party leadership from the rank-and-file by arguing that the Communist leadership organized defense leagues to counter the fascist threat but admits "that their ordinary members often saw things differently and wished to respond to aggressive violence in kind." However, he stops short of exploring this last dimension: why Communists at the grassroots sought independence in developing their own violent offensives. Conan Fischer, *The German Communists and the Rise of Nazism* (New York: St. Martin's Press, 1991), pp. 149–53.

[14] Before 1933, the role of the SA in the workers' districts of Berlin was primarily to challenge leftist activism and not to serve as "anti-Semitic crusaders." For this reason, anti-Semitic violence is not covered in this chapter. On this prioritization of undermining the parties of the left, see the excerpt from a 1927 SA directive in Richard Bessel, *Political Violence and the Rise of Nazism. The Storm Troopers in Eastern Germany, 1925–1934* (New Haven, CT: Yale University Press, 1984), p. 45. For a further example of how the NSDAP used this strategy in its greater goal of gaining and maintaining leadership of the government, see *Sturm 33*. This party publication, the purpose of which was to construct the martyred image of Berlin Sturm leader Hans Maikowski, glorifies the stormtroopers' "protection"

Wessel's SA Sturm-5 had mounted attacks on two Kreuzberg pubs. These and other incidents in surrounding areas made it clear that the Berlin KPD's policy of disinterest toward the Nazis was in need of revision. Over time, the Berlin SA became increasingly brash as a result of its growing popularity and more favorable treatment by the police and courts, putting the left's antifascist street campaign in a more defensive and less effective position, but this fact should not overshadow the willingness and desire of many of Berlin's Communists to engage offensively in street battles.

The assumption that Communists were merely defending themselves also derives from the fact that KPD leaders were never fully comfortable with advocating street violence. The ZK feared that such a stance would further solidify the KPD's reputation as a band of ruffians. After May 1929, the fear of an imminent ban on the party, and the later desire to win over supporters of the SPD, kept them from straying too far from legal political strategies. In addition, an open policy toward individual acts of violence, which the SA had adopted by the late 1920s, meant a great deal of freedom at the local level. The Goebbels-led Berlin NSDAP was willing to risk this independence for a time because their other attempts to strengthen the party in the city had failed. The KPD, on the other hand, already had a strong position in the capital and struggled with the possibility of allowing local initiative, which they feared would foster ideological independence.

Despite these misgivings, the Communist leadership did for a time advocate a physical offensive against Nazi incursion into workers' districts. The phrase, *"Schlagt die Faschisten, wo Ihr sie trefft!"* (Strike the fascists wherever you meet them!), was resurrected from earlier battles against the Stahlhelm and reemployed first in Berlin by the fiery KPD orator and *RF* editor Heinz Neumann in August 1929.[15] Almost immediately, the party leadership, including party chairman Ernst Thälmann, began to doubt the efficacy of this program. The real motivation behind the *"Schlagt die Faschisten"* policy had been to combat NSDAP electoral growth and encourage an inclusive antifascist front. Neither of these goals was furthered by direct violence. Street brawls did nothing to shake the interest or confidence of the great majority of Nazi voters, and the bulk of Berlin's Social Democrats remained reluctant to join a physically dangerous antifascist movement. As the party leaders debated these issues, Communist street fighters continued to battle with local SA units.

In early 1930, the circulars published by the underground RFB leadership were beginning to show signs of discontent with the current path. Local underground factory cells were told to forsake the *"Schlagt die Faschisten"* line in favor "of mass political work to free the working-class elements from

---

of participants at Nazi rallies. *Sturm 33 Hans Maikowski. Geschrieben von Kameraden des Toten* (Berlin: N.S.-Druck und Verlag, 1933).

[15] Rosenhaft, *Beating the Fascists?* (1983), p. 64.

the fascist organizations and win them for the RFB and the revolutionary struggle."[16] In an even more pessimistic memo criticizing the growing independence at the local level, the RFB Reich leadership noted that "the neglect of the political and exaggeration of the physical struggle has led to de-politicization and passivity. The political works called for are carried through only slightly and without enough control."[17] Finally, in June 1930, the party made public its disenchantment with the slogan *"Schlagt die Faschisten, wo Ihr sie trefft!"* The prior stance on violence was reversed, and instead the ZK called for a more structured and unified offensive against the growth of the NSDAP. By stressing propaganda and education, Communist leaders believed they could attract Social Democrats and teach SA members the errors of their leaders' ways.

This about-face was due in part to the ZK's recognition that a good deal of SA support in urban centers like Berlin came from workers. In its rejection of individual violence, therefore, the new policy stressed that physical assaults on SA men were in fact attacks on "class comrades." The goal of expanding the front against fascism by including members of the SA itself, along with workers from the SPD, was a significant change in strategy, which reflected the diversity of the political crisis in these neighborhoods. By disallowing individual acts of violence, however, the RFB and KPD also prioritized regaining administrative control over local cells. The dangers of local initiative had become clear by February 1930. The party was taking its own beating in the Berlin press for the recent death of the popular SA-Sturm leader Horst Wessel.

Despite this change of heart, the ZK's June resolution did not summarily reject violence. The ZK and Berlin-BL tried continuously to explain that the new tactic "meant in no way, that we are 'pacifists,' and reject violence."[18] However, they insisted that party members differentiate between the "individual terror" of gang warfare and "organized mass-struggle," which was to include self-defense, propaganda, and education administered from above. The new concept was especially unwelcome in Berlin, where there was open rebellion against the June resolution.[19] In fact, the change in direction only served to widen the gap between the KPD and its membership in the capital. Through 1930, the number of SA bars in Berlin's workers' districts continued to grow, which meant that the last unchallenged spaces for KPD organizing were dwindling [Plate 11]. Responding to this loss of territory and general discontent with the policy among the ranks, in April 1931 the

---

[16] BA-SAPMO, RY1/I4/2/8, "Resolution concerning the work of the RFB, 1929." No further date is given, but the ZK resolution comes clearly after the May banning of the RFB.

[17] BA-SAPMO, RY1/I4/2/22, "Report of the RFB-Reichsfraktionsleitung," February 23, 1930.

[18] BA, Rep. 15.01, Nr. 26159, "National work plan for the KbgdF," January–March 1932.

[19] Eve Rosenhaft notes that in Berlin people refused to participate in public demonstrations after the June resolution because of their disapproval of the new party policy. See Rosenhaft, *Beating the Fascists?* (1983), p. 67.

Plate 11. On January 30, 1933, Communists allegedly killed Hans Maikowski, the leader of the SA troop that met regularly at this bar. Source: © Bildarchiv Preussischer Kulturbesitz, 2003.

party leadership reiterated more clearly in the *Rote Fahne* that the June resolution supported "mass-terror," if not individual terror, and called for action against SA bars. Pleased by the modification, Berlin Communists led a series of attacks, mostly in the form of small group assaults or drive-by shootings, against key Nazi pubs in workers' districts, leaving a number of people dead by early fall. These attacks were planned by RFB and KbgdF district leaders and were carried out by well-known local rowdies. Among lower-level functionaries, the campaign was seen as a success, but their superiors were shocked by the level of violence and the enthusiasm for it among their men and decided the offensive had not been worth the damage done to public opinion.[20] The party could not live with such a program because it accentuated how much its survival in Berlin depended on neighborhood initiative rather than mass action. The Depression had caused such suspicion, economic vulnerability, and political fragmentation in the city that large-scale

[20] For a detailed analysis of the 1931 campaign against SA taverns in Berlin, see Rosenhaft, *Beating the Fascists?* (1983), Chapter 5. This chapter is most instructive for its description of the interaction between the local and city party leaders, as they debated and planned one attack in particular on Richard Street in Neukölln.

actions, never mind the mass strike, were no longer realistic weapons. Party leaders had been forced by their most radical rank-and-file to try it their way, but the executive soon realized that such methods only scared off peaceful workers and convinced rowdies that they had no real need for the party.

From late 1931 on, leaders of the various Communist organizations sent down instructions reminding low-level functionaries and rank-and-file radicals that "individual terror" was unacceptable. In November 1931, the ZK tried to reinforce its position by quoting a 1916 antiviolence speech by Lenin, coupled with a less theoretical approach: "Attacks on isolated Nazi pubs as individual acts by a workers' group bring us not one step further in the struggle against fascism."[21] This message was repeated a week later in a letter to all factory and street cells in which "the development of terrorist sentiments, the application of individual-terror against the fascists, . . . the carrying out of senseless individual actions and armed attacks, [and] adventurous play with explosives" were highlighted as among the greatest threats to the party.[22]

Despite these instructions, confusion and disagreement between KPD leaders and Berlin's rank-and-file Communists over the value of individual terrorism continued. For example, in the summer of 1932, a meeting was held of the 150 neighborhood functionaries who made up the UBL Northeast. The police were there to report on the proceedings, and from the spy's account we can see the persistence of discord on this issue. The Northeast party secretary, Fritz Otto, began his address by recounting the successes of a united workers' front during the republic: the munitions strike of 1918, resistance to the 1920 Kapp Putsch, the Cuno Strike of 1923 and others. He then called for "mass mobilization" against fascism in this tradition at the workplace and in residential quarters, instead of terror. Otto added that the ZK intended to remove from the party all those "who, with pistol in hand, lead the fight against fascism and [through their actions] encourage the same." This statement was met with loud cries of disapproval from the audience. A second functionary, Gotthard Hoffmann, then spoke on the subject of the upcoming Reichstag election, and tempered his comrade's party line by declaring: "The KPD will not put up with the Nazis moving their propaganda into the workers' quarters in the next few days. One will ruthlessly beat them out of the workers' districts through mass mobilization."[23] The controversy over the meaning of "mass mobilization," and specifically the role of violence, remained heated in Berlin. Even without the party's official support, an offensive struggle was warranted as a way to maintain the integrity of their

---

[21] BA-SAPMO, RY1/I3/1-2/28, "Gegen den individuellen Terror," November 10, 1931.

[22] BA-SAPMO, RY1/I3/1-2/28, memo to all factory and street cells: "Für revolutionären Massenkampf gegen individuellen Terror!" November 17, 1931.

[23] BLHA, Rep. 30, Berlin C, Title 95, Sektion 9, Nr. 191, political police IA spy report dated June 18, 1932, concerning the previous day's meeting of the Northeast UBL at the Weissenseer Gesellschaftshaus.

neighborhoods and prove to the community that they too had the courage and discipline to solve the crises of the day.

The KPD's June 1930 resolution against individual terror, therefore, did little to curb KPD radicals from seeking confrontations with Nazis in their neighborhoods. After this date, we must assume that, for the most part, violent KPD actions were impromptu or planned only by participants. The roots of this turmoil, like the origins of the denunciations discussed in Chapter 4, were found in all manner of disputes, encompassing economic discrimination, personal revenge, and political antagonism. The combatants did not always know each other personally, but they often knew of each other. Street violence was a highly ordered affair that conformed to general patterns of behavior and expectations for the participants. The most active SA and KPD street fighters had reputations and commanded respect and authority in line with their prior deeds, much like their unaffiliated political cousins the clique "bulls," discussed earlier.

It is difficult to judge the extent to which the general population of the workers' districts participated in the unrest. Even though the number of violent activists was small, residents clearly had extensive knowledge of local conflict. Street newspapers were fairly explicit about the political allegiances of Kiez residents. There were also plenty of eyewitnesses to the brawls at rallies, in pubs, and on the streets, and rumors circulated about criminal acts. This information turned up in the numerous anonymous tips sent to the police, including the names and addresses of guilty neighbors, and in the testimony presented at court. Finally, we know from police records that sympathetic neighbors often got involved by harboring suspects or by coming to the aid of "their troops" by pelting opponents and police with objects from windows. The police tried to keep abreast of the rumors circulating about changing neighborhood hierarchies, offenders' street names, and the relationships between various radical groups. However, the *Schutzpolizei* were usually thwarted in their attempts to control violence by the secrecy of radicals and the antagonistic acts of nonviolent sympathizers. They were hindered further by the simple fact that small-scale street violence could erupt anywhere in Berlin, at any time day or night.

The police did have an advantage during campaign seasons because they could be fairly certain that Communists and Nazis would try to disrupt each other's preelection assemblies and marches. In the case of an outdoor march, opponents would usually schedule their own meeting indoors, at a pub or hall in the area and then wait for the approaching parade. For example, in October 1930, the Berlin NSDAP received police permission for a campaign march through the workers' district of Neukölln. The district's Communists "coincidentally" planned a sports competition in the Neuköllner Stadium for the same day. Instead of meeting at the stadium, the Communist athletes were to assemble on a square in nearby Schöneberg and march en masse to the competition site. The police anticipated a confrontation and issued an escort

Plate 12. Hitler Youth corps singing as they march through Berlin under the protection of the police, early 1930s. Source: © Bildarchiv Preussischer Kulturbesitz, 2003.

for the KPD parade. The Communists marched to the sports stadium without incident but did not stay inside. Instead, roughly eighty men left the building and drove back toward Schöneberg, where they formed another parade. Knowing the Nazi marchers were not far away, the police now commanded the Communists to break up their columns. When they resisted, the police cleared the street with the use of their batons. The Communists took refuge in a known KPD bar on Bahn Street. The patrolmen mistakenly assumed that since the crowd was now inside, it was safe to leave the scene. Having reached their station, they were immediately sent back out because the Nazi marchers had just entered Bahn Street. Though initially the *Schutzpolizei* had been ordered to protect the Nazi marchers, they now attempted to ensure that the Communists inside the bar were not attacked. The Communists, who did not want police protection, pelted the arriving officers with beer glasses and coffee cups and barricaded the tavern door.[24] In the end, both sides were thwarted in their attempts to disrupt the other's plans. The Nazi marchers passed the bar, while the police stood between them and their trapped opponents. It was not every day that the *Schutzpolizei* had such luck [Plate 12].

---

[24] GStA, Rep. 84a, 2.5.1., Nr. 10598, "Strafsache beim Schöffengericht Schöneberg," October 4, 1930. From this entire sequence of events, only one man was arrested and charged with leading a riot that demonstrated violent resistance to the police (glasses and a belt buckle were thrown). The forty-three-year-old Schöneberg resident received a six-month jail sentence.

To disturb an indoor rally, one side would encourage as many of its own supporters as possible to attend the scheduled meeting of the opposition. Sometimes more uninvited guests than supporters of the organizers showed up at these assemblies. The campaigning party was then forced to end the rally before it began, since the serious audience members were such a clear and threatened minority. However, when the hosts tried to shut down an event early because of the danger posed by the unwanted guests, a brawl was likely to ensue. In a number of cases, fighting began before the speeches did, as the organizing party attempted to limit the number of political opponents entering the building. Sometimes the evening's speakers were able to begin their presentations without incident, but as the crowd became heated by the provocative rhetoric, catcalls would escalate to physical confrontation. In other cases, organizers invited opposition speakers to participate. Naturally, the combination of debating politicians and a mixed crowd often resulted in fistfights or rushes toward the podium.

The hosts always stocked the room with plenty of bouncers and body-guards for the speakers, but these men were often eager to fight and acted more often as instigators than peacekeepers. Both those who came to render *Saalschutz* (protection for the rally) and those present to disrupt the event expected a physical end to the evening and came lightly armed.[25] Brass knuckles and knives could be smuggled in fairly easily past the weapon searches, but chair and table legs, beer mugs, and ashtrays from the rally site proved to be formidable weapons as well. Beyond checking for weapons, police attended all political assemblies to report on the content of the speeches, size up the audience, and keep the peace if needed. If a physical confrontation erupted, however, they were always far outnumbered by the crowds, which could range from one hundred to several thousand people, depending on the size of the hall. The police, therefore, had little chance of preventing brawls from starting; they could only hope to limit the damage, clear the room, and arrest some of the participants.

In June 1930, the *Vossische Zeitung* reported on a large-scale brawl in the Saalbau Friedrichshain. The NSDAP had organized a public rally in

---

[25] As conditions worsened in Berlin, *Saalschutz* became a more serious endeavor. In early 1932, the Rote Hilfe circulated new rules about conducting *Saalschutz*. The rules were intended to make security more efficient and safer for volunteers. For example, the new instructions prohibited members providing *Saalschutz* from coming to the rallies alone. Instead, the cell functionaries were to coordinate and escort those willing to the assembly and then stay with the volunteers until the end of the event. The rules also suggested that a more systematic network of *Saalschutz* volunteers be set up and controlled by the local level of the KPD. See GStA, Rep. 77, Title 4043, Nr. 225, "Richtlinien für die Durchführung des proletarischer Veranstaltungen von Rote Hilfe Deutschlands," February 19, 1932. When mixed assemblies took place, the police regularly searched for weapons at the entrance, even when the assembly drew a relatively small crowd. For an example of a search and the weapons retrieved, see GStA, Rep. 84a, 2.5.1., Nr. 10619, ministry of justice memo, January 1931.

the hall, which was filled to capacity with about three thousand people. The Communist Party was strongly represented, with perhaps as many as one thousand members in attendance. The Nazi speaker had the floor for ninety minutes, which transpired without incident. A KPD representative was allowed to make a rebuttal, but not long into his speech, the Communist minority began singing the "Internationale," which was countered with whistles from the Nazis. Soon beer glasses and chairs flew through the windows, followed by members of the audience. Expecting just such a disaster, the *Schutzpolizei* had stationed five hundred men at the site, who immediately stormed the hall to break up the mêlée. Afterward, the hall "lay in ruins." Most of the windows were broken, and the floor was smeared with blood. No guns were found, but at least fifty injuries were reported, twelve of which were serious and resulted mostly from being thrown through the building's windows.[26] Police then conducted an extensive search of the surrounding Friedrichshain neighborhood to arrest suspects and contain the expected aftershocks that always followed the initial eruption of violence. Police surveillance was likely welcomed by the bourgeois readers of the VZ, whose assumptions about "dark Friedrichshain" were confirmed by the report.

Once a rally ended or the police forcibly emptied the hall, scuffles frequently developed as the participants made their way home. This category of street brawls forms a transitional group of violent incidents. They were usually much smaller than the coordinated efforts at the assemblies and marches, involving only a small number of men or even one-on-one confrontations. Yet they were provoked by the antagonism of the large-scale rallies because audience members often left intoxicated and emboldened both by alcohol and the calls to action made by the evening's speakers. These fistfights in the streets surrounding the meeting site sometimes only involved those present at the earlier rally, but there were also attacks on pedestrians who fit the stereotypes of various "enemies" targeted in the speeches by party orators. Again the police found it difficult to prevent these outbursts of violence since they could not escort all audience members to their homes or hold each individual in custody until his radical enthusiasm subsided. As a matter of practice, audience members walked home together in order to protect themselves from this very sort of attack. But this use of the buddy system only heightened the likelihood of violence because small groups of men from opposing sides would cross paths as they returned to their shared

---

[26] VZ, "Tumulte im Saalbau Friedrichshain. Etwa 50 Verletzte – Zahlreiche Verhaftungen," Nr. 300, June 28, 1930. Five months earlier a similar brawl had taken place at another Friedrichshain locale. It drew a much smaller crowd, but at least eight serious injuries were reported. The police suspected dozens of lighter injuries but had no way of counting since the men were carried off by their comrades. See VZ, "Die Tumulte am Friedrichshain. Über 50 Waffen gefunden/ Fünf Minuten Kampf: ein Lokal demoliert," January 22, 1930.

neighborhoods, or a group – encouraged by its numbers – might happen upon defenseless bystanders.

For example, around ten o'clock on the evening on July 13, 1932, one of the deadliest months in Germany's ongoing crisis, an SA Sturm attacked a number of Communists returning home from an evening demonstration on Wittenberg Platz in Schöneberg.[27] All but one of the KPD sympathizers were able to escape, but on hearing his calls for help, they returned to rescue their friend. They were able to free him, but the group was followed and the fighting broke out repeatedly. As the police arrived, shots rang out. Five Communists were severely wounded, two of whom died on the way to the hospital. A number of Stormtroopers were apprehended, and the police found them to be heavily armed.[28] The level of violence evident in this case was not uncommon and led to a variety of charges being filed, including disturbing the peace, resistance to the police, weapons violations, manslaughter, and murder.

In one example from the Nostiz Kiez, we get a glimpse of the kinds of people involved in a typical incident of violence. After a citywide HJ demonstration march on November 30, 1930, in which the Gneisenau Sturm took part, about fifteen marchers, including several young women, were heading home along Gneisenau. They turned into Nostiz to drop off one of their compatriots "in order to avoid an attack by members of the KPD." As they arrived at his address, however, "a large number of members of the KPD suddenly appeared from all sides and jumped the [HJ] troops." Some of those waiting to ambush the Nazis allegedly came out of the Lorenz pub. A number of the Nazis were beat up or hit with stones, and nine were taken into custody by the police. Their ages ranged from eighteen to thirty-one years old. Eight of the nine were single. Seven lived with one or both parents. Three reported having fathers who were no longer living; one had "no knowledge of his father." Only four appeared to have some sort of employment.[29]

Sometimes those returning from a rally claimed to the police that they had sensed the danger and sought to avoid the confrontation. In one such incident, the Nazis who left a Schöneberg meeting, only to be followed by a

[27] Berlin always witnessed more violence during the summer months because the warm weather allowed for more outdoor political activity and necessitated escape from the stuffy workers' apartments. July 1932 was especially volatile because the ban on the SA, instituted in April, had been lifted during June. The Berlin SA felt victorious after the quick repeal and responded with increasing bravado and aggression. About half of the politically motivated deaths in Prussia during 1932 occurred in July. See GStA, Rep. 77, Title 4043, Nr. 122, p. 328.

[28] GStA, Rep. 77, Title 4043, Nr. 134, chief of police in Berlin to the Prussian minister of the interior, August 5, 1932.

[29] LAB, Rep. 58, Nr. 161, Film 372, case documents, November 30, 1930. In court records from February 1931, it was noted that the Nazi marchers began receiving threats from residents when they entered Kreuzberg. Witnesses also told police that a whistle had sounded, calling the attackers to the street, when the marchers reached Nostiz. Two shots were also fired before the police arrived. In the same file, see also the indictment of February 3, 1931.

group of Communists in a taxi, sought refuge in a police station and nearby Nazi pub. The Communists demonstrated their strength in the area by waiting patiently for the Nazis to emerge in a KPD pub across the street. Though the Nazis claimed later to have avoided any confrontation, they stood outside their own pub's front door, so as not to appear cowardly. The Communists eventually approached, shots were fired, and stones were thrown, scaring the Nazis back into their tavern. No one was injured, except for an approaching pedestrian, who spent some time in the hospital for two shots he received in the arm and hip. Four Communists, identified by the Nazis, were arrested even though no weapons were found.[30]

In these two incidents and many others like them, some patterns of local violence begin to emerge. It becomes clear, for example, that the chief cause for violence was the perceived breach of territorial boundaries. Certainly many of the perpetrators and victims lived near where they were attacked, and most, especially those traveling in small groups or alone, were probably heading home. Nonetheless, any public demonstration of party allegiance, by carrying posters or literature from the rally, wearing uniforms or political insignia, or discussing the evening's speeches, was an affront to those who believed their standing in the neighborhood was determined by their ability to keep out those deemed enemies. There were additional ways in which this territorialization of Berlin's neighborhoods was manifested in violence. Among the most frequently occurring were attacks on propaganda distributors, including assaults on newspaper dealers stationed on street corners or at transportation hubs to sell the party press and confrontations between residents and bands of activists stuffing mailboxes with invitations to meetings or plastering walls and bulletin boards with posters and slogans.[31] Both types of propaganda distribution could provoke residents' sense of turf by

---

[30] GStA, Rep. 77, Title 4043, Nr. 415, police report of violent incident in Schöneberg, March 12, 1930. The strategy of targeting people returning from political meetings had two inherent problems. Innocent pedestrians were sometimes mistaken for political enemies; and even if a few from the rally were found and attacked, it was impossible to judge how many of their party comrades might be just around the corner. See, for example, GStA, Rep. 77, Title 4043, Nr. 302, interior ministry memo, December 6, 1929. After beating four men who were mistaken for participants returning from a NSDAP rally, a small group of Communists were attacked by some Nazis who had in fact been at the meeting, leaving one KPD member with stab wounds.

[31] From the police witness statements in cases concerning the distribution of illegal KPD party literature, especially the local street newspapers, it appears that women made up a good portion of those serving in this capacity. It made sense to have women circulate pamphlets in the housing blocks and at the markets since this was their daily sphere of activity. Depending on the materials, women could also earn a small amount of money selling party writings. Because it was not considered acceptable political behavior to harm women in public, the large number of Communist women participating in the distribution of propaganda meant that the KPD appears to have roughed up more Nazi propaganda salesmen than the other way around. For examples of females under police questioning for their roles in distributing illegal party literature, see the files in LAB, Rep. 58, Film 734.

invading semiprivate residential areas and Kiez landmarks, thereby upsetting local power structures.[32]

The stabbing death of sixteen-year-old HJ member Herbert Norkus, who was delivering party fliers with comrades when he was killed in Moabit, was one such incident of turf violation. Nazis often planned their propaganda raids for the middle of the night or the early daylight hours, knowing that their public presence in large numbers in workers' neighborhoods would be seen as a threat, even if the pamphleteers were area residents. The most dangerous place to be caught handing out unpopular party literature was inside the apartment buildings themselves. A brawl in the foyer where the mailboxes were located was less likely to be detected by the police, or by other comrades canvassing outside.[33] The fact that Kiez Communists frequently knew ahead of time when and where the NSDAP planned to circulate its propaganda is further illustration of the contact between the two sides. Spies certainly played a role, but so did friends and neighbors held in common. In the other type of propaganda-related violence, newspaper sellers were often the targets of attack. These conflicts often involved only a few people, such as in May 1931, when two men selling *Der Angriff* in front of Neukölln's district city hall, who were "known to the Neuköllner Communists [as Nazis]" were attacked by men who had just taken part in an RJ demonstration. Two were arrested, one of whom had allegedly roughed up this same victim two months earlier.[34]

In both types of attacks, the goal was not just to show that Brown propaganda was unwelcome in these Red strongholds and vice versa. The aim was also to humiliate the victim. Attackers tried to steal the newspapers, which could have economic consequences for the besieged salesman.[35] Along with

[32] In his book on sectarian violence in Northern Ireland, Allen Friedman makes a salient point about territorialization. He remarks that it is not just space that defines turf and leads to violence but also violence that leads to turf-defined space. In conjunction with this observation, Friedman explains how burning members of one religious minority out of their homes in Northern Ireland serves as social engineering. The family eventually returns to a neighborhood of coreligionists, further strengthening ethnic divisions. While the tactics used by Nazis and Communists were different from those cited by Friedman, both groups similarly used violence not only as a means to uphold borders but also as a way to construct territorial borders. Allen Friedman, *Formations of Violence* (Chicago: University of Chicago Press, 1991), p. 26.

[33] An HJ member reported in April 1931 that he was overcome by six or seven men in an apartment house hallway, while he stuffed mailboxes with invitations to a party function. He lost his fliers, HJ belt, and HJ insignia and received a mild beating. The culprits wore no uniforms, but he claimed to recognize them as Schöneberg Communist hooligans, one of whom he knew by name. LAB, Rep. 58, Nr. 172, Film 374, victim's report to the police IA, May 19, 1931.

[34] LAB, Rep. 58, Nr. 169, Film 374, concluding report by the police IA, May 23, 1931, and letter from the prosecuting attorney to the Schöffengericht Neukölln, July 28, 1931.

[35] The strategic downside of stealing an opponent's newspapers was that it was hard for a Communist to explain how "80 copies of *Der Angriff* " ended up in his possession. See LAB,

the literature itself, it was common for both sides to take the political insignia worn by the victim – a cap or a patch worn on the shirt or jacket. These personal trophies were symbols of the courage and physical prowess of the victor.[36] Though the loss or damage of the uniform was a financial burden to the often impoverished young radicals, the theft of an RFB cap or SA patch was more humiliating than a physical injury, which at least denoted combat experience.[37]

Another category of violence, caused largely by the central significance of territory in this political culture, was the high level of brutality frequently exhibited by the police in the Red districts of Berlin. Many members of the *Schutzpolizei* were predisposed by their training and backgrounds to assume that all radical workers were criminal revolutionary Communists. The paranoia that emerged when an officer was caught behind "enemy lines" was enough, at times, to result in hasty violent responses. In July 1931, a brawl broke out on a Neukölln street after an SA assembly. As two policemen approached, a number of men dressed in the uniform of the banned RFB ran from the scene. The police fired five warning shots. When a fleeing Communist grabbed at his trouser pocket, one of the patrolmen wrongly assumed that he had a gun and shot him, fatally wounding the suspect.[38] Even though a man lost his life, no charges were filed. The other RFB members were able to escape the scene, and apparently without further investigation, the actions of the police were accepted as necessary under the circumstances.

Another case exemplifies the violent consequences of both turf-inspired propaganda distribution and fear among police within the borders of Red Berlin. Late in the evening in February 1932, a young man arrived at a Wedding police station asking for protection for his SA comrades, who planned on distributing propaganda in the early morning hours to the apartment houses in the area. They feared for their safety because of a

---

Rep. 58, Nr. 158, Film 371, prosecuting attorney to the Schöffengericht in Neukölln, March 3, 1931.

[36] The "hunt" for insignia was such an important part of localized conflict that one RJ member in Kreuzberg noted in police questioning, that his group's meetings regularly ended with such an outing. The "disarming" of a Nazi's insignia did not necessarily result in serious violence; the securing of political trophies was sometimes an end in itself. See Rosenhaft, *Beating the Fascists?* (1983), p. 144.

[37] Martin Jankowski makes a similar claim about his subjects: "gang members are not absolutely adverse to being injured; to them, injuries can be used as commendations. Scars are displayed like medals, and members who do not have them are always a little envious." Jankowski, *Islands in the Street* (1991), p. 139. There is a long history of scar adulation, see Ute Frevert, *Men of Honour: A Social and Cultural History of the Duel* (Cambridge: Polity Press, 1995).

[38] GStA, Rep. 84a, 2.5.1., Nr. 10888, ministry of justice memo concerning the shooting of an RFB member by a police officer in Berlin during a brawl between the SA and Communists on July 13, 1931.

suspicious-looking group of bicycle riders already circling the neighborhood. By three o'clock in the morning the police had begun their investigation at a KPD pub on Soldiner Street, where they were kept waiting outside for close to ten minutes by the pub's unwelcoming patrons. When they finally received permission to question the thirty people in the tavern, many of the suspects ran out of the building. In the confusion, one of the policemen found himself alone in the kitchen with those who had remained inside. He never claimed the patrons attacked him or held him in any way, but he felt so threatened by their presence that he shot his way out of the room. A twenty-nine-year-old male worker died of his wounds at the hospital four days later. Seventeen were arrested for threatening a police officer, and the officer's actions were deemed appropriate. Those taken in by the police were later found not to be KPD members. The police concluded, however, that they were Communist sympathizers, rounded up from the neighborhood to shield those who really intended to carry out the attack against the Nazi propaganda troops that night.[39]

For radical men, the protection and acquisition of territory was a way to demonstrate their authority in the neighborhood. Through their activism they could control access to the semiprivate neighborhood spaces. That violent battles over territory had more to do with neighborhood authority and masculine prerogatives than differences of political opinion becomes clear when examining the reasons for attacks provided by the participants themselves. Time and time again, street fighters cited personal disputes as the causes for violent incidents. Four men, ages twenty-two to thirty-eight, were arrested in early 1931 for beating a Nazi newspaper distributor and stealing his wares. On questioning, the men declared they had heard from a variety of sources that a female *RF* distributor had been harassed by Nazis that same morning. Assuming the rumor to be true, the men explained to the police that they had set out to find any distributor of Nazi literature to beat up in retaliation.[40] Confrontations that revolved around the "protection" of young women, and fights that developed during attempts to woo them, were fairly common. In another instance, a sixteen-year-old Reichsbanner member from Neukölln was questioned for participating in a brawl with a number of HJ members in a park. In his account of the confrontation, he claimed that the "HJ guys were talking to the girls, which aroused the indignation of the other [leftist] youngsters. Therefore, two of them went to Hohenzollern Square, in order to get some more KPD people." When the reinforcements returned to the park, the entire group, which now consisted of fifteen or so young Communist, Reichsbanner, and unaffiliated workers,

---

[39] GStA, Rep. 77, Title 4043, Nr. 133, police chief in Berlin to the Prussian interior minister, March 19, 1932.

[40] LAB, Rep. 58, Nr. 158, Film 371, prosecuting attorney to the Schöffengericht in Neukölln, March 31, 1931.

went up to the Hitler Youths "to see what they would do."[41] Not surprisingly, a show of physical strength in front of some of the area's young female population was the result.

Sometimes the police were forced to reassess their initial conclusions about local altercations, once the underlying motivations surfaced. In the summer of 1932, a pub on the outskirts of Berlin was attacked by a group of men who threw rocks through the windows and destroyed the tavern's sign. Communists were suspected, and since the majority of guests in the bar at the time were Nazis, it was assumed that the perpetrators' ideological convictions had led them to storm the pub and provoke a brawl with the patrons. On further investigation, however, the police determined that the Communists never attempted to enter the building, and that they were just angry with the proprietor. Ten days earlier the Communists had held a cell meeting in the pub but had since been asked by the proprietor to find another location for future gatherings. In response to this snub, the rejected radicals, assisted by neighborhood Reichsbanner troops, exacted revenge by causing extensive property damage.[42]

Economic discord was another primary cause of violence. As noted in the preceding chapter, Berlin's neighborhoods were economic units as well as social and political communities. The Depression vastly increased the codependence and tension between retail and service providers and their customers. Consequently, conflicts over price, quality, or service sometimes had violent ramifications. For example, in the attack just described, the bar owner may have been forced to reject his Communist customers because the Nazis in this small community had threatened a boycott, or because the KPD could not promise enough beer consumption. Neighborhood economic disagreements were often recounted in each party's street newspapers. The Communists in the previous case swore to the tavern owner that they would publish the news of his betrayal and call for a boycott of the pub. The financial difficulties of many of Berlin's radicals could also cause turmoil within an organization. Information concerning the large profit margin on the potatoes sold at an SA cafeteria in Reinickendorf led the local Sturm members to attack their party comrade who managed the kitchen. When this incident was later reported in the local Communist street newspaper, the perpetrators were not criticized. Rather the kitchen manager's financial greed was used as a symbol of the greater "deception, corruption,

---

[41] LAB, Rep. 58, Nr. 1683, Film 750, eyewitness report to the police by G. S., September 24, 1932.

[42] LAB, Rep. 58, Nr. 1676, Film 750, case file of the assault on the Sachs pub in Oberschöneweide, July 12, 1932. The distinction made by the police between "political" and "personal" had legal significance because "political" crimes carried more severe punishments under the presidential emergency decrees, which were issued periodically beginning in March 1931 to contain political radicalism in the republic.

failure to uphold one's word of honor, and sex crimes" of all NSDAP leaders.[43]

Economic conflict could eventually involve the whole neighborhood, as it did in Prenzlauer Berg in November 1932, when competition between two families who owned bakeries in the same neighborhood escalated to denunciation and violence. The family V., which owned a bakery on Prenzlauer Street, also owned the nearby building in which the family G. ran its bakery. The two businesses had coexisted peacefully for twenty-seven years, until the Depression forced the landlord V. to evict his tenants. The family G. must have been in great debt because the courts sanctioned their removal. The landlord probably also hoped that the disappearance of a competitor would increase his own bakery's declining profits in these difficult economic times.

In the weeks before the planned eviction and auction of the business, the radical residents in the neighborhood came to the aid of family G., even though the family had apparently not been active in party politics nor were they members of the industrial working class. In the days preceding their eviction, a threatening letter appeared at family V.'s home, warning them to retract the order to evict or the area's "Workers' Fighting League" would "take the necessary measures."[44] Other fliers turned up around the neighborhood calling the family V. "nationalist" and "Nazi" and encouraging residents to stay away from the auction.[45] Then the sons of the soon-to-be ex-tenants burst into the bakery of their landlord, demanding to see him. When the target of their anger could not be located, they proceeded to break into the man's living quarters, threaten his wife, and ransack the kitchen. Before leaving, they promised to return with others and threatened: "If anything happens to my mother because of this. . . . Then it will be an eye for an eye and a tooth for a tooth."[46] Despite the uproar, the eviction took place as scheduled. News of the conflict had spread throughout the neighborhood, and over one thousand people came out to support the family G. Large numbers of police were on hand for the family's removal.[47] They struggled to keep the streets clear during the eviction process, and a number of demonstrators were taken into police custody.

---

[43] LAB, Rep. 58, Nr. 1690, Film 750, *Der Rote Beobachter des Nordens*, Vol. 1, Nr. 6, no date.

[44] LAB, Rep. 58, Nr. 1496, Film 741, letter from the "Kampfgemeinschaft der Arbeiter, Angestellten und Mittelständler" to E. V., November 19, 1932.

[45] LAB, Rep. 58, Nr. 1496, Film 741, see the fliers "An die werktätige Bevölkerung rund um den Wörther Platz" and "Arbeiter, Angestellte, Mittelständler!"

[46] LAB, Rep. 58, Nr. 1496, Film 741, concluding report by the chief detective, November 19, 1932.

[47] LAB, Rep. 58, Nr. 1496, Film 741, police report, November 23, 1932. For a KPD account of the eviction and the accompanying demonstration, see the *RF*, Nr. 210, November 22, 1932.

All of these local disturbances were multifaceted. Whether they involved challenges to territorial supremacy, personal and economic disagreements, or a combination of all these elements, what becomes clear is that many neighborhood conflicts led to subsequent acts of violence. After one SA man in southern Berlin was allegedly assaulted by KPD members, "[about twelve] SA men from the area got together to seek revenge." At a nearby street corner, they came across a group of Reichsbanner men returning from a rally and decided that beating up these innocent men would suffice as retaliation for the earlier Communist-led incident. The Nazis could not have mistaken the Social Democrats for Communists because the men had just attended an official rally and were likely wearing their RB uniforms. Even if they had been in street clothes, one member of the group was carrying a conspicuous 1.6 meter RB flag.[48] In fact, the SA men would have been better off had they continued their search for more suitable targets because the flag pole was broken during the battle and used as an effective weapon, severely injuring the eye of one of the Stormtroopers. The SA's attack was less about party politics than it was about regaining the local respect lost in the initial assault on one of their own. Their acceptance of these political foes as adequate victims illustrates that their primary goal after the earlier humiliation was to reestablish their reputation in the neighborhood as good soldiers, which in this case failed due to the RB's use of the convenient wooden flagstaff.

Though some of the main sites for political violence – the assembly halls, residential streets, and squares of the workers' districts – have been mentioned, it is important to examine some of the other locations for conflict in Berlin. These were varied, making it increasingly difficult for police to control violence and for residents to avoid disturbances. Berlin's political pubs have been mentioned numerous times throughout this study. The pub's significance as a Kiez landmark, male oasis, and semiprivate sphere lent it both traditional authority and current relevance in the political upheaval. Its central political function as a meeting site, and the prevalence of alcohol at all social and political gatherings within taverns, made the pubs prime spots for spontaneous violence. At one point in the early 1930s, the *Schutzpolizei* kept watch over 354 known Communist bars in the city, about half of which were located in the six original city districts. Nostiz Street had Walter Lorenz's pub, but some major streets that ran through workers' districts were home to more than one KPD bar. Neukölln's Ziethen Street alone had four. Friedrichshain had the highest individual district total with thirty-nine, two each on Weber, Boxhagener, and Lange Streets.[49] The number of

---

[48] LAB, Rep. 58, Nr. 231, Film 389, report by Police Sergeant-7947, June 28, 1932 and district court indictment, July 27, 1932.

[49] BLHA, Rep. 30, Berlin C, Title 95, Sektion 9, Nr. 164, police list by district of the addresses and proprietors of Communist taverns. No date is given, but the list is likely from 1931 or 1932.

Nazi pubs was smaller, and less meticulously accounted for by the police, but their numbers were growing rapidly, leading to bitter and bloody rivalries around the old city center and North and East Ends. By October 1931, the NSDAP also sponsored twenty-two Berlin party *Heime*, the barrack-like residences for impoverished and single comrades.[50] These *Heime* functioned very similarly to the pubs in terms of their role in political violence.

Almost all acts of political violence in Berlin had some connection to pubs and alcohol. It was over a glass of beer that rumors swirled of the opposition's "crimes" in the neighborhood, and news was shared about the enemy's whereabouts on that given evening. In the relative privacy of the bar, troops gathered, and plans were made for attack. During the fighting, the pub acted as a home base. Rowdies sought it as a defensive fort that could be barricaded against stronger forces. The pub also provided reinforcements, and in desperate situations it could be used secretly to telephone the police in order to break up a losing battle. After the incident, the tavern acted as the site for the victory celebration or as a makeshift triage unit for the wounded. When the police arrived, the back door of the bar was employed as an escape route to the interior courtyards and apartment buildings. The front door was kept closed so that patrons could deny knowledge of the turmoil outside, and the pub's interior frequently served as a hiding place for recently fired weapons.

A pub's location represented a greater sense of territorial supremacy to its patrons than having their residences along the same street, because the pub signified political consensus. In some instances radicals even stationed themselves outside their taverns and demanded to see the identification papers of those strangers who passed by, as if manning their own border patrols. Warnings of "the street belongs to us!" further testified to the sense of political turf created by the pub.[51] In October 1931, a group of leftist sympathizers passed an NSDAP pub allegedly without looking for trouble. A group of Nazis were standing in front of the bar, and one of the passersby was punched in the face by a tavern patron. Because the KPD supporters were outnumbered, they ran, but soon they crossed the path of another man, walking alone. The vengeful Communists assaulted him, after noting, "Yeah, you're a Nazi."[52] Only this second attack brought the notice of the police and courts.

Much of the district of Steglitz in southwest Berlin was considered a Nazi stronghold, yet not devoid of KPD sympathizers. It was not surprising, therefore, when a group of Stormtroopers launched a firestorm of bullets at a

---

[50] BLHA, Rep. 30, Berlin C, Title 95, Sektion 9, Nr. 164, police list of SA *Parteiheime* in Berlin, October 14, 1931.

[51] LAB, Rep. 58, Nr. 233, Film 389. In this case, a brawl broke out in Treptow between Reichsbanner and Nazi men, after the RB members insisted on seeing the identification of the passing Nazis. When additional RB men poured out of the pub "Maus," a pedestrian was asked by the surrounded Nazis to call the police.

[52] LAB, Rep. 58, Nr. 192, Film 379, concluding report by the police IA, October 7, 1931.

contingent of RB and KPD men on their territory. A policeman on the scene claimed to have heard twenty-five shots, and one twenty-two-year-old Communist was rushed to the hospital with serious gunshot wounds. Five SA men stood trial for the shooting, and their statements to the police declaring their innocence illustrate how a violent evening might develop. A twenty-four-year-old SA defendant who had previously been a member of the KPD and was found with two guns after the incident – one of which was still warm – described the evening in the following way:

On June 26th I ate my dinner at the SA-Home around 7 P.M. Afterward I went to the restaurant, "Wiesenschlößchen," which serves as a regular pub for the SA. There I met a whole number of comrades, and also some who belonged to other Steglitz SA-units. No specific plan was issued for this evening. I played skat in the garden and drank my beer. I was not in the pub the entire time. Naturally, with regard to the Communists, who by the way from time to time [watched] our pub and had set up a patrol system on Schloß Street, which means a volunteer service which has the purpose of figuring out if anything is going on [sic]. One cannot really speak of a patrol system [among the SA]. Whoever feels like going out for a while does so and uses this opportunity to see what is up. Nothing had happened, so after midnight, it may have also been 12:30, I and Comrade G. walked along Schloß and Grünewald Streets to the Fichteberg. Neither of us was in uniform. I had a small SA insignia on my jacket and a large one on my tie. When we reached the hill, we heard shots in the vicinity of the district city hall. . . . One of the others questioned, W., is a leader of the KbgdF and also of the RFB. He naturally does not speak very highly of me, especially since I brought over a number of his comrades to the NSDAP. I can't comment on the other witnesses.[53]

From this excerpt, we can draw a number of conclusions about daily life among radicals and the overall context in which this shooting unfolded. First, this defendant spent the evening with his SA friends, in what appears to have been a frequent pattern: dinner at the party home and then beer and cards at the pub. Second, we learn that on some evenings there was a planned attack, the instructions for which would be circulated to all those present at the pub. Third, though there was allegedly no plan for an assault on this night, it was understood that when outside one should keep an eye on any possible activities in the neighborhood. Fourth, he claims that both the leftist organizations as well as his own SA took part in some manner of patrol, and both viewed Schloß Street, a major thoroughfare through Steglitz, as prime territory worth controlling. Finally, membership fluctuation among radicals in Steglitz meant these combatants were familiar with each other. These personal relationships could, as in this case, present more reasons to fight. The RFB leader had already been embarrassed once before by this SA

---

[53] LAB, Rep. 58, Nr. 201, Film 381, concluding report by the police IA, June 28, 1932 and the statement given by E. G. on August 8, 1932. The membership fluctuation in this case is also of significance.

man, who had "stolen" a number of his comrades. After such a humiliation, the RFB fighter would be unlikely to back down from a chance at redemption. The former Communists would also be enthusiastic about a shootout, since victory would prove they had correctly chosen the "superior" – more disciplined, more masculine – organization.

Though the city's drinking establishments were the quintessential sites for violent confrontation, Berlin was also experiencing an advancing politicization of other parts of the social realm previously considered beyond the reaches of politics. While political disagreements did not always result in bloodshed in these areas, there were some cases in which physical conflict appeared. As discussed earlier, Nazis and Communists founded children's organizations that were closely tied to activities at schools. As the political crisis intensified, political campaigns linked to schools and the associated parents' committees took on an especially aggressive tone. School strikes became increasingly common in a number of working-class districts. Parent-led demonstrations were usually conducted peacefully, but the violence of the streets was also reflected in schoolyard animosity among older students. In one instance, a father brought charges against one of his son's classmates for politically motivated physical abuse. The boy had harassed and kicked the man's son for wearing a brown shirt to school. W., the accused seventeen-year-old, made it clear to the police that he saw it as his duty as a representative of the left-wing student group to "suggest" his schoolmate change his wardrobe. In fact, this budding rowdy invoked the same territorial justification for his actions that was used on the street. Allegedly, he told his principal that when a Nazi student appeared at the "purely Marxist Karl-Marx School" in a brown shirt, "the Marxist students had the right to rip the shirt from his body." When the Hitler Youth supporter threatened to have some of his friends confront his attacker the following day, the young left-wing radical had replied: "the issue is not cleared up by such threats" and then kicked his opponent.[54] A number of other students were interviewed by the police and freely noted their individual political positions and/or organizational affiliations. In a long letter to the district attorney, the father of the HJ student showed his displeasure that the SPD-aligned principal refused to act against such activism in this state-run, ostensibly politically neutral space. In fact, the father declared that, since his first complaint to the school, "the terror carried out through obscene language, threats and insults on the part of W. and his like-minded comrades has only intensified."[55]

Violent activism was also aimed at institutions of the state. Feeling frustrated with the failing welfare system and suspicious that the criminal justice

---

[54] LAB, Rep. 58, Nr. 1592, Film 747, police witness report by sixteen-year-old SAJ sympathizer, T. R., November 29, 1932.
[55] Ibid., case file documents including the letter from the alleged victim's father to the state prosecutor's office, August 16, 1932.

system was prejudiced against them, workers lashed out at the state's representatives. There were extensive measures taken during the early 1930s to secure federal offices in Berlin against attack, though violence during the Depression rarely targeted anonymous bureaucrats or high-level administrators. Nonetheless, Reich officials feared armed rebellion against their facilities as much as the mass strike. What they failed to realize was that there was no possibility of mass action because, in addition to the organizational shortcomings of the KPD, the rank-and-file in Berlin did not prioritize the grand goals of the party. Rather, workers' political passions were stirred by the difficulties of daily existence, and they sought immediate, local solutions. As a result, the real threat against state administrators existed at the neighborhood level. The only official "outsiders" who regularly fell victim to worker resistance were police and welfare workers who had daily contact with Berlin's radical residents.

On the evening of the Reichstag elections in September 1930, officers on duty by the police station on Selchower Street in Neukölln were shocked to see a group of about one hundred men armed with sticks and canes heading in their direction. When the patrolmen realized the crowd was readying to storm the station, they ran to alert their colleagues and seek shelter inside. With the doors opened to accept the returning patrolmen, some of the demonstrators were able to push their way into the station's foyer. The police fought back, and the group was pushed back out into the street. They began to run, but from within the crowd, someone yelled: "Stand your ground!" The group, presumed to be Communists, followed the command, and shots were fired at the station and returned by the officers. The demonstrators, some of whom may have taken part in a similar attack on the same police station during the May 1929 unrest, dispersed and could not be immediately apprehended. The police undertook an extensive search of the area and brought in thirty suspects. In the end only three stood trial, two juveniles and one twenty-one year old who was a well-known, previously arrested, Neukölln street fighter.[56]

This example is of interest on many levels, especially because of one proclamation, which emanated from the advancing gang, and which appears more than once in the judicial accounts of the evening's events. As the group of loosely assembled demonstrators first made its way peacefully past the *Schutzpolizei*, one activist yelled: "You can give us your batons, we can still use them; but we have enough pea-shooters [Knarren]."[57] This sort of taunting always accompanied confrontations between police and radicalized workers. Though not physically dangerous, similar shows of disrespect hit the nerves of the embattled police, often leading to the use of

---

[56] GStA, Rep. 84a, 2.5.1., Nr. 10589, district prosecutor to the Prussian minister of justice, October 25, 1930, and indictment at the Schöffengericht Neukölln, October 21, 1930.
[57] Ibid.

violence. As with the violence between political parties on Berlin's streets, the motivations behind this assault on official outsiders were numerous. They included the claim to neighborhood autonomy through the exhibition of courage ("Stand your ground!"), the challenge for territory (in the assault on the police station), and the use of tactics to humiliate the enemy. The jeer about the pea-shooters was pure braggadocio. In fact, the men were carrying only "sticks and canes" and initially ran when the police fought back.

Just as with violence between members of political organizations, the physical attacks on state authorities were often of an individual nature. Berlin's welfare workers were assigned a particularly difficult task during the Depression. Their physical presence in workers' neighborhoods was resented by some as much as the decreasing benefits and message of financial and moral discipline that the social workers represented. One social worker was quite attuned to her clients' response to her presence: 'When we social workers go into a family, we are generally not eagerly awaited guests that people are happy to see. We show up, unannounced, in the middle of situations that cannot really support the presence of a stranger.'[58] It was possible to appeal decisions about public assistance, but the statistics show that appeals did not achieve positive results for most who filed them. In the administrative year 1928–9, requests for reconsideration numbering 1,544 were registered at Berlin's welfare offices, and of these about 60 percent were rejected. The following year, the total number of appeals jumped to 2,098, an increase of about 35 percent.[59]

In order to receive benefits, the needy had to register weekly at their local unemployment office. Without funds for transportation, many were forced to walk long distances to the district bureau. Tired and frustrated, arriving welfare clients were often confronted with infamously long lines for service. Among the most hated and overcrowded was the Neukölln welfare branch, known as the "Unemployed's hell on Sonnenallee," pictured in Plate 2.[60] Those who received the brunt of the unemployed workers' animosity were

[58] This quotation from a Hamburg social worker comes from David F. Crew, *Germans on Welfare* (1998), p. 64.

[59] *Berliner Wohlfahrtsblatt*, 7 Jg., Nr. 4, February 15, 1931, p. 29. This data is also found in Crew, *Germans on Welfare* (1998), p. 72. On the language of appeals and other forms of self-help, see Crew, *Germans on Welfare* (1998), pp. 79–88.

[60] LAB, Rep. 58, Nr. 1746, Film 753, *An der Passage. Sprachrohr der Werktätigen*, June 1932. This Communist street newspaper used the common disgust with the Neukölln welfare office to elicit solidarity among all the jobless, "whether SPD or Nazi supporters." The article noted that forty more welfare clerks had been laid off, which would lead to longer waits for clients. "Don't let yourself be treated like a piece of cattle," warned the author, "which is pushed along by a rod when it is led to slaughter." The deteriorating situation at welfare offices also led the bureaucrats who staffed them to organize themselves. For one week in November 1929, some welfare employees in Neukölln went on strike to protest the conditions at their offices as well as cuts in funding. See LAB, Rep. 214, Nr. 118.

the office employees who had to face them on a daily basis. The occurrence of violence inside these public institutions at first seems unlike the other forms of violence described so far in this chapter. After all, in the earlier examples radicalized workers felt "at home" in the politicized semiprivate spaces of their streets, pubs, apartment buildings, meeting halls, and even school yards. However, on further analysis, the permeation of violence into the welfare offices really does not stray from this pattern. The overwhelming majority of workers in comparison to the number of administrators present, the required regular attendance, and the excessively long waiting periods created a microcommunity similar to that which existed outside the bureau's walls.

Without trivializing the shame felt by many who subsisted on public aid during the Depression, it is safe to say that the welfare offices carried a social meaning for clients. In the welfare line, one heard the latest neighborhood gossip and political news. Party literature was shared, and speakers frequently set up their soapboxes in front of the regular crowd.[61] People met friends at the welfare office and made plans for how to while away the rest of the day.[62] It was in this atmosphere, which fostered courage and distrust of those not allied with this community of the unemployed, that discontented workers could become violent.[63] After the wait and the humiliation of insufficient assistance or the rejection of an application, angered citizens staged sit-ins, bringing the work of the already cramped offices to a standstill. Also increasingly common were individual physical assaults aimed at caseworkers, office cashiers, or the files and office furniture. When such acts took place in front of other clients, additional people might become involved. Early notification of the police often kept large-scale confrontations from developing, but welfare administrators were always fearful that the unruly behavior would get out of control.

---

[61] Police often patrolled the streets in front of welfare and unemployment offices, arresting those who circulated illegal political literature. Limits were also put on political discussion in the waiting rooms of many official agencies. When Erich Kästner's fictional Berliner, Jacob Fabian, first finds himself among the unemployed at a job registry, he passes the time reading various signs on the office wall, some of which prohibit political debate and the wearing of organizational armbands within the building. Erich Kästner, *Fabian. The Story of a Moralist* (Evanston, IL: Northwestern University Press, 1993; original edition, Zurich: Atrium,1931), p. 91.

[62] Statements given to the police about a day's chain of events often began with the trip to the welfare office or job registry. Here a friend or acquaintance was met by chance, and from the offices the two unemployed people would visit others, go to a pub, or participate in political activities. For example, see LAB, Rep. 58, Nr. 147, Film 368, police witness statement by thirty-year-old A. L., August 16, 1930.

[63] See Crew, *Germans on Welfare* (1998), pp. 157–63 for more on violence in welfare offices. Crew refers to the administrators' fear of "contamination" through physical contact with the aid recipients. The caseworkers' perceptions of "dirty" welfare clients stemmed not only from their poverty but also from their presumed support of radical politics.

UPHOLDING ORDER: STREET VIOLENCE AND THE BERLIN COURTS

Clearly violence became an acceptable way for some workers in Berlin to demonstrate control over their lives and communities in this period. Violence was mostly spontaneous or locally organized and conformed to certain patterns consistent with the contours of this radical culture. The political diversity of the neighborhoods made them increasingly susceptible to violence between antagonistic groups fighting for superiority within their neighborhoods. Violent radicalism reflected the desire for territorial control and the belief that achieving such control demonstrated masculine bravery and discipline.

In the rest of this chapter, I will take this analysis of violence as consistent with a particular Depression-era radical culture in Berlin a step further. Without providing an in-depth sociological profile of street fighters, a brief look at the personal lives of violent offenders as represented in investigatory welfare reports does offer us clues to the motives of young radicals.[64] In addition, these reports identify a number of ways state officials viewed radical and violent behavior. We then turn to the ways defendants approached their accusers, both the police and courts. Instead of hiding behind party rhetoric, their own interpretations of the events seem surprisingly honest, and reinforce the importance of certain motivations and patterns of behavior. Finally, the courts and their verdicts in these bloody confrontations will be explored. As explained at the very beginning of this chapter, my intention here is not to revisit the discrepancy between Communist and Nazi indictments or sentencing. It is well known that prosecutors and judges treated right-wing violators with more leniency than those from the left. Rather, my intent is to show how the "rules of the game" were to some extent accepted by the courts, indicating that a dangerous rationalization of violence had spread throughout the city, preparing the way for the Third Reich.

It is ironic and yet fitting that the best sources of information on the lives of the young men involved in Berlin's political violence are the reports issued by welfare agencies about their clients. These men, struggling for independence and control over their own lives, had often been under the long-term care of state or private assistance agencies. It should also be remembered that, though the caseworkers had personal contact with their subjects, the reports were written in light of an arrest for a political crime, the circumstances of which shaped the authors' assessments. Nonetheless, it was considered a

---

[64] For an in-depth sociological look at Berlin's Communist street fighters, see Rosenhaft, *Beating the Fascists?* (1983), pp. 167–207. For a brief analysis of the background of those involved in political violence in Sachsen, see Dirk Schumann, *Politische Gewalt in der Weimarer Republik 1918–1933: Kampf um die Straße und Furcht vor dem Bürgerkrieg* (Essen: Klartext, 2001), pp. 329–31.

sign of the progress embodied in the Weimar *Sozialstaat* that these reports played a role in young offenders' court cases.[65]

These reports, which were sent at the request of the criminal courts in Berlin during the preparation for trial and sometimes during appeals or applications for early release, provide us with two main categories of information. First, they expand our knowledge of the men involved in such crimes. This sampling of subjects from the younger generation of adults born around 1910 reinforces earlier arguments made in this book. These children of the war were reaching adulthood just as the Depression was arriving and were most affected by the generational and gender conflicts it wrought. Second, these reports begin to create a picture of how representatives of the state made sense of the political crimes committed by men with whom they had at least a modicum of personal contact.

Not surprisingly, in almost all of these profiles of young defendants, we find details of a troubled employment history. What is surprising is that many had learned some trade, often completing long-term apprenticeships with good to excellent evaluations by their masters, only to have difficulty finding employment in their chosen fields. One nineteen year old from Schöneberg, having learned the construction of interior moldings under his father, took up employment in Leipzig where he worked for about eight months. By 1929, he had returned to Berlin, and in the following twelve months worked at nine different construction firms. In the first seven months of 1930, he was employed by three different companies. Since that time he had again been unemployed for what amounted to seven months at the time of the report.[66] A twenty year old born outside the city had similar problems. At age fifteen, he had entered a cabinetmaking apprenticeship but switched to another firm because he did not feel he was learning enough. After four years of training, he received a "very good" assessment on his exams. He also scored well at a specialist school for cabinetmakers. However, after completing his training in 1929, he could find no suitable positions. He worked for a time as an unskilled laborer but was laid off. In the following months, he was employed as a household servant, Christmas tree salesman, and messenger. By May 1930, he was again without a job.[67] Though these

---

[65] Though youth services officially defined juveniles as those up to age eighteen, they also assisted in the trials of "young adults," a category which included eighteen to twenty-one year olds. For further analysis of developments in criminology and prison reform in the Weimar Republic, see Richard E. Wetzell, *Inventing the Criminal: A History of German Criminology, 1880–1945* (Durham: University of North Carolina Press, 2000) and Nikolaus Wachsmann, "Between Reform and Repression: Imprisonment in Weimar Germany," in *The Historical Journal* (Vol. 45, No. 2, 2000), pp. 411–32.

[66] LAB, Rep. 58, Nr. 131, Film 364, youth welfare bureau Schöneberg to the district court in Schöneberg, November 10, 1930.

[67] LAB, Rep. 58, Nr. 143, Film 367, youth welfare bureau Schöneberg to the district court in Berlin-Charlottenburg, May 3, 1930.

two men had had disappointments, they were better off than some who went for over a year without any sort of work. In many cases, these were not unskilled or undirected men.

Though the subjects were all old enough to live independently, a good number of them still lived at home out of financial necessity and, in some cases, in order to qualify for public assistance. Another trend seen in the youth welfare reports is the extent to which the Depression shaped the lives of all family members.[68] In one family the twenty-year-old son, though trained as a metal grinder, had been unemployed for six months and was in trouble with the law. His father, who had the same occupation, had lost his job at about the same time. Since then, the father had at least procured temporary work, which was crucial since it was the only paid employment among the five adults in this family of seven.[69] In a number of cases, the families' poverty could be traced back for years. In these instances, the young men had been monitored by the youth office throughout their childhoods, and the long-term impact of Weimar's extensive welfare system becomes evident. The family of one boy had been assisted since 1924. When he was eleven, he and his sisters were found begging. The oldest boy spent three years at a state-run children's facility in the countryside, until he was old enough to go to work. At the time the report was filed in 1931, two younger siblings still lived in a group home in a nearby town, and the family's youngest child lived with foster parents.[70]

Unfortunately for some youngsters, the conditions from which they were removed were better than those to which they were sent. A number of the young defendants reported that they had been treated harshly by foster parents or were matched with unsuitable employers. One twenty-four year old complained in a statement to the police that on the farm where he was sent to work, he had been falsely accused of stealing and had been physically and sexually abused by the farmer.[71] For some families the trouble originated over a decade earlier, during World War I.[72] Many fathers were noted to have fallen in the war, and many mothers were suffering from work-related

---

[68] For more on the youth welfare system, the homes set up for impoverished young males, and the connections to the judicial system, see the report of an instructor in one such facility, Albert Lamm, *Betrogene Jugend: aus einem Erwerbslosenheim* (Berlin: Bruno Cassirer, 1932).

[69] LAB, Rep. 58, Nr. 154, Film 370, youth welfare bureau Neukölln to the district attorney's office, March 3, 1931.

[70] LAB, Rep. 58, Nr. 161, Film 373, youth welfare bureau Kreuzberg to the district attorney's office, February 26, 1931.

[71] LAB, Rep. 58, Nr. 201, Film 381, police witness statement by E. G. to the district court, August 6, 1932.

[72] W. G.'s experiences as a *"Kriegskind"* were noted in a newspaper article out of Dortmund that described the difficulties faced by Berlin's young unemployed. After his father's death in the war and his mother's subsequent illness, he had left home. The real dangers and despair, the article explains, arrived when W. G. turned to the pubs to keep warm and find companionship. Here he learned how to steal from veterans of the streets and began

diseases or were debilitated by "nerves." For those fathers still present during the Weimar Republic, alcoholism was another common problem that limited the chances for childhood stability. One caseworker even began the essay by noting the uniqueness of her subject's father, who "is not a drinker."[73]

The tension between these men and their parents is often palpable in the reports. In some cases, political disagreements had escalated until the youngster left home. By mid 1929, a worker in a candy factory had left his parents' home "because he could not stand his father, who is a Social Democratic Party functionary."[74] Many parents who did not participate in party politics disapproved of their sons' involvement. For unemployed young men, however, leaving the generational discord behind was often not an option. Instead, most tried to hide their political activities from their parents. One mother claimed to be very happy with her twenty-year-old son's behavior. Her son's caseworker, however, recognized the naiveté of both parents: "The parents had not known that he took part in party events. They believed that he only had friends of this political bent [NSDAP]. From the beginning they were against it and after this incident forbade him to participate in a political organization, since they are convinced that he is too young for it and must make something of himself first."[75]

Welfare workers used this information about past and current living conditions within their client's family to decide whether the youngster was a criminal or "politically misled." This differentiation was fundamental to caseworkers' understanding of violent political behavior, and hence to their assessments of each defendant's level of guilt or innocence. While the extent of the client's poverty did play a role in this decision, welfare workers also considered the young man's current moral reputation and the level of his intelligence. One way they investigated these issues was by asking relatives,

---

prostituting himself to the "homosexual men he met [in the bars]." EZA 51/SIIG6. "Gefahr für eine ganze generation!" in *General-Anzeiger für Dortmund*, Nr. 46, February 15, 1931.

[73] Rep. 58, Nr. 183, Film 378, welfare bureau Neukölln to the district attorney's office, report on H. M., August 16, 1931. For an example of the problems caused by alcohol, see LAB, Rep. 58, Nr. 135, Film 364. In this family, the alcoholic father had been sent to numerous treatment centers without success. He had been unemployed for some time, and his wife, who worked as a janitor in their apartment house, was left unable to support her six children, some of whom were removed from her care.

[74] LAB, Rep. 58, Nr. 134, Film 364, youth welfare bureau Neukölln to the district attorney's office, December 13, 1929. Some parents cheered the radical involvement of their sons, even when they did not support the political goals of the organization. The communal living, or at least basic material assistance, provided by radical organizations to their members meant that unemployed sons required less support from their parents' households. Even clique membership meant communal tent living in the warmer months. See Hellmut Lessing and Manfred Liebel, *Wilde Cliquen: Szenen aus einer anderen Arbeiterjugendbewegung* (Bensheim: Pädagogischer Buchverlag, 1981), p. 38.

[75] LAB, Rep. 58, Nr. 143, Film 367, youth welfare bureau Schöneberg report on M. F., July 31, 1930.

friends, and neighbors to judge the young man's standing in his family and community. The first questions were directed toward the parents and focused on behavior at home, particularly whether the subject donated any of his income or weekly public assistance to household costs. Contributing to family expenses was considered an important sign of sociability and respect for elders. It also meant that there would be little left to spend on alcohol and women. Welfare workers also asked whether the son posed discipline problems for his parents. Mothers were consistently reluctant to show their sons in a bad light. More than one mother even conspired to keep the news of the arrest from her intimidating husband as long as possible.[76] Maternal devotion may have inspired these positive reviews, but they were likely also a strategy to maintain dignity and privacy, and to ensure that public assistance would not be withdrawn.

The caseworkers then turned to other apartment house residents. The most convenient interviewee, and often the most willing, was the building superintendent, who was an expert on residents' comings and goings in the tenement. The scope of the investigations makes it clear that the reputation of all family members was important to the assessment of the individual. The parents of one defendant remarked that they were satisfied with his behavior. "They were only dissatisfied with his political engagement," explained the caseworker, "from which they could not distract him. G. donates his public assistance to the house, keeping only two or three marks for himself." When asked about G.'s behavior in the building, the superintendent at 9 Maxstraße agreed that "he is respectful and polite to his parents and the other residents. [The superintendent] also knew his grandparents to be hardworking and honest people."[77]

In judging the family's moral standards, apartment upkeep also played a significant role. One family lived in the least expensive type of basement apartment, which was "officially unheatable." Nonetheless, the welfare worker assessed the dwelling as "clean and orderly," though the possessions were mostly from charity organizations.[78] In another family, the parents were both "afflicted by nerves" and the brother had kidney problems. The

[76] LAB, Rep. 58, Nr. 136, Film 364, youth welfare bureau Neukölln report on E. F., February 26, 1930. In this family, the father was described as "very strict." And it was "out of fear" that the son had not told his father the news. The mother, "who could barely speak through her tears," had also kept the story quiet and had not yet decided how to handle the situation. However, she praised her son as "ambitious and obedient."

[77] LAB, Rep. 58, Nr. 131, Film 364, youth welfare bureau Schöneberg report on G. S., November 10, 1930.

[78] LAB, Rep. 58, Nr. 146, Film 367, Steglitz welfare bureau report on O. S., September 29, 1930. This report was unusual in that it was requested about the family of a forty-eight-year-old man who had been involved with his adult son in an attack on a Nazi newspaper salesman. The report touched on the same issues as those for the younger clients, in this case going back to the early 1900s.

sister had a child out of marriage, but the couple and infant lived together with the rest of the family. They received little from the welfare office and could only count on the sale of flowers and vegetables as additional income. "In spite of all of this," the caseworker reported happily, "the atmosphere is fresh and in no way depressed."[79] Apartment size and quality mattered little, therefore, as long as the family tried to maintain the standards of cleanliness and respectability held by the welfare administrators themselves.

The most important part of the report on young violators, at least as far as the courts were concerned, was the analysis of their political motivations and level of participation. Surprisingly, these welfare reviews did not dwell on party affiliations. For the most part, radical organizations appear to be lumped under one umbrella. The absence of references to specific organizations in these evaluations illustrates a marked difference between these reports and those filed by the police. In police reports, a suspect's political résumé was recorded at the very beginning of the interview. The contrast directs our attention to two separate understandings of radicalism. For the police, Communist activities were viewed primarily as criminal, whereas involvement in the NSDAP, SPD, or even SA and Reichsbanner was considered political. It was crucial, therefore, to make specific reference to the organizational affiliation of the suspect. For the mainly social democratic welfare workers in Berlin, this bifurcation did not apply. In their minds, all radicalism was considered first and foremost antisocial, hence the need to weigh such behavior against a client's other social roles, as family member, worker, and neighbor.

Similarly, caseworkers rarely detailed the political beliefs of their subjects. This information might have simply been considered outside the purview of their expertise, but the omission is also consistent with their sociological and even physical interpretations of radicalism. In a great number of cases, for example, the client's bodily attributes are mentioned. Ailments suffered as a child, operations, and accidental injuries are incorporated into their assessments. In addition, other less specific physical qualities of the defendant are considered: size, level of muscular strength, and any miscellaneous abnormalities such as a limp or scar.[80] The implication is that radicalism resulted not only from the material and moral disadvantages experienced by

---

[79] LAB, Rep. 58, Nr. 160, Film 372, Protestant district welfare and youth welfare bureau Schöneberg, request for pardon of K. K., March 3, 1932. These welfare reports were also used after sentencing, if the guilty party appealed for a pardon out of economic necessity. In this case, the welfare authorities agreed that the young man was the only one in the family capable of bringing in sufficient income to support the others and requested that he be released in order to work.

[80] Cf. LAB, Rep. 58, Nr. 132, Film 364, youth welfare bureau Neukölln to the district attorney's office, report on W. S., November 25, 1929. The first line in this summary of the accused's background and current situation reads: "W. S.: left-side paralysis of the hand and foot – and mentally backward."

many of these men but also from their physical shortcomings. If the accused was a healthy, robust-looking young man, the general tenor of the report improved.

Lastly, the mental capacity of the defendant came under scrutiny. Some clients did impress their caseworkers as "physically and mentally well developed," though, more often than not, the young person was seen as intellectually stunted. Codefendants in one case elicited different reactions from the same welfare investigator. Though twenty-one-year-old L. G. made a "good impression" as a consistently employed unskilled worker, he was assessed as lacking strong mental ability. His partner in crime, fifteen-year-old worker E. Z., also had a job and contributed financially to the household, but "made an intelligent impression."[81] Both assessments could help the defendant seek a milder sentence. For L. G., and many others like him, the fact that he was not believed capable of making good decisions meant that he should not be held fully responsible for his actions. His radicalism was primarily a result of being misled, which meant he did not possess a "criminal nature." Some reports even noted the positive results that presumably would come if the client could extricate himself from the bad influence of friends, who "held him to drinking and loitering about."[82] As in most cases where the caseworker believed the young man had been duped, the investigator recommended probation for L. G. This decision was undoubtedly welcomed by the defendant. However, it is also easy to see how the assessment of L. G. and others fit the stereotype of radicals, especially Communists, in Berlin. "Due to his age and his severe lack of judgment," concluded the caseworker, the accused was vulnerable to the "misuse" of conspiring local leaders.[83] The real discontent of these men was overlooked because of presumptions about poor, unskilled, young laborers and the "string-pullers" of the KPD.

The actions of those, like E. Z., who made a good impression because they did "not look demoralized," had employment, and seemed able to reason sufficiently, were much more difficult for the caseworkers to interpret. In some cases of social and intellectual promise, when there had been no prior arrests, the call for probation came without further explanation.[84] The welfare worker likely assumed that without the sociological or physical factors, which they believed led to radicalism, future run-ins with the law were improbable. Like their less intelligent comrades, these respectable workers were never suspected as the instigators of political violence. One such defendant,

[81] LAB, Rep. 58, Nr. 132, Film 364, youth welfare bureau Neukölln to the district attorney's office, report on L. G. and E. Z., November 16, 1929.

[82] LAB, Rep. 58, Nr. 143, Film 367, youth welfare bureau Schöneberg to the district attorney's office, report on H. R., July 30, 1930.

[83] LAB, Rep. 58, Nr. 135, Film 364, youth welfare bureau Steglitz to the Schöffengericht Schöneberg, report on K. D., May 12, 1930.

[84] For example, see LAB, Rep. 58, Nr. 156, Film 371, Jugendgerichtshilfe report on K. P., February 1931.

E. V., was assessed to be a "calm and orderly youth. In the crime he is to be viewed as a hanger-on. On the grounds of his character and in light of his previous good behavior, it is to be assumed with certainty that in the future he will behave well and will prove worthy of probation."[85] For young men like E. Z. and E. V., probation was not recommended because of their mental naiveté. Rather, their "strong characters" freed them from charges of criminal "string-puller" and convinced the welfare authorities that their political activism was a fluke.

Of course, not all clients received positive evaluations from their welfare workers. First, there were those who had developed a bad reputation among their neighbors. In the case of one twenty year old, the report from the welfare authorities explained that "the influence of protective supervision [from this office] had not been enough in light of the character weaknesses of this youngster to keep him from reckless conduct and associations with bad friends."[86] Though this repeat offender regretted his past mistakes, the investigator thought him insincere and recommended that he serve the punishment for his crimes in prison. Another caseworker could make no recommendations as to the best solution for her client. The unemployed nineteen year old did not have a good reputation among the area's residents. "In general he is known as a 'rowdy.' Furthermore, he is considered one of the worst young people, who mixes with the left radical party." This welfare officer had such a low opinion of the accused that she believed that even time spent in prison would be wasted on him.[87] His codefendant also had a bad reputation among his neighbors because "he was thought to be among the leaders of all rabble unrest [*Pöbeleien*]." Nevertheless, the author of the report noted that he was "a calm, peaceable person when alone." The recommendation was made for probation, since it was deemed that prison "would not have the desired effect." In this case, it was believed that the youngster could still be reformed. His character was not fundamentally flawed. Instead, the "great misery due to the unemployment that has seized his family alongside the political incitement [of the times]" were viewed as the main causes for his criminal behavior.[88] If through a long probation he could be kept apart from radical influences, he might very well be able to stay on the right side of the law.

In general, Berlin's welfare workers were compassionate in their assessments of youthful defendants. Perhaps their frequent willingness to seek

---

[85] LAB, Rep. 58, Nr. 161, Film 373, Tempelhof welfare office to the district court in Tempelhof, report on E. V., July 27, 1931.

[86] LAB, Rep. 58, Nr. 131, Film 364, youth welfare bureau Steglitz to the district court in Schöneberg, report on W. E., February 12, 1931.

[87] LAB, Rep. 58, Nr. 154, Film 370, Jugendgerichtshilfe Neukölln to the district attorney's office, report on O. H., November 19, 1930.

[88] LAB, Rep. 58, Nr. 154, Film 370, Jugendgerichtshilfe Neukölln to the district attorney's office, report on H. P., March 3, 1931.

milder punishments was a result of witnessing firsthand the poverty under which many of Berlin's workers suffered. Perhaps these low-level state authorities, who likely supported the social justice platform of the Weimar *Sozialstaat*, felt some sympathy for these workers whose political enthusiasm, in their opinion, had veered off course. Whatever the reason, their compassion still harbored a specific understanding of radicalism, which failed to identify the complex motivations of their clients. Though they pointed to unemployment and misery, they saw only desocialized youngsters. Where they found political engagement, they blamed a lack of intellectual ability and string-pulling operatives.

We know little about the defense attorneys who represented these men. There were a few star lawyers who came out for the high-profile cases of left-wing leaders, perhaps most prominently Felix Halle, but there were others in Berlin who repeatedly served street fighters. These included Hans Litten, remembered for having once forced Adolf Hitler into a corner on the witness stand; Ludwig Barbasch, Litten's partner in practice; and the team of Fritz Löwenthal and Eduard Alexander.[89] These attorneys all worked with Rote Hilfe Deutschland, which provided legal counsel and raised money to support left-wing defendants.[90] The NSDAP also had a number of lawyers in Berlin who were called on to defend its members in court: Walther Triebel, Georg Horn II, and Dr. Zarnack, among others. It is difficult to know from the documents the extent to which defense attorneys scripted their clients' responses to police interrogation or criminal charges.

Whether they were instructed by legal counsel or not, the accused rarely admitted to the crimes for which they were charged. The confessions that do exist usually came well into the investigation, as a way to secure a lighter sentence. Therefore, radicals did not believe it was necessary to accept the consequences of their actions in order to gain respect among their peers. Furthermore, there is little evidence to support the conclusion that suspects chose brash resistance in the face of police interrogation. Instead, just about every manner of excuse and alibi was presented in the hopes of deflecting suspicion. The most common defense offered was mistaken identity. Others claimed they were simply innocent bystanders or innocently running errands in the area when the violence erupted. A somewhat unusual, though not infrequent, alibi was intoxication. A number of men argued that they were

---

89 For short biographies of Halle and Litten, see Kritische Justiz, ed., *Streitbare Juristen* (Baden-Baden: Nomos, 1988). Horst Göppinger's monograph also has short biographies of many of Weimar's Jewish attorneys and chronicles their persecution after 1933. Having withstood five years of imprisonment, Hans Litten finally committed suicide within Dachau in 1938. See further Horst Göppinger, *Juristen jüdischer Abstammung im "Dritten Reich": Entrechtung und Verfolgung* (Munich: Beck, 1990).

90 On the RHD, see Felix Halle, *Anklage gegen Justiz und Polizei* (Berlin: Mopr Verlag, 1926) and Martin Wagner, ed., *Im Namen des Volkes! Rote Hilfe gegen Polizeiterror und Klassenjustiz* (W. Berlin: Oberbaumverlag, 1976).

too drunk to have participated in a brawl, or if they had been involved should not be held accountable for their actions because of their alcohol-impaired state. Turning to drunkenness as an excuse or alibi shows the centrality of drinking and pub socializing to male workers' sense of camaraderie and demonstrates that creating an image of a disciplined fighting force was not a high priority for individual radicals.

Another explanation for this lack of courageous confessions is that street fighters believed their actions had already proven them to be brave and loyal in their neighborhoods, while it mattered little what police or judges thought of their motivations. The lack of defiant idealism when confronted by the law also further illustrates my contention that the conflicts were incited more by local crises and less so by ideological conviction. When men did explain the chain of events that resulted in their involvement in brawls, they focused on the neighborhood-related causes for their actions and never reproduced a party line about advancing world revolution or ushering in the Third Reich. Not only did Communists omit ideological declarations from their police statements, but when faced with criminal charges, defendants on the left commonly distanced themselves from the KPD as much as possible. Witness after witness noted that up until recently he had been a member of the KJVD, KbgdF, or the party itself but was no longer affiliated. This desire not to be connected too closely to the Communist Party was a reflection of the KPD's unfavorable status in Berlin.[91] Many Nazis, on the other hand, were quick to mention that they had previously been associated with the radical left. The frequency at which men switched sides – and the fact that they so freely admitted this – indicates that there was no shame among radicals in making this change. Furthermore, by demonstrating that over time they had realized the foolish ways of their youth, recently minted Nazis had reason to believe that they gained an added glimmer of respect – even beyond the favorable treatment NSDAP members frequently enjoyed in the judicial system. Lawyers for the SA made explicit use of the respect that accompanied Nazi membership in their clients' defenses, declaring in one case that the fact that the convicted Stormtrooper held "a position of responsibility in the NSDAP stands as proof that he is a peaceful and level-headed person."[92]

---

[91] Felix Halle's instructional pamphlet for workers facing the justice system reiterated the difficulties of receiving a fair trial but also stressed that each worker must safeguard the movement through silence. See Halle's pamphlet for a critical primer of the Weimar justice system, Felix Halle, *Wie verteidigt sich der Proletarier* (third edition, Berlin: Mopr, 1929).

[92] LAB, Rep. 58, Nr. 206, Film 383 Bd. IV, letter from attorney Zarnack to the appeals court, district court II, November 8, 1932. Lawyers for Reichsbanner defendants also tried to use the solid reputation held by this organization in Berlin as a way to argue that their clients were upstanding citizens. One attorney wrote that his client "did not belong to one of the political groups, which through the use of acts of violence hopes to step forward." See LAB, Rep. 58, Nr. 152, Film 370, appeal for clemency by attorney Günther Joachim,

When a man found it impossible to avoid charges for an assault, he often tried to convince his accusers that he had acted only in self-defense. Because many of these attacks took place on public streets where numerous witnesses could testify to the events, it was usually fairly clear who was the aggressor and who was the victim. Therefore, the argument of self-defense was presented in another way. Some argued they were defending others, and therefore the community as a whole. For example, one man maintained that his aggressive actions, which included throwing rocks at the police, came subsequent to the police officer's "brutal handling of two uninvolved young women."[93] In this sense the rock thrower was acting in defense of local females, for whom he felt some responsibility. Others claimed that their violence resulted from months of ill-treatment by the current victims. A Communist and former RFB member admitted, for example, to purchasing a revolver and having used his weapon aggressively. He explained in 1931, however, that "[he] wanted the weapon as protection, because [he] had been attacked by Swastikers many times."[94] Though he had no witnesses for the earlier attacks on himself, he eventually confessed to having shot a Nazi when he felt threatened by what he believed to be a piece of pipe in the victim's hand. Another KPD man, who had been involved in a rather brutal group assault on two Nazis, claimed that he had "long been threatened by Nazis because he wouldn't go over to their side." He added in his defense that in the local Nazi pub his picture had hung on the wall with the caption: "he must die."[95]

The most common defense for violence was lending assistance to friends. Whether providing protection at a rally, guarding a newspaper salesman, or walking someone home, radicals on both sides felt they had the right to defend their friends, even when their presence appeared to have provoked the violence. When protection turned to revenge, camaraderie could have serious consequences. In the early morning of September 10, 1931, an eighteen-year-old man wearing the insignia of the Reichsbanner was on his way to his apprenticeship as a printer near his home in the Nostiz Kiez. He was accompanied by a friend when they came upon two men, wearing "black shirts and dark pants," standing by a parked car. The two youngsters immediately recognized the uniform as that of the NSDAP. They kept to themselves, but as they passed one of the two men yelled: "Well you Reich-whiners, haven't you been beat up enough?" The two apprentices tried to ignore the insult, but the SA man who had spoken punched the young printer in the chin.

August 8, 1931. The appeal board agreed the man was not inspired by "criminal inclinations" but only "recklessness," and he was released early on probation.

[93] LAB, Rep. 58, Nr. 131, Film 364, decision of the Landgericht II, November 29, 1929.

[94] LAB, Rep. 58, Nr. 142, Film 366, witness statement by A. M. to the Landgericht II, May 31, 1931.

[95] LAB, Rep. 58, Nr. 160, Film 372, proceedings of the Schöffengericht Schöneberg, May 9, 1931.

They tried again to continue on their path, when the Nazi added: "Get out of here or you'll get a knife in the ribs." The Nazis then got in their car and followed the Reichsbanner supporters. At the next corner, one of the Nazis reached through the car window and grabbed the printer. Then he picked up a sawed-off table leg from the backseat and began to beat the young man. Though the victim could not free himself from his assailant, the youngster was able to knock away the weapon and save himself from extensive injury. The driver accelerated, forcing the young man to run alongside while he was being punched by the car's passenger. Eventually, after the driver had turned on to another street, the police stopped the car and arrested the two Nazis inside. The primary assailant, a twenty-year-old SA member and resident of the Nostiz Kiez, was charged with inflicting dangerous bodily harm and the illegal use of a weapon.[96]

This case was fairly typical because of the low number of participants, the use of a homemade weapon, the seemingly unprovoked nature of the attack, and the fact that all those involved lived in that very neighborhood. It is also significant for the way the SA man defended his actions. The accused was a member of Berlin's SA Sturm 24, which on the night before had suffered an attack at their Kiez pub "Hochburg" only a block away from where this morning assault took place. The shooting at the pub, which was the first in the string of infamous KPD-organized assaults on SA taverns in workers' districts in 1931, had led to the death of the Sturm leader, Thielsch, and the wounding of three others.[97] Though no evidence was presented that the young Stormtrooper who beat up the apprentice had been present the night before, by the next morning he had already learned of the incident and explained his actions to both the police and the court as the consequence of becoming "infuriated" by the shooting. The defendant could not directly claim he was seeking revenge for the earlier crime by the KPD, since he had targeted a man with the insignia of the Reichsbanner. He argued instead that the symbols of the Reichsbanner represented Marxism, and it was this indirect connection to the perpetrators which "had set him off."[98] What is important in this testimony is that the accused focused on this local conflict. Marxism had come to symbolize the person who shot his commander. Party rallies may have first created the image of Marxism as the enemy in his mind, but it was at the grassroots level that radicalism gained meaning and purpose through daily crises.

---

[96] LAB, Rep. 58, Nr. 186, Film 378, police IA, concluding report, September 29, 1931.

[97] For more detail on the campaign against SA taverns, see Rosenhaft, *Beating the Fascists?* (1983), pp. 111–27.

[98] LAB, Rep. 58, Nr. 186, Film 378, Schöffengericht Tempelhof proceedings, November 4, 1931. A worker and female telephone operator sat as lay assessors in the trial, and the defendant was given a fourteen-week jail sentence. The car's driver was sentenced to three weeks' incarceration for aiding and abetting.

Street fighters were not the only ones who found themselves facing the criminal courts. The owners of Berlin's radical pubs had their own rationales for accepting the violence that broke out in their establishments. The proprietor and patrons of politically aligned pubs were often the first to be questioned about altercations arising in their areas. During police questioning most pub owners described themselves as politically neutral. Even when this claim of indifference was made, no proprietor willingly shared any clues that could hurt his customers. Clearly, many of these owners must have had political sympathies in line with their patrons. However, the fact that all pub owners, even those who chose not to take sides for the record, sought to protect their customers from the police is evidence that some political decisions were dependent on economic exigencies. In order to keep the loyalty of their patrons in these difficult financial times, tavern owners turned a blind eye to their criminal activities.

In February 1932, there was an extensive brawl between the regulars of a Nazi bar and those of its nearby Communist counterpart. The proprietor of the SA tavern gave his statement to the police the following day. He described his business as consisting of one taproom and one meeting room. Local Nazis had been meeting there for about three weeks, and "since then people of other political opinions had stayed away." He was told by the Sturm leader (whose name he claimed not to know) that on the coming Sunday evening a small initiation ceremony was to be held in his establishment. The owner then added: "As concerns myself, I would like to note beforehand, that I belong to no political party. I also sympathize with no party, and am of the opinion that a businessman may not do this." Around sixty people attended the Nazi function between 9 P.M. and 1:30 A.M. They came in and out of the pub and drank a large amount of beer. Around 1 A.M., one patron returned from a walk outside and informed the others that trouble was brewing. A group went back out with him, and later returned splattered in blood. The owner claimed never to have looked outside or to have had any idea what was going on. Soon the police showed up, arrested a number of those inside, and searched the pub. The *Schutzpolizei* found nothing, but on their return visit at 7 A.M., the proprietor explained that in between he had located a pistol behind the oven and had taken it to the cellar for safe keeping, though "in the excitement it was not possible for [him] to know who hid the firearm."[99]

A woman, who was staying with a friend near the tavern, reported that she witnessed the events from her balcony. The two women had been awakened by a terrible racket and saw ten to fifteen SA men, who looked as if they were preparing to storm the Communist bar on the corner of Max and Ebers Streets. Ebersstraße was at the heart of a Schöneberg KPD Kiez and home

---

[99] LAB, Rep. 58, Nr. 206, Film 382, police witness report by E. M., owner of the pub at 7 Max Street, Schöneberg, February 7, 1932. He was seventy years old, married, and had no prior arrests at the time of his statement.

to one family, denounced to police in the previous chapter, for threatening neighbors and organizing local violence. A couple of the men appeared to the witnesses to be leading the charge, but they were very drunk, and their comrades persuaded them to return to their own tavern. The two women were drawn from their beds again by shouting one hour later and saw a large crowd of fifty to one hundred people in the street below, chanting "SA" and "Communists come out!" The Nazis attacked the bar, breaking the door, windows, and lamps inside. She saw at least one firearm.[100] There had been a police unit on watch that night because of the festivities in the SA establishment, but as was often the case, little was done to prevent the violence.

This example is significant first because of the coy, indifferent stance taken by the SA pub owner. He did not want to appear hostile to the police, who could petition to close his pub temporarily as a threat to public security. Nor did he want to betray the radicals who kept his business afloat. Second, we also see the various uses of the pub: social recreation, territorial outpost, and source of alibi. Third, the report by the thirty-year-old female worker illustrates how common such occurrences were. She did not seem shocked or in disbelief, but instead knew how to interpret the scene, and could even describe the weapon she saw as a *Schutzpolizei*-issued gun.

In a similar case, the proprietor of the infamous Communist bar on Nostiz Street, Walter Lorenz, denied having any knowledge of a KPD drive-by shooting of a nearby SA bar. Two men, ages twenty-two and twenty-one, were in custody. Further investigation had linked them to the bar on Nostiz, where a handgun was later found during a police search. A study by the police ballistics unit concluded that the weapon could have been used in the attack, though it did not alone fire the fifteen shots at the bar "von Höhr." Lorenz, thirty-seven years old and married with two children, gave the following statement to police:

I am the propietor of the pub at Nostiz number 16. At my place congregate mostly members of the KPD from the immediate area. Tuesdays and Fridays my clubroom is used by the members of the gymnasts' club Fichte, then on Saturdays after the first and fifteenth of every month it is occupied by the boxing club "Poor Brothers." ... I am not myself politically organized and must, in this sense as a businessman, remain completely neutral. I put no blame on my clientele in this relationship, but I must always have my business interests first in sight. I have said to my guests, that weapons may not be carried, otherwise I prohibit them from the pub. I have also never noticed any weapons with them.[101]

---

[100] LAB, Rep. 58, Nr. 206, Film 382, February 7, 1932, police witness report by B. R., female worker born in 1902.

[101] LAB, Rep. 58, Nr. 162, Film 373, police witness statement from W. L., February 28, 1931. From another document we learn that Thursday evenings at the Lorenz pub belonged to the local KJVD meetings. Thursdays happened to be the same evening the local Stahlhelm gymnasts trained at a club also on Nostiz, which led to a number of confrontations between

Eventually, Lorenz offered to the police a story in which he innocently traded his own pistol for the weapon in question on the day the shooting occurred. Conveniently, he had forgotten the name of the man with whom he had exchanged guns. The police did not believe any of his claims of coincidence or ignorance and concluded that his denial "only served to strengthen the long-held suspicion that all political attacks and shootings in the Kreuzberg area in which Communists are the perpetrators are discussed or organized in L.'s pub."[102] Once he was formally arrested for disturbing the peace, he changed his story again. He demanded anonymity before naming the man who gave him the gun "because otherwise he feared great damage to his business."[103] According to the new story, a twenty-two-year-old resident of the Kiez, E. R., was in the pub with the gun. Lorenz complained about its presence; R. told Lorenz he could put it out of harm's way, and that is where it stayed. Lorenz continued to deny any knowledge of the shooting. He was not, however, willing to risk conviction to shield his patron from prosecution.[104]

Clearly, motivation was prioritized ahead of the violent act itself in accounting for radical political behavior. Though defendants and the social workers who evaluated them focused on different causes for the turmoil, their explanations were similar in that both legitimized political violence under certain circumstances. Caseworkers believed that an individual's background, living standards, and physical and mental abilities, as well as the highly charged political atmosphere were mitigating factors in judging each radical. Defendants themselves chose other explanations. They pleaded for leniency in the language of their radical culture. They pointed out initial provocation by opponents, the duty and right to defend comrades and their

the two groups. See LAB, Rep. 58, Nr. 161, Film 372, concluding report concerning an attack on five Jung Deutsche Orden (Jungdo) members on November 27, 1930. The culprits were presumed to be Communist youth. Two Jungdo victims were shot. It appears from this one document that no one was arrested for the crime.

[102] LAB, Rep. 58, Nr. 162, Film 373, concluding report, police IA, March 12, 1931.

[103] LAB, Rep. 58, Nr. 162, Film 373, indictment of W. L. at the district court Berlin-Mitte, March 13, 1931.

[104] E. R. was questioned. He was single, unemployed, and lived with his parents on Bergmannstraße in the Nostiz Kiez. He told his accusers he was not affiliated with any political organizations. He denied having been in the pub with a pistol or having ever owned a gun. The police, however, described him as the leader of the neighborhood branch of the Communist sports club Fichte, as a "regular" at the Lorenz pub, and as having been involved in other political cases. LAB, Rep. 58, Nr. 162, Film 373, "Verhandelt E. R.," March 28, 1931 and police IA note, March 30, 1931. R. was not one of the two men originally brought in as suspects. In August, both R. and Lorenz were tried in Tempelhof. The former faced charges for possession of a weapon in public "for political purposes," for the firing of the weapon, and for participating in a violent mob. He served six weeks in jail. Lorenz was declared innocent of knowingly aiding a criminal. See in the same file: the indictments of May 13, 1931, and the trial proceedings of the expanded Schöffengericht Tempelhof, August 25, 1931.

neighborhoods from "outsiders," and even alcohol use as a reason for illegal behavior. Court decisions also reflected this emphasis on the circumstances surrounding the violent incident. By issuing judgments determined by the context rather than the actual crime, it becomes clear that to some extent violence was accepted by the courts as a political strategy. More importantly, in some cases, the decisions used the same language and codes employed by the street fighters themselves to regulate radicalism.

In coming to their decisions about the motivations behind various acts of radicalism and violence, the courts were working within a specific, legal definition of politics, which once again emphasized motivation over action. The point at which political activism, such as marches and demonstrations, was subject to prosecution was when it threatened to disturb the peace. For this to be the case under the existing legal codes, there had to be political intent. For example, the wearing of the banned RFB uniform was acceptable as long as it was done in the privacy of one's own home. Even in public an individual wearing the insignia of the RFB was usually exonerated by the courts. However, when the individual appeared with others who were also wearing pieces of the prohibited uniform, the courts interpreted this collective act as a sign of political intent and a declaration that the banned organization was still active.[105] To these ends, the motivations of everyone acting in the public sphere had to be determined.

Some of the bloodiest episodes in the ongoing political crisis took place in the large assembly halls. As shown at the beginning of this chapter, hundreds of people could be involved in brawls that followed provocative statements by a speaker or taunting from the audience. The courts, however, often set the combatants in these cases free or gave them minimal sentences for two reasons. First, it was often impossible to determine who among the hundreds involved should be held responsible for these large-scale battles. Second, the issue of political intent was often difficult to prove. Police witnesses made up a small minority of the audience and often were unable to tell who had struck the first blow or, in general, which side was acting in self-defense. In January 1932, for example, unemployed workers in Berlin staged demonstrations at various locations around the city to protest a set of cuts in welfare benefits, which was to take effect on February 1. About one hundred fifty Nazis showed up at one of the rallies in Neukölln, claiming later that they had been invited, since the posters for the event described the topic of one of the speakers as

---

[105] For an example of the handling of cases concerning the illegal wearing of the RFB uniform and insignia as called for under the Law for the Protection of the Republic, see GStA, Rep. 84a, 2.5.1., Nr. 10884. Men tried to argue that their garment choices were limited by poverty, and that the loose-fitting "Russian" style tunic of the RFB uniform made for a comfortable sporting and outdoor garment. When congregating in similarly attired groups, however, defendants were usually convicted of demonstrating the intent to declare the RFB as an active political force. This crime was not severely punished and usually only carried a small fine.

the "National Socialist Campaign of Terror." Before the rally got under way, a fight broke out between members of the two sides. Coal shovels and chair legs were the primary weapons in the brawl, which took place mostly on the front lawn of the assembly hall and spilled into the street as Communists tried to block the growing Nazi crowd from the entrance. Twenty-four people were arrested, only four of whom were Communists. The police doubted the large Nazi presence had been a coincidence and described the incident as a "planned action" to "break up the rally through force."[106] In the trial that followed, two Nazis, a nineteen and twenty-two year old, were both given six-month sentences for felony disturbance of the peace.

On appeal, however, both were set free. The court listed two main reasons why the original decision could not stand. First, though the provocative statement by a Nazi: "We want to show that the SA still lives in Neukölln" did imply the desire "to act violently against the Communists," it could not be proven that "the other Nazis had this same intention and that they mutually wanted to assault the Communists." Second, because most of the fighting took place outside the meeting hall, and the demonstration went on regardless of the unrest, the actions of the Nazis had not disrupted the political event.[107] In other words, the intentions of the Nazis arrested were not clear, and the fighting could not even be ruled political, since the political event – the rally by the unemployed – was held unimpeded. Sympathies for the Nazi cause may have made this decision easier to hand down for the court, but these same criteria were applied in other cases.[108] The deed itself, unprovoked physical assault, was not on trial.

In a less dramatic trial, a member of the Eiserne Front was charged with leading a number of his comrades in the threatening and physical mishandling of three Nazis. It was a typical story, in that members of both sides were returning home from their respective bars when the tussle broke out after midnight. Witnesses identified a thirty-year-old, previously convicted metal fitter as the instigator. His primary defense was that he was too drunk to have been involved. He claimed to have consumed a bottle of wine, between twenty and thirty small glasses of beer, and a number of shots of schnapps all in celebration of a friend's birthday and the republican Constitution Day.[109] He was found innocent of all charges and did not even receive a fine for his behavior. The court decided that though he was at least guilty of

---

[106] LAB, Rep. 58, Nr. 224, Film 387, concluding report by the police IA, February 15, 1932.

[107] LAB, Rep. 58, Nr. 224, Film 387, decision of the district court II, June 22, 1932.

[108] For an example of a case concerning a Communist attack on a Nazi pub, in which the same criteria concerning political motivation and public versus private space were considered, see GStA, Rep. 84a, 2.5.1., Nr. 10598.

[109] LAB, Rep. 58, Nr. 233, Film 389, indictment of the fitter S. at the district court II, November 7, 1932. This case is also of interest because the defense attorney asked for a list of the lay assessors before the beginning of the trial. Due to the "political nature of the case and the tense atmosphere," he requested information concerning "the personality and outlook"

threatening the Nazis, medical records showing the defendant suffered from a weak heart, as well as his undisputed drunkenness, "without having had anything to eat," were sufficient to show his judgment had been clouded. If his intentions on the night in question (beyond getting drunk) could not be ascertained, he could not be convicted.

One of the primary factors considered by the courts in assessing violent behavior was the age of the defendant. Young people, especially if they were first-time offenders, were treated with more leniency than those considered old enough to know better. Like their counterparts in the local welfare bureaus, officers of the courts saw these young men in part as victims of manipulative veteran party leaders and seasoned street fighters. Because teenagers and those in their early twenties were not held fully responsible for their actions, leaders or instigators who had "misused" their innocent followers were charged with the separate crime of "ringleader," which demanded a lengthier prison sentence.

For a serious riot in which numerous injuries resulted, a sixteen-year-old Communist defendant received three months of jail time, which was then reduced on appeal to a three-year suspended sentence. This decision was not based entirely on his age. In fact, there was "no doubt, that at the time of the incident he was able, according to his mental and moral development, to see that his was an unlawful act and to voice his will. The court is, however, of the opinion that the defendant W. D. can be improved and committed the crime primarily under the influence of his brother and older like-minded comrades."[110] This judgment suggests a very mixed appraisal of the political crisis. On one hand, the Berlin courts misunderstood the level of political discontent of young radicals. For example, in this case the court recognized that the young W. D. was old enough to understand his crime, yet they still doubted he was truly politically motivated. On the other hand, the court correctly understood how powerful camaraderie was for these men. Most importantly, though the court disapproved, the strength of these bonds was accepted as part of the political culture, and acts committed under this powerful force were not considered fully criminal.

This point is illustrated further by the case discussed earlier, in which two young Stormtroopers beat a Reichsbanner member on his way to work. The court had a difficult time weighing two contradictory beliefs about this case. They accepted the defendant's explanation for why he had been so brutal: "In sentencing, the court has allowed for milder punishment, since as a result of the [shooting] on the night of September 9–10, 1931, great excitement existed. G., in particular, is still a young person, who could not remain uninfluenced by the death of his friend Thielsch." "Nevertheless," argued

---

of the assessors. See attorney Bergmann's letter to the chairman of the criminal division, district court II, November 2, 1932.

[110] LAB, Rep. 58, Nr. 159, Film 372, court decision of the criminal division, August 14, 1931.

the judge, "the political incitement must not go so far, that a completely innocent person, unknown to the defendant, can be assaulted on his way to work because the insignia he wears is hated by the accused."[111] It was understandable, therefore, for the SA man to seek physical revenge for the death of his comrade. But there were limits to what the court would tolerate, and in this case, the defendant stepped beyond those bounds by selecting a victim who had played no part in the previous evening's attack.

There were other limits to what the courts would accept, and these reflected the same sort of moral standards that the rowdies used to order their own conduct. The courts found it especially offensive, for example, to attack a small force with a much larger one, to allow women to be victimized, or to attack in the dark without warning. There were incidents in which men transgressed these boundaries, but we know that in such cases the perpetrators were criticized as cowardly by both Nazis and Communists in their neighborhood newspapers and party presses. One antinazi flyer addressed to women in 1932 ran the headline: "Mothers protect your children from the SA!" The text was allegedly written by a woman whose son died at the hands of Stormtroopers. The shocking part of the story was that the murderers were being sought among the comrades of the deceased. The lesson presented to the reader was that of the hypocrisy of a brotherhood, which could strike at one of its own.[112] Whenever certain moral codes were brashly ignored by violent paramilitaries, the acts were publicly condemned. But the basic use of violence as a political strategy was not itself routinely questioned within these communities, or by the courts that tried the offenders.

The fact that judges seemed to accept violence, even if they meted out longer sentences for radicals on the left, has been explained by their own conservatism and disdain for anything connected to socialism, including the republic. Heinrich and Elisabeth Hannover reported in the mid 1960s that only 0.15 percent of Wilhelmine judges (about one in seven hundred) removed themselves from the bench after the revolution because they believed themselves unable to uphold the new constitution. That about 10 percent of higher civil servants chose this path led the Hannovers to conclude that "the great majority of judges" continued to serve even though they were deeply opposed to the new system.[113] This claim is bolstered by the difficulties faced by those judges who did support the young democracy. By 1923 three republicans (one member of the DDP, who joined the SPD in 1929, and

---

[111] LAB, Rep. 58, Nr. 186, Film 378, decision of the Schöffengericht Tempelhof, November 4, 1931.

[112] BA-SAPMO, SgY2/V/DF/VIII/62, "Mütter schützt Eure Kinder vor der SA!," Berlin, 1932/1933.

[113] Hannover and Hannover-Drück, *Politische Justiz* (1966), p. 23. For a sarcastic look at the entire Weimar judicial system, including the judges, see the work of the court reporter "Sling," the pseudonym for Paul Schlesinger, especially his collection *Richter und Gerichtete* (Berlin: Ullstein, 1929).

two members of the SPD) had been named to the highest court in the land, prompting two-thirds of the one hundred who served the *Kammergericht* to protest their appointments. The Prussian Judges Association also cried out against what they perceived to be an unwise politicization of the bench and "a serious danger to the administration of justice."[114] For a variety of causes, German attorneys witnessed the erosion of their political and economic power in the 1920s. These developments, which whittled away the privileges enjoyed by members of this profession and led to "proletarianization" for some, were worsened by the conditions of Depression, not least because a number of the emergency decrees led to cuts in the legal system.[115] This is not to say, however, that decisions taken on cases in the last years of the Weimar Republic can be explained simply as hatred for republicanism. Though these conditions must be recognized, judges were more concerned with the defendant's *Gesinnung*, a difficult to translate legal term that can have several meanings. It was frequently used to describe a person's political sentiments or "leaning." In criminal law, however, where the concept had a long tradition in Germany, the meaning is a bit more complex and can be best described as a defendant's ethical framework or position. *Gesinnung* was frequently cited by Berlin's judges when handing down verdicts and in sentencing the convicted. Though related, it is important not to confuse a defendant's *Gesinnung* with his motive. As one legal theorist explained:

It does not come down to whether the motives for an act are commendable, rather whether the *Gesinnung* of the perpetrator is of a high or low ethical level, which can be determined [by examining] the strength and nature of the motives, ... comparing the transgressed law with the aimed outcome and the manner in which the act was carried out.[116]

---

[114] Kritische Justiz, ed., *Streitbare Juristen* (Baden-Baden: Nomos, 1988), pp. 204–17. The three judges were Arnold Freymuth, Hermann Großmann, and Alfred Orgler. Großmann joined the other two in the SPD after leaving the DDP in 1929.

[115] Kenneth F. Ledford, "Conflict within the Legal Profession: Simultaneous Admission and the German Bar, 1903–1927" in Geoffrey Cocks and Konrad H. Jarausch, eds., *German Professions, 1800–1950* (Oxford: Oxford University Press, 1990), pp. 252–69 and Kenneth F. Ledford, *From General Estate to a Special Interest. German Lawyers, 1878–1933* (Cambridge: Cambridge University Press, 1996), pp. 275–89. See also Fritz Ostler, *Die Deutschen Rechtsanwälte, 1871–1971* (Essen: Juristischer Verlag W. Ellinghaus, 1982), pp. 202–20; and Tillmann Krach, *Jüdische Rechtsanwälte in Preussen: Über die Bedeutung der freien Advokatur und ihre Zerstörung durch den Nationalsozialismus* (Munich: Beck, 1991), pp. 42–52.

[116] Alfred Balzer, *Die ehrlose Gesinnung im geltenden und zukünkftigen Strafrecht* (Diss. juristischen Fakultät der Friedrich-Alexanders-Universität zu Erlangen, 1934), p. 12. Though this dissertation comes from 1934, Balzer is drawing from the major works of the pre-1933 period. The difficulty with evaluating *Gesinnung* is determining the ethical standards by which to judge the actions and motives of the defendant. As Balzer writes, in democratic states like the Weimar Republic there are competing majority and minority opinions. He cheers the new era of national socialism because the ideological worldview provides not only a political framework but also an "ethical" one (Balzer, p. 13). Cf. Philipp Allfeld, *Der*

This concept now became more critical than ever in the judgment of political violence. It was easier for lay assessors and judges to believe the intentions of defendants associated with the far right were well placed because the NSDAP was seen as a more legitimate and ethical political voice than the partially banned Communist movement, whose defendants were often at best loosely associated with the KPD and at the bottom of the socioeconomic scale. When the preceding definition is put to the political test, the same theorist responded:

It cannot be said that someone, who in the political struggle has killed an opponent in order to achieve an advantage for his party, did not act dishonorably, view however this dishonor not in terms of the interests pursued through the act – for these are neither base nor egoistic – rather in the nature and strength of the motive and in the divergence between the transgressed law and the aim.[117]

The following case is an appropriate final example of the role played by political violence in Berlin, its causes, and the extent to which *Gesinnung* was used by the courts to rationalize violence. In January 1932, a thirty-nine-year-old mechanic with no related prior convictions, who was also married and the father of three, was sentenced to nine months in prison for his pivotal role in a riot and physical assault. Though one man was badly beaten, no shots were fired, and no deaths occurred, making this a severe sentence even under the conditions of the emergency decrees against political violence. Like many incidents of street violence, this one unfolded during the hot summer months and in the intensity of a political campaign. The crime occurred in August 1931, when a statewide referendum was held on the question of whether the Prussian parliament should be dissolved. The NSDAP made the campaign in favor of dissolution a major priority, and on the day before the vote, party sections throughout Berlin were busy circulating propaganda.

The accused worker, S., had been a member of the NSDAP from its very beginning, joining soon after World War I. Early in 1931, however, he severed his ties with the party but declined to join other political organizations. Between ten and eleven o'clock on the evening before the vote in Bohnsdorf, on the southeastern edge of the capital, a small scuffle broke out between the propaganda troops of the NSDAP and the local Communists who had been meeting in a pub. One of the Nazis involved in the initial incident left to round up more of his comrades. When they first returned to the scene, everything seemed calm. Soon a number of Communists came out of their pub, and others appeared from the side streets. The defendant S. was among this growing crowd and after drawing attention by blowing a whistle, he walked

Einfluß der Gesinnung des Verbrechers auf die Bestrafung (Leipzig: W. Engelmann, 1909) and Eduard Guckenheimer, *Der Begriff der ehrlosen Gesinnung im Strafrecht* (Hamburg: W. Gente, 1921).

[117] Balzer, *Die ehrlose Gesinnung* (1934), p. 10.

over to the encircled Nazis and identified by name the leader of the local NSDAP troop. He then pointed out another as the party's treasurer, and a third as "the jerk who ... ruined my business." Next he allegedly encouraged the Communists to attack, which they did using canes and fence poles. The accused pleaded not guilty to all charges stemming from the incident.[118]

However, since a number of witnesses identified S. as having led the assault and as having participated in the beating of at least one man, he was convicted on all counts. To his benefit, the court recognized that he had not been arrested since 1920, and, as usual, they took into account the high level of political excitement due to the impending vote. To his detriment, the court declared that such public political violence deserved strong condemnation. To this point, the court's decision reads like hundreds of others in Berlin during this period. However, what led the court to hand down the harsh sentence of nine months to this family man were his specific "reprehensible actions" in this conflict. The reference here was not to the fact that S. held down one Nazi, while a cohort beat the restrained man with a dangerous weapon. Rather, S. deserved an especially severe punishment, "since he led the members of one party, to which he admittedly did not belong, to assault his former party comrades and used his prior knowledge of the organization to these ends."[119] The punishment reflected the court's disgust with his failure to participate within acceptable boundaries. The court was explicit in its disapproval of his involvement in the political scene without officially joining a party or organization, and found it dishonorable that he would then use private, internal knowledge of the NSDAP against his former friends.

Let me interrupt the story at this point to note some similarities between this incident and others referred to earlier in this chapter. To begin, this action was certainly planned at the most local level. All those involved were from the immediate surroundings and knew each other by name. In fact, this personal familiarity was what cost S. the trial. He was identified by numerous witnesses who recognized his voice and knew his name. The early scuffle, followed by the enlistment of friends as reinforcements to seek revenge, was a typical precursor to greater street conflicts. In addition, the importance of pubs and propaganda distribution in the development of the physical confrontation supports my contentions about turf and struggles for Kiez superiority. We also see an element of economic conflict behind this attack. The available sources do not explain further the reasons for the departure of S. from the Nazi Party, to which he belonged for more than a decade. It should be noted that such long-term commitment to either the NSDAP or KPD in this era was uncommon among Berlin's street fighters. However, his own statement that one of the Nazis "ruined his business" implies that some

---

[118] LAB, Rep. 58, Nr. 188, Film 379, proceedings from the case against mechanic P. S. at the Schöffengericht Schöneberg, January 4, 1932.

[119] Ibid.

sort of personal and/or economic motivation was either behind his leaving the party or developed in the course of his departure, which was undoubtedly seen by his former friends as a personal betrayal.

S. was ordered to enter the prison at Plötzensee on March 11, 1932; however, his wife fought for leniency. In a letter to the court which tried S., she explained how desperate her plight, and that of their three children, would become in her husband's absence. She claimed to be chronically ill and unable to care for her children. Since the family belonged to no political party, she added, they could not count on any such assistance and would become fully dependent on the state. She argued that at the very least she would need someone, paid by the state, to assist her at home until her husband was freed. She also wanted police protection since she had been harassed already by one of the wives of the Nazis involved in the August violence.[120] Hers was a very clever argument in these days of state fiscal emergency, and the court gave S. six months of freedom to prepare for his incarceration.

Only a few weeks into his prison term, S. wrote a letter to the district attorney in order to bring a mistake to the prosecutor's attention. Much to his dismay, at Plötzensee he had been housed with the "criminal prisoners" rather than the "political prisoners," and he requested a transfer. Within a week, S. received a response from the district court, which explained that no error had been made. Because he had "acted reprehensibly," he had been placed with other similarly motivated criminals.[121] This exchange is important for two reasons. It shows the importance of reputation to those involved in street fighting. S. did not want to be seen as a common prisoner, but as

---

[120] Ibid., letter from E. S. to the Schöffengericht Schöneberg, March 8, 1932. Her appeal was supported by the report of a private welfare association. The report highlighted the war service and wounds suffered by P. S. as well as his wife's heart and lung ailments. The children, ages two, four, and six, were described as susceptible to illnesses. Their dwelling consisted of a common kitchen/living room and a "sleeping niche." The family's clothing was, "under the impoverished circumstances, clean and orderly." P. S. was thought to have a good relationship to his wife and children, though he was known as a "big talker" who often got involved in political debates. The caseworker recommended probation. See, in the same file, letter from the Bezirksausschuss für Arbeiterwohlfahrt und Kinderschutz e.V. to the Beauftragten der Justizverwaltung für Gerichtshilfe, April 14, 1932. The recommendation for probation was denied. The commissioner who authored the denial for clemency explained that he would have liked to grant the request since the family was facing such dire financial straits. Repeating the decision of the court about his betrayal of former comrades, he declared probation to be impossible owing to the highly censurable actions of the prisoner. See, in the same file, the memo from the Beauftragte für Gnadensache to the Justice Minister, May 20, 1932.

[121] LAB, Rep. 58, Nr. 188, Film 379, letter from P. S. to the district attorney, October 26, 1932 and the response to P. S. from the Amtsgericht Schöneberg, November 2, 1932. S. was given a leave from prison sometime in November in order to complete urgently needed repairs on his home before winter arrived. On December 27, 1932, he was released under the terms of a nationwide amnesty declared for the Christmas holiday. A large number of the prisoners discussed in this chapter benefited from this amnesty.

one who had acted politically. This designation implied courage and support of his family and like-minded neighbors. Importantly, the court clearly upheld this distinction as well. In fact, the distinction was institutionalized by prison procedures and regarded so highly by the court that a guilty participant in a political conflict like S., who was not viewed worthy of this special designation, was denied such treatment.

The goals of this last chapter have been threefold. In the first section, I presented some of the common characteristics of street battles, their causes, and their outcomes. Though these skirmishes and assaults may seem irrational to the present-day observer, as they did to many witnesses at the time, I have argued that in fact there was a certain logic to the unrest. By using this phrase, I offer an explanation of how and why participants may have become involved in political violence. Surely the men involved, like the mechanic S., suffered immensely under the Depression. However, their motivations and actions illustrate a desire to find solutions to the crises that afflicted their individual lives. It was also made clear that political institutions played a minor role in leading these street fights. Party leaders, especially those representing the NSDAP, did encourage and provoke violence through their policies. Yet specific cases show that many other factors came into play, ultimately overshadowing party ideology and discipline.

A second goal was to explore the ways local authorities responded to the increasing unrest. Throughout this project much attention has been focused on the relationship between radical activists and the police, but they were not the only civil servants to come in contact with politicized workers in Berlin. Welfare workers first had a hand at trying to "reform" the young people thought to be most at risk. The files subsequently compiled on young men, particularly those who had run-ins with the law, tell us much about how radicalism and political violence were understood in this society. Preconceptions about politics and the poor led to explanations of radicalism that ignored the real generational and gender conflicts introduced in Chapter 2. Caseworkers emphasized physical and intellectual shortcomings or stressed the controlling presence of the political parties. The courts also misread the threat posed by these self-destructive individuals and their endangered communities. The reasons for their misjudgment were many. Though we know that the conservative bias of many judicial officials led to frequent injustices, I have asserted that we must look beyond party allegiance to understand this process fully. By also looking at the actions of those charged and the reports of caseworkers, who often had social democratic sympathies, we can see that across the board those judging political violence were more interested in intent and *Gesinnung* than deed. As a result, crimes that appeared to champion respect for discipline within an organization, claimed to protect friends or women, or sought revenge for previous injustices were treated lightly. This statement is by no means an apology for injustice. Rather, it is meant to emphasize just how pervasive the acceptance of political violence was throughout Weimar society and to demonstrate how such approval could ultimately undermine the republic.

Finally, this chapter should be seen in the context of the rest of this study. The examples of violence explored here point again to the local nature of the republic's collapse. Structural faults and government infighting may have created an unstable republic, but Berliners in the workers' districts were active in combating the crises. Strategies such as neighborhood boycotts, denunciations, and violence, however, only led to the further growth of instability at the most basic levels of society: families and neighborhoods. Through the examples of violent radicalism discussed here, it is clear that radical workers' own brands of "self-help" were not defined solely by party or class solidarity. Instead local activism, violent and nonviolent, was fueled by personal and moral claims about social status and was shaped by long-standing beliefs about masculinity and neighborhood power structures.

Conclusion

In the days following the May 1929 riots in Berlin, the police received a letter from an "anonymous eyewitness." The letter commended the actions of the Berlin force, which in carrying out its "duty and responsibility" had acted "correctly and blamelessly." However, the author did blame the police for not always taking such a strong stand: "A state may be so poor and in debt, as is unfortunately the case today, but peace and order must be [preserved]."[1] In the end, of course, a sinister kind of order was established in Berlin and elsewhere in Germany. The state was transformed, beginning in 1931 with the first emergency decree designed to fight political radicalism, reaching a new stage with the Papen-led coup in Prussia on July 21, 1932, and culminating in the chancellorship of Adolf Hitler on January 30, 1933, from a republic with a great deal of political freedom to a dictatorship in which order was finally achieved.

This process, which unfolded at the highest levels of political power in the capital, should not be studied in isolation. Rather the *Notverordnungen*, or emergency decrees, should be treated as a response to the culture of radicalism in Berlin. Before January 30, 1933, the decrees were intended to contain not eradicate radicalism. By placing ever-greater limitations on political expression and political space, the presidential cabinets challenged radicals in the city to prove their worth in the intensifying struggle for turf and power. This brings us back to the main claims of the study. The primary motivation of radical workers in Berlin, regardless of party affiliation, was not to overthrow the republic but to defend the sovereignty of their communities. The strategies they chose, however, were incompatible with a bordered public sphere and were seen as challenging to the authority of the state. With the advent of the emergency decrees, this challenge was criminalized.

THE EMERGENCY DECREES

Heinrich Brüning was the first to be granted the power by Hindenburg to act without parliamentary support in mid-July 1930, at which time he issued

---

[1] BLHA, Rep. 30, Berlin C, Title 95, Teil 2, Nr. 174, anonymous letter to police headquarters in Berlin, May 3, 1929, p. 239.

an emergency decree to "safeguard the national economy and finances."[2] Through the following winter, several more uncontested deflationary decrees were issued. These early decrees played a critical role in deepening the economic crisis in Germany.[3] Bypassing the parliament as the nation's sole legislative body, this first set of decrees also set the precedent for authoritarianism, which would be followed into the Third Reich.[4] In 1930, the Reichstag passed ninety-eight laws, and only five emergency decrees were issued. By 1932, the ratio had been reversed: only five laws were enacted by parliament, while sixty-six decrees went into effect.[5]

Though the economic decrees were intended to halt the downward spiral of economic depression, the political urgency behind the laws came from the fear that economic hardship led directly to political radicalism, especially communism. Brüning and even more so his successors in the chancellery, Franz von Papen and Kurt von Schleicher, used the economic crisis and their extended powers to dismantle the republic, which they viewed to be domestically weak and internationally impotent. In doing so, they were also motivated by the opportunity to sideline the SPD and deal a crippling blow to the KPD. When the economic decrees failed to have the desired economic or political results, the Brüning cabinet and those that followed turned to other decrees that targeted radicalism directly.

[2] The SPD and others protested this move, leading Brüning to dissolve parliament. The controversy did not unseat the cabinet, and the new elections yielded disappointing results for prorepublican forces. In light of these developments, the SPD changed its position, declaring in the fall of 1930 that it would "tolerate" the Brüning government and abstain from votes against future emergency decrees.

[3] The long-running debate about the role played by Brüning's economic measures in the collapse of the republic still continues. The argument that the unemployment rate would have never reached the heights that it did in Germany if Brüning had chosen an inflationary instead of deflationary course was challenged by Knut Borchardt beginning in 1978. Borchardt argued first that Brüning was hampered in choosing such a path. Furthermore, Borchardt maintains that even if such policies had been possible, Weimar's fundamental economic problems could not have been overcome simply through job creation. For a concise discussion of both sides of this controversy, see Jürgen von Kruedener, *Economic Crisis and Political Collapse. The Weimar Republic, 1924–1933* (New York: Berg Press, 1990). See also Harold James, *The Great Slump* (Oxford: Clarendon Press, 1986).

[4] For a brief overview of the presidential cabinets and their goals, see Manfred Funke, "Republik im Untergang: Die Zerstörung des Parlamentarismus als Vorbereitung der Diktatur" in Karl-Dietrich Bracher, Manfred Funke, and Hans Adolf Jacobsen, eds., *Die Weimarer Republik, 1918–1933: Politik, Wirtschaft, und Gesellschaft* (Düsseldorf: Droste, 1987), pp. 505–31. Like most historians who have written about the emergency decrees, Funke's emphasis lies on the internal political maneuverings and the ailing economy. See also Karl-Dietrich Bracher, *Auflösung der Weimarer Republik* (Villingen: Ring Verlag, 1955) for a detailed account of the presidential cabinets and emergency decrees. Bracher argues that the death of parliamentarism created a political vacuum into which conservatives with the backing of the army were able to push Hitler.

[5] Eberhard Kolb, *The Weimar Republic* (London: Unwin Hyman, 1988), p. 114.

On March 28, 1931, the first far-reaching presidential decree designed to suppress political radicalism went into effect. The law required all *outdoor* public political assemblies and parades to be registered at least one week in advance with the local police. A public assembly could be prohibited if the police suspected the meeting would break any laws, would offend or act contemptuously toward the state or any of its institutions, would insult any religious community, or would in any other way endanger the public order. A minimum three-month prison sentence was prescribed for those organizers who failed to register an assembly, ignored the prohibition of a proposed meeting, or were involved in any of the previously mentioned illegal activities at an authorized event. Participants in nonregistered assemblies also faced the possibility of jail time. Registered meetings could also be broken up by the police, if any of the foregoing activities took place during the event. In addition, the emergency decree directly aimed at combating violence by setting a minimum jail sentence of six months for using or threatening to use an unauthorized weapon. It strengthened the measures to ban political organizations and made it possible to ban political uniforms. Furthermore, anyone who continued to act as a member of a banned organization by wearing its uniform or participating in events sponsored by an illegal organization would face at least three-months incarceration. Finally, new regulations for political newspapers and other political publications were introduced. All political posters or other writings circulated to the public had to be registered with the police twenty-four hours in advance. The March decree allowed for the confiscation of any political writings not registered with the police as well as those that were thought to incite disorder. Daily newspapers could be banned for up to eight weeks.[6]

Like the Law for the Protection of the Republic and the *Bannmeile*, the decree's restrictions tried to contain radicalism by making political organizations adhere to certain boundaries for political expression prescribed by bourgeois society. Political activities that remained private (i.e., indoor meetings closed to the general public) were not affected by the March decree even if they contained hate-filled speeches or discussions of revolution. Only when engagement extended beyond these confines was it considered a potential threat to public order. The rationale for such proscriptions is not dissimilar to fears about foreign influences spreading from the East or similarly contamination of youthful or feminine minds.

When Prussian Interior Minister Joseph Wirth was forced to defend the decree shortly after its implementation,[7] he delivered the following radio

---

[6] For specifics of the March decree against political excesses, see *Reichsgesetzblatt*, Nr. 11, March 28, 1931, "Verordnung des Reichspräsidenten zur Bekämpfung politischer Ausschreitungen," p. 79.

[7] BA, R43I/2701a, Dr. Rudolf Breitscheid (for the SPD Reichstag faction) to Reich Interior Minister Wirth, April 20, 1931, p. 62.

address to Berlin's police force: "I repeat that the decree is not intended to rule against the freedom of political participation in respectable and objective forms. It does not intend to limit the ability to assemble politically or to engage in political debate through publications. It does not illustrate political understanding, when posters or fliers, which further the interests of all and the good of the state . . . are excluded from circulation."[8] Wirth's statement straddled a very fine line, as did the decree and other official responses to local radicalism. Wirth hoped the decree would contain radical/violent behavior while keeping the public sphere open for political discourse.[9]

After March 28, 1931, the Berlin sections of the Nazi and Communist Parties sent out to their supporters directives that explained what was no longer permissible and gave suggestions on how to circumvent the regulations. In public, both radical parties went on the offensive, issuing antidecree propaganda that combined portrayals of victimization at the hands of a few top officials with calls for resistance to the new restrictions. In one sarcastic KPD caricature, which appeared in *Die Rote Fahne* in April 1931, there is an experiment going on at the "Laboratory for fighting Bolshevism." Chancellor Brüning asks, "So, is the Communist bacillus dying off because of the added emergency decree?" His assistant Carl Severing peers into the microscope and responds in disbelief: "No, it's becoming ever greater."[10]

Data collected by Berlin's police and presented in Figure 8 demonstrate that the March decree had little effect on the number of assemblies requiring police intervention. The initial drop noted at assemblies sponsored by the NSDAP dissipated within a few months.[11] On November 20, 1931, the Prussian interior minister made his own efforts to contain radicalism by issuing a number of new instructions to his police force "to secure peace and order." Henceforth, all assemblies that appeared to incite violence, "even in a veiled form," were to be broken up immediately. Assemblies that invited speakers known to instigate violence were automatically prohibited. Those under

---

[8] BA, R43I/2701a, Reich Interior Minister Wirth radio address to all police departments, April 17, 1931, p. 68.

[9] As the calendar year came to an end, problems with the decree's measures against the political press continued. In December, Reich Interior Minister Groener issued a memo to high-level national and state officials reminding them that censorship of periodicals should not follow in every "legally *permissible*" case, rather only when censorship was "entirely *necessary*" in order to keep the peace. While Groener stressed that it was improper to ban summarily those news sources that "represented the demands of an opposition party," he defended the rights of the government not to be challenged on its decisions. Examples of the type of reporting that would necessitate prohibition were, according to Groener, "false news [stories] suited to excite the population . . . [and] alarming sensationalist news or headlines which thwart the efforts of the Reich government to restore the [nation's] economic, financial and political health." BA, R43I/2701a, memo by Reich Interior Minister Groener, December 16, 1931, p. 306. The emphasis is present in the original.

[10] *RF*, Nr. 91, April 19, 1931, "Im Laboratorium zur Bekämpfung des Bolschewismus."

[11] Statistics from GStA, Rep. 77, Title 4043, Nr. 121.

twenty years of age were prohibited from possessing any weapon that could cause injury through a "blow or stab." Finally, all marches and other types of paramilitary exercise and training were prohibited out of doors between 5 in the evening and 7 in the morning.[12]

A further emergency decree against political excesses was signed in December banning all uniforms of political organizations. This *Uniformverbot* had two flaws: it was unclear what counted as a uniform and what counted as a political organization. Did tying small swastika emblems to your bicycle count as the *wearing* of insignia? Did the youth groups that camped and hiked in uniform count as political organizations? Problems of these sorts had existed on a smaller scale since the first emergency decree, which prohibited people from dressing or acting as a member of an *illegal* political organization (namely the RFB and its affiliates). There were numerous cases in which former members, or currently underground members, of the illegal RFB were arrested in Berlin for wearing insignia or parts of the uniform, usually a cap or wind-breaker. Some men claimed that they had no other clothes or simply wore the uniform pieces out of practicality. What made the crucial difference in applying the new laws was intent. Donning a uniform in public, especially if the wearer was not alone, was seen as a declaration that the banned organization was still active.[13]

[12] *Wolff's Telegraphisches Büro*, Nr. 2446, November 20, 1931. Significantly, trade union activites were allowed to go on outside of the restrictions imposed by the emergency decrees. Unions were considered by the interior ministry "not to ... be political organizations in the sense of the emergency decrees." There were, however, exceptions to the rule because some organizations called themselves unions "but in reality sought other goals, for example the Communist RGO," which was to be held to the letter of the decrees as a political organization. The Reich interior minister recommended that all unions, in order to hold on to their "nonpolitical" status in terms of the decrees, "hold back from questions of public life, which did not concern their specific occupation sector's interests." BA, R15.01, Nr. 25877/2, letter from the Reich interior minister to the Prussian interior minister, March 4, 1932, p. 7. A second decree "against political excesses" was issued on July 17, 1931, and amended on August 10. This decree forced political publications – including newspapers – to publish official state declarations and opinions. The increasingly isolated SPD-led Prussian government took the opportunity on August 6, 1931, to attack the alliance between the KPD and NSDAP in the upcoming plebiscite to dissolve the Prussian parliament. Brüning viewed this as a misuse of the decree and lashed out against the Prussian government for its editorial, which warned that unless voters wanted a fascist or soviet Prussia, they should abstain from the polling stations. This Prussian independence led to the changes of August 10, 1931, which required *Land* governments to seek permission from the Reich interior minister before official declarations could be published. On the reaction by the Brüning cabinet, see BA, R43I/2701a, excerpt from the minutes of the ministers' discussion on August 10, 1931, pp. 159–60. Chancellor Brüning was particularly incensed because the plan to publish such a statement was kept secret from the cabinet for a week. For the amendments made to the July 17 decree, see *Wolff's Telegraphisches Büro*, first early edition, Nr. 1683, August 11, 1931.

[13] To make things easier, the Reich interior ministry presented a nonexhaustive list of forty-one organizations that did fall under the uniform ban. BA, R15.01, Nr. 25894, memo from the Reich minister of the interior to the *Land* governments, December 18, 1931, pp. 170–2.

In 1932, the restrictions of the *Notverordnungen* continued to expand under new names. First came the decree to "safeguard the Christmas peace" from December 20 until January 3, 1932, which forbade all public political assemblies and all outdoor political meetings. In addition, all political posters, fliers, and other circulars issued publicly or posted on public streets were banned. Those who ignored this holiday moratorium faced fines and jail time.[14] The same conditions were implemented between March 20 and April 3 for "the protection of the interior peace," also known as the Easter Peace.[15] These decrees, though stricter than those that had come before, were met with little controversy in the capital.

Controversy, however, did erupt in Berlin in April 1932 when the Reich government issued a decree "to secure state authority," finally dissolving the paramilitary wings of the NSDAP, including SA, SS, SA reserves and barracks, and other smaller troops such as the mounted corps.[16] Ever since the RFB was dissolved in May 1929, the KPD and many in the SPD had argued for inclusion of the Nazi paramilitary organizations in the ban.[17] Yet prior to April 1932, governmental leaders had argued that since SA and SS membership was theoretically restricted to members of the NSDAP, it would be unconstitutional to ban a section of a legitimate political party. The NSDAP used the time under the 1932 ban to extend their image as an oppressed group of martyrs. Insignia was worn on the backside of lapels, and men marched in plain white shirts in order to avoid the penalties for appearing in uniform. If the ban had been enacted earlier or had lasted longer, the SA might have experienced the sort of drop-off in participation that the RFB experienced after 1929. Since many had joined the Berlin SA to take part

[14] BA, R43I/2701a, "Maßnahmen zur Sicherung des Weihnachtsfriedens," December 3, 1931, p. 279.

[15] BA, R43I/2701b, "Verordnung des Reichspräsidenten zum Schutz des inneren Friedens," March 1932, p. 27.

[16] BA, R43I/2701b, "Verordnung des Reichspräsidenten zur Sicherung der Staatsauthorität," April 13, 1932, p. 48.

[17] Berlin had led the way in the summer of 1930 with a ban on the Nazi uniform, dubbed the "pants war" by the party's press. By March 1931, the prohibition had been declared unconstitutional in the district courts for limiting free speech. The Prussian government had hoped that any *public* wearing of a uniform would be considered *political* and therefore a threat to public order. The court did not see it this way, arguing that if a person was incited to disorder by the sight of an individual wearing a uniform then that agitated person was the guilty party in disrupting the peace. Prussian Interior Minister and Social Democrat Carl Severing was unwilling to support a uniform ban as part of a presidential decree because it would include the SPD-supported Reichsbanner. The possibility for uniform prohibition was incorporated into the text of the March 28, 1931, decree to curb political radicalism. For more on this initial uniform ban, see GStA, Rep. 77, Title 4043, Nr. 294. See also Dirk Schumann, *Politische Gewalt in der Weimarer Republik 1918–1933: Kampf um die Straße und Furcht vor dem Bürgerkrieg* (Essen: Klartext, 2001), p. 311 and Peter Leßmann, *Die Preußische Schutzpolizei in der Weimarer Republik: Streifendienst und Straßenkampf* (Düsseldorf: Droste, 1989), pp. 336–41.

Conclusion

in the public showmanship or spend time among comrades in the *Heime*, the reduced activities after April 1932 would quickly have grown tiresome. However, because the ban was lifted in June, this attempt to curb the growth of the SA probably worked more to the organization's benefit. The SA was able to return triumphantly during the summer – the warm months always meant more marching and public assemblies. The reversal of fortunes also confirmed the Berlin SA's claim that they had been unfairly victimized by a Marxist-supporting government, which was of course far from the truth during the Brüning era. Brüning did in fact face criticism for his support of the ban, adding to Hindenburg's growing dissatisfaction with his chancellor and leading in part to Brüning's resignation. The KPD paramilitary organizations remained illegal, leaving the SA to flaunt its strength in the capital throughout the critical summer and fall of 1932.

After the SA ban was lifted in the decree of June 14, 1932, a number of states acted on their own to ban uniforms. The variety of laws that emerged led to legal confusion and contributed to the public perception of a collapsing republic. The tension between the Reich and its states was clear. During cabinet meetings, there was talk of "separatism," and Papen's ministers expressed concern about the image of a state in which there was conflict over who held responsibility for national security.[18] This instability led to a bold move from Papen's cabinet in the form of the June 28, 1932, decree. It placed all power to determine whether assemblies or uniforms were to be forbidden in the hands of the Reich interior minister. In other words, state governments lost all authority in dealing with radicalism, except insofar as they still controlled their respective police forces.[19] Even then, police activities were determined largely at the Reich level.

This move was clearly a strike against the remaining SPD *Land* governments, namely the Prussian administration of Otto Braun. It served, therefore, as a step toward the executive decree that dissolved the Prussian government on July 20 and replaced it with an individual overseer, Reich Commissar Franz Bracht, appointed by Papen. The wording of the July 20 decree is explicit in its criticism of the SPD Prussian government. Ironically the SPD was blamed for allegedly allowing the KPD to continue its revolutionary preparations unimpeded:

The bloody unrest called for by the Communist side has laid the difficult task of caring for the peace and security of Germany's largest state in front of the Reich government. In the other German states, in which the police are strongly led, there is no fear that the Communist machinations will succeed. . . . In Prussia the Reich government must

---

[18] BA, R43I/2701b, excerpt from the minutes of the ministers' discussion in the Reich Chancellery, June 18, 1932, pp. 125–6.

[19] For the decree of June 14, 1932, see *Reichsgesetzblatt*, Teil I, Nr. 36, June 16, 1932, p. 297. For the decree of June 28, 1932, see its publication in *Wolff's Telegraphisches Büro*, first afternoon edition, Nr. 1366, June 29, 1932, which comes with an analysis of the law's significance.

recognize that the method and decisiveness of the leadership is lacking [in the fight] against the Communist movement.[20]

On July 20, along with the dismissal of Braun and Severing, Chief of Police Albert Grzesinski and others were arrested, and control of all security forces was handed over to the military. Reminiscent of the days following the rioting of May 1, 1929, certain neighborhoods in the capital were put under strict police surveillance until fears of an SPD- or KPD-led revolt subsided.[21]

While there was no large-scale protest of the newly appointed Prussian administrator, local activism and street violence continued. In August, with temperatures and death tolls rising in Berlin, a new presidential decree was issued in the capital. In this decree "against the terror," the death penalty was introduced for sentencing in premeditated political murders, nonpremeditated political acts that led to the death of police or soldiers, and deaths caused by politically motivated use of explosives and arson.[22] A companion decree was also issued on August 9, 1932, calling for the creation of special courts. These *Sondergerichte* were set up in political hot spots, such as Berlin, to deal with those brought to trial under the many statutes of the emergency decrees.

The emergency decrees follow an important path of progression. In the beginning, the hope was to contain political activism by ensuring that it was regulated by the police and restricted to indoor, members-only functions. When these measures failed, there were further attempts to discipline radical Berliners by expanding censorship and raising the levels of punishment meted out to those who disobeyed. Limits on political freedom eventually extended to all political parties and politically oriented associations. State governments too lost power, culminating in the dissolution of the Prussian government.

The presidential decrees against radicalism did little to curb the political tide because they strove only to combat radicalism without properly understanding its causes. The course taken – a path between political freedom with positive reinforcement of republicanism and total suspension of all political rights – may have been the most dangerous course in the long run. These disciplining measures – more police, new courts, more trials – coupled with the limited effectiveness of the decrees to bring an end to violence, made the republic's future seem more doubtful than ever. Berliners recognized that a

---

[20] *Wolff's Telegraphisches Büro*, first afternoon edition, Nr. 1529, July 20, 1932, "Reichskommissar in Preussen. Verordnung des Reichspräsidenten betreffend der Wiederherstellung der öffentlichen Sicherheit und Ordnung im Gebiete des Landes Preussen."

[21] For more detail on the *Preussenschlag*, see Hans Mommsen, *The Rise and Fall of Weimar Democracy* (Chapel Hill: University of North Carolina Press, 1996), pp. 445–50.

[22] *Wolff's Telegraphisches Büro*, evening edition, Nr. 1700, "Verordnung des Reichspräsidenten zur Sicherung des inneren Friedens," August 9, 1932. For the full description of the new decrees of August 9, see *Reichsgesetzblatt*, Teil I, Nr. 54, August 9, 1932, pp. 403–7. The August decrees were not the last to be signed by Hindenburg, but there were few other major changes.

state that needed to go to such lengths to control the streets in its own capital city was no longer a legitimate state.

THE CULTURE OF RADICALISM

Political radicalism was foremost a local response to the erosion of cultural norms and power structures in Berlin's neighborhoods rather than the product of party control and ideology. This independence fostered strategies that, though their intention was to reestablish neighborhood power hierarchies, served to undermine community cohesiveness and ultimately eroded any chance for democratic stability. Violence, as one such local strategy, became an acceptable tool for political change. Though the Nazi solution was not inevitable, this society's familiarity with violence, and indeed acceptance of certain forms of violence during the last years of the Weimar Republic, clearly aided the expansion and institutionalization of brutality after January 30, 1933.

Throughout the Weimar period, change was a constant in Berlin. The republic was new and so was the city's emerging identity as a democratic capital. Economic conditions remained unstable throughout the decade, as did the relationship between Berlin and its neighborhoods. Increasing disparity between the living conditions in the bourgeois West End and industrial East Side intensified mutual distrust. Though Red Berlin was not isolated from the rest of the city in any real sense, long-held perceptions about life in the workers' districts affected the ways western Berliners, the police, and other state agencies viewed events in these areas. Such bias against workers is not surprising. However, this divisiveness contributed to the growing sense of neighborhood autonomy. As republican welfare measures failed to alleviate the poverty of half the city, Berlin's workers rallied around the independent social and political structures of their East End neighborhoods.

Especially after 1929, these residents clung desperately to this independence. The desire to sustain autonomous Kieze was a direct response to the conditions of crisis under which many of these people lived. World War I, economic instability, industrial rationalization, changing relations between the sexes, and the emergence of a modern urban consumer culture made the daily struggle and future prospects of many Berliners seem forbidding. By the early 1930s, many had become radicalized by these pressures, deciding to defend their sphere of power – family, street, and neighborhood – with all means available to them.

Though both gender and generational conflict had long-term causes, it was during the post-1929 period that this turmoil thoroughly altered the political culture of the day. The popularity of militaristic values and paramilitary organizations by the late 1920s should not be read simply as "front generation" nostalgia for the camaraderie and discipline of World War I. Most of those who were active in Berlin's radical politics were too young to have served. Rather, radical enthusiasm and the militarism that accompanied it were manifestations of rebellion against the previous generation's reformism and against male disempowerment at home and in society. The political culture that emerged out of this rebellion was similar on the extreme right and left. Nazis and Communists discouraged and even forbade the involvement of women in certain party activities, conducted similar rites of passage, and glorified the authority of a patriarchal hierarchy and sense of brotherhood within the paramilitary organizations. By 1930, these structures served as male-only substitute families for Berlin's discontented young men.

The development of these extended familial communities cannot be separated from the Depression because the economic crisis most exacerbated young males' sense of alienation from their fathers' lifestyles and political traditions. In confronting the social and economic crises, social democratic policy appeared static, and its leadership seemed ossified. Many of Berlin's young people were unable to find the sort of stable industrial work that ensured entrance to the trade unions. Members of the younger generation were forced to delay starting their own families, and many remained financially dependent on their parents. The Depression also provided the impetus for radicalism, because it sped up changes to gender norms and further intensified some men's feelings of failure. In some cases, women became primary breadwinners, while men looked for jobs or sat at home. The loss of fathers and brothers in the war seemed further evidence that a lack of patriarchal authority was to blame for the erosion of families and neighborhood autonomy. Disconnected from paternal traditions and unable to begin families of their own, some men sought these male-only familial units that provided intimacy and reaffirmed their social importance. Political radicalism promised action instead of patience and self-initiated change instead of representative reform as a response to these individual and collective problems.

Though radical in practice, therefore, the intentions of those on the streets, even those affiliated with the far left, were often quite conservative. This is not just a story about young men, fearful of a changing world; it is a story of communities in crisis. Young men may have felt they had more at stake, and they certainly had more opportunity for involvement, but men and women of all ages were mobilized in these years by the desire to combat what they saw as declining power over their own lives. Beginning at home and extending to the courtyards, streets, and immediate neighborhood, politicized workers sought to mark boundaries, regulate behavior within this prescribed territory, and exclude outsiders.

The brewing discontent and suspicion in the city boiled over first in the May Day riots of 1929. I have argued that this tragedy revealed more than the brutality of the Prussian police or the willingness of the KPD to sacrifice lives in order to demonstrate the state's "betrayal" of workers. Rather, the importance of the *Blutmai* rebellions lies in the local nature of the fighting. The police had specific preconceptions about the dangers lurking in certain northern and eastern districts, and their strategies targeted these neighborhoods alone. We also learned of the willingness among the protesters to act in defense of "their streets," which went far beyond the calls for resistance issued by the KPD. This territorialism would characterize later street fighting in the capital. The 1929 riots are also significant because they demonstrated the inability of the KPD to handle crisis in Berlin. The party enjoyed its strongest support in the capital, but rank-and-file Communists were increasingly dissatisfied with their leaders' handling of the political situation. Local political independence was, in this way, partly a product of the party's own ineffectiveness. Finally, the May tragedy begins to bring into focus the new political culture as it developed in Berlin at the end of the Weimar Republic. The riots were mainly spontaneous, residentially based, violent outbursts. Participants were attempting to protect neighborhood sovereignty from the incursion of state authorities. Women were again unwelcome in this struggle, which legitimated local nonparty political hierarchies and highlighted the prejudice and brutality of the city's police force.

The three parties that sought the support of the city's workers wanted to harness this aggression for their own political goals. The parties and their paramilitary organizations provided a convenient structure for the local desires of Berlin's young radicals. Men were attracted to the camaraderie, material benefits, glorification of masculinity, and active lifestyle provided by the RFB, SA, and to a lesser extent RB. The private, clublike political atmosphere of the early 1920s was giving way to an environment in which political organizations took to the streets to proclaim their goals and demands.[23] Of the three parties in Berlin that appealed to workers, the SPD struggled most in this new climate. Their members too were moved by the generational tensions and local problems, which seemed so distant from the legislative reformism of their leaders. By 1931, the social democratic leadership was forced to recognize its dwindling ability to compete with the more action-oriented organizations and retain loyalty among the capital's workers. The creation of the Eiserne Front and the attempts to transform the RB into a more convincing fighting force were their chief responses to the growth of radicalism.

The parties demanded discipline in exchange for the material benefits and organizational structures they offered workers, but they rarely got it. Respect for leaders' authority and the larger aims of the parties were not priorities for many in these movements. This study attempts to offer an alternative understanding of political motivations and participation at the end of the Weimar Republic. First, we must rethink our understanding of class identity. Friends and enemies were fluid categories, determined much more by local events

[23] This trend was seen among all political parties, not just the three considered here. Peter Fritzsche makes this point most convincingly in *Rehearsals for Fascism: Populism and Political Mobilization in Weimar Germany* (New York: Oxford University Press, 1990).

and concerns than by party rhetoric or propaganda. These parties were not well-organized, disciplined ideological machines. All three parties had major problems, especially the KPD and NSDAP, which faced astronomical growth in these years. These two parties, as well as the SPD, were confronted with growing local independence, undermining attempts to construct cohesive policies and programs. Berlin's workers, even under the strain of the Depression, cannot be said to have surrendered themselves to party hierarchies or institutional regulations. Rather there was a great deal of give and take at the neighborhood level between local functionaries and their supporters. Parties were most successful when they incorporated the demands and desires of their rank-and-file members into their broader programs, but despite the virulent propaganda and calls for ideological discipline, some activists found nothing irregular about switching sides in the political struggle when the opportunity presented itself. This statement does not depoliticize these actions. Fluctuation was not a sign of indifference. To the contrary, these workers were responding to a set of political issues and motivations, but their priorities were often different from those the parties chose to emphasize. Radical workers were making choices that reflected their daily political needs, and when their local unit no longer seemed equipped to handle these issues – through its public activities, material resources, or physical prowess – young men did not hesitate to join a more "successful" group or reject all party affiliation. Though the electoral successes and failures of the SPD, KPD, and NSDAP have not played a significant role in this project, a look at voting statistics shows that all three parties were largely unable to negotiate consistently the space between local activism and national platform. Between 1928 and 1933, all three parties saw dramatic increases and declines in their national electoral tallies, and none was able to secure continued levels of support until the chancellorship gave Hitler the power to eliminate other options.[24]

The use of denunciation was another sign of heightened activity at the grassroots level. In the case of the Berlin KPD, it is particularly clear that standards of moral and political behavior were defined and judged in the neighborhoods. While the KPD tried to make use of their supporters' willingness to root out "criminals" in their midst, the motivation behind the

---

[24] The Social Democrats dropped from a high of 153 Reichstag seats won in the May 1928 elections down to 121 by the end of 1932. The Communists had only forty-five representatives in parliament in 1928 but by 1932 had gained fifty-five more. The Nazi Party only received enough votes in the May 1928 elections to send fourteen representatives to Berlin. After the July 1932 elections, however, the NSDAP boasted 230 Reichstag members, but by the end of the year, the number had fallen to 196. For a complete table of Reichstag election results between 1920 and 1933, see Volker R. Berghahn, *Modern Germany: Society, Economy and Politics in the Twentieth Century* (Cambridge: Cambridge University Press, 1987). For the results in Kreuzberg and Berlin, see Figures 6 and 7.

local denunciations was quite different. Those denouncing neighbors were seeking to expose men and women who were, in the minds of their accusers, threatening neighborhood stability. The denounced were seen as traitors, not to the party or the workers' movement per se but to their communities. By punishing those who appeared to bring disorder to their neighborhoods through sexual indiscretion, price gouging, inappropriate violence, or excessive drunkenness, the perpetrators would desist, others would be deterred, and these threats to the social fabric would be eliminated. Though the KPD hoped to use denunciations to limit ideological independence, political nonconformity was not seen as a priority among the party's rank-and-file. The sources show a surprising amount of political diversity in these neighborhoods. Communists were familiar with those who supported other parties and only judged outsiders harshly when their actions were perceived to worsen the daily neighborhood crises.

The problem with denunciation as a strategy for rebuilding neighborhood autonomy was that it introduced more suspicion and tension into these communities than it dispelled. Nonetheless, this form of grassroots activism should be viewed the way the denouncers intended it – as a way to assert local power. Political violence in Berlin should be studied in the same manner, as an example of political independence with great significance for the collapse of the republic. Violence became socially acceptable as a means to political change by many more than the few hundred Communists and Nazis who participated in the turmoil. By pitting neighbors against each other, by necessitating an increase in police surveillance, and by creating more fear and suspicion of the districts of Red Berlin, street fighting undermined any vestiges of community solidarity and autonomy. Moreover, the acceptance of physical conflict was not restricted to the neighborhoods that experienced most of Berlin's street violence. In statements by court officials and news articles, it is clear that violence came to be expected among other sectors of society, preparing the way for an institutionalization of political violence after 1933.

The phrase "the logic of violence" is admittedly an oxymoron. Its use as a chapter heading is not meant to imply that this violence was somehow justified or necessary. However, if the larger goal behind the study of violent societies is to understand how they got that way, it is not enough to conclude that desperation causes irrational behavior. Instead, we must seek to comprehend why and how violence in each specific context comes to be viewed as a legitimate strategy for creating change. The reasoning behind Berlin's street violence, and the ways it was regulated and accepted, constitute the behavior's logic. In other words, violence became an attractive alternative, particularly for young men, because they believed its use assisted in the maintenance of order and confirmed their own status as local authorities.

Only a few thousand in this city of roughly four million ever participated in political violence during the final years of the Weimar Republic. The small number of activists, however, does not mean the unrest was any less of a threat to political and social stability. At the height of their popularity in mid 1932, the KPD and NSDAP attracted 56 percent of the electorate for greater Berlin – a higher percentage than in any other metropolitan area in the country.[25] Large numbers of nonviolent supporters likely sympathized with "their" side in the struggle. Others too supported the police in their attempts to contain the "political excesses," even by violent means. By the early 1930s, few in Berlin could imagine a nonviolent end to the political crisis. Denunciation and violence weakened these communities by instilling fear, anger, and suspicion among residents. Because violence also drew extensive attention from the press at home and abroad, the press coverage also meant greater fear in the western half of the city, which led to greater support for the NSDAP. The emergency decrees that followed and the accompanying police surveillance meant further intrusion of outsiders. These state efforts not only sidestepped the parliamentary process but also increasingly curtailed political expression, and thereby laid the groundwork for dictatorship. Berlin's radical neighborhood culture – though not aimed at toppling the government or instigating a revolution – did much to precipitate the early collapse of the republic.

It is wrong to equate the violence from 1929 to 1933 with the state-sanctioned brutality that followed during the Third Reich. Under the veil of officialdom, the violence of the Nazi state could be systematized, and its targets isolated, in ways not possible before 1933. The local, multidimensional, violent struggle was replaced after 1933 by a single-minded racist political hunt under the mandate of the government. Nonetheless, it is clearly wrong to conclude that there was only minimal connection between the two eras, particularly with respect to violence. West German oral histories of the mid 1930s are helpful in this regard. Historians have found that many Germans, even after the devastation of World War II, had generally positive reviews of Hitler's prewar Reich.[26] Of course, these memories were likely made more prominent by the destruction, defeat, and division that followed in the 1940s. However, the positive evaluation of this period was also aided by the misery of the years between 1929 and 1933. Berliners were exhausted by 1933, tired of the long-term political and economic instability of the republic. As a result, many middle-class Berliners not directly targeted by the regime more easily accepted, or at least resigned themselves to, an authoritarian government in 1933. They hoped that the new system would finally

[25] The electoral support for the NSDAP and KPD in the entire Reich was just under 52 percent. These statistics come from the results of the July 31, 1932, parliamentary elections. See Alexander Wilde, "Republikfeindschaft in der Berliner Bevölkerung und der Wandel der kommunalen Selbstverwaltung um 1931" in Otto Büsch, ed., Beiträge zur Geschichte der Berliner Demokratie 1919–1933/1945–1985 (Berlin: Colloquium Verlag, 1988), p. 109.

[26] Cf. Lutz Niethammer, ed., "Die Jahre weiss man nicht, wo man die heute hinsetzen soll": Faschismuserfahrungen im Ruhrgebiet (Berlin: Dietz, 1983).

deliver on the promises to create economic stability and bring order to the streets, and they had learned to rationalize the use of violence to achieve these goals.

Workers too were not prepared to mount any sort of rebellion. Their lack of resistance should not be explained solely by the ideological division between Social Democrats and Communists. There was distrust between the two parties, but the alienation *within* each party, between the party hierarchies and their constituents, played an even larger role. Socialist and Communist leaders were rounded up in the early days of the regime, but it is unlikely that these institutions could have mobilized or coordinated significant resistance to Hitler. It was not just the failures of the Weimar Republic that encouraged a local radical culture but the freedoms of the republic as well. Though workers did not articulate it as such and their actions worked largely to weaken democracy, they were fighting to defend a local sense of power that could have only developed during the republican period. By 1933, the freedoms that had allowed for local radicalism no longer existed.

After Hitler's appointment as chancellor, violence for the NSDAP was not just a means to the end of securing power: it was a necessary and continuous way to demonstrate order. Party leaders presumed correctly that under governmental control, violence could be more effectively harnessed to serve the movement's racist objectives. Once in power, the new regime increasingly depended on violence, even among its own organizations, to demonstrate the authority of its dictatorial reign.[27] The street violence of late Weimar Berlin had inured workers to this harsh new reality. They had grown to accept violence, but now the Nazis alone possessed the power to use it in defining local order.

[27] With regard to the radicalization of violence in the Third Reich, Detlev Peukert argues that the Nazi regime consistently sought to "'conquer the only remaining unsolved problem' by creating a new and bigger problem." Detlev Peukert, *Inside Nazi Germany. Conformity, Opposition, Racism in Everyday Life* (New Haven, CT: Yale University Press, 1987a), p. 45.

Bibliography

Unpublished Archival Material

Brandenburgisches Landeshauptarchiv (BLHA), Potsdam
Rep. 30, Berlin C, Title 95: Polizeipräsidium
    Sektion 9: Kommunistische Bewegung
    Sektion 9 Teil II: Überwachung der öffentlichen Ordnung
    Sektion 10: Sozialistische Bewegung nach 1918
Rep. 30, Berlin C, Title 90: Schutzpolizei
Rep. 61: NSDAP und ihre Gliederungen

Bundesarchiv (BA), Berlin – Lichterfelde
NS 18: Reichspropaganda
NS 22: Organisationsleitung
NS 23: Sturmabteilung
NS 26: NSDAP Hauptarchiv
NS 28: Hitler Jugend
R 32: Reichskunstwart
R 43I, II: Reichskanzlei 1918–33
R15.01: Reichsministerium des Innern VF II
R15.07: Überwachung der öffentlichen Ordnung
R8034 II: Reichslandbund – Pressearchiv

Bundesarchiv-Außenstelle Filmarchiv, Berlin – Wilmersdorf
Newsreel Collection, 1929–33

Evangelisches Zentralarchiv (EZA), Berlin
Bestand 51: Ökumenische Archiv

Geheimes Staatsarchiv Preussischer Kulturbesitz (GStA), Berlin – Dahlem
Rep. 77, Title 4043: Polizeiabteilung
Rep. 84a (2.5.1.): Justizministerium

Institut für Zeitgeschichte (IFZ), Munich
Db203.07, Fa88

Landesarchiv Berlin (LAB)
Rep. 58: Akten des Generalstaatsanwalts beim Landgericht, Berlin
Rep. 214: Bezirksamt Neukölln
Flugblättersammlung

Landesarchiv Berlin-Außenstelle
Rep. 01–02 Magistrat von Berlin: Generalburo

Rathaus Neukölln, Berlin-Neukölln
Files Nr. 407, 1890

Stiftung Archiv der Parteien und Massenorganisationen der DDR im Bundesarchiv (BA-
SAPMO), Berlin – Lichterfelde
RY1/I4/1–RY1/I4/16, Band VI: KPD, Revolutionäre Massenorganisationen
RY1/I3/1-2–RY1/I3/2, Band IV: Bezirk Berlin-Brandenburg-Lausitz-Grenzmark der KPD
RY1/I2/701–RY1/I2/706, Band III, Teil II: Schriftgut des Apparates des ZK (Abteilungen)
SgY2/V/DF: Flugblättersammlung

Periodicals

8-Uhr Abendblatt
Der Angriff
Arbeiter Illustrierte Zeitung (AIZ)
Berliner Börsen-Zeitung
Berliner Tageblatt (BT)
Berliner Wohlfahrtsblatt
Deutsche Tageszeitung
Deutsche Zeitung
Neuköllner Tageblatt
New York Times
Die Rote Fahne (RF)
Völkischer Beobachter (VB)
Vorwärts
Vossische Zeitung (VZ)
Die Welt am Abend

Other Published Contemporary and Secondary Sources

10 Jahre Weimarer Verfassung. *Die Verfassungsreden bei den Verfassungsfeiern der Reichs-
regierung.* (Berlin: Reichszentrale für Heimatdienst, 1929).
Abrams, Lynn, and Elizabeth Harvey, eds. *Gender Relations and German History.* (Durham,
NC: Duke University Press, 1997).
Allfeld, Philipp. *Der Einfluß der Gesinnung des Verbechers auf die Bestrafung.* (Leipzig: W.
Engelmann, 1909).
Applegate, Celia. *A Nation of Provincials. The German Idea of Heimat.* (Berkeley: University
of California Press, 1990).
   "Democracy or Reaction? The Political Implications of Localist Ideas in Wilhelmine and
Weimar Germany." In Larry Eugene Jones and James Retallack, eds. *Elections, Mass Poli-
tics, and Social Change in Modern Germany.* (Washington, DC: German Historical Institute
and Cambridge University Press, 1992).
Asmus, Gesine, ed. *Hinterhof, Keller, und Mansarde: Einblicke in Berliner Wohnungselend
1901–1920.* (Reinbek: Rowohlt, 1982).
Bahne, Siegfried. *Die KPD und das Ende von Weimar.* (Frankfurt a. M.: Campus, 1976).
Balzer, Alfred. *Die ehrlose Gesinnung im geltenden und zukünkftigen Strafrecht.* (Diss. der
juristischen Fakultät der Friedrich-Alexanders-Universität zu Erlangen, 1934).
Behrenbeck, Sabine. "The Nation Honours the Dead: Remembrance Days for the Fallen in the
Weimar Republic and Third Reich." In Karin Friedrich, ed. *Festival Culture in Germany
and Europe.* (Lampeter: Mellen, 2000).
Benenowski, Hans. *Nicht nur für die Vergangenheit. Streitbare Jugend in Berlin um 1930.*
(Berlin: Verlag in Kreuzberg, 1983).

Berghahn, Volker R. *Modern Germany: Society, Economy and Politics in the Twentieth Century.* (Cambridge: Cambridge University Press, 1987).

Berg-Schlosser, Dirk, and Ralf Rytlewski, eds. *Political Culture in Germany.* (London: Macmillan, 1993).

Bessel, Richard. *Political Violence and the Rise of Nazism. The Storm Troopers in Eastern Germany, 1925–1934.* (New Haven, CT: Yale University Press, 1984).

"Die Erblast des verlorenen Krieges." In Frank Bajohr et al., eds. *Zivilisation und Barbarei: Die widersprüchliche Potentiale der Moderne.* (Hamburg: Christians, 1991a).

"Policing, Professionalisation and Politics in Weimar Germany." In Clive Elmsley and Barbara Weinberger, eds. *Policing Western Europe. Politics, Professionalism, and Public Order, 1850–1940.* (New York: Greenwood Press, 1991b).

"Militarisierung und Modernisierung: Polizeiliches Handeln in der Weimarer Republik." In Alf Lüdtke, ed. *Sicherheit und Wohlfahrt. Polizei, Gesellschaft und Herrschaft im 19. und 20. Jahrhundert.* (Frankfurt a. M.: Suhrkamp, 1992).

Germany after the First World War. (Oxford: Clarendon, 1993).

"The 'Front Generation' and the Politics of Weimar Germany." In Mark Roseman, ed. *Generations in Conflict.* (Cambridge: Cambridge University Press, 1995).

Beyer, Hans. *Die Frau in der politischen Entscheidung.* (Stuttgart: F. Enke, 1933).

Birkenfeld, Günther. *Dritter Hof Links.* (Berlin: Bruno Cassirer, 1929).

Bleek, Stephan. "Das Stadtviertel als Sozialraum. Innerstädtische Mobilität in München 1890 bis 1933." In Klaus Tenfelde, ed. *Soziale Räume in der Urbanisierung: Studien zur Geschichte Münchens im Vergleich 1850 bis 1933.* (Munich: Oldenbourg, 1990).

Boak, Helen. "Women in Weimar Germany: The *Frauenfrage* and the Female Vote." In R. Bessel and E. J. Feuchtwanger, eds. *Social Change and Political Development in Weimar Germany.* (London: Croom Helm, 1981).

"National Socialism and Working-Class Women Before 1933." In Conan Fischer, ed. *The Rise of National Socialism and the Working Classes in Weimar Germany.* (Providence: Berghahn Books, 1996).

Boberg, Jochen, Tilman Fichter, and Eckhart Gillen, eds. *Exerzierfeld der Moderne. Industriekultur in Berlin im 19. Jahrhundert.* (Munich: Beck, 1984).

Boberg, Jochen, Tilman Fichter, and Eckhart Gillen, eds. *Die Metropole. Industriekultur in Berlin im 20. Jahrhundert.* (Munich: Beck, 1986).

Bock, Gisela. *Zwangssterilisation im Nationalsozialismus: Studien zur Rassenpolitik und Frauenpolitik.* (Opladen: Westdeutscher Verlag, 1986).

Bock, Gisela, and Pat Thane, eds. *Maternity and Gender Policies: Women and the Rise of the European Welfare States, 1880s–1950s.* (London: Routledge, 1991).

Borchardt, Knut. *Wachstum, Krisen, Handlungsspielräume der Wirtschaftspolitik.* (Göttingen: Vandenhoeck & Ruprecht, 1982).

Borchert, James. *Alley Life in Washington: Family, Community, Religion, and Folklife in the City, 1850–1970.* (Urbana: University of Illinois Press, 1980).

Böß, Gustav. *Berlin von Heute.* (Berlin: Gsellius, 1929).

Bowlby, Chris. "Blutmai 1929: Police, Parties and Proletarians in a Berlin Confrontation." In *The Historical Journal* (Vol. 29, No. 1, 1986), pp. 137–58.

Bracher, Karl-Dietrich. *Die Auflösung der Weimarer Republik.* (Villingen: Ring Verlag, 1955).

The German Dictatorship. (New York: Praeger, 1970).

Bracher, Karl-Dietrich, Manfred Funke, and Hans Adolf Jacobsen, eds. *Die Weimarer Republik, 1918–1933: Politik, Wirtschaft, und Gesellschaft.* (Düsseldorf: Droste, 1987).

Braune, Rudolf. *Die Geschichte einer Woche* (Berlin: Verlag Neues Leben, 1978; original edition, 1930).

Das Mädchen an der Orga Privat. (Frankfurt a. M: Societäts-Verlag, 1930; Munich: Damnitz, 1975).

Bredel, Willi. *Maschinenfabrik N. & K. Ein Roman aus dem proletarischen Alltag.* (Berlin: Aufbau Verlag, 1982; original edition, Vienna: Internationaler Arbeiter-Verlag, 1930).

Breitman, Richard. *German Socialism and Weimar Democracy.* (Chapel Hill: University of North Carolina Press, 1981).

Bridenthal, Renate, Atina Grossmann, and Marion Kaplan, eds. *When Biology Became Destiny.* (New York: Monthly Review Press, 1984).

Broszat, Martin. *Hitler and the Collapse of Weimar Germany.* (New York: Berg, 1987).

Brückner, Eva. "Soziale Fragmentierung und kollektives Gedächtnis. Nachbarschaftsbeziehungen in einem Berliner Arbeiterviertel 1920–1980." In Wolfgang Hofmann and Gerd Kuhn, eds. *Wohnungspolitik und Städtebau, 1900–1930.* (Berlin: Technische Universität, 1993).

"Wohnen und Leben in SO 36, zum Beispiel in der Wiener Straße 10–12." In Helmut Engel, Stefi Jersch-Wenzel, and Wilhelm Treue, eds. *Geschichtslandschaft Berlin: Orte und Ereignisse. Band 5: Kreuzberg.* (Berlin: Nicolai, 1994).

"Und ich bin heil da 'rausgekommen': Gewalt und Sexualität in einer Berliner Arbeiternachbarschaft zwischen 1916/17 und 1958." In Thomas Lindenberger und Alf Lüdtke, eds. *Physiche Gewalt.* (Frankfurt a. M.: Suhrkamp, 1995).

Brustein, William. *The Logic of Evil: The Social Origins of the Nazi Party, 1925–1933.* (New Haven, CT: Yale University Press, 1996).

Busch, Bernd. "Nur politische... denn hast doch keene Freizeit mehr." In Kunstamt Kreuzberg, ed., *Kreuzberg 1933. Ein Bezirk erinnert sich.* (Berlin: Durchschlag, 1983).

Büsch, Otto, and Wolfgang Haus. *Berlin als Hauptstadt der Weimarer Republik, 1919–1933.* (Berlin: de Gruyter, 1987).

Büttner, Eva. *Hamburg in der Staats- und Wirtschaftskrise 1928–1931.* (Hamburg: Christians, 1982).

Caldwell, Peter. *Popular Sovereignty and the Crisis of German Constitutional Law: The Theory and Practice of Weimar Constitutionalism.* (Durham, NC: Duke University Press, 1997).

Campbell, Anne. *The Girls in the Gang.* (Oxford: Basil Blackwell, 1984).

Campbell, Bruce. *The SA Generals and the Rise of Nazism.* (Lexington: University of Kentucky Press, 1998).

Carsten, Francis L. *The Reichswehr and Politics, 1918 to 1933.* (Berkeley: University of California Press, 1973).

The German Workers and the Nazis. (London: Scolar Press, 1995).

Clark, Anna. *Women's Silence, Men's Violence: Sexual Assault in England, 1770–1845.* (London: Pandora, 1987).

The Struggle for the Breeches: Gender and the Making of the British Working Class. (Berkeley: University of California Press, 1995).

Cohen, Deborah. *The War Come Home: Disabled Veterans in Britain and Germany, 1914–1939.* (Berkeley: University of California Press, 2001).

Confino, Alon. *The Nation as a Local Metaphor: Württemberg, Imperial Germany, and National Memory, 1871–1918.* (Chapel Hill: University of North Carolina Press, 1997).

Corner, Paul. *Fascism in Ferrara 1915–1925.* (New York: Oxford University Press, 1975).

Crew, David F. "The Pathologies of Modernity: Detlev Peukert on Germany's Twentieth Century." In *Social History.* (Vol. 17, No. 2, May 1992), pp. 319–28.

"Who's Afraid of Cultural Studies? Taking a 'Cultural Turn' in German History." In Scott Denham, Irene Kacandes, and Jonathan Petropoulos, eds. *A User's Guide to German Cultural Studies.* (Ann Arbor: University of Michigan, 1997).

Germans on Welfare: From Weimar to Hitler. (New York: Oxford University Press, 1998).

Daniel, Ute. *Arbeiterfrauen in der Kriegsgesellschaft: Beruf, Familie und Politik im Ersten Weltkrieg.* (Göttingen: Vandenhoeck & Ruprecht, 1989).

The War from Within: German Working-Class Women in the First World War. Margaret Ries., trans. (New York: Berg, 1997).

Davis, Belinda. "Food Scarcity and the Empowerment of the Female Consumer in World War I Berlin." In Victoria de Grazia, ed. *The Sex of Things. Gender and Consumption in Historical Perspective.* (Berkeley: University of California Press, 1996).

Home Fires Burning: Food, Politics, and Everyday Life in World War I Berlin. (Chapel Hill: University of North Carolina Press, 2000).

Della Porta, Donatella. *Social Movements, Political Violence and the State. A Comparative Analysis of Italy and Germany.* (Cambridge: Cambridge University Press, 1995).

Diehl, James. *Paramilitary Politics in the Weimar Republic.* (Bloomington: Indiana University Press, 1977).

Döblin, Alfred. *Berlin Alexanderplatz. Die Geschichte von Franz Bieberkopf.* (Berlin: Fischer, 1929).

Berlin Alexanderplatz. The Story of Franz Bieberkopf, Eugene Jolas, trans. (New York: F. Ungar, 1983).

Domansky, Elisabeth. "Militarization and Reproduction in WWI Germany." In Geoff Eley, ed. *Society, Culture and the State in Germany, 1870–1930.* (Ann Arbor: University of Michigan Press, 1996).

Dudek, Peter. *Erziehung durch Arbeit. Arbeitslagerbewegung und Freie Arbeitsdienst, 1920–35.* (Opladen: Westdeutscher Verlag, 1988).

Erhardt, Justus. *Straßen ohne Ende.* (Berlin: Agis, 1931).

Eksteins, Modris. *The Limits of Reason. The German Democratic Press and the Collapse of Weimar Democracy.* (London: Oxford University Press, 1975).

Rites of Spring: The Great War and the Birth of the Modern Age. (New York: Doubleday, 1989).

Eley, Geoff. "Labor History, Social History, *Alltagsgeschichte*: Experience, Culture, and the Politics of the Everyday – A New Direction for German Social History?" In *Journal of Modern History.* (Vol. 61, No. 2, 1989), pp. 297–343.

Elmsley, Clive, and Barbara Weinberger, eds. *Policing Western Europe. Politics, Professionalism and Public Order, 1850–1940.* (New York: Greenwood Press, 1991).

Engel, Helmut, Stefi Jersch-Wenzel, and Wilhelm Treue, eds. *Geschichtslandschaft Berlin. Orte und Ereignisse, Band 5: Kreuzberg.* (Berlin: Nicolai, 1994).

Engelbrechten, Julius, and Hans Volz. *Wir wandern durch das nationalsozialistische Berlin: Ein Führer durch die Gedenkstätten des Kampfes um die Reichshauptstadt.* (Munich: Zentralverlag der NSDAP, 1937).

Ermath, Michael, ed. *America and the Shaping of German Society.* (Providence: Berg, 1993).

Evans, Richard J. *Kneipengespräche im Kaiserreich: Die Stimmungsberichte der Hamburger politischen Polizei, 1892–1914.* (Reinbek bei Hamburg: Rowohlt, 1989).

"Die Todesstrafe in der Weimarer Republik." In Frank Bajohr, Werner Johe, and Uwe Lohalm, eds. *Zivilisation und Barbarei. Die widersprüchlichen Potentiale der Moderne.* (Hamburg: Christians, 1991).

Rituals of Retribution. Capital Punishment in Germany, 1600–1987. (New York: Oxford University Press, 1996).

Evans, Richard J., and Dick Geary, eds. *The German Unemployed.* (New York: St. Martin's Press, 1987).

Fallada, Hans. *Kleiner Mann – Was Nun?* (Rheinbek bei Hamburg: Rowohlt, 1992; original edition, 1932).

Little Man, What Now? Eric Sutton, trans. (Chicago: Academy Chicago Publishers, 1992).

Falter, Jürgen. "Die Jungmitglieder der NSDAP zwischen 1925 und 1933." In Wolfgang Krabbe, ed. *Politische Jugend in der Weimarer Republik.* (Bochum: Universitätsverlag, 1993).

Falter, Jürgen, Thomas Lindenberger, and Siegfried Schumann, eds. *Wahlen und Abstimmungen in der Weimarer Republik: Materialien zum Wahlverhalten, 1919–1933.* (Munich: Beck, 1986).

Fiebig, Irma. "Die Gefährtin des Arbeitslosen." In *Die Berliner Front.* (October 29, 1932).

Fink, Georg. *Mich Hungert!* (Berlin: Bruno Cassirer, 1930).

Fischer, Conan. *Stormtroopers: A Social, Economic and Ideological Analysis, 1929–1935.* (London: Allen and Unwin, 1983).

"Class Enemies or Class Brothers? Communist-Nazi Relations in Germany, 1929–1933." In *European History Quarterly* (Vol. 15, No. 3, 1985), pp. 259–79.

The German Communists and the Rise of Nazism. (New York: St. Martin's Press, 1991).

"Gab es am Ende der Weimarer Republik einen marxistischen Wählerblock?" In *Geschichte und Gesellschaft.* (Vol. 21, Nr. 1, 1995), pp. 63–79.

ed. *The Rise of National Socialism and the Working Classes in Weimar Germany.* (Providence: Berghahn Books, 1996).

Fischer, Josepha. *Die Mädchen in den deutschen Jugendverbänden.* (Leipzig: R. Voigtländer, 1933).

Fitzpatrick, Sheila, and Robert Gellately, eds. *Accusatory Practices: Denunciation in Modern European History, 1789–1989.* (Chicago: University of Chicago Press, 1996).

Fitzpatrick, Sheila. "Signals from Below: Soviet Letters of Denunciation of the 1930s." In *Journal of Modern History.* (Vol. 68, No. 4, 1996b), pp. 831–66.

Flemming, Jens, Klaus Saul, and Peter-Christian Witt, eds. *Familienleben im Schatten der Krise. Dokumente und Analyse zur Sozialgeschichte der Weimarer Republik.* (Düsseldorf: Droste, 1988).

Fowkes, Ben. *Communism in Germany under the Weimar Republic.* (New York: St. Martin's Press, 1984).

Fraenkel, Ernst. *Zur Soziologie der Klassenjustiz und Aufsätze zur Verfassungskrise, 1931–1932.* (Berlin: E. Verlagsbuchhandlung, 1927; second edition, Darmstadt: Wissenschaftliche Buchgesellschaft, 1968).

Franken, Paul. *Vom Werden einer neuen Kultur: Aufgaben der Arbeiter-Kultur-und-Sportorganisationen.* (Berlin: E. Laubsche, 1930).

Franzoi, Barbara. *At the Very Least She Pays the Rent. Women and German Industrialization, 1871–1914.* (Westport, CT: Greenwood Press, 1985).

Frevert, Ute. "Traditionelle Weiblichkeit und moderne Interessenorganisation: Frauen im Angestelltenberuf 1918–1933." In *Geschichte und Gesellschaft.* (Vol. 3/4, 1981), pp. 507–33.

Women in German History. (Oxford: Berg, 1989).

Men of Honour: A Social and Cultural History of the Duel. (Cambridge: Polity Press, 1995).

Friedman, Allen. *Formations of Violence.* (Chicago: University of Chicago Press, 1991).

Friedrich, Otto. *Before the Deluge: A Portrait of Berlin in the 1920s.* (second edition, New York: Harper, 1995).

Friedrich, Thomas. *Berlin Between the Wars.* (New York: Vendome Press, 1991).

Fritzsche, Peter. *Rehearsals for Fascism: Populism and Political Mobilization in Weimar Germany.* (New York: Oxford University Press, 1990).

"Did Weimar Fail?" In *The Journal of Modern History.* (Vol. 68, No. 3, 1996a), pp. 629–56.

Reading Berlin 1900. (Cambridge, MA: Harvard University Press, 1996b).

Germans into Nazis. (Cambridge, MA: Harvard University Press, 1997).

Fromm, Erich. *The Working Class in Weimar Germany: A Psychological and Sociological Study.* (Oxford: Berg, 1984; original edition 1929).

Funke, Manfred. "Republik im Untergang: Die Zerstörung des Parlamentarismus als Vorbereitung der Diktatur." In Karl-Dietrich Bracher, Manfred Funke, and Hans Adolf Jacobsen, eds., *Die Weimarer Republik, 1918–1933: Politik, Wirtschaft, und Gesellschaft.* (Düsseldorf: Droste, 1987).

Gailus, Manfred, and Heinrich Volkmann, eds. *Der Kampf um das tägliche Brot, 1770–1990.* (Opladen: Westdeutscher Verlag, 1994).

Ganz, Cornelia. "Wohnen hinter Stuckfassaden." In Geschichtskreis Kreuzberg, ed. *Nostitzritze. Ein Straße in Kreuzberg.* (Berlin: Gericke, 1992).

Gassert, Philipp. *Amerika im Dritten Reich. Ideologie, Propaganda und Volksmeinung, 1933–1945.* (Stuttgart: Franz Steiner, 1997).

Gay, Peter. *Weimar Culture. The Outsider as Insider.* (New York: Harper & Row, 1968).

Geist, Johann Friedrich, and Klaus Kürvers. *Das Berliner Mietshaus, Volume 2, 1862–1945.* (Munich: Prestel, 1980).

Gellately, Robert. *The Gestapo and German Society: Enforcing Racial Policy, 1933–1945.* (New York: Oxford University Press, 1990).

  Backing Hitler: Consent and Coercion in Nazi Germany. (New York: Oxford University Press, 2001).

Gill, Anton. *A Dance Between Flames: Berlin Between the Wars.* (London: J. Murray, 1993).

Glaeser, Ernst. *Class of 1902,* Willa and Edwin Muir, trans. (New York: Viking, 1929; original German edition, 1928).

Glass, Derek, Dietmar Rösber, and John J. White, eds., *Berlin: Literary Images of a City.* (Berlin: Schmidt, 1989).

Goebbels, Joseph. *Kampf um Berlin.* (Munich: Zentralverlag der NSDAP, 1939).

Göppinger, Horst. *Juristen jüdischer Abstammung im "Dritten Reich": Entrechtung und Verfolgung.* (Munich: Beck, 1990).

Gordon, Linda. *Heroes of Their Own Lives: The Politics of Family Violence, Boston, 1880–1960.* (Urbana: University of Illinois, 2002).

Gotschlich, Helga. *Zwischen Kampf und Kapitulation.* (E. Berlin: Dietz, 1987).

Gottwaldt, Alfred. *Berliner Fernbahnhöfe: Erinnerungen an ihre Große Zeit.* (Düsseldorf: Alba, 1983).

Gräser, Marcus. *Das blockierte Wohlfahrtsstaat: Unterschichtjugend und Jugendfürsorge in der Weimarer Republik.* (Göttingen: Vandenhoeck & Ruprecht, 1995).

Grimm, Jacob, and Wilhelm Grimm. *Deutsches Wörterbuch.* (Leipzig: S. Hirzel, 1873).

Grossmann, Atina. "*Girlkultur* or Thoroughly Rationalized Female: A New Woman in Weimar Germany?" In Judith Friedlander et al., eds. *Women in Culture and Politics.* (Bloomington: Indiana University Press, 1986).

  Reforming Sex: The German Movement for Birth Control and Abortion Reform, 1920–1950. (New York: Oxford University Press, 1995).

Guckenheimer, Eduard. *Der Begriff der ehrlosen Gesinnung im Strafrecht.* (Hamburg: W. Gente, 1921).

Guérin, Daniel. *The Brown Plague: Travels in Late Weimar and Early Nazi Germany,* Robert Schwartzwald, trans. (Durham, NC: Duke University Press, 1994, from the original 1933 Paris edition, *La peste brune a passé par là...*).

Guttsman, W. L. *The German Social Democratic Party, 1875–1933.* (London: Allen and Unwin, 1981).

Habedank, Heinz. *Geschichte der revolutionären Berliner Arbeiterbewegung, II, 1917–1945.* (E. Berlin: Dietz, 1987).

Haben, Michael. "'Die Waren so unter sich': Über Kneipen, Vereine und Politik in Berlin Kreuzberg." In Karl-Heinz Fiebig, Dieter Hoffmann-Axthelm, and Eberhard Knödler-Bunte, eds. *Kreuzberger Mischung: Die innerstädtische Verflechtung von Architektur, Kultur und Gewerbe.* (Berlin: Äesthetik und Kommunikation, 1984).

Haffner, Ernst. *Jugend auf der Landstraße.* (Berlin: Bruno Cassirer, 1932).

Halle, Felix. *Anklage gegen Justiz und Polizei.* (Berlin: Mopr Verlag, 1926).

  Wie verteidigt sich der Proletarier. (third edition, Berlin: Mopr, 1929).

Hagemann, Karen. *Frauenalltag und Männerpolitik: Alltagsleben und gesellschaftliches Handeln von Arbeiterfrauen in der Weimarer Republik.* (Bonn: Dietz, 1990).

Hamilton, Richard. *Who Voted for Hitler?* (Princeton, NJ: Princeton University Press, 1982).

Hannover, Heinrich, and Elisabeth Hannover-Drück. *Politische Justiz, 1918–1933.* (Frankfurt a. M.: Fischer, 1966).

Harlander, Tilman, Katrin Hater, and Franz Meiers, eds. *Siedeln in der Not. Umbruch von Wohnungspolitik und Siedlungsbau am Ende der Weimarer Republik.* (Hamburg: Christians, 1988).

Harsch, Donna. *German Social Democracy and the Rise of Nazism.* (Chapel Hill: University of North Carolina Press, 1993).

Häring, Dieter. *Zur Geschichte und Wirkung staatlicher Interventionen im Wohnungssektor.* (Hamburg: Hammonia, 1974).

Harvey, Elizabeth. *Youth and the Welfare State in Weimar Germany.* (Oxford: Clarendon Press, 1993).

Hauptamt für Statistik, ed. *Berlin in Zahlen.* (Berlin: Berlin Kulturbuchverlag, 1947).

Hauschild, Peer. "Bahnhöfe in Berlin." In Wolfgang Gottschalk, ed. *Bahnhöfe in Berlin: Photografen von Max Missmann.* (Berlin: Argon, 1991).

Hausen, Karin. "The Nation's Obligations to the Heroes' Widows of World War One." In Margaret R. Higgonet, ed., *Behind the Lines. Gender and the Two World Wars.* (New Haven, CT: Yale University Press, 1987).

Hausen, Karin, and Heide Wunder, eds. *Frauengeschichte – Geschlechtergeschichte.* (Frankfurt a. M.: Campus, 1992).

Heffen, Annegret. *Der Reichskunstwart, Kunstpolitik in den Jahren 1920–1933: zu den Bemühungen um eine offizielle Reichskunstpolitik in der Weimarer Republik.* (Essen: Die Blaue Eule, 1986).

Hegemann, Werner. *Das Steinerne Berlin. Geschichte der grössten Mietskasernenstadt der Welt.* (Berlin: Gustav Kiepenheuer, 1930).

Heilbronner, Oded. *Catholicism, Political Culture, and the Countryside: A Social History of the Nazi Party in Southern Germany.* (Ann Arbor: University of Michigan Press, 1998).

Hermand, Jost, and Frank Trommler. *Die Kultur der Weimarer Republik.* (Munich: Nymphenburger Verlagshandlung, 1978).

Hermanns, Manfred. *Jugendarbeitslosigkeit seit der Weimarer Republik.* (Opladen: Leske & Budrich, 1990).

Higgonet, Margaret R., ed. *Behind the Lines. Gender and the Two World Wars.* (New Haven, CT: Yale University Press, 1987).

Hipp, Hermann, ed. *Wohnstadt Hamburg. Mietshäuser der zwanziger Jahre zwischen Inflation und Weltwirtschaftskrise.* (Hamburg: Christians, 1982).

Hochstadt, Steve. *Mobility and Modernity: Migration in Germany, 1820–1989.* (Ann Arbor: University of Michigan Press, 1999).

Hofmann, Wolfgang, and Gerd Kuhn, eds. *Wohnungspolitik und Städtebau, 1900–1930.* (Berlin: Technische Universität, 1993).

Homburg, Heidrun. *Rationalisierung und Industriearbeit. Arbeitsmarkt–Management–Arbeiterschaft im Siemens-Konzern Berlin 1900–1939.* (Berlin: Haude and Spener, 1991).

Hong, Young-Sun. *Welfare, Modernity, and the Weimar State, 1919–1933.* (Princeton, NJ: Princeton University Press, 1998).

Hüber-Koller, Maria. *Gewerkschaften und Arbeitslose: Erfahrungen der Massenerwerbslosigkeit und Aspekte freigewerkschaftlicher Arbeitslosenpolitik in der Endphase der Weimarer Republik*, 2 vols. (Pfaffenweiler: Centaurus, 1992).

Hunt, Richard. *German Social Democracy, 1918–1933.* (New Haven, CT: Yale University Press, 1964).

Huyssen, Andreas. *After the Great Divide. Modernism, Mass Culture and Postmodernism.* (Bloomington: Indiana University Press, 1986).

Jahoda, Marie, Paul F. Lazarsfeld, and Hans Zeisel. *Die Arbeitslosen von Marienthal.* (Leipzig: S. Hirzel, 1933).

    Marienthal. The Sociography of an Unemployed Community. Translation by the authors with John Reginall and Thomas Elsaesset. (Chicago: Aldine, 1971).

James, Harold. *The Great Slump*. (Oxford: Clarendon Press, 1986).

Jankowski, Martin Sanchez. *Islands in the Street: Gangs and American Urban Society*. (Berkeley: University of California Press, 1991).

Jarausch, Konrad H., and Larry Eugene Jones, eds. *In Search of a Liberal Germany, Studies in the History of German Liberalism from 1789 to the Present*. (Oxford: Berg, 1990).

Jasper, Gotthard. *Der Schutz der Republik: Studien zur staatlichen Sicherung der Demokratie in der Weimarer Republik, 1922–1930*. (Tübingen: J. C. B. Mohr, 1963).

"Justiz und Politik in der Weimarer Republik." In *Vierteljahrshefte für Zeitgeschichte*. (Vol. 30, No. 2, 1982), pp. 167–205.

Jellonnek, Burkhard. *Homosexuelle unter dem Hakenkreuz: Die Verfolgung von Homosexuellen im Dritten Reich*. (Padeborn: F. Schöningh, 1990).

Jones, Larry Eugene. "German Liberalism and the Alienation of the Younger Generation in the Weimar Republic." In Konrad H. Jarausch and Larry Eugene Jones, eds. *In Search of a Liberal Germany: Studies in the History of German Liberalism from 1789 to the Present*. (Oxford: Berg, 1990).

Jones, Larry Eugene, and James Retallack. *Elections, Mass Politics, and Social Change in Modern Germany*. (New York: Cambridge University Press, 1992).

Kaak, Heinrich. *Geschichte der Berliner Verwaltungsbezirke Band 2: Kreuzberg*. (Berlin: Colloquium Verlag, 1988).

Kaelble, Hartmut. "Soziale Mobilität in Deutschland, 1900–1960." In Hartmut Kaelble, ed. *Probleme der Modernisierung*. (Opladen: Westdeutscher Verlag, 1978).

Kaes, Anton, Wolfgang Jacobsen, and Hans Helmut Prinzler. *Geschichte des deutschen Films*. (Stuttgart: Metzler, 1993).

Kähler, Gert, ed. *Geschichte des Wohnens. Vol. 4: 1918–1945: Reform, Reaktion, Zerstörung*. (Stuttgart: Deutsche Verlagsanstalt, 1996).

Kähler, Hermann. *Berlin – Asphalt und Licht*. (W. Berlin: das europäische Buch, 1986).

Kästner, Erich. "Besuch vom Lande." In *Ein Mann gibt Auskunft*. (Zurich: Atrium Verlag, 1930; second edition, Munich: DTV, 1988).

Fabian: Die Geschichte eines Moralisten (Zurich: Atrium, 1931).

Fabian. The Story of a Moralist. Cyrus Brooks, trans. (Evanston, IL: Northwestern University Press, 1993).

Kaplan, Michael. "New York City Tavern Violence and the Creation of a Working-Class Male Identity." In *Journal of the Early Republic*. (Vol. 15, Winter 1995), pp. 591–619.

Kater, Michael. *The Nazi Party. A Social Profile of Members and Leaders, 1919–1945*. (Oxford: Basil Blackwell, 1983).

"Generationskonflikt als Entwicklungsfaktor in der NS-Bewegung vor 1933." In *Geschichte und Gesellschaft*. (Vol. 11, No. 2, 1985), pp. 217–43.

"Review of *The Logic of Evil*." In *Central European History*. (Vol. 30, No. 2, 1997), pp. 339–40.

Katz, Jack. *Seductions of Crime: Moral and Sensual Attractions in Doing Evil*. (New York: Basic Books, 1988).

Kaufmann, Bernd, ed. *Der Nachrichtendienst der KPD, 1919–1937*. (Berlin: Dietz, 1993).

Kaufmann, Günter. *Das kommende Deutschland: Die Erziehung der Jugend im Reich Adolf Hitlers*. (Berlin: Junker und Dünnhaupt, 1940).

Kele, Max. *Nazis and Workers. National Socialist Appeals to German Labor, 1919–33*. (Chapel Hill: University of North Carolina Press, 1972).

Kerbs, Diethart, and Henrick Stahr, eds. *Berlin 1932. Das letzte Jahr der Weimarer Republik*. (Berlin: Hentrich, 1992).

Kershaw, Ian. *The 'Hitler Myth', Image and Reality in the Third Reich*. (Oxford: Oxford University Press, 1987).

ed. *Weimar: Why Did German Democracy Fail?* (New York: St. Martin's Press, 1990).

Keun, Irmgard. *Gilgi – eine von uns*. (Düsseldorf: Claassen, 1979; original edition, 1931).

Das kunstseidene Mädchen. (Munich: dtv, 1989; original edition, 1932).

Klage, Rita. "Proletarische Fluchtburgen oder letzte Widerstandsorte? Zeltstädte und Laubenkolonien in Berlin." In Berliner Geschichtswerkstatt, ed., *Projekt: Spurensicherung. Alltag und Widerstand im Berlin der 30er Jahre.* (Berlin: Elefanten, 1983).

Knickerbocker, H. R. *The German Crisis.* (New York: Farrar & Rinehart, 1932a). *Deutschland so oder so?* (Berlin: Rowohlt, 1932b).

Kniesche, Thomas, and Stephen Brockmann, eds. *Dancing on the Volcano: Essays on the Culture of the Weimar Republic.* (Columbia, SC: Camden House, 1994).

Kolb, Eberhard. *The Weimar Republic.* (London: Unwin Hyman, 1988). *Umbrüche deutscher Geschichte.* Dieter Langewiesche and Klaus Schönhoven, eds. (Munich: Oldenbourg, 1993).

König, Gerhard. *Berlin – Kreuzberg und seine Nostizstraße.* (Berlin: Druckerei der pbw, no date).

Koonz, Claudia. *Mothers in the Fatherland: Women, the Family and Nazi Politics.* (New York: St. Martin's Press, 1987).

Korff, Gottfried. "Rote Fahnen und geballte Faust. Zur Symbolik der Arbeiterbewegung in der Weimarer Republik." In Dietmar Petzina, ed. *Fahnen, Fäuste, Körper. Symbolik und Kultur der Arbeiterbewegung.* (Essen: Klartext, 1986).

Koshar, Rudy. *Social Life, Local Politics and Nazism: Marburg, 1880–1935.* (Chapel Hill: University of North Carolina Press, 1986).

Krabbe, Wolfgang, ed. *Politische Jugend in der Weimarer Republik.* (Bochum: Universitätsverlag, 1993).

Kracauer, Siegfried. *From Caligari to Hitler: A Psychological History of German Film.* (Princeton, NJ: Princeton University Press, 1947).

Krach, Tillmann. *Jüdische Rechtsanwälte in Preussen: Über die Bedeutung der freien Advokatur und ihre Zerstörung durch den Nationalsozialismus.* (Munich: Beck, 1991).

Kratzenberg, Volker. *Arbeiter auf dem Weg zu Hitler? Die Nationalsozialistische Betriebszellen-Organisation. Ihre Entstehung, ihre Programmatik, ihr Scheitern, 1927–1934.* (Frankfurt a. M.: Peter Lang, 1989).

Kritische Justiz, ed. *Streitbare Juristen.* (Baden-Baden: Namos, 1988).

Krohn, Manfred. *Die deutsche Justiz im Urteil der Nationalsozialisten, 1920–1933.* (Frankfurt a. M.: Peter Lang, 1991).

Krolzig, Günter. *Der Jugendliche in der Großstadtfamilie.* (Berlin: F. A. Herbig, 1930).

Künkel, Fritz. *Krisenbriefe. Die Beziehung zwischen Wirtschaftskrise und Charakterkrise.* (Schwerin: Bahn, 1933).

Kurz, Thomas. *Blutmai.* (Berlin: Dietz, 1988).

Lacey, Kate. *Feminine Frequencies: Gender, German Radio and the Public Sphere, 1923–1945.* (Ann Arbor: University of Michigan Press, 1998).

Ladd, Brian. *Urban Planning and Civic Order in Germany, 1860–1914.* (Cambridge, MA: Harvard University Press, 1990). *Ghosts of Berlin. Confronting German History in the Urban Landscape.* (Chicago: University of Chicago Press, 1997).

Lambertz, Jan, and Pat Ayers. "Eheliche Beziehungen, Geld und Gewalt in Liverpool, 1919–1939." In Jutta Dahlhoff, Uschi Frey, and Ingrid Schöll, eds. *Frauenmacht in der Geschichte.* (Düsseldorf: Schwann, 1986).

Lamm, Albert. *Betrogene Jugend: aus einem Erwerbslosenheim.* (Berlin: Bruno Cassirer, 1932).

Lanwer, Agnes. "Das Berliner Zeitungsviertel." In Helmut Engel, Stefi Jersch-Wenzel, and Wilhelm Treve, eds. *Geschichtslandschaft Berlin: Orte und Ereignisse. Band 5: Kreuzberg.* (Berlin: Nicolai, 1994). "Marheineke-Markthalle." In Helmut Engel, Stefi Jersch-Wenzel, and Wilhelm Treue, eds. *Geschichtslandschaft Berlin: Orte und Ereignisse. Band 5: Kreuzberg.* (Berlin: Nicolai, 1994).

Ledford, Kenneth F. "Conflict within the Legal Profession: Simultaneous Admission and the German Bar, 1903–1927." In Geoffrey Cocks and Konrad H. Jarausch, eds. *German Professions, 1800–1950*. (Oxford: Oxford University Press, 1990).

From General Estate to a Special Interest. German Lawyers, 1878–1933. (Cambridge: Cambridge University Press, 1996).

Leed, Eric. *No Man's Land*. (New York: Oxford University Press, 1979).

Lees, Andrew. *Cities Perceived*. (New York: Columbia University Press, 1985).

"Berlin and Modern Urbanity in German Discourse, 1845–1945." In *Journal of Urban History*. (Vol. 17, No. 2, 1991), pp. 153–80.

Lehnert, Detlef, and Klaus Megerle, eds. *Politische Identität und nationale Gedenktage. Zur politischen Kultur der Weimarer Republik*. (Opladen: Westdeutscher Verlag, 1989).

"Problems of Identity and Consensus in a Fragmented Society: The Weimar Republic." In Dirk Berg-Schlosser and Ralf Rytlewski, eds. *Political Culture in Germany*. (New York: St. Martin's Press, 1993).

Lessing, Hellmut, and Manfred Liebel. *Wilde Cliquen. Szenen aus einer anderen Arbeiterjugendbewegung*. (Bensheim: Pädagogischer Buchverlag, 1981).

Leßmann, Peter. *Die Preussische Schutzpolizei in der Weimarer Republik: Streifendienst und Straßenkampf*. (Düsseldorf: Droste, 1989).

Leyden, Friedrich. *Groß-Berlin. Geographie der Weltstadt*. (Berlin: Gebr. Mann Verlag, 1933; reprinted 1995).

Liang, Hsi-Huey. *The Berlin Police Force in the Weimar Republic*. (Berkeley: University of California Press, 1970).

Lidtke, Vernon. *The Alternative Culture*. (Oxford: Oxford University Press, 1985).

Lindenberger, Thomas. *Straßenpolitik. Zur Sozialgeschichte der öffentlichen Ordnung in Berlin 1900–1914*. (Bonn: Dietz, 1995).

Lindenberger, Thomas, and Alf Lüdtke, eds. *Physische Gewalt: Studien zur Geschichte der Neuzeit*. (Frankfurt a. M.: Suhrkamp, 1995).

Loewenberg, Peter. "The Psychohistorical Origins of the Nazi Youth Cohort." In *The American Historical Review*. (Vol. 76, No. 5, 1971), pp. 1457–502.

Longerich, Peter. *Die braune Bataillone. Geschichte der SA*. (Munich: Beck, 1989).

Lüdtke, Alf. "Cash, Coffee-Breaks, Horseplay: *Eigensinn* and Politics among Factory Workers in Germany circa 1900." In Michael Hanagan and Charles Stephenson, eds. *Confrontation, Class Consciousness and the Labor Process. Studies in Proletarian Class Formation*. (New York: Westport Press, 1986).

"Hunger in der Großen Depression: Hungererfahrung und Hungerpolitik am Ende der Weimarer Republik." In *Archiv für Sozialgeschichte*. (Vol. 27, 1987), pp. 145–76.

ed. *"Mein Arbeitstag – Mein Wochenende." Arbeiterinnen berichten von ihrem Alltag 1928*. (Hamburg: Ergebnisse Verlag, 1991).

ed. *Sicherheit und Wohlfahrt. Polizei, Gesellschaft und Herrschaft im 19. und 20. Jahrhundert*. (Frankfurt a. M.: Suhrkamp, 1992).

Eigen-Sinn. Fabrikalltag, Arbeitererfahrungen und Politik vom Kaiserreich bis in den Faschismus. (Hamburg: Ergebnisse Verlag, 1993).

ed. *The History of Everyday Life: Reconstructing Historical Experiences and Ways of Life*. William Templer, trans. (Princeton, NJ: Princeton University Press, 1995).

Lyttelton, Adrian. *The Seizure of Power. Fascism in Italy, 1919–1929*. (second edition, Princeton, NJ: Princeton University Press, 1987).

Mai, Gunther. "Die NSBO. Zum Verhältnis von Arbeiterschaft und Nationalsozialismus." In *Vierteljahrshefte für Zeitgeschichte*. (Vol. 31, No. 4, 1983), pp. 573–613.

Mallmann, Klaus-Michael. "Milieu, Radikalismus und lokale Gesellschaft." In *Geschichte und Gesellschaft*. (Vol. 21, No. 1, 1995), pp. 5–31.

Kommunisten in der Weimarer Republik: Sozialgeschichte einer revolutionären Bewegung. (Darmstadt: Wissenschaftliche Buchgesellschaft, 1996).

Mannheim, Karl. "Das Problem der Generationen." In *Kölner Vierteljahrshefte für Soziologie*. (Vol. 7, 1928), pp. 157–85 and 309–30.

"The Problem of Generations." In *Essays on the Sociology of Knowledge*. (New York: Oxford University Press, 1952).

Mason, Tim. "Women in Germany, 1925–1940: Family, Welfare and Work." In Jane Caplan, ed. *Fascism and the Working Class*. (Cambridge: Cambridge University Press, 1995).

McElligott, Anthony. "'. . . und so kam es zu einer schweren Schlägerei': Strassenschlachten in Altona und Hamburg am Ende der Weimarer Republik." In Maike Bruhns, Claudia Preuschoft, and Werner Skrentny, eds. "*Hier war doch alles nicht so schlimm*." (Hamburg: VSA-Verlag, 1984).

Contested City: Municipal Politics and the Rise of Nazism in Altona. (Ann Arbor: University of Michigan Press, 1998).

The German Urban Experience, 1900–1945. (London: Routledge, 2001).

Merkl, Peter. *The Making of a Stormtrooper.* (Princeton, NJ: Princeton University Press, 1980).

Miller Lane, Barbara. *Architecture and Politics in Germany, 1918–1945.* (Cambridge, MA: Harvard University Press, 1968, 1985).

Möbius, Hanno. "Der Rote Eine-Mark-Roman." In *Archiv für Sozialgeschichte*. (Vol. 14, 1974), pp. 157–71.

Mommsen, Hans. "Generationskonflikt und Jugendrevolte in der Weimarer Republik." In Thomas Koebner, Rolf-Peter Janz, and Frank Trommler, eds. "*Mit uns zieht die neue Zeit*": *Der Mythos Jugend.* (Frankfurt a. M.: Suhrkamp, 1985).

The Rise and Fall of Weimar Democracy. (Chapel Hill: University of North Carolina Press, 1996).

Mosse, George L., ed. *Police Forces in History.* (London: Sage, 1975).

Fallen Soldiers: Reshaping the Memory of the World Wars. (New York: Oxford University Press, 1990).

Muer, H. "Kino und Jugend." In *Jugendführung*. (No. 15, 1928).

Die neue Reichsverfassung. (Berlin: C. Heymann, 1919).

Neukrantz, Klaus. *Barrikaden am Wedding.* (Berlin: Oberbaumverlag, 1931).

Barricades in Wedding. (Chicago: Banner Press, 1933).

Newman, Oscar. *Defensible Space: Crime Prevention through Urban Design.* (New York: Macmillan, 1973).

Niemeyer, Annemarie. *Zur Struktur der Familie. Statistischen Materialen.* (Berlin: F. A. Herbig, 1931).

Niethammer, Lutz, ed. "*Die Jahre weiss man nicht, wo man die heute hinsetzen soll*": *Faschismuserfahrungen im Ruhrgebiet.* (Berlin: Dietz, 1983).

Nitsche, Rainer, ed. *Häuserkämpfe, 1872, 1920, 1945, 1982.* (Berlin: Transit, 1981).

Nolan, Mary. *Visions of Modernity: American Business and the Modernization of Germany.* (New York: Oxford University Press, 1994).

Noth, Ernst Erich. *Die Mietskaserne.* (Frankfurt: Societätsverlag, 1931).

Orthmann, Rosemary. *Out of Necessity. Women Working in Berlin at the Height of Industrialization, 1874–1913.* (New York: Garland Publishing, 1991).

Ostler, Fritz. *Die Deutschen Rechtsanwälte, 1871–1971.* (Essen: Juristischer Verlag W. Ellinghaus, 1982).

Paul, Gerhard. *Aufstand der Bilder: Die NS-Propaganda vor 1933.* (Bonn: Dietz, 1990).

"Krieg der Symbole. Formen und Inhalte des symbolpublizistischen Bürgerkriegs 1932." In Diethart Kerbs and Henrich Stahr, eds. *Berlin 1932. Das letzte Jahr der Weimarer Republik.* (Berlin: Hentrich, 1992).

Petro, Patrice. *Joyless Streets. Women and Melodramatic Representation in Weimar Germany.* (Princeton, NJ: Princeton University Press, 1989).

Petzina, Dietmar, ed. *Fahnen, Fäuste, Körper. Symbolik und Kultur der Arbeiterbewegung.* (Essen: Klartext, 1986).

Peukert, Detlev. *Die KPD im Widerstand: Verfolgung und Untergrundarbeit an Rhein und Ruhr 1933 bis 1945.* (Wuppertal: Hammer, 1980).

"Die 'Wilden Cliquen' in den zwanziger Jahren." In Wilfried Breyvogel, ed. *Autonomie und Widerstand. Zur Theorie und Geschichte des Jugendprotestes.* (Essen: Rigodon, 1983).

"Die Erwerbslosigkeit junger Arbeiter in der Weltwirtschaftskrise in Deutschland 1929–1933." In *Vierteljahrschrift für Sozial- und Wirtschaftsgeschichte.* (Vol. 72, No. 3, 1985), pp. 305–28.

Grenzen der Sozialdisziplinierung: Aufstieg und Krise der deutschen Jugendfürsorge 1878–1932. (Cologne: Bund-Verlag, 1986).

Inside Nazi Germany. Conformity, Opposition, Racism in Everyday Life. (New Haven, CT: Yale University Press, 1987a).

Jugend zwischen Krieg und Krise. (Cologne: Bund-Verlag, 1987b).

The Weimar Republic: The Crisis of Classical Modernity. (New York: Hill and Wang, 1989).

Posse, Ernst H. *Die Politischen Kämpferbünde Deutschlands.* (Berlin: Junker und Dünnhaupt, 1930).

Rabinbach, Anson. *The Human Motor. Energy, Fatigue, and the Origins of Modernity.* (Berkeley: University of California Press, 1992).

Raynsford, Anthony. "Swarm of the Metropolis: Passenger Circulation at Grand Central Terminal and the Ideology of the Crowd Aesthetic." In *Journal of Architectural Education.* (Vol. 50, No. 1, 1996), pp. 2–14.

Redslob, Edwin. *Bekenntnis zu Berlin. Reden und Aufsätze.* (Berlin: Stapp, 1964).

Reese, Dagmar, ed. *Rationale Beziehungen? Geschlechterverhältnisse im Rationalisierungsprozess.* (Frankfurt a. M.: Suhrkamp, 1993).

Reibe, Axel. "Mit den Sturmabteilungen der NSDAP fängt es an." In Kunstamt Kreuzberg, ed., *Kreuzberg 1933. Ein Bezirk erinnert sich.* (Berlin: Dürchschlag, 1983).

"Zwischen Arbeitsamt und Volksküche." In Kunstamt Kreuzberg, ed. *Kreuzberg 1933. Ein Bezirk erinnert sich.* (Berlin: Dürchschlag, 1983).

Reichardt, Sven. "Gesellschaften im Übergang. Überlegungen zum Vergleich faschistischer Kampfbünde in Italien und Deutschland." In Armin Triebel, ed. *Die Pragmatik des Gesellschaftsvergleichs.* (Leizpig: Leipziger Universitätsverlag, 1997).

Reiche, Erich. *The Development of the SA in Nürnberg 1922–1934.* (Cambridge: Cambridge University Press, 1986).

Reichszentrale für Heimatdienst, ed. *Zum Verfassungstag: Eine Materialsammlung.* (Berlin: Reichszentrale für Heimatdienst, 1928).

Richie, Alexandra. *Faust's Metropolis: A History of Berlin.* (New York: Carroll and Graf, 1998).

Rohe, Karl. *Das Reichsbanner Schwarz-Rot-Gold.* (Düsseldorf: Droste, 1966).

"Party Cultures and Regional Traditions: The SPD in the Ruhr." In Eva Kolinsky, ed. *The Federal Republic of Germany. The End of an Era.* (New York: Berg, 1991).

Röhl, Klaus Rainer. *Nähe zum Gegner. Kommunisten und Nationalsozialisten im Berliner BVG-Streik von 1932.* (Frankfurt: Campus Verlag, 1992).

Roseman, Mark, ed. *Generations in Conflict. Youth Revolt and Generation Formation in Germany, 1770–1968.* (Cambridge: Cambridge University Press, 1995).

Rosenbaum, Heidi. *Proletarische Familien. Arbeiterfamilie und Arbeiterväter im frühen 20. Jahrhundert zwischen traditioneller, sozialdemokratischer und kleinbürgerlicher Orientierung.* (Frankfurt a. M.: Suhrkamp, 1992).

Rosenhaft, Eve. "Working-class Life and Working-class Politics: Communists, Nazis, and the State in the Battle for the Streets, Berlin 1928–1933." In Richard Bessel and E. J. Feuchtwanger, eds. *Social Change and Political Development in the Weimar Republic.* (London: Croom Helm, 1981).

Beating the Fascists? The German Communists and Political Violence, 1929–1933. (Cambridge: Cambridge University Press, 1983).

"Links gleich rechts? Militante Straßengewalt um 1930." In Thomas Lindenberger and Alf Lüdtke, eds. *Physische Gewalt.* (Frankfurt a. M.: Suhrkamp, 1995).

Rück, Fritz. *Der Wedding in Wort und Bild.* (Berlin: E. Laubsche, 1931).

Rühle-Gerstel, Alice. *Das Frauenproblem der Gegenwart.* (Leipzig: S. Hirzel, 1932).

Sachse, Carola. *Industrial Housewives: Women's Social Work in the Factories of Nazi Germany.* (New York: The Haworth Press, 1987).

Saunders, Thomas J. *Hollywood in Berlin: American Cinema and Weimar Germany.* (Berkeley: University of California Press, 1994).

Scarpa, Ludovica. *Martin Wagner und Berlin. Architektur und Städtebau in der Weimarer Republik.* (Braunschweig: F. Viewig & Sohn, 1986).

Schellack, Fritz. *Nationalfeiertage in Deutschland von 1871–1945.* (Frankfurt a. M.: Peter Lang, 1990).

Scheringer, Richard. *Erwachendes Volk. Briefe an Leutnant a. D. Scheringer.* (Berlin: Agis Verlag, 1931).

Schilde, Fritz, and Lothar Uebel. "Fleisch vom Ross." In Geschichtskreis Kreuzberg, ed. *Nostitzritze. Ein Straße in Kreuzberg.* (Berlin: Gericke, 1992).

Schiller, Joachim. *Schulerselbstmorde in Preussen: Spiegelungen des Schulsystems.* (Frankfurt a. M.: Peter Lang, 1992).

Schirmann, Leon. *Blutmai Berlin 1929.* (Berlin: Dietz, 1991).

Schirmer, Dietmar. *Mythos – Heilshoffnung – Modernität. Politisch-kulturelle Deutungscodes in der Weimarer Republik.* (Opladen: Westdeutscher Verlag, 1992).

Schivelbusch, Wolfgang. *The Railway Journey.* (New York: Berg, 1986).

Schönstedt, Walther. *Kämpfende Jugend.* (Berlin: Oberbaumverlag, 1972; original edition, Berlin: Internationalen-Arbeiter Verlag, 1932).

Schumann, Dirk. *Politische Gewalt in der Weimarer Republik 1918–1933: Kampf um die Straße und Furcht vor dem Bürgerkrieg.* (Essen: Klartext, 2001).

Schuster, Kurt. *Der Rote Frontkämpferbund, 1924–1929.* (Düsseldorf: Droste, 1975).

Schütz, Erhard. *Romane der Weimarer Republik.* (Munich: W. Fink, 1986).

Schwan, Bruno. *Die Wohnungsverhältnisse in der Berliner Altstadt.* (Berlin: Deutscher Verein für Wohnungsreform, 1932).

ed., *Städtebau und Wohnungswesen der Welt – Town Planning and Housing throughout the World – L'Urbanisme et L'Habitation dans tous les Pays.* (Berlin: Verlag Ernst Wasmuth, 1935).

Severing, Carl. *Mein Lebensweg. Band II.* (Cologne: Greven Verlag, 1950).

Sling (pseud. Paul Schlesinger). *Richter und Gerichtete.* (Berlin: Ullstein, 1929).

Sneeringer, Julia. *Winning Women's Votes: Propaganda and Politics in Weimar Germany.* (Chapel Hill: University of North Carolina Press, 2002).

Snowden, Frank M. *The Fascist Revolution in Tuscany, 1919–1922.* (Cambridge: Cambridge University Press, 1989).

Soder, Martin. *Hausarbeit und Stammtischsozialismus. Arbeiterfamilie und Alltag im Deutschen Kaiserreich.* (Giessen: Focus Verlag, 1980).

Solomon, Alice, and Marie Baum. *Das Familienleben in der Gegenwart.* (Berlin: F. A. Herbig, 1930).

Splanemann, Andreas. "Berliner Wahl- und Sozialstatistik, 1919–1933." In Otto Büsch and Wolfgang Haues, eds. *Berlin als Hauptstadt der Weimarer Republik, 1919–1933.* (Berlin: de Gruyter, 1987).

"Bewährung und Begrenzung der Berliner Demokratie. Die erste Magistratsbildung der neuen Stadtgemeinde Berlin 1920." In Otto Büsch, ed. *Beiträge zur Geschichte der Berliner Demokratie, 1919–1933/1945–1985.* (Berlin: Colloquium Verlag, 1988).

Spode, Hasso. "Die Schultheiss-Brauerei auf dem Kreuzberg." In Helmut Engel, Stefi Jersch-Wenzel, and Wilhelm Treue, *Geschichtslandschaft Berlin. Orte und Ereignisse, Band 5: Kreuzberg.* (Berlin: Nicolai, 1994).

Stachura, Peter. *Nazi Youth in the Weimar Republic.* (Santa Barbara, CA: Clio, 1975).

ed. *Unemployment and the Great Depression in Weimar Germany*. (New York: St. Martin's Press, 1986).

The Weimar Republic and the Younger Proletariat. (New York: St. Martin's Press, 1989).

Staewen-Ordemann, Gertrud. *Menschen der Unordnung*. (Berlin: Furche Verlag, 1933).

Stahr, Henrik. "'Erst Essen – dann Miete!' Mieterkrawalle, Mieterstreiks und ihre bildliche Repräsentation." In Diethart Kerbs und Henrik Stahr, eds. *Berlin 1932. Das letzte Jahr der Weimarer Republik*. (Berlin: Hentrich, 1992).

Statistischen Amt der Stadt Berlin, ed. *Statistisches Jahrbuch der Stadt Berlin*. Jg. 1 (1924), Jg. 2 (1926)–Jg. 9 (1933).

Stephenson, Jill. *The Nazi Organisation of Women*. (London: Croom Helm, 1981).

Striefler, Christian. *Kampf um die Macht*. (Frankfurt a. M.: Propyläen, 1993).

Stier-Somlo, Fritz, Alexander Elster, Erich Volkmar, and Günther Küchenhoff, eds. *Handwörterbuch der Rechtswissenschaft*. Bände I–VI. (Berlin: de Gruyter, 1926).

Sturm 33 Hans Maikowski. Geschrieben von Kameraden des Toten. (Berlin: N.S.-Druck und Verlag, 1933).

Stürzbecher, Manfred. "Stadthygiene." In J. Boberg, T. Fichter, and E. Gillen, eds. *Exerzierfeld der Moderne*. (Munich: C. H. Beck, 1984).

Tammen, Werner, and Lothar Uebel. "Freizeit im Kiez." In Kunstamt Kreuzberg, ed. *Kreuzberg 1933. Ein Bezirk erinnert sich*. (Berlin: Dürschlag, 1983).

Tannenbaum, Edward T. *1900: The Generation before the Great War*. (New York: Anchor Press, 1976).

Taylor, Robert. *Berlin and its Culture*. (New Haven, CT: Yale University Press, 1997).

Theweleit, Klaus. *Male Fantasies, Vol 1: Women, Floods, Bodies, History*. (Cambridge: Polity Press, 1987).

Tilly, Charles, Louise Tilly, and Richard Tilly. *The Rebellious Century, 1830–1930*. (Cambridge, MA: Harvard University Press, 1975).

Tjaden, K. H. *Struktur und Funktion der 'KPD-Opposition' (KPO)*. (Meisenheim am Glan: A. Hain, 1964).

Totomianz, Vacan. *Konsumentenorganisationen. Theorie, Geschichte und Praxis der Konsumgenossenschaften*. (Berlin, 1929).

Turner, Henry A. *Hitler's Thirty Days to Power: January 1933*. (New York: Addison Wesley, 1996).

Uebel, Lothar. "Jugend auf der Straße." In Kunstamt Kreuzberg ed. *Kreuzberg 1933. Ein Bezirk erinnert sich*. (Berlin: Dürschlag, 1983).

"Lieber draußen als zu Hause." In Kunstamt Kreuzberg, ed. *Kreuzberg 1933. Ein Bezirk erinnert sich*. (Berlin: Dürschlag, 1983).

Viel Vergnügen. Die Geschichte der Vergnügungsstätten rund um den Kreuzberg und die Hasenheide. (Berlin: Nishen, 1985).

"Ein heisses Pflaster." In Geschichtskreis Kreuzberg, ed. *Nostitzritze. Ein Straße in Kreuzberg*. (Berlin: Gericke, 1992).

"Milch vom Hinterhof." In Geschichtkreis Kreuzberg, ed. *Nostitzritze. Ein Straße in Kreuzberg*. (Berlin: Gericke, 1992).

"Verkehrslokale und andere Budiken." In Geschichtskreis Kreuzberg, ed. *Nostitzritze. Ein Straße in Kreuzberg*. (Berlin: Gericke, 1992).

Usborne, Cornelia. *The Politics of the Body in Weimar Germany: Women's Reproductive Rights and Duties*. (Basingstoke: Macmillan, 1992; Ann Arbor: University of Michigan Press, 1992).

Vogelsang, Thilo. *Die Reichswehr und die Politik, 1918–1934*. (Hannover: Niedersächsischen Landeszentrale für Heimatdienst, 1959).

von Ankum, Katharina. "Gendered Urban Spaces in Irmgard Keun's *Das kunstseidene Mädchen*." In Katharina von Ankum, ed. *Women in the Metropolis*. (Berkeley: University of California Press, 1997).

von Kruedener, Jürgen. *Economic Crisis and the Political Collapse: The Weimar Republic, 1924–1933*. (New York: Berg, 1990).

von Repkow, Eike (pseud. Robert M. W. Kempner). *Justiz-Dämmerung. Auftakt zum Dritten Reich*. (Berlin: Volksfunk Verlag, 1932; second edition, 1963).

von Saldern, Adelheid. "Arbeiterkulturbewegung in Deutschland in der Zwischenkriegszeit." In Friedhelm Boll, ed. *Arbeiterkulturen zwischen Alltag und Politik*. (Vienna: Europa-Verlag, 1986).

Voß, Angelika, Ursula Büttner, and Hermann Weber. *Vom Hamburger Aufstand zur politischen Isolierung. Kommunistischen Politik 1923–33 in Hamburg und im Deutschen Reich*. (Hamburg: Landeszentrale für politische Bildung, 1983).

Wachsmann, Nikolaus. "Between Reform and Repression: Imprisonment in Weimar Germany." In *The Historical Journal*. (Vol. 45, No. 2, 2002), pp. 411–32.

Wagenführ, Rolf. "Die Industriewirtschaft: Entwicklungstendenzen der deutschen und internationalen Industrieproduktion 1860 bis 1932." In *Vierteljahreshefte zur Konjunkturforschung*. (Berlin: Sonderheft 31, 1933).

Wagner, Martin, ed. *Im Namen des Volkes! Rote Hilfe gegen Polizeiterror und Klassenjustiz*. (W. Berlin: Oberbaumverlag, 1976).

Weber, Hermann. *Die Wandlung des deutschen Kommunismus: Die Stalinisierung der KPD in der Weimarer Republik*, 2 vols. (Frankfurt a. M.: Europäische Verlagsanstalt, 1969).

Hauptfeind Sozialdemokratie: Strategie und Taktik der KPD 1929–1933. (Düsseldorf: Droste, 1981).

Weiland, Ruth. *Die Kinder der Arbeitslosen*. (Berlin: E. & C. Müller, 1933).

Weindling, Paul. *Health, Race and German Politics between National Unification and Nazism, 1870–1945*. (Cambridge: Cambridge University Press, 1989).

Weisbrod, Bernd. "Gewalt in der Politik. Zur politischen Kultur in Deutschland zwischen den beiden Weltkriegen." In *Geschichte in Wissenschaft und Unterricht*. (Vol. 43, No. 7, 1992), pp. 391–404.

"Die Krise der bürgerlichen Gesellschaft und die Machtergreifung von 1933." In Hans-Ulrich Wehler, ed. *Scheidewege der deutschen Geschichte*. (Munich: Beck, 1995).

"The Crisis of Bourgeois Society in Interwar Germany." In Richard Bessel, ed. *Fascist Italy and Nazi Germany. Comparisons and Contrasts*. (Cambridge: Cambridge University Press, 1996).

Weitz, Eric D. *Popular Communism: Political Strategies and Social Histories in the Formation of the German, French and Italian Communist Parties, 1919–1948*. (Ithaca, NY: Cornell University Press, 1992).

Creating German Communism, 1890–1990: From Popular Protests to Socialist State. (Princeton, NJ: Princeton University Press, 1996).

Wetzell, Richard F. *Inventing the Criminal: A History of German Criminology, 1880–1945*. (Durham: University of North Carolina Press, 2000).

Whalen, Robert. *Bitter Wounds: German Victims of the Great War, 1914–1939*. (Ithaca, NY: Cornell University Press, 1984).

Wiedenhoeft, Ronald. *Berlin's Housing Revolution. German Reform in the 1920s*. (Ann Arbor, University of Michigan Research Press, 1985).

Wilde, Alexander. "Republikfeindschaft in der Berlin Bevölkerung und der Wandel der kommunalen Selbstverwaltung um 1931." In Otto Büsch, ed. *Beiträge zur Geschichte der Berliner Demokratie 1919–1933/1945–85*. (Berlin: Colloquium Verlag, 1988).

Willett, John. *Art and Politics in the Weimar Period: The New Sobriety*. (New York: Pantheon, 1980).

Willmann, Heinz. *Geschichte der Arbeiter-Illustrierten Zeitung, 1921–1938*. (Berlin: Dietz, 1975).

Winkler, Heinrich August. *Der Schein der Normalität. Arbeiter und Arbeiterbewegung in der Weimarer Republik 1924 bis 1930*. (Berlin: Dietz, 1988).

Der Weg in die Katastrophe. Arbeiter und Arbeiterbewegung in der Weimarer Republik 1930 bis 1933. (Berlin: Dietz, 1987).

ed. *Die Deutsche Staatskrise 1930–1933.* (Munich: Oldenbourg, 1992).

Wise, Michael Z. *Capital Dilemma: Germany's Search for a New Architecture of Democracy.* (New York: Princeton Architectural Press, 1998).

Wohl, Robert. *The Generation of 1914.* (Cambridge, MA: Harvard University Press, 1979).

Woytinski, Emma. *Sozialdemokratie und Kommunalpolitik. Gemeindearbeit in Berlin.* (Berlin: E. Laubsche, 1929).

Wruck, Peter, ed. *Literarisches Leben in Berlin 1871–1933.* (Berlin: Akademie-Verlag, 1987).

Zollitsch, Wolfgang. *Arbeiter zwischen Weltwirtschaftskrise und Nationalsozialismus.* (Göttingen: Vandenhoeck & Ruprecht, 1990).

Index

Page references in italics indicate the presence of an illustration.

8-Uhr Abendblatt, 117

activism. *See* radicalism (political) and
    radical activism
alcohol
    alcoholism, 264
    drunkenness, 86, 181, 224, 277–278
    and political violence, 255, 269,
        277–278
Alexander, Eduard, 129, 269
Alexanderplatz, 36, 68, 122
Allgemeine Elektrizitäts-Gesellschaft
    (AEG), 55, 67, 93
Allgemeiner Deutscher
    Gewerkschaftsbund (ADGB),
    141
Angriff, Der, 59, 114, 144, 209, 249
Anhalter station, 54, 66
Antifaschistische Aktion (Antifa
    Aktion), 163
Antifaschistische Junge Garde (Antifa,
    Young Antifascist Guard), 163,
    228
anti-Semitism
    against Löwenstein, 66
    in propaganda, 167, 174
    against publishers, 58
    violent attacks, 63, 238
    See also Jews and Judaism
Anti-Socialist Laws (1878–1890), 91,
    97
apartment buildings. *See* tenements and
    communities
Applegate, Celia, 64

Arbeiter Illustrierte Zeitung (AIZ), 25,
    68, 116, 193
    on housing shortage, 2, 53
    on May 1929 violence, 127
    on the *Scheunenviertel*, 54
    on unemployment, 85
    on women, 93–94
Arndt Street, 30, 140
assemblies, rallies, and marches
    banning of (May 1929), 121, 134, 232
    decree banning (1931), 237–238,
        288–290
    for elections, 243–248
    at government buildings, 56, 62,
        155–156
    HJ marches, 35
    KPD instructions for, 237
    KPD sites for, 56
    at markets, 198–199
    NSDAP sites for, 56
    police intervention at, 233, *233*
    in Red Berlin, 56
    violence with, 233, 243–248,
        276–277
Auguste-Viktoria-Platz, 68

Bahn Street, 244
Balzer, Alfred, 280
Bannmeile, 62, 155–156, 288
Barbasch, Ludwig, 269
bars. *See* pubs
Beer Hall Putsch (Munich, 1923), 169,
    172
Behrenbeck, Sabine, 153

Belle-Alliance Street, 30
Bergmann Street, 40
Berlin
  building heights in, 47
  as "city of millions," 65
  districts of, *xvi*, 53, 64, 65
  East-West contrasts in, 56–57, 59, 62,
    78, 133, 294
  election results for, *143*
  issues of unity and structure in, 64,
    76–77
  legislation expanding (*Gross-Berlin-
    Gesetz*, 1920), 64–66, 76, 298
  Nazi disdain for, 166
  population density, 45, 46
  portrayal in literary works, 2–5
    See also specific authors
  pre-1918, 4
  in Weimar period, 6–7, 24–25, 64
  West End shopping district, 62–63
  as *Zeitungsstadt*, 58
  See also Red Berlin
Berlin, Sinfonie der Großstadt (film),
  69
Berliner Börsen-Zeitung, 58, 60–61, 63,
  209
Berliner Front, Die, 174, 175
Berliner Illustrierte Zeitung, 58
Berliner Lokal-Anzeiger, Der, 58, 178
Berliner Morgenpost, 84
Berliner Tageblatt (BT), 58, 59, 63
  on May 1929 violence, 130
  on Norkus murder, 119–120
Berliner Verkehrsgesellschaft (BVG,
    Berlin Transport Company), 61,
    68, 70, 209
Berliner Volkszeitung, 118
Berlin Sports Palace, 56
Berlin Stadium, 151
Bessel, Richard, 36
Beussel Street station, 67
Birkenfeld, Günther
  Dritter Hof Links, 3, 4, 104
BL (Bezirksleitung). *See under*
    Kommunistische Partei
    Deutschlands
blacklisting, 221–222

bodyguards, 245
Bohnsdorf, 281
Borchardt, Knut, 9, 287
Borchert, James, 35, 202, 230
Borsig factory, 55
Böß, Gustav, 48, 50, 77, 155
boycotts, 221
Bracher, Karl-Dietrich
  *Die Auflösung der Weimarer
    Republik*, 9
Bracht, Franz, 292
Brandler, Heinrich, 191
Braun, Otto, 124, 140, 293
Braune, Rudolf
  Die Geschichte einer Woche, 3
  Das Mädchen an der Orga Privat, 3,
    165–166
Britz, 49, 55
Broszat, Martin, 169
Brot, Arbeit und Freiheit (bread, work
    and freedom), 167
Brücker, Eva, 38, 39, 87
Brüning, Heinrich, 141, 143, 189, 190,
    289, 290
  economic policies, 9, 286–287
  and SA, 189, 292
BT. *See Berliner Tageblatt*
building cooperatives, 49
Bülowplatz, 54, 56, 157
Bund deutscher Mädel (BDM, League
    of German Girls), 172, 180, 194

Catholic Center Party, 141, 142, 159,
    167
Catholic Church, 13, 38–39, 106
Chakhotin, Sergei, 145
Charlottenburg, 38, 55, 65
  Siemensstadt, 50, 55
children
  during Depression, 104–106
  early maturation of, 106
  during First World War, 102, 104,
    263
  in foster care or institutions, 263
  illegitimate, 106
  Josephskinder, 104
  politicization of, *118*, 137, 206, 257

school strikes, 116–117, *118*, 257
in tenements, 43
as wage-earners, 105
war orphans, 104
in youth movements, 103–104
See also youth
cliques, 200–202, 243, 264
Cölln, 64
communism. *See* specific Communist
organizations (KPD, RFB, etc.)
Confino, Alon, 18, 148
Constitution Day. *See Verfassungstag*
Cöpenick, 53
courts and justice system
ages of juveniles and young adults,
262
appeals in, 277
assesment of political intent,
276–278, 284
bank and court authorities, 90
bias against political left, 279–280
decisions in, 276–284
decisions involving large groups,
276–277
defendants' statements, 236,
269–276
Gesinnung, 280–281, 284
Halle's instruction pamphlet for,
270
lawyers in, 269
political *vs.* personal crimes, 252
probation, 267, 268
Sondergerichte, 293
welfare reports on young offenders,
236, 261–269, 275, 284

dairies (in tenement courtyards), 31
defensible space, 230
demonstrations. *See* assemblies, rallies,
and marches
denunciation, 21, 214–231
archival records of, 217, 218, 222
blacklisting, 221–222
and breakdown of order, 216
fear and suspicion created by, 217,
221, 231
house searches, 226–227

for ideological reasons, 222–223
informants *(Achtgroschenjungen)*,
214–215
within KPD, 216, 217–218, 222–227,
297–298
of landlords, 219–220
for leniency from police, 215–216
neighborhood focus of, 214, 216,
297–298
and party discipline, 216, 230–231
payment for, 214, 230
to police, 214–216, 217
political impact of, 229–231
within political parties, 216
and pubs, 99
for social behavior, 223–224
Deutsche demokratische Partei (DDP,
German Democratic Party), 64, 66,
117, 279
Deutsches Lichtspiel-Syndikat AG, 148
Deutsche Tageszeitung, 59
Deutsche Volkspartei (DVP, German
People's Party), 65
Deutsche Zeitung, 62, 217
Deutschnationale Volkspartei (DNVP,
German National People's Party),
65, 66, 226
discipline (political), 185–187
in cliques, 201–202
and denunciation, 216, 230–231
faction discipline, 181
of KPD, 180–181, 185, 191–192
and local focus of members, 296–297
of NSDAP, 178–180, 193–194,
197
proletarian *vs.* bourgeois, 180
of RB, 156–157, 159
republican, 185
of RFB, 178, 180–185
of SA, 177–178
Distress and Struggle (women's
newspaper), 84
Döblin, Alfred
Berlin Alexanderplatz, 54
Doppelverdiener (double earners),
83–85
Drei Pfeile (three arrows), 145

Ebersstraße, 273
Ebert, Friedrich, 51
economic decrees, 287
economic issues, 194, 228, 252–253,
    282
Eden Hotel, 182
Eigensinn, 27, 28
Eiserne Front (EF, Iron Front),
    145–146, 190, 277, 296
Eksteins, Modris, 58
election returns, *142, 143*
    in 1928, 53, 55, 140, 297
    in 1930, 212
    in 1932, 29, 297
    for KPD, 29, 53, 55, 212, 297,
        299
    for NSDAP, 9, 29, 212, 297, 299
    for SPD, 29, 65–66, 140, 212, 297
elections
    for Berlin assembly (1920), 65–66
    election gimmicks, 177
    electoral fluctuation, 211, 297
    propaganda for, 137, 145–146,
        167–168, 177, 184–185, 193
    rallies and marches for, 243–248
Emergency decrees *(Notverordnungen)*,
    252, 280, 286–294
    economic, 287
    link with authoritarianism, 287,
        299
    number of, 287
    political, 288–294
    progression of, 293–294
    as response to radicalism, 286,
        293–294
    specific decrees
        1931 March, 237–238, 288–290,
            291
        1931 June, 109
        1931 July, 290, 291
        1931 Christmas, 291
        1931 December, 290
        1932 April, 291–292
        1932 Easter, 291
        1932 June, 292
        1932 August, 293
    See also Weimar Republic
Emmerich, Paul, 51

Erhardt, Justus
    Strassen ohne Ende, 42, 87
evictions, 52, 90, 204, 220, 253

factories
    industrial neighborhoods, 54, 55
    as Kiez focal points, 28
    KPD organizing in, 164–165, 181,
        218
    NSAD organizing in, 170–171
    rationalization of production, 27–28,
        49
    workers' hierarchies in, 27–28
    See also specific factories (Borsig,
        Siemens)
Fallada, Hans
    *Kleiner Man – Was Nun? (Little Man,
        What Now?)*, 2, 3, 35, 52, 113,
        202
Falter, Jürgen, 207, 211
Familienkneipen (family pubs), 32
families
    generational tensions, 112–113
    impact of First World War on, 104
    marriage prevented by
        unemployment, 110
    poverty of, 263–264
fear(s)
    created by denunciation, 217, 221,
        231, 299
    of radical youth, 115–116
film, 148
Fink, Georg
    Mich Hungert!, 4, 105
First World War
    front generation, 101–102, 294
    German defeat and Versailles Peace
        Treaty, 10, 137–138
    impact on women, children, and
        families, 4, 81, 102, 104, 263
    political violence associated with,
        135
    RB view of, 160
    veterans of, 81, 161, 169
Fischer, Conan, 207, 238
    *The German Communists and the
        Rise of Nazism*, 11–12
Fischer, Ruth, 191

flag, republican, 153
Flammenwerfer, Der (The Flame-thrower), 182
fluctuation (of political party membership), 210–213
  and interparty contacts, 39–40
  and local focus of members, 270, 297
  and voting patterns, 211
Fontane, Theodore, 30
Frau und Sport, 184
Free Trade Unions, 170
Freikorps (Free Corps), 135, 137, 169
Freymuth, Arnold, 280
Friedman, Allen, 249
Friedrichshain, 65, 70, 91
  political violence in, 122, 245–246
  pubs in, 162, 210, 254
  as a workers' district, 54
Friedrichstraße, 54
Friesenstraße, 101
Fritzsche, Peter, 13
Fromm, Erich, 27, 81, 86
front generation, 101–102, 294

gangs, 20, 91, 214, 230, 236, 250
garden allotments, 52, 72–73
Gayle, Wilhelm von, 159
Gellately, Robert, 217
Gemeinnützige Heimstätten-Aktiengesellschaft (Gehag), 49
gender relations. *See* men; women
generational tensions, 21, 100–120
  in families, 112–113
  front generation, 101–102, 294
  historical cohorts, 100
  in KPD, 114
  link with radical youth, 294–295
  political disagreements, 264
  in SPD, 103, 112–113, 190
  younger generation, 101, 262
German Academy for Social and Pedagogical Women's Work, 44
German Society for Housing Reform, 43
Geschke, Ottomar, 130

Gesetz über Arbeitsvermittlung und Arbeitslosenversicherung (AVAVG), 109
Gesinnung, 280–281, 284
Gesundbrunner (clique), 201
Glaeser, Ernst
  Class of 1902, 101
Gneisenau Street, 40, 52
  as a boundary, 30, 34
  May 1929 violence in, 123
  pubs on, 31, 168
Goebbels, Joseph, 95, 146, 177
  and *Der Angriff*, 59, 114
  "struggle for Berlin," 100, 166–167, 168, 238
Goldschmidt, Alfons, 130
Gollnow Street, 95
Görlitzer station, 66–67
government buildings and Reichstag
  Bannmeile, 62, 155–156
  demonstrations at, 56, 62, 155–156
Groener, Wilhelm, 289
Gropius, Walter, 49
Großman, Hermann, 280
Grosse Schauspielhaus, 130
Gross-Siedlung Friedrich Ebert, 51
Gross-Siedlung Reinickendorf, 49
Grzesinski, Albert, 121, 124, 158–159, 161, 293

Haben, Thomas, 32
Hagemann, Karen, 16
Hakescher Markt, 122
Halle, Felix, 269
Hallesches Tor, 122, 140
Hamilton, Richard, 53
Hannover, Heinrich and Elisabeth, 279
Harsch, Donna, 140
Harvey, Elizabeth, 109
Haussmann, Georges Eugène, 41
Havel River, 64
Heidelberger Krug (SPD pub on Arndt Street), 140
Heilbronner, Oded
  Catholicism, Political Culture, and the Countryside, 13
Heimat, 18, 148

Heime (SA barracks), 176, 179, 220, 221, 255, 291
Hermann Street, 124
Himmler, Heinrich, 197
Hindenburg, Paul von, 5, 9, 151, 185, 193, 286
Hitler, Adolf
  and the *Bannmeile*, 156
  as chancellor, 5, 22–23, 25, 286, 297
  and Hans Litten, 269
  and the NSBO, 170
  and the NSDAP, 179, 193, 197
  propaganda against, 95, 185
  and the SA, 172
  and Walter Stennes, 169–170
Hitler Jugend (HJ, Hitler Youth), 114, 115, *116*, 180, 257
  goal of, 113
  marches of, 35
  and Norkus murder, 119–120
  and political violence, 238, 247, 249, 251
  strength of, 171
  See also Nationalsozialistische Deutsche Arbeiterpartei (NSDAP, National Socialist Party)
Hitlerjunge Quex (film), 115, *116*
Hochstadt, Steve, 26
Hoffmann, Gotthard, 242
Hohenzollern Square, 251
homelessness, 73, *108*
homosexuality, 48, 94, 95
Hong, Young-Sun, 15, 106
Horn II, Georg, 269
horse butchers, 31
Hörsing, Otto, 155, 159
hospitals, 206–207
housing, 40–53
  building cooperatives, 49
  contemporary descriptions of, 25–41, 42, 52–53
  crisis in, 78
  effect on radicalism, 42, 227
  frequency of moving, 202
  high rents, 52, 202
  homelessness, 52–53, 73, *108*
  land control legislation, 47

large developments, 47, 49–51, 202
  and moral collapse, 42
  photographs of, 43
  reforms of, 41, 43–44
  row houses, 48–49
  tents and shacks *(Laubenkolonie)*, 52, 73
  See also tenements and communities
Hufeisen Siedlung, 49
Hugenberg, Alfred, 58

ideology, 270
  focus of KPD, 173, 191–192, 219, 222–223
  and local issues, 214, 296–297
  of NSDAP, 173–174
industrial culture, 27
informers *(Achtgroschenjungen)*, 214–215
Italy, 13, 197

Jahn, Martha and Alfred, 94
Jankowski, Martin Sanchez, 230, 236, 250
Jews and Judaism, 54, 58, 66, 269
  See also anti-Semitism
Jugendämter, 106, 107
Jungdeutsche Orden (Jungdo), 162, 275
Jungfernheide, 49
justice system. *See* courts and justice system

Kampfbund gegen den Faschismus (KbgdF, Fighting League against Fascism), 163, 164, 165, 198–199, 212
  attacks on SA pubs, 241
  newspaper of, 95
Kampfgemeinschaft für Rote Sporteinheit (Fighting Association for Red Sport Unity), 183–184
Kampfmai 1929 (film), 130
Kapp Putsch, 70, 242
Karl-Friedrich-Platz, 38–39
Karl Liebknecht House, 54, 56, 157

Kästner, Erich
  Fabian, 3, 4, 5, 34, 69, 260
Katz, Jack, 20, 91
Keun, Irmgard
  Gilgi – eine von uns, 69
  Das kunstseidene Mädchen, 3, 5, 75
Kieze, 25–42
  as autonomous, 294
  competition within, 38–39
  definition and character of, 26–27
  landmarks as focal points of, 28–29,
    34, 39, 235
  non-residents in, 35, 88
  police presence in, 35–37, 90–91
  radicalism within, 28, 31, 38
  semi-private space in, 32, 35, 45, 87,
    120, 199, 251, 260
  See also neighborhoods and
    neighborhood identity;
    Nostizstrasse Kiez
Klausener, Erich, 38
Kleinarbeit, 56, 194, 197
Knickerbocker, H. R., 24, 133, 182
Knobelsdorffstraße, 38
Kohn, Albert, 43
Kollwitz, Käthe, 166
kommunistische Agitator, Der, 208,
  219
Kommunistische Jugendverband
  Deutschlands (KJVD, Communist
  Youth League), 114, 158, 164, 228,
  274
Kommunistische Partei Deutschlands
  (KPD, German Communist Party),
  10–12, 160–166
  appeal of to youths, 102, 111,
    112–113
  attacks on police, 258–259
  and attacks on SA pubs, 240–241,
    272
  Bezirksleitung (BL, District
    Leadership), 164, 193, 218, 219,
    228, 240
  and BVG strike, 70, 209
  and cliques, 200–202
  compared to NSDAP, 168–169
  "Conciliators," 191

conservatism of, 164–165
criticism of SPD, 161
deaths from political violence,
  234–235, 238, 250
demonstration instructions, 237
denunciations within, 216, 217–218,
  222–227, 297–298
discipline of, 180–181, 185, 191–192
dissension within, 114, 135, 191–193
education and training, 182–183,
  192, 193
election returns for, 29, 53, 55, 212,
  297, 299
expulsion from, 191–192, 223
extra-party organizations, 163
financial problems of, 175, 191, 211
Hunger-march (1932), 62–63
ideology of, 173
Intelligence Service, 218
and the judicial system, 270
Karl Liebknecht House, 54, 56, 157
leader/member gap, 192–193
leadership and structure of, 164,
  181–182, 191, 212, 228–229
legal status of, 186
links with NSDAP, 209–210
links with SPD, 39–40, 120, 208
and looting, 195
male worker image of, 11, 165
and May 1929 violence, 120,
  121–122, 123, 124, 126–127, 128,
  129, 132, 135, 296
and membership fluctuation,
  211–213
middle-class fear of, 173
National Committee for Working
  Women, 185
and Norkus murder, 119
paid positions with, 177
police surveillance of, 132, 218
policy on alcohol, 181
policy on factory organizing,
  164–165, 181, 218
policy on violence, 12, 238–243
press coverage of, 60–61, 62–64
propaganda against, 95–96, 167,
  168

Kommunistische Partei (*cont.*)
pubs used by, 99, 132, 137, 228, 251,
254, 273–274
"*Schlagt die Faschisten*" (Strike the
facists), 239–240
and school strike, 117
sites for demonstrations, 56
social activities of, 183
sport groups, 183–184
Stennes revolt and, 170
street cells and individual activism,
198–199, 212, 218–219, 223, 229,
240–243
and tenants' issues, 45–46, 204
Unterbezirksleitung (UBL, local
leadership), 164, 212, 218, 223,
228, 242
vagabonds and criminals in,
225–226
and *Verfassungstag* (1929), 157–158
women, policies on and roles of. *See
under* women
Zentralkomitee (ZK, Central
Committee), 135, 161, 164–165,
212, 239
Kommunistische Partei-Opposition
(KPO, Communist Party of
Germany Opposition), 191,
223
Köpenicker Street, 205
Kösliner Street, 122, 123, 133
Köster, Helmut, 168
Kranz, Paul, 94
Kreuzberg
character of, 54
district of, 65, 122
election returns for, 29, 142
employment offices, 138
as middle-class district, 30
Nazi activities in, 168, 239
police presence in, 91
political violence in, 233
population of, 26
publishing houses in, 58
pubs in, 140
unemployment in, 88
Kreuz-Zeitung, 61

Kurfürstendamm, 63
Kurz, Thomas, 127

Lane, Barbara Miller, 50
Law for the Protection of the Republic
(*Gesetz zum Schutz der Republik*),
131–132, 276, 288
lawyers, 269, 270
Lehrlingsarbeit, 114
Lehrter station, 66
Leipziger-Platz, 68
Lenin, Vladimir Ilyich, and Leninist
theory, 92, 161, 181, 191, 242
Ley, Robert, 194
Lichtenberg, 53
Liebknecht, Karl, 1, 166, 181, 182
Lindenberger, Thomas, 17, 19
Straßenpolitik, 133
Lindenhof, 48
Lindenstrasse, 56, 101
Lipinski's pub (Nostizstrasse), 31
Litten, Hans, 269
Loewenberg, Peter, 102
looting, 195–197
Lorenz, Walter (Othello), and Lorenz
pub
and KPD, 31, 168, 209, 232, 247,
254, 274
role of in Kiez, 31, 32
trial of, 275
Löwenstein, Kurt, 66
Löwenthal, Fritz, 129, 269
Lüdtke, Alf, 27, 28
Lustgarten, 56, 122, 155, 157
Luxemburg, Rosa, 166, 181, 182

Magdeburg, 142
Magenfrage (stomach question), 176
Maikowski, Hans, 238, 241
Mallmann, Klaus-Michael, 12, 40
Mannheim, Karl, 100
marches. *See* assemblies, rallies, and
marches
Marheinekeplatz, 32, 195
Marienthal Austria study, 82,
85–86
market demonstrations, 198–199

Marx, Karl, and Marxism, 30, 181, 272
Maslow, Arkadi, 191
May 1929 violence *(Blutmai)*, 21, 120–136
  as alleged Communist conspiracy, 126
  arrests and trials, 126, 129
  deaths and injuries in, 96, 122, 124, 125–126, 129–130, 134
  events of, 122–125
  KPD blamed for, 126, 127, 128, 135
  neighborhood focus of, 127, 134, 295–296
  police actions during, 56, 123–124, 125, 134, 141, 286
  political impact of, 120–121, 133–134
  press coverage of, 127–128
  public hearings following, 130
  restrictions during, 55, 124–125
  significance of, 79–80, 232, 295–296
  weapons used in, 123, 127
Mebes, Paul, 51
men
  and domestic work, 85–86
  feminization of, 21, 83, 175
  First World War veterans, 81, 161, 169
  front generation, 101–102, 294
  hyper-masculinity, 17
  loss of patriarchal authority, 86, 105–106, 295
  male worker image, 11, 165
  occupational identities of, 82, 83
  in paramilitary organizations, 295, 296
  pubs as male spaces, 97–100
  stepfathers, 104–105
  unemployed, 21, 82–83, 85–86, 89, 108, 174–175
  and welfare system, 88
Meyers-Hof (tenement), 55
middle class
  districts of Berlin, 30, 53, 55
  domestic ideal of, 147
  Doppelverdiener (double earners), 83–85

fear of KPD, 173
and murders of youth, 93–94
and radical youths, 115–116, 117–119
role in Weimar Republic, 8
as white collar workers, 3
Mietskasernen, 41, 55
milieu(s), 13–14, 40
  Communist, 29
  workers', 200
mimeograph machines, 215
Mitte, 53–54, 65, 122, 124, 219, 226
Moabit, 53, 54, 55, 119, 124, 204, 249
Mosse publishing house, 58
movie houses, 73–76
Müller, Hermann, 109, 121, 140
murders and other deaths
  of children and youth, 59–60, 93–94, 119–120
  in May 1929 violence, 96, 124, 125–126, 129–130, 134
  of Rathenau, 131
  of women, 92–94, 96, 129–130, 134
Muthow (horse butcher), 31

Nachbarschaft, 26
National Committee for Working Women (KPD), 185
Nationalsozialistische Betriebszellen Organisation (NSBO), 170–171, 209
Nationalsozialistische Deutsche Arbeiterpartei (NSDAP, National Socialist Party), 166–173
  anti-Semitic policies. *See* anti-Semitism
  and BVG strike, 70, 209
  and Catholics in South Germany, 13
  and cliques, 201
  concept of order, 174, 177
  conflict with SA, 169–170
  deaths from political violence, 176, 234, 235
  denunciation within, 216–217
  discipline of, 178–180, 193–194, 197
  dissension and discontent within, 193–194
  education and training in, 179

Nationalsozialistische Deutsche
Arbeiterpartei (*cont.*)
election returns for, 9, 29, 212, 297,
299
financing of, 175
growth of, 5, 11–15
and housing, 50
ideology of, 173–174
and industrial workers, 53, 167–168
and interparty contacts, 209–210
and judicial system, 269, 270
leadership of, 175, 193, 197
and looting, 196–197
loyalty to Hitler, 179, 197
masculinity and, 17
material compensation for members,
175–176, 238
membership dues, 213
and membership fluctuation, 212–213
membership in, 168–169, 170,
178–179
newspaper press of, 58–59
police members, 221
pubs used by, 99–100, 168, 228, 255
as *Sammelbewegung*, 167
and sexual deviance, 94–95
sites for demonstrations, 56
structure of, 171
use of Communist tactics, 60
use of violence, 117–118, 300
view of Berlin, 166–167
Volksgemeinschaft, 13
women, views on and roles of. *See
under* women
working-class support for, 228
youths in, 102
See also Hitler Jugend (HJ, Hitler
Youth); Sturmabteilung (SA, Storm
troops)
neighborhoods and neighborhood
identity
codes of behavior, 194
competition in, 39
and denunciation, 214–231, 297–298
distrust of police, 215, 216
ideology *vs.* local issues, 214, 296–297
justice forms within, 216–218, 230

landmarks in, 28–29, 34, 39, 235
local *vs.* central power, 8
and May 1929 violence, 127, 134,
295–296
networks in, 202
political diversity in, 227–228, 298
and political fluctuation, 211
and political violence, 243, 251–252,
270, 282
and radical activism, 91, 203–204
resistance to political "outsiders,"
199
social role of welfare offices, 260
and transportation system, 28, 34,
70–72, 78
See also Kieze; tenements and
communities
Neukölln
district of, 45, 53, 54–55
HJ march in (1930), 35
housing in, 44, 49
KPD strength in, 56, 223, 228, 254
May 1929 violence in, 55, 122,
123–124
political activism in, 203, 206
political violence in, 91, 241, 243,
249, 250, 258, 276
pubs in, 254
welfare office in, 89, 259
Neuköllner Stadium, 243
Neukrantz, Klaus
Barrikaden am Wedding, 120
Neumann, Heinz, 191, 239
newspaper press, 57–64
attacks on sellers, 249
extent of, 58
foreign, 6, 150
and July 1931 decree, 290, 291
and March 1931 decree, 288
portrayals of radicalism in, 59–63,
119
readers' trust of, 57
street newspapers (*Straßenzeitungen*),
218–222, 252
newspaper press coverage
of looting, 196
of May 1929 violence, 127–128

of Nazi violence, 63
of school strikes, 116–117
of women's political activism, 96–97,
   203–204
of women's suicide and murder,
   92–93, 94
newsreels, 74, 76, 148
New York Times, 6, 150, 159
Niemeyer, Annemarie, 44–45
Norkus, Herbert, 119–120, 249
Nostitz, General Graf August von, 30
Nostizstrasse, 30–32, 124, 254
Nostizstrasse Kiez, 20, 29–42, 122, 123,
   140, 232, 247
   contemporary descriptions of, 41
   See also Kieze
Noth, Ernst Erich (pseud. Paul Kranz),
   94
Die Mietskaserne,
November Revolution, 135
NS-Frauenschaft (Women's Corps),
   172, 194
NS-Mädchenschaft (Girls' Corps), 194

Oktober, 237
order/disorder
   and denunciations, 216
   Nazi concept of order, 174, 177
   and police control, 286
Orgler, Alfred, 280
Ossietzky, Karl von, 130
Otto, Fritz, 242

pacifism, 86, 144, 240
Pankow, 53
Pank Street, 124
Panzerkreuzer battleship, 140–141
Papen, Franz von, 140, 159, 286, 287,
   292
paramilitary organizations
   banning of, 291–292
   as male communities, 295, 296
   vs. cliques, 200
   See also specific organizations (RB,
      RFB, SA)
Peukert, Detlev, 15, 19, 106, 200, 300
Plötzensee prison, 283

Poelzig, Hans, 41
police
   and 1929 *Verfassungstag*, 154, 158
   blacklisting of, 221
   brutality of, 129–130, 141, 250–251
   criticisms of, 36, 37, 59
   denunciations to, 214–216
   fear of radical activists, 250
   Gestapo, 217
   inefficiency of, 36
   injuries to, 126, 235
   KPD attacks on, 258–259
   links with SPD and government,
      208
   and looting, 195–196
   and May 1929 violence, 122,
      123–124, 125, 134, 286
   neighborhood distrust of, 215, 216
   NSDAP members in, 221
   political (IA), 232
   presence in workers' districts, 35–37,
      90–91
   public views of, 132–133
   at rallies and marches, 233, *233*
   Reich-level control of, 292
   role in controlling violence, 243–244,
      245
   shootings by, 250, 251
   size of force, 221
   and street newspapers, 222
   surveillance of KPD, 157–158
   surveillance of train passengers, 72
   taunting of, 258
   view of radical youth, 266
   at welfare offices, 260
population
   of Berlin, 26, 43, 46
   of Charlottenburg, 38
   of Kreuzberg, 26
   migration to cities, 25
   of youths, 107
Potsdamer Platz, 66, 68, 69
Prenzlauer Berg, 55, 65, 90, 135,
   253
press. *See* newspaper press
Prinz Handjery Street, 123
probation, 267, 268

propaganda
and membership fluctuation, 213
mimeograph machines, 215
and political violence, 248–250
theatrical displays as, 152
Protestant church, 106
Prügelfreitag (beating Friday), 86
Prussian parliament
and 1931 decree, 290, 291
and ban of RFB, 130–131
dissolution of, 281, 292, 293
and expansion of Berlin, 65, 66
Papen coup in, 286, 292
pubs
absence of liquor in, 32
as focus for political violence, 61,
100, 168, 252, 254–257, 273–275
as male spaces, 97–100
owners' protection of clients, 273,
275
police surveillance in, 97, 254
as political spaces, 98, 99, 205, 228
as political turf, 255, 282
as semi-private spaces, 32
social function of, 31–32
types of, 31–32
women in, 98–99
See also under specific political
organizations (NSDAP, KPD, RFB,
SA, etc.)

radicalism (political) and radical
activism, 160–187
as antisocial, 266
appeal of, 18–19, 113–114
conservatism of individuals, 295
as criminal *vs.* political, 266
culture of, 8, 18, 29, 79, 217, 227,
286, 290, 294
extra-party organizations, 163
family rhetoric of, 113–114, 295
interparty contacts, 39–40, 207–213
Kleinarbeit, 56, 194, 197
link with male authority, 91, 251–252
link with physical attributes, 266–267
link with unemployment, 111,
174–175

as a local response, 293–294, 295
material compensation for
participants, 175–176, 194, 238,
264
negative impact on social order and
stability, 18, 134, 232, 285
neighborhood focus of, 91, 194,
203–204, 211
police view of, 266
as product of Weimar Republic, 300
Reich-level control of, 292
right/left similarities in, 295
welfare workers' views of, 266,
268–269
women's role in, 203–204
youth as "misled" or "misused,"
117–119, 264, 267, 278–279
See also violence, political; specific
parties and organizations (KPD,
NSDAP, etc.)
radio, 77
rallies. *See* assemblies, rallies, and
marches
Rathenau, Walther, 131
Red Berlin (workers' districts), 53–78
alleged link with USSR, 59, 133
borders of, 53
characteristics and contrasts of, 53–55
police brutality in, 250–251
sites for demonstrations in, 56
West Berlin's fear of, 134, 294
See also Berlin; workers (industrial)
Redslob, Edwin, 149, 151, 152–153,
154
Reichskunstwart office, 151
*Reichsausschuss der deutschen
Jugendverbände*, 103
Reichsbanner Schwarz-Rot-Gold (RB),
112, 142–145, *150*
attacks on, 190, 238, 254, 271–273
and the *Bannmeile*, 155–156
cartoon on membership fluctuation,
211
deaths from political violence, 234
discipline of, 156–157, 159
dissension and dissatisfaction within,
143, 159, 190–191

link to republican government, 144,
159–160
as a military organization, 144
as a multi-party organization,
142–143
pubs of, 140
reorganization of, 143–144, 190
and republican flag, 153
Schufos, 143, 144, 178
Stafos, 143
and *Verfassungstag*, 155–157, 159
See also Sozialdemokratische Partei
Deutschlands (SPD, Social
Democratic Party)
Reichsjugendwohlfahrtsgesetz (RJWG,
National Youth Welfare Law),
106–107
Reichskunstwart office, 151
Reichstag. *See* government buildings
and Reichstag
Reichszentrale für Heimatdienst,
149
Reinickendorf, 53, 55, 64, 252
republicanism
and anti-republican judges, 279
discipline of, 159, 185
German flag, 153
RB as organization of, 144, 159–160
role of *Verfassungstag*, 139, 148–149,
159
state propaganda for, 147–148
Revolutionäre Gewerkschafts-
Opposition (RGO, Revolutionary
Trade Union Opposition), 170,
290
Richard Street, 241
Rohe, Karl, 13
Röhm, Ernst, 95, 176, 178
Röhm Putsch (1934), 38
Rosenbaum, Heidi, 105
Rosenhaft, Eve
Beating the Fascists?, 10–11
Rote Einheitsfront, Die, 208
Rote Fahne, Die (RF), 58, 62, 63, 93,
226
and KPD attacks on SA pubs, 241
and March 1931 decree, 289

and May 1929 violence, 127, *128*,
130, 135
Rote Hilfe Deutschland (RHD), 245,
269
Rote Jugend, 158
Rote Jungfront (RJ, Red Youth Front),
131, 192, 249, 250
Rote Jungsturm, 60
Rote Pfingsttreffen, *162*
Roter Frauen- und Mädchenbund
(RFMB, Red League of Women
and Girls), 165
Roter Frontkämpferbund (RFB, Red
Front-fighters' League), 161–163
attacks on SA pubs, 241
banning of, 121, 124, 125, 130–131,
132, 192, 276, 290
and denunciation, 216
discipline of, 178, 180–185
family rhetoric of, 113–114
First World War veterans in, 161
founding and purpose of, 161
as a male organization, 163, 165
and May 1929 violence, 122, 126,
127, 130
and membership fluctuation, 211, 213
members of, 162–163
as a military organization, 178
and Pankow murder, 59–60
policy on violence, 239–240
pubs used by, 162, 168
as underground organization, 99, 163
uniforms of, 162, 276, 290
Roter Massenselbstschutz (Red Mass
Self-Defense), 92, 163
Rummel (Fortuna amusement park),
32–34
Ruttman, Walter, 69

SA. *See* Sturmabteilung (SA,
Stormtroops)
Saalbau Friedrichshain, 54, 245–246
Saalschutz, 144, 245
St. Kamillus Catholic parish, 39
Scharoun, Hans, 49
Scheidemann, Philip, 1
Scheller family, 94

Scheringer, Richard, 213
Schering factory, 38
Scheunenviertel, 54
Schivelbusch, Wolfgang, 71
"Schlagt die Faschisten" (Strike the
      fascists), 239–240
Schleicher, Kurt von, 287
Schleiermacher Street, 168
Schlesinger, Paul (Sling), 279
Schloßstraße, 38, 256
Schöneberg, 45, 48, 65, 117, 247, 273
      Lindenhof development, 48
Schönstedt, Walter, 29, 191
      Kämpfende Jugend, 5, 28, 31, 34, 42,
         98, 112, 115, 174, 195, 200–201
schools, 206, 257
school strikes, 116–117, *118*, 257
Schufos (of RB, Schutzformationen),
      143, 144, 178
Schultheiss brewery, 34, 41
Schulze, Hagen, 9
Schumann, Dirk, 14
Schutzstaffel (SS, Protective Squads),
      146, 172, 291
Schwan, Bruno, 43–44, 50, 52
Selchower Straße, 258
Severing, Carl, 61, 161, 289
      and 1929 *Verfassungstag*, 153–154,
         155
      and banning of RFB, 121, 124
      dismissal of, 293
      on Law for the Protection of the
         Republic, 131–132
      and Panzerkreuzer controversy, 140
      and the RB, 144, 291
      and Ruhr labor dispute, 141
sexual behavior, 80, 94–95
Siemens factory, 38, 49, 55, 67
Siemensstadt, 50, 55
Simeon Bogen, 221
Sino-Japanese war, 74
Sklarek brothers, 161
Soldiner Street, 251
Solms Street, 40, 52, 168
Sondergerichte, 293
Sonnenallee, 89
Sophiensälle, 124

Sozialdemokratische Partei
      Deutschlands (SPD, Social
      Democratic Party), 139–149
   and Berlin expansion, 64, 66
   and Brüning government, 159
   compromise with conservative right,
      137
   corruption within, 161
   discontent and dissension within,
      103, 112–113, 159, 189–190, 191
   election returns for, 29, 65–66, 140,
      212, 297
   historical studies of, 10
   and KPD, 39–40, 60–61, 120, 208
   KPD criticisms of, 161
   links with police, 208
   and May 1929 violence, 121, 122,
      132
   Nazi propaganda against, 167
   pub used by, 140
   reform of architectural standards, 41
   republican discipline, 185
   responses to radicalism, 296, 299
   role in May 1929 riots, 120
   strength of, 140, 142
   views of KPD, 190
   women, policies on and roles for. *See
      under* women
   workers' support, 17–18
   See also Reichsbanner
      Schwarz-Rot-Gold (RB)
Sozialistische Arbeiter-Jugend (SAJ,
      Social Democratic Youth), 140
Sozialrepublikanische Partei
      Deutschland, 159
Spandau, 53, 67
Spandauer Damm, 38
Spartacus League, 1, 101, 138
Spieker, Karl, 147–148
spies, political, 186, 225, 226–227,
      249
sports clubs, 183–184
      Fichte, 32, 73, 114–115, 164, 183,
         274, 275
sports events, 39, 74
Spree River, 64
Stachura, Peter, 106

Stafos (of RB, Stammformationen), 143
Stahlhelm, 59, 121, 162, 169, 213, 234,
   238, 274
Stalin, Joseph, 181, 182, 191
Steglitz, 45, 65, 255, 256
Steinhoff, Hans, *116*
Stennes, Walter, 169, 170, 193, 202
Stephan, Hans, 94
Stinnes, Claerenore, 74
Strasser, Gregor, 176
Strasser, Otto, 193
street cells (of KPD). *See*
   Kommunistische Partei
   Deutschlands
street elites, 20
street newspapers *(Straßenzeitungen)*,
   218–222, 252
Stresemann, Gustav, 138
Striefler, Christian, 10
strikes
   at BVG (1932), 61, 70, 209
   general strike (1920), 70
   mass strike (1929), 129
   press coverage of, 61–62
   school strikes, 116–117
   tenants', 45–46, 95, 204, *205*
   of welfare workers, 259
Sturmabteilung (SA, Stormtroops),
   168–170
   attacks on Jews, 63, 238
   attacks on RB, 254, 271–273
   banning of (1932), 132, 247,
      291–292
   barracks *(Heime)*, 176, 179, 220,
      221, 255, 291
   conflict with NSDAP, 169–170
   contact with KPD members, 210
   discipline of, 177–178
   family rhetoric of, 113–114
   First World War veterans in, 169
   image of male worker, 11
   leadership (Oberste
      SA-Führer/Führung), 177, 197
   link with Hitler, 172
   looting by, 196–197
   material compensation for members,
      175–176

and membership fluctuation, 211,
   213
membership of, 168–169
military emphasis of, 169
political legitimacy of, 172–173
propaganda insulting, 94–96
pubs used by, 168, 240–241, *241*,
   256, 272, 273–274
Sturm 24, 168, 272
Sturm 27, 168
travel, 197
uniforms of, 177–178, 196, 197
use of violence, 238–239
view of Marxism, 238, 272
See also Nationalsozialistische
   Deutsche Arbeiterpartei (NSDAP,
   National Socialist Party)
Südpol (clique), 200
suicide, 92–93

Tag, Der, 58
Tante Emma (pub), 168, 177
Taut, Bruno, 41, 48, 49, 51
taverns. *See* pubs
Tegel, 64
Tegel Lake, 64
Tempelhof airport, 54
tenants' strikes *(Mieterstreiks)*, 45–46,
   95, 204, *205*
tenement communities, 30
tenements and communities, 41–46
   apartment subdivision, 30
   building heights, 47
   children in, 43
   communal toilets, 44, 87
   contemporary descriptions of, 25–41,
      42
   crowded conditions in, 38, 41, 43,
      44–45, 55, 227
   denunciation of landlords, 219–220
   evictions, 52, 90, 204, 220, 253
   familiarity among neighbors, 25, 227
   families' reputations in, 265–266
   on Nostizstrasse, 30
   as political spaces, 206
   semi-private space in, 32, 35, 45, 87,
      120, 199, 251, 260

tenements and communities (*cont.*)
  superintendents, 265
  tenants' strikes, 45–46, 95, 204, 205
  turnover rates in, 25
  violence in, 87, 249
  See also housing; neighborhoods
territorialization
  and masculine authority, 251–252
  and police brutality, 250–251
  and political violence, 248–249, 252,
    295
  and pubs, 255, 282
Thalheimer, August, 191
Thälmann, Ernst, 160, 182, 185, 193,
    239
Thielsch, Herman, 168, 272, 278
Third Reich
  Germans' view of, 299–300
  lack of workers' resistance to, 300
  violence and authoritarianism, 12,
    294, 299, 300
Tiergarten, 53, 54, 55, 56, 65, 204
trade unions, 141, 170, 290
transportation system, 66–72
  for commuting workers, 57, 67
  growth of, 28, 66–68
  impact of strikes on, 70
  and neighborhood identification, 28,
    34, 70–72, 78
  noise of, 68–69
  as political focus, 69–70, 72
  stations, 3–4, 68–69, 71–72
  underground network, 67–68
  use of electric trams, 67, 68
  viaduct architecture, 67, 71
Treptow, 53, 65
Triebel, Walther, 269
Trommel, Die, 105
Turner, Henry A., 9

UBL (Unterbezirksleitung). *See under*
    Kommunistische Partei
    Deutschlands
Ullstein (publishing house), 58
Unabhängige Sozialdemokratische
    Partei Deutschlands (USPD,
    Independent Social Democratic
    Party), 64, 65–66

unemployment, 21, 89
  assistance programs for, 51, 109–110,
    141
  effects of on men, 21, 82–83, 85–86,
    89, *108*, 174–175
  effects of on youth, 103, 107–109,
    110–111, 262–263, 295
  impact on housing developments, 51
  link with radicalism, 111, 174–175
  literary portrayals of, 3
  statistics on, 88, *108*, 138
uniforms (of paramilitary
    organizations)
  banning of, 288, 290, 291
  insignia taken from, 250
  and political intent, 276
  of RFB, 162, 276, 290
  of SA, 177–178, 196, 197
United States of America, 74, 75
Unter den Linden, 56, *150*, 155
Urban Street, 34
USSR and Soviet Communism, 59, 60,
    126, 133, 173

Verband sozialer Baubetriebe, 48
Verfassungstag (Constitution Day),
    148–159
  budget for, 152
  mass spectacles for, 151–152, 153
  police role in, 154, 157–158, 159
  RB role in, *150*, 155–157, 159
  republican role of, 77, 139, 148–149,
    159
  tenth anniversary celebrations
    (1929), 148, 150–158
  Verfassungsrede (speeches), 153–154,
    159
Versailles Peace Treaty, 10, 137–138
Viktoriapark, 32
violence
  acceptance of, 11, 276, 279, 284,
    294–298, 300
  domestic, 81, 86–87
  militaristic values, 294
violence, political
  accusations of cowardice, 95–96
  and alcohol, 255, 269, 277–278
  attacks on pedestrians, 246, 248

avoiding confrontation, 247–248
bravery ritualized in, 236
broad support for, 299
as class warfare, 238
codes of behavior in, 232, 236, 243, 279, 282
combatants' knowledge of each other, 243, 282
of Communists, 238
contemporary description of, 256–257
as criminal *vs.* political, 264, 266, 283–284
deaths from, 168, 234–235, 250
as economic disputes, 252–253, 282
generational differences in, 112–113
humiliation of victims, 250, 257
as individual actions, 229, 240–243
injury as commendation, 250
and inter-party meetings, 210
large brawls, 276–277
link with Third Reich, 294, 299, 300
local focus of. *See under* neighborhoods and neighborhood identity
logic of, 284, 298
as male activity, 103
and male camaraderie, 278–279
motivation of, 275–276
national *vs.* neighborhood, 135–136
neighborhood participation in, 243
in Nostizstrasse Kiez, 29
personal disputes, 251
police roles in. *See under* police
political intent in, 276–278, 284
political parties' role in, 237–238, 284
at political rallies and marches. *See* assemblies, rallies, and marches
press coverage of, 59
and propaganda distribution, 248–250
for revenge, 252, 254, 271–273
role of pubs in. *See under* pubs
role of women in. *See under* women
Saalschutz, 144, 245
in schools, 257
as self-defense, 239, 271
against state institutions, 257–260

statistics on, 233, 234–235
street violence, 22, 246–247
in summer months, 247
and territory. *See under* territorialization
weapons used in, 245, 256, 274, 277
in Weimar society, 19–20
against welfare system, 88, 260
See also radicalism (political) and radical activism
Völkischer Beobachter (VB), 58
Volksgemeinschaft, 13
Volkspark, 54
von Ankum, Katharina, 75
Vorwärts, 58, 96, 97, 128, 159
building of, 101
"Constraint and Freedom" (Severing), 131
Vossische Zeitung (VZ), 58, 59, 60, 97, 118, 217, 245–246

Wagner, Martin, 48, 49
Waldsiedlung (forest development), 49
Wandervogel movement, 103, 171
Wedding
Beussel Street station, 67
clique in, 201
contemporary description of, 57
housing in, 51, 55
KPD strength in, 56, 212
May 1929 violence in, 120, 122, 123–124, 129, 133
school strike in, 116
as workers' district, 53, 55, 65, 91
Weg der Frau, Der, 184
Wehrwolf, 162
Weiland, Ruth, 86
Weimar Republic
and anti-republican judges, 279
Berlin as focus for, 6–7, 64
constitution, 47, 64
Crisis Period, 5, 9
and culture of political radicalism, 300
establishment of (1918), 1, 137–138
fall of, 1, 8–12, 285, 299

Weimar Republic *(cont.)*
　Law for the Protection of the
　　Republic *(Gesetz zum Schutz der
　　Republik)*, 131–132, 276, 288
　state governments, 292–293
　uniqueness of, 14
　as welfare state, 87, 106
　See also Emergency decrees
Weindling, Paul, 106
Weisbrod, Bernd, 12, 14
Weissensee, 53, 65
Weitz, Eric D., 12
　*Creating German Communism,
　　1890–1990*, 12
welfare system, 87–88, 259–260
　attacks on, 88, 260
　clients' resentment of, 259
　contemporary description of, 88
　demands of Depression on, 87–88
　offices, 89, 138, 259–260
　provisions for youth, 106–107,
　　109–110, 262
　unemployment assistance, 51,
　　109–110, 138
welfare workers, 259
　court reports on young offenders,
　　236, 261–269, 275, 284
　fear of clients, 260
　strikes of, 259
　view of radicalism, 266, 268–269
　violence against, 88, 260
　visits of, 88
Welt am Abend, Die, 145
Weltanschauung, 179
Wermuth, Adolf, 66
Wessel, Horst, 238, 240
white collar workers *(Angestellten)*,
　3
Wiedenhoeft, Ronald, 50
Wiener Garten, 168
Wiesen Street, 124
Willibald-Alexis Street, 140
Wilmersdorf, 45, 65
Wirth, Joseph, 111, 149, 155,
　288–289
Wittenberg Platz, 247
women, *33*
　abortion, 80, 203

Doppelverdiener (double earners),
　83–85
　effects of unemployment on, 110
　employment opportunities for, 27,
　　75, 80, 81, 83
　family role of, 80–81, 85, 180, 184,
　　265
　female gangs, 91
　impact of First World War on, 81,
　　104, 263
　killed in May 1929 violence, 96,
　　129–130, 134
　KPD roles for and views on, 84,
　　92–94, 164, 165–166, 184–185,
　　198, 199, 224–225, 248
　legal equality of, 16
　and make-up, 82
　murder and suicide by, 92–94
　the "new woman," 17, 75, 165
　NSDAP views and policies on, 83–84,
　　92, 146, 171–172, 180
　political roles of, 16–17, 81,
　　98–99
　and political violence, 96–97, 125,
　　129–130, 251–252, 271
　as radical activists, 91, 98–99, 172,
　　203–204, 232, 290
　and sexual freedom, 80
　as single parents, 104–105
　SPD roles for and views of, 84, 92,
　　146, 147
　in sport, 184
　and tenants' strikes, 45–46, 204
　as unpaid workers, 85
　violence against, 81, 86–87, 90
　as wage-earners for families, 83, 85,
　　295
workers (industrial)
　convervative views of women's roles,
　　82, 91–92, 199
　factory hierarchies, 27–28
　family traditions in trades, 111–112
　images of, 11
　and Nazism, 53, 167–168, 300
　neighborhood focus of, 286
　self-interest of, 27
　transportation system for, 57, 67
　See also Red Berlin

youth
  apprentices, 109
  effects of unemployment on, 103,
    107–109, 110–111, 262–263, 295
  and family traditions, 111–112
  generation of, 101, 262
  involvement in political violence, 103,
    247
  justice system for, 107
  legislation affecting, 106–107,
    109–110
  living with parents, 263
  in May 1929 violence, 134
  as "misled" or "misused," 117–119,
    264, 267, 278–279
  moral reputation, 264–266
  population of, 107
  street elites, 20
  as threat to middle class, 115–116
  vagrants, 107
  welfare court reports on, 236,
    261–269, 275, 284
  youth movements, 103–104, 171
  See also children

Zarnack, Dr., 269
Zehlendorf, 65
  Waldsiedlung (forest development) in,
    49
ZK (Zentralkomittee). *See under*
  Kommunistische Partei
  Deutschlands
Zörgiebel, Karl, 121, 128, 132
Zossener Street, 30, 40
Zur Hochburg (pub), 168, 209,
  272

The normal distribution is frequently used as a standard against which the peakedness of other distributions is compared.

For an exponentially distributed variate

$$\mu_4' = E(t^4) = \int_0^\infty t^4 \lambda e^{-\lambda t}\, dt = \frac{24}{\lambda^4}.$$

Consequently, from (2-47) and the preceding results,

$$\mu_4 = \frac{24}{\lambda^4} - 4\left(\frac{6}{\lambda^3}\right)\left(\frac{1}{\lambda}\right) + 6\left(\frac{2}{\lambda^2}\right)\left(\frac{1}{\lambda}\right)^2 - 3\left(\frac{1}{\lambda}\right)^4 = \frac{9}{\lambda^4}, \tag{2-49}$$

and from (2-48)

$$\beta_2 = \frac{9/\lambda^4}{(1/\lambda^2)^2} = 9. \tag{2-50}$$

Thus the value of β_2 for an exponentially distributed variate does not involve λ, and the exponential density is more peaked than a normal density.

ESTIMATION OF CENTRAL MOMENTS FROM DATA

If we do not know the form and parameters of the probability density function, the estimated central moments, denoted by m_k, may be calculated by replacing μ_k' by $(1/n)\sum_{i=1}^n x_i^k$ in the preceding expressions, where x_i, $i = 1, 2, \ldots, n$, are the values of n given observations.* Thus

$$m_2 = \frac{1}{n}\sum_{i=1}^n x_i^2 - \frac{1}{n^2}\left(\sum_{i=1}^n x_i\right)^2 \tag{2-51}$$

is an estimate of μ_2 or σ^2 and is often denoted as $\hat{\sigma}^2$.

This equation leads to what statisticians call a "biased estimate." The corresponding unbiased formula is

$$s^2 = \frac{n\sum_{i=1}^n x_i^2 - \left(\sum_{i=1}^n x_i\right)^2}{n(n-1)}. \tag{2-51a}$$

Equation 2-51a is frequently used instead of (2-51) as an estimate of the variance. A data estimate for σ is obtained either as the square root of $\hat{\sigma}^2$ or as the square root of s^2.

---

* For grouped data the mid-point of each frequency class is used to represent all observations in that class. Some correction factors, which may be especially applicable when the grouping is coarse, are discussed in Reference 2-8 (pages 75–79).

The data estimates of μ_3 and μ_4 are

$$m_3 = \frac{\sum_{i=1}^{n} x_i^3}{n} - 3 \frac{\sum_{i=1}^{n} x_i^2}{n} \frac{\sum_{i=1}^{n} x_i}{n} + 2\left(\frac{\sum_{i=1}^{n} x_i}{n}\right)^3 \tag{2-52}$$

and

$$m_4 = \frac{\sum_{i=1}^{n} x_i^4}{n} - 4 \frac{\sum_{i=1}^{n} x_i}{n} \frac{\sum_{i=1}^{n} x_i^3}{n} + 6\left(\frac{\sum_{i=1}^{n} x_i}{n}\right)^2 \frac{\sum_{i=1}^{n} x_i^2}{n} - 3\left(\frac{\sum_{i=1}^{n} x_i}{n}\right)^4. \tag{2-53}$$

These equations are in the form that is most convenient for calculation. However, they may be subject to appreciable round-off errors if sufficient care is not taken. Therefore it is sometimes advisable to use the equivalent expressions

$$m_2 = \hat{\sigma}^2 = \frac{\sum_{i=1}^{n}(x_i - \bar{x})^2}{n}, \tag{2-51b}$$

$$s^2 = \frac{\sum_{i=1}^{n}(x_i - \bar{x})^2}{n - 1}, \tag{2-51c}$$

$$m_3 = \frac{\sum_{i=1}^{n}(x_i - \bar{x})^3}{n}, \tag{2-52a}$$

$$m_4 = \frac{\sum_{i=1}^{n}(x_i - \bar{x})^4}{n}, \tag{2-53a}$$

where $\bar{x}$ is the data mean.

The estimates of $\sqrt{\beta_1}$ and β_2 denoted as $\sqrt{b_1}$ and b_2, respectively, are

$$\sqrt{b_1} = \frac{m_3}{(m_2)^{3/2}} \tag{2-54}$$

and

$$b_2 = \frac{m_4}{(m_2)^2}. \tag{2-55}$$

To illustrate, we calculate the values m_2, m_3, m_4, $\sqrt{b_1}$, and b_2 for the data shown in Table 2-4.

From the data,

$$\sum_{i=1}^{n} x_i = -0.40, \qquad \sum_{i=1}^{n} x_i^2 = 0.044, \qquad \sum_{i=1}^{n} x_i^3 = -0.005122,$$

$$\sum_{i=1}^{n} x_i^4 = 0.000661,$$

and $n = 10$.

Therefore, from (2-51) to (2-55),

$$m_2 = \frac{0.044}{10} - \frac{1}{10^2}(-0.40)^2 = 0.0028,$$

$$m_3 = \frac{-0.005122}{10} - 3(0.0044)(-0.04) + 2(-0.04)^3 = -0.0001122,$$

$$m_4 = \frac{0.000661}{10} - 4(-0.04)(-0.0005122) + 6(-0.04)^2(0.0044)$$

$$- 3(-0.04)^4 = 0.00001871,$$

$$\sqrt{b_1} = \frac{-0.0001122}{(0.0028)^{3/2}} = \frac{-0.0001122}{0.000148} = -0.76,$$

$$b_2 = \frac{0.00001871}{(0.0028)^2} = \frac{0.00001871}{0.00000784} = 2.38.$$

These estimates thus suggest that the distribution is skewed to the left and is less peaked than a normal distribution.

2-10. Fractiles, Percentiles, and Related Measures

A further way of summarizing information about a distribution is by its *fractiles*. The αth fractile is that value of the random variable that has a proportion α of the cumulative distribution below it. Thus, for a continuous random variable with probability density $f(x)$, the αth fractile is that point $z(\alpha)$ such that

$$\int_{-\infty}^{z(\alpha)} f(x) \, dx = \alpha. \qquad (2\text{-}56)$$

For example, the 0.10 fractile, $z(0.10)$, of the exponential distribution is the solution to

$$\int_0^{z(0.10)} \lambda e^{-\lambda t} \, dt = 0.10 \qquad \text{or} \qquad z(0.10) = -\frac{\ln 0.9}{\lambda}.$$

The definition for a discrete random variable is similar, except that integration is replaced by summation and most of the time an exact solution is not obtained.

We have already encountered one fractile, namely, the median, in discussing measures of central tendency. In many problems we are interested in points in the tail of the distribution, such as the 0.01 or the 0.99 fractile (see Fig. 2-22). For example, the 0.01 fractile of the distribution of failure time is that time at which the chances are one out of 100 that a randomly chosen unit will have failed.

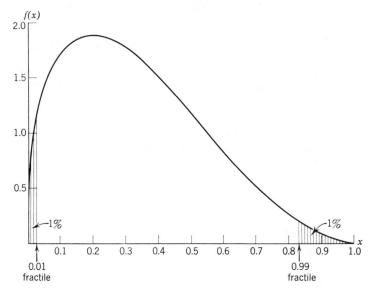

Fig. 2-22   Probability density function with 0.01 and 0.99 fractiles shown.

The term *quantile* is on occasion used instead of fractile. Also the term *percentile* or *percentage point* is used frequently to refer to the 0.01, 0.02, 0.03, etc., fractiles when expressed in per cent form. We shall make frequent use of these terms. Similarly, the first *decile* corresponds to the tenth percentile, the second decile is the twentieth percentile, and so on.

Differences between two percentiles are on occasion used as measures of dispersion. Thus the difference between the first and ninth deciles, sometimes known as the *interdecile range*, is a measure of distribution spread. The difference between the values of the largest and smallest observations, known as the *range*, is also frequently used to characterize the spread of a given set of data.

The α 100th *data percentile* is calculated from *n* observations as the

$\alpha(n + 1)$th ranked value. For example, if $n = 99$, the 5th and 95th data percentiles are the values, respectively, of the 0.05(100)th or the 5th and the 0.95(100)th or the 95th ranked observations. Frequently, this procedure requires interpolation between two values. Thus, if $n = 89$, the fifth data percentile is the mean of the fourth and fifth ranked observations and the ninetieth data percentile is the mean of the 85th and the 86th values. Note that this procedure is consistent with the rule already given for obtaining the data median.

Procedures for estimating percentiles by probability plotting are indicated in Chapter 8.

2-11. Bivariate and Multivariate Distributions

GENERAL CONCEPT

A sample point may be defined in one or more dimensions. For example, tossing two dice yielded 36 sample points, each of the type {result of first toss, result of second toss}—that is, a set of two-dimensional values. The *sum* of the outcomes is a one-dimensional random variable defined on the two-dimensional sample space. Except for the latter part of Section 2-8, our discussion so far has dealt only with one-dimensional random variables—that is, the so-called *univariate* case.

Frequently, however, we are concerned with multivariate situations that simultaneously involve two or more functions defined on the same sample space. We shall consider principally the *bivariate* case, involving two random variables; more complex multivariate situations are straightforward generalizations.

The prior example of the two-dice experiment is an elementary example of a two-dimensional random variable; in this case the values of the random variable are identical with the points in the sample space. In a hand of 13 cards selected at random from a standard deck, the number of aces and the number of hearts are two discrete random variables defined on the sample space of all deals. In an industrial situation, defects may be classified as electrical, mechanical, or both. The weekly totals in each of these categories is a three-dimensional random variable.

Multivariate situations may involve continuous, as well as discrete, random variables. A men's clothing store, in determining its optimum inventory, is concerned with both the height and the waist length of its customers. A ladies' garment store has a more complicated problem, because more than two dimensions are generally required for an adequate specification. In characterizing an alloy, we are typically concerned with a number of properties, such as stress elongation, impact strength, and creep rupture, each of which is a random variable.

In the multivariate as in the univariate case we often associate a probability function with discrete random variables and a probability density function with continuous random variables. We shall consider the discrete case first.

The *joint probability function* of two *discrete random variables*, x and y, is an expression $p(x_i, y_j)$ that gives the probability associated with all possible pairs of values of the random variable—that is,

$$p(x_i, y_j) = \Pr(x = x_i \text{ and } y = y_j)$$

for all possible combinations of x_i and y_j, where

$$p(x_i, y_j) \geq 0 \qquad \text{for all } i, j \tag{2-57}$$

and

$$\sum_i \sum_j p(x_i, y_j) = 1. \tag{2-58}$$

The function $F(x_i, y_j)$ that gives the joint probability that the first random variable takes on a value less than or equal to x_i *and* that the second takes on a value less than or equal to y_j is known as the *joint cumulative distribution* or the *joint distribution function* for the two random variables—that is,

$$F(x_i, y_j) = \Pr(x \leq x_i \text{ and } y \leq y_j). \tag{2-59}$$

For example, the tossing of two dice can give rise to the following two random variables:

$x =$ outcome of first toss,

$$y = \begin{cases} 0 \text{ if value of second toss is less than that of first toss,} \\ 1 \text{ otherwise.} \end{cases} \tag{2-60}$$

Since tossing two dice leads to an experiment with 36 equally likely sample points, the joint probability function for x and y shown in Table 2-5 and Fig. 2-23 is obtained by determining the proportion of sample points associated with each (x_i, y_j). The corresponding cumulative distribution is shown in Table 2-6.

The concepts of a joint probability function and of a joint distribution function for three or more random variables are completely analogous to those for the two-dimensional case. In Chapter 4 we shall encounter an important discrete multivariate distribution, known as the multinomial distribution.

Two *continuous random variables*, x and y, are said to have the *bivariate (or joint) probability density function* $f(x, y)$ if, for two pairs of values (x_1, x_2) and (y_1, y_2),

$$\Pr(x_1 < x \leq x_2 \text{ and } y_1 < y \leq y_2) = \int_{y_1}^{y_2} \int_{x_1}^{x_2} f(x, y) \, dx \, dy. \tag{2-61}$$

Table 2-5   Joint Probability Function for Random Variables x and y in Dice-Tossing Example

		y = Outcome of Second Toss Relative to First Toss[a]	
		0 Value of Second Toss Less Than Value of First Toss	1 Value of Second Toss Equal to or More Than Value of First Toss
	1	0	$\dfrac{6}{36}$ $\begin{bmatrix} 1,1 \\ 1,2 \\ 1,3 \\ 1,4 \\ 1,5 \\ 1,6 \end{bmatrix}$
	2	$\dfrac{1}{36}$ [2, 1]	$\dfrac{5}{36}$ $\begin{bmatrix} 2,2 \\ 2,3 \\ 2,4 \\ 2,5 \\ 2,6 \end{bmatrix}$
x = Outcome of First Toss	3	$\dfrac{2}{36}$ $\begin{bmatrix} 3,1 \\ 3,2 \end{bmatrix}$	$\dfrac{4}{36}$ $\begin{bmatrix} 3,3 \\ 3,4 \\ 3,5 \\ 3,6 \end{bmatrix}$
	4	$\dfrac{3}{36}$ $\begin{bmatrix} 4,1 \\ 4,2 \\ 4,3 \end{bmatrix}$	$\dfrac{3}{36}$ $\begin{bmatrix} 4,4 \\ 4,5 \\ 4,6 \end{bmatrix}$
	5	$\dfrac{4}{36}$ $\begin{bmatrix} 5,1 \\ 5,2 \\ 5,3 \\ 5,4 \end{bmatrix}$	$\dfrac{2}{36}$ $\begin{bmatrix} 5,5 \\ 5,6 \end{bmatrix}$
	6	$\dfrac{5}{36}$ $\begin{bmatrix} 6,1 \\ 6,2 \\ 6,3 \\ 6,4 \\ 6,5 \end{bmatrix}$	$\dfrac{1}{36}$ [6, 6]

[a] Values shown in brackets indicate sample points representing results of first and second tosses respectively.

53

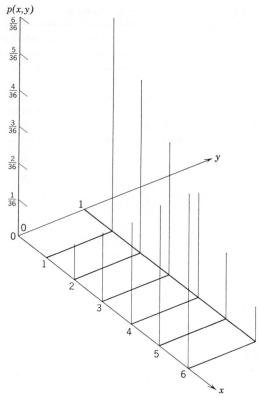

Fig. 2-23   Joint probability function for random variables x and y of Table 2-5.

The requirements on $f(x, y)$, analogous to those of (2-57) and (2-58) for $p(x, y)$, are

$$f(x, y) \geq 0 \qquad \text{for all } x \text{ and } y \tag{2-62}$$

and

$$\int_{-\infty}^{\infty} \int_{-\infty}^{\infty} f(x, y) \, dx \, dy = 1. \tag{2-63}$$

The *bivariate (or joint) cumulative distribution* or *distribution function* for continuous random variables x and y is defined as

$$F(x_1, y_1) = \Pr (x \leq x_1 \text{ and } y \leq y_1) = \int_{-\infty}^{x_1} \int_{-\infty}^{y_1} f(x, y) \, dx \, dy. \tag{2-64}$$

Similar definitions apply for the more general case involving three or more random variables.

Consider the following example. A shipment of merchandise has been guaranteed to arrive some time during a particular day. It is known that a

*Table 2-6   Cumulative Distribution Corresponding to
Joint Probability Function of Table 2-5*

		y = Outcome of Second Toss Relative to First Toss	
		0	1
	1	0	$\dfrac{6}{36}$
	2	$\dfrac{1}{36}$	$\dfrac{12}{36}$
x = Outcome of First Toss	3	$\dfrac{3}{36}$	$\dfrac{18^a}{36}$
	4	$\dfrac{6}{36}$	$\dfrac{24}{36}$
	5	$\dfrac{10}{36}$	$\dfrac{30}{36}$
	6	$\dfrac{15}{36}$	$\dfrac{36}{36}$

[a] Example calculation: $F(3, 1) = \frac{18}{36} = 0 + \frac{6}{36} + \frac{1}{36} + \frac{5}{36} + \frac{2}{36} + \frac{4}{36}$.

specific customer will request this merchandise during the same day. Let x = time of receipt of merchandise, expressed in fraction of a day—that is, $0 \le x \le 1$; let y = time of request for merchandise, expressed in fraction of a day—that is, $0 \le y \le 1$.

Judging by past experience it appears as likely that the merchandise will be received during any short interval of time during the day as during any other interval of equal length. All request-time intervals are also equally likely. It can easily be shown that the joint probability density function for x and y is

$$f(x, y) = 1, \quad \text{where } 0 \le x \le 1 \text{ and } 0 \le y \le 1 \qquad (2\text{-}65)$$

(see Fig. 2-24).

This is a bivariate generalization of the uniform or rectangular distribution mentioned briefly in Section 2-9 and to be discussed in more detail in Chapter 3. The requirements of (2-62) and (2-63) are clearly met.

We can now answer some practical questions about the probabilities associated with the relative times of receiving and requiring the merchandise. In doing so, it will be convenient to show diagrammatically the area in the (x, y) plane over which we need to integrate $f(x, y)$.

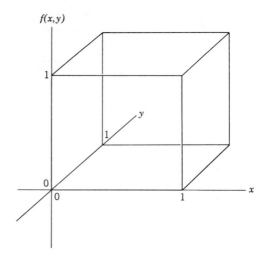

Fig. 2-24   Bivariate probability density function $f(x, y)$ for merchandise receipt time (x) and request time (y).

QUESTION 2-1.   What is the probability that both receipt and request will occur during the first half of the day?

ANSWER. From (2-64) and (2-65)

$$\Pr\left(0 \leq x \leq \frac{1}{2} \text{ and } 0 \leq y \leq \frac{1}{2}\right) = \int_0^{\frac{1}{2}} \int_0^{\frac{1}{2}} 1 \, dx \, dy = \frac{1}{4}.$$

(See Fig. 2-25a for region over which integration is performed.)

QUESTION 2-2.   What is the probability that the request for the merchandise will occur *after* its receipt?

ANSWER.

$$\Pr\left(0 \leq x \leq 1 \text{ and } y > x\right) = \int_0^1 \int_0^x 1 \, dy \, dx = \frac{1}{2}$$

(see Fig. 2-25b).

QUESTION 2-3.   What is the probability that the request for the merchandise will occur within half a day *after* its receipt? (This would be of importance if the merchandise is highly perishable.)

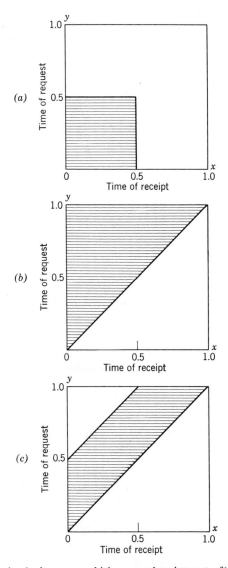

Fig. 2-25   Area in (x, y) plane over which we need to integrate $f(x, y)$ to obtain the probability of (a) both receipt (x) and request (y) of merchandise during first half day; (b) request occurring after receipt; and (c) request occurring within one half day after receipt.

57

ANSWER. From Fig. 2.25c it is clear that the problem need be broken down into two parts. Thus

$$\Pr \left(0 \leq x \leq 1 \text{ and } x \leq y \leq x + \frac{1}{2} \leq 1 \right)$$

$$= \Pr \left(0 \leq x \leq \frac{1}{2} \text{ and } x \leq y \leq x + \frac{1}{2} \right) + \Pr \left(\frac{1}{2} < x \leq 1 \text{ and } x \leq y \leq 1 \right)$$

$$= \int_0^{\frac{1}{2}} \int_x^{x+\frac{1}{2}} 1 \, dy \, dx + \int_{\frac{1}{2}}^1 \int_x^1 1 \, dy \, dx$$

$$= \frac{1}{4} + \frac{1}{8} = \frac{3}{8}.$$

We shall consider another joint distribution of two random variables, namely, the bivariate normal distribution, in Chapter 3.

MARGINAL DISTRIBUTIONS

On occasion, we are given the joint distribution of two random variables and would like to obtain the distribution of one of the variables alone. This can be done by summing over or integrating out the variable that is no longer of interest. Thus, if $p(x_i, y_j)$ is the probability function for two discrete random variables, x and y, we obtain the probability function $p_1(x_i)$ for x as

$$p_1(x_i) = \sum_j p(x_i, y_j) \tag{2-66}$$

and the probability function $p_2(y_j)$ for y as

$$p_2(y_j) = \sum_i p(x_i, y_j). \tag{2-67}$$

Similarly, if x and y are continuous variates with joint probability density function $f(x, y)$, the probability density function for x is

$$f_1(x) = \int_{-\infty}^{\infty} f(x, y) \, dy \tag{2-68}$$

and the probability density function for y is

$$f_2(y) = \int_{-\infty}^{\infty} f(x, y) \, dx. \tag{2-69}$$

More generally, when dealing with the joint distribution of s variates we may obtain the joint distribution of a subset of k variables by summing over or integrating out those variables that are no longer required. The resulting expression is called the *marginal probability function* (for discrete random variables) or the *marginal probability density function* (for continuous random variables) of the subset of the remaining variables.

For example, in the dice-tossing example that was introduced earlier the marginal probability distributions for x and y are obtained by summing respectively over the columns and rows of Table 2-5. The results are shown in Table 2-7. We note that $p_1(x)$ is the probability function that we would construct to describe the result in tossing a single die; $p_2(y)$ gives the probability of the second toss yielding a value less than the first toss—that is, $p_2(0)$—or a value equal to or greater than that of the first toss—that is, $p_2(1)$.

Table 2-7   Marginal Probability Functions for
Random Variables x and y with Joint Probability
Functions Shown in Table 2-5

x	1	2	3	4	5	6
$p_1(x)$	$\frac{1}{6}$	$\frac{1}{6}$	$\frac{1}{6}$	$\frac{1}{6}$	$\frac{1}{6}$	$\frac{1}{6}$
y	0	1				
$p_2(y)$	$\frac{5}{12}$	$\frac{7}{12}$				

In the merchandise-shipment problem the marginal density functions for the time of receipt and for the time of request are

$$f_1(x) = \int_0^1 1 \, dy = 1, \qquad 0 \le x \le 1 \tag{2-70}$$

and

$$f_2(y) = \int_0^1 1 \, dx = 1, \qquad 0 \le y \le 1, \tag{2-71}$$

respectively. It is seen in Chapter 3 that (2-70) and (2-71) are univariate uniform distributions.

INDEPENDENCE OF RANDOM VARIABLES

Earlier in this chapter we indicated that the joint probability of two independent events A and B is the product of their individual probabilities—that is,

$$\Pr(AB) = \Pr(A) \Pr(B). \tag{2-9}$$

We now define two *random variables* as *independent* if and only if their joint probability function (or probability density function) is the product

of their marginal probability functions (or probability density functions)—
that is, the random variables x and y are independent if and only if

$$p(x_i, y_j) = p_1(x_i)\, p_2(y_j) \quad \text{for all } x_i \text{ and } y_j \text{ in the discrete case,} \quad (2\text{-}72)$$

and

$$f(x, y) = f_1(x) f_2(y) \qquad \text{for all values of } x \text{ and } y \text{ in the continuous case,} \quad (2\text{-}73)$$

where $p(x_i, y_j)$ and $f(x, y)$ are joint probability and probability density
functions, and $p_1(x_i)$, $p_2(y_j)$, $f_1(x)$ and $f_2(y)$ represent the corresponding
marginal probability and probability density functions.

The variates x and y defined by (2-60) are *not* independent, because

$$p(x_i, y_j) \neq p_1(x_i)\, p_2(y_j)$$

for every x_i and y_j. For example, $p_1(4) = \frac{1}{6}$ and $p_2(0) = \frac{5}{12}$, but

$$p(4, 0) = \frac{3}{36} \neq \left(\frac{1}{6}\right)\left(\frac{5}{12}\right)$$

(see Tables 2-5 and 2-7).

On the other hand, x and y in the merchandise-receipt and -request
problem are independent, for

$$\begin{aligned}
f(x, y) &= 1 & &\text{for } 0 \le x \le 1 \quad \text{and} \quad 0 \le y \le 1, \\
f_1(x) &= 1 & &\text{for } 0 \le x \le 1, \\
f_2(y) &= 1 & &\text{for } 0 \le y \le 1,
\end{aligned}$$

and thus

$$f(x, y) = f_1(x) f_2(y), \quad \text{for } 0 \le x \le 1 \quad \text{and} \quad 0 \le y \le 1.$$

CONDITIONAL DISTRIBUTIONS

In Section 2-5 we discussed nonindependent events and introduced the
subject of conditional probability. In particular, we found

$$\Pr(B \mid A) = \frac{\Pr(AB)}{\Pr(A)}, \quad (2\text{-}12)$$

where $\Pr(B \mid A)$ denotes the conditional probability of B, given A.

In dealing with nonindependent random variables, an analogous concept
is provided by the conditional distribution. Say x and y are two *discrete*
random variables with joint probability function $p(x_i, y_j)$. The *conditional
probability function* of y, given x, denoted by $p(y_j \mid x_i)$, is then the probability function of y, *given* that x is known to take on the value x_i. In a

manner similar to (2-12) it follows that

$$p(y_j \mid x_i) = \frac{p(x_i, y_j)}{p_1(x_i)}, \tag{2-74}$$

where $p_1(x)$ is the marginal probability function of x. Also, if x and y are two *continuous* random variables, the *conditional probability density* of y given x is

$$g(y \mid x) = \frac{f(x, y)}{f_1(x)}. \tag{2-75}$$

The joint conditional probability function and joint conditional density of $(s - k)$ random variables, given the values of the remaining k random variables, are defined in a similar manner.

Let us return to the dice-tossing example dealing with the random variables x and y, defined by (2-60). Say we know that the result of the first toss is a 2—that is, $x_i = 2$. Now, from Table 2-7,

$$p_1(2) = \frac{1}{6}.$$

Thus, using (2-74), the conditional probability function of y, given $x_i = 2$, is

$$p(y_j \mid 2) = \frac{p(2, y_j)}{1/6}.$$

From Table 2-5

$$p(2, 0) = \frac{1}{36},$$

and

$$p(2, 1) = \frac{5}{36}.$$

Therefore

$$p(0 \mid 2) = \frac{1/36}{1/6} = \frac{1}{6}$$

and

$$p(1 \mid 2) = \frac{5/36}{1/6} = \frac{5}{6}.$$

Thus, *after* the first toss has yielded a 2, the chances are one in six that the second toss will yield a smaller value and five in six that it will yield the same or a larger value. This result could have been arrived at more directly by the methods discussed earlier in this chapter.

We note that if x and y are independent random variables the conditional probability function (or conditional probability density) of y, given x, equals the marginal probability function (or marginal probability density) of y; that is

$$p(y_j \mid x_i) = p_2(y_j)$$

for the discrete case and

$$g(y \mid x) = f_2(y)$$

for the continuous case. These expressions are analogous to our previous definition of independent events (see Section 2-3).

DESCRIPTIVE MEASURES FOR MULTIVARIATE DISTRIBUTIONS

Expected values can also be defined for random variables in more than one dimension. In particular, if $h(x, y)$ is a function of the random variables x and y, then

$$E[h(x, y)] = \begin{cases} \displaystyle\int_{-\infty}^{\infty} \int_{-\infty}^{\infty} h(x, y) f(x, y)\, dx\, dy & \begin{array}{l} \text{if } x \text{ and } y \text{ are continuous} \\ \text{random variables with} \\ \text{joint probability density} \\ \text{function } f(x, y), \end{array} \\[1em] \displaystyle\sum_i \sum_j h(x_i, y_j)\, p(x_i, y_j) & \begin{array}{l} \text{if } x \text{ and } y \text{ are discrete} \\ \text{random variables with} \\ \text{joint probability function} \\ p(x_i, y_j). \end{array} \end{cases} \quad (2\text{-}76)$$

For the simple case in which $h(x, y) = x$, (2-76) reduces to

$$E(x) = \begin{cases} \displaystyle\int_{-\infty}^{\infty} \int_{-\infty}^{\infty} x f(x, y)\, dx\, dy = \int_{-\infty}^{\infty} x \int_{-\infty}^{\infty} f(x, y)\, dy\, dx = \int_{-\infty}^{\infty} x f_1(x)\, dx \\ \qquad\qquad\qquad\qquad \text{for the continuous case,} \\[1em] \displaystyle\sum_i \sum_j x_i\, p(x_i, y_j) = \sum_i x_i \sum_j p(x_i, y_j) = \sum_i x_i\, p_1(x_i) \\ \qquad\qquad\qquad\qquad \text{for the discrete case.} \end{cases} \quad (2\text{-}77)$$

This result is in accordance with (2-28).

We now verify (2-36) and (2-36a) for two continuous random variables x and y with joint probability density function $f(x, y)$.

First let $h(x, y) = x + y$.
Then

$$E[x + y] = \int_{-\infty}^{\infty} \int_{-\infty}^{\infty} (x + y) f(x, y)\, dx\, dy$$

$$= \int_{-\infty}^{\infty} \int_{-\infty}^{\infty} x f(x, y)\, dx\, dy + \int_{-\infty}^{\infty} \int_{-\infty}^{\infty} y f(x, y)\, dx\, dy$$

$$= E(x) + E(y).$$

Next let $h(x, y) = b_1 x + b_2 y$.
Then

$$E[h(x, y)] = \int_{-\infty}^{\infty} \int_{-\infty}^{\infty} [b_1 x + b_2 y] f(x, y) \, dx \, dy$$

$$= \int_{-\infty}^{\infty} \int_{-\infty}^{\infty} b_1 x f(x, y) \, dx \, dy + \int_{-\infty}^{\infty} \int_{-\infty}^{\infty} b_2 f(x, y) \, y \, dx \, dy$$

$$= b_1 \, E(x) + b_2 \, E(y).$$

The derivations are the same for the discrete case, except that the integrations are replaced by appropriate summations.

Equations 2-76 and 2-77 can be generalized to more than two dimensions. The resulting expressions may then be used to establish (2-36) and (2-36a) for an arbitrary number of random variables.

We note that when x and y are independent random variables,

$$E(xy) = E(x) \, E(y), \tag{2-78}$$

since in the continuous case we obtain, through (2-73), (2-76), and (2-77),

$$E(xy) = \int_{-\infty}^{\infty} \int_{-\infty}^{\infty} xy \, f(x, y) \, dx \, dy$$

$$= \int_{-\infty}^{\infty} \int_{-\infty}^{\infty} xy \, f_1(x) \, f_2(y) \, dx \, dy$$

$$= \int_{-\infty}^{\infty} x f_1(x) \, dx \int_{-\infty}^{\infty} y f_2(y) \, dy$$

$$= E(x) \, E(y),$$

where the notation is the same as before. A similar result can be obtained for two independent discrete random variables.

In a manner analogous to the variance of a single random variable we define the *covariance* between two variates x and y as

$$\text{Cov}(x, y) = E\{[x - E(x)][y - E(y)]\} \tag{2-79}$$

or

$$\text{Cov}(x, y) = E(xy) - E(x) \, E(y). \tag{2-79a}$$

Note that if x and y are independent,

$$\text{Cov}(x, y) = E(x) \, E(y) - E(x) \, E(y) = 0. \tag{2-80}$$

A standardized measure of the linear relationship between two variates is the *coefficient of correlation*,

$$\rho = \frac{\text{Cov}(x, y)}{[\text{Var}(x) \, \text{Var}(y)]^{1/2}} = \frac{\text{Cov}(x, y)}{\sigma(x) \, \sigma(y)}. \tag{2-81}$$

The covariance has been divided by the standard deviation of each of the variables to obtain a value that is independent of units of measurement. When $\rho = 1.0$, the variates are positively perfectly correlated—that is, $y = kx + c$, where k and c are constants. If $\rho = -1$ the variates are perfectly negatively correlated—that is, $y = -kx + c$. If $\rho = 0$, the

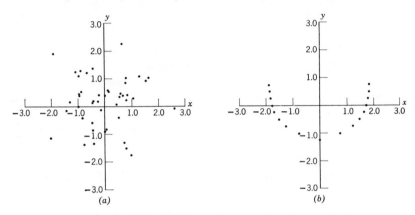

Fig. 2-26   Two plots of data with r approximately equal to 0.

variates are said to be uncorrelated. ρ is estimated from n pairs of observations (x_1, y_1), (x_2, y_2), . . . , (x_n, y_n) as follows:

$$\hat{\rho} = \frac{\sum_{i=1}^{n} (x_i - \bar{x})(y_i - \bar{y})}{\left[\sum_{i=1}^{n} (x_i - \bar{x})^2 \sum_{i=1}^{n} (y_1 - \bar{y})^2\right]^{1/2}}$$

$$= \frac{\sum_{i=1}^{n} x_i y_i - \dfrac{\left(\sum_{i=1}^{n} x_i\right)\left(\sum_{i=1}^{n} y_i\right)}{n}}{\left\{\left[\sum_{i=1}^{n} x_i^2 - \dfrac{\left(\sum_{i=1}^{n} x_i\right)^2}{n}\right]\left[\sum_{i=1}^{n} y_i^2 - \dfrac{\left(\sum_{i=1}^{n} y_i\right)^2}{n}\right]\right\}^{1/2}}. \tag{2-82}$$

$\hat{\rho}$ is also frequently denoted by r. Plots of data with r's of approximately 0 are shown in Figs. 2-26a and -b. The second plot illustrates the fact that the correlation coefficient measures only the *linear* relationship between two variables. Thus, although independence implies zero correlation, the reverse is not true. Data with r's of $+1.0$, -1.0, $+0.9$, $+0.66$, and $+0.33$ are plotted in Fig. 2-27a, -b, -c, -d, and -e, respectively.

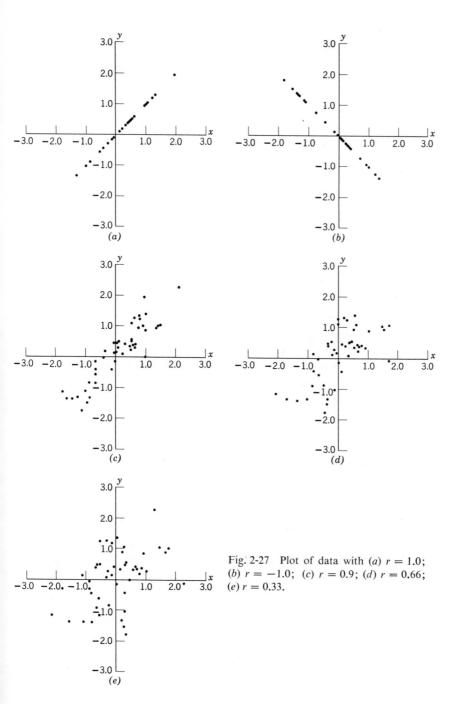

Fig. 2-27 Plot of data with (a) $r = 1.0$; (b) $r = -1.0$; (c) $r = 0.9$; (d) $r = 0.66$; (e) $r = 0.33$.

2-12. *Variance of a Linear Function of a Random Variable*

We frequently desire the variance of a function of one or more random variables, without finding the distribution of the function itself. Approximate procedures for doing this are presented in Chapter 7. In this section we indicate an exact result for a linear function.

Let $x_1, x_2, \ldots, x_n$ be n random variables with expected values $E(x_1)$, $E(x_2), \ldots, E(x_n)$ and variances Var (x_1), Var $(x_2), \ldots,$ Var (x_n), respectively, and with a typical covariance denoted as Cov (x_i, x_j). Then the variance of a linear function of these random variables is

$$\text{Var}\left[\sum_{j=1}^{n} b_j x_j\right] = \sum_{j=1}^{n} b_j^2 \,\text{Var}\,(x_j) + 2 \sum_{\substack{i \ j \\ i<j}} b_i b_j \,\text{Cov}\,(x_i, x_j), \quad (2\text{-}83)$$

where $b_1, b_2, \ldots, b_n$ are constants.

The proof of this result for two random variables, using (2-35), (2-39), and (2-79a), is as follows:

$$\begin{aligned}
\text{Var}\,(b_1 x_1 + b_2 x_2) &= E(b_1 x_1 + b_2 x_2)^2 - [E(b_1 x_1 + b_2 x_2)]^2 \\
&= E(b_1^2 x_1^2 + b_2^2 x_2^2 + 2 b_1 b_2 x_1 x_2) - [b_1 E(x_1) + b_2 E(x_2)]^2 \\
&= b_1^2 \{E(x_1^2) - [E(x_1)]^2\} + b_2^2 \{E(x_2^2) - [E(x_2)]^2\} \\
&\quad + 2 b_1 b_2 [E(x_1 x_2) - E(x_1) E(x_2)] \\
&= b_1^2 \,\text{Var}\,(x_1) + b_2^2 \,\text{Var}\,(x_2) + 2 b_1 b_2 \,\text{Cov}\,(x_1, x_2).
\end{aligned}$$

Generalization of the proof to a linear function of n random variables follows directly from the two-variable case.

The preceding result could be used in the equipment-breakdown example at the end of Section 2-8 to obtain the variance of the total cost per breakdown, assuming that the variances and covariances for delay penalty, material repair cost, and labor repair cost are known.

Note that when the n random variables are uncorrelated, (2-83) reduces to

$$\text{Var}\left[\sum_{j=1}^{n} b_j x_j\right] = \sum_{j=1}^{n} b_j^2 \,\text{Var}\,(x_j). \quad (2\text{-}84)$$

Some additional special cases of (2-83) corresponding to (2-34), (2-35), and (2-36) for expected values are

$$\text{Var}\,(c) = 0, \quad (2\text{-}85)$$

where c is a constant,

$$\text{Var}\,(cx) = c^2 \,\text{Var}\,(x), \quad (2\text{-}86)$$

and

$$\text{Var}\left(\sum_{j=1}^{n} x_j\right) = \sum_{j=1}^{n}\text{Var}\,(x_j) + 2\sum_{\substack{i \\ i<j}}^{n}\sum_{j}^{n}\text{Cov}\,(x_i, x_j). \qquad (2\text{-}87)$$

We are now in a position to consider specific probability distributions in some detail.

References

2-1 W. Feller, *An Introduction to Probability Theory and Its Applications*, rev. ed., John Wiley and Sons, New York, 1957.

2-2 E. Parzen, *Modern Probability Theory and Its Applications*, John Wiley and Sons, New York, 1960.

2-3 A. M. Mood, and F. Graybill, *Introduction to the Theory of Statistics*, rev. ed., McGraw-Hill Book Co., New York, 1963.

2-4 P. G. Hoel, *Introduction to Mathematical Statistics*, 3rd ed., John Wiley and Sons, New York, 1962.

2-5 R. V. Hogg and A. T. Craig, *Introduction to Mathematical Statistics*, 2nd ed., Macmillan Co., New York, 1965.

2-6 D. V. Lindley, *Introduction to Probability and Statistics from a Bayesian Viewpoint*, 2 vols., Cambridge University Press, Cambridge, 1965.

2-7 R. Schlaifer, *Probability and Statistics for Business Decisions*, McGraw-Hill Book Co., New York, 1959.

2-8 M. G. Kendall and A. Stuart, *The Advanced Theory of Statistics*, Vol. 1, Hafner Publishing Co., New York, 1958.

Chapter 3

Continuous Statistical Distributions

This chapter deals with distributions for continuous random variables, used to describe engineering phenomena. Distributions for discrete random variables are discussed in Chapter 4.

The normal or Gaussian distribution is the best known statistical model, and we consider its application in both univariate and bivariate situations. However, many phenomena cannot be adequately described by a normal distribution. Therefore two more versatile models, the gamma and the beta distributions, are introduced. Some special cases—namely the Erlangian, the chi-square, the exponential, the uniform, the right triangular, and the parabolic distributions—are discussed.

Next, three models closely related to the normal distribution—the lognormal, the Rayleigh, and the Cauchy distributions—are described. A discussion of distributions used to represent the life of components and systems follows. These distributions include some of the previous models and also the Weibull and the Type I extreme value distributions. The chapter concludes with a summary of the shapes and applications of continuous distributions, including a list of their means, variances, and third and fourth standardized moments ($\sqrt{\beta_1}$ and β_2).

The choice of a distribution to represent a physical system is generally motivated by an understanding of the nature of the underlying phenomenon and is verified by the available data. After a model has been chosen, its parameters must be determined. We shall be dealing with continuous distributions involving three types of parameters related, respectively, to the location, scale, and shape of the distribution. The Greek letter μ is used to denote location parameters, σ and λ to represent scale parameters, and η and γ for shape parameters. Not all distributions involve one of each of these parameters. For example, the normal distribution has no shape parameter, and the beta distribution has two such parameters. Methods for estimating parameters from given data are indicated for some of the

68

distributions. Tests for the adequacy of the chosen model are discussed in Chapter 8. Empirical distributions, which are sometimes useful in representing data when there is no physical justification for using one of the models discussed in this chapter, are described in Chapter 6.

3-1. The Normal Distribution

NATURE OF MODEL

The *normal (or Gaussian) distribution* is the most frequently used statistical model. Its probability density function is

$$f(x; \mu, \sigma) = \frac{1}{\sigma\sqrt{2\pi}} \exp\left[-\frac{(x-\mu)^2}{2\sigma^2}\right],$$

$$-\infty < x < \infty, -\infty < \mu < \infty, \sigma > 0,$$

(3-1)

where μ and σ are location and scale parameters respectively of the distribution.

The mean or expected value of the normal distribution is, from (2-28),

$$E(x) = \int_{-\infty}^{\infty} x f(x; \mu, \sigma) \, dx$$

$$= \int_{-\infty}^{\infty} x \frac{1}{\sigma\sqrt{2\pi}} \exp\left[-\frac{(x-\mu)^2}{2\sigma^2}\right] dx = \mu.$$

(3-2)

Similarly, from (2-38) or (2-39), we obtain

$$\text{Var}(x) = \sigma^2.$$

(3-2a)

Thus the standard deviation of x is σ. Consequently, the two parameters of the normal distribution, μ and σ, are its mean and standard deviation, respectively. Normal distributions with differing values of μ and a common σ and with different values of σ for a common μ are shown in Figs. 3-1 and 3-2, respectively. All normal distributions are symmetric and have the same shape—that is, the distribution has no shape parameter. Thus the shewness measure μ_3 is zero, irrespective of the value of μ and σ, as can be verified from (2-42). All normal distributions have a relative kurtosis β_2 of 3, as noted in Chaper 2.

From (2-25) the cumulative normal distribution is

$$F(x; \mu, \sigma) = \int_{-\infty}^{x} \frac{1}{\sigma\sqrt{2\pi}} \exp\left[-\frac{(z-\mu)^2}{2\sigma^2}\right] dz.$$

(3-3)

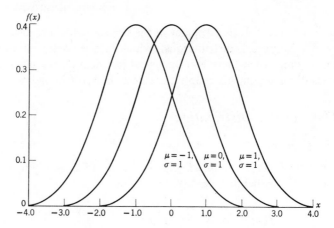

Fig. 3-1 Normal distributions with different values of μ and same σ.

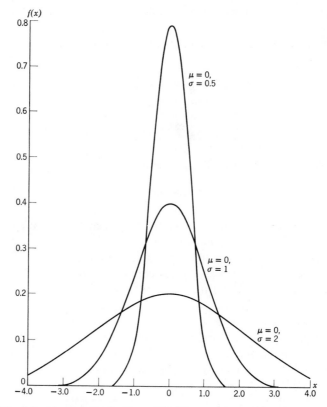

Fig. 3-2 Normal distributions with different values of σ and same μ.

70

This expression gives the probability of a randomly selected value from a normal distribution with parameters μ and σ being less than x. Equivalently, it yields the proportion of observations in the population with values less than x.

Equation 3-3 can be evaluated by approximate methods. The results could be tabulated as a function of μ and σ; however only the tabulation of $F(x)$ for the normal distribution with $\mu = 0$ and $\sigma = 1$, given in Table I at the end of this book, is required. This table can be use to evaluate cumulative probabilities for *any* normal distribution, for, as shown in Chapter 5, if x is normally distributed with arbitrary μ and σ, the random variable

$$y = \frac{x - \mu}{\sigma} \tag{3-4}$$

is normally distributed with $\mu = 0$ and $\sigma = 1$. The variate, y, is known as a *standardized* or *standard normal* variate.

The tables give $F(y; 0, 1)$ for points in the right tail of the distribution only—that is, for $y \geq 0$. The corresponding values for $y < 0$ are obtained from the symmetry of the normal distribution by the relationship

$$F(-y; 0, 1) = 1 - F(y; 0, 1). \tag{3-5}$$

For example, the probability that y is less than 2.5—that is, $F(+2.5; 0, 1)$—is found from Table I to be 0.9938. Consequently, from (3-5)

$$F(-2.5; 0, 1) = 1 - 0.9938 = 0.0062.$$

The use of this table is further illustrated by the following example. Specifications require the length of a part to be between 24 and 25 cm. If part length is a normally distributed random variable with $\mu = 24.6$ cm and $\sigma = 0.4$ cm, what proportion of manufactured units will, on the average, be outside the specification limits?

The problem can be changed by use of (3-4) to one of determining the probability that an observation from a normal distribution with $\mu = 0$ and $\sigma = 1$ either exceeds $(25.0 - 24.6)/0.4 = 1$ or is less than $(24.0 - 24.6)/0.4 = -1.5$ (see Fig. 3-3). From Table I we find $F(1.0; 0, 1) = 0.841$. This is the probability of a value *below* 1.0. Thus the probability of a value *above* 1.0 is $1 - 0.841 = 0.159$. Likewise, $F(1.5; 0, 1) = 0.933$. Then, from (3-5),

$$F(-1.5; 0, 1) = 1 - 0.933 = 0.067,$$

which is the probability of a value *below* -1.5. Consequently, 15.9 and 6.7 per cent of manufactured units will, in the long run, be above and below the specification limits, respectively, and there will be, on the average, a total of 22.6 per cent unacceptable units.

The table of the cumulative normal distribution may be used to verify the statement in Chapter 2 that 68.3, 95.5, and 99.7 per cent of the area under a normal distribution are located, respectively, in the ranges $\mu \pm 1\sigma$, $\mu \pm 2\sigma$, and $\mu \pm 3\sigma$. For example, the chances are about 997 out of 1000 that a randomly selected observation from a normal distribution is within the range $\mu \pm 3\sigma$. (See Fig. 2-20.)

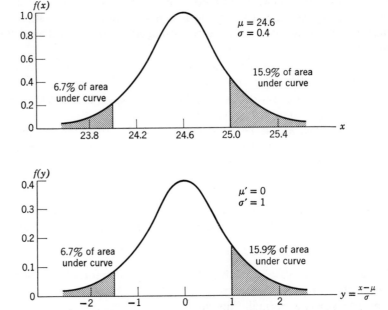

Fig. 3-3   Area in selected tails of normal distribution with $\mu = 24.6$ and $\sigma = 0.4$ and corresponding tails of standardized normal distribution. [From H. Chestnut, *Systems Engineering Tools*, John Wiley and Sons, New York, 1965 (Fig. 6.2-9).]

ADEQUACY OF NORMAL DISTRIBUTION AS A PHYSICAL MODEL

The normal is the most widely used of all distributions. For a long time its importance was exaggerated by the misconception that it was the underlying distribution of nature, and that according to the "Theory of Errors" it was supposed to govern all measurements. With the advent of statistical tests about the year 1900, this assumption was shown not to be universally valid.

Instead, the theoretical justification for the role of the normal distribution is the *central limit theorem*,* one of the most important results of

---

* More precisely, *a* central limit theorem, since there are a number of such theorems in statistics.

mathematical statistics. This theorem states that the distribution of the *mean* of n independent observations from *any distribution*, or even from up to n different distributions, with finite mean and variance approaches a normal distribution as the number of observations in the sample becomes large—that is, as n approaches infinity. The result holds, ir-respective of the distribution of each of the n elements making up the average.

Although the central limit theorem is concerned with large samples, the sample mean tends to be normally distributed even for relatively small n as long as no single element or small group of elements has a dominating variance and the element distributions do not deviate extremely from a normal distribution.

In fact the central limit theorem is used as a technique for generating random normal variates. One such scheme averages seven uniform de-viates—that is, seven random samples from a uniform distribution (see Section 3-3)—to obtain a random deviate that is approximately normally distributed. The use of the central limit theorem is illustrated in Chapter 7 in an example dealing with the total time required to check out a system in a multistation test and repair facility.

When a random variable represents the total effect of a large number of independent "small" causes, the central limit theorem thus leads us to expect the distribution of that variable to be normal. Furthermore, *empirical evidence* has indicated that the normal distribution provides a good representation for many physical variables. Examples include measurements on living organisms, molecular velocities in a gas, scores on an intelligence test, average temperatures in a given locality, and random electrical noise. Instrumentation error is also often normally distributed either around the true value or around some average bias. The normal distribution has the further advantage for many problems that it is tract-able mathematically. Consequently, many of the techniques of statistical inference, such as the method known as the "analysis of variance," have been derived under the assumption that the data come from a normal distribution.

Because of the prominence, and perhaps the name, of the normal dis-tribution, it is sometimes assumed that a random variable is normally distributed unless proven otherwise. Therefore it should be clearly recog-nized that many random variables *cannot* be reasonably regarded as the sum of many small effects, and consequently there is no theoretical reason for expecting a normal distribution. This could be the case when one nonnormal effect is predominant.

Further, the range of a normally distributed variate is minus to plus infinity; however, most physical variables have upper or lower limits and sometimes both.* This does not preclude using a normal distribution to represent such variables as adult height, where the average value is many standard deviations removed from the value zero and the error in asuming plus and minus infinity as bounds is negligible. However, there are other variables for which values concentrated close to some physical boundary are quite common—for example, per cent yield in a manufacturing process or time to failure of a system. In such cases the normal distribution, or any other symmetrical representation, is inadequate. Finally, it should be noted that for some random variables a normal distribution provides a reasonable approximation in the center, but *is inadequate at one or both tails of the distribution.*

The errors of incorrectly assuming normality depend upon the use to which this assumption is put. Many statistical methods derived under this assumption remain valid under moderate deviations and are thus said to be *robust.* The analysis of variance is an example of a method that is robust under deviations from normality. On the other hand, if the normality assumption were used incorrectly in such problems as determining the proportion of manufactured items above or below some extreme design limit at the tail of the distribution, serious errors might result.

ESTIMATION OF NORMAL DISTRIBUTION PARAMETERS AND
CONFIDENCE INTERVAL ON μ

In many problems μ and σ are not known and must be estimated from the available data. Since, for the normal distribution, the parameter μ is the population mean, (2-31) may be used to estimate μ—that is,

$$\hat{\mu} = \bar{x} = \frac{\sum_{i=1}^{n} x_i}{n}, \tag{2-31}$$

where $x_i, i = 1, 2, \ldots, n$, are the values of the n data points, and the hat on the μ denotes an estimate.

Also, since the parameter σ is the standard deviation of the normal distribution, we obtain from (2-51) the estimate

$$\hat{\sigma} = \sqrt{m_2} = \left[\frac{\sum_{i=1}^{n} (x_i - \bar{x})^2}{n} \right]^{1/2} = \left[\frac{\sum_{i=1}^{n} x_i^2}{n} - \frac{\left(\sum_{i=1}^{n} x_i \right)^2}{n^2} \right]^{1/2}, \tag{3-6}$$

---

* In some applications we encounter a truncated normal distribution—that is, a normal distribution with one or both tails removed. Such a model would apply, for example, in sampling from a normal process from which all elements below and/or above some specification limits have been removed initially. See References 3-49 and 3-52 for further details.

or, using (2-51*a*),

$$s = \left[\frac{\sum\limits_{i=1}^{n} (x_i - \bar{x})^2}{n - 1} \right]^{1/2} = \left[\frac{n \sum\limits_{i=1}^{n} x_i^2 - \left(\sum\limits_{i=1}^{n} x_i \right)^2}{n(n - 1)} \right]^{1/2}. \tag{3-7}$$

Because of theoretical considerations (see Chapter 2), (3-7) is used more frequently than (3-6). For large n it makes little difference which expression is used.

An alternate graphical procedure for estimating μ and σ is given in Chapter 8 in conjunction with the discussion of probability plotting.

The value $\bar{x}$ is a random variable whose variance depends on n, the number of observations, and on the population variance, as estimated by s^2. A measure of the precision of $\bar{x}$ as an estimate of the unknown parameter μ can be obtained from a *confidence interval*. A precise definition of a $(1 - \alpha)100$ per cent confidence interval for μ would involve the following statement: "If in a series of very many repeated experiments an interval such as the one calculated were obtained, we would in the long run be correct $(1 - \alpha)100$ per cent of the time in claiming that μ is located in the interval (and wrong 100α per cent of the time)." Unfortunately, such a statement is sometimes difficult to comprehend for the nonstatistician and awkward to interpret operationally. Therefore we shall consider a $(1 - \alpha)100$ per cent confidence interval as a range within which we are $(1 - \alpha)100$ per cent sure that the true parameter is contained, recognizing that this interpretation takes liberties with the strict classical definition (because the true parameter is not normally regarded as a random variable). The values of $1 - \alpha$ most commonly used are 0.90, 0.95, and 0.99, and these are known as the *confidence levels* associated with the interval.

Returning to the problem of determining the precision of our estimate of the normal distribution parameter μ, a confidence interval for μ is calculated as

$$\bar{x} \pm (t_{CL,n-1}) \frac{s}{\sqrt{n}}, \tag{3-8}$$

where $\bar{x}$ and s are obtained from the n observations by (2-31) and (3-7), respectively, and where $t_{CL,n-1}$ is given in Table II at the end of the book for different values of $n - 1$ for the confidence levels, $CL = 1 - \alpha = 0.90$, 0.95, and 0.99.* The following example illustrates the procedure.

Viscosity is determined for a random sample of nine test units. From the data an average $\bar{x} = 10$ and a standard deviation $s = 2$ are calculated.

---

* These values are obtained from the percentiles of a probability density function known as Student's t distribution; see Chapter 6.

Assuming that viscosity is a normally distributed variate, a 95 per cent confidence interval for the unknown true mean μ is desired.

Referring to Table II for $n - 1 = 8$ and a confidence level $CL = 1 - \alpha = 0.95$, we obtain $t_{CL,n-1} = t_{0.95,8} = 2.31$. Equation 3-8 thus yields the interval $10 \pm 2.31(2/\sqrt{9})$. The 95 per cent confidence interval for μ is therefore $(8.46, 11.54)$—that is, we are 95 per cent sure that μ is between 8.46 and 11.54. If tighter limits were desired, additional observations would be required.

If we are interested in only a lower bound, $\bar{x}_L$—that is, a value that we are $(1 - \alpha)100$ per cent sure the true mean does not fall below—or an upper bound $\bar{x}_U$, the appropriate formulae are

$$\bar{x}_L = \bar{x} - (t'_{CL,n-1}) \frac{s}{\sqrt{n}} \tag{3-9}$$

and

$$\bar{x}_U = \bar{x} + (t'_{CL,n-1}) \frac{s}{\sqrt{n}}, \tag{3-10}$$

where $t'_{CL,n-1}$ is tabulated in Table III at the back of the book for different values of $n - 1$ and confidence levels $CL = 1 - \alpha = 0.90, 0.95,$ and 0.99. Equations 3-9 and 3-10 thus provide intervals on one side of the mean, in contrast to the two-sided interval given by (3-8).

In the preceding example we find from Table III that $t'_{0.95,8} = 1.86$. Consequently, from (3-9), the 95 per cent *lower* confidence bound on μ is $10 - 1.86(2/\sqrt{9})$—that is, the one-sided 95 per cent confidence interval is found to be $(8.76, \infty)$. Thus we are 95 per cent sure that μ is *at least* 8.76. In a similar fashion, a 95 per cent *upper* confidence bound on μ is found from (3-10) to be 11.24, leading to the one-sided 95 per cent confidence interval $(-\infty, 11.24)$.

We shall not show the calculation of confidence intervals for the parameters of all the distributions discussed in this and the following chapter, but shall consider only the simpler and more important cases.* The subject is treated in detail and more precisely in texts on statistical methods, such as References 3-1 to 3-6.

The preceding discussion deals with an interval concerning the information about some *parameter*. For example, in the viscosity problem we were 95 per cent confident that the true value of μ was between 8.46 and 11.54. This is clearly *not* the same as saying that 95 per cent of the observations in the population are located within this interval. In fact, as can be seen from (3-8), the interval for μ can be made as small as desired by increasing the sample size sufficiently. Thus increased precision in our knowledge

---

* For example, we do not indicate how to obtain a confidence interval for the normal distribution parameter σ.

of a parameter should not be confused with improvement of the product. By obtaining more viscosity readings, the estimate of average viscosity is improved, but the distribution of viscosity remains the same. An interval within which we can state with a given probability of being correct that at least a prespecified proportion of values from a sampled distribution are located, is known as a *statistical tolerance interval.* Tabulations of factors to calculate such intervals for a normal distribution based on an $\bar{x}$ and s calculated from n observations are given in References 3-5 and 3-50. A procedure for obtaining a tolerance interval when *no* assumptions about the form of the underlying population is made is described in Section 3-3.

THE HALF-NORMAL DISTRIBUTION

In some applications we deal with a normally distributed variate in which only the absolute deviations around the mean are known. By the methods of Chapter 5 it can be shown that this leads to the following probability density function, known as the *half-normal distribution*:

$$f(x; \sigma) = \begin{cases} [2/(\pi\sigma^2)]^{1/2} e^{-x^2/2\sigma^2} & x \geq 0, \sigma > 0, \\ 0 & \text{elsewhere,} \end{cases} \tag{3-10a}$$

where σ is a scale parameter which, however, does *not* equal the distribution standard deviation. This distribution is plotted in Fig. 3-4.

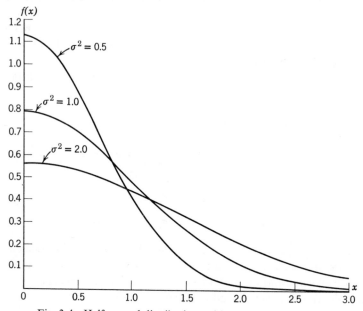

Fig. 3-4 Half-normal distributions with various values of σ^2.

The following example illustrates a typical use of the half-normal distribution. A flywheel of a motor is assembled from two parts of the same type. It is important that these parts have approximately the same weight so that the wheel will be balanced. Thus we desire to know the distribution of the difference in the weight of the two parts. Because the parts are arbitrarily paired, only the magnitude of their difference in weights is recorded. If the weights of the original parts are normally distributed, the absolute value of the weight difference follows a half-normal distribution.

Other examples of the use of the half-normal distribution are given in Reference 3-51, together with tables of cumulative probabilities and methods of parameter estimation. This reference discusses the more general *folded normal distribution*, for which the recorded deviations occur about an arbitrary point, rather than about the mean of the original distribution. This leads to a "folding" of one tail of the original distribution on to the rest of the distribution. A folded normal distribution would have resulted in the preceding problem if the two parts whose difference in weight is of interest came from normal distributions with *different* means.

THE BIVARIATE NORMAL DISTRIBUTION

A multivariate extension of the univariate normal distribution, known as the *multivariate normal distribution*, is frequently used to describe the joint behavior of two or more variables. A detailed discussion of this distribution is beyond the scope of this book; the interested reader is referred to Reference 3-46. However a brief description of the two-variate or *bivariate normal distribution* is given below.

The bivariate normal probability density function for the random variables x and y is

$$f(x, y; \mu_x, \mu_y, \sigma_x, \sigma_y, \rho) = [4\pi^2 \sigma_y^2 \sigma_x^2 (1 - \rho^2)]^{-\frac{1}{2}}$$

$$\times \exp\left\{-\frac{1}{2(1 - \rho^2)}\left[\left(\frac{x - \mu_x}{\sigma_x}\right)^2 - \frac{2\rho(x - \mu_x)(y - \mu_y)}{\sigma_x \sigma_y} + \left(\frac{y - \mu_y}{\sigma_y}\right)^2\right]\right\},$$

$$-\infty < x < \infty, \; -\infty < y < \infty, \; -\infty < \mu_x < \infty,$$

$$-\infty < \mu_y < \infty, \; \sigma_x > 0, \; \sigma_y > 0, \; -1 \leqslant \rho \leqslant 1. \tag{3-10b}$$

A bivariate normal distribution is shown in Fig. 3-5. The significance of the parameters μ_x, μ_y, σ_x, σ_y, and ρ is as follows. From (3-2) and (3-2a), the expected value and variance of a random variable following a univariate normal distribution were found to equal μ and σ^2, respectively. If x and y are jointly distributed according to a bivariate normal distribution, μ_x

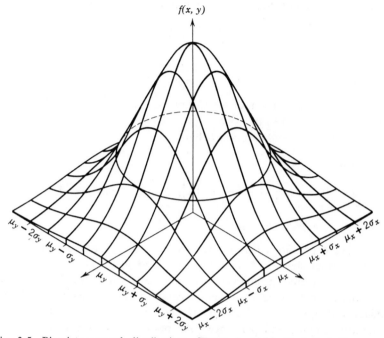

$f(x, y)$

Fig. 3-5 Bivariate normal distribution. [From A. Hald, *Statistical Theory with Engineering Applications*, John Wiley and Sons, New York, 1952 (Fig. 19.1).]

and μ_y are the expected values of these two variates—that is, using (2-77),

$$E(x) = \int_{-\infty}^{\infty} \int_{-\infty}^{\infty} x f(x, y; \mu_x, \mu_y, \sigma_x, \sigma_y, \rho) \, dx \, dy = \mu_x$$

and

$$E(y) = \int_{-\infty}^{\infty} \int_{-\infty}^{\infty} y f(x, y; \mu_x, \mu_y, \sigma_x, \sigma_y, \rho) \, dx \, dy = \mu_y.$$

Similarly, σ_x^2 and σ_y^2 are the variances of x and y—that is, by applying (2-76),

$$\text{Var}(x) = E[(x - E(x))^2]$$

$$= \int_{-\infty}^{\infty} \int_{-\infty}^{\infty} (x - \mu_x)^2 f(x, y; \mu_x, \mu_y, \sigma_x, \sigma_y, \rho) \, dx \, dy = \sigma_x^2$$

and

$$\text{Var}(y) = E[(y - E(y))^2]$$

$$= \int_{-\infty}^{\infty} \int_{-\infty}^{\infty} (y - \mu_y)^2 f(x, y; \mu_x, \mu_y, \sigma_x, \sigma_y, \rho) \, dx \, dy = \sigma_y^2.$$

It can also be shown that the covariance between x and y [see (2-79)] is

$$\text{Cov}(x, y) = \rho \sigma_x \sigma_y,$$

and thus

$$\rho = \frac{\text{Cov}(x, y)}{\sigma_x \sigma_y}$$

—that is, ρ is the coefficient of correlation between x and y [see (2-81)], and measures the relationship between the two variates.

When $\rho = 0$, (3-10b) can be written

$$f(x, y; \mu_x, \mu_y, \sigma_x, \sigma_y, 0)$$

$$= \left\{ (2\pi\sigma_x^2)^{-\frac{1}{2}} \exp\left[-\frac{1}{2}\left(\frac{x - \mu_x}{\sigma_x}\right)^2 \right] \right\} \left\{ (2\pi\sigma_y^2)^{-\frac{1}{2}} \exp\left[-\frac{1}{2}\left(\frac{y - \mu_y}{\sigma_y}\right)^2 \right] \right\}$$

$$= f_1(x; \mu_x, \sigma_x) f_2(y; \mu_y, \sigma_y).$$

The above expressions $f_1(x; \mu_x, \sigma_x)$ and $f_2(y; \mu_y, \sigma_y)$ are seen to be univariate normal densities. Thus, when x and y are bivariate normally distributed random variables with $\rho = 0$, their joint probability density function equals the product of their marginal densities—that is, x and y are independent if and only if $\rho = 0$. Hence for a *normal* distribution zero correlation implies independence. As pointed out in Chapter 2, zero correlation does not *in general* imply independence for jointly distributed variates.

The parameters μ_x and σ_x may be estimated from data, using (2-31) and (3-7), with μ_y and σ_y obtained similarly, using the observed values of y. Equation 2-82 is generally used to estimate ρ.

The joint distribution of the height and weight of individuals, the distribution in the x and y coordinates of bullets aimed at a target, and the distribution of the real and imaginary components of a sum of electrical impedances are several examples of the practical applications of the bivariate normal distribution.

Probability statements concerning variates that follow a bivariate normal distribution can be made with the help of appropriate tabulations. For example, we might want to determine the following:

1. That value $1 - \alpha$ which satisfies

$$\Pr\left[(b_1(x - \mu_x)^2 + b_2(y - \mu_y)^2) \leq k\right] = 1 - \alpha$$

for specified b_1, b_2, and k. This yields the probability that a randomly selected value from a given bivariate normal distribution will be located within a specified ellipse that is centered at the point (μ_x, μ_y) in the x-y plane.

2. That value k which yields an ellipse such that $\Pr\,[(b_1(x - \mu_x)^2 + b_2(y - \mu_y)^2) \leq k] = 1 - \alpha$ for given b_1 and b_2, where $1 - \alpha$ is a value such as 0.50, 0.75, 0.90, or 0.99. This yields an ellipse centered at (μ_x, μ_y) within which we can state with a specified probability that a randomly selected value from a given bivariate normal distribution will be located.

Tabulations for these two situations are given in Sections 8.3 and 8.4 of Reference 3.50 respectively.* These tabulations are applicable to such problems as determining the probability that a bullet aimed at a target will fall within a specified ellipse or finding a circle around the target point (in this case, $b_1 = b_2 = 1$) so that the chances are 9 out of 10 that the bullet will be located within it. References to other tabulations, including those dealing with an offset ellipse [i.e., one that is *not* centered at (μ_x, μ_y)], are also given in Reference 3.50.

In other situations we would like to find

$$\Pr\,(x_1 \leq x \leq x_2 \text{ and } y_1 \leq y \leq y_2) = \int_{y_1}^{y_2} \int_{x_1}^{x_2} f(x, y; \mu_x, \mu_y, \sigma_x, \sigma_y, \rho)\,dx\,dy$$

—that is, to determine the probability of an observation from a bivariate normal distribution being within a specified rectangle or, more generally, within a specified polygon. Such probabilities can be obtained from tabulations given in References 3-50 (Section 8-5) and 3-59.

Consider the following example. The reverse breakdown voltage (x) and forward voltage (y) at some designated measurement points for a particular type of semiconductor diode follow a bivariate normal distribution with $\mu_x = 100$ volts, $\mu_y = 0.7$ volt, $\sigma_x = 5$ volts, $\sigma_y = 0.07$ volt, $\rho = 0.5$. The values of a sample of 100 diodes are shown in Fig. 3-6.

Suppose that all diodes with reverse breakdown voltages below 95 volts and/or forward voltage below 0.65 volt are rejected, and it is desired to determine the proportion of process rejects. This requires finding the relative area under a bivariate normal distribution in the rejection region shown in Fig. 3-6.

This probability is found to be 0.08 with the aid of the tabulations in Section 8-5 of Reference 3-50. It can be seen that a bivariate distribution is required in this problem on account of the correlation between the two variables. An erroneous result would have been obtained if we had determined the proportion of rejects due to reverse breakdown voltage and forward voltage *separately*, using two univariate normal distributions, and then combined the results under the incorrect assumption of independence.

* When $b_1\sigma_x^2 = b_2\sigma_y^2 = 1$ and $\rho = 0$, more direct methods are applicable, for in this special case $b_1(x - \mu_x)^2 + b_2(y - \mu_y)^2$ follows a chi-square distribution with two degrees of freedom; see later discussion in this chapter and Chapter 5 and References 3-1 and 3-52.

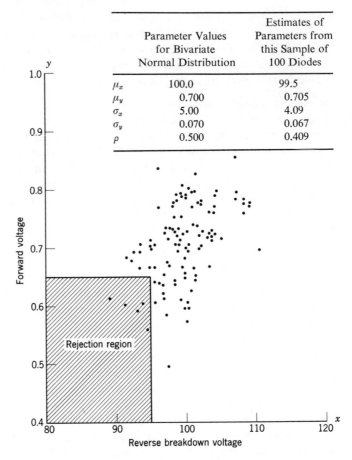

	Parameter Values for Bivariate Normal Distribution	Estimates of Parameters from this Sample of 100 Diodes
μ_x	100.0	99.5
μ_y	0.700	0.705
σ_x	5.00	4.09
σ_y	0.070	0.067
ρ	0.500	0.409

Fig. 3-6   Random sample of 100 semiconductor diodes from bivariate normal distribution for reverse breakdown voltage and forward voltage, with rejection region shown.

From the preceding discussion of the bivariate normal distribution, the generalization to multivariate normal distributions for three or more random variables should be evident. For example, the trivariate normal distribution for the random variables x, y, and z involves the nine parameters μ_x, μ_y, μ_z, σ_x, σ_y, σ_z, ρ_{xy}, ρ_{xz}, and ρ_{yz}.

This model is frequently applicable in describing the location of objects in space whose precise position is subject to random variations, as in determining the trajectory of a space vehicle, or for problems involving three performance properties, as would be the case in the preceding example if a third property, such as resistivity, were added to the specifications. Probabilities for the trivariate normal distribution, similar to those for the bivariate normal distribution, may be obtained from tabulations given in Sections 8-7, 8-8 and 8-9 of Reference 3-50.

3-2. The Gamma and Related Distributions

NATURE OF MODEL

The *gamma distribution* is used to describe random variables bounded at one end. The *beta distribution*, which is discussed in the next section, can represent variates that vary over an interval.

The gamma probability density function is

$$f(x; \eta, \lambda) = \begin{cases} \dfrac{\lambda^\eta}{\Gamma(\eta)} x^{\eta-1}e^{-\lambda x}, & x \geq 0, \qquad \lambda > 0, \eta > 0, \\ 0 & \text{elsewhere.} \end{cases} \tag{3-11}$$

where $\Gamma(\eta)$ is the well known gamma function

$$\Gamma(\eta) = \int_0^\infty x^{\eta-1}e^{-x}\,dx \tag{3-12}$$

and $\Gamma(\eta) = (\eta - 1)!$ when η is a positive integer.

Plots of the gamma probability density function for various values of η and a common λ are shown in Fig. 3-7. It is seen that a wide variety of shapes are obtained. In particular, the distribution is a reverse J-shaped curve for $\eta \leq 1$ and is single peaked, with the peak at $x = (\eta - 1)/\lambda$, for $\eta > 1$. The effect of changing λ for a constant η is illustrated in Fig. 3-8. Varying λ does not change the form of the distribution, but only its scaling. Consequently, η and λ are shape and scale parameters respectively.

The gamma distribution is the appropriate model for the time required for a total of exactly η independent events to take place if events occur at a constant rate λ. This suggests numerous applications. For example, if a part is ordered in *lots* of size η and demand for individual *parts* arises independently and at a constant rate λ per week, the time between lot depletions is a gamma variate. Similarly, system time to failure is gamma distributed if system failure occurs as soon as exactly η subfailures have taken place and if subfailures occur independently at a constant rate λ. (See Section 3-5 for further discussion of the gamma distribution in life testing.) Also, the time between consecutive maintenance operations for an instrument that needs recalibration after exactly η uses, or for an airplane that is inspected after every η missions, is a gamma variate under the appropriate conditions. Thus the gamma distribution plays an important role in statistical queueing theory, which deals with waiting lines and customer servicing problems (see References 3-7 to 3-9).

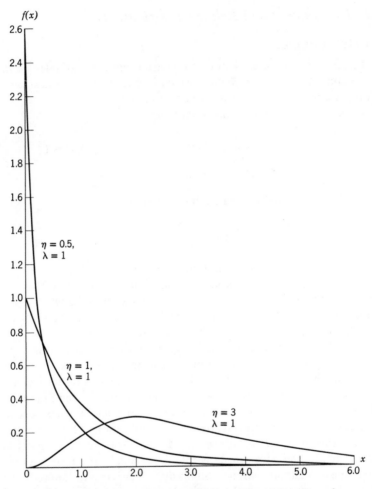

Fig. 3-7   Gamma distributions with $\lambda = 1$ and various values of η.

Many phenomena that cannot be justified theoretically as gamma variates have been found *empirically* to be well approximated by this model. Examples include the distribution of family income and the time to failure for capacitors. The gamma distribution is also used frequently in Bayesian analyses as a prior model to describe initial uncertainty concerning the rate of occurrence of some process, such as the failure rate of a system. For further details, see Reference 3-10.

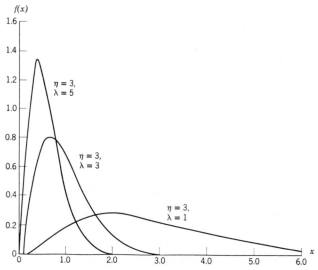

Fig. 3-8   Gamma distributions with $\eta = 3$ and various values of λ.

The wide variety of gamma-distribution shapes might account for the frequent use of this model.

We shall see in Chapter 6, however, that the gamma distribution is only a special case of an even wider family of distributions.

The cumulative gamma distribution

$$F(x; \eta, \lambda) = \begin{cases} \dfrac{\lambda^{\eta}}{\Gamma(\eta)} \displaystyle\int_{0}^{x} t^{\eta-1} e^{-\lambda t}\, dt, & x \geq 0, \\ 0, & x < 0, \end{cases} \tag{3-13}$$

known as the *incomplete gamma function*, is tabulated in References 3-15 and 3-54. In using these tables to determine the probability that a random value from a gamma distribution with parameters λ and η takes on a value less than x, we first determine

$$u = \frac{\lambda x}{\sqrt{\eta}}, \tag{3-14}$$

and then let

$$p = \eta - 1. \tag{3-15}$$

We then find $I(u, p)$ from the tables. This value is the desired cumulative probability, $F(x; \eta, \lambda)$. The following example illustrates the use of the tables.

A ferry boat departs for a trip across a river as soon as exactly nine automobiles have arrived at a terminal. During a given period, automobiles arrive independently at an average rate of six per hour. Determine

(a) the probability that the time between consecutive trips will be less than one hour, and (b) the time t between departures that has a 1 per cent probability of being exceeded.

From the previous discussion, it follows that the time between ferry boat departures is a gamma variate with $\eta = 9$ and $\lambda = 6$. The first part of the problem thus requires evaluation of $F(1; 9, 6)$ in (3-13). From (3-14),

$$u = \frac{\lambda x}{\sqrt{\eta}} = \frac{6(1)}{\sqrt{9}} = 2.0,$$

and setting $p = \eta - 1 = 8$, we find from the tables in Reference 3-15 or 3-54 that

$$I(2.0, 8) = F(1; 9, 6) = 0.153.$$

Thus the probability is 0.153 that the time between consecutive departures is less than one hour.

The second question requires determining the 99th percentile of the distribution—that is, finding that value of x that satisfies

$$0.99 = F(x; 9, 6) = \frac{6^9}{\Gamma(9)} \int_0^x t^8 e^{-6t} \, dt.$$

This requires working backward from the tabulated values. In particular, we find $I(u, 8) = 0.99$ when $u = 5.8$. Thus from (3-14), $5.8 = (6x/\sqrt{9})$ and $x = 2.90$ hours—that is, the chances are one in a hundred that time between departures will exceed 2.9 hours. It would also have been possible to obtain this value directly from a tabulation of percentiles of the gamma distribution given in Reference 3-11.

NORMAL-DISTRIBUTION APPROXIMATION TO THE GAMMA DISTRIBUTION

From the formulation of the gamma distribution as a model for the time required for exactly η events to take place, assuming events occur independently at a constant rate, it can be shown by a cental limit theorem that the gamma distribution approaches a normal distribution as η increases. The expected value and variance of a gamma variate x are η/λ and η/λ^2, respectively; thus it follows that

$$y = \frac{x - \eta/\lambda}{\eta^{1/2}/\lambda}$$

is approximately a standardized normal variate for large η. Thus in the preceding problem the probability of a delay of less than one hour is seen from (3-3) to be approximately

$$F\left(1; \mu = \frac{\eta}{\lambda}, \sigma = \frac{\eta^{1/2}}{\lambda}\right) = \int_{-\infty}^{1} \frac{\lambda}{\sqrt{2\pi\eta}} \exp\left[-\frac{\lambda^2(z - \eta/\lambda)^2}{2\eta}\right] dz.$$

Because $\eta = 9$ and $\lambda = 6$, the standardized normal variate is

$$y = \frac{1 - 9/6}{(9)^{1/2}/6} = -1.$$

Thus from Table I the desired probability is approximately $F(-1; 0, 1) = 0.159$, which differs only slightly from the previous more exact result.

In the second part of the problem the 99th percentile of the distribution for time between departures is required. Using the normal distribution approximation, we set $F(y; 0, 1) = 0.99$. From Table I we find $y = 2.33$. Hence the desired time x is the solution to

$$2.33 = \frac{x - (9/6)}{(9)^{1/2}/6},$$

or $x = 3.16$ hours, which differs by about 10 per cent from the previous exact answer. Better agreement would be expected at a condition that is not as far in the distribution tails.

ESTIMATION OF GAMMA-DISTRIBUTION PARAMETERS

Frequently, one or both parameters of the gamma distribution have to be estimated from engineering data. There are several methods for doing this. The first, based on the method of maximum likelihood, is explained in Reference 3-12, where charts to simplify the calculations and a method for obtaining confidence intervals for the parameters are also given. For many engineering problems the following simpler, less precise expressions,* based on the method of matching moments, can be used:

$$\hat{\lambda} = \frac{\bar{x}(n-1)}{\sum\limits_{i=1}^{n} (x_i - \bar{x})^2} = \frac{\bar{x}}{s^2} \tag{3-16}$$

where $\bar{x}$ and s^2 are defined by (2-31) and (2-51a) and the x_i, $i = 1, 2, \ldots,$ n, are the observed values.

---

* The method of maximum likelihood involves taking as the estimate for each unknown parameter the value that appears most probable on the basis of the given data. The method of matching moments requires expression of the distribution parameters in terms of low distribution moments, substitution of the moments estimated from the given data, and a solution to obtain parameter estimates. For the gamma distribution the mean and variance equal η/λ and η/λ^2, respectively. Setting these equal to the data mean and variance (we have used the unbiased estimate of the variance, see Equation 2-51a) yields two equations that are solved to obtain estimates for λ and η. If the distribution involved three parameters, a third equation would be obtained by setting the third distribution moment equal to the corresponding calculated moment, and so on.

Equivalently,

$$\hat{\lambda} = (n-1) \left[\frac{\sum\limits_{i=1}^{n} x_i}{n \sum\limits_{i=1}^{n} x_i^2 - \left(\sum\limits_{i=1}^{n} x_i \right)^2} \right]. \qquad (3\text{-}16a)$$

The estimate of η is

$$\hat{\eta} = \frac{\bar{x}^2(n-1)}{\sum\limits_{i=1}^{n} (x_i - \bar{x})^2} \qquad (3\text{-}17)$$

or

$$\hat{\eta} = \hat{\lambda}\bar{x}. \qquad (3\text{-}17a)$$

The following example illustrates the above procedure.

The elapsed time between the placement of an order and its receipt is believed to follow a gamma distribution. The elapsed times for 20 random orders are shown in Table 3-1. From this information estimates of the parameters η and λ are desired.

Table 3-1   Elapsed Time Between Day of Order
and Day of Receipt for 20 Orders

Order Number	Elapsed Time in Days
1	10
2	10
3	6
4	11
5	8
6	7
7	11
8	12
9	12
10	6
11	10
12	6
13	13
14	8
15	12
16	7
17	6
18	16
19	9
20	5

From the given data,

$$n = 20, \qquad \sum_{i=1}^{n} x_i = 185, \qquad \sum_{i=1}^{n} x_i^2 = 1875.$$

Thus from (3-16a) and (3-17a)

$$\hat{\lambda} = 19 \frac{185}{20(1875) - (185)^2} = 1.07$$

and

$$\hat{\eta} = \frac{185}{20}(1.08) = 9.99.$$

In many applications of the gamma distribution η is known and only λ need be estimated from the data. For example, in representing the time required for η independent events to take place, only the rate of occurrence λ might be unknown. When the gamma distribution is used as a time-to-failure model, η might be the same for all types of a component and might be known from theoretical considerations or past experience. In such situations, λ may be estimated by (3-17a) or by probability plotting (see Chapter 8).

Occasionally, the exact values of all data points beyond some limit are unknown, as in a life test when all unfailed units are removed at a predetermined time T, or when testing is terminated as soon as exactly k failures have taken place. Such samples are said to be *censored*.* Procedures for estimating the gamma distribution parameters from censored data are given in Reference 3-13.

GENERALIZED FORM OF GAMMA DISTRIBUTION

A gamma variate has so far been assumed to take on values from zero to infinity. However, it is possible to define this distribution over some other interval, say μ to infinity. This leads to the three-parameter gamma distribution,

$$f(x; \eta, \lambda, \mu) = \begin{cases} \dfrac{\lambda^{\eta}}{\Gamma(\eta)} (x - \mu)^{\eta-1} e^{-\lambda(x-\mu)}, & x \geq \mu, \lambda > 0, \eta > 0, \\ 0 & \text{elsewhere.} \end{cases} \tag{3-18}$$

---

* A subtle difference exists between censored data and data from a truncated distribution. In the truncated case the distribution ends at the truncation point. It is therefore impossible to obtain samples beyond this point. When dealing with censored data, there is, in addition to the samples whose values have been recorded, a known number of points about which nothing is known *other than* that they are beyond some value(s). Thus in a manufacturing process in which readings are taken for all units within specification limits and items outside limits are rejected, keeping a count only of the number of such rejects, censored data are obtained. The customer who receives shipment only of the accepted units and takes their readings is dealing with a truncated distribution.

Cumulative probabilities may be obtained for this distribution by letting $x' = x - \mu$ and proceeding as for the two-parameter gamma distribution.

SPECIAL CASES OF THE GAMMA DISTRIBUTION: THE ERLANGIAN, CHI-SQUARE AND EXPONENTIAL DISTRIBUTIONS

In the definition of the gamma distribution (3-11) η can take on any positive value, although the formulation of the gamma distribution as the time required for η events to occur implied that η is a positive integer. When η is restricted to integers, the gamma distribution has been referred to as the *Erlangian distribution*. This nomenclature is most generally encountered in queueing theory.

The chi-square distribution is a special case of the gamma distribution when $\lambda = \frac{1}{2}$ and η is a multiple of $\frac{1}{2}$. This distribution thus has only a single parameter, the integer $\gamma = 2\eta$, generally referred to as its *degrees of freedom*. Applications of this distribution arise from the fact that the sum of the squares of the values of γ random observations from a standardized normal distribution has a chi-square distribution with γ degrees of freedom. This result is derived in Chapter 5.

The exponential distribution (or more precisely, the negative exponential distribution) introduced in Chapter 2 and shown in Fig. 3-7 is a gamma distribution with $\eta = 1$. Its probability density function is thus

$$f(x; \lambda) = \lambda e^{-\lambda x}, \qquad x \geq 0, \lambda > 0. \tag{3-19}$$

The cumulative distribution function is

$$F(x; \lambda) = \int_0^x \lambda e^{-\lambda t}\, dt = 1 - e^{-\lambda x}, \tag{3-20}$$

which is easily evaluated using negative exponential tables.

From the development of the gamma distribution, it follows that the exponential distribution is the model for the time for a *single* outcome to take place if events occur independently at a constant average rate. Equivalently, it is the distribution of the time between occurrences of independent random events that arise at a constant average rate. For example, if particles arrive independently at a counter at an average rate λ of two per second, then the probability that a particle will arrive within one second of the previous particle is found from (3-20) to be

$$F(1) = 1 - e^{-2(1)} = 0.865.$$

The exponential distribution is used frequently as a time-to-failure model for a component or a system when a constant failure rate is assumed. This application is discussed in detail in Section 3-5.

The exponential distribution parameter λ is estimated from given data by setting $\eta = 1$ in (3-17a)—that is,

$$\hat{\lambda} = \frac{1}{\bar{x}} = \frac{n}{\sum\limits_{i=1}^{n} x_i} .$$
(3-21)

3-3. The Beta and Related Distributions

NATURE OF MODEL

Just as the gamma distribution permits representation of a wide diversity of distributional shapes over the interval from zero, or some arbitrary origin, to infinity so the beta distribution is a useful model for variates whose values are limited to a finite interval. The beta probability density function defined over the interval (0, 1) is

$$f(x; \gamma, \eta) = \begin{cases} \dfrac{\Gamma(\gamma + \eta)}{\Gamma(\gamma)\Gamma(\eta)} x^{\gamma-1}(1 - x)^{\eta-1}, & 0 \le x \le 1, 0 < \gamma, 0 < \eta \\ 0 & \text{elsewhere.} \end{cases}$$
(3-22)

Plots of beta distributions for different combinations of the two parameters γ and η are shown in Fig. 3-9. Note that

1. When $\gamma > 1$ and $\eta > 1$ the distribution is single peaked with peak at $x = (\gamma - 1)/(\gamma + \eta - 2)$.
2. When $\gamma < 1$ and $\eta < 1$ the distribution is U shaped.
3. When $\gamma < 1$ and $\eta \ge 1$, the distribution is reverse J shaped, and when $\eta < 1$ and $\gamma \ge 1$, it is J shaped.
4. When $\gamma = \eta$ the distribution is symmetrical. The special case $\gamma = \eta = 1$ is discussed later in this section.

The values of both parameters thus affect the distribution shape—that is, both are shape parameters.

The cumulative beta distribution

$$F(x; \gamma, \eta) = \begin{cases} 0, & x < 0, \\ \dfrac{\Gamma(\gamma + \eta)}{\Gamma(\gamma)\Gamma(\eta)} \displaystyle\int_0^x t^{\gamma-1}(1 - t)^{\eta-1}\, dt, & 0 \le x \le 1, \\ 1, & x > 1, \end{cases}$$
(3-23)

is known as the *incomplete beta function* and is tabulated in Reference 3-14. To use these tables when $\gamma \ge \eta$, we set

$$p = \gamma \quad \text{and} \quad q = \eta$$
(3-24)

and then find $I_x(p, q) = F(x; \gamma, \eta)$ from the tables. When $\gamma < \eta$, we set

$$p = \eta, \quad q = \gamma, \quad \text{and} \quad x' = 1 - x$$
(3-25)

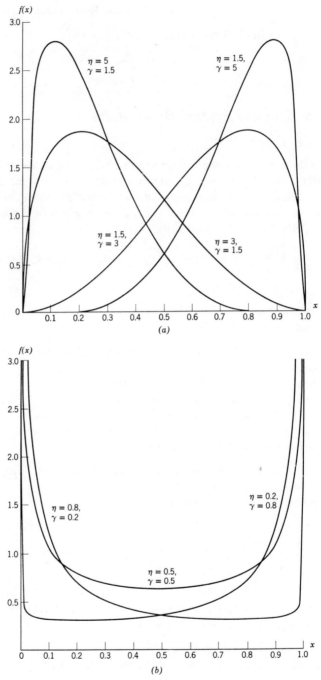

Fig. 3-9 Beta distributions with different parameter values.

92

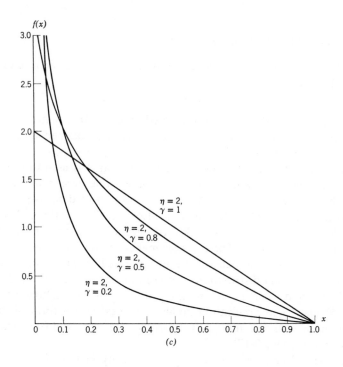

(c)

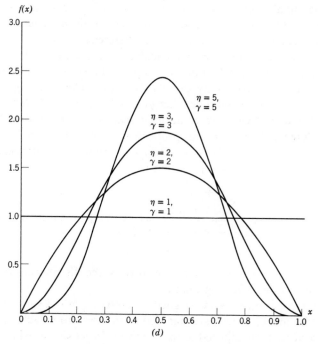

(d)

Fig. 3-9 Beta distributions with different parameter values.

93

and then read $I_{x'}(p, q)$ from the tabulation. The desired cumulative probability is

$$F(x; \gamma, \eta) = 1 - I_{x'}(p, q). \tag{3-26}$$

The use of this table will be illustrated shortly. In situations in which only percentiles are required, they may also be obtained directly from Reference 3-15 or 3-16.

Because of its many shapes, the beta distribution is used to represent a large number of physical variables whose values are restricted to an identifiable interval, such as the daily proportion of defective units on a production line. This distribution also describes estimated time to complete a project phase in PERT (Program Evaluation and Reporting Technique) scheduling. The engineer makes optimistic (o), pessimistic (p) and most likely (m) estimates of the time required for each task. From this information a beta distribution over the interval (o, p), with modal value equal to m and standard deviation equal to $\frac{1}{6}(p - o)$ is assumed for completion time. This application involves the generalized form of the beta distribution over the interval (μ_0, μ_1) (see below). Further details are given in Reference 3-17.

The beta distribution is also used frequently in Bayesian analyses to describe initial knowledge concerning probability of success such as the probability that a space vehicle will successfully complete a specified mission. The procedure is described in Reference 3-10.

The beta distribution is also applicable in the following situation. Suppose n independent random observations are taken on some phenomenon y with arbitrary probability density function. The resulting values are ranked in order of magnitude. Let y_r and y_{n-s+1} be the values of the rth smallest and sth largest observations respectively. It can then be shown (see Reference 3-18) that the proportion x of the original population between y_r and y_{n-s+1} follows a beta distribution with parameters $\gamma = n - r - s + 1$ and $\eta = r + s$—that is

$$f(x; n - r - s + 1, r + s)$$

$$= \frac{\Gamma(n + 1)}{\Gamma(n - r - s + 1)\,\Gamma(r + s)}\, x^{n-r-s}(1 - x)^{r+s-1}, \tag{3-27}$$

$$0 \leqslant x \leqslant 1.$$

This result holds irrespective of the form of the distribution of y and is illustrated by the following example.

A radio receiver has been designed to receive signals of varying voltages. Fifty independent signals are sampled at random from each new source. The receiver is then adjusted to receive those future signals whose voltages fall between the lowest and highest sample values. What is the probability that the receiver, after adjustment, will receive at least 95 per cent of a large number of signals from a given source?

From the preceding discussion the proportion x of the population between the lowest and highest observations in a random sample of size 50 is a beta variate with $\gamma = 50 - 1 - 1 + 1 = 49$, and $\eta = 1 + 1 = 2$. Consequently, the probability that the accepted proportion *exceeds* 0.95 is

$$\Pr(x > 0.95) = 1 - F(0.95; 49, 2)$$

$$= 1 - \frac{\Gamma(51)}{\Gamma(49)\,\Gamma(2)} \int_0^{0.95} t^{49-1}(1 - t)^{2-1}\, dt. \qquad (3\text{-}28)$$

Because $\gamma \geq \eta$, (3-24) is applicable for finding $F(0.95; 49, 2)$; thus $p = 49$ and $q = 2$. From Reference 3-14 we obtain

$$I_{0.95}(49, 2) = F(0.95; 49, 2) = 0.279.$$

The probability that at least 95 per cent of the signals will be received is therefore 0.721.

Similar applications of the beta distribution arise frequently in quality control and reliability. For example,

1. A measuring device allows the lengths of only the shortest and longest units in a sample to be recorded. Fifteen units are selected at random from a very large lot. What is the probability that at least 90 per cent of the units in the lot have lengths between the two recorded values?

2. Twenty electron tubes are tested until that time t when the first one fails. What is the probability that at least 75 per cent of the tubes from this process will survive beyond t? In this problem $r = 1$ and $s = 0$.

These applications of the beta distribution involve finding a tolerance interval (see Section 3-1) without requiring the assumption that the underlying population is normally distributed.

ESTIMATION OF BETA-DISTRIBUTION PARAMETERS

As in the case of the gamma distribution, the maximum-likelihood estimates of the beta distribution parameters are difficult to obtain. Again, for large samples, the method of matching moments is simpler to use and the loss in precision is small. This method leads to the following equations:

$$\hat{\eta} = \frac{(1 - \bar{x})}{s^2} [\bar{x}(1 - \bar{x}) - s^2] \qquad (3\text{-}28a)$$

$$\hat{\gamma} = \frac{\bar{x}\hat{\eta}}{1 - \bar{x}}, \qquad (3\text{-}28b)$$

where $\bar{x}$ and s^2 are obtained from (2-31) and (2-51a).

GENERALIZED FORM OF BETA DISTRIBUTION

The beta distribution can be generalized to cover the interval (μ_0, μ_1). This leads to the probability density function

$$f(x; \gamma, \eta, \mu_0, \mu_1) = \begin{cases} \dfrac{1}{(\mu_1 - \mu_0)} \dfrac{\Gamma(\gamma + \eta)}{\Gamma(\gamma)\,\Gamma(\eta)} \left(\dfrac{x - \mu_0}{\mu_1 - \mu_0}\right)^{\gamma-1} \left(1 - \dfrac{x - \mu_0}{\mu_1 - \mu_0}\right)^{\eta-1}, \\ \qquad\qquad \mu_0 \leq x \leq \mu_1,\, 0 < \gamma,\, 0 < \eta, \\ 0 \qquad \text{elsewhere.} \end{cases} \tag{3-29}$$

Cumulative probabilities can be obtained by transforming to a beta variate over $(0, 1)$ by letting $x' = (x - \mu_0)/(\mu_1 - \mu_0)$ and using the procedures for the two-parameter beta distribution. The justification of this transformation, as well as of (3-29), is indicated in Chapter 5.

A SPECIAL CASE OF THE BETA DISTRIBUTION: THE UNIFORM DISTRIBUTION

When $\gamma = \eta = 1$, the beta distribution reduces to

$$f(x; 1, 1) = \begin{cases} 1, & 0 \leq x \leq 1, \\ 0 & \text{elsewhere.} \end{cases} \tag{3-30}$$

In generalizing this probability density function to the interval (μ_0, μ_1), we obtain

$$f(x; \mu_0, \mu_1) = \begin{cases} \dfrac{1}{\mu_1 - \mu_0}, & \mu_0 \leq x \leq \mu_1, \\ 0 & \text{elsewhere.} \end{cases} \tag{3-31}$$

This is the *uniform* or *rectangular distribution*, whose probability density function is a horizontal line (see Fig. 3-9d).

The probability that a uniformly distributed variate takes on some value in an interval (x_1, x_2) where $x_1 \geq \mu_0$ and $x_2 \leq \mu_1$ is directly proportional to the relative length of the interval—that is,

$$\begin{aligned} \Pr\,(x_1 \leq x \leq x_2) &= \int_{x_1}^{x_2} f(x; \mu_0, \mu_1)\, dx \\ &= \int_{x_1}^{x_2} \frac{1}{\mu_1 - \mu_0}\, dx = \frac{x_2 - x_1}{\mu_1 - \mu_0}. \end{aligned} \tag{3-32}$$

Consequently, the uniform distribution is the appropriate model for the time of occurrence of an event that is equally likely to occur at any time during an interval. For example, if it is equally likely that a signal will be received at any time x during a five second period, the probability density function of x is

$$f(x; 0, 5) = \frac{1}{5}, \qquad 0 \le x \le 5.$$

The probability of the signal being received during the *first second* is

$$F(1; 0, 5) = \int_0^1 \frac{1}{5} \, dx = 0.2.$$

An example of the use of a bivariate generalization of the uniform distribution was discussed in Section 2-11. The use of a discrete approximation to the uniform distribution to generate random values from any probability density function will be indicated in Chapter 7.

SPECIAL CASES OF THE BETA DISTRIBUTION: THE RIGHT-TRIANGULAR AND PARABOLIC DISTRIBUTIONS

Two additional special cases of the beta distribution are the right-triangular and parabolic distributions. The *right-triangular distribution* is obtained by setting $\gamma = 2$ and $\eta = 1$, yielding the probability density function

$$f(x; 2, 1) = \begin{cases} 2x, & 0 \le x \le 1, \\ 0 & \text{elsewhere}; \end{cases} \qquad (3\text{-}32a)$$

or by setting $\gamma = 1$ and $\eta = 2$, yielding*

$$f(x; 1, 2) = \begin{cases} 2(1 - x), & 0 \le x \le 1, \\ 0 & \text{elsewhere}. \end{cases} \qquad (3\text{-}32b)$$

This distribution is shown in Fig. 3-9c.

The *parabolic distribution* is obtained by setting $\gamma = \eta = 2$ in (3-22) and is shown in Fig. 3-9d. Its density function is

$$f(x; 2, 2) = \begin{cases} 6x(1 - x), & 0 \le x \le 1, \\ 0 & \text{elsewhere}. \end{cases} \qquad (3\text{-}32c)$$

These distributions are sometimes used to give simple approximations to more complex symmetric or asymmetric distributions. Thus the parabolic distribution can be used as a very simple approximation to the normal distribution, whereas a right-triangular distribution provides a very rough representation for certain gamma variates.

* This form has also been referred to as the semi-triangular distribution.

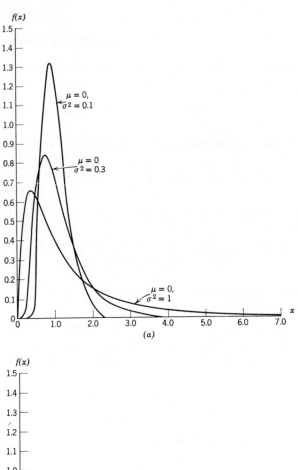

Fig. 3-10 Log-normal distributions with various values of μ and σ^2.

98

3-4. *Statistical Models Related to the Normal Distribution: The Log-Normal, Rayleigh, and Cauchy Distributions*

GENERAL NATURE OF MODELS

The normal distribution has led to various related distributions that are useful in many engineering situations. Three such models—the log-normal, the Rayleigh, and the Cauchy distributions—are discussed in this section. Their derivation is not given here, but the general technique is explained in Chapter 5.

THE LOG-NORMAL DISTRIBUTION

The *log-normal distribution* is the model for a random variable whose logarithm follows the normal distribution with parameters μ and σ. Thus the probability density function for $y = \ln x$ is

$$g(y) = \frac{1}{\sigma\sqrt{2\pi}} \exp\left[-\frac{1}{2\sigma^2}(y - \mu)^2 \right]; \quad -\infty < y < \infty. \quad (3\text{-}33)$$

By the methods of Chapter 5 the resulting probability density function for x is

$$f(x;\mu,\sigma) = \begin{cases} \dfrac{1}{\sigma x\sqrt{2\pi}} \exp\left[-\dfrac{1}{2\sigma^2}(\ln x - \mu)^2 \right], \\[4pt] \qquad\qquad x > 0,\ -\infty < \mu < \infty,\ \sigma > 0, \\[4pt] 0 \qquad \text{elsewhere.} \end{cases} \quad (3\text{-}34)$$

This distribution has many different shapes for non-negative variates, as can be seen from the plots of log-normal distributions with different values of μ and σ in Fig. 3-10. It is skewed to the right, the degree of skewness increasing with increasing values of σ. Note that μ and σ are scale and shape parameters respectively and *not* location and scale parameters as in the normal distribution. We are thus making an exception from the notational scheme for parameters established at the beginning of the chapter.

The log-normal distribution may be generalized to cover an interval other than $(0, \infty)$ by introducing the location parameter ϵ. Thus

$$f(x;\mu,\sigma,\epsilon) = \frac{1}{\sigma(x - \epsilon)\sqrt{2\pi}} \exp\left[-\frac{1}{2\sigma^2}(\ln(x - \epsilon) - \mu)^2 \right],$$

$$x \geqslant \epsilon,\ -\infty < \mu < \infty,\ \sigma > 0,\ -\infty < \epsilon < \infty. \quad (3\text{-}34a)$$

The log-normal distribution can be derived as the model for a process whose value results from the *multiplication* of many small errors in a manner similar to that for the normal distribution for the *addition* of errors. In fact, by a central limit theorem, it can be shown that the distribution of the *product* of n independent positive variates approaches a log-normal distribution under very general conditions. The derivation is given in Reference 3-19, where the theory and applications of the distribution are discussed in detail.

The log-normal distribution has been used in a variety of applications, from economics to biology, for processes in which the observed value is a random proportion of the previous value. Examples include the distribution of personal incomes, inheritances, and bank deposits, and the distribution of the size of an organism whose growth is subject to many small impulses, the effect of each of which is proportional to the momentary size of the organism. The log-normal has also been used to represent the distribution of particle sizes obtained from breakage processes (see Reference 3-20). Its use in life testing will be indicated in Section 3-5.

The popularity of the log-normal distribution is in part due to the ease in obtaining its percentiles, since cumulative values for $y = \ln x$ can be obtained from the tabulation of the standardized normal distribution and the corresponding values of x are found by taking antilogs. Methods for estimating the parameters of the log-normal distribution from given data are indicated in Chapters 6 and 8.

THE RAYLEIGH DISTRIBUTION

The Rayleigh is used to represent the distribution of radial error in a plane where the errors in each axis are independent and normally distributed with equal variance and zero mean. Thus, if y_1 and y_2 are values of independent random samples from normal distributions, each with $\mu = 0$ and identical values of σ, then the random variable

$$x = \sqrt{y_1^2 + y_2^2} \tag{3-35}$$

follows the Rayleigh distribution

$$f(x; \sigma) = \begin{cases} \dfrac{x}{\sigma^2} \exp\left[-\dfrac{x^2}{2\sigma^2}\right], & x \geq 0, \sigma > 0, \\ 0 & \text{elsewhere.} \end{cases} \tag{3-36}$$

This probability density involves only the scale parameter σ. A plot is shown in Fig. 3-11.

The main applications of the Rayleigh distribution are for such problems as determining the distribution of the distance of actual bomb hits from an aimed-at target when the sighting errors in the x and y directions are independent and normally distributed with equal variances. A second application arises in statistical communication theory. It is shown in

Reference 3-21 that when random noise is detected by a linear detector the amplitude of the envelope of noise is distributed according to the Rayleigh distribution.

The cumulative Rayleigh distribution

$$F(x; \sigma) = \begin{cases} \int_0^x \left(\frac{y}{\sigma^2}\right) \exp\left[\frac{-y^2}{2\sigma^2}\right] dy = 1 - \exp\left[\frac{-x^2}{2\sigma^2}\right], & x \geqslant 0, \\ 0 & \text{elsewhere,} \end{cases} \tag{3-37}$$

can be easily evaluated.

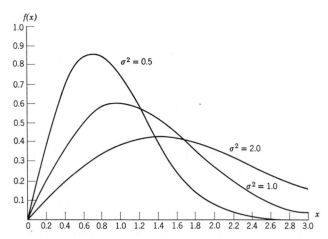

Fig. 3-11   Rayleigh distributions with various values of σ^2.

THE CAUCHY DISTRIBUTION

The Cauchy probability density function is

$$f(x; \mu, \sigma) = \frac{1}{\sigma\pi} \frac{1}{1 + [(x - \mu)^2/\sigma^2]},$$

$$-\infty < x < \infty, -\infty < \mu < \infty, \sigma > 0, \tag{3-38}$$

where μ and σ are location and scale parameters respectively.

The cumulative distribution is

$$F(x; \mu, \sigma) = \frac{1}{\sigma\pi} \int_{-\infty}^x \left[1 + \frac{(y - \mu)^2}{\sigma^2}\right]^{-1} dy = \frac{1}{2} + \frac{1}{\pi} \arctan \frac{(x - \mu)}{\sigma}. \tag{3-39}$$

The *ratio* of two independent variates from a normal distribution with zero mean follow a Cauchy distribution with $\mu = 0$ and $\sigma = 1$. Furthermore, the ratio x/y of two independent normal variates with zero mean and parameter values σ_x and σ_y respectively is Cauchy distributed with $\mu = 0$ and $\sigma = \sigma_x/\sigma_y$.

Consider the following example. Two independent readings, w_1 and w_2, are obtained at random from a transmission device that is generating normally distributed noise at an average level of 20 dB with a standard deviation of 2 dB. The standardized ratio

$$x = \frac{(w_1 - 20)/2}{(w_2 - 20)/2} = \frac{z_1}{z_2}$$

is calculated. What is the probability that this ratio has a value between -1 and 1?

From the preceding discussion x is a Cauchy variate with $\mu = 0$ and $\sigma = 1$. Thus we obtain

$$\Pr\,[-1 \leqslant x \leqslant 1] = F(1; 0, 1) - F(-1; 0, 1)$$

$$= \frac{1}{\pi} \int_{-1}^{+1} \frac{1}{1 + y^2}\,dy = \frac{1}{\pi} \arctan x \,\Big|_{-1}^{1} = 0.50.$$

The Cauchy is a symmetric long-tailed distribution, as can be seen from Fig. 3-12, where it is plotted with a normal distribution. Hence, this model is used to represent variables for which it is possible to obtain values extremely far in either direction from the distribution center μ. For example, if θ is uniformly distributed on $(-\pi/2, \pi/2)$ it can be shown by the methods of Chapter 5 that $\tan \theta$ follows a Cauchy distribution.

The Cauchy distribution does not have any finite moments. Thus applying (2-28) to obtain the expected value of a Cauchy variate results in an expression that does not converge. For this reason the sample median

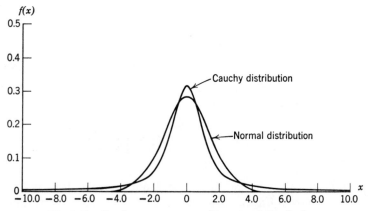

Fig. 3-12   Cauchy versus comparable normal distribution.

is used to estimate the location parameter μ from given data. In this respect, the Cauchy differs from the other distributions considered in this book.

3-5. Statistical Models Used in Life Testing and Reliability

NATURE OF PROBLEM

An important application of probability distributions is as time-to-failure models for components or systems. The number of hours or years or cycles of satisfactory operation is a random variable whose exact value depends on many factors, such as variations due to manufacturing tolerances and materials and changes in the environmental conditions. Once an appropriate probabilistic model for time to failure has been constructed and its parameters estimated, this information may be used to predict life, develop optimum initial burn-in procedures, establish part-replacement schedules and inventory rules, plan future reliability test programs, and so on. An extensive review of the statistical literature pertaining to life testing is given in Reference 3-47.

In this section we are concerned with distributions for time to failure. Some of these—the exponential, gamma, and log-normal distributions—have already been discussed. Two others—the Weibull and the Type I extreme-value distributions—are introduced for the first time.

THE HAZARD FUNCTION

It is frequently meaningful to consider a function that gives the probability of failure during a very small time increment, assuming that no failure occurred before that time. This function, known as the *hazard function* (also as the conditional failure function or intensity function or force of mortality) is

$$h(t) = \frac{f(t)}{1 - F(t)}, \qquad (3\text{-}40)$$

where $f(t)$ and $F(t)$ are the probability density and distribution functions for time to failure. Consequently, $[1 - F(t)]$ is the probability of survival to time t, and $h(t)\,dt$ represents the proportion of the items surviving at time t that fail during the interval $(t, t + dt)$.

A hazard function appropriate for many phenomena, including human life, is the so-called "bathtub curve" shown in Fig. 3-13. For an initial period up to time t_0, $h(t)$ is relatively large, but decreasing in value, because of "infant mortality"—that is, early failures often attributable to manufacturing defects. Subsequently, $h(t)$ remains approximately constant until time t_1, after which it increases because of wear-out failures. We can

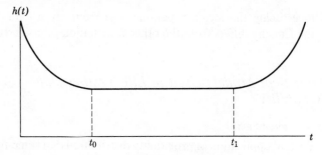

Fig. 3-13   Typical hazard function.

optimize "in usage" reliability for products with this hazard function by (a) initial burn-in until time t_0 to weed out early failures, and (b) replacement at time t_1 to avoid wear-out failures.

The hazard function corresponding to a specified probability density function can be found directly from (3-40). For example, for the uniform distribution

$$f(t; 0, 10) = \frac{1}{10}, \qquad 0 \leq t \leq 10,$$

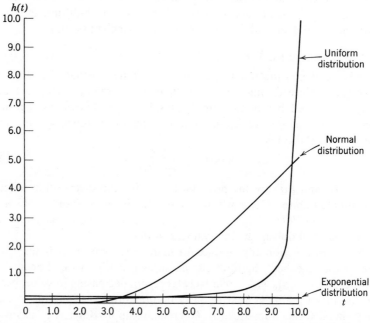

Fig. 3-14   Hazard functions for normal, uniform, and exponential distributions.

the hazard function is

$$h(t) = \frac{0.1}{1 - \int_0^t 0.1\, dy} = \frac{0.1}{1 - 0.1t}.$$

The following hazard functions are shown in Fig. 3-14: (a) normal distribution with $\mu = 5$ and $\sigma = 1$; (b) uniform distribution over interval $(0, 10)$; (c) exponential distribution with $\lambda = 0.2$. The normal distribution may not be applicable as a time-to-failure model, because a normally distributed variate can take on negative values, whereas time to failure, which may be close to zero due to infant mortality, cannot be negative. The uniform distribution is limited as a time-to-failure model, because there is a specified upper limit before which the failure *must* occur. Therefore its hazard rate approaches infinity as t approaches the upper limit, since all units that have not yet failed must fail in a smaller and smaller time interval.

The hazard function for an exponentially distributed variate is a constant. This result and its implications are discussed below.

THE EXPONENTIAL DISTRIBUTION AS A TIME-TO-FAILURE MODEL

The exponential probability density function (see Section 3-2)

$$f(t; \lambda) = \begin{cases} \lambda e^{-\lambda t}, & t \geq 0, \quad \lambda > 0 \\ 0 & \text{elsewhere}, \end{cases} \tag{3-41}$$

is the most commonly used time-to-failure distribution. It plays a central role in reliability, comparable to that of the normal distribution in other applications.

From (3-40) and (3-41), the hazard function for an exponentially distributed variate is

$$h(t) = \frac{\lambda e^{-\lambda t}}{1 - \int_0^t \lambda e^{-\lambda y} dy} = \frac{\lambda e^{-\lambda t}}{e^{-\lambda t}} = \lambda. \tag{3-42}$$

Thus the probability of failure during a specified time interval is a constant depending only on the length of the interval and is the same irrespective of whether the unit in question is in its first hour of operation or has previously survived 100 hours, 1000 hours, or 10^6 hours. The parameter λ is referred to as the failure rate.

From the discussion in Section 3-2, it follows that time to failure for a unit is exponentially distributed if the unit fails as soon as some single event, such as the disintegration of a particle, occurs, assuming such events happen independently at a constant rate. Frequently, although the time-to-failure distribution for a component is not exponential over its *entire* life, the in-usage portion is. Assume, for example, that a motor whose hazard function can be represented as in Fig. 3-13 is installed in a system only after it has been successfully "burned in" until time t_0. Also the motor is replaced after $(t_1 - t_0)$ hours by another motor from the same population, which had been previously exposed to the same burn in. This process is continued indefinitely. The time to failure for the *motors in system usage* is then exponentially distributed, because the applicable hazard function is constant. This is so, even if the time-to-failure distribution over the *total life* of the motor is far from exponential.

The exponential distribution is more appropriate as a time-to-failure model for complex systems than it is for components. It is shown in Reference 3-22 that this distribution is the "in-the-limit" model for time-to-failure for a system with a large number of in-series components, none of which individually contributes very heavily to the total failure probability, even if the distributions for the individual components are not exponential. This result corresponds to the central limit theorem which establishes the normal distribution as the appropriate model in many nonlife-test situations. It also applies to the distribution of the *time between failures* for such systems if each failed component is replaced immediately by another omponent of the same type.

The use of the exponential distribution has also been justified in reliability problems on strictly empirical grounds. A series of examples, dealing with electron tubes, resistors, capacitors, and so on, are given in Reference 3-23. However, the simplicity of the theory and of the required calculations (see later discussion) should not delude the engineer into believing that the time-to-failure distribution for all elements is exponential. For many components there is no physical reason to expect a constant hazard rate. Such an assumption could be as erroneous as the assumption of normality for all nonlife-test data, or even more so, since the exponential distribution in many instances does not enjoy the robust properties of the normal distribution. In Chapter 8 procedures for evaluating the validity of the exponential distribution assumption are discussed.

Cumulative probabilities for an exponential variate can be obtained from (3-20). For example, if the time to failure for an equipment follows an exponential distribution with $\lambda = 0.1$ per year, the probability of failure during the first year is

$$F(1; 0.1) = 1 - e^{-0.1} = 0.095.$$

Note that

$$F(t; \lambda) = 1 - e^{-\lambda t} \approx \lambda t$$

if λt is small, as is the case in most reliability problems.

In some situations the parameter λ is known from physical considerations, but more frequently its value must be estimated from the test data by the following expression (obtained by the method of maximum likelihood):

$$\lambda = \frac{\text{total number of failures } (F)}{\text{total test time on failed and unfailed units } (T)}. \tag{3-43}$$

Assume, for example, that in a life test of four batteries, failures were observed after 10, 40, and 60 hours. The fourth battery was tested 70 hours without failure, at which time the test was terminated. Thus $F = 3$, $T = 180$, and

$$\hat{\lambda} = \frac{3}{180} = \frac{1}{60}. \tag{3-44}$$

The expected value of time to failure t, known as mean time to failure and denoted by θ, is also frequently of interest. From (2-29),

$$E(t) = \theta = \frac{1}{\lambda}.$$

The appropriate estimate from sample data is

$$\hat{\theta} = \frac{1}{\hat{\lambda}}. \tag{3-45}$$

Thus in the above example the estimated mean time to failure is

$$\hat{\theta} = \left(\frac{1}{60}\right)^{-1} = 60 \text{ hours.}$$

Assuming that the total test time is predetermined (and thus that the observed number of failures is the only random variable), the lower confidence bound on θ at the $(1 - \alpha)100$ per cent confidence level is

$$\theta_L = \frac{2T}{\chi^2_{1-\alpha,\gamma}}, \tag{3-46}$$

where $\gamma = 2F + 2$ and where $\chi^2_{1-\alpha,\gamma}$ is given in Table IV at the end of this book for various values of α*.

In the preceding example $\gamma = 8$. From Table IV, $\chi^2_{0.95,8} = 15.5$. The lower 95 per cent confidence bound on mean time to failure is

$$\theta_L = \frac{2(180)}{15.5} = 23.2 \text{ hours.}$$

* The values in Table IV are percentiles of the chi-square distribution with γ degrees of freedom (see Section 3-2).

Thus, assuming an exponential distribution for failure time, the one point estimate for mean time to failure based on the data is 60 hours; however, we may be 95 per cent confident that the mean time to failure is *at least* 23.2 hours.

In some situations the value of γ in (3-46) is slightly different, depending on the specific rule governing the termination of the test. See References 3-24 and 3-25 for further details.

Note that in applying (3-43), (3-45), and (3-46) it does not matter how many test units are involved in accumulating the total time T. For example, if three failures occurred during a total test time of 100 hours, $\hat{\lambda} = 3/100$, irrespective of whether the 100 hours were obtained on 100 units tested an average of one hour each or 10 units tested for an average of 10 hours each. This is a direct consequence of assuming an exponential distribution for time to failure, with the resulting implication that probability of future failure for an unfailed unit is independent of its history.

The simplicity of these expressions has been a contributing factor to the popular use (and misuse) of the exponential distribution. It is thus possible to obtain the same information about reliability for a single mission of 100 hours duration by testing 100 units each for a single hour or by testing one unit for 100 hours, assuming failed units are immediately replaced by good ones. This procedure is valid if the exponential model for time to failure is correct, but can lead to crroneous results otherwise.

We now turn to some more general models for life testing. These are frequently more realistic, though more complex, than the exponential distribution.

THE WEIBULL DISTRIBUTION

In many cases the inadequacy of the exponential distribution as a model for time to failure is due to the restrictive assumption of a constant hazard function. Consequently, more general distributions are needed for cases where the failure probability varies with time.

The *Weibull distribution* results from the hazard function

$$h(t) = \frac{\eta}{\sigma}\left(\frac{t}{\sigma}\right)^{\eta-1}. \tag{3-47}$$

Its probability density function is

$$f(t; \eta, \sigma) = \begin{cases} \dfrac{\eta}{\sigma}\left(\dfrac{t}{\sigma}\right)^{\eta-1} \exp\left[-\left(\dfrac{t}{\sigma}\right)^{\eta}\right], & t \geq 0, \sigma > 0, \eta > 0, \\ 0 & \text{elsewhere,} \end{cases} \tag{3-48}$$

where σ is the scale parameter and η is the shape parameter. The hazard function and the probability density function for the Weibull distribution have a wide variety of shapes, as can be seen from the plots for differing values of η in Fig. 3-15 and 3-16. In particular, when $\eta > 1$, the Weibull probability density function is single-peaked and the hazard function increases with t; for $\eta < 1$ the probability density function is reverse J shaped and the hazard function decreases with t. When $\eta = 1$ the hazard function is a constant and the Weibull distribution is equivalent to the exponential distribution; in this case the Weibull scale parameter σ

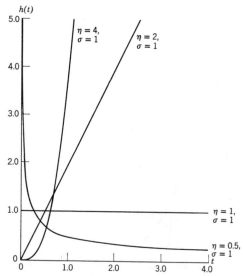

Fig. 3-15   Hazard functions for Weibull distributions with $\sigma = 1$ and various values of η.

equals the reciprocal of the exponential distribution parameter λ. The Rayleigh distribution, (3-36), is a Weibull distribution with $\eta = 2$. It is apparent from (3-47) that the corresponding hazard function is a linear increasing function of t.

The Weibull distribution has been frequently suggested as a time-to-failure model on empirical grounds, and satisfactory representations have been obtained for electron tubes, relays, and ball bearings (see References 3-26 to 3-31). The years to failure for some businesses have also been found to follow a Weibull distribution.

A theoretical justification for the Weibull distribution based on extreme-value theory will be indicated in the next Section.

The cumulative Weibull distribution

$$F(t; \eta, \sigma) = \int_0^t \frac{\eta}{\sigma}\left(\frac{y}{\sigma}\right)^{\eta-1} \exp\left[-\left(\frac{y}{\sigma}\right)^{\eta}\right] dy = 1 - \exp\left[-\left(\frac{t}{\sigma}\right)^{\eta}\right], \qquad t \geq 0,$$

$$(3\text{-}49)$$

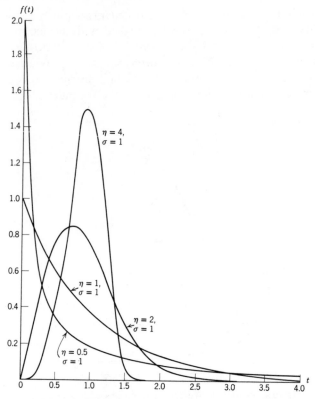

Fig. 3-16 Weibull distributions for $\sigma = 1$ and various values of η.

can be easily evaluated. For example, assume that the time to failure for a particular type of electron tube follows a Weibull distribution with $\eta = 2$ and $\sigma = 8$, with test time expressed in years. Then the probability of a failure during the first two years is

$$\Pr(t \leq 2) = F(2; 2, 8) = 1 - \exp\left[-\left(\frac{2}{8}\right)^2\right] = 0.06.$$

The Weibull distribution can be generalized to take into account an arbitrary origin by introducing the location parameter μ. Thus the three-parameter Weibull probability density function is

$$f(t; \eta, \sigma, \mu) = \begin{cases} \dfrac{\eta}{\sigma}\left(\dfrac{t-\mu}{\sigma}\right)^{\eta-1} \exp\left[-\left(\dfrac{t-\mu}{\sigma}\right)^{\eta}\right] \\ \qquad\qquad t \geq \mu, \; -\infty < \mu < \infty, \sigma > 0, \eta > 0, \\ 0 \qquad \text{elsewhere.} \end{cases} \tag{3-50}$$

In life testing μ represents an initial period during which no failures can take place.

Estimation of the Weibull distribution parameters from test data generally involves solution of nonlinear equations. The method is described in References 3-34 and 3-35. A simpler graphical procedure, frequently adequate for practical problems, is discussed in Chapter 8. Methods for obtaining confidence limits are given in References 3-60 and 3-61.

THE TYPE I AND OTHER EXTREME VALUE DISTRIBUTIONS

Failure of a component or system may frequently be linked to extremal phenomena dependent directly on either the smallest or largest value in a sample from a particular distribution. Consider, for example, two circuits, each comprised of n components randomly chosen from the same manufacturing lot. If, in the first circuit, the components are connected in series, a failure occurs when the *first* component fails. If in the second circuit the components are connected in parallel, a circuit failure takes place only when *all* components have failed. In fatigue tests at a constant stress, failure may be directly dependent on the strength of the weakest of many "elements" in the given material. In the analysis of paper capacitors it has been hypothesized that a very large number of flaws are randomly distributed throughout the material and that breakdown voltage depends directly on the size of the largest flaw.

In these cases we are interested in the distribution of the smallest element (minimum value) or largest element (maximum value) in a sample from some initial distribution. Frequently this initial distribution is not known and cannot be sampled directly, such as in the fatigue and breakdown voltage examples, where only minimum or maximum values are observed. The distribution of the smallest or largest element will in general depend on the sample size n and on the nature of the initial distribution. However, if n is large, we can use certain general asymptotic results that depend on some limited assumptions concerning the initial distribution.

Three types of asymptotic distributions have been developed for both minimum and maximum values based on different (but not all possible) initial distributions. The following cases are of special interest:

1. Type I asymptotic distribution for maximum values.
2. Type I asymptotic distribution for minimum values.
3. Type III asymptotic distribution for minimum values.

The Type I asymptotic distribution has been referred to as the "Type I extreme value distribution," "Gumbel's extreme value distribution," or simply "*the* extreme value distribution." The Type III asymptotic distribution for minimum values is the Weibull distribution. These three cases are now discussed.

A Type I asymptotic distribution for maximum values is the limiting model as n approaches infinity for the distribution of the maximum of n independent values from an initial distribution whose right tail is unbounded and which is "exponential type"; that is, the initial cumulative distribution approaches unity with increasing values at least as rapidly as an exponential distribution function (for a more complete definition see References 3-36 and 3-37). Because the gamma (exponential, special case), normal, and log-normal distributions are all unbounded to the right and exponential type, this leads to a wide choice of possible initial distributions.

The Type I asymptotic distribution for maximum values may thus be used to represent time to failure for the circuit with n elements in parallel; assuming that n is a large number, the component failure times come from the same exponential-type distribution and failures occur independently. This model, however, is not limited to life test and reliability situations. For example, the Type I asymptotic distribution has been used successfully to represent the distribution of the yearly maximum of daily water discharges for a particular river at a specified measuring point. As pointed out by Gumbel in Reference 3-37, this application assumes the following:

1. The values of the daily discharges follow an exponential-type distribution.

2. The original number of elements, 365 days, is sufficiently large for the asymptotic theory to be applicable.

3. The daily discharges are independent.

Although the last assumption clearly does not hold, probability plots of actual data (see Chapter 8) have suggested that the Type I asymptotic distribution does provide a reasonable representation, and this model has been used in designing dams.

Other phenomena which have been represented by the Type I asymptotic distribution for maximum values include gust velocities encountered by airplanes, extinction times for bacteria, the maxima of stock market indices over a given year and depths of corrosion pits (see References 3-36 to 3-41, 3-62 and 3-63).

The Type I asymptotic distribution for minimum values is the limiting model as n approaches infinity for the distribution of the minimum of n independent values from an initial distribution whose left tail is unbounded and which is exponential type for decreasing values. The normal distribution, which as already stated, is exponential type unbounded to the right is clearly the same to the left. Thus the Type I asymptotic distribution for minimum values is applicable as a time to failure model in the circuit example given a large number of components in series, assuming the times to failure for the individual components are independently and identically normally distributed.

The hazard functions and probability density functions for the Type I asymptotic distributions for the largest and smallest elements respectively are

$$h(t) = \frac{\exp\left[-(1/\sigma)(t - \mu)\right]}{\sigma\{\exp\left[e^{-(1/\sigma)(t-\mu)}\right] - 1\}}, \tag{3-51a}$$

$$h(t) = \frac{1}{\sigma} \exp\left(\frac{t - \mu}{\sigma}\right), \tag{3-51b}$$

$$f(t; \mu, \sigma) = \frac{1}{\sigma} \exp\left[-\frac{1}{\sigma}(t - \mu) - e^{-(1/\sigma)(t-\mu)}\right],$$

$$-\infty < t < \infty, -\infty < \mu < \infty, \sigma > 0, \tag{3-52a}$$

$$f(t; \mu, \sigma) = \frac{1}{\sigma} \exp\left[\frac{1}{\sigma}(t - \mu) - e^{(1/\sigma)(t-\mu)}\right],$$

$$-\infty < t < \infty, -\infty < \mu < \infty, \sigma > 0. \tag{3-52b}$$

Plots for $\mu = 5$ and $\sigma = 1$ are given in Figs. 3-17 and 3-18.

It is clear from (3-52a) and (3-52b) and Fig. 3-18 that the Type I asymptotic probability density functions for the largest and smallest elements are mirror images of one another. The former is skewed to the right, the latter to the left. The hazard function for the smallest element increases exponentially with time; for the largest element the increase is at a decreasing rate approaching a constant value asymptotically (see Fig. 3-17).

Note that, just as for the normal distribution, the Type I asymptotic distribution parameters μ and σ are location and scale parameters, respectively, but in this case they are *not* the distribution mean and standard deviation. The parameter μ is the mode of the distribution and is related to the mean as follows:

Mean for Type I asymptotic distribution for largest element:

$$\mu + 0.577\sigma.$$

Mean for Type I asymptotic distribution for smallest element:

$$\mu - 0.577\sigma.$$

The distribution standard deviation equals 1.283σ for both largest and smallest elements. Because the distribution has no shape parameter, there is only a single shape. Consequently, this distribution does not lead to as diverse hazard functions as does the Weibull distribution. Note also that the distribution is not limited to non-negative variates (although in life-test applications $h(t)$ is meaningless for $t < 0$).

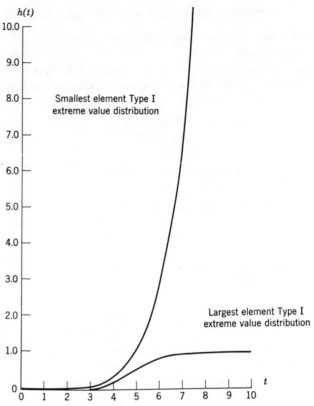

Fig. 3-17 Hazard functions for Type I extreme-value distributions for smallest and largest elements with $\mu = 5$ and $\sigma = 1$.

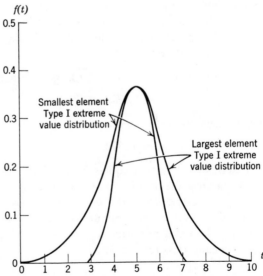

Fig. 3-18 Type I extreme value distributions for smallest and largest elements with $\mu = 5$ and $\sigma = 1$.

Values of the largest element Type I asymptotic probability density function and the corresponding cumulative probability distribution

$$F(y; 0, 1) = \int_{-\infty}^{y} \exp\left[-(x + e^{-x})\right] dx = \exp\left[-e^{-y}\right] \qquad (3\text{-}53a)$$

for the standardized or "reduced" variate

$$y = \frac{t - \mu}{\sigma} \qquad (3\text{-}54)$$

are tabulated in Reference 3-48. Distribution percentiles, that is, values of

$$y(\alpha) = -\ln\left[\ln\left(\frac{1}{\alpha}\right)\right]$$

[see (2-56) and (3-53a)] for various α are also given. These tabulations can be used for the Type I asymptotic distribution for smallest elements using $-y$ in place of y in the probability density function and $1 - F(-y)$ in place of $F(y)$ in the cumulative probability distribution. The latter substitution follows from the fact that the cumulative distribution function for the Type I asymptotic reduced variate for the smallest element is

$$F(y) = 1 - \exp\left(-e^{y}\right). \qquad (3\text{-}53b)$$

The use of the tables is illustrated by the following example.

The maximum demand for electric power at any time during a year in a given locality is related to extreme weather conditions and follows a Type I largest element asymptotic distribution with $\mu = 2000$ and $\sigma = 1000$. A power station, in evaluating the adequacy of a new generator, needs to determine (a) the probability that demand will exceed 4000 kW at any time in a year; (b) the kW demand that has only a one-in-twenty chance of being exceeded in a given year.

From (3-54) the value of y corresponding to $t = 4000$ kW is

$$y = \frac{4000 - 2000}{1000} = 2.0,$$

and from Table 1 of Reference 3-48

$$F(2; 0, 1) = 0.873.$$

Thus the chances are about one in eight that demand will exceed 4000 kW.

To answer the second part of the question we need determine the 95th percentile for yearly demand; that is, that y for which

$$F(y; 0, 1) = 0.95.$$

From the inverse use of Table 1 (or the direct use of Table 2) of Reference 3-48 we obtain $y = 2.97$. Using (3-54), the 95th percentile is

$$t = \sigma y + \mu = 4970 \text{ kW}.$$

Estimates of the parameters of the extreme-value distribution from given data may be obtained graphically by probability plotting (see Chapter 8). Alternately, the previously stated relationships between the mean and standard deviation of the distribution and its parameters may be used by matching moments; that is, the distribution mean and standard deviation are set equal to the corresponding sample values leading to the estimates

$$\hat{\sigma} = 1.283s, \tag{3-55}$$

$$\hat{\mu} = \bar{x} - 0.577\hat{\sigma}, \tag{3-56a}$$

for the distribution of the largest element and

$$\hat{\mu} = \bar{x} + 0.577\hat{\sigma} \tag{3-56b}$$

for the distribution of the smallest element, where $\bar{x}$ and s are obtained from the data using (2-31) and (2-51a). Some more precise estimation methods, which are applicable when there are few observations or censored samples, are described in References 3-27, 3-37, 3-38, 3-42, and 3-43.

As indicated, the Type III asymptotic distribution for the smallest element is equivalent to the Weibull distribution (see above). This is the limiting model as n approaches infinity for the distribution of the minimum of n values from various initial distributions bounded at the left. The gamma is one such initial distribution. Thus, if in a circuit identical components are connected in series and if their time to failure distribution is gamma, the circuit time to failure follows a Type III asymptotic or Weibull distribution rather than a Type I asymptotic distribution, as would have been the case if the initial distribution were normal (see Reference 3-55). The use of the Weibull distribution to represent the distribution of the breaking strength of materials has been justified by using extreme value theory in Reference 3-33. This model has also been used in drought analyses in a manner similar to flood studies. However, in droughts minimum rather than maximum values are of interest.

We conclude this discussion with the following general observations concerning extreme value distributions:

1. The gamma distribution illustrates the fact that the asymptotic distribution for minimum and maximum values from the same initial distribution are not necessarily of the same type. Thus, as stated above,

the asymptotic distribution for minimum values from a gamma distribution is Type III and that for maximum values is Type I.

2. Selection of the minimum value in a sample from a Type I or Type III asymptotic distribution for minimum values leads to an asymptotic distribution of the same type, and a similar result holds in taking the maximum value in a sample from an asymptotic distribution for maximum values. However, the asymptotic distribution of the minimum value from a maximum value asymptotic distribution and the distribution of the maximum value from a minimum value asymptotic distribution are Type I (minimum and maximum value, respectively), regardless of whether the initial distribution is Type I or Type III.

3. The various type extreme value distributions are themselves closely related. For example, it can be easily shown by the methods of Chapter 5 that the logarithm of a Weibull variate is distributed as minimum value Type I. This result has been used in developing procedures for estimating the parameters of the Weibull distribution (see, for example, Reference 3-27 and 3-43).

4. The preceding discussion has dealt with the asymptotic distribution of the minimum and maximum values. The asymptotic distribution for the mth largest and mth smallest values have also been considered in the literature. Percentiles of the Type I asymptotic distribution for the mth largest value are given in Reference 3-48.

5. The preceding results are asymptotic, that is, they are derived for the case in which n approaches infinity. The rate of convergence to this asymptotic result, that is, the extent to which it is applicable for moderate size n, depends on the initial distribution. For example, fewer observations are required for the distribution of the largest value to approach the Type I asymptotic distribution if the initial distribution is exponential than if it is normal. Thus Gumbel (Reference 3-37) gives plots that indicate that good convergence to the asymptotic distribution is obtained for as few as 10 samples from an initial exponential distribution, whereas the agreement at the tails of the asymptotic distribution is questionable for the extreme of as many as 100 observations from a normal distribution. On the other hand, if the initial distribution is already extreme value and of the same type as the asymptotic distribution, the asymptotic result is applicable for all n.

The theory underlying the exact (as opposed to the asymptotic) distribution of the largest or smallest or mth largest observation from a sample of size n is well known (see, for example, References 3-36, 3-37 and 3-55) and useful tabulations have been obtained for some distributions. Most notable of these are the tables of percentiles of the distribution for maximum values from a normal distribution for samples of size $n = 3, 5,$

10, 20, 30, 50, 100, (100), 1000, given in Reference 3-57 and graphed in part in Reference 3-37, and the tabulations of percentiles of the distribution of the mth value in samples of size 1 to 10 from gamma distributions with $\eta = 1(1)5$, given in References 3-56 and 3-58. Thus, when n is relatively small and the nature of the underlying distribution is known, it is preferable to use exact results, whenever possible. This would, for example, be the case in evaluating time to failure in the circuit problem if there were a total of five components whose time to failure is known to follow the same normal or gamma distribution with specified values of the parameters.

However, in many cases the initial distribution is neither known nor can be observed, and we must frequently resort to the asymptotic theory.

6. In addition to the Type I asymptotic distributions and the Type III asymptotic distribution for minimum values discussed in this section, there are also Type II asymptotic distributions and a Type III asymptotic distribution for maximum values. The latter is related to the Type III asymptotic distribution for minimum values in a manner similar to the relationship between the minimum value and maximum value Type I asymptotic distributions. Thus it is the limiting model for the distribution of maximum values from many initial distributions bounded to the right. The Type II asymptotic distributions for minimum and maximum values arise from initial distributions, such as the Cauchy distribution, for which all moments do not exist. Because the required initial distributions do not arise frequently in practice, the applications of the Type I asymptotic distribution for maximum values and the Type II asymptotic distributions are limited (see Reference 3-37 for further details).

THE GAMMA AND LOG-NORMAL DISTRIBUTIONS AS TIME TO
FAILURE MODELS

As seen in earlier sections, the gamma and log-normal distributions provide diverse representations for random variables with values from zero to infinity. This property makes these distributions natural candidates as time-to-failure models.

Like other life-test models, the gamma and log-normal distributions have been advanced as time-to-failure distributions on both theoretical and empirical grounds. The gamma distribution may be thought of as a generalization of the exponential distribution where failure takes place as soon as exactly k events have occurred, assuming events take place independently at a constant rate. This distribution is thus an appropriate time-to-failure model for a system with one operating unit and $k - 1$ standby units, where a new unit goes into operation as soon as the preceding unit has failed and where each of the units has an exponential time-to-failure distribution during operation. System failure then occurs when the last unit fails. As k increases, the gamma distribution approaches a normal distribution (see Section 3-2). In this case the system time to failure would generally not be peaked near zero, and hence the earlier objection to the normal distribution as a time-to-failure model is not applicable.

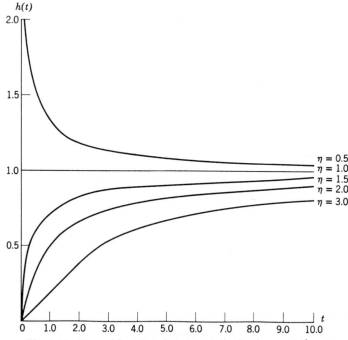

Fig. 3-19   Hazard functions for gamma distributions with $\lambda = 1$.

The justification of the log-normal distribution to represent time to failure is based on the multiplicative-effect properties of that distribution (see previous discussion). However, this property leads more directly to a log-normal distribution for the degree of deterioration by a specified time than for the time-to-failure.

The theory supporting the gamma and log-normal distributions as time to failure models has been supported by empirical results. For example, Reference 3-45 gives an example in which a log-normal distribution closely fitted the observed failure times for transistors.

Comparison of the hazard functions for the gamma and log-normal distributions (see Figs. 3-19 and 3-20) indicate that for some cases the two are similar. Given data may thus on occasion be represented about equally well by either model, or possibly by one of the other distributions discussed earlier. Therefore it is important that the choice of the time to failure distribution is based upon an understanding of the underlying physical failure mechanisms, especially when the model is to be used for extrapolation beyond the range of the available data.

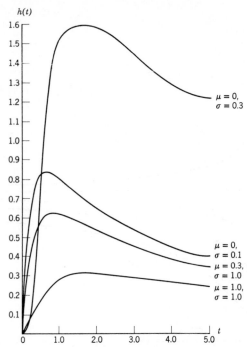

Fig. 3-20   Hazard functions for log-normal distributions with different parameter values.

3-6. Summary of Continuous Distributions

Information concerning the distributions discussed in this chapter is summarized in Fig. 3-21 and Table 3-2. The figure also gives the expected value, variance, and standardized third and fourth moments ($\sqrt{\beta_1}$ and β_2) for each of these models.

Normal

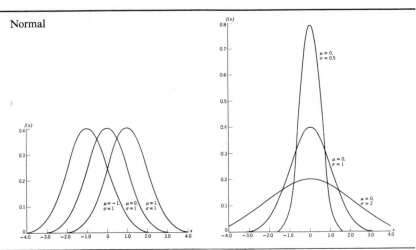

Half-Normal

Gamma

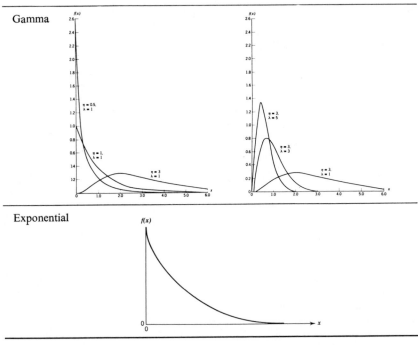

Exponential

Fig. 3-21 Summary of important

Parameters	Probability Density Function
$-\infty < \mu < \infty,$ $\sigma > 0$	$f(x) = \dfrac{1}{\sigma\sqrt{2\pi}}\, e^{-(x-\mu)^2/2\sigma^2},$ $-\infty < x < \infty$
$\sigma > 0$	$f(x) = \begin{cases} \left(\dfrac{2}{\pi\sigma^2}\right)^{\!1/2} e^{-x^2/2\sigma^2}, & x \ge 0 \\ 0 & \text{elsewhere} \end{cases}$
$\lambda > 0,$ $\eta > 0$	$f(x) = \begin{cases} \dfrac{\lambda^\eta}{\Gamma(\eta)}\, x^{\eta-1} e^{-\lambda x}, & x \ge 0 \\ 0 & \text{elsewhere} \end{cases}$
$\lambda > 0$	$f(x) = \begin{cases} \lambda e^{-\lambda x}, & x \ge 0 \\ 0 & \text{elsewhere} \end{cases}$

continuous distributions

Expected Value	Variance	$\sqrt{\beta_1}$	β_2
μ	σ^2	0	3
0.798σ	$0.363\sigma^2$	0.995	3.869
$\dfrac{\eta}{\lambda}$	$\dfrac{\eta}{\lambda^2}$	$\dfrac{2}{\sqrt{\eta}}$	$\dfrac{3(\eta + 2)}{\eta}$
$\dfrac{1}{\lambda}$	$\dfrac{1}{\lambda^2}$	2.0	9.0

Fig. 3.21 (*continued*)

124

Beta

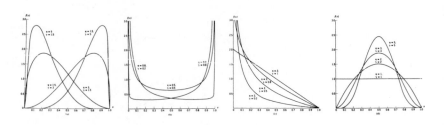

Uniform

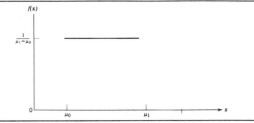

Log-Normal

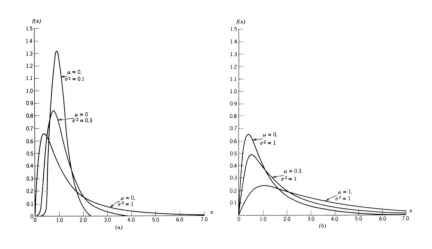

Fig. 3.21

126

Parameters	Probability Density Function
$\eta > 0, \gamma > 0$	$f(x) = \begin{cases} \dfrac{\Gamma(\eta + \gamma)}{\Gamma(\eta)\Gamma(\gamma)}\, x^{\gamma-1}\,(1-x)^{\eta-1}, & 0 \le x \le 1 \\[2mm] 0 & \text{elsewhere} \end{cases}$
$\mu_0, \mu_1,$ where $\mu_0 < \mu_1$	$f(x) = \begin{cases} \dfrac{1}{\mu_1 - \mu_0}, & \mu_0 \le x \le \mu_1 \\[2mm] 0 & \text{elsewhere} \end{cases}$
$-\infty < \mu < \infty;$ $\sigma > 0$	$f(x) = \dfrac{1}{\sigma x \sqrt{2\pi}}$ $\exp\left[-\dfrac{1}{2\sigma^2}\,(\log x - \mu)^2 \right],$ $x \ge 0$

(*continued*)

Expected Value	Variance	$\sqrt{\beta_1}$	β_2
$\dfrac{\gamma}{\eta + \gamma}$	$\dfrac{\eta\gamma}{(\eta + \gamma)^2(\eta + \gamma + 1)}$	*	†
$\dfrac{\mu_0 + \mu_1}{2}$	$\dfrac{(\mu_1 - \mu_0)^2}{12}$	0	1.8
$e^{\mu + \frac{1}{2}\sigma^2}$	$e^{2\mu + \sigma^2}(e^{\sigma^2} - 1)$	$(e^{\sigma^2} - 1)^{\frac{1}{2}}(e^{\sigma^2} + 2)$	‡

$* \ \sqrt{\beta_1} = \dfrac{2(\eta - \gamma)(\gamma + \eta + 1)^{\frac{1}{2}}}{(\eta\gamma)^{\frac{1}{2}}(\gamma + \eta + 2)}$

$† \ \beta_2 = \dfrac{3(\eta + \gamma + 1)[2(\gamma + \eta)^2 + \eta\gamma(\eta + \gamma - 6)]}{\eta\gamma(\eta + \gamma + 2)(\eta + \gamma + 3)}$

$‡ \ \beta_2 = 3 + (w - 1)(w^3 + 3w^2 + 6w + 6); \ w = e^{\sigma^2}$

Fig. 3.21 (*continued*)

128

Distribution Name

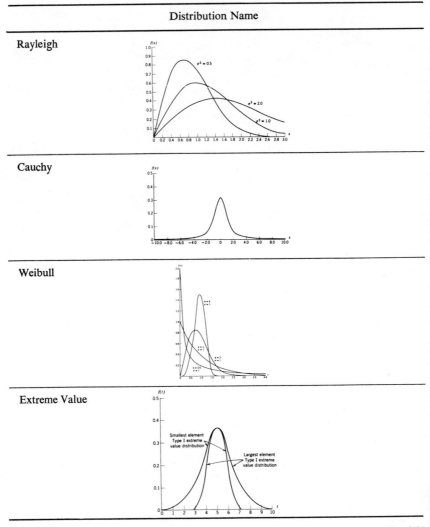

Rayleigh

Cauchy

Weibull

Extreme Value

Fig. 3.21

130

Parameters	Probability Density Function
$\sigma > 0$	$f(x) = \begin{cases} \left(\dfrac{x}{\sigma^2}\right) e^{-x^2/2\sigma^2}, & x \geq 0 \\ 0 & \text{elsewhere} \end{cases}$
$-\infty < \mu < \infty,$ $\sigma > 0$	$f(x) = \dfrac{1}{\sigma\pi}\left[1 + \dfrac{(x-\mu)^2}{\sigma^2}\right]^{-1},$ $-\infty < x < \infty$
$\eta > 0, \sigma > 0$	$f(x) = \begin{cases} \left(\dfrac{\eta}{\sigma}\right)\left(\dfrac{x}{\sigma}\right)^{\eta-1} \exp\left[-\left(\dfrac{x}{\sigma}\right)^{\eta}\right], & x \geq 0 \\ 0 & \text{elsewhere} \end{cases}$
$-\infty < \mu < \infty,$ $\sigma > 0$	Largest element: $f(x) = \dfrac{1}{\sigma}\exp\left[-\dfrac{1}{\sigma}(x-\mu) - e^{-(1/\sigma)(x-\mu)}\right],$ Smallest element: $f(x) = \dfrac{1}{\sigma}\exp\left[\dfrac{1}{\sigma}(x-\mu) - e^{(1/\sigma)(x-\mu)}\right],$ $-\infty < x < \infty$

(*continued*)

Expected Value	Variance	$\sqrt{\beta_1}$	β_2
$\dfrac{(\sigma^2\pi)^{\frac{1}{2}}}{\sqrt{2}}$	$0.429\sigma^2$	0.63	3.26
No finite value	No finite value	No finite value	No finite value
$\sigma\Gamma\left(\dfrac{1}{\eta}+1\right)$	$\sigma^2\left\{\Gamma\left(\dfrac{2}{\eta}+1\right)-\left[\Gamma\left(\dfrac{1}{\eta}+1\right)\right]^2\right\}$	*	**
Largest element: $\mu+0.577\sigma$, Smallest element: $\mu-0.577\sigma$	$1.645\sigma^2$	Largest element: 1.14, Smallest element: -1.14	5.4

$$* \ \sqrt{\beta_1} = \frac{\Gamma\left(1+\dfrac{3}{\eta}\right)-3\Gamma\left(1+\dfrac{2}{\eta}\right)\Gamma\left(1+\dfrac{1}{\eta}\right)+2\left[\Gamma\left(1+\dfrac{1}{\eta}\right)\right]^3}{\left\{\Gamma\left(1+\dfrac{2}{\eta}\right)-\left[\Gamma\left(1+\dfrac{1}{\eta}\right)\right]^2\right\}^{3/2}}$$

$$** \ \beta_2 = \frac{\Gamma\left(1+\dfrac{4}{\eta}\right)-4\Gamma\left(1+\dfrac{3}{\eta}\right)\Gamma\left(1+\dfrac{1}{\eta}\right)+6\Gamma\left(1+\dfrac{2}{\eta}\right)\left[\Gamma\left(1+\dfrac{1}{\eta}\right)\right]^2-3\left[\Gamma\left(1+\dfrac{1}{\eta}\right)\right]^4}{\left\{\Gamma\left(1+\dfrac{2}{\eta}\right)-\left[\Gamma\left(1+\dfrac{1}{\eta}\right)\right]^2\right\}^2}$$

Fig. 3.21 (*continued*)

Table 3-2 Summary: Applications of Continuous Statistical Distributions

Distribution	Application	Example	Comments
Normal	A basic distribution of statistics. Many applications arise from central limit theorem (average of values of n observations approaches normal distribution, irrespective of form of original distribution under quite general conditions). Consequently, appropriate model for many—but not all—physical phenomena.	Distribution of physical measurements on living organisms, intelligence test scores, product dimensions, average temperatures, and so on.	Tabulation of cumulative values of standardized normal distribution readily available. Many methods of statistical analysis presume normal distribution.
Gamma	A basic distribution of statistics for variables bounded at one side—for example, $0 \leq x < \infty$. Gives distribution of time required for exactly k independent events to occur, assuming events take place at a constant rate. Used frequently in queueing theory, reliability, and other industrial applications.	Distribution of time between recalibrations of instrument that needs recalibration after k uses; time between inventory restocking; time to failure for a system with standby components.	Cumulative distribution values have been tabulated. Erlangian, exponential, and chi-square distributions are special cases.
Exponential	Gives distribution of time between independent events occurring at a constant rate. Equivalently, probability distribution of life, presuming constant conditional failure (or hazard) rate. Consequently, applicable in many—but not all—reliability situations.	Distribution of time between arrival of particles at a counter. Also life distribution of complex nonredundant systems, and usage life of some components—in particular, when these are exposed to initial burn-in, and preventive maintenance eliminates parts before wear-out.	Special case of both Weibull and gamma distributions.
Beta	A basic distribution of statistics for variables bounded at both sides—for example $0 \leq x \leq 1$. Useful for both theoretical and applied problems in many areas.	Distribution of proportion of population located between lowest and highest value in sample; distribution of daily per cent yield in a manufacturing process; description of elapsed times to task completion (PERT).	Cumulative distribution values have been tabulated. Uniform, right triangular, and parabolic distributions are special cases.

133

Table 3-2 (continued)

Summary: Applications of Continous Statistical Distributions

Uniform	Gives probability that observation will occur within a particular interval when probability of occurrence within that interval is directly proportional to interval length.	Used to generate random values.	Special case of beta distribution.
Log-normal	Permits representation of random variable whose logarithm follows normal distribution. Model for a process arising from many small multiplicative errors. Appropriate when the value of an observed variable is a random proportion of the previously observed value.	Distribution of sizes from a breakage process; distribution of income size, inheritances and bank deposits; distribution of various biological phenomena; life distribution of some transistor types.	
Rayleigh	Gives distribution of radial error when the errors in two mutually perpendicular axes are independent and normally distributed around zero with equal variances.	Bomb-sighting problems; amplitude of noise envelope when a linear detector is used.	Special case of Weibull distribution.
Cauchy	Gives distribution of ratio of two independent standardized normal variates.	Distribution of ratio of standardized noise readings; distribution of tan θ when θ is uniformly distributed.	Has no moments.
Weibull	General time-to-failure distribution due to wide diversity of hazard-rate curves, and extreme-value distribution for minimum of N values from distribution bounded at left.	Life distribution for some capacitors, ball bearings, relays, and so on.	Rayleigh and exponential distributions are special cases.
Extreme value	Limiting model for the distribution of the maximum or minimum of N values selected from an "exponential-type" distribution, such as the normal, gamma, or exponential.	Distribution of breaking strength of some materials, capacitor breakdown voltage, gust velocities encountered by airplanes, bacteria extinction times.	Cumulative distribution has been tabulated.

134

References

3-1 C. A. Bennett and N. L. Franklin, *Statistical Analysis in Chemistry and the Chemical Industry*, John Wiley and Sons, New York, 1954.

3-2 A. H. Bowker and G. J. Lieberman, *Engineering Statistics*, Prentice-Hall, Englewood Cliffs, New Jersey, 1959.

3-3 K. A. Brownlee, *Statistical Theory and Methodology in Science and Engineering*, 2nd ed., John Wiley and Sons, New York, 1965.

3-4 O. L. Davies (Ed.), *Statistical Methods in Research and Production*, 3rd ed., Hafner Publishing Co. New York, 1961.

3-5 W. J. Dixon and F. J. Massey, Jr., *Introduction to Statistical Analysis*, 2nd ed., McGraw-Hill Book Co., New York, 1957.

3-6 W. Volk, *Applied Statistics for Engineers*, McGraw-Hill Book Co., New York, 1958.

3-7 D. R. Cox and W. L. Smith, *Queues*, John Wiley and Sons, New York, 1961.

3-8 P. M. Morse, *Queues, Inventories and Maintenance*, John Wiley and Sons, New York, 1958.

3-9 T. L. Saaty, *Elements of Queueing Theory with Applications*, McGraw-Hill Book Co., New York, 1961.

3-10 R. Schlaifer, *Probability and Statistics for Business Decisions*, McGraw-Hill Book Co., New York, 1959.

3-11 M. B. Wilk, R. Gnanadesikan, and M. J. Huyett, "Probability Plots for the Gamma Distribution," *Technometrics*, **4**, 1 (1962).

3-12 J. A. Greenwood and D. Durand, "Aids for Fitting the Gamma Distribution by Maximum Likelihood," *Technometrics*, **2**, 55 (1960).

3-13 M. B. Wilk, R. Gnanadesikan, and M. J. Huyett, "Estimation of Parameters of the Gamma Distribution Using Order Statistics," *Biometrika*, **49**, 525 (1962).

3-14 K. Pearson, *Tables of the Incomplete Beta-Function*, Biometrika Office, University College, London, 1948.

3-15 H. L. Harter, *New Tables of the Incomplete Gamma-Function Ratio and of Percentage Points of the Chi-square and Beta Distributions*, Aerospace Research Laboratories, U.S. Air Force, 1964 (Available from Superintendent of Documents, U.S. Govt. Printing Office, Washington, D.C.)

3-16 E. S. Pearson and H. O. Hartley, *Biometrika Tables for Statisticians*, Vol. I, Cambridge University Press, Cambridge 1954.

3-17 D. G. Malcolm, J. H. Roseboom, C. E. Clark, and W. Fazar, "Application of a Technique for Research and Development Program Evualuation," *Operations Res.*, **7**, 646 (1959).

3-18 S. Wilks, "Statistical Prediction with Special Reference to the Problem of Tolerance Limits," *Ann. Math. Statist.*, **13**, 400 (1942).

3-19 J. Aitchison and J. A. C. Brown, *The Log-normal Distribution*, Cambridge University Press, Cambridge, 1957.

3-20 B. Epstein, "The Mathematical Description of Certain Breakage Mechanisms Leading to the Logarithmic-Normal Distribution," *J. Franklin Inst.*, **244**, 471 (1947).

3-21 D. Middleton, *An Introduction to Statistical Communication Theory*, McGraw-Hill Book Co., New York, 1960.

3-22 R. F. Drenick, "The Failure Law of Complex Equipment," *J. Soc. Ind. Appl. Math.*, **8**, 680 (1960).

136   Continuous Statistical Distributions

3-23 D. J. Davis, "An Analysis of Some Failure Data," *J. Am. Statist. Assoc.*, **47**, 113 (1952).

3-24 B. Epstein, "Estimation from Life Test Data," *Technometrics*, **2**, 447 (1960).

3-25 I. Bazovsky, *Reliability Theory and Practice*, Prentice-Hall, Englewood Cliffs, New Jersey, 1961.

3-26 W. Weibull, "A Statistical Distribution Function of Wide Applicability," *J. Appl. Mech.*, **18**, 293 (1951).

3-27 J. Lieblein, and M. Zelen, "Statistical Investigation of the Fatigue Life of Deep-Groove Ball Bearings," *J. Res. Nat. Bur. St.*, **57**, 273 (1956).

3-28 J. H. K. Kao, "A New Life Quality Measure for Electron Tubes," *IRE Trans. Reliability Quality Control*, **7**, 1 (1956).

3-29 J. H. K. Kao, "A Summary of Some New Techniques on Failure Analysis," *Proc. 6th Nat. Symp. Reliability Quality Control in Electron.*, pp. 190–201, 1960.

3-30 J. N. Perry, "Semiconductor Burn-in and Weibull Statistics," *Semiconductor Reliability*, Vol. 2, Engineering Publishers, Elizabeth, New Jersey, 1962, pp. 80–90.

3-31 A. Procassini and A. Romano, "Weibull Distribution Function in Reliability Analysis, *Semiconductor Reliability*, Vol. 2, Engineering Publishers, Elizabeth, New Jersey, 1962, pp. 29–34.

3-32 R. A. Fisher and L. H. C. Tippett, "Limiting Forms of the Frequency Distribution of the Largest or Smallest Member of a Sample," *Proc. Cambridge Phil. Soc.*, **24**, (2), 180 (1928). Reprinted in R. A. Fisher, *Contributions to Mathematical Statistics*, John Wiley and Sons, New York, 1950.

3-33 A. M. Freudenthal and E. J. Gumbel, "On the Statistical Interpretation of Fatigue Tests," *Proc. Royal Soc.* (A) **216**, 309 (1953).

3-34 J. H. K. Kao, "Computer Methods for Estimating Weibull Parameters in Reliability Studies," *IRE Trans. Reliability Quality Control*, **13**, 15, (1958).

3-35 G. J. Hahn and J. T. Godfrey, "Estimation of Weibull Distribution Parameters with Differing Test Times for Unfailed Units," *Technometrics* **6**, 118 (1964) (Abstract).

3-36 E. J. Gumbel, *Statistical Theory of Extreme Values and Some Practical Applications*, Nat. Bur. Std., Appl. Math. Ser. 33.

3-37 E. J. Gumbel, *Statistics of Extremes*, Columbia University Press, New York, 1958.

3-38 J. Lieblein, *A New Method for Analysing Extreme Value Data*, National Advisory Committee for Aeronautics Technical Note 3053, January 1954.

3-39 H. Press, *The Application of Statistical Theory of Extreme Values to Gust-Load Problems*, Nat. Advisory Comm. Aeron., Rept. 991, 1950.

3-40 B. Epstein, "Application of the Theory of Extreme Values in Fracture Problems," *J. Amer. Statist. Assoc.*, **43**, 403 (1948).

3-41 B. Epstein and H. Brooks, "The Theory of Extreme Values and Its Implications in the Study of the Dielectric Strength of Paper Capacitors," *J. Appl. Phys.*, **19**, 544 (1948).

3-42 B. F. Kimball, "Sufficient Statistical Estimation Functions for the Parameters of the Distribution of Maximum Values," *Ann. Math. Statist.*, **17**, 299 (1946).

3-43 F. Downton, "Linear Estimates of Parameters in the Extreme Value Distribution," *Technometrics*, **8**, 3 (1966).

3-44 K. Mather, "The Analysis of Extinction Time Data in Bioassay," *Biometrics*, **5**, 127 (1949).

3-45 D. S. Peck, "Uses of Semiconductor Life Distributions," *Semiconductor Reliability*, Vol. 2, Engineering Publishers, Elizabeth, New Jersey, 1962 pp. 10–28.

3-46 T. W. Anderson, *An Introduction to Multivariate Statistical Analysis*, John Wiley and Sons, New York, 1958.

3-47 W. R. Buckland, *Statistical Assessment of the Life Characteristic*, Griffin's Statistical Monographs and Courses, No. 13, Hafner Publishing Co., New York, 1964.

3-48 *Probability Tables for the Analysis of Extreme-Value Data*, Nat. Bur. Std., Appl. Math. Ser. 22.

3-49 N. L. Johnson and F. C. Leone, *Statistics and Experimental Design in Engineering and the Physical Sciences*, Vol. 1, John Wiley and Sons, New York, 1964.

3-50 D. Owen, *Handbook of Statistical Tables*, Addison-Wesley Publishing Co., Reading, Massachusetts, 1962.

3-51 F. C. Leone, L. S. Nelson, and R. B. Nottingham, "The Folded Normal Distribution," *Technometrics*, 3, 543 (1961).

3-52 A. Hald, *Statistical Theory with Engineering Applications*, John Wiley and Sons, New York, 1952.

3-53 B. Epstein, "Elements of the Theory of Extreme Values," *Technometrics*, 2, 27 (1960).

3-54 K. Pearson, *Tables of the Incomplete Γ-Function*, Biometrika Office, University College, London, 1957.

3-55 E. Pieruschka, *Principles of Reliability*, Prentice-Hall, Inc., Englewood Cliffs, New Jersey, 1963.

3-56 A. E. Sarhan, and B. G. Greenberg, *Contributions to Order Statistics*, John Wiley and Sons, New York, 1962.

3-57 K. Pearson, *Tables for Statisticians and Biometricians*, Vol. II, Cambridge University Press, Cambridge, 1931.

3-58 S. S. Gupta, "Order Statistics from the Gamma Distribution," *Technometrics*, 2, 243 (1960).

3-59 *Tables of the Bivariate Normal Distribution Function and Related Functions*, Nat. Bur. Std. Appl. Math. Ser. 50.

3-60 M. V. Johns, Jr., and G. J. Lieberman, "An Exact Asymptotically Efficient Confidence Bound for Reliability in the Case of the Weibull Distribution," *Technometrics*, 8, 135 (1966).

3-61 N. R. Mann, "Exact Three-Order-Statistic Confidence Bounds on Reliability Parameters under Weibull Assumptions," Paper presented to 126th Annual Meeting of the American Statistical Association, Los Angeles, California, 1966.

3-62 P. M. Aziz, "Application of the Statistical Theory of Extreme Values to the Analysis of Maximum Pit Depth Data for Aluminum," *Corrosion*, 12, 495 (1956).

3-63 G. G. Eldredge, "Analysis of Corrosion Pitting by Extreme-Value Statistics and Its Application to Oil Well Tubing Caliper Surveys," *Corrosion*, 13, 51 (1957).

Chapter 4

Discrete Statistical Distributions

In this chapter we consider models for random variables defined on a discrete sample space. As indicated in Chapter 2, the probability function $f(x_i)$ for a discrete random variable x gives the probability that x takes on the value x_i.*

The nature and application of the following distributions will be discussed: binomial, multinomial, hypergeometric, geometric, Pascal, negative binomial, and Poisson. Methods for estimating distribution parameters and establishing confidence intervals from given data will be shown for the two most important cases—the binomial and the Poisson. The mean, variance, and standardized moments for each of the distributions are given in the summary at the end of the chapter.

4-1. The Binomial and Multinomial Distributions

THE BINOMIAL DISTRIBUTION

Many engineering problems involve independent repeated trials, known as *Bernoulli trials*, in which each trial results in one of two possible outcomes, frequently referred to as success and failure, and where the probability of success, p, remains constant from one trial to the next. The best known example occurs in repeat tossings of a coin. If the coin is "fair," p has a value of 0.5. We frequently want to know the probability of getting exactly x (or at least x) successes in n independent trials. Some examples are:

1. Ten space shots are planned. Each has a probability of success of 0.95. What are the chances that at least nine shots will be successful?

---

* In Chapter 2 the notation $p(x_i)$ was used to designate a probability function of a discrete random variable. In this chapter it will be convenient to use $f(x_i)$ instead.

2. The register of a digital computer is instructed to round up or down to the nearest integer. In processing 10 random digits, what is the probability that exactly half will be rounded up and half will be rounded down?

3. Twenty sales presentations are planned. The probability of receiving an order in each case has been estimated as one out of three. What are the chances of getting 10 or more orders?

From the multiplication law for independent events (2-9a), the probability of a *specific sequence* of x successes and $(n - x)$ failures in n trials is $p^x(1 - p)^{n-x}$, where p is the probability of success on a single trial. From the simple rules of combinations and permutations (see Reference 4-1) there are $n!/[x!\,(n - x)!]$ equally likely sequences in which x successes and $(n - x)$ failures can occur in n trials. The notation

$$\binom{n}{x} = \frac{n!}{x!\,(n - x)!}$$

is used. Consequently, from the addition law for mutually exclusive events (2-5b), the probability of exactly x successes in n independent trials, given a probability of success p in a single trial, is given by the *binomial probability function*:

$$f(x; p, n) = \binom{n}{x}p^x(1 - p)^{n-x}, \qquad x = 0, 1, 2, \ldots, n; 0 \leq p \leq 1. \quad (4\text{-}1)$$

Using the binomial expansion, we note that

$$\sum_{x=0}^{n} f(x; p, n) = \sum_{x=0}^{n}\binom{n}{x}p^x(1 - p)^{n-x}$$

$$= (1 - p)^n + np(1 - p)^{n-1} + \binom{n}{2}p^2(1 - p)^{n-2} + \cdots + p^n$$

$$= (1 - p + p)^n = 1,$$

as is required for a probability function.* Plots of the binomial probability function for different values of the parameters n and p are shown in Fig. 4-1.

The probability of r *or fewer* successes in n independent trials, given a probability of success p in a single trial, is given by the cumulative binomial distribution—that is,

$$\Pr(x \leq r) = F(r; p, n) = \sum_{x=0}^{r}\binom{n}{x}p^x(1 - p)^{n-x}. \quad (4\text{-}2)$$

---

* We shall leave the verification of this property for the remaining distributions of this chapter to the reader.

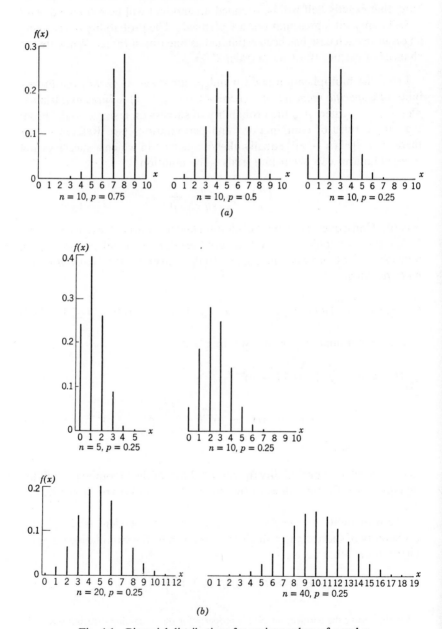

Fig. 4-1   Binomial distributions for various values of *n* and *p*.

Values of the cumulative binomial distribution are tabulated as a function of p, n, and r in the following references:

1. Reference 4-2 for
   $r = 0\,(1)\,n;$†
   $n = 1\,(1)\,50\,(2)\,100\,(10)\,200\,(20)\,500\,(50)\,1000;$
   $p = 0.01\,(0.01)\,0.50;\ \frac{1}{16},\ \frac{1}{12},\ \frac{1}{8},\ \frac{1}{6},\ \frac{3}{16},\ \frac{5}{16},\ \frac{1}{3},\ \frac{3}{8},\ \frac{5}{12},\ \frac{7}{16}.$
2. Reference 4-3 for
   $r = 0\,(1)\,n;$
   $n = 2\,(1)\,49;$
   $p = 0.01\,(0.01)\,0.50.$
3. Reference 4-4 for
   $r = 0\,(1)\,n;$
   $n = 50\,(5)\,100;$
   $p = 0.01\,(0.01)\,0.50.$
4. Reference 4-16 for
   $r = 0\,(1)\,n$
   $n = 1\,(1)\,100$
   $p = 0.0001\,(0.0001)\,0.0009;\ 0.001\,(0.001)\,0.100.$

A sample page from Reference 4-2 is shown in Table 4-1. This table gives $\Pr\{x \geq r\}$. To obtain $\Pr\{x \leq r\} = F(r;p,n)$ we note that

$$\Pr\{x \leq r\} + \Pr\{x \geq r+1\} = 1.$$

Hence

$$\Pr\{x \leq r\} = 1 - \Pr\{x \geq r+1\}.$$

For example,

$$\Pr\{x \leq 3\} = 1 - \Pr\{x \geq 4\}.$$

In many problems it is convenient to refer to these tabulations instead of evaluating (4-2) directly.

A typical application of the binomial distribution is as follows. Items are manufactured in large lots, from each of which twenty units are selected at random. The lot is accepted if the sample contains three or fewer defective units. If the production process yields on the average 10 per cent defectives, what is the probability of lot acceptance?

The problem may be rephrased as, "What is the probability of three or fewer successes in 20 independent Bernoulli trials, each having a probability of success 0.1?" From (4-2) with $p = 0.1$ and $n = 20$, we obtain

$$\Pr(x \leq 3) = F(3; 0.1, 20) = \sum_{x=0}^{3} \binom{20}{x}(0.1)^x(0.9)^{20-x} = 0.867.$$

† i.e., for all integer values of r from 0 to n.

Table 4-1　Sample Page from Harvard University Press, Tables of Cumulative Binomial Probability

$$\text{Distribution showing } \sum_{x=r}^{n} \binom{n}{x} p^{x}(1-p)^{n-x} \text{ for } n = 16, 17, \ldots, 20 \text{ and Various Values of } p$$

n	r	p = 0.09	p = 0.10	p = 0.11	p = 0.12	p = $\frac{1}{8}$	p = 0.13	p = 0.14	p = 0.15	p = 0.16	p = $\frac{1}{6}$
16	0	1.00000	1.00000	1.00000	1.00000	1.00000	1.00000	1.00000	1.00000	1.00000	1.00000
	1	0.77886	0.81470	0.84503	0.87066	0.88193	0.89228	0.91047	0.92575	0.93856	0.94591
	2	0.42893	0.48527	0.53858	0.58847	0.61207	0.63473	0.67727	0.71610	0.75130	0.77283
	3	0.16937	0.21075	0.25451	0.29987	0.32292	0.34611	0.39255	0.43862	0.48380	0.51321
	4	0.04957	0.06841	0.09066	0.11621	0.13016	0.14484	0.17625	0.21011	0.24602	0.27090
	5	0.01106	0.01700	0.02485	0.03482	0.04066	0.04710	0.06182	0.07905	0.09882	0.11339
	6	0.00192	0.00330	0.00533	0.00818	0.00998	0.01205	0.01711	0.02354	0.03153	0.03779
	7	0.00026	0.00050	0.00090	0.00152	0.00194	0.00245	0.00376	0.00559	0.00803	0.01007
	8	0.00003	0.00006	0.00012	0.00023	0.00030	0.00040	0.00066	0.00106	0.00164	0.00215
	9	0.00000	0.00001	0.00001	0.00003	0.00004	0.00005	0.00009	0.00016	0.00027	0.00037
	10		0.00000	0.00000	0.00000	0.00000	0.00001	0.00001	0.00002	0.00003	0.00005
	11						0.00000	0.00000	0.00000	0.00000	0.00001
	12										0.00000
17	0	1.00000	1.00000	1.00000	1.00000	1.00000	1.00000	1.00000	1.00000	1.00000	1.00000
	1	0.79876	0.83323	0.86208	0.88618	0.89669	0.90628	0.92300	0.93689	0.94839	0.95493
	2	0.46042	0.51821	0.57229	0.62234	0.64580	0.66821	0.70992	0.74755	0.78126	0.80168
	3	0.19273	0.23820	0.28576	0.33450	0.35906	0.38363	0.43241	0.48024	0.52660	0.55648
	4	0.06035	0.08264	0.10869	0.13825	0.15425	0.17100	0.20654	0.24439	0.28406	0.31128
	5	0.01453	0.02214	0.03209	0.04459	0.05185	0.05981	0.07784	0.09871	0.12237	0.13964
	6	0.00274	0.00467	0.00747	0.01138	0.01381	0.01660	0.02337	0.03187	0.04230	0.05039
	7	0.00041	0.00078	0.00139	0.00232	0.00295	0.00369	0.00563	0.00828	0.01179	0.01469
	8	0.00005	0.00011	0.00021	0.00038	0.00051	0.00066	0.00110	0.00174	0.00266	0.00347
	9	0.00000	0.00001	0.00002	0.00005	0.00007	0.00010	0.00017	0.00030	0.00049	0.00066
	10		0.00000	0.00000	0.00001	0.00001	0.00001	0.00002	0.00004	0.00007	0.00010
	11				0.00000	0.00000	0.00000	0.00000	0.00000	0.00001	0.00001
	12									0.00000	0.00000
18	0	1.00000	1.00000	1.00000	1.00000	1.00000	1.00000	1.00000	1.00000	1.00000	1.00000
	1	0.81688	0.84991	0.87725	0.89984	0.90960	0.91846	0.93378	0.94635	0.95665	0.96244
	2	0.49088	0.54972	0.60417	0.65400	0.67716	0.69916	0.73975	0.77595	0.80805	0.82722
	3	0.21682	0.26620	0.31728	0.36904	0.39491	0.42062	0.47126	0.52034	0.56735	0.59735
	4	0.07226	0.09820	0.12816	0.16180	0.17986	0.19865	0.23816	0.27976	0.32287	0.35215
	5	0.01865	0.02819	0.04051	0.05583	0.06465	0.07426	0.09586	0.12056	0.14824	0.16825
	6	0.00380	0.00642	0.01018	0.01536	0.01857	0.02222	0.03099	0.04190	0.05511	0.06527
	7	0.00062	0.00117	0.00206	0.00341	0.00430	0.00537	0.00812	0.01182	0.01667	0.02064
	8	0.00008	0.00017	0.00034	0.00061	0.00081	0.00106	0.00173	0.00272	0.00412	0.00534
	9	0.00001	0.00002	0.00005	0.00009	0.00012	0.00017	0.00030	0.00051	0.00083	0.00113

n	c	0.00000	0.00000	0.00000	0.00001	0.00002	0.00002	0.00004	0.00008	0.00014	0.00020
	10			0.00000	0.00001	0.00002	0.00002	0.00004	0.00008	0.00014	0.00020
	11			0.00000	0.00000	0.00000	0.00000	0.00000	0.00001	0.00002	0.00003
	12			0.00000	0.00000	0.00000	0.00000	0.00000	0.00000	0.00000	0.00000
19	0	1.00000	1.00000	1.00000	1.00000	1.00000	1.00000	1.00000	1.00000	1.00000	1.00000
	1	0.83336	0.86491	0.89075	0.91186	0.92090	0.92906	0.94305	0.95440	0.96358	0.96870
	2	0.52022	0.57974	0.63421	0.68350	0.70622	0.72767	0.76691	0.80151	0.83179	0.84976
	3	0.24148	0.29456	0.34883	0.40324	0.43019	0.45683	0.50885	0.55868	0.60585	0.63566
	4	0.08527	0.11500	0.14897	0.18667	0.20674	0.22750	0.27079	0.31585	0.36199	0.39301
	5	0.02347	0.03519	0.05016	0.06854	0.07905	0.09043	0.11578	0.14444	0.17618	0.19890
	6	0.00514	0.00859	0.01352	0.02022	0.02433	0.02899	0.04007	0.05370	0.07001	0.08243
	7	0.00091	0.00170	0.00295	0.00484	0.00609	0.00756	0.01132	0.01633	0.02282	0.02808
	8	0.00013	0.00027	0.00053	0.00095	0.00125	0.00162	0.00262	0.00408	0.00613	0.00789
	9	0.00002	0.00004	0.00008	0.00015	0.00021	0.00028	0.00050	0.00084	0.00136	0.00183
	10	0.00000	0.00000	0.00001	0.00002	0.00003	0.00004	0.00008	0.00014	0.00025	0.00035
	11			0.00000	0.00000	0.00000	0.00000	0.00001	0.00002	0.00004	0.00006
	12							0.00000	0.00000	0.00000	0.00001
	13										0.00000
20	0	1.00000	1.00000	1.00000	1.00000	1.00000	1.00000	1.00000	1.00000	1.00000	1.00000
	1	0.84836	0.87842	0.90277	0.92244	0.93079	0.93829	0.95103	0.96124	0.96941	0.97392
	2	0.54840	0.60825	0.66243	0.71090	0.73305	0.75385	0.79157	0.82444	0.85287	0.86958
	3	0.26657	0.32307	0.38022	0.43687	0.46469	0.49204	0.54498	0.59510	0.64200	0.67134
	4	0.09933	0.13295	0.17095	0.21266	0.23467	0.25732	0.30412	0.35227	0.40100	0.43345
	5	0.02904	0.04317	0.06102	0.08272	0.09501	0.10825	0.13748	0.17015	0.20591	0.23125
	6	0.00679	0.01125	0.01755	0.02602	0.03117	0.03697	0.05067	0.06731	0.08700	0.10184
	7	0.00129	0.00239	0.00411	0.00669	0.00837	0.01035	0.01534	0.02194	0.03037	0.03714
	8	0.00020	0.00042	0.00079	0.00142	0.00185	0.00239	0.00384	0.00592	0.00880	0.01125
	9	0.00003	0.00006	0.00013	0.00025	0.00034	0.00046	0.00080	0.00133	0.00212	0.00284
	10	0.00000	0.00001	0.00002	0.00004	0.00005	0.00007	0.00014	0.00025	0.00043	0.00060
	11		0.00000	0.00000	0.00000	0.00001	0.00001	0.00002	0.00004	0.00007	0.00011
	12			0.00000	0.00000	0.00000	0.00000	0.00000	0.00000	0.00001	0.00002
	13									0.00000	0.00000

(The value 0.13295 for n = 20, c = 4 is circled in the original.)

From Computation Laboratory, Harvard University, Tables of the Cumulative Binomial Probability Distribution, Harvard University Press, Cambridge, Mass., 1955 (page 59).

The same result could have been found directly from the tabulation in Reference 4-2, which shows

$$\Pr{(x \geq 4)} = \sum_{x=4}^{20} \binom{20}{x}(0.1)^x(0.9)^{20-x} = 1 - F(3; 0.1, 20) = 0.133$$

(see circled value in Table 4-1). Therefore $F(3; 0.1, 20) = 0.867$.

The binomial distribution has applications in quality control, reliability, survey sampling, and many other fields.

MEAN AND VARIANCE OF BINOMIAL-DISTRIBUTION AND NORMAL-DISTRIBUTION APPROXIMATION

It is shown in Appendix 4A that the mean and variance for a binomial variate are

$$E(x) = np$$

and

$$\text{Var}(x) = np(1 - p).$$

The binomial probability function is symmetric for $p = 0.5$ (see Fig. 4-1). When $p \neq 0.5$ the distribution approaches symmetry as n becomes larger, the approach being more rapid when p is close to 0.5. Also as n increases, the binomial distribution can be approximated by a normal distribution with the same mean and variance—that is, $\mu = np$ and $\sigma^2 = np(1 - p)$, see References 4-5, 4-11, and 4-12. This approximation gives reasonable results if np and $n(1 - p)$ are both at least 5.

The percentiles of the normal distribution are more readily available and more convenient to use than the cumulative binomial tables, because only one table is needed for the normal as compared to a book of tables for the binomial. Hence the normal distribution approximation is frequently used in problems such as the following.

Forty per cent of the employees in a large plant are union members. In a newspaper survey, 100 employees have been randomly selected. What are the chances that the sample includes 50 or more union members?

This problem is essentially equivalent to conducting 100 Bernoulli trials with $p = 0.4$. Since $np = 40$ and $n(1 - p) = 60$, a normal distribution with $\mu = np = 40$ and $\sigma^2 = np(1 - p) = 24$, or $\sigma = 4.9$, will provide a satisfactory approximation. We need find the probability of obtaining a value above 49.5 in sampling from a normal distribution with $\mu = 40$ and $\sigma = 4.9$. The value 49.5 is used, instead of 50, since to achieve continuity in approximating the discrete binomial by the continuous normal distribution the point $x = 50$ is replaced by the interval $x_1 = 49.5$ to $x_2 = 50.5$. Equivalently, we desire the proportion of area to the *right* of

$$\frac{x_1 - \mu}{\sigma} = \frac{49.5 - 40}{4.9} = 1.939$$

for a standard normal distribution—that is, one for which $\mu = 0$ and $\sigma = 1$. From Table 1 at the end of the book, this value is 0.0263. Thus the chances are about three out of 100 that 50 or more union members will be included in the sample.

The result obtained from the tabulation in Reference 4-2 is

$$\Pr(x \geq 50) = \sum_{x=50}^{100} \binom{100}{x}(0.4)^x(0.6)^{100-x} = 0.0271,$$

which is close to that using the normal-distribution approximation. If we had desired the probability of 50 *or fewer* union members in the sample, we would require the proportion of area to the left of $(x_2 - \mu)/\sigma = (50.5 - 40)/4.9 = 2.14$ for a standard normal distribution.

The normal-distribution approximation can be used similarly to establish bounds on the number of union members to be expected in the sample. Since 90 per cent of the area under a normal distribution curve lies within the interval $\mu \pm 1.645\sigma$, the chances are about 90 out of 100 that the number of union members in the sample will be in the range $40 \pm 1.645(4.9)$, or approximately between 32 and 48 members. Equivalently, the probability is about 0.95 that the number of union members will not exceed 48 and about 0.05 that *fewer* than 32 union members will be in the sample. This result could also have been obtained by using the tables in References 4-2, 4-3, or 4-4 in an inverse manner—that is, by searching in the column for $p = 0.4$ and $n = 100$ for the values r_1 and r_2 such that

$$\sum_{x=r_1}^{100} \binom{100}{x}(0.4)^x(0.6)^{100-x} \approx 0.95$$

and

$$\sum_{x=r_2}^{100} \binom{100}{x}(0.4)^x(0.6)^{100-x} \approx 0.05.$$

These expressions involve approximate equalities, because in dealing with a discrete distribution it is unlikely that we would be able to find values r_1 and r_2 that yield the exact specified probabilities. In particular,

$$\sum_{x=32}^{100} \binom{100}{x}(0.4)^x(0.6)^{100-x} = 0.960$$

and

$$\sum_{x=33}^{100} \binom{100}{x}(0.4)^x(0.6)^{100-x} = 0.939.$$

Also

$$\sum_{x=48}^{100} \binom{100}{x}(0.4)^x(0.6)^{100-x} = 0.064$$

and

$$\sum_{x=49}^{100} \binom{100}{x}(0.4)^x(0.6)^{100-x} = 0.042,$$

which again agrees closely with the results using the normal-distribution approximation. The above procedure may be used when the normal-distribution approximation does not hold. An alternative, the Poisson-distribution approximation, which is frequently applicable when the normal-distribution approximation is not, is discussed in Section 4-4.

ESTIMATION OF BINOMIAL PARAMETER p

Frequently, instead of knowing p and anticipating the number of successes in n trials, we are in the reverse situation—that is, the experimental data yields x successes in n trials, and from this information we would like to estimate p. For example, in sampling from a large lot, three out of 10 parts have been found defective. What can be said about the per cent defective in the lot?

The estimate for p is

$$\hat{p} = \frac{\text{number of successes}}{\text{number of trials}} = \frac{x}{n}. \tag{4-3}$$

Confidence bounds on p may be found by interpolating in References 4-2, 4-3, or 4-4, or by using the normal-distribution approximation to the binomial distribution, when applicable. Alternatively, we may use the curves of Figs. 4-2a and 4-2b, which have been constructed from such tables for confidence levels of $1 - \alpha = 0.95$ and 0.99, as in the following example.

In a market survey 34 out of 100 randomly selected individuals indicated they would consider buying a new model television set. From this information, what can be said about the proportion p of individuals in the population who would consider buying the new model? A sample of size $n = 100$ has been taken from a binomial distribution and $x = 34$ "successes" have resulted. From (4-3),

$$\hat{p} = \frac{x}{n} = \frac{34}{100} = 0.34.$$

The 95 per cent confidence limits on p can be found from Fig. 4-2a by reading the left ordinate corresponding to the curves for $n = 100$ with abscissa $x/n = 0.34$. This leads to a 95 per cent confidence interval on p of 0.25 to 0.44—that is, the chances are 95 out of 100 that we would be correct in asserting that the per cent of individuals in the population that would consider buying the set is between 25 and 44. If tighter limits were desired,

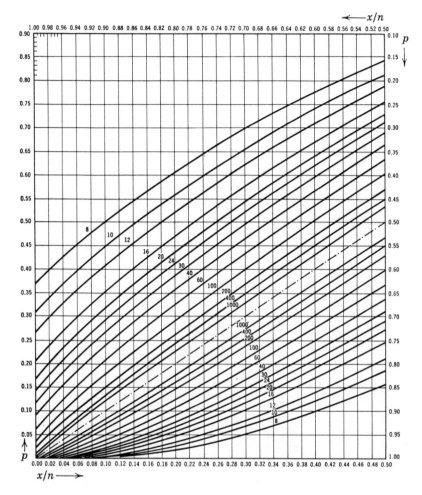

Fig. 4-2a   Chart providing 95 per cent confidence limits for p in binomial sampling, given a sample fraction x/n. Different curves represent different sample sizes n. Values on ordinate represent 95 per cent confidence bounds on p. [From E. S. Pearson and H. O. Hartley, *Biometrika Tables for Statisticians*, Vol. 1, 1954, Cambridge University Press, Cambridge, England (Table 41).]

additional samples would have to be taken. A one-sided bound may be calculated in a similar manner.

An application of these methods to Monte Carlo analysis and a further discussion of the sample size required to estimate p with a predetermined degree of precision are given in Chapter 7.

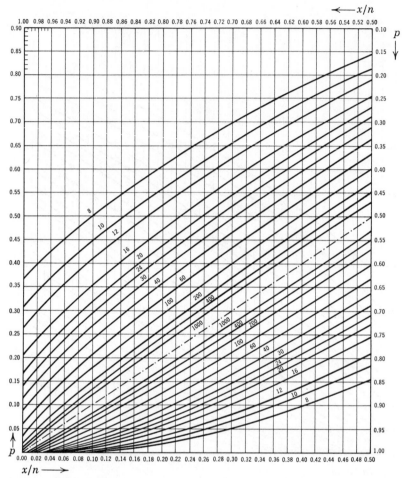

Fig. 4-2b Chart providing 99 per cent confidence limits for p in binomial sampling, given a sample fraction x/n. Different curves represent different sample sizes n. Values on ordinate represent 99 per cent confidence bounds on p. [From E. S. Pearson and H. O. Hartley, *Biometrika Tables for Statisticians*, Vol. 1, 1954, Cambridge University Press, Cambridge, England (Table 41).]

EFFECT OF POPULATION SIZE

The binomial distribution gives the probability of obtaining a specified number of successes in sampling from an infinite population. In each of the three examples at the beginning of this section, the population can be regarded as infinite. For example, the 10 space shots represent a sample from an infinite number of possible shots, the 10 random digits are a sample from all random digits, and so on.

In cases in which there are only a finite number of objects an infinite universe is obtained by "sampling with replacement." For example, say there are 20 tools of a particular type in a tool shop. Each morning a worker picks a tool at random and returns it that evening. The tool selected the following day is taken at random from the replenished supply. In this case the universe is infinite, because the process may be continued arbitrarily many times. If four of the tools have been made by manufacturer A and 16 by manufacturer B, the binomial distribution is applicable in determining the probability that a tool made by manufacturer A will be used on more than 25 of 100 days. Since the selected tool is replaced before the next sample is taken, the binomial parameter p remains constant at $\frac{4}{20}$.

In many practical applications the population size is *not* infinite. If the worker does not replace the tool, but submits it for servicing at the end of each day, the "experiment" must end after 20 days. In this case the results are no longer independent from day to day. The probability of picking a tool made by manufacturer A on the second day is either $\frac{4}{19}$ or $\frac{3}{19}$, depending on whether the tool selected on the first day had been made by manufacturer A. The outcome on the twentieth day is completely determined by the outcomes of the 19 preceding days. Consequently, the value of p varies from day to day, and clearly the requirements for the use of the binomial distribution—a constant value of p and independent trials—are no longer satisfied.

Nevertheless, the binomial distribution provides an adequate *approximation* for practical purposes when the sample size n is small compared to the population size. If there were 2000 tools in inventory, 400 of which were from manufacturer A and 1600 from manufacturer B, and if we are concerned with the selection for 20 consecutive days, the change in p from day to day and the consequent lack of independence are so small that they could, for practical purposes, be ignored. For that reason we were able to use the binomial distribution in the example dealing with the survey of 100 employees from all the workers at a large industrial plant and in evaluating the results of interviews with 100 potential purchasers of television sets in a particular area. It is generally reasonable to use the binomial distribution in sampling from a finite universe as long as the sample is not more than about 10 per cent of the population.

The irrelevance of population size, within the restrictions indicated, is not generally appreciated in such situations as national pre-election polls and television audience surveys. For example, a *random sample* of size 1000 is essentially as precise in estimating the proportion of votes for a candidate for office from a district with 100,000 voters as for one with a constituency of 100 million. The only practical difference is the greater difficulty in getting a random sample from the larger group. The confidence bounds are read in both cases directly from Fig. 4-2a or -b and are *independent of population size.*

GENERALIZATION TO k POSSIBLE OUTCOMES: THE MULTINOMIAL DISTRIBUTION

In many problems, instead of only two possible results, any one of $k > 2$ outcomes may occur. Units selected from a production line may be good, marginal, or unacceptable. The respondents in the newspaper survey may be classified as union members, salaried nonunion members, and non-salaried nonunion members. The responses concerning the new television model might have been categorized as (a) definitely would buy, (b) probably would buy, (c) probably would not buy, (d) definitely would not buy.

In general, let there be k distinct outcomes with associated probabilities $p_1, p_2, \ldots, p_k$, where $\sum_{i=1}^{k} p_i = 1$. Then for n independent trials, we would like to find the probability of exactly x_1 occurrences of outcome 1, x_2 occurrences of outcome 2, $\ldots$, and x_k occurrences of outcome k. From (2-9a), the probability of a *specified sequence* of outcomes is

$$p_1{}^{x_1} p_2{}^{x_2} \cdots p_k{}^{x_k}.$$

There are $n!/(x_1! \, x_2! \cdots x_k!)$ equally likely ways in which such a sequence can occur. Because these ways are mutually exclusive, we find from (2-5b) that the probability of exactly x_1 occurrences of outcome 1, x_2 occurrences of outcome 2, $\ldots$, and x_k occurrences of outcome k in n trials is

$$f(x_1, x_2, \ldots, x_k; n, p_1, p_2, \ldots, p_k) = \frac{n!}{x_1! \, x_2! \cdots x_k!} p_1{}^{x_1} p_2{}^{x_2} \cdots p_k{}^{x_k},$$

$$x_1, x_2, \ldots, x_k = 0, 1, 2, \ldots n; \quad 0 \leq p_1, p_2, \ldots, p_k \leq 1 \quad (4\text{-}4)$$

where $x_k = n - \sum_{i=1}^{k-1} x_i$ and $p_k = 1 - \sum_{i=1}^{k-1} p_i$. This multivariate generalization of the binomial distribution is known as the *multinomial probability function.*

For example, the probabilities of companies A, B, and C obtaining a particular type of order equal 0.4, 0.4, and 0.2 respectively. Four orders are to be awarded independently. What is the probability that a single company will receive all four orders? There are three mutually exclusive ways that this can occur; hence from (4-4), the desired probability is

$f(4, 0, 0; 4, 0.4, 0.4, 0.2) + f(0, 4, 0; 4, 0.4, 0.4, 0.2)$

$$+ f(0, 0, 4; 4, 0.4, 0.4, 0.2)$$

$$= \frac{4!}{4!\,0!\,0!} (0.4)^4(0.4)^0(0.2)^0 + \frac{4!}{0!\,4!\,0!} (0.4)^0(0.4)^4(0.2)^0$$

$$+ \frac{4!}{0!\,0!\,4!} (0.4)^0(0.4)^0(0.2)^4$$

$$= 0.0256 + 0.0256 + 0.0016 = 0.0528.$$

4-2. The Hypergeometric Distribution

The hypergeometric distribution gives the probability of exactly x successes in n trials when n is *not* small relative to the population size. This distribution is frequently applicable in problems involving sampling from a small production lot. Thus the *hypergeometric probability function* gives the probability of exactly x defective units in randomly selecting n units from a lot of N units, of which exactly k are defective. The n units may be obtained from N units in a total of $\binom{N}{n}$ ways, each of which is equally likely. Similarly, x of k defective units may be chosen in $\binom{k}{x}$ different ways. For *each* such combination, there are also $\binom{N-k}{n-x}$ different ways to select $(n - x)$ of the $(N - k)$ good elements. Therefore, the *total* number of ways of obtaining x defective units and $(N - k)$ good units is $\binom{k}{x}\binom{N-k}{n-x}$.

Because we are dealing with equally likely events, the first definition of probability of Chapter 2 is applicable. The total number of points in the reference set—that is, the number of possible outcomes—is $\binom{N}{n}$, and the number of points corresponding to the event "selecting x out of k defective and $(n - x)$ good units out of $(N - k)$ units" is $\binom{k}{x}\binom{N-k}{n-x}$. Thus, according to (2-8), the probability of this event is given by the hypergeometric probability function

$$f(x; N, n, k) = \frac{\binom{k}{x}\binom{N-k}{n-x}}{\binom{N}{n}}, \quad x = 0, 1, 2, \ldots, n; x \le k, n - x \le N - k.$$

$$(4-5)$$

A plot of this distribution for $N = 25$, $n = 10$, and $k = 8$ is shown in Fig. 4-3. A tabulation of individual and cumulative probabilities is given in Reference 4-6 for various combinations of N, n, k, and x; an abridged version may be found in Reference 4-7. The use of the hypergeometric distribution is illustrated by the following example.

From an order for 25 high-reliability electron tubes, five are selected at random and life tested. If fewer than two tubes fail this test, the remaining 20 tubes will be accepted. Otherwise, the complete lot will be rejected.

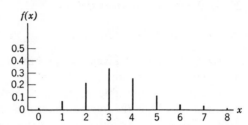

Fig. 4-3   Hypergeometric distribution with $N = 25$, $n = 10$, and $k = 8$.

What is the probability of lot acceptance if four of 25 submitted tubes are defective?

The lot will be accepted if the selected sample contains either zero or one defective unit. The corresponding probability is found from (4-5) to be

$$\sum_{x=0}^{1} f(x; 25, 5, 4) = \frac{\binom{4}{0}\binom{25-4}{5-0}}{\binom{25}{5}} + \frac{\binom{4}{1}\binom{25-4}{5-1}}{\binom{25}{5}} = 0.834.$$

Therefore the chances are about five out of six that the lot will be accepted.

The hypergeometric distribution approaches the binomial distribution with parameters n and $p = k/N$ as n/N becomes small. If, in the above example, the binomial distribution with $p = \frac{4}{25} = 0.16$ had been used, the probability of acceptance would have been found to be 0.817, instead of the correct value of 0.834. Because, in this example, the sample is 20 per cent of the population, we would not expect the binomial distribution to provide a very good approximation.

4-3. The Geometric, Pascal, and Negative-Binomial Distributions

In some problems we desire the probability that *exactly* x independent Bernoulli trials, each with a probability of success p, will be required until the first success is achieved.

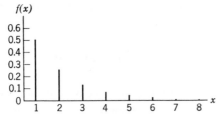

Fig. 4-4   Geometric distribution with $p = \frac{1}{2}$

From (2-9a), the probability of a sequence of exactly $(x - 1)$ failures, each with a probability $(1 - p)$, is $(1 - p)^{x-1}$. Thus the probability that $(x - 1)$ failures will be followed by a success is $(1 - p)^{x-1}p$. The resulting probability function

$$f(x; p) = (1 - p)^{x-1}p, \qquad x = 1, 2, 3, \ldots ; 0 \le p \le 1 \qquad (4\text{-}6)$$

is known as the *geometric distribution*. A plot of this probability function for $p = \frac{1}{2}$ is shown in Fig. 4-4. If we were interested in the probability that the first *failure* occurs on the xth trial, we would obtain

$$f(x; 1 - p) = p^{x-1}(1 - p), \qquad x = 1, 2, 3, \ldots ; 0 \le p \le 1. \qquad (4\text{-}7)$$

Consider the following example. Five space vehicles have been built. Four of them are to be selected randomly and sent into unmanned flights. If all four shots are successful, the remaining vehicle will be used for a manned flight. What is the probability as a function of p, the probability of a success on any one shot, that four successful shots will be followed by an unsuccessful one?

From (4-7) the probability of a failure after four successes is $f(5; 1 - p) = p^4(1 - p)$. A plot of $f(5; 1 - p)$ versus p is shown in Fig. 4-5. Note that $f(5; 1 - p) = 0$ for both $p = 0$ and $p = 1$, for if $p = 0$ the unmanned shots will fail and a manned shot will not take place, and if $p = 1$ both the unmanned and the manned shots will be successful.

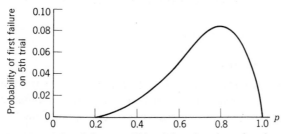

Fig. 4-5   Probability of first failure on fifth trial as function of p, the probability of success on any one shot.

The probability that four successful shots will be followed by an unsuccessful one is largest when p is the solution to

$$\frac{d}{dp}[p^4(1 - p)] = 0,$$

which yields $p = 0.8$. Thus the sequence of four successes followed by one failure is more likely if $p = 0.8$ than if p takes any other value; from (4-7) the resulting probability is $f(5; 1 - 0.8) = (0.8)^{5-1}(0.2) = 0.082$.

The *Pascal distribution* gives the probability that if one conducts independent Bernoulli trials, each with a probability of success p, until exactly s successes are obtained one will encounter x failures (or equivalently, require a total of $x + s$ trials). The probability function is

$$f(x; s, p) = \binom{x + s - 1}{x} p^s(1 - p)^x; \qquad x = 0, 1, 2, \ldots; s = 1, 2, \ldots,$$

$$0 \leq p \leq 1. \quad (4.8)$$

The geometric distribution is a special case of the Pascal distribution for which $s = 1$. Note, however, that for the geometric distribution the random variable refers to $(x - 1)$ failures, whereas in the definition of the Pascal distribution x failures are involved. For example, the probability that the third success will occur on the tenth trial when the probability of success p on a single trial is 0.4 is found from (4-8) to be

$$f(7; 3, 0.4) = \binom{7 + 3 - 1}{7}(0.4)^3(0.6)^7 = 0.0645.$$

A tabulation of individual and cumulative probabilities is given in Reference 4-18.

The generalization of the Pascal distribution when s is not an integer and the factorials in (4-8) are replaced by gamma functions is known as the *negative binomial distribution*.* An application of the negative binomial distribution is suggested briefly in Section 4-4.

4-4. *The Poisson Distribution*

THE STATISTICAL MODEL

The probability that exactly x customers will arrive at a store during a particular time interval cannot be handled by the binomial distribution. One reason is that there is no clear-cut specification of the "sample size";

* However, many authors do not differentiate between the Pascal and negative binomial distributions.

this could be all the inhabitants in the town in which the store is located, in the town plus the neighboring community, or even all the inhabitants in the state or nation. Also, some individuals might come to the store more than once. Thus, instead of the probability "per trial" and the total number of trials, the available data might be the average number of arrivals in a specified interval. It is this information that is used to specify a statistical model known as the *Poisson distribution*. This distribution

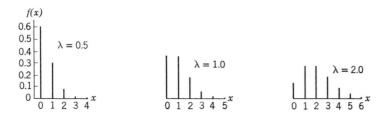

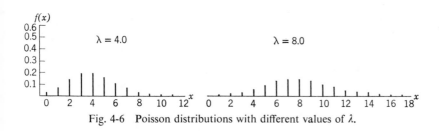

Fig. 4-6   Poisson distributions with different values of λ.

represents the number of events that occur over equal intervals of time or space, assuming that events occur independently at a constant *average rate*.

The Poisson probability function is derived in Appendix 4B as

$$f(x; \lambda) = \frac{\lambda^x}{x!} e^{-\lambda}, \qquad x = 0, 1, 2, 3, \ldots ; \lambda > 0, \tag{4-9}$$

where $f(x; \lambda)$ is the probability of exactly x events in a specified interval, and the parameter λ is the rate of occurrence. Poisson probability functions for different values of λ are shown in Fig. 4-6.

The Poisson distribution is used in the time domain as a model for the number of alpha particles emitted from a radioactive source in a specified time interval, the number of insurance claims per year, and the number of incoming calls per minute on a switchboard during a particular time of day. Events over constant areas or volumes, represented by the Poisson distribution include the number of flaws in similar pieces of material, the number of bacteria on a series of slides, and the number of flying bombs falling on equal areas of London during World War II.

The Poisson distribution is tabulated in the following references:

1. Reference 4-8. Individual and cumulative terms are given for
   $\lambda = 0.001\ (0.001)\ 0.01\ (0.01)\ 0.3\ (0.1)\ 15\ (1)\ 100$.
2. Reference 4-9. Individual and cumulative terms are given for
   $\lambda = 0.00000010\ (0.0000001)\ 0.0000015\ (0.0000005)\ 0.000015$
   $(0.000001)\ 0.00005\ (0.000005)\ 0.0005\ (0.00001)\ 0.001\ (0.00005)$
   $0.005\ (0.0001)\ 0.01\ (0.0005)\ 0.2\ (0.001)\ 0.4\ (0.005)\ 0.5\ (0.01)$
   $1\ (0.05)\ 2\ (0.1)\ 5\ (0.5)\ 10\ (1)\ 100\ (5)\ 205$.
3. Reference 4-10. Individual terms are given for
   $\lambda = 0.0005\ (0.0005)\ 0.005\ (0.005)\ 0.05\ (0.05)\ 1.0\ (0.1)\ 5\ (0.25)\ 10\ (0.5)$
   $20\ (1)\ 60$.
   and cumulative terms are given for $\lambda = 0.1\ (0.1)\ 15$.

Alternatively, cumulative Poisson probabilities for values of λ from 0.1 to 30 may be read from Fig. 4-7.

The following example illustrates the use of the Poisson distribution. Flaws in a particular type weld arise independently at a rate of two flaws per weld. What is the probability that a weld has $0, 1, 2, 3, \ldots$ defects? By setting $\lambda = 2$ and substituting $x = 0, 1, 2, 3, \ldots$ in (4-9), the probabilities shown in the accompanying tabulation are obtained.

Number of Defects x	Probability	Cumulative Probability
0	0.1353	0.1353
1	0.2707	0.4060
2	0.2707	0.6767
3	0.1804	0.8571
4	0.0902	0.9473
5	0.0361	0.9834
6	0.0121	0.9955
7	0.0034	0.9989
8	0.0009	0.9998
9	0.0002	0.99995

The cumulative probabilities of x or fewer defects are also shown. These values could also have been found from the tabulations in References 4-8, 4-9, or 4-10, or from the cumulative probabilities on the ordinate of Fig. 4-7 corresponding to the curves for $x = 0, 1, 2, \ldots$ and an abscissa value of $\lambda = 2$.

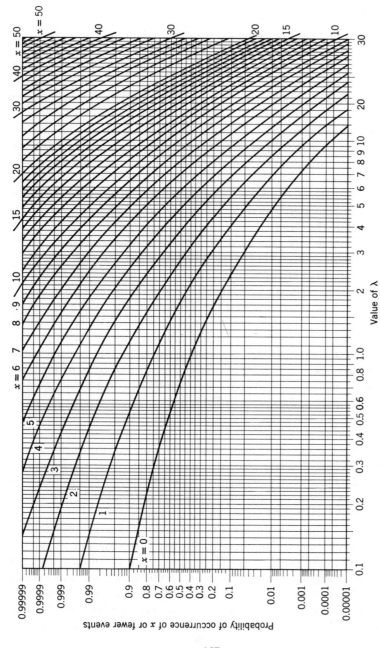

Fig. 4-7 Curves showing cumulative probabilities for Poisson distribution. [From H. F. Dodge and H. G. Romig, *Sampling Inspection Tables*, John Wiley, and Sons, New York, 1944 (Fig. 6).]

157

The mean and variance of a Poisson variate both equal λ—that is, $E(x) = \lambda$ and Var $(x) = \lambda$. This result is derived in Appendix 4C.

ESTIMATION OF λ

The value of λ may be estimated from given data as

$$\hat{\lambda} = \frac{k}{n}, \tag{4-10}$$

where k is the observed number of occurrences in n intervals (or pieces of material).

Confidence bounds on λ at various confidence levels can be obtained from Table 4-2, as in the following example. In 10 random railroad runs from Chicago to San Francisco a total of 15 separate and independent delays were recorded. It is assumed that the number of delays is a Poisson variate, whose parameter λ is the average number of delays *per run*. The railroad company claims that the long-run or true value of λ is 1.2. Do the data refute the claim?

From Table 4-2 the two-sided 99 per cent confidence bounds on the average number of delays *in 10 runs*, based on $x = 15$, are 6.89 and 28.16. Therefore 99 per cent confidence bounds on λ, the average number of delays in *a single run*, are $6.89/10 = 0.689$ and $28.16/10 = 2.816$ that is, we may be 99 per cent sure that the unknown "true" value is between 0.689 and 2.816. The data consequently do not refute the company's claim that $\lambda = 1.2$, because this value is contained within the 99 per cent confidence interval (0.689, 2.816). A company claim that $\lambda = 0.5$ *would*, however, have been rejected as unreasonable on the basis of the data. One-sided confidence bounds on λ may be obtained in a similar manner by using the indicated columns in Table 4-2.

ADEQUACY OF THE POISSON MODEL

The Poisson distribution may be used to represent the occurrence of *independent events* that take place at a constant rate. If these requirements are not met, (e.g., when customers arrive in groups, or defects are more likely in some environments than in others) the probabilities obtained assuming a Poisson model are no longer correct.

Frequently, when we do not know whether the assumptions for a Poisson distribution are appropriate, the available data can be used to evaluate this model (see Chapter 8). If the Poisson distribution does not provide an adequate representation, we must search for an alternate model. Although a detailed discussion is beyond the scope of this book, it is noted that one possible alternative is the negative binomial distribution introduced in Section 4-3. This model arises when the occurrence rate λ is *not* constant. An example is the distribution of the number of dental cavities per individual, since some individuals are more prone to cavities than others—that is, the cavity rate λ differs from one individual to the next. When the λ's for different individuals may be regarded as a random variable which follows a gamma distribution, it can be shown (see References 4-13, 4-14 and 4-17) that the negative binomial, rather than the Poisson, is the appropriate distribution for the number of occurrences.

POISSON DISTRIBUTION APPROXIMATION TO THE BINOMIAL DISTRIBUTION AND OTHER RELATIONSHIPS

It is shown in Appendix 4D that the binomial distribution approaches the Poisson distribution with $\lambda = np$ as n becomes large and p or $(1 - p)$ approaches zero. This result can be used to evaluate binomial probabilities when the normal distribution approximation is not adequate and tables of the binomial distribution are either not available or the required values of p are not tabulated. The method is illustrated by the following example.

A communications channel transmits an incorrect signal, on the average, once every 100 times. What is the probability of five or more errors in 200 independently transmitted messages?

This problem is equivalent to asking what the chances are of five or more "successes" in $n = 200$ Bernoulli trials when each trial has a success probability $p = 0.01$.

Using the Poisson distribution approximation with $\lambda = np = (200)(0.01) = 2$, we find from the tabulation in Reference 4-8 that

$$\Pr(x > 4) \approx \sum_{x=5}^{\infty} \frac{2^x}{x!} e^{-2} = 0.0527.$$

Direct application of the tables for the binomial distribution in Reference 4-2 yields

$$\Pr(x > 4) = 1 - F(4; 0.01, 200) = \sum_{x=5}^{200} \binom{200}{x}(0.01)^x(0.99)^{200-x} = 0.0518.$$

The result obtained by the Poisson distribution approximation agrees closely with the value calculated by exact methods. If p had been 0.005 rather than 0.01, the exact tabulations in Reference 4-2 could not have been used, because the binomial probabilities corresponding to $p = 0.005$ are not tabulated there. The approximation has been found to give adequate results for $p \leq 0.1$ or $p \geq 0.9$, irrespective of n.

The Poisson distribution is related to the exponential distribution of Chapter 3. If the time between consecutive events follows an exponential distribution with parameter λ, the number of events occurring in a fixed

Table 4-2 Table Showing Confidence Limits for $n\lambda$ in Sampling from a Poisson Distribution

Two-sided confidence level	0.998		0.99		0.98		0.95		0.90	
One-sided confidence level	0.999		0.995		0.99		0.975		0.95	
x	Lower Bound	Upper Bound	Lower Bound	Upper Bound	Lower Bound	Upper Bound	Lower Bound	Upper Bound	Lower Bound	Upper Bound
0	0.00000	6.91	0.00000	5.30	0.0000	4.61	0.0000	3.69	0.0000	3.00
1	0.00100	9.23	0.00501	7.43	0.0101	6.64	0.0253	5.57	0.0513	4.74
2	0.0454	11.23	0.103	9.27	0.149	8.41	0.242	7.22	0.355	6.30
3	0.191	13.06	0.338	10.98	0.436	10.05	0.619	8.77	0.818	7.75
4	0.429	14.79	0.672	12.59	0.823	11.60	1.09	10.24	1.37	9.15
5	0.739	16.45	1.08	14.15	1.28	13.11	1.62	11.67	1.97	10.51
6	1.11	18.06	1.54	15.66	1.79	14.57	2.20	13.06	2.61	11.84
7	1.52	19.63	2.04	17.13	2.33	16.00	2.81	14.42	3.29	13.15
8	1.97	21.16	2.57	18.58	2.91	17.40	3.45	15.76	3.98	14.43
9	2.45	22.66	3.13	20.00	3.51	18.78	4.12	17.08	4.70	15.71

160

x										
10	2.96	24.13	3.72	21.40	4.13	20.14	4.80	18.39	5.43	16.96
11	3.49	25.59	4.32	22.78	4.77	21.49	5.49	19.68	6.17	18.21
12	4.04	27.03	4.94	24.14	5.43	22.82	6.20	20.96	6.92	19.44
13	4.61	28.45	5.58	25.50	6.10	24.14	6.92	22.23	7.69	20.67
14	5.20	29.85	6.23	26.84	6.78	25.45	7.65	23.49	8.46	21.89
15	5.79	31.24	6.89	28.16	7.48	26.74	8.40	24.74	9.25	23.10
16	6.41	32.62	7.57	29.48	8.18	28.03	9.15	25.98	10.04	24.30
17	7.03	33.99	8.25	30.79	8.89	29.31	9.90	27.22	10.83	25.50
18	7.66	35.35	8.94	32.09	9.62	30.58	10.67	28.45	11.63	26.69
19	8.31	36.70	9.64	33.38	10.35	31.85	11.44	29.67	12.44	27.88
20	8.96	38.04	10.35	34.67	11.08	33.10	12.22	30.89	13.25	29.06
21	9.62	39.38	11.07	35.95	11.82	34.36	13.00	32.10	14.07	30.24
22	10.29	40.70	11.79	37.22	12.57	35.60	13.79	33.31	14.89	31.42
23	10.96	42.02	12.52	38.48	13.33	36.84	14.58	34.51	15.72	32.59
24	11.65	43.33	13.25	39.74	14.09	38.08	15.38	35.71	16.55	33.75
25	12.34	44.64	14.00	41.00	14.85	39.31	16.18	36.90	17.38	34.92
26	13.03	45.94	14.74	42.25	15.62	40.53	16.98	38.10	18.22	36.08
27	13.73	47.23	15.49	43.50	16.40	41.76	17.79	39.28	19.06	37.23
28	14.44	48.52	16.24	44.74	17.17	42.98	18.61	40.47	19.90	38.39
29	15.15	49.80	17.00	45.98	17.96	44.19	19.42	41.65	20.75	39.54
30	15.87	51.08	17.77	47.21	18.74	45.40	20.24	42.83	21.59	40.69
35	19.52	57.42	21.64	53.32	22.72	51.41	24.38	48.68	25.87	46.40
40	23.26	63.66	25.59	59.36	26.77	57.35	28.58	54.47	30.20	52.07
45	27.08	69.83	29.60	65.34	30.88	63.23	32.82	60.21	34.56	57.69
50	30.96	75.94	33.66	71.27	35.03	69.07	37.11	65.92	38.96	63.29

x is the observed frequency or count. The lower and upper confidence limits for $n\lambda$ are shown in the body of the table. [From E. S. Pearson and H. O. Hartley, *Biometrika Tables for Statisticians*, Vol. 1, Cambridge University Press, 1954 (Table 40).]

period of time T is Poisson-distributed with parameter λT and conversely (see Reference 4-15).

It can also be shown that for a Poisson variate with parameter μ

$$\Pr(x \le x_1) = \frac{1}{\Gamma(x_1 + 1)} \int_\mu^\infty e^{-t} t^{x_1} \, dt. \tag{4-11}$$

From (3-13) we see that the right-hand side of this expression is the probability that a gamma variate with parameters $\eta = x_1 + 1$ and $\lambda = 1$ exceeds μ. A similar relationship exists between the binomial and beta distributions. If x is a binomial variate with parameters p and n, then

$$\Pr(x \le x_2) = \frac{\Gamma(n + 1)}{\Gamma(n - x_2)\Gamma(x_2 + 1)} \int_0^{1-p} t^{n-x_2-1}(1 - t)^{x_2} \, dt. \tag{4-12}$$

From (3-23) we note that the right-hand side of this expression is the probability that a beta variate with parameters $\gamma = n - x_2$ and $\eta = x_2 + 1$ takes on a value less than $1 - p$.

Equations 4-11 and 4-12 may be used to obtain cumulative probabilities for Poisson and binomial variates from the tabulations of the cumulative gamma and beta distributions. These results may also be used in reverse to obtain cumulative probabilities for gamma and beta variates with integer-valued shape parameters from the generally more accessible tabulations of the cumulative Poisson and binomial distributions.

4-5. Summary of Discrete Distributions

Information concerning the distributions discussed in this chapter is summarized in Fig. 4-8 and Table 4-3. The figure also indicates the expected value, variance, and standardized moments for each distribution.

Table 4-3 Summary: Applications of Discrete Statistical Distributions

Distribution	Application	Example	Comments
Binomial	Gives probability of exactly x successes in n independent trials, when probability of success p on *single* trial is a constant. Used frequently in quality control, reliability, survey sampling, and other industrial problems.	What is the probability of 7 or more "heads" in 10 tosses of a fair coin?	Can sometimes be approximated by normal or by Poisson distribution.
Multinomial	Gives probability of exactly x_i outcomes of event i, for $i = 1, 2, \ldots, k$ in n independent trials when the probability p_i of event i in a *single* trial is a constant. Used frequently in quality control and other industrial problems.	Four companies are bidding for each of three contracts, with specified success probabilities. What is the probability that a single company will receive all the orders?	Generalization of binomial distribution for more than 2 outcomes.
Hypergeometric	Gives probability of picking exactly x good units in a sample of n units from a population of N units when there are k bad units in the population. Used in quality control and related applications.	Given a lot with 21 good units and four defectives. What is the probability that a sample of five will yield not more than one defective?	May be approximated by binomial distribution when n is small relative to N.
Geometric	Gives probability of requiring exactly x binomial trials before the first success is achieved. Used in quality control, reliability, and other industrial situations.	Determination of probability of requiring exactly five test firings before first success is achieved.	
Pascal	Gives probability of exactly x failures preceding the sth success.	What is the probability that the third success takes place on the 10th trial?	
Negative Binomial	Gives probability similar to Poisson distribution (see below) when events do not occur at a constant rate and occurrence rate is a random variable that follows a gamma distribution.	Distribution of number of cavities for a group of dental patients.	Generalization of Pascal distribution when s is not an integer. Many authors do not distinguish between Pascal and negative binomial distributions.
Poisson	Gives probability of exactly x independent occurrences during a given period of time if events take place independently and at a constant rate. May also represent number of occurrences over constant areas or volumes. Used frequently in quality control, reliability, queueing theory, and so on.	Used to represent distribution of number of defects in a piece of material, customer arrivals, insurance claims, incoming telephone calls, alpha particles emitted, and so on.	Frequently used as approximation to binomial distribution.

163

Distribution Name

Binomial

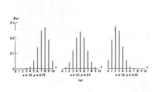

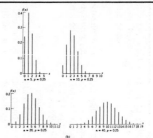

Multinomial

Hypergeometric

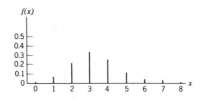

Fig. 4.8. Summary of important

164

Parameters	Probability Function
Positive integer n, $0 \le p \le 1$	$\binom{n}{x} p^x (1-p)^{n-x}, \quad x = 0, 1, 2, \ldots, n$
Positive integer n, $p_1 \ge 0, p_2 \ge 0, \ldots, p_k \ge 0,$ where $\sum_{i=1}^{k} p_i = 1$	$\dfrac{n!}{x_1! \, x_2! \cdots x_k!} p_1^{x_1} p_2^{x_2} \cdots p_k^{x_k}, \quad x_1 = 0, 1, 2, \ldots ;$ $x_2 = 0, 1, 2, \ldots ; \ \ldots x_k = 0, 1, 2, \ldots ; \ \sum_{i=1}^{k} x_i = n$
Positive integers N, n and k.	$\dfrac{\binom{k}{x}\binom{N-k}{n-x}}{\binom{N}{n}}, \quad x = 0, 1, 2, \ldots n, x \le k, n - x \le N - k$

discrete distributions

Expected Value	Variance	$\sqrt{\beta_1}$	β_2
np	$np(1-p)$	$\dfrac{1-2p}{[np(1-p)]^{1/2}}$	$3 + \dfrac{1-6p(1-p)}{np(1-p)}$
np_i for $i = 1, 2, \ldots, k$	$np_i(1-p_i)$ for $i = 1, 2, \ldots, k$	$\dfrac{1-2p_i}{[np_i(1-p_i)]^{1/2}}$ for $i = 1, 2, \ldots, k$	$3 + \dfrac{1-6p_i(1-p_i)}{np_i(1-p_i)}$ for $i = 1, 2, \ldots, k$
$\dfrac{nk}{N}$	$\dfrac{nk(N-k)(N-n)}{N^2(N-1)}$	$\dfrac{(N-2k)(N-2n)(N-1)^{1/2}}{(N-2)[nk(N-k)(N-n)]^{1/2}}$	*

$$* \quad \frac{N^2(N-1)}{(N-2)(N-3)nk(N-k)(N-n)} \left\{ N(N+1) - 6n(N-n) + 3\frac{k}{N^2}(N-k)[N^2(n-2) - Nn^2 + 6n(N- \right.$$

Fig

Distribution Name

Geometric

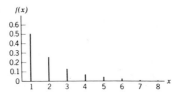

Negative Binomial and Pascal

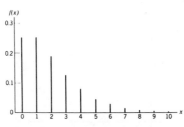

Poisson

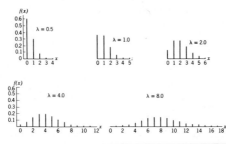

(*continued*)

Parameters	Probability Function
$0 \leq p \leq 1$	$(1 - p)^{x-1} p, \quad x = 1, 2, \ldots$
$0 \leq p \leq 1$; Negative Binomial if $s \geq 0$. Pascal if s is a positive integer.	$\begin{pmatrix} x + s - 1 \\ x \end{pmatrix} p^s (1 - p)^x, \quad x = 0, 1, 2, \ldots$
$\lambda > 0$	$\dfrac{\lambda^x e^{-\lambda}}{x!}, \quad x = 0, 1, 2, \ldots$

Fig. 4.8

xpected value	Variance	$\sqrt{\beta_1}$	β_2
$\dfrac{1}{p}$	$\dfrac{1-p}{p^2}$	$\dfrac{2-p}{(1-p)^{1/2}}$	$\dfrac{p^2 - 9p + 9}{1 - p}$
$\dfrac{s(1-p)}{p}$	$\dfrac{s(1-p)}{p^2}$	$\dfrac{2-p}{[s(1-p)]^{1/2}}$	$\dfrac{p^2 - 6p + 6}{s(1-p)} + 3$
λ	λ	$\dfrac{1}{\sqrt{\lambda}}$	$\dfrac{1 + 3\lambda}{\lambda}$

inued)

References

4-1   W. Volk, *Applied Statistics for Engineers*, McGraw-Hill Book Co., New York, 1958.

4-2   Staff of the Computation Laboratory, *Tables of the Cumulative Binomial Probability Distribution*, Harvard University Press, Cambridge, Massachusetts, 1955.

4-3   *Tables of the Binomial Probability Distribution*, Nat. Bur. Std., Appl. Math. Ser. 6, 1950.

4-4   H. G. Romig, 50–100 *Binomial Tables*, John Wiley and Sons, New York 1953.

4-5   H. Cramer, *Mathematical Methods of Statistics*, Princeton University Press, Princeton, New Jersey, 1946.

4-6   G. J. Lieberman and D. B. Owen, *Tables of the Hypergeometric Probability Distribution*, Stanford University Press, Stanford, California, 1961.

4-7   D. B. Owen, *Handbook of Statistical Tables*, Addison-Wesley Publishing Co., Reading, Massachusetts, 1962.

4-8   E. C. Molina, *Poisson's Exponential Binomial Limit*, D. Van Nostrand Co., Princeton, New Jersey, 1949.

4-9   Defense Systems Department, General Electric Co., *Tables of the Individual and Cumulative Terms of Poisson Distribution*, D. Van Nostrand Co., Princeton, New Jersey, 1962.

4-10 E. S. Pearson and H. O. Hartley, *Biometrika Tables for Statisticians*, Vol. 1, Cambridge University Press, Cambridge, 1954.

4-11 K. A. Brownlee, *Statistical Theory and Methodology in Science and Engineering*, 2nd ed., John Wiley and Sons, New York, 1965.

4-12 W. Feller, *An Introduction to Probability Theory and Its Applications*, Vol. 1, 2nd ed., John Wiley and Sons, New York, 1957.

4-13 H. Freeman, *Introduction to Statistical Inference*, Addison-Wesley Publishing Co., Reading, Massachusetts, 1963.

4-14 N. L. Johnson and F. C. Leone, *Statistics and Experimental Design in Engineering and the Physical Sciences*, Vol. I, John Wiley and Sons, New York, 1964.

4-15 E. Parzen, *Stochastic Processes*, Holden-Day, Inc., San Francisco, 1962.

4-16 S. Weintraub *Tables of the Cumulative Binomial Probability Distribution for Small Values of p*, Free Press of Glencoe, The Macmillan Co., New York, 1963.

4-17 A. Hald, *Statistical Theory with Engineering Applications*, John Wiley and Sons, New York, 1952.

4-18 E. Williamson and M. H. Bretherton, *Tables of the Negative Binomial Probability Distribution*, John Wiley and Sons, New York, 1963.

Appendix 4A: Derivation of the Expected Value and the Variance of a Binomial Variate

Let x be a random value from a binomial distribution with parameters n and p—that is,

$$f(x; p, n) = \binom{n}{x} p^x (1 - p)^{n-x}, \qquad x = 0, 1, 2, \ldots, n, 0 \leq p \leq 1.$$

Then, from (2-28)

$$E(x) = \sum_{x=0}^{n} x f(x) = \sum_{x=0}^{n} x \binom{n}{x} p^x (1 - p)^{n-x}$$

$$= \sum_{x=0}^{n} x \frac{n!}{x! \, (n - x)!} p^x (1 - p)^{n-x}.$$

Since the first term of the sum is zero, let us start the summation at 1 and factor out an n and a p. Thus

$$E(x) = np \sum_{x=1}^{n} \frac{(n - 1)!}{(x - 1)! \, (n - x)!} p^{x-1} (1 - p)^{n-x}.$$

Changing the index of summation by letting $y = x - 1$ and $m = n - 1$, we obtain

$$E(x) = np \sum_{y=0}^{m} \frac{m!}{y! \, (m - y)!} p^y (1 - p)^{m-y} = np \sum_{y=0}^{m} \binom{m}{y} p^y (1 - p)^{m-y} = np,$$

since this summation is over all terms of a binomial distribution. From (2-39),

$$\text{Var} \, (x) = E(x^2) - [E(x)]^2$$

Now

$$E(x^2) = \sum_{x=0}^{n} x^2 f(x) = \sum_{x=0}^{n} x(x - 1) f(x) + \sum_{x=0}^{n} x f(x)$$

and

$$\sum_{x=0}^{n} x f(x) = E(x) = np.$$

Proceeding as above,

$$\sum_{x=0}^{n} x(x - 1) \frac{n!}{x! \, (n - x)!} p^x (1 - p)^{n-x}$$

$$= n(n - 1)p^2 \sum_{x=2}^{n} \frac{(n - 2)!}{(x - 2)! \, (n - x)!} p^{x-2} (1 - p)^{n-x}$$

$$= n(n - 1)p^2 \sum_{y=0}^{m} \binom{m}{y} p^y (1 - p)^{m-y} = n(n - 1)p^2.$$

Thus

$$E(x^2) = n(n - 1)p^2 + np$$

and

$$\text{Var} \, (x) = n(n - 1)p^2 + np - n^2 p^2 = np - np^2 = np(1 - p).$$

Appendix 4B: Derivation of the Poisson Distribution

We want to show that the Poisson distribution is the appropriate model for the number of events occurring over a fixed period of time, assuming events occur independently at a constant rate. The derivation is identical for the number of events over constant areas or volumes.

Let λ^* represent the rate of occurrence of some event. Thus the probability of a single event taking place in a small time interval dt is $\lambda^* \, dt$, provided that dt has been chosen sufficiently small that the probability of two or more events during dt is negligible. The probability $\Pr_x (t + dt)$ that exactly x events will have taken place at an arbitrary time $(t + dt)$ is the sum of the probabilities for the following two mutually exclusive occurrences:

1. x events take place by time t, with probability $\Pr_x (t)$, and no events occur during the interval dt, the latter probability being $(1 - \lambda^* \, dt)$. Because of independence, the joint probability of this occurrence is $(1 - \lambda^* \, dt) \Pr_x (t)$,

2. $(x - 1)$ events take place by time t, with probability $\Pr_{x-1} (t)$, and one event occurs during the interval dt, the latter probability being $\lambda^* \, dt$. Because of independence, the joint probability of this occurrence is $\lambda^* \, dt \, \Pr_{x-1} (t)$.

Thus

$$\Pr_x (t + dt) = (1 - \lambda^* \, dt) \Pr_x (t) + \lambda^* \, dt \, \Pr_{x-1} (t)$$

or

$$\frac{\Pr_x (t + dt) - \Pr_x (t)}{dt} = \lambda^* [\Pr_{x-1} (t) - \Pr_x (t)].$$

Letting $dt \to 0$ yields

$$\Pr_x' (t) = \lambda^* (\Pr_{x-1} (t) - \Pr_x (t)).$$

Setting $x = 0$ gives

$$\Pr_0' (t) = -\lambda^* \, \Pr_0 (t)$$

since $\Pr_{-1} (t) \equiv 0$.

The solution of the preceding differential equation with the boundary condition $\Pr_0 (0) = 1$ is

$$\Pr_0 (t) = e^{-\lambda^* t}.$$

Similarly, solution of the differential equation

$$\Pr_1' (t) = \lambda^* [\Pr_0 (t) - \Pr_1 (t)] = \lambda^* [e^{-\lambda t} - \Pr_1 (t)]$$

with boundary condition $Pr_1(0) = 0$ gives

$$Pr_1(t) = \lambda^* t e^{-\lambda^* t}.$$

Continuing this process, we easily see that

$$Pr_x(t) = \frac{(\lambda^* t)^x e^{-\lambda^* t}}{x!}.$$

Letting $\lambda^* t = \lambda$ thus leads us to the Poisson probability function

$$f(x; \lambda) = \frac{\lambda^x e^{-\lambda}}{x!}.$$

Appendix 4C: Derivation of the Expected Value and the Variance of a Poisson Variate

Let x be a random variable from a Poisson distribution with parameter λ—that is,

$$f(x; \lambda) = \frac{\lambda^x e^{-\lambda}}{x!}, \qquad x = 0, 1, 2, 3 \cdots; \lambda > 0.$$

Then, from (2-28)

$$E(x) = \sum_{x=0}^{\infty} x \frac{\lambda^x e^{-\lambda}}{x!} = \lambda \sum_{x=1}^{\infty} \frac{\lambda^{x-1} e^{-\lambda}}{(x-1)!},$$

since the first term in the series is zero. Let $y = x - 1$. Then

$$E(x) = \lambda \sum_{y=0}^{\infty} \frac{\lambda^y e^{-\lambda}}{y!} = \lambda,$$

since the summation is over all terms of a Poisson distribution.
Now from (2-39),

$$\mathrm{Var}\,(x) = E(x^2) - [E(x)]^2,$$

and from (2-32) and (4-9),

$$E(x^2) = \sum_{x=0}^{\infty} x^2 \frac{\lambda^x e^{-\lambda}}{x!}$$

$$= \sum_{x=0}^{\infty} x(x-1) \frac{\lambda^x e^{-\lambda}}{x!} + \sum_{x=0}^{\infty} x \frac{\lambda^x e^{-\lambda}}{x!}.$$

Now

$$\sum_{x=0}^{\infty} x \frac{\lambda^x e^{-\lambda}}{x!} = \lambda,$$

and since the first two terms in the sum are zero,

$$\sum_{x=0}^{\infty} \frac{x(x-1)\lambda^x e^{-\lambda}}{x!} = \lambda^2 \sum_{x=2}^{\infty} \frac{\lambda^{x-2} e^{-\lambda}}{(x-2)!} = \lambda^2 \sum_{y=0}^{\infty} \frac{\lambda^y e^{-\lambda}}{y!} = \lambda^2.$$

Thus

$$E(x^2) = \lambda^2 + \lambda,$$

and therefore

$$\text{Var}(x) = \lambda.$$

Appendix 4D: Derivation of the Poisson Distribution as an Approximation to the Binomial Distribution

The binomial distribution approaches the Poisson distribution as n becomes arbitrarily large and p becomes arbitrarily small, np remaining constant. The proof of this result follows.

From (4-1), the binomial probability function is

$$f(x; n, p) = \binom{n}{x} p^x (1-p)^{n-x} = \frac{n(n-1)\cdots(n-x+1)}{x!} p^x (1-p)^{n-x}.$$

Multiplying and dividing by n^x and letting $np = \lambda$ yields

$$f(x; n, p) = \frac{n(n-1)\cdots(n-x+1)}{n^x} \frac{\lambda^x}{x!} (1-p)^{n-x}$$

$$= \left(1 - \frac{1}{n}\right)\left(1 - \frac{2}{n}\right) \cdots \left(1 - \frac{x-1}{n}\right) \frac{\lambda^x (1-p)^n}{x! (1-p)^x}.$$

Now

$$(1-p)^n = [(1-p)^{-1/p}]^{-np} = [(1-p)^{-1/p}]^{-\lambda},$$

and

$$\lim_{p \to 0} [(1-p)^{-1/p}]^{-\lambda} = e^{-\lambda}.$$

Also

$$\lim_{\substack{n \to \infty \\ p \to 0}} \frac{\left[\left(1 - \frac{1}{n}\right)\left(1 - \frac{2}{n}\right) \cdots \left(1 - \frac{x-1}{n}\right)\right]}{(1-p)^x} = 1.$$

Thus

$$\lim_{\substack{n \to \infty \\ p \to 0}} f(x; n, p) = \frac{e^{-\lambda} \lambda^x}{x!}$$

which is the Poisson probability function with $\lambda = np$.

Chapter 5

The Transformation of Variables

In the two preceding chapters we have discussed distributions to represent simple outcomes. However, the performance of a system is frequently due to many phenomena, each of which can be represented by one of the basic distributions and which combine together in a known way. For example, the output of a physical system may be a *function of the basic component variables*. Our interest now turns to determining the distribution of a function.

An example is the distribution of the total time required for a machine to perform a certain job. Say this time depends on the sum of the times to complete two tasks, each of which can be represented by independently distributed exponential variates, x and y, with probability densities $f(x) = \lambda_1 e^{-\lambda_1 x}$ and $g(y) = \lambda_2 e^{-\lambda_2 y}$. The distribution of the total time is the distribution of $(x + y)$.

The results of combining functions of basic random variables have been stated in Chapter 3; for example, in the motivation for the Rayleigh, gamma, and log-normal distributions, and also in the discussion of the central limit theorem. This chapter describes a technique known as the transformation of variables, which was used to obtain these results and which is applicable to finding the distribution of simple functions of random variables. The method is feasible only for relatively simple situations; for more complex cases approximate techniques, such as generation of system moments and Monte Carlo simulation (see Chapter 7), must be used.

Parts of this chapter require more mathematics than the remainder of the book. Some readers might wish to omit these parts which are mostly near the end of the chapter, on a first reading. Those who would like further examples of the methods should consult References 5-1 to 5-9.

5-1. Functions of Discrete Random Variables

Let x be a discrete random variable defined over some specified sample space for which the distribution of a function of x, to be denoted $w = h(x)$, is desired. Since x is a random variable, so is w. The following steps are necessary to determine the distribution* $p(w)$ of w: (a) establish the sample space for w, and (b) find the values of $p(w)$ corresponding to each point in the new sample space.

Consider the following example. A manufacturer incurs warranty charges for each breakdown during the first year of system life as follows: $C for the first failure, C^2 for the second failure, and, in general, C^x for the xth failure, where $C > 1$. The time between system failures is exponentially distributed with parameter λ, and consequently the number of failures during any constant time period T is a Poisson variate with parameter λT (see Chapter 4). The manufacturer would like to determine the probability distribution of warranty costs for $T = 1$ year.

The problem may be restated as follows: x is a random variable following the Poisson distribution

$$f(x) = \frac{e^{-\lambda}}{x!} \lambda^x, \qquad x = 0, 1, 2, \ldots. \tag{5-1}$$

Find the probability distribution $p(w)$ of

$$w = h(x) = \begin{cases} 0, & x = 0, \\ C^x, & x = 1, 2, \ldots; \quad C > 1. \end{cases} \tag{5-2}$$

The sample space for the penalty costs consists of the points $w = h(x) = 0$, $C, C^2, C^3, \ldots$ and is related to the sample space for x as follows:

$$
\begin{aligned}
x &\to w \\
0 &\to 0 \\
1 &\to C \\
2 &\to C^2 \\
3 &\to C^3
\end{aligned}
$$

and so on. The points in the new sample space have the same probabilities as the corresponding points in the old sample space; thus, the probability of incurring a cost of $0 is the same as the probability of zero breakdowns, the probability of incurring a cost of $C is the same as the probability of one breakdown, and so on. Consequently, the probability function for

---

* In this chapter it is convenient to designate probability functions (or probability density functions) of the original and transformed variables respectively by $f(x)$ and $p(w)$.

the manufacturer's warranty cost is obtained by substituting for x in (5-1) the equivalent value in terms of w.

From (5-2),

$$\begin{cases} x = 0, & \text{if } w = 0, \\ x = \dfrac{\ln w}{\ln C}, & \text{if } w = C, C^2, \ldots, \end{cases} \tag{5-3}$$

hence

$$p(w) = \begin{cases} e^{-\lambda}, & w = 0 \\ \dfrac{e^{-\lambda}}{(\ln w/\ln C)!} \lambda^{\ln w/\ln C}, & w = C, C^2, C^3, \ldots. \end{cases} \tag{5-4}$$

Equation 5-4 can be generalized for any one-to-one transformation $w = h(x)$ for a discrete random variable x distributed as $f(x)$ by the expression

$$p(w) = f[x(w)], \tag{5-5}$$

where the sample space for w is found from the sample space for x by the expression $w = h(x)$. Equation 5-5 requires determining the inverse function $x(w)$ of the transformation $w = h(x)$ and substituting this into the probability function in place of the original random variable x.

When the transformation is not one to one in that there are a number of values of x in the original sample space corresponding to the same point w in the new sample space, the probabilities for the corresponding x's must be added to obtain the probability for w. This procedure is illustrated for the similar situation of a continuous random variable in the next section.

Details are not given for the procedure of finding a function of *more than one* discrete random variable. The method is analogous to the case of the continuous random variable covered in detail in Section 5-3.

5-2. *Function of a Single Continuous Random Variable*

Say x is a continuous random variable with probability density function $f(x)$ defined over some sample space. Let $w = h(x)$ be a strictly increasing or a strictly decreasing function of x over the sample space. The probability density function of w is then

$$p(w) = f[x(w)] \left| \frac{dx}{dw} \right|, \tag{5-6}$$

where the sample space for w is determined from the sample space for x from $w = h(x)$, $f[x(w)]$ means that $x(w)$ [the inverse of the function $h(x)$] is substituted for x in $f(x)$, and $|dx/dw|$ denotes the absolute value of dx/dw.

Note that (5-5) for a function of a discrete random variable and (5-6) for a function of a continuous random variable are identical except for the factor $|dx/dw|$ in the latter equation. This factor, called the Jacobian of the transformation, is required for the mapping of a continuous function in order that the new probability density function will integrate to 1 over its sample space. The procedure is illustrated by the following example.

In Chapter 3 we considered the function

$$w = h(x) = \frac{x - \mu}{\sigma}, \tag{5-7}$$

where x is normally distributed with mean μ and standard deviation σ—that is,

$$f(x) = \frac{1}{\sigma\sqrt{2\pi}} \exp\left[\frac{-(x - \mu)^2}{2\sigma^2}\right], \quad -\infty < x < \infty. \tag{5-8}$$

In finding the distribution for w, we first note that w is a strictly increasing function of x. From (5-7) it is seen that the range of w is the same as that of x—that is, $-\infty$ to $+\infty$—and also that

$$x(w) = \sigma w + \mu. \tag{5-9}$$

Consequently

$$\left|\frac{dx}{dw}\right| = \sigma. \tag{5-10}$$

Therefore from (5-6) the probability density function for w is

$$p(w) = \frac{1}{\sigma\sqrt{2\pi}}\left[\exp\left(\frac{-(\sigma w + \mu - \mu)^2}{2\sigma^2}\right)\right]\sigma, \quad -\infty < w < \infty$$

or

$$p(w) = \frac{1}{\sqrt{2\pi}} e^{-w^2/2}, \quad -\infty < w < \infty. \tag{5-11}$$

We note that $p(w)$ is a normal probability density function with $\mu = 0$ and $\sigma = 1$. Thus we have verified our claim of Chapter 3 that the standard variate $w = (x - \mu)/\sigma$ is normally distributed with $\mu = 0$ and $\sigma = 1$ if x is normally distributed with arbitrary μ and σ.

Proceeding in the same manner, we can derive the following more general result. If x is a random variable with probability density function $f(x)$ and a and b are constants, then

$$w = \frac{x - a}{b} \tag{5-12}$$

is distributed as

$$p(w) = |b| f(bw + a), \tag{5-12a}$$

where the sample space for w is determined from the sample space for x and (5-12). It follows, for example, that the function $w = cx$ is distributed as

$$p(cx) = \left| \frac{1}{c} \right| f \left(\frac{w}{c} \right). \tag{5-12b}$$

Equation 5-12a verifies the use of a standard gamma distribution with location parameter $\mu = 0$ to find cumulative probabilities for any three-parameter gamma distribution with arbitrary μ, and the use of the standard beta distribution to find cumulative probabilities for any three-parameter beta distribution with arbitrary μ_0 and μ_1 (see Chapter 3). In fact, the constants a and b of 5-12 and 5-12a are defined as the location and scale parameters respectively for the distribution of a random variable x.

Equation 5-6 can also be used to show that if x is normally distributed with parameters μ and σ and

$$w = h(x) = e^x, \tag{5-13}$$

then

$$p(w) = \frac{1}{\sigma w \sqrt{2\pi}} \exp \left[\frac{-(\ln w - \mu)^2}{2\sigma^2} \right], \qquad w \geq 0, \tag{5-14}$$

which is the log-normal distribution discussed in Chapter 3.

When $h(x)$ is a strictly increasing function over parts of its range and a strictly decreasing function over other parts, then $p(w)$ can be obtained by handling each of these parts separately and adding together the values of x corresponding to a particular w. This procedure is illustrated by the following example.

The scrap due to a flaw in the interior of long rectangular strips of sheet material can be thought of as a line segment of constant length L, which appears randomly within the material (see Fig. 5-1). Let θ be the angle that the line segment for a given flaw makes with a line perpendicular to the sides of the strip. Since flaws appear randomly within the material, the random variable θ is uniformly distributed from 0 to π; that is,

$$f(\theta) = \frac{1}{\pi}, \qquad 0 \leqslant \theta \leqslant \pi \tag{5-15}$$

according to (3-31).*

Whenever a flaw occurs, it is necessary to cut out a strip of material defined by lines perpendicular to the sides of the sheet from one end to the other end of the flaw segment, as shown by the dashed lines of Fig. 5-1.

* Note that this problem could have been simplified by restricting θ to the interval $(0, \pi/2)$; this would have led to a one-to-one transformation.

Thus the scrap length w can vary from 0 if the flaw segment is perpendicular to the sides of the sheet (and assuming essentially 0 width) to L if the flaw segment is parallel to the sides of the sheet. In particular,

$$w = h(\theta) = L \sin \theta. \tag{5-16}$$

The problem is to determine $p(w)$, the probability density function for w, the scrap length for a flaw of length L.

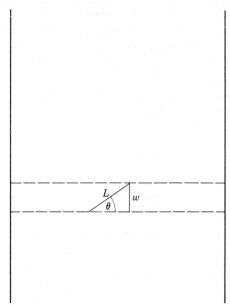

Fig. 5-1   Diagram of flaw of length L in material making angle θ with line perpendicular to sides of material, showing strip that must be removed because of flaw.

Equation 5-16 maps the sample space defined by the interval $0 \leq \theta \leq \pi$ into the sample space defined by the interval $0 \leq w \leq L$. For each value of w, however, there are two values of θ; w is a strictly increasing function of θ for the range $0 \leq \theta < \pi/2$ and a strictly decreasing function of θ for the range $\pi/2 \leq \theta \leq \pi$, as shown in Fig. 5-2. Thus the intervals $0 \leq \theta < \pi/2$ and $\pi/2 \leq \theta \leq \pi$ must be handled separately and the results added for corresponding values of w.

From (5-16), we obtain

$$\theta(w) = \sin^{-1}\left(\frac{w}{L}\right). \tag{5-17}$$

Thus

$$\left|\frac{d\theta}{dw}\right| = \frac{1}{L}\left\{\left[1 - \left(\frac{w}{L}\right)^2\right]^{-\frac{1}{2}}\right\} = (L^2 - w^2)^{-\frac{1}{2}}. \tag{5-18}$$

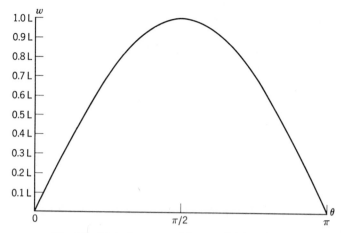

Fig. 5-2   Plot of w versus θ in material-flaw problem.

Using (5-6), (5-15), and (5-18) for the interval $0 \leqslant \theta < \pi/2$ gives

$$p_1(w) = \frac{1}{\pi}(L^2 - w^2)^{-\frac{1}{2}}, \qquad 0 \leq w \leq L, \tag{5-19}$$

and for the interval $\pi/2 \leqslant \theta \leqslant \pi$,

$$p_2(w) = \frac{1}{\pi}(L^2 - w^2)^{-\frac{1}{2}}, \qquad 0 \leq w \leq L. \tag{5-20}$$

The probability density function for the scrap corresponding to a random flaw is found, by summing (5-19) and (5-20) for equivalent values of w, to be

$$p(w) = p_1(w) + p_2(w) \tag{5-21}$$

or

$$p(w) = \frac{2}{\pi}(L^2 - w^2)^{-\frac{1}{2}}, \qquad 0 \leq w \leq L. \tag{5-22}$$

When integrated over its sample space, $p(w)$ should equal 1. Thus

$$\int_0^L p(w)\,dw = \int_0^L \frac{2}{\pi}(L^2 - w^2)^{-\frac{1}{2}}\,dw = \frac{2}{\pi}\sin^{-1}\left(\frac{w}{L}\right)\Big|_0^L = 1 \tag{5-23}$$

as required.

An expression equivalent to (5-6) that is sometimes easier to use is

$$p(w) = f[x(w)]\left|\frac{dw}{dx}\right|^{-1}. \tag{5-6a}$$

Applying (5-6a) in the preceding example would have given

$$\frac{dw}{d\theta} = L \cos \theta = \frac{L(L^2 - w^2)^{\frac{1}{2}}}{L}.$$ (5-24)

Thus

$$\left| \frac{dw}{d\theta} \right|^{-1} = (L^2 - w^2)^{-\frac{1}{2}},$$ (5-25)

and

$$p_1(w) = \frac{1}{\pi} (L^2 - w^2)^{-\frac{1}{2}}, \qquad 0 \leq w \leq L,$$

as before.

5-3. Functions of More Than One Continuous Random Variable

BASIC METHOD

In many cases, such as the one suggested at the beginning of this chapter, a function of *more than one* continuous random variable is required. The resulting methods are generalizations of those for a single variable.

The discussion in this book is limited to cases in which (a) there are as many variables after the transformation as before—(as will be seen, unnecessary variables will be removed by integration), and (b) the transformation is one to one—that is, every combination of values of the original variables defines a unique combination of values of the new variables, and vice versa. These assumptions should become clearer in the treatment that follows. The reader should consult References 5-1 for a discussion of more complex cases.

The case of two random variables is discussed first. The extension to three or more variables is straightforward and is illustrated later. Let

$$w = h(x, y)$$ (5-26)

denote the desired function of two random variables x and y with marginal probability density functions $f(x)$ and $g(y)$, respectively, over specified sample spaces. Also let $m(x, y)$ denote the joint probability density function of x and y. If x and y are independent, it follows from (2-73) that

$$m(x, y) = f(x) g(y).$$ (5-27)

The following steps lead to the probability density for w:

1. Select a second function of x and y to be denoted

$$z = k(x, y),$$ (5-28)

where z is an auxiliary variable that will bring the number of variables after the transformation up to the number with which we started, namely two. Because z will subsequently be eliminated, its choice is arbitrary and it is selected to facilitate the integration.

2. Determine the sample space for w and z from the sample space for x and y and (5-26) and (5-28). These sample spaces or regions will be referred to as D and R respectively.

3. Solve (5-26) and (5-28) for x and y in terms of w and z—that is, find $x(w, z)$ and $y(w, z)$.

4. Obtain the joint probability density function of w and z as

$$n(w, z) = m[x(w, z), y(w, z)]\,|J|, \qquad w \in D, z \in R, \qquad (5\text{-}29)$$

where $m[x(w, z), y(w, z)]$ is (5-27) with x replaced by $x(w, z)$ and y replaced by $y(w, z)$; $w \in D$ and $z \in R$ denote the points in the sample spaces D and R, respectively, and J, the Jacobian of the transformation, is the determinant

$$J = \begin{vmatrix} \dfrac{\partial x}{\partial w} & \dfrac{\partial x}{\partial z} \\[2ex] \dfrac{\partial y}{\partial w} & \dfrac{\partial y}{\partial z} \end{vmatrix}. \qquad (5\text{-}30)$$

In limiting ourselves to transformations that are strictly one to one, we shall obtain a Jacobian that will not change sign over the sample spaces of w and z. This is a generalization of the "strictly increasing" and "strictly decreasing" requirement discussed at the beginning of Section 5-2. The Jacobian J of (5-30) is a generalization of the term dx/dw of (5-6). Note also that the absolute value of J is used in (5-29). In some problems it will be more convenient to calculate

$$J^{-1} = \begin{vmatrix} \dfrac{\partial w}{\partial x} & \dfrac{\partial z}{\partial x} \\[2ex] \dfrac{\partial w}{\partial y} & \dfrac{\partial z}{\partial y} \end{vmatrix} \qquad (5\text{-}31)$$

and use the relationship $J = 1/J^{-1}$.

5. Once the joint probability density of w and z—that is, (5-29)—is obtained, the distribution of w is found by integrating out z. Thus the probability density function for w is given by

$$p(w) = \int_R n(w, z)\, dz, \qquad w \in D. \qquad (5\text{-}32)$$

In some cases, by proper choice of z, the variables z and w can be made independent. In this event

$$n(w, z) = m[x(w, z), y(w, z)]\,|J| = p^*(w)\,q(z), \quad w \in D, z \in R, \quad (5\text{-}33)$$

where $p^*(w)$ and $q(z)$ are functions of w and z, respectively.
Application of (5-32) then yields

$$p(w) = p^*(w) \int_R q(z)\,dz, \qquad w \in D \qquad (5\text{-}34)$$

as the probability density function for w.

SAMPLE PROBLEM

Consider the simple circuit of Fig. 5-3 with two resistors, A and B, connected in series. For any such circuit total resistance is the sum of the

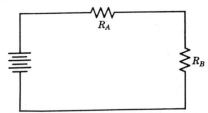

Fig. 5-3   Circuit with two resistors in series.

resistances of A and B. The two resistors used in a given circuit are selected randomly from two large batches with average resistances of 10 and 20 ohms. For both batches the resistances follow a normal distribution with $\sigma = 1$ ohm. We would like to determine the distribution for circuit resistance.

Using previous notation, the function of interest is

$$w = h(x, y) = x + y. \qquad (5\text{-}26a)$$

The choice of the second variable is arbitrary, but by selecting

$$z = k(x, y) = x - y \qquad (5\text{-}28a)$$

w and z will be made independent, as subsequently shown, and thus the calculations will be easier. Because x and y are independent, their joint probability density is

$$m(x, y) = f(x)\,g(y) = \frac{1}{2\pi}\exp\left\{-\tfrac{1}{2}[(x - 10)^2 + (y - 20)^2]\right\}, \quad (5\text{-}27a)$$

using

$$f(x) = (2\pi)^{-\frac{1}{2}} \exp\{-\tfrac{1}{2}(x - 10)^2\}, \qquad -\infty < x < \infty, \qquad (5\text{-}35)$$

and

$$g(y) = (2\pi)^{-\frac{1}{2}} \exp\{-\tfrac{1}{2}(y - 20)^2\}, \qquad -\infty < y < \infty. \qquad (5\text{-}35a)$$

Equation 5-27a is a bivariate normal distribution with $\rho = 0$ (see Chapter 3). Because x and y both range from $-\infty$ to $+\infty$, it follows from (5-26a) and (5-28a) that w and z can take on values from $-\infty$ to $+\infty$ independently.

Solving (5-26a) and (5-28a) for x and y in terms of w and z, we obtain

$$x(w, z) = \frac{w + z}{2} \qquad (5\text{-}36)$$

and

$$y(w, z) = \frac{w - z}{2}. \qquad (5\text{-}37)$$

Consequently, from (5-29) the joint probability density function of w and z is

$$n(w, z) = \frac{1}{2\pi} \exp\left\{-\frac{1}{2}\left[\left(\frac{w + z}{2} - 10\right)^2 + \left(\frac{w - z}{2} - 20\right)^2\right]\right\} |J|, \qquad (5\text{-}29a)$$

$$-\infty < w < \infty, -\infty < z < \infty.$$

Also

$$\frac{\partial x}{\partial w} = \frac{1}{2}, \qquad \frac{\partial x}{\partial z} = \frac{1}{2}, \qquad \frac{\partial y}{\partial w} = \frac{1}{2}, \qquad \frac{\partial y}{\partial z} = -\frac{1}{2}$$

and thus

$$J = \begin{vmatrix} \frac{1}{2} & \frac{1}{2} \\ \frac{1}{2} & -\frac{1}{2} \end{vmatrix} = -\tfrac{1}{2} \qquad (5\text{-}30a)$$

and $|J| = \tfrac{1}{2}$.

By substituting $|J|$ into (5-29a), expanding the terms in the exponent, and forming separate terms in w and z we obtain

$$n(w, z) = \frac{1}{4\pi} \exp\left\{-\frac{1}{2}\left[\frac{(w - 30)^2}{2} + \frac{(z + 10)^2}{2}\right]\right\}, \qquad (5\text{-}38)$$

$$-\infty < w < \infty, -\infty < z < \infty.$$

This expression can be written as

$$n(w, z) = \frac{1}{4\pi} \exp\left[-\frac{1}{2}\frac{(w - 30)^2}{2}\right] \exp\left[-\frac{1}{2}\frac{(z + 10)^2}{2}\right] = c\, p^*(w)\, q(z),$$

$$-\infty < w < \infty, -\infty < z < \infty, \qquad (5\text{-}39)$$

thus verifying that w and z are independent.

The final step is to eliminate z by integrating out this variable [see (5-34)]. This yields

$$p(w) = \frac{1}{4\pi} \exp\left[-\frac{1}{2}\frac{(w-30)^2}{2} \right] \int_{-\infty}^{\infty} \exp\left[-\frac{1}{2}\frac{(z+10)^2}{2} \right] dz, \tag{5-40}$$
$$-\infty < w < \infty.$$

From the definition of the normal probability density function and the fact that the area under any probability distribution equals unity,

$$\int_{-\infty}^{\infty} (2\pi\sigma^2)^{-\frac{1}{2}} \exp\left[-\frac{1}{2}\left(\frac{v-\mu}{\sigma}\right)^2 \right] dv = 1. \tag{5-41}$$

Letting $z = v$ and setting $\mu = -10$ and $\sigma = \sqrt{2}$ in (5-41) gives

$$\int_{-\infty}^{\infty} \exp\left[-\frac{1}{2}\left(\frac{z+10}{\sqrt{2}}\right)^2 \right] dz = (4\pi)^{\frac{1}{2}} \tag{5-42}$$

Substituting (5-42) into (5-40) yields

$$p(w) = (4\pi)^{-\frac{1}{2}} \exp\left[-\frac{1}{2}\frac{(w-30)^2}{2} \right], \qquad -\infty < w < \infty. \tag{5-43}$$

This is a normal probability density function with $\mu = 30$ and $\sigma = \sqrt{2}$, that is, the circuit resistance is normally distributed, with a mean of 30 ohms and a standard deviation of $\sqrt{2}$ ohms.

The preceding example can be generalized to show that the sum of independent normally distributed random variables is normally distributed, with a mean equal to the sum of the individual means and a variance equal to the sum of the individual variances. The central limit theorem (see Chapter 3) states that for large samples from any probability density function, the sum is normally distributed. We now find that if the individual variates are themselves normally distributed, their sum is normally distributed for *any* sample size. This result holds even for non-independent variates, except that in this case the variance must be adjusted for correlation among the variables [see (2-87)].

ALTERNATE PROCEDURE FOR ELIMINATING z

In the preceding example integrating out z in (5-40) was simple. It may not be so in other problems. Consequently, the following alternate way of eliminating z when this variable has been chosen so that it is independent of w is sometimes used. Because $\int_R q(z)\, dz$ in (5-34) is not a function of w, it can be treated as a constant in determining the distribution of w.

Thus let

$$K = \int_R q(z)\, dz \tag{5-44}$$

and write (5-34) as

$$p(w) = K p^*(w), \qquad w \in D. \tag{5-45}$$

K may be determined from the fact that

$$\int_D p(w)\, dw = 1, \tag{5-46}$$

where D is the region over which w is defined; hence

$$K \int_D p^*(w)\, dw = 1, \tag{5-47}$$

and

$$K = \left[\int_D p^*(w)\, dw \right]^{-1}. \tag{5-47a}$$

Applying this procedure to the circuit example, (5-40) would be rewritten as

$$p(w) = K \exp\left[-\frac{1}{2}\left(\frac{w - 30}{\sqrt{2}}\right)^2 \right], \qquad -\infty < w < \infty. \tag{5-48}$$

Then, from (5-47),

$$K \int_{-\infty}^{\infty} \exp\left[-\frac{1}{2}\left(\frac{w - 30}{\sqrt{2}}\right)^2 \right] dw = 1. \tag{5-49}$$

Setting $\mu = 30$ and $\sigma = \sqrt{2}$ in (5-41), we obtain

$$(4\pi)^{-\frac{1}{2}} \int_{-\infty}^{\infty} \exp\left[-\frac{1}{2}\left(\frac{v - 30}{\sqrt{2}}\right)^2 \right] dv = 1. \tag{5-50}$$

Consequently,

$$K = \frac{1}{\sqrt{4\pi}}. \tag{5-51}$$

Thus, from (5-48) and (5-51),

$$p(w) = \frac{1}{\sqrt{4\pi}} \exp\left[-\frac{1}{2}\frac{(w - 30)^2}{2} \right], \qquad -\infty < w < \infty, \tag{5-43}$$

as before. K is thus an adjustment factor to assure that a legitimate probability density function has been obtained—that is, one that integrates to unity over the sample space.

The advantage of selecting z so that it is independent of w should now be clear. If w and z are not independent, the procedure we have described is not applicable and some difficult integration might be required. Finding a particular z that is independent of w might require trial and error and may not be possible in some cases. In our example we established that z was indeed independent of w only after obtaining (5-39).

Finally, it is important to note that independence of w and z requires independence of their ranges of variation. When this is not the case, the procedure suggested by (5-44) through (5-47) is not applicable even if factorization of (5-34) is possible, and we must be careful in seeing that the proper sample space is used in setting up the limits for integrating out z (see example at the end of this chapter).

EXAMPLE INVOLVING A FUNCTION OF THREE VARIABLES

The extension of the above procedure to obtaining the distribution of a function of three or more random variables is straightforward. If we are interested in a function w of r variables, we introduce $r - 1$ auxiliary variables so that there are r variables after transformation. The joint distribution of the new variables is obtained by a generalization of (5-29). The new sample space is found from the definition of the new variables and the sample space for the old variables. For the same reasons as before, it is desirable, whenever possible, to have the auxiliary variables independent of w. The auxiliary variables are then removed by integration or by other means, and we are left with the probability density function for w. The procedure is illustrated by the following example.

It is desired to evaluate the precision of an antisubmarine weapon system. The system is designed so that the average detonation error in each of the three coordinates—depth, longitude, and latitude—is zero and the standard deviation is one measurement unit. It appears from preliminary tests that a normal distribution adequately approximates the distribution of the errors from the target for each coordinate and that the errors are independent of one another. We desire the distribution of the radial distance r from the point of detonation to the target for this system—that is, we wish to find the distribution of

$$r = \sqrt{x^2 + y^2 + z^2}, \qquad (5\text{-}52)$$

where x, y, and z are the errors from target in depth, longitude and latitude respectively, and are independent and normally distributed, each with $\mu = 0$ and $\sigma = 1$. Thus

$$f_1(x) = \frac{1}{\sqrt{2\pi}} e^{-x^2/2}, \qquad -\infty < x < \infty,$$

$$f_2(y) = \frac{1}{\sqrt{2\pi}} e^{-y^2/2}, \qquad -\infty < y < \infty,$$

and

$$f_3(z) = \frac{1}{\sqrt{2\pi}}\, e^{-z^2/2}, \qquad -\infty < z < \infty.$$

Because of independence, the joint probability density function of x, y, and z is

$$m(x, y, z) = [f_1(x)][f_2(y)][f_3(z)] = \left(\frac{1}{2\pi}\right)^{3\!/\!2} e^{-\frac{1}{2}(x^2+y^2+z^2)},$$

$$-\infty < x < \infty, \ -\infty < y < \infty, \ -\infty < z < \infty.$$

This is a trivariate normal distribution with all ρ's equal to zero. The first step in finding the distribution of r is to choose two auxiliary variables. Because we are interested in radial distance, it is advisable to change to polar coordinates and use θ and ϕ—the angles associated with the radius vector—as the two additional variates. Because r is independent of θ and ϕ, this choice will facilitate the necessary integrations. The range for r is from 0 to infinity, and θ and ϕ both vary between 0 and π. The ranges of variation of the three new variables are clearly independent.

The original variables are written as functions of the new variables as follows:

$$x(r, \theta, \phi) = r \cos \theta$$
$$y(r, \theta, \phi) = r \sin \theta \cos \phi$$
$$z(r, \theta, \phi) = r \sin \theta \sin \phi.$$

Thus

$$J = \begin{vmatrix} \dfrac{\partial x}{\partial r} & \dfrac{\partial x}{\partial \theta} & \dfrac{\partial x}{\partial \phi} \\[2mm] \dfrac{\partial y}{\partial r} & \dfrac{\partial y}{\partial \theta} & \dfrac{\partial y}{\partial \phi} \\[2mm] \dfrac{\partial z}{\partial r} & \dfrac{\partial z}{\partial \theta} & \dfrac{\partial z}{\partial \phi} \end{vmatrix} = \begin{vmatrix} \cos \theta & -r \sin \theta & 0 \\[2mm] \sin \theta \cos \phi & r \cos \theta \cos \phi & -r \sin \theta \sin \phi \\[2mm] \sin \theta \sin \phi & r \cos \theta \sin \phi & r \sin \theta \cos \phi \end{vmatrix}$$

$$= r^2 \sin \theta,$$

since $\sin^2 \theta + \cos^2 \theta = 1$.

Also

$$|J| = J = r^2 \sin \theta$$

for $0 \le \theta \le \pi$.

Using the generalized form of (5-29) and the fact that $x^2 + y^2 + z^2 = r^2$, the joint probability density function of r, θ, and ϕ is

$$n(r, \theta, \phi) = m[x(r, \theta, \phi), y(r, \theta, \phi), z(r, \theta, \phi)]\, |J| = \left(\frac{1}{2\pi}\right)^{3\!/\!2} e^{-r^2/2}\, r^2 \sin \theta,$$

$$0 \le r < \infty,\ 0 \le \theta \le \pi,\ 0 \le \phi \le \pi. \qquad (5\text{-}54)$$

Now by generalizing (5-32) we obtain

$$p(r) = \left(\frac{1}{2\pi}\right)^{3/2} e^{-r^2/2} r^2 \int_0^\pi \int_0^\pi \sin\theta \, d\theta \, d\phi, \qquad 0 \leq r < \infty. \qquad (5\text{-}55)$$

Since θ and ϕ are independent of r, we can use (5-45) to write

$$p(r) = Ke^{-r^2/2} r^2, \qquad 0 \leq r < \infty. \qquad (5\text{-}56)$$

Thus from (5-47a)

$$K = \left(\int_0^\infty e^{-r^2/2} r^2 \, dr\right)^{-1}. \qquad (5\text{-}57)$$

From integration by parts

$$K = \sqrt{\frac{2}{\pi}}.$$

Thus

$$p(r) = \sqrt{\frac{2}{\pi}} \, e^{-r^2/2} r^2, \qquad 0 \leq r < \infty, \qquad (5\text{-}58)$$

which is the probability density function for the radial distance of system error.

In Chapter 3 it was stated that the Rayleigh distribution is used to represent radial error in two dimensions. The preceding example led to a generalization in three dimensions of a Rayleigh distribution, with $\sigma = 1$.

EXTENSION OF PRECEDING EXAMPLE TO THE DERIVATION OF
CHI-SQUARE DISTRIBUTION

The distribution of r^2, the square of the variate whose distribution was found in the previous section, is of special interest in many problems. In particular, starting with the probability density function for r, as obtained in (5-58), and making a change of variables $u = r^2$, we obtain by the method given earlier in this chapter

$$f(u) = \frac{1}{\sqrt{2\pi}} e^{-\frac{1}{2}u} u^{1/2}, \qquad 0 \leq u < \infty. \qquad (5\text{-}59)$$

This can also be written as

$$f(u) = [(2)^{3/2}\Gamma(3/2)]^{-1} e^{-\frac{1}{2}u} u^{3/2-1}, \qquad 0 \leq u < \infty. \qquad (5\text{-}60)$$

This distribution is the chi-square distribution with three degrees of freedom (see Chapter 3). More generally, it can be shown that for

$$u = \sum_{i=1}^{\nu} x_i^2, \qquad (5\text{-}61)$$

where $x_1, x_2, \ldots, x_\nu$ are ν independent variates from a normal distribution with mean 0 and standard deviation 1, u is distributed as

$$f(u) = \left[(2)^{\nu/2} \, \Gamma\!\left(\frac{\nu}{2}\right) \right]^{-1} e^{-\frac{1}{2}u} u^{(\nu/2)-1}, \qquad 0 \le u < \infty. \tag{5-62}$$

This is the chi-square distribution with ν degrees of freedom.

EXAMPLE INVOLVING NONINDEPENDENT AUXILIARY VARIABLES

In the previous examples it was possible to use (5-45) to avoid integrating out the auxiliary variables, since these were independent of the variable whose distribution was desired. In the following example it will not be possible to find simple auxiliary variables for which this is true.

In a preventive-maintenance program a repairman inspects and, if necessary, repairs k machines. From past records it is known that the time required to service a single machine is an exponential variate with parameter λ—that is,

$$f(t_i) = \lambda e^{-\lambda t_i}, \qquad 0 \le t_i < \infty, \text{ for } i = 1, 2, \ldots, k.$$

It is desired to determine the distribution of the total time to service k machines—that is, to find the distribution of the sum of k exponential variates.

Let

$$w = t_1 + t_2 + \cdots + t_k. \tag{5-63}$$

Because of independence, the joint distribution of the k exponential variates is

$$m(t_1, t_2, \ldots, t_k) = \lambda^k \exp\left[-\lambda \sum_{i=1}^{k} t_i \right]. \tag{5-64}$$

We now introduce the $k - 1$ auxiliary variables

$$\begin{aligned}
z_1 &= t_1 \\
z_2 &= t_1 + t_2 \\
&\;\cdot \\
&\;\cdot \\
&\;\cdot \\
z_{k-1} &= t_1 + t_2 + \cdots + t_{k-1}.
\end{aligned} \tag{5-65}$$

Using a generalization of (5-31) the Jacobian of the transformation is easily seen to equal one.

Thus from (5-63) and (5-64) and the generalization of (5-29), we obtain the joint distribution of $w, z_1, z_2, \ldots, z_{k-1}$ to be

$$n(z_1, z_2, \ldots, z_{k-1}, w) = \lambda^k e^{-\lambda w}, \tag{5-66}$$
$$0 \le z_1 \le z_2 \le \cdots \le z_{k-1} \le w < \infty.$$

Note that the auxiliary variables do not appear explicitly in the expression for the joint probability density function, but they *still* must be integrated out. Also note that the range of variation for each variable is dependent on the other variates, and hence the variables are not independent. The required integration is conducted in order from the smallest extraneous variate, z_1, to the largest, z_{k-1}. The limits of integration are determined from the inequality in (5-66). Thus the limits for z_1 are 0 to z_2, the limits for z_2, after z_1 has been eliminated, are 0 to z_3, and so forth until z_{k-1} is reached. The limits of z_{k-1} are 0 to w.

Thus by generalizing (5-32)

$$p(w) = \lambda^k e^{-\lambda w} \int_0^w \int_0^{z_{k-1}} \cdots \int_0^{z_3} \int_0^{z_2} dz_1 \, dz_2 \cdots dz_{k-1}. \qquad (5\text{-}67)$$

Therefore

$$p(w) = \lambda^k e^{-\lambda w} \int_0^w \int_0^{z_{k-1}} \cdots \int_0^{z_3} z_2 \, dz_2 \, dz_3 \cdots dz_{k-1},$$

and continuing the integration,

$$p(w) = \frac{\lambda^k e^{-\lambda w} w^{k-1}}{(k-1)!}, \qquad 0 \le w < \infty. \qquad (5\text{-}68)$$

For example, if $\lambda = 2$, the probability density for the time to service 10 machines is

$$p(w) = \frac{(2)^{10}}{9!} e^{-2w} w^9, \qquad 0 \le w < \infty. \qquad (5\text{-}69)$$

We can rewrite (5-68) as

$$p(w) = \frac{\lambda^k e^{-\lambda w} w^{k-1}}{\Gamma(k)}, \qquad 0 \le w < \infty,$$

and recognize this to be a gamma probability density function with parameters λ and $\eta = k$. In fact, by the above example we have proven the assertion in Chapter 3 that the time required for a total of η independent events to take place is a gamma variate if each event occurs at a constant rate λ.

5-4. Some Useful General Results

Expressions from which the distribution of frequently occurring functions of a single continuous random variable and of two independent continuous random variables can be obtained are summarized in Table 5-1. The sample space over which the new variable is defined needs to be determined from the sample space of the original variable and the definition of the transformation. For example, if x has the probability

Table 5-1   Expressions for Obtaining the Probability Density Functions for Frequently Occurring Functions of Independent Continuous Random Variables. [f(x) and g(y) are marginal probability densities of x and y, respectively]

Function of Interest	Resulting Probability Density Function
$w = a + bx$ (a and b are constants)	$p(w) = \left\lvert \dfrac{1}{b} \right\rvert f\!\left(\dfrac{w-a}{b} \right)$
$w = \dfrac{1}{x}$	$p(w) = \dfrac{1}{w^2} f\!\left(\dfrac{1}{w} \right)$
$w = e^x$	$p(w) = \left\lvert \dfrac{1}{w} \right\rvert f(\ln w)$
$w = \ln x$	$p(w) = e^w f(e^w)$
$w = x^2$	$p(w) = \dfrac{1}{2\sqrt{w}} [f(+\sqrt{w}) + f(-\sqrt{w})]$
$w = x + y$	$p(w) = \displaystyle\int f(z)\,g(w-z)\,dz = \int f(w-z)\,g(z)\,dz$
$w = xy$	$p(w) = \displaystyle\int \left\lvert \dfrac{1}{z} \right\rvert f(z)\,g\!\left(\dfrac{w}{z} \right) dz$ $= \displaystyle\int \left\lvert \dfrac{1}{z} \right\rvert f\!\left(\dfrac{w}{z} \right) g(z)\,dz$
$w = \dfrac{x}{y}$	$p(w) = \displaystyle\int \lvert z \rvert\, f(wz)\,g(z)\,dz$ $= \displaystyle\int \left\lvert \dfrac{z}{w^2} \right\rvert f(z)\,g\!\left(\dfrac{z}{w} \right) dz$

density function

$$f(x) = \begin{cases} 2x, & 0 \le x \le 1, \\ 0, & \text{otherwise,} \end{cases}$$

using the first result of Table 5-1 [given previously as (5-12a)], it follows that the function $w = 2x + 3$ has the probability density function

$$p(w) = \begin{cases} \dfrac{1}{2}\left[(2)\left(\dfrac{w-3}{2} \right) \right] = \dfrac{w-3}{2}, & 3 \le w \le 5, \\ 0, & \text{otherwise} \end{cases}$$

To check that $p(w)$ is a legitimate probability density function, we obtain

$$\int_3^5 f(w)\, dw = \int_3^5 \left(\frac{w-3}{2}\right) dw = 1.$$

The expressions that involve two variables require integration over the sample space of the variable to be removed. In many cases this cannot be done explicitly.

The density of $x + y$ is known as the *convolution* of these two variables and will be familiar to those acquainted with mathematical transform theory. The convolution of n random variables is obtained by repeated application of the result shown, again assuming that the required integration can be performed. As n increases, we know from the central limit theorem that the resulting distribution should approach a normal distribution.

References

5-1 R. V. Hogg and A. T. Craig, *Introduction to Mathematical Statistics*, 2nd ed., Macmillan Co., New York, 1965.

5-2 G. P. Wadsworth and J. G. Bryan, *Introduction to Probability and Random Variables*, McGraw-Hill Book Co., New York, 1960.

5-3 M. E. Munroe, *Theory of Probability*, McGraw-Hill Book Co., New York, 1951.

5-4 H. Freeman, *Introduction to Statistical Inference*, Addison-Wesley, Reading, Massachusetts, 1963.

5-5 T. C. Fry, *Probability and Its Engineering Uses*, D. Van Nostrand Co., 2nd ed., Princeton, New Jersey, 1965.

5-6 N. L. Johnson and H. Tetley, *Statistics, An Intermediate Text*, Vol. 2, Cambridge University Press, Cambridge, 1950.

5-7 A. M. Mood and F. A. Graybill, *Introduction to the Theory of Statistics*, 2nd ed., McGraw-Hill Book Co., New York, 1963.

5-8 P. L. Meyer, *Introductory Probability and Statistical Applications*, Addison-Wesley, Reading, Massachusetts, 1965.

5-9 Z. W. Birnbaum, *Introduction to Probability and Mathematical Statistics*, Harper and Brothers, New York, 1962.

Chapter 6

Approximation by Empirical
Distributions

In previous chapters we have given theoretical justifications for specific distributions to represent physical phenomena. Systems that may be represented by a normal, gamma, or extreme-value distribution, for example, have been indicated. Frequently, the engineer has insufficient theoretical grounds for selecting a model. He obtains data and by empirical methods must draw conclusions concerning the phenomenon under study. Sometimes it is sufficient to represent the available information by a histogram and perhaps refine this by freehand smoothing. There are other situations in which it is desirable to represent the data formally by an empirical distribution. Some reasons for doing this are the following:

1. The desire for objectivity. A freehand "fit" to the same data will differ from person to person. The use of an empirical distribution eliminates such arbitrariness. Objectivity might, for example, be important to vendors presenting data to a customer or to a government agency. A mathematical expression is sometimes also required for other reasons, such as when random values are to be selected from the resulting distribution for a Monte Carlo simulation (see Chapter 7) or when distribution percentiles are required for further statistical analysis, such as for the W tests to evaluate distributional assumptions (see Chapter 8).
2. The need for automating the data analysis. When similar sets of data are to be analyzed frequently, and especially when interpolation at a number of specified points is required, it might be more economical to fit the data using a high-speed computer than by freehand methods.
3. Interest in the values of the distribution parameters. The estimated parameters of the fitted distributions often provide important summary

information and can be useful for interpolation. Say, for example, that in fatigue testing, data on cycles to failure are obtained at several stress levels. If the number of cycles to failure at each stress can be represented by the same distribution family, it is possible to obtain estimates of the parameters of the empirical distribution at each stress, and plot these against stress. From such plots information about the parameters of the distribution for cycles to failure for *intermediate* stresses is obtained, and hence predictions for such intermediate stresses can be made, as well as better estimates at the given stress levels.

The use of empirical distributions in evaluating system performance when only data on component performance are available will be indicated in Chapter 7. Such distributions also provide approximations in situations where some of the moments of the distribution have been determined theoretically, but the exact distribution is unknown. An example is given in Reference 6-1.

The fitting of distributions to data has a long history, and many different procedures have been advocated. The most common of these is the use of a normal distribution. As indicated in Chapter 3, the central limit theorem leads one to expect this distribution to provide a reasonable representation for many, but not all, physical phenomena. The gamma and log-normal distributions have similarly been used to represent variables bounded at one end, as has been the beta distribution for variables bounded from above and below. Although these models do lead to a wide diversity of distribution shapes, they still do not provide the degree of generality that is frequently desirable. This is illustrated by Fig. 6-1. This chart shows the regions in the (β_1, β_2) plane for different normal, beta (uniform special case), gamma (exponential special case) and log-normal distributions, where β_1 and β_2 are respectively the square of the standardized measure of skewness and the standardized measure of peakedness (see Chapter 2). The Student t distribution, a symmetric distribution that approaches the normal as its parameter (degrees of freedom) becomes arbitrarily large, is also included.

For all normal distributions $\beta_1 = 0$ and $\beta_2 = 3$. Therefore this distribution is represented in Fig. 6-1 by a *single point*, as are also the exponential and uniform distributions. This is reasonable, since these distributions do not have a shape parameter and therefore involve only a single shape. The gamma, log-normal, and Student t distributions involve curves. Thus gamma distributions can be fitted for all values of β_1 and β_2 that fall on the curve shown near the center of the chart. Note also that the curve for the gamma distribution is close to that for the log-normal distribution. This helps explain the fact that empirical data can frequently be fitted equally well (or equally poorly) by either the gamma or the log-normal distribution.

The beta distribution, which has two shape parameters, occupies a *region* in Fig. 6-1 and thus provides greater generality than any of the other distributions. However, there is a large region of values of β_1 and β_2 that is not covered by any of the above distributions. A purpose of this chapter

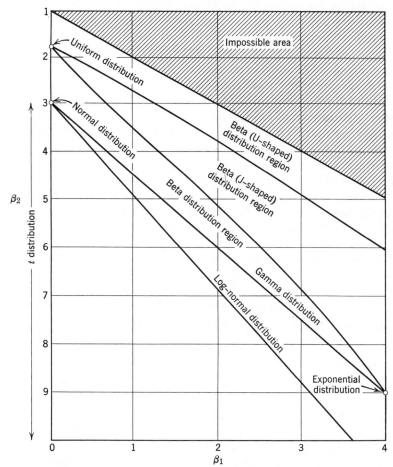

Fig. 6-1   Regions in (β_1, β_2) plane for various distributions. (From Professor E. S. Pearson, University College, London.)

is to discuss distribution families that permit representation over the whole possible region shown in the chart.

To use Fig. 6-1 we need to know the values of β_1 and β_2, which are usually unknown. This chart might, however, be used to provide an indication of whether or not given data might be appropriately represented by one of the distributions shown. This is done by obtaining the sample estimates b_1 and b_2, using (2-51) to (2-55), and plotting this point on Fig. 6-1. If the plotted point is reasonably close to a point, curve, or region corresponding to one of the models we have named, this distribution can be used to represent the data. We might then proceed to obtain estimates for the distribution parameters, using the appropriate formulas, some of which are given in Chapter 3. A similar procedure is used later in this chapter for the more general models.

In applying this method, two important limitations must be recognized. First we note that for any given set of data, b_1 and b_2 are only estimates of β_1 and β_2 and are subject to sampling fluctuations. In fact, from examining (2-51) to (2-55) it is clear that these estimates are very sensitive to a few extreme observations. Thus the methods of this chapter must be used cautiously, especially when there are few observations—say less than 200. Second, the shape of a distribution is not in general uniquely defined by its standardized measures of skewness and peakedness. Thus fitting a given set of data by the distribution suggested by Fig. 6-1 and its later extensions does *not ensure* an adequate fit. It is generally desirable to set up a frequency table to compare the fitted distribution with the actual data. Statistical procedures for evaluating the adequacy of a fitted model are described in Chapter 8.

More general techniques for representing data are the use of Johnson or Pearson distributions, the Cornish–Fisher expansion, Gram–Charlier series, and Edgeworth series. This chapter will be limited to a consideration of Johnson and Pearson distributions. The interested reader should consult Reference 6-2 for a discussion of other methods.

6-1. Johnson Distributions

GENERAL

Johnson (Reference 6-3) proposed basing empirical distributions on the transformation of a standard normal variate. An advantage of such a transformation is that estimates of the percentiles of the fitted distribution can be obtained using a table of areas under a standard normal distribution, such as Table I at the end of the book. Let x be the variable to be fitted by a Johnson distribution. Then the general form of the transformation is

$$z = \gamma + \eta \tau(x; \epsilon, \lambda), \qquad \eta > 0, -\infty < \gamma < \infty, \lambda > 0, -\infty < \epsilon < \infty$$

$$(6-1)$$

where τ is an arbitrary function, γ, η, ϵ, and λ are four parameters, and z is a standard normal variate. The following three alternate forms or families for τ were proposed by Johnson:

(a) $\tau_1(x; \epsilon, \lambda) = \ln\left(\dfrac{x - \varepsilon}{\lambda}\right),$ $x \geq \epsilon,$ (6-2)

(b) $\tau_2(x; \epsilon, \lambda) = \ln\left(\dfrac{x - \epsilon}{\lambda + \epsilon - x}\right),$ $\epsilon \leq x \leq \epsilon + \lambda,$ (6-3)

(c) $\tau_3(x; \epsilon, \lambda) = \sinh^{-1}\left(\dfrac{x - \epsilon}{\lambda}\right),$ $-\infty < x < \infty.$ (6-4)

For the first of these functions we find from (6-1) and (6-2) that

$$x = \lambda \exp\left(\frac{z - \gamma}{\eta}\right) + \epsilon.$$ (6-5)

Applying the methods of Chapter 5 and recalling that z is a standard normal variate, we obtain the following probability density function:

$$f_1(x) = \frac{\eta}{\sqrt{2\pi}(x - \epsilon)} \exp\left\{-\frac{1}{2}\left[\gamma + \eta \ln\left(\frac{x - \epsilon}{\lambda}\right)\right]^2\right\}, \qquad x \geq \epsilon,$$

$$\eta > 0, -\infty < \gamma < \infty, \lambda > 0, -\infty < \epsilon < \infty. \quad (6\text{-}6)$$

Setting

$$\gamma^* = \gamma - \eta \ln \lambda \qquad (6\text{-}7)$$

yields

$$f_1(x) = \frac{\eta}{\sqrt{2\pi}(x - \epsilon)} \exp\left\{-\frac{1}{2}\eta^2\left[\frac{\gamma^*}{\eta} + \ln(x - \epsilon)\right]^2\right\}, \qquad x \geq \epsilon,$$

$$\eta > 0, -\infty < \gamma^* < \infty, -\infty < \epsilon < \infty. \quad (6\text{-}8)$$

This is the three-parameter log-normal distribution, given by (3-34a), with

$$\eta = \frac{1}{\sigma} \qquad \text{and} \qquad \gamma^* = -\frac{\mu}{\sigma} \qquad (6\text{-}9)$$

and is also known as the *Johnson S_L family.*

For the function defined by (6-3) we find similarly

$$f_2(x) = \frac{\eta}{\sqrt{2\pi}} \frac{\lambda}{(x - \epsilon)(\lambda - x + \epsilon)} \exp\left\{-\frac{1}{2}\left[\gamma + \eta \ln\left(\frac{x - \epsilon}{\lambda - x + \epsilon}\right)\right]^2\right\},$$

$$\epsilon \leq x \leq \epsilon + \lambda, \eta > 0, -\infty < \gamma < \infty, \lambda > 0, -\infty < \epsilon < \infty. \quad (6\text{-}10)$$

This four-parameter expression is the *Johnson S_B family* of distributions. Finally, for the function defined by (6-4),

$$f_3(x) = \frac{\eta}{\sqrt{2\pi}} \frac{1}{\sqrt{(x-\epsilon)^2 + \lambda^2}}$$

$$\times \exp\left[-\frac{1}{2}\left(\gamma + \eta \ln\left\{\left(\frac{x-\epsilon}{\lambda}\right) + \left[\left(\frac{x-\epsilon}{\lambda}\right)^2 + 1\right]^{\frac{1}{2}}\right\}\right)^2\right],$$

$$-\infty < x < \infty, \eta > 0, -\infty < \gamma < \infty, \lambda > 0, -\infty < \epsilon < \infty. \quad (6\text{-}11)$$

This four-parameter expression is the *Johnson S_U family* of distributions.

The region in the (β_1, β_2) plane for the three Johnson families is shown in Fig. 6-2. Thus distributions whose values of β_1 and β_2 fall close to the S_L

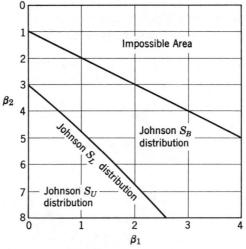

Fig. 6-2 Chart for determining appropriate Johnson distribution approximation. (From N. L. Johnson, *Systems of Frequency Curves Generated by Methods of Translation*, Biometrika, 1949, Vol. 36, p. 148–176.)

curve in the chart may be represented by a log-normal distribution, those with values above the curve by a Johnson S_B family, and those with values below the curve by a Johnson S_U family. Comparing Fig. 6-2 with Fig. 6-1 indicates the broader scope of distributional shapes that can be accommodated by the Johnson families than by the distributions presented in Chapter 3.

Note that the Johnson S_B and S_U families both have two shape parameters γ and η, one location parameter ϵ and one scale parameter λ. Plots of the probability density functions for Johnson S_B and S_U distributions with various parameter values are shown in Figs. 6-3 and 6-4, respectively. Plots of log-normal probability density functions were previously shown in Fig. 3-10.

From (6-11), (6-8), and (6-10) note that the Johnson S_U, S_L, and S_B distributions are defined, respectively, for unbounded variates, variates

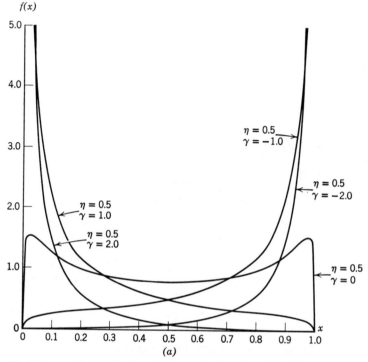

Fig. 6-3   Johnson S_B distributions with $\epsilon = 0$, $\lambda = 1$, and various values of the parameters η and γ.

bounded at one end, and variates bounded from both above and below. These limitations, however, need not be strictly adhered to. For example, the Johnson S_U family might provide a satisfactory approximation to the distribution of a bounded variate. This is analogous to the common use of the normal distribution, which is also unbounded, to represent physical measurements, such as the height of individuals.

The following steps are involved in fitting a Johnson distribution to a set of data: (a) determine which of the three distribution families is applicable, and (b) estimate the parameters of the chosen family and obtain the expected frequencies for the fitted distribution.

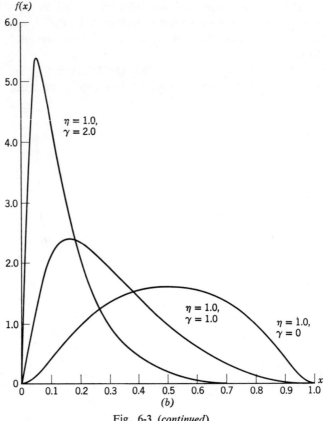

Fig. 6-3 (*continued*)

SELECTION OF JOHNSON DISTRIBUTION FAMILY

To decide which of the three Johnson families should be used for a given set of data, the usual procedure is to obtain the data estimates b_1 and b_2 from (2-51) to (2-55) and use these for β_1 and β_2 in Fig. 6-2. Hence, if the (b_1, b_2) point is close to the curve shown in Fig. 6-2, the S_L family is chosen. If it is in the region above the curve, the S_B family is chosen; and if it is below the curve, the S_U family is used.

The range of the curve in Fig. 6-2 can be extended by use of the parametric equations

$$\begin{aligned}
\beta_1 &= (\omega - 1)(\omega + 2)^2, \\
\beta_2 &= \omega^4 + 2\omega^3 + 3\omega^2 - 3.
\end{aligned} \tag{6-12}$$

Thus additional points are obtained by choosing values of ω and solving for the corresponding values of β_1 and β_2.

The following example illustrates the procedure for determining the appropriate Johnson family. A total of 500 one-half–ohm resistors were subjected to a corrosive environment for 100 hours, and at the end of the test the resistance was measured on each unit. The resulting observations are summarized in Table 6-1. Using (2-51) to (2-55) we obtained the following values: $\sqrt{b_1} = 0.976$ and $b_2 = 4.68$. Thus $b_1 = 0.953$.

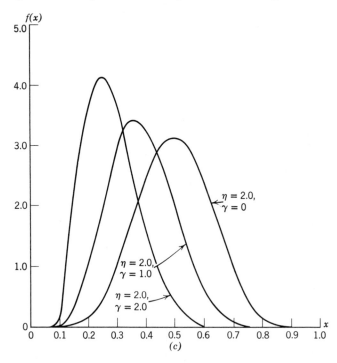

Fig. 6-3 (*continued*)

The (b_1, b_2) point, when used in place of (β_1, β_2), falls close to the dividing curve in Fig. 6-2, and the S_L family should be used to represent the data.

ESTIMATION OF THE PARAMETERS OF THE JOHNSON S_L
(LOG-NORMAL) FAMILY

We shall consider two cases: one in which the location parameter ϵ is known, and the other in which it is not known and must be estimated from the data. Since ϵ is the lower bound on the random variable whose distribution is being fitted, it is often known from physical considerations. For example, in the analysis of life test data ϵ often equals zero. A more detailed discussion of the following and other estimation methods is given in References 6-3 and 6-4.

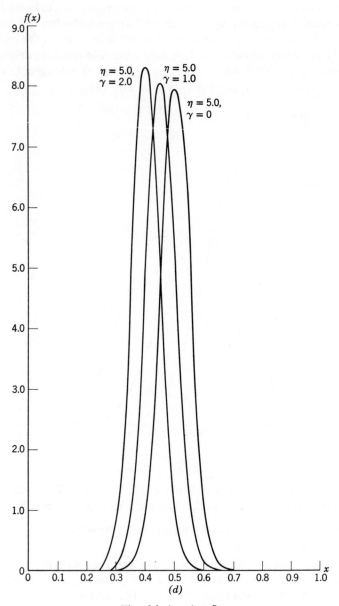

Fig. 6-3 *(continued)*

204

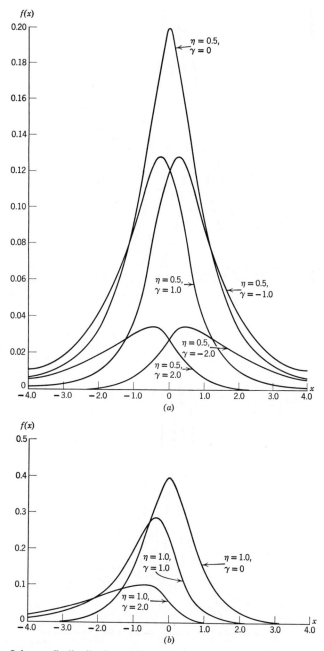

Fig. 6-4 Johnson S_U distributions with $\epsilon = 0$, $\lambda = 1$, and various values of the parameters η and γ.

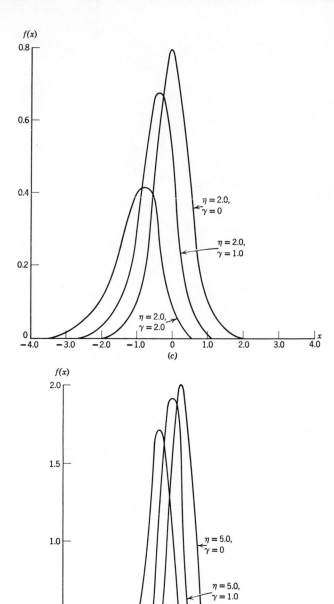

Fig. 6-4 (*continued*)

Table 6-1   Resistances of 500 One-Half–Ohm Resistors after 100 Hours of Environmental Testing, Summarized in Frequency Distribution

Resistance in Ohms	Number of Units
below 0.350	1
0.350 to 0.374	1
0.375 to 0.399	2
0.400 to 0.424	9
0.425 to 0.449	24
0.450 to 0.474	34
0.475 to 0.499	44
0.500 to 0.524	43
0.525 to 0.549	56
0.550 to 0.574	41
0.575 to 0.599	46
0.600 to 0.624	44
0.625 to 0.649	32
0.650 to 0.674	22
0.675 to 0.699	29
0.700 to 0.724	21
0.725 to 0.749	11
0.750 to 0.774	14
0.775 to 0.799	7
0.800 to 0.824	4
0.825 to 0.849	3
0.850 to 0.874	4
0.875 to 0.899	1
0.900 to 0.924	2
0.925 to 0.949	1
0.950 to 0.974	0
0.975 to 0.999	1
over 1.000	3

Value of ϵ Known. Expressing the log-normal probability density function in the form of (3-34a) with parameters μ and σ, then in a manner analogous to that for estimating the parameters of the normal distribution [see (2-31), (3-6), and (3-7)], the following estimates are obtained:

$$\hat{\mu} = \frac{1}{n} \sum_{i=1}^{n} \ln (x_i - \epsilon), \tag{6-13a}$$

$$\hat{\sigma} = \left\{ \frac{\sum_{i=1}^{n} [\ln (x_i - \epsilon)]^2}{n} - \left[\frac{\sum_{i=1}^{n} \ln (x_i - \epsilon)}{n^2} \right]^2 \right\}^{\frac{1}{2}}, \tag{6-13b}$$

or

$$s = \left\{ \frac{n \sum_{i=1}^{n} [\ln (x_i - \epsilon)]^2 - \left[\sum_{i=1}^{n} \ln (x_i - \epsilon) \right]^2}{n(n-1)} \right\}^{\frac{1}{2}}, \qquad (6\text{-}13c)$$

where x_i, $i = 1, 2, \ldots, n$, are the observed values. The estimates of γ^* and η in (6-8) are then

$$\hat{\eta} = \frac{1}{\hat{\sigma}} \qquad \text{or} \qquad \hat{\eta} = \frac{1}{s} \qquad (6\text{-}14)$$

and

$$\hat{\gamma}^* = -\frac{\hat{\mu}}{\hat{\sigma}} \qquad \text{or} \qquad \hat{\gamma}^* = -\frac{\hat{\mu}}{s}. \qquad (6\text{-}15)$$

An alternate procedure for obtaining $\hat{\mu}$ and $\hat{\sigma}$ by probability plotting is described in Chapter 8.

The expected proportion of observations within specified frequency classes—that is, the fitted distribution—may be obtained using the estimated parameters, and the results may be compared with the actual data. The method will be described and illustrated for the situation in which all three parameters of the log-normal distribution need be estimated from the data.

Value of ϵ Unknown. Using (6-2) and (6-7) we rewrite (6-1) as

$$z = \gamma^* + \eta \ln (x - \epsilon), \qquad (6\text{-}16)$$

where z is a standard normal variate.

Estimates of the three unknown parameters γ^*, η, and ϵ of the log-normal distribution are obtained by setting three percentiles calculated from the data equal to the three corresponding percentiles for the normal variate z in (6-16). The three resulting equations are then solved for the unknown parameters, yielding the desired estimates. Thus three equations are obtained of the form

$$z_\alpha = \gamma^* + \eta \ln (x_\alpha - \epsilon), \qquad (6\text{-}17)$$

where z_α is the α 100th percentile for a standard normal variate and x_α is the corresponding percentile calculated from the data. For example, if the 5th, 50th and 95th percentiles are used for this purpose the three equations are

$$-1.645 = \gamma^* + \eta \ln (x_{0.05} - \epsilon),$$
$$0 \;\;= \gamma^* + \eta \ln (x_{0.50} - \epsilon), \qquad (6\text{-}18)$$

and

$$1.645 = \gamma^* + \eta \ln (x_{0.95} - \epsilon),$$

since $z_{0.05} = -1.645$, $z_{0.50} = 0$, and $z_{0.95} = 1.645$.

Solution of these equations yields

$$\hat{\eta} = 1.645 \left[\ln \left(\frac{x_{0.95} - x_{0.5}}{x_{0.5} - x_{0.05}} \right) \right]^{-1}, \tag{6-19}$$

$$\hat{\gamma}^* = \hat{\eta} \ln \left(\frac{1 - e^{-1.645/\hat{\eta}}}{x_{0.5} - x_{0.05}} \right), \tag{6-20}$$

and

$$\hat{\epsilon} = x_{0.5} - e^{-\hat{\gamma}^*/\hat{\eta}}. \tag{6-21}$$

More generally, if any two symmetric percentiles—say, the α 100th and the $(1 - \alpha)$ 100th percentiles—were used instead of the 5th and 95th percentiles, the resulting equations would become

$$\hat{\eta} = z' \left[\ln \left(\frac{x_{1-\alpha} - x_{0.5}}{x_{0.5} - x_{\alpha}} \right) \right]^{-1}, \tag{6-22}$$

$$\hat{\gamma}^* = \hat{\eta} \ln \left(\frac{1 - e^{-z'/\hat{\eta}}}{x_{0.5} - x_{\alpha}} \right), \tag{6-23}$$

and

$$\hat{\epsilon} = x_{0.5} - e^{-\hat{\gamma}^*/\hat{\eta}}, \tag{6-24}$$

where $z' = z_{1-\alpha} = -z_{\alpha}$ is the 100 αth percentile of a normal distribution, and x_{α} and $x_{1-\alpha}$ are respectively the α 100th and $(1 - \alpha)$ 100th percentiles calculated from the data. When the chosen percentiles are not symmetric, the equation for $\hat{\eta}$ takes on the following nonlinear form:

$$\frac{x_{1-\alpha'} - x_{0.5}}{x_{0.5} - x_{\alpha}} = \frac{e^{z_{1-\alpha'}/\hat{\eta}} - 1}{1 - e^{z_{\alpha}/\hat{\eta}}}, \tag{6-25}$$

where $z_{1-\alpha'}$ and $x_{1-\alpha'}$ are the $(1 - \alpha')$100th percentiles for a standard normal variate and for the given data, respectively. The expressions for $\hat{\gamma}^*$ and $\hat{\epsilon}$ remain the same except that $-z'$ in (6-23) is replaced by z_{α}.

The selection of specific percentiles is somewhat arbitrary. Use of different values will lead to somewhat different estimates of the parameters, although the discrepancies are generally expected to be small. When we are interested in obtaining a close approximation in the tails of the distribution, it is recommended that tail values, such as the 5th and 95th percentiles, be chosen. However, use of too extreme a percentile would lead to loss of precision in the fit because of the high variance in the estimate of the percentile.

Note that the α 100th data percentiles are obtained as the $\alpha(n + 1)$th ranked values from the n observations, using interpolation if necessary (see Chapter 2).

The above procedure is applied to fitting a distribution to the resistances summarized in Table 6-1. A log-normal distribution was suggested as an approximation, and the parameters need now be estimated by matching the 5th, 50th, and 95th percentiles of the data with the corresponding fitted distribution percentiles.

Since $n = 500$, the 5th percentile is estimated by interpolating between the values of the 25th and 26th ranked observations; the 50th percentile, or median, is the mean of the values of the 250th and 251st observations;

Table 6-2   Values of Selected Ranked Resistances for 500 One-Half-Ohm Resistors After 100 Hours of Environmental Testing

Rank	Resistance in Ohms
25	0.439
26	0.440
100	0.488
101	0.488
250	0.568
251	0.570
400	0.675
401	0.678
475	0.776
476	0.777

and the 95th percentile is obtained by interpolating between the 475th and 476th ranked observations. From the values shown in Table 6-2 we thus obtain

$$x_{0.05} = 0.439,$$
$$x_{0.50} = 0.569,$$

and

$$x_{0.95} = 0.777.$$

Substituting into (6-19) to (6-21) yields

$$\hat{\eta} = 1.645\left[\ln\left(\frac{0.777 - 0.569}{0.569 - 0.439}\right)\right]^{-1} = 3.5,$$

$$\hat{\gamma}^* = 3.5\ln\left(\frac{1 - e^{-1.645/3.5}}{0.569 - 0.439}\right) = 3.707,$$

and

$$\hat{\epsilon} = 0.569 - e^{-3.707/3.5} = 0.222.$$

The approximating log-normal distribution for the resistance x is thus

$$f_1(x) = \frac{3.5}{\sqrt{2\pi}\,(x - 0.222)} \exp\left\{-\frac{1}{2}(3.5)^2\left[\frac{3.707}{3.5} + \ln(x - 0.222)\right]^2\right\}.$$

If the 20th, 50th, and 80th percentiles instead of the 5th, 50th, and 95th percentiles were matched, the following percentiles would be obtained from Table 6-2:

$$x_{0.20} = 0.488,$$
$$x_{0.50} = 0.569,$$

and

$$x_{0.80} = 0.677.$$

Substituting these in (6-22) to (6-24) and using $z' = z_{0.80} = -z_{0.20} = 0.842$, we have

$$\hat{\eta} = 2.975,$$
$$\hat{\gamma}^* = 3.311,$$

and

$$\hat{\epsilon} = 0.240.$$

To fit the distribution, we obtain the expected proportion (or number) of observations within specified frequency classes, using the estimated parameter values. These may be compared with the *actual* proportion (or number) within these classes. The expected proportion of observations *below* some value x is obtained by using $\hat{\gamma}^*$, $\hat{\eta}$, $\hat{\epsilon}$, and x in place of γ^*, η, ϵ, and x_α to estimate z_α in (6-17) and then finding the proportion of area α under a standard normal curve to the left of z_α from Table I. The expected proportion of observations within a given frequency class is the difference between the expected proportions below each of the end points of the class. Thus, using the fitted distribution based on matching the 5th, 50th, and 95th percentiles in the previous example, the expected proportion of resistances below $x = 0.40$ is equivalent to the proportion of area under a normal curve to the left of the point $z_\alpha = 3.707 + 3.5 \ln(0.4 - 0.222) = -2.333$, or a proportion of 0.010.

Similarly, the expected proportion of resistances below $x = 0.45$ is found to be 0.071. Therefore the expected proportion of resistances between 0.40 and 0.45 is 0.061, as compared to the observed proportion of 0.066. A comparison of actual versus expected per cent frequencies, based on the two sets of parameter estimates that were obtained previously, is given in Table 6-3 and plotted in Figs. 6-5 and 6-6, respectively. In both cases the log-normal distribution appears to provide an excellent approximation to the data. A more objective evaluation of the adequacy of the fit may be obtained by conducting a chi-squared test (see Chapter 8).

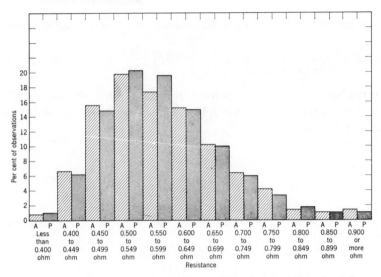

Fig. 6-5 Actual (A) versus predicted (P) per cent of observations for Johnson S_L (log-normal) distribution fit to resistor data based on matching 5th, 50th, and 95th percentiles. (All three parameters are assumed to be unknown.)

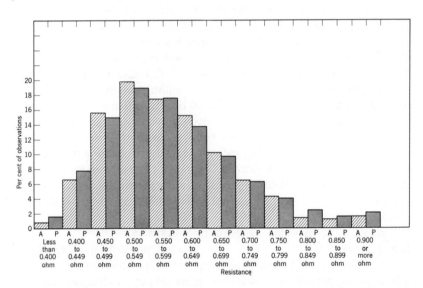

Fig. 6-6 Actual (A) versus predicted (P) per cent of observations for Johnson S_L (log-normal) distribution fit to resistor data based on matching 20th, 50th, and 80th percentiles. (All three parameters are assumed to be unknown.)

Table 6-3   Comparison of Actual Versus Predicted Per Cent Observations by Frequency Classes for Johnson S_L (Log-Normal) Distribution Fits[a] to Resistor Data

Resistance in Ohms	Actual Per Cent of Observations	Predicted Per Cent of Observations, Based on Matching 5th, 50th, and 95th Percentiles	Predicted Per Cent of Observations, Based on Matching 20th, 50th, and 80th Percentiles
Less than 0.400	0.8	1.0	1.6
0.400 to 0.449	6.6	6.1	7.8
0.450 to 0.499	15.6	14.8	14.9
0.500 to 0.549	19.8	20.3	18.9
0.550 to 0.599	17.4	19.6	17.5
0.600 to 0.649	15.2	15.0	13.7
0.650 to 0.699	10.2	10.0	9.7
0.700 to 0.749	6.4	6.0	6.3
0.750 to 0.799	4.2	3.4	4.0
0.800 to 0.849	1.4	1.8	2.3
0.850 to 0.899	1.0	1.0	1.4
0.900 or more	1.4	1.0	1.9

[a] Assuming all three parameters unknown.

ESTIMATION FOR THE JOHNSON S_B FAMILY

A Johnson S_B variate is theoretically bounded by ϵ and $\epsilon + \lambda$. This leads to the following situations:

1. The values of both end points are known. This would be the case, for example, in fitting a distribution to the daily per cent of acceptable units from a given process.

2. The value of only one end point is known, as in life testing in which case failure time cannot be less than zero.

3. The value of neither end point is known.

Methods for estimating parameters for each of these three cases are discussed here. Further details may be found in References 6-3 and 6-5.

Range of Variation Known. Since ϵ, the smallest possible value, and $\epsilon + \lambda$, the largest possible value for the variate are known, we need only estimate γ and η. Their values are estimated by equating two percentiles calculated from the data with the corresponding percentiles of the normal distribution in (6-1) and solving the resulting two equations for γ and η.

Proceeding as for the three-parameter log-normal distribution, we obtain

$$\hat{\eta} = \frac{z_{1-\alpha'} - z_\alpha}{\ln\left[\dfrac{(x_{1-\alpha'} - \epsilon)(\epsilon + \lambda - x_\alpha)}{(x_\alpha - \epsilon)(\epsilon + \lambda - x_{1-\alpha'})}\right]} \qquad (6\text{-}26)$$

and

$$\hat{\gamma} = z_{1-\alpha'} - \hat{\eta}\ln\left(\frac{x_{1-\alpha'} - \epsilon}{\epsilon + \lambda - x_{1-\alpha'}}\right), \qquad (6\text{-}27)$$

where z_α and $z_{1-\alpha'}$ are the α 100th and $(1 - \alpha')$ 100th percentiles of a standard normal distribution, and x_α and $x_{1-\alpha'}$ are the corresponding data percentiles. Thus x_α is the value of the $\alpha(n + 1)$th ranked value obtained from the data, using interpolation if necessary.

This procedure is used, for example, to fit a Johnson S_B distribution to data for the time to complete the manufacture of a part in an automated production process. This time varies from unit to unit because of differences in material quality and hardness. Suppose the minimum cycle time is one half minute for ideal material. The upper bound is two minutes, at which time the material is automatically rejected. The time required for successful completion of 1000 randomly selected units is summarized in the first two columns of Table 6-4.

From the original observations, $b_1 = 0.406$ and $b_2 = 3.28$ are calculated from (2-51) to (2-55). The plot of these values in place of β_1 and β_2 in Fig. 6-2 suggests a Johnson S_B distribution approximation. It is decided to match the 9th and 91st data percentiles with the corresponding fitted values (the choice of percentiles is somewhat arbitrary). Thus we obtain $x_{0.09} = 0.84$, $x_{0.91} = 1.42$, and $-z_{0.09} = z_{0.91} = 1.34$. From the problem statement $\epsilon = 0.5$ and $\lambda = 2.0 - 0.5 = 1.5$. Substitution of these values into (6-26) and (6-27) yields

$$\hat{\eta} = \frac{1.34 + 1.34}{\ln\left[\dfrac{(1.42 - 0.5)(0.5 + 1.5 - 0.84)}{(0.84 - 0.5)(0.5 + 1.5 - 1.42)}\right]} = 1.587$$

and

$$\hat{\gamma} = 1.34 - 1.587\ln\left(\frac{1.42 - 0.5}{0.5 + 1.5 - 1.42}\right) = 0.608.$$

Let us investigate the effect of the bounds on the estimates of the parameters and on the resulting fit. Suppose lower and upper bounds of 0 and 3 minutes respectively rather than 0.5 and 2 minutes were used. Thus $\epsilon = 0$ and $\lambda = 3.0$.

Table 6-4 Comparison of Actual versus Predicted Per Cent Observations by Frequency Classes for Johnson S_B Distribution Fits to Production Time for 1000 Randomly Selected Units

Production Time in Minutes	Actual Per Cent of Observations	Predicted[a] Per Cent of Observations Assuming Bounds of 0.5 and 2.0	Predicted[a] Per Cent of Observations Assuming Bounds of 0 and 3.0	Predicted[b] Per Cent of Observations, Assuming Lower Bound of 0.5, Upper Bound Unknown
Less than 0.70	0.9	0.9	1.7	0.4
0.70 to 0.79	3.7	4.7	4.3	4.5
0.80 to 0.89	12.6	10.3	9.2	12.8
0.90 to 0.99	18.4	15.2	14.4	18.7
1.00 to 1.09	18.8	17.4	17.7	19.1
1.10 to 1.19	15.8	16.9	17.6	15.7
1.20 to 1.29	12.2	13.9	14.5	11.3
1.30 to 1.39	7.6	10.2	10.1	7.4
1.40 to 1.49	5.0	6.1	5.9	4.5
1.50 to 1.59	2.8	3.1	2.8	2.6
1.60 to 1.69	1.1	1.0	1.2	1.4
1.70 to 1.79	0.9	0.3	0.5	0.8
1.80 or more	0.2	0.0	0.1	0.8

[a] Based on matching 9th and 91st observed and predicted percentiles.
[b] Based on matching 9th, 50th, and 91st observed and predicted percentiles.

The resulting parameter estimates are $\hat{\eta} = 3.199$ and $\hat{\gamma} = 1.681$.

Using the relationship between the normal and the Johnson S_B distributions [see (6-1) and (6-3)] the proportion of observations expected within specified frequency classes can be determined as before. The resulting comparison between the observed proportions and those expected from each of the two distribution fits is shown in the first four columns of Table 6-4 and is plotted in Figs. 6-7 and 6-8. The two fits yield very similar predictions, despite the difference in the estimates of the parameters, and both appear to represent the data quite well.

One End Point Known. To estimate the parameters of a Johnson S_B distribution when only the lower bound ϵ is known we supplement (6-26) and (6-27) with an additional equation obtained by matching the median of the data, $x_{0.5}$, with the median of the normal distribution, $z_{0.5} = 0$.

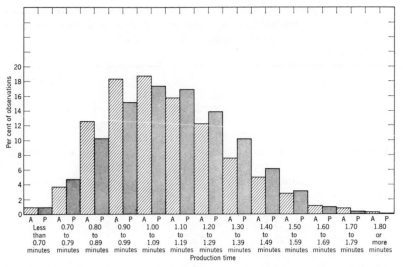

Fig. 6-7 Actual (A) versus predicted (P) per cent of observations for Johnson S_B distribution fit to production time data, based on matching 9th and 91st percentiles and assuming bounds of 0.5 and 2.0.

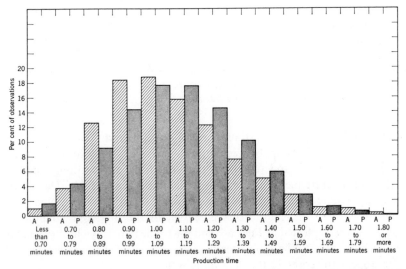

Fig. 6-8 Actual (A) versus predicted (P) per cent of observations for Johnson S_B distribution fit to production time data, based on matching 9th and 91st percentiles and assuming bounds of 0 and 3.0.

216

When symmetric percentiles are used—that is, when $\alpha = \alpha'$—this yields

$$\hat{\lambda} = (x_{0.5} - \epsilon)$$

$$\times \frac{(x_{0.5} - \epsilon)(x_\alpha - \epsilon) + (x_{0.5} - \epsilon)(x_{1-\alpha} - \epsilon) - 2(x_\alpha - \epsilon)(x_{1-\alpha} - \epsilon)}{(x_{0.5} - \epsilon)^2 - (x_\alpha - \epsilon)(x_{1-\alpha} - \epsilon)}.$$

(6-28)

If $\alpha \neq \alpha'$, it is necessary to solve the following equation for $\hat{\lambda}$:

$$\left[\frac{(x_{0.5} - \epsilon)(\epsilon + \hat{\lambda} - x_{1-\alpha'})}{(\epsilon + \hat{\lambda} - x_{0.5})(x_{1-\alpha'} - \epsilon)}\right]^{-z_\alpha/z_{1-\alpha'}} = \left(\frac{x_\alpha - \epsilon}{\epsilon + \hat{\lambda} - x_\alpha}\right)\left(\frac{\epsilon + \hat{\lambda} - x_{0.5}}{x_{0.5} - \epsilon}\right).$$

(6-29)

In both cases estimates for η and γ are obtained by substituting $\hat{\lambda}$ for λ in (6-26) and (6-27).

If the upper bound for the data of Table 6-4 were not known, the procedure just described would be required to estimate this value. The median of the data was found to be $x_{0.50} = 1.07$. Thus, using the 9th, 50th, and 91st data percentiles in (6-28) and taking $\epsilon = 0.5$, we obtain

$$\hat{\lambda} = (1.07 - 0.5)$$

$$\times \frac{\begin{array}{c}(1.07 - 0.5)(0.84 - 0.5) + (1.07 - 0.5)(1.42 - 0.5) \\ - 2(0.84 - 0.5)(1.42 - 0.5)\end{array}}{(1.07 - 0.5)^2 - (0.84 - 0.5)(1.42 - 0.5)} = 4.36;$$

substitution of this value for λ in (6-26) and (6-27) yields $\hat{\eta} = 2.328$ and $\hat{\gamma} = 4.411$.

The resulting predicted percentages are shown in the last column of Table 6-4 and are plotted against the observed proportions in Fig. 6-9. Again an excellent fit is obtained.

Neither End Point Known. For the case in which neither end point is known four data percentiles have to be matched with corresponding percentiles of the standard normal distribution.

The resulting four equations

$$z_i = \hat{\gamma} + \hat{\eta} \ln\left(\frac{x_i - \hat{\epsilon}}{\hat{\epsilon} + \hat{\lambda} - x_i}\right), \qquad i = 1, 2, 3, 4 \qquad (6\text{-}30)$$

are nonlinear in form and must be solved by numerical methods.

Fortunately, in most engineering situations one end point, such as the lower limit of zero, is known, and the simpler methods apply.

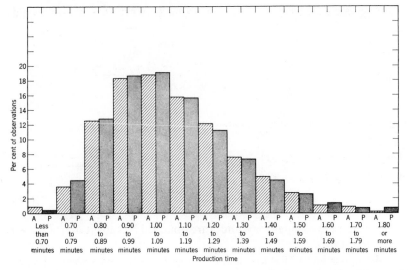

Fig. 6-9   Actual (A) versus predicted (P) per cent of observation for Johnson S_B distribution fit to production-time data, based on matching 9th, 50th, and 91st percentiles and assuming lower-bound of 0.5 and unknown upper bound.

ESTIMATION FOR THE JOHNSON S_U FAMILY

A Johnson S_U variate is theoretically unbounded, and in general the four parameters γ, η, λ, and ϵ are unknown. However, these can be estimated with the help of Table V at the back of the book*. The procedure based on the method of moments (that is, the first four moments of the fitted distribution are set equal to those of the data) is as follows:

1. Obtain $\bar{x}$, $\hat{\sigma}$, $\sqrt{b_1}$ and b_2 from the data, using (2-31) and (2-51) to (2-55). The last two values were obtained previously in selecting the appropriate Johnson distribution family.

2. Use Table V to obtain the estimates $\hat{\gamma}$ (the actual tabulated value is $-\hat{\gamma}$) and $\hat{\eta}$ from $\sqrt{b_1}$ and b_2, interpolating where necessary. If greater accuracy is desired when there are many observations (and the estimates are statistically more precise), an iterative method described in Reference 6-6 can be used.

3. Calculate

$$\hat{\lambda} = \frac{\hat{\sigma}}{\left[\frac{1}{2}(\omega - 1)\left(\omega \cosh\left(2\frac{\hat{\gamma}}{\hat{\eta}}\right) + 1\right)\right]^{1/2}} \qquad (6\text{-}31)$$

* This table was published originally in Reference 6-6.

and

$$\hat{\epsilon} = \bar{x} + \hat{\lambda}\omega^{\frac{1}{2}} \sinh\left(\frac{\hat{\gamma}}{\hat{\eta}}\right),$$ (6-32)

where

$$\omega = e^{1/\hat{\eta}^2}.$$ (6-33)

The following problem illustrates this method. Measurements of the coefficient of friction for a metal were obtained on 250 samples. The resulting values are summarized in the first two columns of Table 6-5. It

Table 6-5 Comparison of Actual versus Predicted Per Cent Observations by Frequency Classes for Johnson S_U Distribution Fit to Coefficient of Friction for 250 Samples

Coefficient of Friction	Actual Per Cent of Observations	Predicted Per Cent of Observations
Less than 0.0150	0.4	0.7
0.0150 to 0.0199	3.6	3.3
0.0200 to 0.0249	12.0	10.8
0.0250 to 0.0299	17.6	20.0
0.0300 to 0.0349	23.2	22.5
0.0350 to 0.0399	18.0	17.9
0.0400 to 0.0449	11.6	11.5
0.0450 to 0.0499	6.8	6.4
0.0500 to 0.0549	3.6	3.5
0.0550 to 0.0599	1.6	1.7
0.0600 or more	1.6	1.7

was decided to approximate the data by a Johnson distribution. The following values were calculated from the original data: $\bar{x} = 0.0345$, $\hat{\sigma} = 0.0098$, $\sqrt{b_1} = 0.87$, and $b_2 = 4.92$.

Plotting the point (b_1, b_2) on Fig. 6-2 suggests the use of a Johnson S_U distribution, in spite of the fact that the observed variate can take on only positive values and thus is bounded at one end.

Based on $\sqrt{b_1}$ and b_2, the following values are obtained by interpolating in Table V: $\hat{\eta} = 2.433$ and $\hat{\gamma} = -1.783$.

Equations 6-31 to 6-33 yield

$$\omega = \exp\left[(2.433)^{-2}\right] = 1.184,$$

$$\hat{\lambda} = \frac{0.0098}{\left[\frac{1}{2}(1.184 - 1)\left\{1.184 \cosh\left[2\left(\frac{-1.783}{2.433}\right)\right] + 1\right\}\right]^{\frac{1}{2}}} = 0.0169,$$

and

$$\hat{\epsilon} = 0.0345 + (0.0169)(1.184)^{\frac{1}{2}} \sinh\left(\frac{-1.783}{2.433}\right) = 0.0198.$$

The comparison of the expected and observed percentages in selected frequency classes, using these estimates, shows excellent agreement (see Table 6-5 and Fig. 6-10).

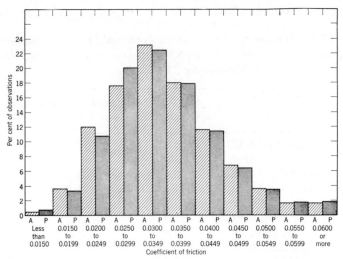

Fig. 6-10   Actual (A) versus predicted (P) per cent of observations for Johnson S_U distribution fit to coefficient of friction data.

6-2. Pearson Distributions

Another group of distribution families are those proposed by Karl Pearson. Each family in the *Pearson system* can be generated as a solution to the differential equation

$$\frac{df(x)}{dx} = \frac{(x - \phi_3)f(x)}{\phi_0 + \phi_1 x + \phi_2 x^2} \qquad (6\text{-}34)$$

for the random variable x with probability density function $f(x)$ by proper choice of the four parameters ϕ_0, ϕ_1, ϕ_2, and ϕ_3. The solution of this equation leads to a large number of distribution families, including the normal, beta (Pearson Type I), and gamma (Pearson Type III) distributions discussed in Chapter 3. A plot of the regions in the (β_1, β_2) plane corresponding to various Pearson distributions is shown in Fig. 6-11. This chart is similar to Figs. 6-1 and 6-2. It indicates the wide diversity of Pearson distribution shapes and may be used to select the appropriate approximation for a given variate, based on knowledge or estimates of β_1 and β_2. The expressions for the probability density functions for the various Pearson distributions are given in References 6-7, 6-9 and 6-10.

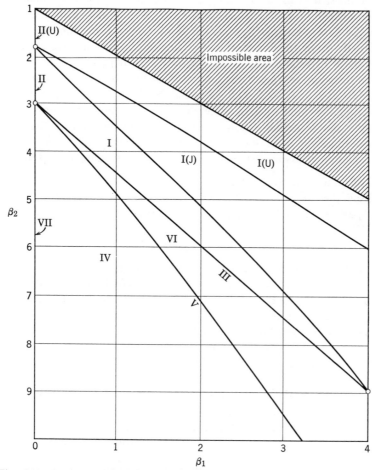

Fig. 6-11   Region in (β_1, β_2) plane for various type Pearson distributions. Letters U and J denote U-shaped and J-shaped distributions. (From E. S. Pearson, Seminars, Princeton University, 1960.)

The descriptions of the procedures for fitting Pearson distributions to data are lengthy, since each family requires solution of a different set of equations. The underlying principles are reviewed in Reference 6-2 and formulae for each family are given in Reference 6-7. These expressions, together with those for estimating the first four moments and β_1 and β_2, may be used to develop a computer program to fit a Pearson distribution to a given set of data. The resulting fit can then be compared with the actual data, in a manner similar to that described above for the Johnson distributions.

Sometimes, instead of obtaining the expression for the approximating Pearson distribution, it is sufficient to estimate only its percentiles. This can be done from knowledge or estimates of the first four moments, without actually fitting the distribution, by using tables given in Reference 6-8. These allow determination of the following α 100th percentiles of the Pearson distribution approximation: 0.25, 0.50, 1.0, 2.5, 5.0, 10.0, 25.0, 50.0, 75.0, 90.0, 95.0, 97.5, 99.0, 99.5, and 99.75. A less extensive tabulation, originally published in Reference 6-9 and involving only eight percentiles and a smaller region in the (β_1, β_2) plane, is given in Table VI. The procedure for using these tabulations to estimate percentiles of the approximating Pearson distribution based on given data is as follows:

1. Calculate $\bar{x}$, $\hat{\sigma}$, b_1, and b_2.
2. Find the tabulated standardized percentile z_α for the chosen α by using b_1 and b_2 instead of β_1 and β_2 in the tabulations of Reference 6-8 or Table VI.
3. Determine the estimated α 100th percentile as $\hat{\sigma} z_\alpha + \bar{x}$.   (6-35)

Reference 6-8 includes a discussion of procedures for using the tabulations to obtain percentiles other than those tabulated and indicates their possible use for the inverse problem of estimating cumulative probabilities corresponding to specified values of the random variable.

These methods are illustrated for the coefficient-of-friction data summarized in the first two columns of Table 6-5. The following values were calculated from the data: $b_1 = 0.76$, $b_2 = 4.92$, $\bar{x} = 0.0345$, and $\hat{\sigma} = 0.0098$.

Interpolation in the tables of Reference 6-8* and use of (6-35) yield the values in the following tabulation.

100α	z_α	α 100th Percentile Estimated by Pearson Distribution Approximation
5	−1.405	0.021
10	−1.148	0.023
50	−0.116	0.033
95	1.797	0.052
99	2.961	0.064

* The values to estimate the 5th, 95th and 99th percentiles could equivalently have been obtained from our Table VI.

The actual per cent of observations falling below these calculated percentiles is shown in Table 6-6. (The corresponding values based on the previous Johnson S_U distribution fit are also shown.) The table shows the Pearson distribution approximation to be quite adequate in this case and to give results close to those obtained using a Johnson S_U distribution.

Table 6-6   Comparison of Cumulative Percentages from Actual Data and Pearson and Johnson S_U Distribution Approximations for Coefficient of Friction Data

Cumulative Percentages from Actual Data	Corresponding Cumulative Percentages Predicted by Pearson Distribution Approximation	Corresponding Cumulative Percentages Predicted by Johnson S_U Distribution Approximation
6.4	5.0	5.4
11.2	10.0	9.3
47.6	50.0	48.5
94.8	95.0	94.8
99.2	99.0	99.0

6-3.   Some Final Comments

This chapter has dealt principally with fitting empirical distributions to engineering data. This differs from the discussion in earlier chapters, where we attempted to show the theoretical basis for various statistical models. Empirical distributions provide a useful mechanism for summarizing data when no clear-cut theoretical explanation is available.

A Johnson distribution can be fitted with relative ease, using the expressions of Section 6-1. If we are interested only in percentiles of a fitted distribution, without requiring the explicit distribution form, they can be obtained very simply by means of a Pearson distribution approximation with the aid of the tabulations given in Reference 6-8 and Table VI.

It should be clearly recognized that an empirical approximation to a given set of data is generally not as satisfactory as a well founded theoretical representation. The limitations indicated at the beginning of the chapter— the sensitivity of the data estimates to sampling fluctuations and the possible errors in selecting an approximation based on only the lower moments of the distributions—must be kept clearly in mind. It is generally desirable to compare fitted values with observed values to evaluate the adequacy of the approximation. Procedures for testing whether these values differ by more than chance variations are presented in Chapter 8.

References

6-1   M. Merrington and E. S. Pearson, "An Approximation to the Distribution of Non-central t," *Biometrika*, **45**, 484 (1958).

6-2   M. G. Kendall and A. Stuart, *The Advanced Theory of Statistics*, Vol. 1, Hafner Publishing Company, New York, 1958.

6-3   N. L. Johnson, "Systems of Frequency Curves Generated by Methods of Translation," *Biometrika*, **36**, 149 (1949).

6-4   J. Aitchison and J. A. C. Brown, *The Lognormal Distribution*, Cambridge University Press, Cambridge, 1957.

6-5   J. Draper, "Properties of Distributions Resulting from Certain Simple Transformations of the Normal Distribution," *Biometrika*, **39**, 290 (1952).

6-6   N. L. Johnson, "Tables to Facilitate Fitting S_U Frequency Curves," *Biometrika*, **52**, 547 (1965).

6-7   W. P. Elderton, *Frequency Curves and Correlation*, 4th ed., Cambridge University Press, Cambridge, 1953.

6-8   N. L. Johnson, E. Nixon and D. E. Amos, "Table of Percentage Points of Pearson Curves, for Given $\sqrt{\beta_1}$, β_2, Expressed in Standard Measure," *Biometrika*, **50**, 459 (1963).

6-9   E. S. Pearson and H. O. Hartley, *Biometrika Tables for Statisticians*, Vol. 1, Cambridge University Press, Cambridge, 1954.

6-10 H. Jeffreys, *Theory of Probability*, 3rd ed. Oxford University Press (Clarendon), Oxford, 1961.

Chapter 7

Drawing Conclusions About System Performance from Component Data

Many engineering situations involve complex systems whose performance fluctuates because of variations in their components. From a knowledge of these variations and an understanding of the system structure, it is desired to draw conclusions about system performance. The systems may be quite general and are not limited to mechanical or electrical configurations. Some examples are:

1. A test and repair facility consisting of six stations is used to check out systems. Each system has to pass through each station. The time spent at a particular station is a random variable whose distribution has been estimated from available data and is independent of the times at other stations. An estimate, based on this information, of the maximum time to check a randomly chosen system is desired.

2. Engine life depends upon (a) mechanical properties of the engine, such as material tensile strength; (b) the environment in which the engine is run, such as operating temperature; and (c) the frequency of maintenance, as measured by time between lubrications. A theoretical expression relating these variables to engine life has been developed. If the statistical model for each of these factors is postulated, what conclusions concerning engine failure times can be drawn?

3. Three resistors with nominal resistances R_A, R_B, and R_C are connected in parallel across a battery with nominal voltage V, as shown in Fig. 7-1. The nominal value of total current drawn is, from Ohm's law,

$$I = V\left(\frac{1}{R_A} + \frac{1}{R_B} + \frac{1}{R_C}\right).$$

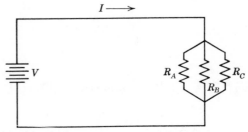

Fig. 7-1   Sketch of circuit with battery and three resistors.

The current drawn by a particular circuit differs from its nominal value because the actual resistances and voltage vary from their nominal values. If information is available about these component variations—say, from component test data—and the components are selected at random for assembly into circuits, within what range may we expect the actual current of 95 per cent of all assembled circuits?

4. Yearly profit on a particular product line can be expressed roughly as

Profit = (total industry sales)(per cent share of market)(unit sales price − unit manufacturing cost) − fixed cost.

Each component on the right-hand side of this expression is a random variable whose probability distribution has been estimated. From this information, what can be said about the variation in profit?

Because of their complexity, such problems can rarely be solved by direct analytic methods, such as the transformation of variables discussed in Chapter 5. This chapter therefore deals with three other methods, which, though approximate, are often adequate for the desired purpose.

7-1. Application of Central Limit Theorem for Linear Systems

The central limit theorem (introduced in Chapter 3) states that the distribution of the average—and therefore the sum—of independent observations from distributions with finite mean and variance approaches a normal distribution as the number of observations becomes large. Consequently, this theorem is applicable for linear systems such as the test-and-repair facility of the preceding section, where total checkout time is the sum of the times at each of the n stations, for the case in which n is large.

It was also seen in Chapter 3 that the normal distribution is completely specified once its mean, μ, and standard deviation, σ, are known. These can be obtained from (2-36) and (2-87); thus for any random variables $x_1, x_2, \ldots, x_n$

$$E(x_1 + x_2 + \cdots + x_n) = E(x_1) + E(x_2) + \cdots + E(x_n) = \mu, \quad \text{(7-1)}$$

and if the variables are uncorrelated

$$\text{Var}\,(x_1 + x_2 + \cdots + x_n) = \text{Var}\,(x_1) + \text{Var}\,(x_2) + \cdots + \text{Var}\,(x_n) = \sigma^2. \quad \text{(7-2)}$$

In the problem of the test-and-repair facility assume, for example, that the distribution for the time in hours spent at the ith station ($i = 1, 2, \ldots, 6$) is as given in Table 7-1. The normal, gamma, exponential, and

Table 7-1   Assumed Distributions for Test and Repair Time in Hours at Each of Six Stations

Station No. 1	$f_1(x_1) = \dfrac{1}{\sqrt{2\pi}}\, e^{-\frac{1}{2}(x_1-10)^2}$	(normal distribution with $\mu = 10$ and $\sigma = 1$)
Station No. 2	$f_2(x_2) = \dfrac{1}{\sqrt{2}\,\sqrt{2\pi}}\, e^{-\frac{1}{2}[(x_2-20)^2/2]}$	(normal distribution with $\mu = 20$ and $\sigma = \sqrt{2}$)
Station No. 3	$f_3(x_3) = \dfrac{(6)^9}{\Gamma(9)}\,(x_3)^8\, e^{-6x_3}$	(gamma distribution with $\eta = 9$ and $\lambda = 6$)
Station No. 4	$f_4(x_4) = \dfrac{1}{\Gamma(10)}\,(x_4)^9\, e^{-x_4}$	(gamma distribution with $\eta = 10$ and $\lambda = 1$)
Station No. 5	$f_5(x_5) = 5e^{-5x_5}$	(exponential distribution with $\lambda = 5$)
Station No. 6	$f_6(x_6) = \dfrac{1}{2^5\Gamma(5)}\,(x_6)^4\, e^{-x_6/2}$	(chi-square distribution with $\nu = 10$)

chi-square distributions have been used as models for the checkout time at individual stations, and the parameter values have been specified in each case. (For plots of the distributions, see Fig. 7-3.)

We are interested in the distribution of total time $T = x_1 + x_2 + x_3 + x_4 + x_5 + x_6$ spent by a system at the facility. The means and variances shown in the tabulation were obtained for hours at each station from the expressions given in Chapter 3. For example, from Fig. 3-21 the mean and variance of a gamma variate are η/λ and η/λ^2, respectively. Thus the mean and variance of checkout time at station 3 are 1.5 hours and 0.25, respectively.

	Station No. 1	Station No. 2	Station No. 3	Station No. 4	Station No. 5	Station No. 6
Mean	10	20	1.5	10	0.2	10
Variance	1	2	0.25	10	0.04	20

Substitution of the station means and variances into (7-1) and (7-2) yields a system mean of $(10 + 20 + 1.5 + 10 + 0.2 + 10) = 51.7$ hours and a variance of $1 + 2 + 0.25 + 10 + 0.04 + 20 = 33.29$. From the central limit theorem the total test and repair time can thus be approximated by a normal distribution with a mean, μ, of 51.7 hours and a standard deviation σ of $\sqrt{33.29} = 5.8$ hours. From the properties of the normal distribution we can now say that the chances are nine out of ten that the checkout time for a random system will not exceed $\mu + 1.28\sigma$ hours, 95 out of 100 that it will not exceed $\mu + 1.65\sigma$ hours, and 99 out of 100 that it will not exceed $\mu + 2.33\sigma$ hours. Hence the approximate 90, 95, and 99 per cent upper limits are 59.1, 61.2, and 65.2 hours, respectively.

This problem involved a six-element system, rather than one with "very many" elements. More important, the variances of the individual elements are far from equal, and the total variance is highly dominated by the variances of the times at stations 4 and 6. (It will be recalled from Chapter 3 that one of the factors affecting the rate of convergence to normality is the relative magnitude of the component variances.) Therefore the applicability of the central limit theorem in this problem is questionable. Fortunately, we shall be able to evaluate the adequacy of the normal distribution approximation by comparing our results with those obtained by more precise methods later in this chapter.

Finally, we note that exact knowledge of the distribution for each of the component variables is not essential, since all that is needed to use (7-1) and (7-2) are the means and variances.

7-2. Generation of System Moments

PROBLEM STATEMENT

It was indicated in Chapter 6 that, based upon estimates of the first four moments, a Pearson distribution approximation can be used to estimate percentiles of the distribution of a variable under study. Since the Pearson system includes many diverse distribution shapes, this method frequently leads to adequate approximations. Thus if the moments for system performance can be obtained, the same approach may be used for problems of this chapter. The method for the *generation of system moments,* sometimes referred to as *statistical error propagation* or the *delta method,* will now be described.

Let the relationship between system performance z and the component variables $x_1, x_2, \ldots, x_n$ be given by the function $z = h(x_1, x_2, \ldots, x_n)$. For example, in the case of the six-station test-and-repair facility $z = x_1 + x_2 + x_3 + x_4 + x_5 + x_6$—that is, total checkout time is the sum of the times at each of the stations.

Let $E(x_i)$ be the mean or expected value for the ith component variable and let $\mu_k(x_i)$ denote its kth central moment (or moment about the mean). Similarly, $E(z)$ and $\mu_k(z)$ denote the expected value and the kth moment about the mean for system performance, respectively. The problem is to obtain an estimate of $E(z)$ and $\mu_k(z)$ for $k = 2, 3$, and 4, based on (a) data on the component variables from which estimates of $E(x_i)$ and $\mu_k(x_i)$ for $i = 1, 2, \ldots, n$ can be obtained and (b) knowledge of the system structure $h(x_1, x_2, \ldots, x_n)$.

CALCULATION OF MEAN SYSTEM PERFORMANCE

The method consists of expanding $h(x_1, x_2, \ldots, x_n)$ about $[E(x_1), E(x_2), \ldots, E(x_n)]$, the point at which each of the component variables takes on its expected value, by a multivariable Taylor series. An equation for the expected value of system performance is then obtained by taking expected values in the resulting expression and applying some simple algebra. The complete derivation is given in Appendix 7A. Assuming that the component variables are uncorrelated, the final expression for mean system performance, retaining terms up to second order,* is

$$E(z) = h[E(x_1), E(x_2), \ldots, E(x_n)] + \frac{1}{2} \sum_{i=1}^{n} \frac{\partial^2 \bar{h}}{\partial x_i^2} \text{Var} (x_i), \qquad (7\text{-}3)$$

where $\partial^2 \bar{h}/\partial x_i^2$ denotes $\partial^2 h/\partial x_i^2$ evaluated at $E(x_r)$—that is, with the $E(x_r)$ substituted for x_r for $r = 1, 2, \ldots, n$. For example, if $h(z) = x_1 x_2^2 x_3^3$,

$$\frac{\partial^2 \bar{h}}{\partial x_3^2} = [E(x_1)][E(x_2)]^2[6E(x_3)].$$

---

* By the statement "retaining terms up to kth order" we mean that in the derivation all terms whose powers of the expected value sum to k or less are retained and those whose powers sum to more than k are dropped, that is, for a term involving

$$E\{[x_i - E(x_i)]^r[x_j - E(x_j)]^s \cdots [x_m - E(x_m)]^t\}$$

to be retained we require $r + s + \cdots + t \leq k$. The resulting equations are thus approximate rather than strict equalities.

Henceforth, $\partial^2 \bar{h}/\partial x_i^2$ is written without the bar on h—that is, as $\partial^2 h/\partial x_i^2$.

Equation 7-3 requires knowledge or estimates of the means and variances for each of the component variables.

Note that estimating mean performance by substituting the component means into the system equation—that is, setting

$$E(z) = h[E(x_1), E(x_2), \ldots, E(x_n)]$$

—provides an exact result when all second and higher order partial derivatives are zero; for example, when system performance is a linear function of the component variables, as in the test-and-repair facility problem. However, the expression is only approximate in the general case.

EXAMPLE OF FINDING MEAN SYSTEM PERFORMANCE

The estimation of mean system performance is illustrated by the circuit problem presented at the beginning of the chapter and shown in Fig. 7-1. Assume that the mean and variance for each component have been estimated from data by (2-31) and (2-51a) as follows:

	Mean	Variance
V	120	15
R_A	10	1
R_B	15	1
R_C	20	2

Now

$$I = h(V, R_A, R_B, R_C)$$

$$= V\left(\frac{1}{R_A} + \frac{1}{R_B} + \frac{1}{R_C}\right).$$

Then

$$\frac{\partial h}{\partial V} = \sum_{i=A,B,C} \frac{1}{R_i} \, ; \qquad \frac{\partial^2 h}{\partial V^2} = 0 \tag{7-4}$$

and

$$\frac{\partial h}{\partial R_i} = \frac{-V}{R_i^2} \, ; \qquad \frac{\partial^2 h}{\partial R_i^2} = \frac{2V}{R_i^3}, \tag{7-5}$$

where $i = A, B, C$.

Using these values in (7-3), we obtain

$$E(I) = E(V) \sum_{i=A,B,C} \left[\frac{1}{E(R_i)}\right] + \frac{1}{2} \sum_{i=A,B,C} \frac{2E(V)}{[E(R_i)]^3} \, \text{Var}\,(R_i).$$

Substitution of the estimated means and variances into the preceding expressions for the corresponding parameters yields

$$\text{estimated } E(I) = 120\left(\frac{1}{10} + \frac{1}{15} + \frac{1}{20}\right) + \left(\frac{1}{2}\right)\frac{2(120)}{10^3} \quad (1)$$

$$+ \left(\frac{1}{2}\right)\frac{2(120)}{15^3}(1) + \left(\frac{1}{2}\right)\frac{2(120)}{20^3} \quad (2)$$

$$= 26.19 \text{ amperes.}$$

Note that if only the first term had been retained in (7-3), an estimate of 26.00 amperes, instead of 26.19 amperes, would have resulted.

CALCULATION OF THE VARIANCE OF SYSTEM PERFORMANCE

The Taylor-series expansion for the variance of system performance, assuming the component variables to be uncorrelated, is derived in Appendix 7A. The resulting equation, retaining terms up to third order, reduces to

$$\text{Var}(z) = \sum_{i=1}^{n} \left(\frac{\partial h}{\partial x_i}\right)^2 \text{Var}(x_i) + \sum_{i=1}^{n} \left(\frac{\partial h}{\partial x_i}\right)\left(\frac{\partial^2 h}{\partial x_i^2}\right)\mu_3(x_i), \quad (7\text{-}6)$$

where $\mu_3(x_i)$ is the third central moment for the ith variate and, as before, all derivatives are evaluated at their mean values. Most texts that deal with this subject, such as References 7-1 to 7-4, omit the last term in (7-6) and give only the expression

$$\text{Var}(z) = \sum_{i=1}^{n} \left(\frac{\partial h}{\partial x_i}\right)^2 \text{Var}(x_i), \quad (7\text{-}7)$$

which is frequently a satisfactory approximation.

In the circuit example, assume that the third and fourth central moments (the latter will be used shortly) have been estimated from observations on n components by (2-52) and (2-53), respectively, as follows:

x_i	$m_3(x_i)$	$m_4(x_i)$
V	25	100
R_A	1	5
R_B	-1	3
R_C	5	5

Substitution of (7-4) and (7-5) into (7-6) gives

$$\text{Var}(I) = \left\{\sum_{i=A,B,C} \frac{1}{E(R_i)}\right\}^2 \text{Var}(V) + \sum_{i=A,B,C} \left\{\frac{-E(V)}{[E(R_i)]^2}\right\}^2 \text{Var}(R_i)$$

$$+ \sum_{i=A,B,C}\left\{\frac{-E(V)}{[E(R_i)]^2}\right\}\left\{\frac{2E(V)}{[E(R_i)]^3}\right\}\mu_3(R_i).$$

Using the values estimated from the data for the component expected values, variances, and third central moments yields

$$\text{estimated Var}(I) = \left[\frac{1}{10} + \frac{1}{15} + \frac{1}{20}\right]^2 (15) + \left[\frac{(-120)}{10^2}\right]^2 (1)$$

$$+ \left[\frac{(-120)}{15^2}\right]^2 (1) + \left[\frac{(-120)}{20^2}\right]^2 (2)$$

$$+ \left[\frac{(-120)}{10^2}\right]\left[\frac{(2)(120)}{10^3}\right](1) + \left[\frac{(-120)}{15^2}\right]\left[\frac{2(120)}{15^3}\right](-1)$$

$$+ \left[\frac{(-120)}{20^2}\right]\left[\frac{2(120)}{20^3}\right](5) = 2.32.$$

If the less accurate expression, (7-7), rather than (7-6), had been used, only the first four values in this calculation would have been required. This leads to an estimated variance of circuit current of 2.61 rather than 2.32.

CALCULATION OF THIRD AND FOURTH CENTRAL MOMENTS OF SYSTEM PERFORMANCE

Expressions for the third and fourth central moments for system performance—that is, $\mu_3(z)$ and $\mu_4(z)$—may be derived in a manner analogous to that for the variance. The resulting expressions, retaining only the lowest-order non-zero terms, are

$$\mu_3(z) = \sum_{i=1}^{n} \left(\frac{\partial h}{\partial x_i}\right)^3 \mu_3(x_i), \tag{7-8}$$

$$\mu_4(z) = \sum_{i=1}^{n} \left(\frac{\partial h}{\partial x_i}\right)^4 \mu_4(x_i) + 6 \sum_{i} \sum_{\substack{j \\ i>j}} \left(\frac{\partial h}{\partial x_i}\right)^2 \left(\frac{\partial h}{\partial x_j}\right)^2 \text{Var}(x_i)\,\text{Var}(x_j). \tag{7-9}$$

All derivatives are again evaluated at the mean values of the variates.

In the circuit problem substitution of (7-4) and (7-5) into (7-8) yields

$$\mu_3(I) = \left[\sum_{i=A,B,C} \frac{1}{E(R_i)}\right]^3 \mu_3(V) + \sum_{i=A,B,C} \left\{\frac{-E(V)}{[E(R_i)]^2}\right\}^3 \mu_3(R_i).$$

Use of the values calculated from the data to estimate the component parameters in the preceding expression gives estimated $\mu_3(I) = -1.457$. The estimate of the standardized measure of skewness $\sqrt{\beta_1}$ (see Chapter 2) is $(-1.457)/(2.32)^{3/2} = -0.41$. Thus the distribution for circuit current is estimated to be skewed to the left.

Similarly, from (7-4), (7-5), and (7-9),

$$\mu_4(I) = \left[\sum_{i=A,B,C} \frac{1}{E(R_i)}\right]^4 \mu_4(V) + \sum_{i=A,B,C} \left[\frac{-E(V)}{[E(R_i)]^2}\right]^4 \mu_4(R_i)$$

$$+ 6 \sum_{i=A,B,C}\left\{\sum_{j=A,B,C} \frac{1}{E(R_j)}\right\}^2 \left\{\frac{-E(V)}{[E(R_i)]^2}\right\}^2 \text{Var}\,(V)\,\text{Var}\,(R_i)$$

$$+ 6 \sum_{\substack{i=A,j=B \\ i=A,j=C \\ i=B,j=C}} \left\{\frac{-E(V)}{[E(R_i)]^2}\right\}^2 \left\{\frac{-E(V)}{[E(R_j)]^2}\right\}^2 \text{Var}\,(R_i)\,\text{Var}\,(R_j),$$

and substitution of the values calculated from the data for the component parameters gives estimated $\mu_4(I) = 23.24$. Consequently, the estimate of the standardized measure of peakedness β_2 is $23.20/(2.32)^2 = 4.34$. Thus the distribution for circuit current appears to be more peaked than a normal distribution.

The hazards of using estimates of $\mu_3(x_i)$ and $\mu_4(x_i)$ based on limited data were pointed out in Chapter 6. These could lead to poor estimates of $\mu_3(z)$ and $\mu_4(z)$.

DISTRIBUTION OF CIRCUIT CURRENT

In summary, the estimated mean, variance, standardized skewness, and standardized peakedness for circuit current are as follows:

$$\begin{aligned}
\text{estimated mean} &= 26.19, \\
\text{estimated variance} &= 2.32, \\
\text{estimated } \sqrt{\beta_1} &= -0.41, \\
\text{estimated } \beta_2 &= 4.34.
\end{aligned}$$

The methods of Chapter 6 can now be used to estimate distribution percentiles. Using the Pearson distribution approximation we find from our Table VI that the chances are about 95 out of 100 that current for a randomly assembled circuit is between 22.92 and 29.01 amperes. Similarly, the chances are about 99 out of 100 that the circuit current is between 21.36 amperes and 30.03 amperes. If we had assumed circuit current to be normally distributed, a 95 per cent range of 23.24 to 29.22 amperes and a 99 per cent range of 22.30 to 30.16 amperes would have been obtained. In this instance, therefore, assuming a normal distribution apparently would not have been greatly in error.

By locating values of $\beta_1 = 0.17$ and $\beta_2 = 4.34$ in Fig. 6-2 it is also seen that the distribution of circuit current may be approximated by a Johnson S_U distribution, and the methods of Chapter 6 for estimating the parameters for this distribution based on the calculated moments can be used. If, instead, it had turned out that Fig. 6-2 suggested a Johnson S_B distribution, the methods of Chapter 6 could *not* be applied directly to estimate the parameters, because these would have required some knowledge of the percentiles of system performance. Estimates of the parameters could be obtained by matching the calculated moments with the theoretical S_B moments, as suggested by Johnson in Reference 6-3. However, this procedure is quite arduous.

APPLICATION TO CHECKOUT EXAMPLE

The preceding methods are now applied to the test-and-repair facility problem. Total checkout time z is represented by the linear function $z = x_1 + x_2 + x_3 + x_4 + x_5 + x_6$, where x_i is the time at the ith station $(i = 1, 2, \ldots, 6)$ with assumed statistical distributions given in Table 7-1. Then

$$\frac{\partial z}{\partial x_i} = 1, \qquad i = 1, 2, \ldots, 6,$$

and

$$\frac{\partial^2 z}{\partial x_i^2} = 0 \qquad i = 1, 2, \ldots, 6.$$

Thus (7-3), (7-6), (7-8), and (7-9) reduce to

$$E(z) = \sum_{i=1}^{6} E(x_i),$$

$$\text{Var}(z) = \sum_{i=1}^{6} \text{Var}(x_i),$$

$$\mu_3(z) = \sum_{i=1}^{6} \mu_3(x_i),$$

and

$$\mu_4(z) = \sum_{i=1}^{6} \mu_4(x_i) + 6 \sum_{\substack{i \ j \\ i > j}} \text{Var}(x_i)\,\text{Var}(x_j).$$

The third and fourth central moments for the distributions of time at each station can be obtained from Table 7-1 by the methods of Chapter 2. The resulting values, together with the means and variances are

	Station No. 1	Station No. 2	Station No. 3	Station No. 4	Station No. 5	Station No. 6
Mean	10	20	1.5	10	0.2	10
Variance	1	2	0.25	10	0.04	20
$\mu_3(x_i)$	0	0	0.08	20	0.02	80
$\mu_4(x_i)$	3	12	0.23	360	0.01	1680

Thus

$$E(z) = 10 + 20 + 1.5 + 10 + 0.2 + 10 = 51.7,$$
$$\text{Var}\,(z) = 1 + 2 + 0.25 + 10 + 0.04 + 20 = 33.3,$$
$$\mu_3(z) = 0 + 0 + 0.08 + 20 + 0.02 + 80 = 100.1,$$
$$\mu_4(z) = (3 + 12 + 0.23 + 360 + 0.01 + 1680)$$
$$+ 6[1(2 + 0.25 + 10 + 0.04 + 20) + 2(0.25 + 10 + 0.04 + 20)$$
$$+ 0.25(10 + 0.04 + 20) + 10(0.04 + 20) + 0.04(20)]$$
$$= 3864.7,$$

and

$$\sqrt{\beta_1} = \frac{100.1}{(33.3)^{3/2}} = 0.52,$$

$$\beta_2 = \frac{3864.7}{(33.3)^2} = 3.49.$$

Using only the upper tail in a Pearson distribution approximation we find from Reference 6-8 that total checkout and repair time will exceed (a) 59.4 hours 10 per cent of the time, (b) 62.0 hours 5 per cent of the time, (c) 67.4 hours 1 per cent of the time.

These results compare with the corresponding values of 59.1 hours, 61.2 hours, and 65.2 hours that were obtained in Section 7-1, where, by invoking the central limit theorem, total time had been assumed to be normally distributed. It is noted that although there is a close correspondence for the 90th and 95th percentiles, the divergence increases for the 99th percentile, thus illustrating the fact, mentioned in Chapter 3, that the normal-distribution approximation is frequently least adequate at the extreme tails of a distribution.

CORRELATED VARIABLES

Up to this point the component variables have been assumed to be uncorrelated. Correlation between components occurs when the random value taken by one or more components in a system is related to the random value of one or more other components in the *same* system. For example, in the test-and-repair problem the times are correlated if a defect that causes above-average checkout time at one station also leads to above-average times at other stations.

Expressions for system performance when component variables are correlated can be obtained in a fashion analogous to the uncorrelated case. The results are given in Appendix 7B.

The method of generating system moments is an approximate, rather than an exact, procedure, because of the omission of higher-order terms in the Taylor series expansion. (In the special case of a linear function the expression becomes exact because all higher order derivatives are zero, as in the system checkout example.) A study of the general adequacy of the method (Reference 7-5) concluded that the approximation "turns out to be better than expected" and that the retention of only the lowest order terms is frequently adequate. This paper also gives expressions which include additional higher order terms for the mean and for the second, third, and fourth central moments for both the uncorrelated and correlated cases. These expressions can be used when still greater precision is required. In the circuit example it was found that omission of the first higher-order terms for the mean did not substantially affect the answer. Thus the omission of *additional* Taylor series terms in this expression was inconsequential. However, the error in the variance would have been 10 per cent if the higher order terms had been omitted. In this example the mean, variance, and central moments were estimated from test data, adding further sampling error. Unless a great many observations are forthcoming, such an error might well exceed that introduced by the omission of higher-order terms. This might frequently be the case in practical problems.

Conclusions about system performance based on component information may thus be drawn from the method of generation of system moments when used in conjunction with the techniques of Chapter 6. However, the method is limited to functions for which a Taylor series expansion about the mean exists and the resulting expression is not too cumbersome—that is, the partial derivatives are not too difficult to obtain and are moderate in number. In this case it is often possible to obtain the derivatives by numerical methods with the help of an electronic computer.

7-3. Monte Carlo Simulation

GENERAL CONCEPT

Monte Carlo simulation is another method for obtaining information about system performance from component data. This method has also been referred to as *synthetic sampling* or *empirical sampling*. It consists of "building" many systems by computer calculations and evaluating the performance of such synthesized systems.

Consider a system made up of many components. Say, for the moment, that there are available 1000 of each of the components that make up the system. We could then build 1000 systems and obtain 1000 measurements of system performance. If, however, the system structure—that is, the relationship between the component variables and system performance— is known, system performance can be calculated from the component measurements *without* actually building the systems. Also, if instead of having 1000 samples of each component, we know the distribution for each

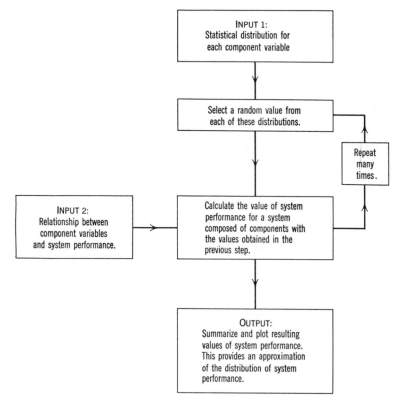

Fig. 7-2   Flow chart of Monte Carlo simulation method.

component variable, it is possible to obtain synthetic measurements on these components by drawing 1000 random values from each distribution. These random values can then be used to calculate the performance of 1000 synthetic systems. This procedure, the so-called Monte Carlo method, is shown graphically in Fig. 7-2. The availability of high-speed computers that can economically and rapidly synthesize the performance of complex systems has led to the popularization of Monte Carlo procedures.

Before we discuss the details for obtaining random values from designated distributions, we apply the method to the six-station test-and-repair

1. A random value is generated for test and repair time from distribution at each station.

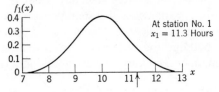

At station No. 1
$x_1 = 11.3$ Hours

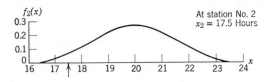

At station No. 2
$x_2 = 17.5$ Hours

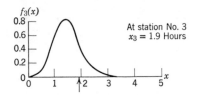

At station No. 3
$x_3 = 1.9$ Hours

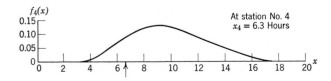

At station No. 4
$x_4 = 6.3$ Hours

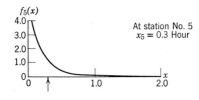

At station No. 5
$x_5 = 0.3$ Hour

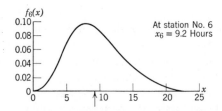

At station No. 6
$x_6 = 9.2$ Hours

2. System checkout time is . . . . 46.5 Hours
3. Procedure is repeated many times. Resulting plot of system checkout times approximates true distribution.

Fig. 7-3   Steps in system simulation for checkout problem.

238

facility problem. The distribution of checkout time at the first station was assumed to be normal, with a mean of 10 hours and a standard deviation of one hour. A random value is selected from this distribution—say, 11.3 hours. This represents the checkout time for the first synthetic system at station 1. Random values are similarly obtained to represent checkout

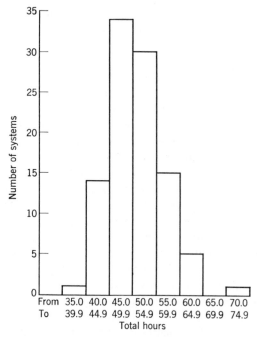

Fig. 7-4   Checkout times for 100 simulated systems.

times at each of the remaining stations, as follows: station 2, 17.5 hours; station 3, 1.9 hours; station 4, 6.3 hours; station 5, 0.3 hours; and station 6, 9.2 hours.

The total checkout time for the first simulated system is thus 46.5 hours. The process is illustrated in Fig. 7-3. This procedure is followed a total of 100 times, each time drawing new random values. The resulting values obtained by a high-speed computer are summarized in Fig. 7-4. This histogram provides an approximation to the distribution of system check-out time. From the generated values, estimates of maximum checkout time can be obtained. For example, the 90th and 91st longest checkout times are 58.8 and 59.4 hours, and hence the estimate of the 90th percentile obtained in the manner described in Section 2-10 is 59.3 hours. The 95th percentile is similarly estimated as 61.0 hours. These values compare closely with the corresponding values calculated by the methods of the previous two sections.

It is also possible to estimate the moments for checkout time from the Monte Carlo values and use these in a Pearson or a Johnson distribution approximation—that is, to obtain an empirical fit to Fig. 7-4. Actually, the moments calculated from the Monte Carlo values are very close to those obtained by the method of generating system moments, and therefore a similar approximation would be obtained.

METHODS FOR GENERATING RANDOM VALUES

Random values from the uniform distribution over the interval (0, 1) and from the normal distribution with parameters $\mu = 0$ and $\sigma = 1$ are tabulated in References 7-6 and 7-7 and are also available on computer punch cards and tapes. Five hundred numbers from these two distributions are given in Tables VII and VIII at the end of this book.

The random values were originally generated by various mechanical or electronic devices. Thus the uniform variates in References 7-6 and 7-7 were obtained respectively by a disk, spun many times by a motor operating in a fashion similar to a roulette wheel, and by an electronic device whose input was a random noise source. A detailed discussion of methods for generating random numbers is given in Reference 7-8.

Despite the availability of uniform and normal variates on cards and tape, it is sometimes more economical of both computer time and memory to obtain such values directly, and programs have been developed for this purpose. The resulting values are frequently called "pseudorandom" since they are obtained by a deterministic mathematical expression rather than by some physical mechanism. The underlying theory is given in References 7-8 and 7-9.

Statistical tests (see Chapter 8) can be applied to the generated values to determine whether they represent the desired distribution adequately. Such tests have demonstrated that the tables in References 7-6 and 7-7 are satisfactory for most practical purposes.

To obtain a value $Y_U (\mu_0, \mu_1)$ from a uniform distribution over the interval (μ_0, μ_1) from a given uniform variate R_U over the interval (0, 1) the following transformation is applied:

$$Y_U(\mu_0, \mu_1) = (\mu_1 - \mu_0)R_U + \mu_0. \tag{7-10}$$

The validity of this transformation can be easily verified by the method of Chapter 5.

In a similar fashion, a random value, $Y_N(\mu, \sigma)$, from a normal distribution with parameters μ and σ is obtained as

$$Y_N(\mu, \sigma) = \sigma R_N + \mu, \tag{7-11}$$

where R_N is a random value from a normal distribution with parameters $\mu = 0$ and $\sigma = 1$.

Procedures for obtaining random values for other distributions from the standard uniform and normal variates are summarized in Table 7-2. These methods were used to generate random values from the gamma, chi-square, and exponential distributions in the system-checkout problem. For example, the checkout time at station 3 was assumed to be gamma distributed with $\eta = 9$ and $\lambda = 6$. To generate a random value from this distribution, nine independent uniform variates over the interval $(0, 1)$, denoted by $R_{U1}, R_{U2}, \ldots, R_{U9}$, are selected. The desired gamma variate is then $-1/6 \sum_{i=1}^{9} \ln(1 - R_{Ui})$. The procedure is repeated using nine new uniform variates for each additional required gamma variate. The theory underlying the procedures of Table 7-2 is outlined in Appendix 7C.

SAMPLE SIZE AND ERROR BANDS

Because Monte Carlo simulation involves random values, the results are subject to statistical fluctuations. Thus any estimate will not be exact but will have an associated error band. The larger the number of trials in the simulation, the more precise will be the final answer, and we can obtain as small an error as desired by conducting sufficient trials. In practice, the allowable error is generally specified, and this information is used to determine the required trials.

Consider again the system-checkout problem. Say we want to know the proportion p of systems that require a checkout of 60 hours or more. This is typical of many Monte Carlo problems where we wish to make an estimate of the proportion of the population between two limits or above or below some specified value, based on the results of n trials. This problem is the same as estimating the parameter p of a binomial distribution, see Chapter 4. From Fig. 7-4 it is seen that in 100 Monte Carlo trials six simulated systems had checkout times of 60 hours or more. Thus, from (4-3), the estimate $\hat{p}$ is 6/100 or 0.06. Confidence bounds around this estimate may be obtained from Fig. 4-2a or -b. For example, from Fig. 4-2a the 95 per cent confidence interval for p is the range $(0.02, 0.13)$. Additional Monte Carlo trials would be required if p is to be estimated more precisely.

We may also use Figs. 4-2a and -b "in reverse" to determine the approximate sample size for a Monte Carlo study. In doing so we must initially specify E, the maximum allowable error in estimating p; $1 - \alpha$, the desired probability or confidence level that the estimated proportion $\hat{p}$ does not differ from p by more than $\pm E$; and p', an initial estimate of p.

For example, we might want to conduct sufficient Monte Carlo trials

Table 7-2 Generation of Random Values from Various Distributions Given Random Standard Normal (R_N) and Random Standard Uniform (R_U) Values[a]

Distribution To Be Simulated	Probability Density Function	Procedure to Obtain Random Value y'
Exponential	$f(y) = \lambda e^{-\lambda(y-\mu)}, \quad \mu \leq y < \infty$	$y' = -\dfrac{1}{\lambda}\ln(1 - R_U) + \mu$
Gamma (integral values of η)	$f(y) = \dfrac{\lambda^\eta}{\Gamma(\eta)}\, e^{-\lambda y} y^{\eta-1}, \quad 0 \leq y < \infty$	$y' = -\dfrac{1}{\lambda}\sum_{i=1}^{\eta}\ln(1 - R_{Ui})$
Chi-square	$f(y) = \dfrac{1}{2^{\gamma/2}\,\Gamma(\gamma/2)}\, y^{(\gamma/2)-1} e^{-y/2}, \quad 0 \leq y < \infty$	$y' = \sum_{i=1}^{\gamma} R_N^{i2}$
Log-normal	$f(y) = \dfrac{1}{\sqrt{2\pi}\,\sigma y}\exp\left\{-\dfrac{1}{2}\left[\left(\dfrac{\ln y - \mu}{\sigma}\right)^2\right]\right\}, \quad 0 \leq y < \infty$	$y' = e^{\sigma R_N + \mu}$
Johnson S_B	$f(y) = \dfrac{\eta}{\sqrt{2\pi}}\dfrac{\lambda}{(y-\epsilon)(\lambda - y + \epsilon)} \cdot$ $\exp\left\{-\dfrac{1}{2}\left[\gamma + \eta \ln\left(\dfrac{y-\epsilon}{\lambda - y + \epsilon}\right)\right]^2\right\}, \quad \epsilon \leq y \leq \epsilon + \lambda$	$y' = \dfrac{\epsilon + (\epsilon + \lambda)\exp\left(\dfrac{R_N - \gamma}{\eta}\right)}{1 + \exp\left(\dfrac{R_N - \gamma}{\eta}\right)}$
Johnson S_U	$f(y) = \dfrac{\eta}{\sqrt{2\pi}}\dfrac{1}{[(y-\epsilon)^2 + \lambda^2]^{1/2}} \cdot$ $\exp\left\{-\dfrac{1}{2}\left(\gamma + \eta \ln\left\{\dfrac{y-\epsilon}{\lambda} + \left[\left(\dfrac{y-\epsilon}{\lambda}\right)^2 + 1\right]^{1/2}\right\}\right)^2\right\}, \quad -\infty < y < \infty$	$y' = \dfrac{\lambda\left(\exp\left[2\left(\dfrac{R_N - \gamma}{\eta}\right)\right] - 1\right)}{2\exp\left(\dfrac{R_N - \gamma}{\eta}\right)} + \epsilon$

242

Beta (integral values of η and γ) $f(y) = \dfrac{\Gamma(\gamma + \eta)}{\Gamma(\gamma)\Gamma(\eta)} y^{\gamma-1}(1 - y)^{\eta-1}$, $0 \le y \le 1$

$$y' = \frac{\displaystyle\sum_{i=1}^{2\gamma} R_{Ni}^2}{\displaystyle\sum_{i=1}^{2\gamma} R_{Ni}^2 + \sum_{i=2\gamma+1}^{2\gamma+2\eta} R_{Ni}^2}$$

Weibull $f(y) = \dfrac{\eta}{\sigma^\eta} y^{\eta-1} \exp\left[-\left(\dfrac{y}{\sigma}\right)^\eta\right]$, $0 \le y < \infty$

$$y' = -\sigma[\ln(1 - R_{Ui})]^{1/\eta}$$

Poisson $f(y) = \dfrac{e^{-\lambda}}{y!}\lambda^y$, $y = 0, 1, 2, \cdots$

$y' = k$, where k is the lowest integer such that

$$\sum_{i=1}^{k+1} -\frac{1}{\lambda}\ln(1 - R_{Ui}) > 1$$

Binomial $f(y) = \dbinom{n}{y} p^y (1 - p)^{n-y}$, $y = 0, 1, \cdots, n$

$$y' = \sum_{i=1}^{n} k_i$$

where $k_i = \begin{cases} 0 & \text{if } R_{Ui} < p \\ 1 & \text{if } R_{Ui} \ge p \end{cases}$
$i = 1, 2, \cdots, n$

---

[a] R_N is random value from normal distribution with $\mu = 0$ and $\sigma = 1$. R_U is random value from uniform distribution over interval (0, 1). When more than one value is required, a typical value is designated as R_{Ni} or R_{Ui}. All values are taken independently of one another.

to be 95 per cent sure—that is, to make $1 - \alpha = 0.95$—that the proportion p of the population between two specified values (or above or below some specified value) does not differ by more than $E = 0.05$ from the final estimated value, assuming an initial estimate $p' = 0.80$. A trial-and-error procedure for determining n would then be as follows.

If 1000 Monte Carlo trials had been conducted and 800 of these, or 80 per cent, fell within the initially specified range, the resulting 95 per cent confidence interval for p is 0.775 to 0.825 from Fig. 4.2a. Similar intervals for 400 trials and 200 trials, each with 80 per cent of the resulting observations within the specified range, are 0.755 to 0.84 and 0.74 to 0.85 respectively. Because we wish to estimate p within ± 0.05 with 95 per cent confidence, somewhat more than 200 trials are required. Note that the length of the error range is smaller if the sample percentage is above 80 per cent and larger if it is between 50 and 80 per cent. Thus the chosen sample size might be found to be either slightly too conservative or slightly too liberal after the trials have actually been conducted (see later discussion).

Figures 4-2a and -b frequently require interpolation and do not include curves for n larger than 1000. The following expression, based on the normal distribution approximation to the binomial distribution (see Chapter 4), may also be used to estimate the number of trials:

$$n = \frac{p'(1 - p')}{E^2} z_{1-\alpha/2}^2,$$ (7-12)

where E and p' have been previously defined and $z_{1-\alpha/2}$ designates the $(1 - \alpha/2)100$ per cent point of a standard normal distribution. For example, if the desired confidence level is $1 - \alpha = 0.95$, then $\alpha = 0.05$ and $z_{1-\alpha/2} = 1.96$; and if $1 - \alpha = 0.99$, then $\alpha = 0.01$ and $z_{1-\alpha/2} = 2.58$. Thus in the preceding example the estimate of the required sample size is

$$n = \frac{(0.2)(0.8)}{(0.05)^2} (1.96)^2 = 246.$$

This approximation is generally adequate, except when np or $n(1 - p)$ is less than 5.

Both the inverse use of Figs. 4-2a and -b and the use of (7-12) to determine n require an initial estimate of p, the very quantity to be determined by the Monte Carlo study. This is because the size of the confidence interval is a function of p, as can be seen from examining Figs. 4-2a and -b. It is evident from the charts and from (7-12) that the largest sample size is required when $p = 0.5$. Thus, when nothing is known initially about the magnitude of p, the estimate $p' = 0.5$ leads to the most conservative sample size. Sometimes it might instead be advantageous to conduct some preliminary Monte Carlo trials to obtain an estimate p', which would then be used to determine the additional required number of trials.

In some problems only a one-sided bound on p is desired. In such cases only the difference of the upper (or lower) curve from the diagonal line of Fig. 4-2a or -b is used to select n. If the sample size is to be determined by (7-12), the value $z_{1-\alpha/2}$ is replaced by $z_{1-\alpha}$—that is, 1.65 for 95 per cent confidence and 2.33 for 99 per cent confidence.

After the required Monte Carlo trials have been conducted the previous methods are used directly to establish the appropriate error band.

If instead of estimating a proportion p, we evaluate the true process average μ from the estimated mean $\bar{x}$ of the Monte Carlo trials, (3-8) may be used to obtain a confidence band. To determine initially the required number of trials we must specify

E: the maximum allowable error in estimating μ

$1 - \alpha$: the desired probability or confidence level that $\bar{x}$ does not differ
    from μ by more than $\pm E$,

σ': an initial estimate of the process standard deviation.

The approximate number of Monte Carlo trials is then found as

$$ n = \left[\frac{z_{1-\alpha/2}\sigma'}{E} \right]^2 \tag{7-12a} $$

where $z_{1-\alpha/2}$, as previously, is the $(1 - \alpha/2)$ 100 per cent point of a standard normal distribution.

The adequacy of this expression depends on how close the estimate σ' is to the true standard deviation σ, in the same way as (7-12) depends on the initial estimate p' of p.*

If a one-sided error band is required on μ, rather than a two-sided one, we would use $z_{1-\alpha}$ instead of $z_{1-\alpha/2}$ in (7-12a) and use (3.9) or (3.10) to obtain the confidence interval.

From the preceding discussion it is evident that the usual statistical methods for obtaining confidence bands on estimates of parameters and determining the required number of observations to obtain a desired degree of precision are directly applicable in a Monte Carlo analysis.

7-4. Comparison of Methods

The transformation of variables, discussed in Chapter 5, has the advantage that it is an exact method—that is, it provides the exact distribution for system performance when the component distributions are known. Its drawback is that it can be applied to only simple problems and consequently would not be practical for most of the situations we have been

---

* Equation 7-12a is obtained from (3-8) under the assumption that the required number of Monte Carlo trials n is sufficiently large so that the normal variate $z_{1-\alpha/2}$ may be used in place of $t_{1-\alpha/2}$. The error resulting from this assumption is slight if $n \geq 50$.

considering. For example, the checkout problem would be very involved if handled by transformation of variables, because of the varied distributions of time to failure at each station.

The assumption of normality of system performance, based on the central limit theorem, is strictly applicable only when system performance is the *sum* of the effects of *many* component variables, with no single one having a dominant variance. For the checkout example this assumption was seen to be satisfactory except in the extreme tails of the distribution, such as at the 99 per cent point. Even for nonadditive systems, (7-3) and (7-6) or (7-7) are often used to calculate the average and variance for system performance, which is then assumed to be normally distributed. This assumption is sometimes reasonable when performance is affected by a number of variables whose effect on system performance are of similar magnitude and the functional relationship is not "too nonlinear." In the circuit example the results obtained by assuming current to be normally distributed were similar to those using a more complex Pearson distribution approximation. However, indiscriminate assumptions of normality could lead to erroneous conclusions. In a particular case it is not always clear whether a normal distribution will yield a reasonable approximation without generating higher system moments.

Monte Carlo simulation has more intuitive appeal than does the generation of system moments and consequently is easier to understand. The desired precision can be obtained by conducting sufficient trials. Also, the Monte Carlo method is very flexible and can be applied to many highly complex situations for which the method of generation of system moments becomes too difficult. This is especially true when there are interrelationships between the component variables.

A major drawback of the Monte Carlo method is that there is frequently no way of determining whether any of the variables are dominant or more important than others. Furthermore, if a change is made in one variable, the entire simulation must be redone. Also, the method generally requires developing a complex computer program; and if a large number of trials are required, a great deal of computer time may be needed to obtain the necessary answers.

Consequently, the generation of system moments, in conjunction with a Pearson or Johnson distribution approximation, is sometimes the most economical approach. Although the precision of the answers usually cannot be easily assessed for this method, the results of the study referred to in Section 7-2 suggest that this approach often does provide an adequate approximation. In addition, the generation of system moments allows us to analyze the relative importance of each component variable by examining the magnitude of its partial derivative. As a result, it might be desirable to set more stringent tolerances on those components that contribute most heavily to the system variance.

Also, unlike Monte Carlo, the generation of system moments does not necessarily require any assumptions concerning the form of the component distributions. For example, in the circuit problem only the estimates of the moments of the component variables were required, rather than the complete component performance distributions.

For these reasons the practicality of the procedure described in Section 7-2 should be examined before resorting to Monte Carlo methods in evaluating system performance from component data. Perhaps a given situation is so complex that Monte Carlo simulation provides the only workable tool. On the other hand, when the method of generation of system moments can be applied, it provides a cheaper and more refined approach.

7-5. Other Uses of Monte Carlo Simulation

One important application of Monte Carlo simulation has been in the estimation of the reliability of complex systems. Consider again the system shown in Fig. 7-5, which was discussed previously in Chapter 2. All

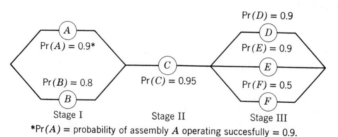

*Pr(A) = probability of assembly A operating succesfully = 0.9.

Fig. 7-5 System with parallel and series elements. From H. Chestnut, *Systems Engineering Tools*, John Wiley and Sons, 1965 (Fig. 6.1-1).

three stages must work to have a successful operation. A failure occurs at stage I only when *both* components A and B, with reliabilities of 0.9 and 0.8 respectively, fail. Stage II fails when component C, which has a reliability of 0.95, fails. A failure at stage III occurs only when components D, E, and F *all* fail. These components have reliabilities of 0.9, 0.9, and 0.5 respectively. By conventional probability analysis, system reliability was found in Chapter 2 to be 0.926.

The same problem could have been solved by Monte Carlo simulation, using a computer to "build" a large number of synthetic systems. For each system, the performance of each component is evaluated by picking a uniform variate over the interval (0, 1) and comparing it with the required reliability. For example, a reliability of 0.9 is synthesized by denoting a failure every time a random value of 0.9 or above is obtained and otherwise denoting a success. After doing this for each component, the three stages and then the whole system are classified as failures or successes. The procedure is repeated many times, and the estimated reliability is the proportion of successful systems to the total number simulated.

Table 7-3   Results of First Five Monte Carlo Trials to Estimate Reliability of System Shown in Fig. 7-5

Random Value Generated for Component		Result for Stage I[a]	Random Value Generated for Component	Result for Stage II	Random Value Generated for Component			Result for Stage III	Result for System
A	B		C		D	E	F		
0.22	0.17	S	0.68	S	0.65	0.84	0.68	S	S
0.93[b]	0.22	S	0.53	S	0.64	0.39	0.07	S	S
0.78	0.76	S	0.58	S	0.54	0.74	0.92	S	S
0.58	0.71	S	0.96	F	0.30	0.24	0.18	S	F
0.18	0.87	S	0.01	S	0.42	0.31	0.57	S	S

[a] S = Success, F = Failure.
[b] Underlined values indicate failures.

The procedure for evaluating the reliability of the system of Fig. 7-5 by Monte Carlo simulation is thus as follows:

1. Generate six independent uniform variates in the interval (0, 1). Designate their values A, B, C, D, E, and F.
2. If $A \geq 0.9$ *and* $B \geq 0.8$, there is a failure in stage I.
3. If $C \geq 0.95$, there is a failure in stage II.
4. If $D \geq 0.90$ *and* $E \geq 0.90$ *and* $F \geq 0.50$, there is a failure in stage III.
5. The simulated system fails if stage I fails *or* stage II fails *or* stage III fails. If none of the stages fails, the system operation is a success.
6. Steps 1 to 5 are repeated many times and a system failure or success is recorded each time. Reliability is then estimated as

$$\frac{\text{number of system successes}}{\text{total number of Monte Carlo trials}}.$$

These rules can be programmed simply on a high-speed computer. The result of five trials is shown in Table 7-3. After these five simulations the estimate of system reliability was $\frac{4}{5}$ or 0.8. After a total of 100 Monte Carlo trials, the estimate was $\frac{91}{100}$ or 0.91 (as compared with the exact value of

0.926). A confidence interval can also be calculated in the manner described previously.

The preceding example is artificial, for the exact result can easily be found analytically. If, however, there were 6000 components, rather than six, and if the performances of some were not independent, the analytic approach might be very complex and the problem might *have to be* handled by Monte Carlo methods.

Monte Carlo simulation is frequently applied to the analysis of problems involving customer service and waiting lines. Statistical queueing theory is the analytic (that is, nonsimulation) method for handling such problems, but this technique has not been developed to the point that it can provide solutions to many complex practical problems. For example, it is often necessary to assume in the theory that the elapsed time between the arrivals of consecutive customers follows an exponential distribution. When such assumptions are not met in practice, we often must resort to Monte Carlo simulation.

An example of the use of Monte Carlo methods in a waiting-line problem arises in simulating a job shop. In such an operation we are interested in processing diverse customer orders on schedule and at a minimum cost. Customer orders enter a waiting line and are processed according to some priority rule such as "first come, first served." The waiting time that a particular order encounters depends upon, among other things, the availability of machines and operators to handle the order. If there are many machines, the orders will generally be processed on time, but the tie-up of investment might be costly. With fewer machines, investment cost goes down, but the chances of not meeting customer demand increases. The problem is complicated by the fact that different kinds of machines are required for different jobs at different work stations. Statistical variations are introduced by fluctuations in the number and types of customer orders, machine breakdowns, allowable lag times between order and delivery, and so on.

The shop manager desires an optimum policy for running the shop. For example, he has to decide how many machines should be available at each stage of operation. The situation may be so complicated that the consequence of many decisions can be evaluated only by trial and error.

Instead of making the comparison under actual operating conditions—which in general would not be practical on a large scale—the manager can use a computer to simulate his operation. Randomly generated numbers from the distribution of orders would then replace actual orders. Machine breakdowns, lead times, and other random variables would be generated by the computer. Each set of trials might represent a year's operation and provide simulated data on idle time, lost orders, and so on.

Many years of synthetic information could be obtained in this manner and a distribution of job-shop performance for the designated machine setup developed. A different setup would then be studied by changing the parameters in the computer program. Thus the consequences of different policies can be compared. The procedure is summarized in Fig. 7-6.

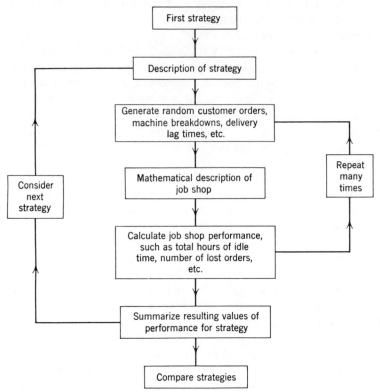

Fig. 7-6   Flow chart of Monte Carlo simulation of job shop.

There are many other applications of Monte Carlo simulation in analyzing complex operational situations, such as in the evaluation of inventory-management rules and the operation of transportation facilities.

Such methods are also used in theoretical statistical studies when it is not possible to find the distribution of some variable directly. For example, the distribution of the W statistics, described in Chapter 8, were approximated by Monte Carlo methods.

This chapter has provided a brief introduction to Monte Carlo methods. This subject is discussed in more detail in References 7-8, 7-10, and 7-11. Specific applications are described in References 7-12 to 7-15.

A bibliography on the use of simulation in management analysis is given in Reference 7-16. Further examples may be found in recent issues of technical journals such as *Operations Research, Management Science,* and *Management Technology.* Procedures for reducing the required number of Monte Carlo trials to obtain a specified degree of precision are discussed in References 7-8, 7-10, 7-11, and 7-17 to 7-19. Computer routines and languages to perform general simulations, such as GPSS (see References 7-20 and 7-21) and SIMSCRIPT (see Reference 7-22), may also frequently be found very useful and should be explored before embarking on the development of a simulation program.

Monte Carlo simulation can clearly be a powerful tool. As in any other method, the validity of the answers depends on the adequacy of the input data. Therefore careful attention must be given to the development of a realistic description of the underlying physical situation to serve as input to the Monte Carlo analysis.

References

7-1   O. L. Davies (ed.), *Statistical Methods in Research and Production,* Hafner Publishing Co., New York, 1957.

7-2   D. S. Villars, *Statistical Design and Analysis of Experiments for Development Research,* William C. Brown Co., Dubuque, Iowa, 1951.

7-3   W. Volk, *Applied Statistics for Engineers,* McGraw-Hill Book Co., New York, 1958.

7-4   W. E. Deming, *Some Theory of Sampling,* John Wiley and Sons, New York, 1950.

7-5   J. W. Tukey, Statistical Techniques Research Group, Princeton University, Princeton, New Jersey, Technical Reports 10, 11, and 12: (10) "The Propagation of Errors, Fluctuations and Tolerances—Basic Generalized Formulas"; (11) "The Propagation of Errors, Fluctuations and Tolerances—Supplementary Formulas"; (12) "The Propagation of Errors, Fluctuations and Tolerances—An Exercise in Partial Differentiation."

7-6   M. G. Kendall and B. Babington-Smith, *Tracts for Computers,* No. 24, Cambridge University Press, Cambridge, 1939.

7-7   The RAND Corporation, *One Million Random Digits and* 100,000 *Normal Deviates,* The Free Press, Glencoe, Illinois, 1955.

7-8   K. D. Tocher, *The Art of Simulation,* D. Van Nostrand Company, Princeton, New Jersey, 1963.

7-9   T. E. Hull and A. R. Dobell, "Random Number Generators," *SIAM Rev.,* **4,** 230 (1962).

7-10   J. M. Hammersley and D. C. Handscomb, *Monte Carlo Methods,* John Wiley and Sons, 1964

7-11   Yu A. Schreider, *Method of Statistical Testing—Monte Carlo Method,* Elsevier Publishing Company, Amsterdam, 1964.

7-12   B. E. Goetz, "Monte Carlo Solution of Waiting Line Problems," *Management Technology,* **1,** 2 (1960).

7-13   J. Harling, "Simulation Techniques in Operations Research—A Review," *J. Oper. Res. Soc. Amer.,* **6,** 307 (1958).

7-14 W. N. Jessop, "Monte Carlo Methods and Industrial Problems," *Appl. Stat.*, **5**, 156 (1956).

7-15 P. V. Youle, K. D. Tocher, J. W. Jessop, and F. I. Musk, "Simulation Studies of Industrial Operations," *J. Roy. Statist. Soc.* **A**, **122**, 484 (1959).

7-16 D. G. Malcolm, "Bibliography on the Use of Simulation in Management Analysis," *J. Oper. Res. Soc. America*, **8**, 169 (1960).

7-17 H. Kahn and A. W. Marshall, "Methods of Reducing Sample Size in Monte Carlo Computation," *J. Oper. Res. Soc. Amer.*, **1**, 263 (1953).

7-18 J. Moshman, "The Application of Sequential Estimation to Computer Simulation and Monte Carlo Procedures," *J. Assoc. Comp. Mach.*, **5**, 343 (1958).

7-19 C. E. Clark, "The Utility of Statistics of Random Numbers," *J. Oper. Res. Soc. Amer.*, **8**, 185 (1960).

7-20 R. Efron and G. Gordon, "A General Purpose Digital Simulator and Examples of Its Application, Part I, Description of the Simulator," *IBM Systems J.*, **3**, 22 (1964).

7-21 H. Herscovitch and T. Schneider, "GPSS III—An Expanded General Purpose Simulator," *IBM Systems J.*, **4**, 174 (1966).

7-22 H. M. Markovitz, "Simulating with SIMSCRIPT," *Management Science*, **12**, B-395 (1966).

Appendix 7A: Derivation of Equations (7-3) and (7-6)

Let the relationship between system performance z and the component variables $x_1, x_2, \ldots, x_n$ be given by

$$z = h(x_1, x_2, \ldots, x_n).$$

Let

$E(x_i) =$ expected value for ith component variable $(i = 1, 2, \ldots, n)$;

$E[x_i - E(x_i)]^r = r$th moment about mean for ith component variable $(i = 1, 2, \ldots, n; r = 2, 3, 4)$;

$E(z) =$ expected value for system performance;

$E[z - E(z)]^r = r$th moment about mean for system performance $(r = 2, 3, 4)$.

Assume the component variables are uncorrelated. Hence by proceeding as in the verification of (2-78) we can easily show that

$$E\{[x_i - E(x_i)]^r [x_j - E(x_j)]^s\}$$
$$= E[x_i - E(x_i)]^r E[x_j - E(x_j)]^s, \qquad i \neq j. \quad (7A\text{-}1)$$

First expand $h(x_1, x_2, \ldots, x_n)$ in a multivariable Taylor series up to second order* about $[E(x_1), E(x_2), \ldots, E(x_n)]$—the point at which each of

* This will assure retention of terms up to second order in the sense defined previously.

the component variables take on its average value. Thus

$$h(x_1, x_2, \ldots, x_n) = h[E(x_1), E(x_2), \ldots, E(x_n)]$$

$$+ \sum_{i=1}^{n} \frac{\partial h}{\partial x_i} [x_i - E(x_i)] + \frac{1}{2}\left\{ \sum_{i=1}^{n} \frac{\partial^2 h}{\partial x_i^2} [x_i - E(x_i)]^2 \right.$$

$$+ 2 \sum_{\substack{i \\ i<j}} \sum_j \frac{\partial^2 h}{\partial x_i\, \partial x_j} [x_i - E(x_i)][x_j - E(x_j)] \bigg\}, \qquad (7A\text{-}2)$$

where all derivatives are evaluated at their expected values—that is, $\partial h/\partial x_i$ represents $\partial h(z)/\partial x_i$ with the $E(x_k)$ substituted for x_k for $k = 1, 2, \ldots, n$. Taking expected values of both sides of (7A-2) yields

$$E[h(x_1, x_2, \ldots, x_n)] = E\{h[E(x_1), E(x_2), \ldots, E(x_n)]\}$$

$$+ E\left\{ \sum_{i=1}^{n} \frac{\partial h}{\partial x_i} [x_i - E(x_i)] \right\}$$

$$+ E\left\{ \frac{1}{2} \sum_{i=1}^{n} \frac{\partial^2 h}{\partial x_i^2} [x_i - E(x_i)]^2 \right\}$$

$$+ E\left\{ \sum_{\substack{i \\ i<j}} \sum_j \frac{\partial^2 h}{\partial x_i\, \partial x_j} [x_i - E(x_i)][x_j - E(x_j)] \right\}.$$

$$(7A\text{-}3)$$

In (7A-3) the following property of the expectation operator, established in Chapter 2, was used:

$$E(y_1 + y_2 + \cdots + y_n) = E(y_1) + E(y_2) + \cdots + E(y_n). \quad (7A\text{-}4)$$

In Chapter 2 it was also found for any constant c and random variable x that

$$E(c) = c \qquad\qquad\qquad (7A\text{-}5)$$

and

$$E(cx) = cE(x). \qquad\qquad\qquad (7A\text{-}6)$$

Therefore

$$E\{h[E(x_1), E(x_2), \ldots, E(x_n)]\} = h[E(x_1), E(x_2), \ldots, E(x_n)] \quad (7A\text{-}7)$$

and

$$E\left\{ \sum_{i=1}^{n} \frac{\partial h}{\partial x_i} [x_i - E(x_i)] \right\} = \sum_{i=1}^{n} E\left\{ \frac{\partial h}{\partial x_i} [x_i - E(x_i)] \right\}$$

$$= \sum_{i=1}^{n} \frac{\partial h}{\partial x_i} \{E[x_i - E(x_i)]\} = 0. \qquad (7A\text{-}8)$$

Similarly,

$$E\left\{\frac{1}{2}\sum_{i=1}^{n}\frac{\partial^2 h}{\partial x_i^2}[x_i - E(x_i)]^2\right\} = \frac{1}{2}\sum_{i=1}^{n}\frac{\partial^2 h}{\partial x_i^2}E[x_i - E(x_i)]^2$$

$$= \frac{1}{2}\sum_{i=1}^{n}\frac{\partial^2 h}{\partial x_i^2}\text{Var}\,(x_i), \qquad (7A\text{-}9)$$

since, by definition

$$E[x_i - E(x_i)]^2 = \text{Var}\,(x_i).$$

Also

$$E\left\{\sum_{\substack{i \ j \\ i<j}}\sum\frac{\partial^2 h}{\partial x_i\,\partial x_j}[x_i - E(x_i)][x_j - E(x_j)]\right\}$$

$$= \sum_{\substack{i \ j \\ i<j}}\sum\frac{\partial^2 h}{\partial x_i\,\partial x_j}E\{[x_i - E(x_i)][x_j - E(x_j)]\} = 0. \quad (7A\text{-}10)$$

since, from (7A-1),
$$E\{[x_i - E(x_i)][x_j - E(x_j)]\} = E[x_i - E(x_i)]E[x_j - E(x_j)] = 0.$$
Substitution of (7A-7), (7A-8), (7A-9), and (7A-10) into (7A-2) yields

$$E(z) = h[E(x_1), E(x_2), \ldots, E(x_n)] + \frac{1}{2}\sum_{i=1}^{n}\frac{\partial^2 h}{\partial x_i^2}\text{Var}\,(x_i),$$

which is (7-3).

Next we derive (7-6). In Chapter 2 it was found that $\text{Var}\,(z) = E(z^2) - [E(z)]^2$. Substitution of $z = h(x_1, x_2, \ldots, x_n)$ yields

$$\text{Var}\,[h(x_1, x_2, \ldots, x_n)] = E\{[h(x_1, x_2, \ldots, x_n)]^2\}$$

$$- \{E[h(x_1, x_2, \ldots, x_n)]\}^2. \quad (7A\text{-}11)$$

To obtain an approximation to the first term on the right-hand side of (7A-11) we square (7A-2), take expected values on a term-by-term basis and retain terms up to the third order. This leads to

$$E\{[h(x_1, x_2, \ldots, x_n)]^2\} = \{h[E(x_1), E(x_2), \ldots, E(x_n)]\}^2$$

$$+ \sum_{i=1}^{n}\left(\frac{\partial h}{\partial x_i}\right)^2 E[x_i - E(x_i)]^2$$

$$+ h[E(x_1), E(x_2), \ldots, E(x_n)]$$

$$\times \sum_{i=1}^{n} \frac{\partial^2 h}{\partial x_i^2} E[x_i - E(x_i)]^2$$

$$+ \sum_{i=1}^{n} \left(\frac{\partial h}{\partial x_i}\right)\left(\frac{\partial^2 h}{\partial x_i^2}\right) E[x_i - E(x_i)]^3, \qquad (7A\text{-}12)$$

for the missing terms all drop out.

The second term on the right-hand side of (7A-11) is the square of (7-3). Thus

$$\{E[h(x_1, x_2, \ldots, x_n)]\}^2$$

$$= \left\{h[E(x_1), E(x_2), \ldots, E(x_n)] + \frac{1}{2}\sum_{i=1}^{n} \frac{\partial^2 h}{\partial x_i^2} \, \mathrm{Var}\,(x_i)\right\}^2$$

$$= \{h[E(x_1), E(x_2), \ldots, E(x_n)]\}^2$$

$$+ h[E(x_1), E(x_2), \ldots, E(x_n)] \sum_{i=1}^{n} \frac{\partial^2 h}{\partial x_i^2} E[x_i - E(x_i)]^2 \quad (7A\text{-}13)$$

if terms up to the third order only are retained.

Substituting (7A-12) and (7A-13) in (7A-11) gives

$$\mathrm{Var}\,[h(x_1, x_2, \ldots, x_n)] = \sum_{i=1}^{n} \left(\frac{\partial h}{\partial x_i}\right)^2 E[x_i - E(x_i)]^2$$

$$+ \sum_{i=1}^{n} \left(\frac{\partial h}{\partial x_i}\right)\left(\frac{\partial^2 h}{\partial x_i^2}\right) E[x_i - E(x_i)]^3.$$

Equivalently, since $E[x_i - E(x_i)]^3 = \mu_3(x_i)$,

$$\mathrm{Var}\,(z) = \sum_{i=1}^{n} \left(\frac{\partial h}{\partial x_i}\right)^2 \mathrm{Var}\,(x_i) + \sum_{i=1}^{n} \left(\frac{\partial h}{\partial x_i}\right)\left(\frac{\partial^2 h}{\partial x_i^2}\right)\mu_3(x_i),$$

which is (7-6).

Appendix 7B: Expressions for Moments for System Performance When Component Variables Are Correlated

In developing (7-3), (7-6), (7-8), and (7-9) for obtaining moments of system performance from component moments it was assumed that the component variables were uncorrelated. The corresponding expressions for correlated component variables are given by (7B-1) to (7B-4),

$$E(z) = h[E(x_1), E(x_2), \ldots, E(x_n)] + \frac{1}{2}\sum_{i=1}^{n} \frac{\partial^2 h}{\partial x_i^2} \, \text{Var}\,(x_i)$$

$$+ \sum_i \sum_{\substack{j \\ i<j}} \frac{\partial^2 h}{\partial x_i \, \partial x_j} \, E\{[x_i - E(x_i)][x_j - E(x_j)]\}. \tag{7B-1}$$

$$\text{Var}\,(z) = \sum_{i=1}^{n} \left(\frac{\partial h}{\partial x_i}\right)^2 \text{Var}\,(x_i)$$

$$+ 2\sum_i \sum_{\substack{j \\ i<j}} \left(\frac{\partial h}{\partial x_i}\right)\left(\frac{\partial h}{\partial x_j}\right) E\{[x_i - E(x_i)][x_j - E(x_j)]\}$$

$$+ \sum_{i=1}^{n} \left(\frac{\partial h}{\partial x_i}\right)\left(\frac{\partial^2 h}{\partial x_i^2}\right)\mu_3(x_i) + \sum_i \sum_{\substack{j \\ i \neq j}} \left(\frac{\partial h}{\partial x_i}\right)\left(\frac{\partial^2 h}{\partial x_j^2}\right)$$

$$\times E\{[x_i - E(x_i)][x_j - E(x_j)]^2\} \tag{7B-2}$$

$$+ 2\sum_i \sum_{\substack{j \\ i \neq j}} \left(\frac{\partial h}{\partial x_i}\right)\left(\frac{\partial^2 h}{\partial x_i \, \partial x_j}\right) E\{[x_i - E(x_i)]^2[x_j - E(x_j)]\}$$

$$+ 2\sum_i \sum_j \sum_{\substack{s \\ i \neq j \neq s}} \left(\frac{\partial h}{\partial x_i}\right)\left(\frac{\partial^2 h}{\partial x_j \, \partial x_s}\right) E\{[x_i - E(x_i)][x_j - E(x_j)][x_s - E(x_s)]\}.$$

$$\mu_3(z) = \sum_{i=1}^{n} \left(\frac{\partial h}{\partial x_i}\right)^3 \mu_3(x_i)$$

$$+ 3\sum_i \sum_{\substack{j \\ i \neq j}} \left(\frac{\partial h}{\partial x_i}\right)^2\left(\frac{\partial h}{\partial x_j}\right) E\{[x_i - E(x_i)]^2[x_j - E(x_j)]\} \tag{7B-3}$$

$$+ 6\sum_i \sum_j \sum_{\substack{s \\ i<j<s}} \left(\frac{\partial h}{\partial x_i}\right)\left(\frac{\partial h}{\partial x_j}\right)\left(\frac{\partial h}{\partial x_s}\right)$$

$$\times E\{[x_i - E(x_i)][x_j - E(x_j)][x_s - E(x_s)]\}.$$

$$\mu_4(z) = \sum_{i=1}^{n} \left(\frac{\partial h}{\partial x_i}\right)^4 \mu_4(x_i)$$

$$+ 4\sum_i \sum_{\substack{j \\ i \neq j}} \left(\frac{\partial h}{\partial x_i}\right)^3\left(\frac{\partial h}{\partial x_j}\right) E\{[x_i - E(x_i)]^3[x_j - E(x_j)]\}$$

$$+ 6\sum_i \sum_{\substack{j \\ i<j}} \left(\frac{\partial h}{\partial x_i}\right)^2\left(\frac{\partial h}{\partial x_j}\right)^2 E\{[x_i - E(x_i)]^2[x_j - E(x_j)]^2\}$$

$$+ 12 \sum_{i} \sum_{j} \sum_{s} \left(\frac{\partial h}{\partial x_i}\right)^2 \left(\frac{\partial h}{\partial x_j}\right) \left(\frac{\partial h}{\partial x_s}\right)$$
$$\scriptstyle i \neq j \neq s$$

$$\times E\{[x_i - E(x_i)]^2[x_j - E(x_j)][x_s - E(x_s)]\}$$

$$+ 24 \sum_{i} \sum_{j} \sum_{s} \sum_{t} \left(\frac{\partial h}{\partial x_i}\right) \left(\frac{\partial h}{\partial x_j}\right) \left(\frac{\partial h}{\partial x_s}\right) \left(\frac{\partial h}{\partial x_t}\right)$$
$$\scriptstyle i < j < s < t$$

$$\times E\{[x_i - E(x_i)][x_j - E(x_j)][x_s - E(x_s)][x_t - E(x_t)]\}. \quad (7B\text{-}4)$$

The terms in these expressions can be estimated from available data in the usual manner. For example,

$$E\{[x_i - E(x_i)]^2[x_j - E(x_j)]^2\}$$

is estimated from R observations by determining

$$\frac{\sum_{r=1}^{R}(x_{ir} - \bar{x}_i)^2(x_{jr} - \bar{x}_j)^2}{R},$$

which can also be written in a form that is more suitable for calculational purposes.

Appendix 7C: Methods for Generating Random Values from Common Distributions Based upon Tabulations of Random Standard Uniform and Normal Variates

Procedures for generating variates from common distributions are summarized in Table 7-2. These methods make use of random values from a standard uniform distribution over $(0, 1)$ and from a standard normal distribution with $\mu = 0$ and $\sigma = 1$. As indicated in this chapter, such random values are tabulated or can be computer generated. In addition, the procedures of Table 7-2 rely upon one or both of two approaches to be described.

The first technique, known as the *uniform probability transformation*, uses the fact that the cumulative probability function for *any* continuous variate is uniformly distributed over the interval $(0, 1)$—that is, for any random variable y with probability density $f(y)$ the variate

$$F(y) = \int_{-\infty}^{y} f(x)\,dx \qquad (7C\text{-}1)$$

is uniformly distributed over $(0, 1)$, or $F(y)$ has the probability density function

$$g[F(y)] = 1, \qquad 0 \le y \le 1.$$

Thus a random value y from an arbitrary probability density function $f(y)$ can be obtained as follows:

1. Generate a random value R_U from a uniform distribution over $(0, 1)$.
2. Set $R_U = F(y)$ in (7C-1).
3. Solve the resulting expression for y.

The procedure is illustrated in Fig. 7C-1.

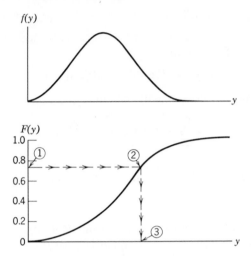

$f(y)$ = probability density function for variate y.
$F(y)$ = cumulative distribution of y.

Procedure
1. Generate random uniform variate R_U over $(0, 1)$.
2. Set $F(y) = R_U$.
3. Determine y corresponding to $F(y)$.

Fig. 7C-1 Generation of random variate by uniform probability transformation.

As an example, consider the generation of a variate from the two parameter exponential probability density function (see Chapter 8),

$$f(y; \lambda, \mu) = \lambda e^{-\lambda(y-\mu)}; \qquad \mu \leq y < \infty.$$

Thus

$$F(y) = \int_\mu^y \lambda e^{-\lambda(x-\mu)}\, dx = 1 - e^{-\lambda(y-\mu)}$$

and therefore

$$\ln\left[1 - F(y)\right] = -\lambda(y - \mu)$$

or

$$y = -\frac{1}{\lambda} \ln\left[1 - F(y)\right] + \mu.$$

Since $F(y)$ is uniformly distributed over (0, 1) we take a random standard uniform variate R_U and obtain the desired exponential variate as

$$y = -\frac{1}{\lambda}[\ln(1 - R_U)] + \mu.$$

The uniform probability transformation is particularly appropriate when, as in the example, the required integration can be explicitly performed and the resulting equation easily solved. In other cases we must resort to numerical methods to solve (7C-1) for y.

The second approach is to use known relationships between the variate to be generated and normal and uniform variates.

For example, the gamma probability density function

$$f(y; \eta, \lambda) = \frac{\lambda^\eta}{\Gamma(\eta)} e^{-\lambda y} y^{\eta-1}, \qquad 0 \le y < \infty$$

was derived in Chapter 5 as a sum of η exponential variates, each with parameter λ. Consequently, this variate may be obtained by generating η appropriate independent exponential variates in the manner described previously and summing these. Weibull, chi-square, beta, Poisson, binomial, log-normal, and Johnson S_B and S_U variates are obtained from similar relationships.

Chapter 8

Probability Plotting and Testing of

Distributional Assumptions

In the preceding chapters the major concern has been the selection of statistical models to represent physical phenomena. This chapter deals with techniques to assess the reasonableness of a selected model on the basis of the given data. Such assessments are especially important when the model is to be used for prediction. For example, if the assumption of an exponential distribution as a model for time to failure in predicting the probability of mission success is incorrect, the prediction can be seriously in error. (See the example in Section 8-2.)

Two different approaches are considered: probability plotting and statistical tests. Probability plotting is a subjective method in that the determination of whether or not the data contradict the assumed model is based on a visual examination, rather than a statistical calculation. The method is very simple and can provide a great deal of useful information in addition to an evaluation of the appropriateness of the chosen model. Statistical tests are more objective and provide a probabilistic framework in which to evaluate the adequacy of the model. Thus they frequently are useful in supplementing the probability plots, especially when the plots fail to provide a clear-cut decision. Two types of tests are discussed: the *W* tests, which have been found very effective in evaluating the normal, log-normal, and exponential distribution assumptions, and the chi-squared test, which can be used to evaluate the adequacy of *any* assumed model.

One might conclude from the discussion in this chapter that a proper procedure for selecting a distribution is to consider a wide variety of possible models, evaluate each by the methods here described, and assume as correct the one that provides the best fit to the data. However, *no* such approach is being suggested. Wherever possible, the selection of the model

260

should be based on an understanding of the underlying physical phenomena, using the criteria suggested in earlier chapters. The distributional test then provides a useful mechanism for evaluating the adequacy of the physical interpretation. Only as a last resort is the reverse procedure warranted, and then, only with much care, for, although many models might appear appropriate within the range of the data, they might well be in error in the range for which predictions are desired.

8-1. Probability Plotting

INTRODUCTION

There is a saying that one picture is worth a thousand words. This applies particularly to probability plotting. The technique provides a pictorial representation of the data, as well as (a) an evaluation of the reasonableness of the assumed probability model, (b) estimates of the percentiles of the distribution, and (c) estimates of the distribution parameters.

This information can be obtained even when the values of only k of n observations are known—that is, for censored samples. As indicated in Chapter 3, such samples arise in life tests that are terminated after k failures, or in using an instrument where values above some reading are unknown because they are beyond the measurement scale of the instrument.

The technique is very simple to use. For a given distributional model the data are plotted on special graph paper designed for that distribution. If the assumed model is correct, the plotted points will tend to fall in a straight line. If the model is inadequate, the plot will not be linear and the extent and type of departures can be seen. Once a model appears to fit the data reasonably well, percentiles and parameter values can be estimated from the plot. The procedure is first illustrated for the normal distribution. Next, probability plots to evaluate some other models are considered. A discussion of the underlying theory is given at the end of the section.

OPERATIONAL PROCEDURE USING THE NORMAL DISTRIBUTION

The following steps are involved in preparing a probability plot from a given set of data:

Step 1.   Obtain graph paper, known as probability paper, designed for the distribution under examination. Paper for the normal distribution is shown in Fig. 8-1 and is readily available. Probability paper for other distributions may be obtained from various sources.* The

---

* A wide diversity of probability paper is available from Technical and Engineering Aids for Management, 104 Belrose Ave., Lowell, Massachusetts.

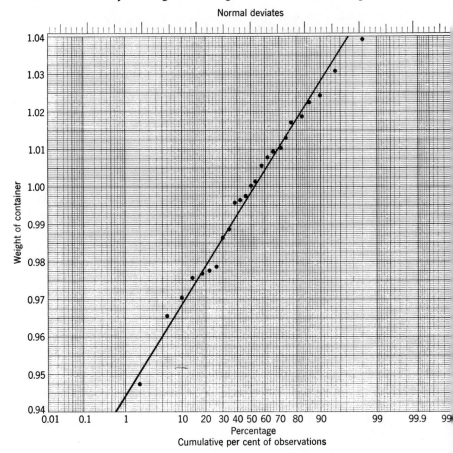

Fig. 8-1   Normal probability plot for weights of 1-pound containers of chemical additive.

procedure for making up this paper when it is not available is suggested later.

Step 2.   Rank the observations from smallest to largest in magnitude. Thus, if $x_{(1)}, x_{(2)}, \ldots, x_{(n)}$ are the original unordered observations then the *ordered observations*, to be denoted $x_1, x_2, \ldots, x_n$, are such that $x_1 \leq x_2 \leq \cdots \leq x_n$.

Step 3.   Plot the x_i's on the probability paper versus $(i - \frac{1}{2})100/n$ or $(i - \frac{1}{2})/n$, depending on whether the marked axis on the probability paper refers to the per cent or the proportion of observations. We shall henceforth assume that we have paper that requires the plot of per cent observations. Thus the lowest observation is plotted versus $(\frac{1}{2})100/n$; the second lowest, versus $(\frac{3}{2})100/n$, and so on.

For censored data, n represents the total number of samples, irrespective of whether or not all their values are known. The axis of the graph paper on which the x_i's are plotted will be referred to as the *observational scale*, and the axis for $(i - \frac{1}{2})100/n$ as the *cumulative scale*. Whether the observational or cumulative scale appears on the abscissa differs for the various probability papers. However, the cumulative scale is easily recognized by the fact that its values range from a small positive number, such as 0.01 per cent (or 0.0001) to some value close to 100 per cent (or 1.0), such as 99.99 per cent (or 0.9999). Thus in Fig. 8.1 it is evident that the cumulative values are plotted on the abscissa and the observational values on the ordinate.

Step 4.   If a straight line appears to fit the data, draw such a line on the graph "by eye."

If the chosen model is correct, the points should cluster around the line, although there will be some deviations because of random-sampling fluctuations. If the plot deviates appreciably from linearity, the chosen model does not adequately describe the given data. Systematic departures are indications that the model is inadequate. The determination of what can and cannot be considered a straight line is a subjective matter, and two people looking at the same plot might arrive at different conclusions. However, the larger the number of samples, and the greater the divergence from the assumed model, the easier it will be to detect a true, as opposed to a random, departure.

As a guide for the evaluation of normal probability plots, five sets each of random samples of size 20 and 50 have been selected from a standard normal distribution. Figures 8-2 and 8-3 show the corresponding normal probability plots. These provide some indication of the divergence from linearity for random samples of size 20 and 50 from a normal distribution. In contrast, Figs. 8-4 and 8-5 show plots on normal probability paper for samples of size 20 and 50, respectively from a uniform distribution—a distribution that is symmetric, just as is the normal, but which is flat. Finally, Figs. 8-6 and 8-7 show normal probability plots for samples of size 20 and 50 from an exponential distribution—a distribution whose shape differs radically from that of the normal distribution. These plots thus indicate typical deviations from linearity of plots on normal probability paper for each of two different sized samples from two distributions with varying divergences from normality. Note that for some of the samples from a *normal distribution*, especially those of size 20, the plots appear to diverge from linearity appreciably due to random variations.

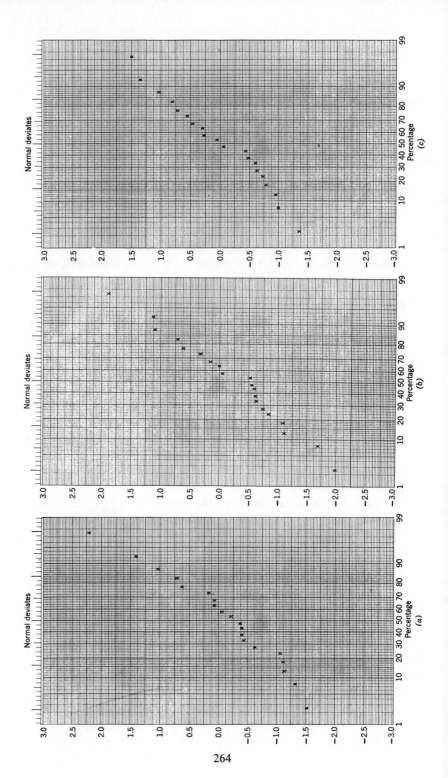

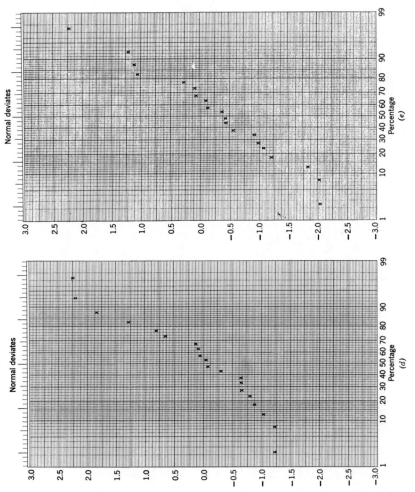

Fig. 8-2 Normal probability plots of five sets of 20 random samples from a normal distribution.

265

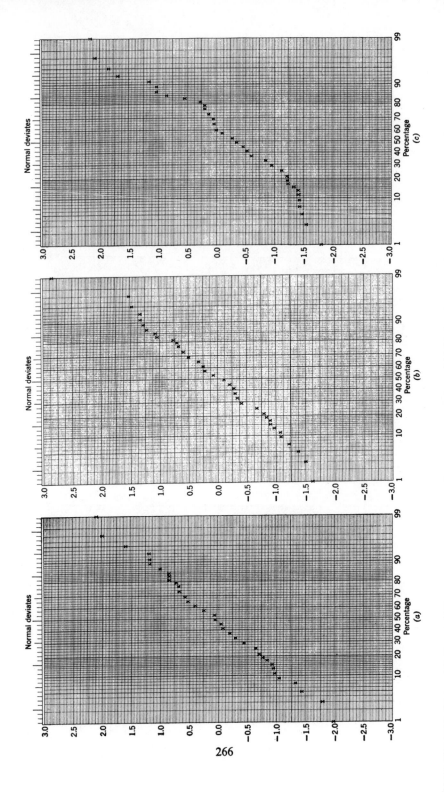

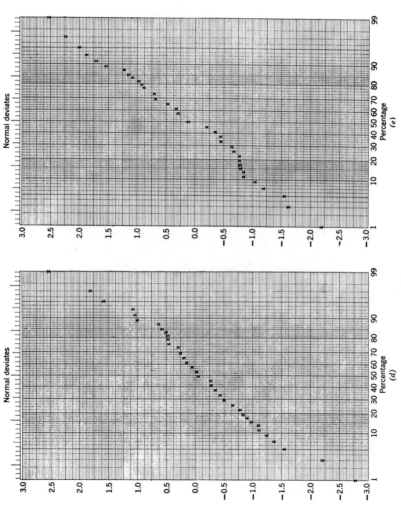

Fig. 8-3 Normal probability plots of five sets of 50 random samples from a normal distribution. (Not all points are plotted.)

267

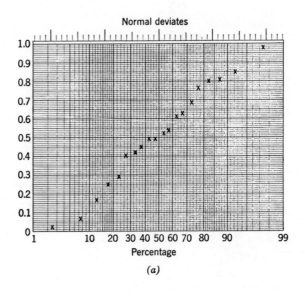

(a)

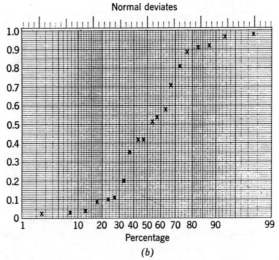

(b)

Fig. 8-4   Normal probability plots for five sets of 20 random samples from a uniform distribution.

268

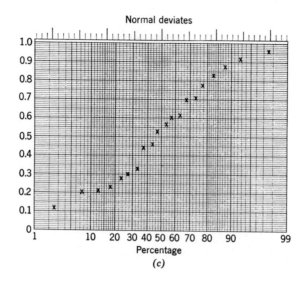

Normal deviates

Percentage

(c)

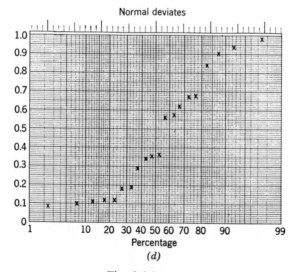

Normal deviates

Percentage

(d)

Fig. 8-4 (continued)

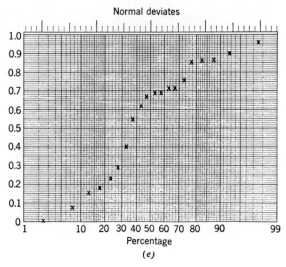

Normal deviates

Percentage

(e)

Fig. 8-4 (continued)

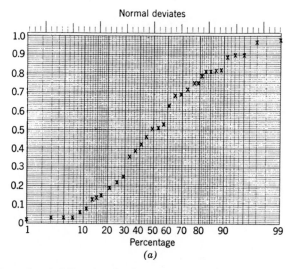

Normal deviates

Percentage

(a)

Fig. 8-5 Normal probability plots for five sets of 50 random samples from a uniform distribution. (Not all points are plotted.)

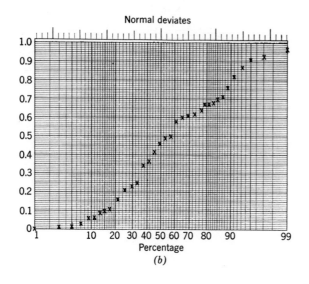

Normal deviates

Percentage

(b)

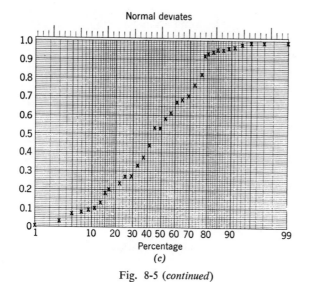

Normal deviates

Percentage

(c)

Fig. 8-5 (continued)

271

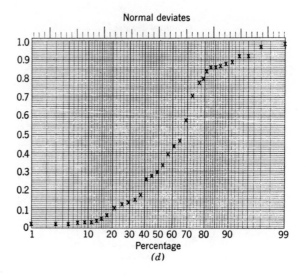

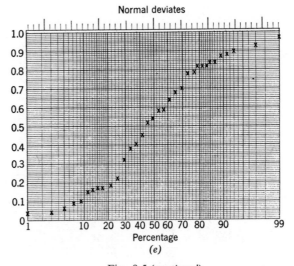

Fig. 8-5 *(continued)*

272

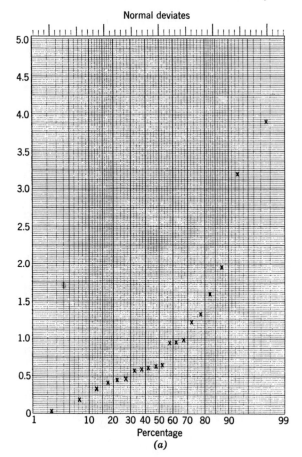

Fig. 8-6   Normal probability of five sets of 20 random samples from an exponential distribution.

However, almost all the plots for the samples from the *exponential distribution* diverge more than those from a normal distribution. The plots for the samples from the *uniform distribution* in general do not deviate from linearity quite as much as do those from the exponential distribution, but at least for samples of size 50, they can be differentiated from the plots of the normal variates.

In examining Figs. 8-2 to 8-7, the following should also be noted:

1. The variance of the points in the tails (extreme low or high plotted values) will be larger than that of the points at the center of the distribution. Thus the relative linearity of the plot near the tails of the distribution will

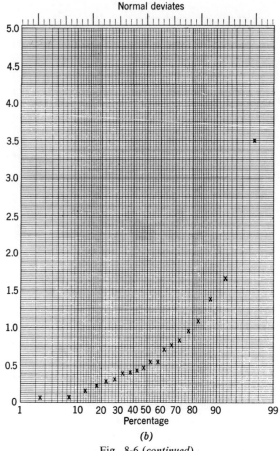

Fig. 8-6 (*continued*)

often seem poorer than at the center of the distribution even if the correct model has been chosen.*

2. The plotted points are ordered and hence are *not* independent. Thus we should not expect them to be *randomly* scattered about a line. For example, the points immediately following a point above the line are also likely to be above the line. Hence, even if the chosen model is correct, the plot may consist of a series of successive points (known as runs) above and below the line.

3. A model can never be *proven* to be adequate on the basis of sample data. Thus the probability plot of a small sample taken from a near-normal distribution will frequently not differ appreciably from that of a

* This does not apply for a bounded distribution tail.

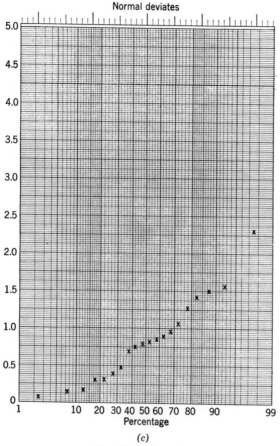

Fig. 8-6 (*continued*)

sample from a normal distribution, as illustrated by the plots we have shown for samples from a uniform distribution.

With these guides and some experience it should generally be possible to draw one of the following three conclusions from the plot: (a) the chosen model *appears* adequate, (b) the model is questionable, or (c) it is inadequate. The procedures described later in this chapter can be used in conjunction with the probability plot if an objective assessment is desired.

An examination of a plot when there is a systematic departure from a straight line can give some information about the shape of a more appropriate model. For example, the plots in Figs. 8-4 and 8-5 generally indicate that the plotted lower points are too large and the upper points are too small, compared with those expected from the chosen model. Thus the

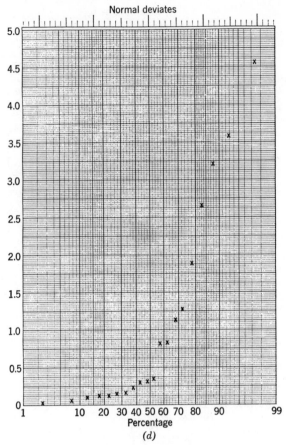

Fig. 8-6 (*continued*)

data indicate the use of a distribution which is less peaked than a normal distribution. Normal probability paper plots resembling those of Figs. 8-4 and 8-5 would also be obtained from a truncated normal distribution, such as in sampling from a normally distributed process where all values below and above specified limits have been removed initially. If the truncation occurred only at one tail of the distribution, the non-linearity in the probability plot would clearly be evident at that tail only.

In Figs. 8-6 and 8-7 the values in both tails are too large. Thus, the data suggest that a model skewed to the right should be chosen. If the values in both tails of the normal probability plot had been too *small* a distribution skewed to the left would be suggested. The technique of probability plotting will now be illustrated.

A chemical additive is packed in one-pound containers. This product

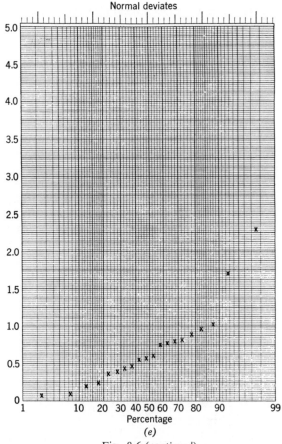

Fig. 8-6 *(continued)*

is quite expensive, and it is important to hold the weight close to one pound. The ordered values of the weights of 25 randomly selected containers are shown in Table 8-1.

Because variations in weight arise as the sum of the effects of many small deviations, a normal distribution is expected to provide a reasonable representation. In order to assess the adequacy of this model, a normal probability plot was prepared and is shown in Fig. 8-1. The ordered container weights are plotted against $(i - \frac{1}{2})100/n$; that is, the smallest value, 0.9473, is plotted on the observational scale versus 2.0 on the cumulative scale, the second ordered value, 0.9655, is plotted versus 6.0, and so on. The highest value, 1.0396, is plotted versus 98.0. The plotted points fall close to the line drawn, and hence a normal distribution does not appear to be an unreasonable model.

Table 8-1   Ordered Weights of One-Pound Containers of Chemical Additive

0.9473	0.9775	0.9964	1.0077	1.0182
0.9655	0.9788	0.9974	1.0084	1.0225
0.9703	0.9861	1.0002	1.0102	1.0248
0.9757	0.9887	1.0016	1.0132	1.0306
0.9770	0.9958	1.0058	1.0173	1.0396

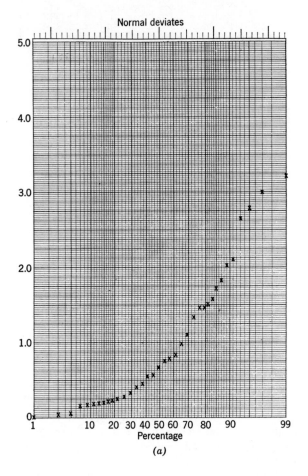

Fig. 8-7   Normal probability plots of five sets of 50 random samples from an exponential distribution. (Not all points are plotted.)

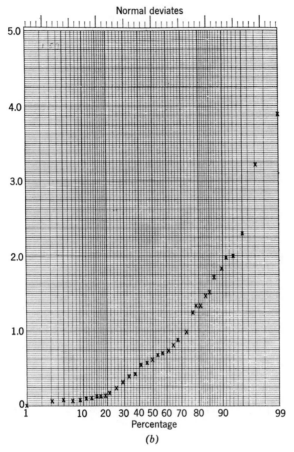

Fig. 8-7 (*continued*)

Distribution percentiles can be estimated from the plot. For example, the 50th percentile or median, is estimated as follows:

1. Locate 50 per cent on the cumulative distribution scale.
2. Find the intersection of the line obtained from the plot and the 50 per cent line.
3. Read the corresponding value on the observational scale.

For example, from Fig. 8-1 the median container weight is estimated to be 0.998 pound.

In a similar manner any other percentile can be estimated, even ones that are outside the range of the plotted points. For example, by extending

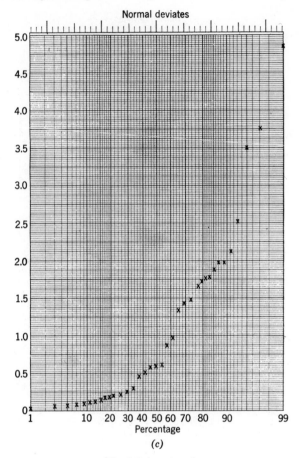

Fig. 8-7 (*continued*)

the line in the lower portion of Fig. 8-1, it is estimated that only 0.5 per cent of the containers would have weights less than 0.939 pound. We could have obtained even more extreme values, such as the 0.01 per cent point. However, it should be emphasized that extrapolation is valid *only* if the assumed model is correct beyond the range of the available data. Unfortunately, it is often possible to find several models that will fit the data in the central region of the distribution but that will vary radically in the tails. Thus we cannot be certain that the model chosen is appropriate at extreme values, even though a reasonably straight line can be drawn on the probability plot. Hence conclusions based on extrapolating probability plots must be viewed very critically.

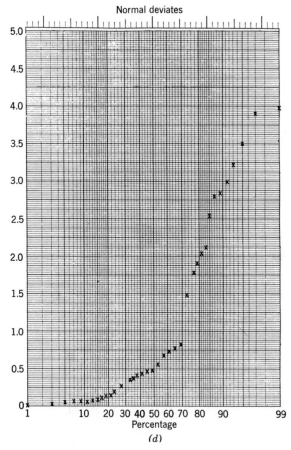

Fig. 8-7 (*continued*)

The plot may also be used in an inverse manner to estimate the probability that a specified value will be exceeded. For example, the probability of a container weight exceeding 1.02 pounds is estimated from Fig. 8-1 to be 0.18.

The procedure for estimating parameters from a probability plot for various distributions is discussed below. For a normal probability plot, the median estimates the location parameter or distribution mean μ, since for symmetric distributions the mean and median coincide. Thus in the container problem the estimate $\hat{\mu}$ is 0.998. The estimate of σ is obtained by using the fact that for *any* normal distribution the standard deviation equals approximately two-fifths of the difference between the 90th and the

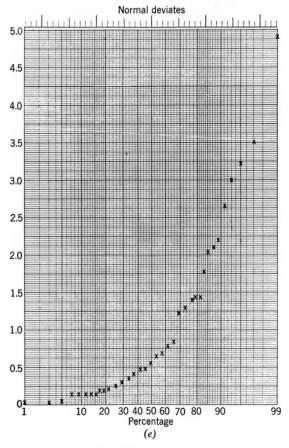

Fig. 8.7 (*continued*)

10th percentiles. In the container problem these points are estimated, from Fig. 8-1, to be 0.968 and 1.028, respectively, and thus $\hat{\sigma} = \frac{2}{5}(1.028 - 0.968) = 0.024$; $\hat{\sigma}$ could have been obtained in a similar manner from other percentiles.

PROBABILITY PLOTS FOR OTHER DISTRIBUTIONS

The Log-Normal Distribution. Probability paper for the log-normal distribution differs from that for the normal distribution in that the axis for the observational scale is logarithmic instead of arithmetic (see Fig. 8-8). A log-normal probability plot can also be prepared on normal probability paper by using the logarithms of the observations and plotting these against $(i - \frac{1}{2})100/n$. The procedure for estimating the parameters is similar to that for the normal distribution, except that the logarithms of the observed values are used. Thus the log-normal distribution parameter μ is estimated as the logarithm of the plotted 50th percentile, and σ is estimated as two fifths of the difference between the logarithms of the plotted 90th and 10th percentiles. The following problem illustrates the technique.

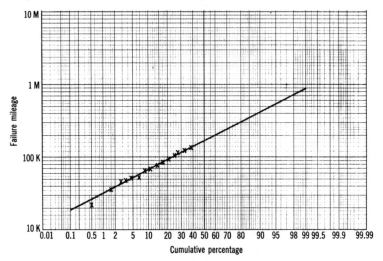

Fig. 8-8   Log-normal probability plot of failure mileage for locomotive control device. (Not all points are plotted.)

A new control device was tested on 96 diesel locomotives. Whenever a device failed, the mileage was recorded and the device was returned to the factory for failure analysis. After 135,000 miles of service each unfailed device was removed from its locomotive. It was felt that if the device could be warranted for 80,000 miles, it could be readily marketed. The underlying failure mechanism suggested a log-normal distribution for time to failure. The ordered times for the 37 units that failed are shown in Table 8-2. The data are censored, for the values of the largest 59 observations are known only to be above 135,000 miles. The log-normal probability plot is shown in Fig. 8-8. The value of the smallest observation is plotted against $(1 - 1/2)100/96$, the second smallest value against $(2 - 1/2)100/96$, and the highest value against $(37 - 1/2)100/96$.

Figure 8-8 suggests the log-normal distribution to be a reasonable choice, since the plotted points fall close to the line drawn (not all the points are plotted).

The probability of a failure in less than 80,000 miles is estimated from the cumulative scale as the value corresponding to the intersection of the 80,000-mile value on the observational scale and the plotted line. This value is approximately 15 per cent or 0.15. Thus the estimated reliability (probability of no failure) in the first 80,000 miles is 0.85. Also, from the 50th percentile, we obtain $\hat{\mu} = \ln(165,000) = 12.01$, and from the logarithms of the 90th and 10th percentiles $\hat{\sigma} = \frac{2}{5}[\ln(400,000) - \ln(66,000)] = 0.72$.

This evaluation indicated that the device was not capable of economically meeting the warranty requirements and that a thorough failure analysis and redesign was needed.

Table 8-2   Thousands of Miles to Failure for Diesel Locomotive Control Device[a]

22.5	69.5	93.5	120.0
37.5	76.5	102.5	122.5
46.0	77.0	107.0	123.0
48.5	78.5	108.5	127.5
51.5	80.0	112.5	131.0
53.0	81.5	113.5	132.5
54.5	82.0	116.0	134.0
57.5	83.0	117.0	
66.5	84.0	118.5	
68.0	91.5	119.0	

[a] Fifty-nine additional devices operated for 135,000 miles without failure.

The preceding analysis was not complicated by the fact that the data were censored. This is a general property of probability plotting, in contrast to statistical estimation techniques, which frequently become quite cumbersome for censored data.

The Gamma, Chi-Square and Exponential Distributions. The gamma distribution was discussed in Chapter 3. Its probability density function is

$$f(x; \eta, \lambda) = \frac{\lambda^{\eta}}{\Gamma(\eta)} x^{\eta-1} e^{-\lambda x}, \qquad 0 \leq x < \infty, \lambda > 0, \eta > 0. \qquad (8\text{-}1)$$

Because the shape of this distribution depends on η, there is no general probability paper on which samples from all gamma distributions plot as straight lines. Thus gamma probability plots can be prepared only for known values of η. Special probability paper is available for the cases where η equals 0.5, 1.0, 1.5, 2.0, 3.0, 4.0, or 5.0. Since the chi-square distribution is a special case of the gamma distribution, with scale parameter $\lambda = \frac{1}{2}$ and shape parameter γ (known as its degrees of freedom), equal to 2η (see Chapter 3), this paper is also applicable for plotting chi-square variates with 1, 2, 3, 4, 6, 8, and 10 degrees of freedom. In fact the paper is known as chi-square probability paper, rather than gamma probability paper. Thus to plot a gamma variate with $\eta = \frac{1}{2}$, we use one-degree-of-freedom chi-square probability paper. An exponential variate may be plotted on chi-square probability paper with two degrees of freedom, since the exponential distribution is a special case of the gamma distribution with $\eta = 1$.

Data plotted on chi-square probability paper should fall approximately on a straight line if the gamma distribution and the preselected value of η do in fact describe the data correctly. Divergence from linearity could be due either to the data not following a gamma distribution or to the true value of η differing from the one chosen.

When the required probability paper is not available—that is, when η has a value other than those indicated above—a technique for constructing gamma probability plots described in Reference 8-1 can be used.

The parameter λ of a gamma distribution with known η is estimated from a chi-square probability plot as half the slope of the plotted line—that is,

$$\hat{\lambda} = \frac{z_2 - z_1}{2(y_2 - y_1)}, \tag{8-2}$$

where y_1 and y_2 are two values on the observational scale and z_1 and z_2 are the corresponding values from the line as obtained from the special scale at the top of the paper. Note that for the special case where the gamma variate is also a chi-square variate, the slope of the plotted line should be approximately one, for $\lambda = \frac{1}{2}$.

The following example illustrates the technique. In a chemical analysis, a given contaminant can be measured analytically for amounts of 0.01 per cent or more. A sample is chosen from each of 16 lots and the per cent contaminant is found to be more than 0.01 per cent for 12 of the 16 analyses. Thus this is a censored sample with the four smallest observations missing. The data after ordering are shown in Table 8-3.

From experience it was thought that the distribution of per cent contaminant is exponential—that is, a gamma distribution with $\eta = 1$. The probability plot for the given data is shown in Fig. 8-9. The first plotted point corresponds to the fifth ordered sample and is plotted versus $(5 - \frac{1}{2})100/16$; the next value is plotted against $(6 - \frac{1}{2})100/16$, and so on.

The closeness of the plotted points to a straight line indicates that the model appears to represent the data reasonably well. The values of the

Table 8-3   Per Cent of Contaminant in a Chemical Compound

Ordered Observation Number	Per Cent Contaminant	Ordered Observation Number	Per Cent Contaminant	Ordered Observation Number	Per Cent Contaminant
1, 2, 3, 4	less than 0.0100	9	0.0231	14	0.0503
5	0.0120	10	0.0250	15	0.0689
6	0.0128	11	0.0305	16	0.0968
7	0.0139	12	0.0363		
8	0.0171	13	0.0402		

censored observations can be estimated by determining values on the plotted line corresponding to $(i - \frac{1}{2})100/n$, for $i = 1, 2, 3$, and 4—that is, the values on the observational scale corresponding to 3.1, 9.4, 15.6, and 21.9 on the cumulative scale. The resulting estimates are 0.0005, 0.0028, 0.0045, and 0.0065 per cent. The distribution scale parameter is estimated from two points on the line by (8-2) as

$$\hat{\lambda} = \frac{1}{2}\left(\frac{3.80 \ - \ 1.82}{0.053 - 0.026}\right) = 36.7.$$

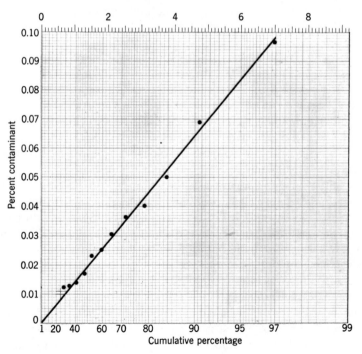

Fig. 8-9   Gamma probability plot of per cent of contaminant in a chemical compound plotted on two-degree-of-freedom chi-square probability paper.

The Weibull Distribution.   In Chapter 3 the Weibull cumulative distribution function was defined as

$$F(x) = 1 - \exp\left[-\left(\frac{x}{\sigma}\right)^{\eta}\right], \qquad 0 \le x < \infty, \eta > 0, \sigma > 0, \quad (8\text{-}3)$$

where σ and η are the scale and shape parameters respectively. It was implied earlier that there is no general probability paper for distributions that contain a shape parameter. However for the Weibull distribution the shape and scale parameters may be transformed, in effect, into scale and location parameters, respectively, and it is thus possible to construct a graph paper that can be used for all Weibull probability plots. From (8-3) we obtain

$$\frac{1}{1 - F(x)} = \exp\left[\left(\frac{x}{\sigma}\right)^{\eta}\right] \qquad (8\text{-}4)$$

and

$$\ln \ln \left[\frac{1}{1 - F(x)}\right] = \eta \ln x - \eta \ln \sigma. \qquad (8\text{-}5)$$

Thus for any Weibull variate $\ln \ln \{1/[1 - F(x)]\}$ will plot as a straight line against the natural logarithms of the observations. To avoid the need for computing $\ln \ln \{1/[1 - F(x)]\}$ and $\ln x$, the axes of the probability paper are scaled so that $(i - \frac{1}{2})100/n$ can be plotted on the ordinate, corresponding to $\ln \ln \{1/[1 - F(x)]\}$, and the observed values can be plotted on the abscissa, corresponding to $\ln x$. A sample of Weibull probability paper is shown in Fig. 8-10.

Equation 8-5 may be written as

$$W = a + bz, \qquad (8\text{-}6)$$

where

$$W = \ln \ln \left[\frac{1}{1 - F(x)}\right] \qquad (8\text{-}7)$$

$$z = \ln x \qquad (8\text{-}8)$$

$$b = \eta \qquad (8\text{-}9)$$

and

$$a = -\eta \ln \sigma. \qquad (8\text{-}10)$$

We can use (8-9) and (8-10) to estimate the Weibull distribution parameters from the probability plot as

$$\hat{\eta} = b, \qquad (8\text{-}11)$$

$$\hat{\sigma} = e^{-a/b}, \qquad (8\text{-}12)$$

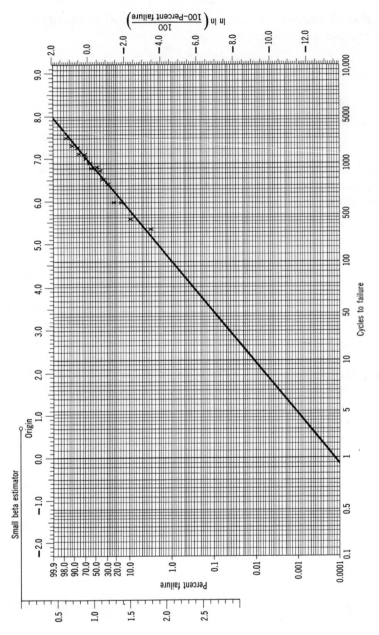

Fig. 8-10 Weibull probability plot of cycles to failure for carbide inserts.

288

where the values a and b are obtained as the y intercept and slope of the plotted line. The slope is

$$b = \frac{W_2 - W_1}{z_2 - z_1},$$ (8-13)

where W_2 and W_1 are two values of $\ln \ln \{1/[1 - F(x)]\}$ and where z_2 and z_1 are the corresponding values of $\ln x$ on the plotted line. These values are read, respectively, from the two auxiliary scales on the right ordinate and the top abscissa of Fig. 8-10.* The intercept is obtained as the value on the right-hand ordinate scale corresponding to the point where $\ln x = 0$ on the top abscissa scale. This procedure is illustrated by the following example.

Table 8-4   Failure Times for 16 Carbide Inserts (Cycles to Failure)

210	619	904	1256
271	698	1008	1417
396	811	1130	1500
402	900	1230	1621

The number of cycles to failure in a life test of 16 carbide inserts are shown in Table 8-4. We believe this variable might be Weibull distributed, hence the test results are plotted on Weibull probability paper in Fig. 8-10. The closeness of the plot to a straight line indicates that this model does appear to provide a reasonable representation of the data.

To estimate the slope of the plotted line values of $W_2 = 2.0$ and $W_1 = -8.0$ were chosen for $\ln \ln \{1/[1 - F(x)]\}$. The corresponding values of $\ln x$ obtained from the line are $z_2 = 7.98$ and $z_1 = 2.88$. Thus from (8-13)

$$\hat{\eta} = b = \frac{2.0 - (-8.0)}{7.98 - 2.88} = 1.96.$$

The intercept of the plotted line is estimated to be -13.5. Thus from (8-12)

$$\hat{\sigma} = e^{-(-13.5)/1.96} = 980.$$

Further details concerning Weibull distribution probability plots are given in Reference 8-2.

---

* The paper in Fig. 8-10 has a supplementary scale in the upper left-hand corner, which can be used to estimate η directly by laying a straightedge parallel to the plotted line through the point marked "origin" at the top and reading the slope from the extreme left-hand scale.

The Type I Extreme Value Distribution.   The cumulative extreme value distribution function for largest elements is

$$F(x) = \exp\left\{-e^{-[(x-\mu)/\sigma]}\right\} \quad -\infty < x < \infty, -\infty < \mu < \infty, \sigma > 0,$$

$$(8\text{-}14)$$

where μ and σ are location and scale parameters, respectively. Thus the reduced variate

$$y = -\ln\left[-\ln F(x)\right] = \frac{x-\mu}{\sigma}, \qquad (8\text{-}15)$$

will plot as a straight line against observations from this distribution. Extreme value probability paper is scaled so that $(i - \frac{1}{2})100/n$, can be plotted directly against the values of the ordered observations. Such paper is shown in Fig. 8-11, which also includes the line around which plotted points from a Type I extreme value distribution for largest elements with $\mu = 5$ and $\sigma = 1$ are scattered.

Equation 8-15 can be written as

$$y = bx - a, \qquad (8\text{-}16)$$

where

$$b = \frac{1}{\sigma} \qquad (8\text{-}17)$$

and

$$a = \frac{\mu}{\sigma}. \qquad (8\text{-}18)$$

Thus estimates of the extreme value distribution parameters can be obtained from the slope b and the intercept a of the plotted line as

$$\hat{\sigma} = \frac{1}{b} \qquad (8\text{-}19)$$

and

$$\hat{\mu} = \frac{-a}{b}. \qquad (8\text{-}20)$$

To obtain b the far left-hand ordinate y, corresponding to

$$-\ln\left\{-\ln\left[F(x)\right]\right\},$$

is used. Thus two values of y, y_1 and y_2, are selected and the corresponding observed values x_1 and x_2 are determined from the plotted line. Then

$$b = \frac{y_2 - y_1}{x_2 - x_1}. \qquad (8\text{-}21)$$

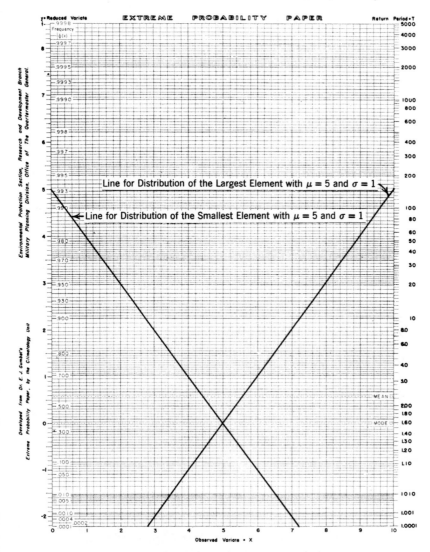

Fig. 8-11   Example of Type I extreme value probability paper.

The intercept is obtained as the value of y on the plotted line corresponding to $x = 0$. This might sometimes require extrapolation. Thus, for the line on Fig. 8-11, by setting $y_2 = 2$ and $y_1 = 0$, reading the corresponding values of $x_2 = 7$ and $x_1 = 5$, and obtaining the extrapolated intercept $a = -5$, we find $\hat{\sigma} = 1$ and $\hat{\mu} = 5$ from (8-19) to (8-21).

Because the Type I extreme value distribution for smallest elements is the mirror-image of that for largest elements the same probability paper is applicable for both. However, in preparing the plot for smallest elements the observations need be ranked in reverse order; that is, the highest observation is plotted against $(1 - \frac{1}{2})100/n$, the second highest against $(2 - \frac{1}{2})100/n$, and so on. The distribution parameters are estimated from the resulting plot as

$$\hat{\sigma} = \frac{-1}{b} \qquad (8\text{-}19a)$$

and

$$\hat{\mu} = \frac{-a}{b}, \qquad (8\text{-}20a)$$

again using the values of y on the furthest left-hand ordinate (in this case b will be negative). In examining the resulting probability plot and estimating percentiles, we must keep in mind that the plot shows $1 - F(x)$, the probability of a value *larger* than x rather than $F(x)$.

The line around which plotted points from a Type I extreme value distribution for smallest elements with $\mu = 5$ and $\sigma = 1$ are scattered is shown in Fig. 8-11. In checking the method for estimating parameters, we set $y_1 = 4$ and $y_2 = 0$, obtaining $x_1 = 1$ and $x_2 = 5$, read the intercept value $a = 5$, and from (8-19a), (8-20a) and (8-21) find $\hat{\sigma} = 1$ and $\hat{\mu} = 5$.

A further discussion of probability plots for the Type I extreme value distribution is given in Reference 8-3.

Beta and Uniform Distributions. Because the beta distribution has two shape parameters, no general probability paper can be constructed except when the values of both parameters are known. One such case is the uniform distribution, for which probability plots can be prepared on arithmetic paper. For this distribution it is preferable to plot the ordered observations against $100i/(n + 1)$, rather than against $(i - \frac{1}{2})100/n$, for reasons that will be indicated shortly.

FUNDAMENTALS OF PROBABILITY PLOTTING

A discussion of the basic principles of probability plotting requires an understanding of the meaning of *the expected value of an ordered obser-vation*. Assume a large number of samples of size n are selected from a population with probability density function $f(x)$ and cumulative distri-bution function $F(x)$. After each sample, the observations are ordered and relabeled x_i, $i = 1, 2, \ldots, n$, where x_i is the value of the ith smallest observation. For example, x_3 is the value of the third lowest observation in a particular sample.

Because x_i is a random variable, its value fluctuates from one sample to the next according to some probability distribution whose expected value, denoted $E(x_{i,n})$, is known as the expected value of the ith ordered observation from a sample of size n. It can be shown that

$$E(x_{i,n}) = \frac{n!}{(i-1)!\,(n-i)!} \int_0^1 x_i\,[F(x_i)]^{i-1}[1-F(x_i)]^{\,n-i}\,dF(x_i),$$

$$i = 1, 2, \ldots, n; \; -\infty < x_1 \le x_2 \le \cdots \le x_n < \infty. \quad (8\text{-}22)$$

For example, if x is a uniform variate over the interval $(0, 1)$—that is,

$$F(x) = x, \qquad 0 \le x \le 1$$

—then (8-22) reduces to

$$E(x_{i,n}) = \frac{i}{n+1}, \qquad i = 1, 2, \ldots, n.$$

The expected values of ordered observations have been tabulated for many distributions; see Reference 8-18. For distributions for which $E(x_{i,n})$ cannot be determined exactly, the following approximation is frequently used:

$$E(x_{i,n}) = F^{-1}\!\left(\frac{i-c}{n-2c+1}\right), \qquad i = 1, 2, \ldots, n, \quad (8\text{-}23)$$

where $F^{-1}\!\left(\dfrac{i-c}{n-2c+1}\right)$ is the value of x, such that

$$\frac{i-c}{n-2c+1} = \int_{-\infty}^x f(u)\,du,$$

that is, it is the $\left(\dfrac{i-c}{n-2c+1}\right)$-th fractile of the distribution, and c is a number which depends on n and $f(x)$ (see below).

For a single sample of size n, the first ordered observation x_1 is a one-sample estimate of $E(x_{1,n})$, x_2 is a one-sample estimate of $E(x_{2,n})$, and so on. Thus the ordered observed values, when plotted against their expected values,* would lie on approximately a straight line through the origin with slope 1.† The deviations about the line would be due to sampling fluctuations. For example, the ordered observations in a sample from a uniform distribution would plot on approximately a straight line against $i/(n+1)$. If the sample had been taken from some distribution other than the uniform, the plot would not be expected to be linear, because $i/(n+1)$ would

---

* Other central values of the distribution, such as the median or mode, are sometimes used instead of the expected value.

† The origin and slope of the plot will change if the variable is linearly transformed for plotting convenience, but the plot will remain a straight line.

no longer be the expected value of the ith ordered observation. Thus the linearity of the plot of the observations versus their expected values provides an evaluation of the adequacy of a chosen model.

The construction of specially scaled graph paper has obviated the need for actually calculating expected values for many distributions. This paper is scaled in such a fashion that the ordered observations can be plotted directly against $\dfrac{(i - c)100}{n - 2c + 1}$, without the need of determining $E(x_{i,n})$. In the previous discussion the use of $c = \frac{1}{2}$ has been implied, except when dealing with a uniform distribution. In general, the correct value of c depends on $f(x)$ and n, but $c = \frac{1}{2}$ has been found generally acceptable for a wide variety of distributions and sample sizes. There is, however, some controversy surrounding the choice of c and some authors prefer $c = 0$, which also has some desirable statistical properties (see References 8-3 to 8-7 for further details).

Occasionally the method of least squares is suggested for fitting a straight line to the plotted data, rather than fitting by eye. The simple least-squares method as described in most standard texts on statistics (see References 8-8 and 8-9) is not strictly applicable in this situation, because the ordered observations are not independent on account of the constraint that $x_{i+1} \geq x_i$ for all i. A more laborious technique, known as generalized least squares (see References 8-10 and 8-18), should be used. In general, this additional effort is not justified, because in the end a subjective decision must still be made.

8-2. Tests for Distributional Assumptions

INTRODUCTION

A statistical test of a distributional assumption provides an objective technique for assessing whether an assumed model provides an adequate description of observed data. The following basic steps are usually involved:

Step 1.   A number known as a *test statistic* is calculated from the observed data.

Step 2.   The probability of obtaining the calculated test statistic, assuming the selected model is correct, is determined. This is frequently done by referring to a table of percentiles of the distribution of the test statistic.

Step 3.   If the probability of obtaining the calculated test statistic is "low," we conclude that the assumed model does *not* provide an adequate representation. The definition of "low" depends on the user's preferences and the consequences of rejecting the model. A probability of 0.10 or 0.05 or less is frequently said to be "low." If the probability associated with the test statistic is not "low," then the data provide *no evidence* that the assumed model is inadequate.

It should be clearly understood that, although this procedure permits us to reject a model as inadequate, it *never* allows us to *prove* that the model is correct. In fact, the outcome of a statistical test depends highly upon the amount of available data—the more data there are, the better are the chances of rejecting an inadequate model. If too few data points are available, even a model that deviates grossly from the assumed model frequently cannot be established as inadequate.

A myriad of statistical tests to evaluate distributional assumptions have been evolved. Some are valid for specific models; others are applicable for a wide range of distributions. Many of the procedures require exact knowledge of the values of each of the parameters in the model. Because in most engineering problems the parameters are not known, but must be estimated, such tests will not be considered here. Of the remaining procedures, only two will be discussed: a series of tests developed by Shapiro and Wilk, known as W tests, and the chi-squared goodness-of-fit test. Reference 8-11 provides a bibliography of other tests.

The W tests to evaluate the assumption of a normal (or log-normal) and an exponential distribution, will be presented. The chi-squared test can be used for *any* distributional model, including the normal and exponential. However for these two cases the W tests are generally more powerful—that is, they provide a better chance of rejecting an incorrect model. Thus, when the data are limited, it is generally advisable to use the appropriate W test, rather than the chi-squared test, to evaluate the assumption of normality or of exponentiality.

THE W TESTS

Test to Evaluate the Assumption of a Normal or Log-Normal Distribution. The W test is shown in Reference 8-11 to be an effective procedure for evaluating the assumption of normality against a wide spectrum of nonnormal alternatives, even if only a relatively small number of observations are given. For example, if 20 samples are taken from a process that is actually exponentially distributed, the chances are about 80 out of 100 that by applying the W test we shall correctly conclude that the normal distribution does *not* give a reasonable representation.*

* This result is for a 5 per cent test—that is, we are ready to take a one-in-twenty chance of wrongly claiming the model inadequate when the underlying distribution is in fact normal.

To use the test for a random sample of size n, when $n \leq 50$ with observed values $x_{(1)}, x_{(2)}, \ldots, x_{(n)}$, we proceed as follows:

Step 1. Rearrange the observations to obtain the ordered sample $x_1, x_2, \ldots, x_n$, where $x_1 \leq x_2 \leq \cdots \leq x_n$.

Step 2. Compute

$$S^2 = \sum_{i=1}^{n} (x_i - \bar{x})^2 = \sum_{i=1}^{n} x_i^2 - \frac{\left(\sum_{i=1}^{n} x_i\right)^2}{n}, \tag{8-24}$$

where $\bar{x}$ is the data mean.

Step 3. If n is even, set $k = n/2$; if n is odd, set $k = (n-1)/2$. Then compute

$$b = a_n(x_n - x_1) + a_{n-1}(x_{n-1} - x_2) + \cdots + a_{n-k+1}(x_{n-k+1} - x_k)$$
$$= \sum_{i=1}^{k} a_{n-i+1}(x_{n-i+1} - x_i), \tag{8-25}$$

where the values of a_{n-i+1} for $i = 1, \ldots, k$, are given in Table IX at the end of the book for $n = 3, \ldots, 50$. Note that when n is odd, x_{k+1} does not enter into this computation.

Step 4. Compute the test statistic

$$W = \frac{b^2}{S^2}. \tag{8-26}$$

Step 5. Compare the calculated value of W with the percentiles of the distribution of this test statistic shown in our Table X. This table gives the minimum values of W that we would obtain with 1, 2, 5, 10, and 50 per cent probability as a function of n, if the data actually came from a normal distribution. Thus small values of W indicate non-normality. For example, if the value of W obtained from (8-26) is *less than* the five per cent tabulated value, there is less than one chance in 20 that the sample could have been drawn from a normal distribution. We might then conclude that the assumption of a normal distribution does not appear to be reasonable.

Step 6 (optional). The approximate probability of obtaining the calculated value of W, assuming a normally distributed variable, can be obtained by finding

$$z = \gamma + \eta \ln \left(\frac{W - \epsilon}{1 - W}\right) \tag{8-27}$$

using the values of γ, η, and ϵ given in Table XI at the back of the book for the appropriate sample size and then using Table I to determine the probability of obtaining a value less than or equal to z from a standardized normal distribution. The resulting value is the approximate probability that a sample such as the one obtained could have been drawn from a normal distribution.*

The following illustrates the use of the test. The amount of gasoline required by a random sample of 10 standard-size automobiles in a round trip from New York to San Francisco following a standard route were found to be as follows: 474, 303, 461, 457, 583, 469, 406, 515, 338, and 489 gallons. The W test is applied to evaluate the assumption that the distribution from which this sample of gasoline consumption values was obtained is normal.

Step 1. Ordering the observations according to magnitude yields $x_1 = 303$, $x_2 = 338, x_3 = 406, x_4 = 457, x_5 = 461, x_6 = 469, x_7 = 474, x_8 = 489$, $x_9 = 515, x_{10} = 583$.

Step 2. From (8-24), compute

$$S^2 = 2081131 - \frac{(4495)^2}{10} = 60628.$$

Step 3. Because $n = 10$, we set $k = 5$. From Table IX, $a_{10} = 0.5739$, $a_9 = 0.3291, \ldots, a_6 = 0.0399$. Using (8-25),
$b = 0.5739(583-303) + 0.3291(515-338) + \cdots + 0.0399(469-461)$
$= 239.113$.

Step 4. From (8-26), $W = \dfrac{(239.113)^2}{60628} = 0.943.$

Step 5. The calculated W *exceeds* the tabulated 50 per cent value of $W = 0.938$ obtained from Table X for $n = 10$.

Step 6. Alternatively, for $n = 10$ we find from Table XI that $\gamma = -3.262$, $\eta = 1.471$ and $\epsilon = 0.3660$. Thus, substituting in (8-27),

$$z = -3.262 + 1.471 \ln \left\{ \frac{0.943 - 0.366}{1 - 0.943} \right\} = 0.143.$$

From Table I,

$$\Pr \{z \le 0.143\} = 0.557.$$

The approximate probability of obtaining a value *as low as* the calculated W, if the sample were drawn from a normal distribution, is therefore found to be 0.557. Since this probability is high, we conclude that on the basis

* The reader will note from the given expressions that this procedure makes use of a Johnson S_B approximation (see Chapter 6) to the distribution of the W statistic.

of the *limited available data* there is no reason to reject the assumption that the normal distribution provides an adequate representation of the amount of gasoline required by different cars for the specified trip.

The W test may also be used to evaluate the assumption of a log-normal model. In this case the test is applied to either the common or the natural logarithms of the observations. This follows because if the logarithms of the values follow a normal distribution, then the original observations are log-normally distributed (see Chapter 3). An example of the application of the W test to evaluate the assumption of a log-normal distribution will be given later. The theory underlying the W test for normality and its relationship to probability plotting are described in Reference 8-11.

Test to Evaluate the Assumption of an Exponential Distribution—Origin Known (WE_0 Test).* The exponential probability density function [see (3-19)] can be generalized into a two-parameter model where one parameter, λ, scales the distribution and the second parameter, μ, defines the distribution origin—that is, the point above which all observations lie. The resulting probability density function is

$$f(x; \lambda, \mu) = \lambda e^{-\lambda(x-\mu)}, \qquad \mu \le x < \infty, -\infty < \mu < \infty, \lambda > 0. \quad (8\text{-}28)$$

In the following discussion it will be assumed that μ is known to equal zero. This leads to no loss of generality. If $\mu \ne 0$, but is known, we subtract μ from each observation. The resulting variable will have an origin of zero and the following results will hold. The test for the case where μ is not known will be discussed subsequently.

The procedure for assessing whether a random sample of from 7 to 35† observations could reasonably have been drawn from an exponential distribution with an origin of zero, known as the WE_0 *test*, is as follows.

Step 1.   Calculate the test statistic

$$WE_0 = \frac{\sum_{i=1}^{n}(x_i - \bar{x})^2}{\left(\sum_{i=1}^{n} x_i\right)^2} = \frac{\sum_{i=1}^{n} x_i^2 - \dfrac{\left(\sum_{i=1}^{n} x_i\right)^2}{n}}{\left(\sum_{i=1}^{n} x_i\right)^2} \quad (8\text{-}29)$$

where x_i, $i = 1, \ldots, n$, are the n observed values and $\bar{x}$ is the data mean.

Step 2.   Determine whether the computed value WE_0 lies outside the tabulated 95 per cent and 90 per cent ranges shown in Table XII as a

---

* The test described here is identical, except for a constant, to that suggested by Bartholomew in Reference 8-13.

† Percentiles of the distribution of WE_0 have not yet been tabulated for other sample sizes.

function of n. This test is two-sided, in that too-low or too-high values indicate nonexponentiality.* Thus if the computed value of WE_0 falls *outside* the 95 per cent range, the chances are less than one in twenty that the observed sample was drawn from an exponential distribution with the *assumed origin*. Values of WE_0 outside the 90 per cent range are similarly interpreted, but refer to a chance of one in ten or less.

Consider the following example. In 10 runs for a servosystem used for tracking objects, the errors in degrees were 0.09, 0.10, 0.13, 0.15, 0.16, 0.19, 0.20, 0.21, 0.23 and 0.27. It was desired to determine whether the assumption that this variable is exponentially distributed appears reasonable, on the basis of the data. Since the smallest possible error is zero, we set $\mu = 0$ and apply the WE_0 test. From the data,

$$\sum_{i=1}^{n} x_i = 1.73, \qquad \sum_{i=1}^{n} x_i^2 = 0.3291 \qquad \text{and } n = 10.$$

Using (8-29) yields

$$WE_0 = \frac{0.3291 - (1.73)^2/10}{(1.73)^2} = 0.010.$$

From Table XII for $n = 10$, it is seen that $WE_0 = 0.010$ is well below 0.025, the lower bound of the 95 per cent range. Thus, the chances are less than one in twenty that the location error is exponentially distributed *with an origin of zero*.

Further details about this test and its theoretical foundations are given in Reference 8-17.

Test to Evaluate the Assumption of an Exponential Distribution—Origin Unknown (WE Test). The following procedure, known as the *WE test*, can be used to test the assumption that a given sample of 7 to 35† observations came from the exponential distribution, (8-28), when the values of both parameters μ and λ are unknown.

Step 1.   Calculate the test statistic

$$WE = \frac{(\bar{x} - x_1)^2}{\sum_{i=1}^{n}(x_i - \bar{x})^2} = \frac{\left(\sum_{i=1}^{n} x_i/n - x_1\right)^2}{\sum_{i=1}^{n} x_i^2 - \frac{\left(\sum_{i=1}^{n} x_i\right)^2}{n}}, \qquad (8\text{-}30)$$

---

* The 90% range is the interval between the 5th and 95th percentiles of the distribution of the test statistic given the data came from an exponential distribution.

† Percentiles of the distribution of WE have not yet been tabulated for other sample sizes.

where x_i, $i = 1, \ldots, n$, are the n observed values, x_1 is the smallest value, and $\bar{x}$ is the data mean.

Step 2.   Compare the computed value WE with the 95 per cent and 90 per cent ranges given in Table XIII (at the back of the book). This is a two-sided test—that is, both too-high and too-low values indicate nonexponentiality. Thus, if the computed value falls *outside* the 95 or 90 per cent range, then the chances are less than one in 20 or one in 10, respectively, that the observed sample was drawn from an exponential distribution.

Using the tracking-system example, we wish to determine whether an exponential distribution with an arbitrary origin could be used as a model for location error. From (8-30),

$$WE = \frac{[(1.73/10) - 0.09]^2}{0.3291 - [(1.73)^2/10]} = 0.231.$$

Using Table XIII, we see that the upper bound of the 90 per cent range for WE is 0.231—that is, the probability is only about one in ten that the data came from an exponential distribution. A two-parameter exponential distribution thus also appears inadequate as a model for the distribution of location error.

Table 8-5   Time to Failures in Hours
for 20 Guidance Systems

1	20	95	268
4	40	106	459
5	40	125	827
6	60	151	840
15	93	200	1089

The theoretical details concerning this test are given in Reference 8-17.

Further Example.   The following example illustrates the use of the exponential and log-normal W tests and emphasizes the importance of testing for distributional assumptions.

The times to failure in hours for 20 guidance systems are given in Table 8-5. It was planned to determine system reliability for a 10-hour mission from the data, assuming an exponential distribution with $\mu = 0$ for the time to failure. Before conducting this analysis it was decided to use the WE_0 test to evaluate the adequacy of the distributional assumption.

From the data we obtain

$$\sum_{i=1}^{n} x_i^2 = 2,972,794, \qquad \sum_{i=1}^{n} x_i = 4444, \qquad n = 20.$$

Using (8-29) yields

$$WE_0 = \frac{2,972,794 - (4444)^2/20}{(4444)^2} = 0.100.$$

The 95 per cent range for $n = 20$ is found from Table XII to be 0.021 to 0.090. Because the calculated value of WE_0 is outside this range, the chances are less than one in 20 that the given data could have come from an exponential distribution.

If system reliability were predicted for a 10-hour mission assuming an exponential distribution, its value would have been calculated as

$$\text{Pr (survival for 10 hours)} = 1 - F(10; \lambda) = 1 - \int_0^{10} \lambda e^{-\lambda t}\, dt = e^{-10\lambda}.$$

In this equation the estimate $\hat{\lambda}$ calculated from the data is used in place of the unknown parameter. This estimate, obtained from (3-43), is

$$\hat{\lambda} = \frac{\text{total number of failures}}{\text{total test time}} = \frac{20}{4444} = 0.0045.$$

Thus the estimated reliability is $e^{-(0.0045)10} = 0.9560$. However, this result is invalid, because it is based on an assumed model that has been found to be unreasonable. An examination of the data, in fact, indicated that four out of 20 failures occurred in less than 10 hours.

Let us examine another model. It is thought from physical considerations that a log-normal distribution might be appropriate in representing the time to failure. This hypothesis may be evaluated by the W test for normality, using the common or natural logarithms of the failure times instead of the original observations.

Thus (8-24) to (8-26) yield

$$W = \frac{\left[\sum\limits_{i=1}^{10} a_{20-i+1}(y_{20-i+1} - y_i)\right]^2}{\sum\limits_{i=1}^{20} y_i^2 - \dfrac{\left(\sum\limits_{i=1}^{20} y_i\right)^2}{n}},$$

where y_i is the logarithm of the ith ordered observation and the a_i's are given in Table IX. For the given data we find $W = 0.9625$.

The approximate probability of obtaining a value of W as low as that observed assuming the true distribution to be log-normal is obtained by substitution in (8-27), using the values $\gamma = -5.153$, $\eta = 1.802$, and $\epsilon = 0.2359$ obtained from Table XI for $n = 20$. This yields $z = 0.19$. From Table I, the desired probability is found to be Pr $(z < 0.19) = 0.57$.

Thus, on the basis of the data, the log-normal distribution appears to be a reasonable model for time to failure. System reliability for a 10-hour mission based on this model is

$$\text{Pr (survival for 10 hours)} = 1 - F(\ln 10; \mu, \sigma)$$

$$= 1 - \int_{-\infty}^{\ln 10} (2\pi\sigma^2)^{-\frac{1}{2}} \exp\left[-\frac{1}{2}\left(\frac{y-\mu}{\sigma}\right)^2\right] dy.$$

The sample estimates are used in place of the unknown parameters μ and σ. From the data and (6-13a) and (6-13c) we obtain $\hat{\mu} = 4.15$ and $s = 1.93$. Thus we require the probability of a standard normal deviate taking on a value more than

$$z = \frac{\ln 10 - 4.15}{1.93} = -0.96,$$

which is found to be 0.83 from Table I. This estimate of the 10-hour system reliability differs appreciably from that obtained assuming an exponential distribution for time to failure, and appears to be in better agreement with the given data.

THE CHI-SQUARED GOODNESS-OF-FIT TEST*

Introduction. The oldest, most commonly used, and perhaps most versatile procedure for evaluating distributional assumptions is the *chi-squared goodness-of-fit test*. To use this test, the given data are grouped into frequency cells and compared to the expected number of observations based on the proposed distribution. From this comparison a test statistic that approximately follows a chi-square distribution (see Chapter 3) *only* if the assumed model is correct is calculated. The test statistic will tend to exceed a chi-square variate if the assumed model is *not* correct. Thus Table IV (at the back of the book), which gives percentiles for the chi-square distribution, may be used to determine whether the data provide evidence contrary to the assumed model. The specific calculational procedure is described below; the reader interested in a more detailed discussion, including the underlying theory, should consult Reference 8-14.

The major advantage of the chi-squared test is its versatility. · It can be applied simply to test *any* distributional assumption, without our having to know the values of the distribution parameters. Its major drawbacks are its lack of sensitivity in detecting inadequate models when few observations are available, and the frequent need to arrange the data into arbitrary cells, which can affect the outcome of the test.

---

* Both the terms chi-square and chi-squared are in frequent usage. We have chosen to speak of the *chi-square* distribution and the *chi-squared* test.

Operational Instructions.   The chi-squared test is used as follows.

Step 1.   Estimate each of the unknown parameters of the assumed distribution. To be theoretically correct, the method of maximum likelihood should be used after the data have been arranged in frequency cells. For practical convenience, however, the various techniques indicated in this book for estimating parameters may be applied to the original data.

Step 2.   Divide the data into k classes or cells and determine the probability of a random value from the assumed model falling within each class. We shall consider two methods for doing this: the first is applicable if the data are initially arranged in frequency classes or can be naturally assigned to such classes. This would be the case when the observations are from a discrete distribution, such as the Poisson. The second method applies when the data are not initially tabulated in classes.

Method a.   The number of cells, k, will be the number of classes of the tabulated data subject to the restriction that the expected number of observations in each cell under the assumed model (see below) is at least five. If this number turns out to be less than five for any cell, the cell should be combined with an adjoining cell or cells so that the expected number in the combined cell is at least five.*

Let CL_i and CU_i denote the lower and upper bounds of the ith frequency cell. The distribution of the assumed model (using the estimated parameters) is then used to estimate

$$\Pr (CL_i \leq x < CU_i), \qquad i = 1, 2, \ldots, k \qquad (8\text{-}31)$$

—that is, the probability of a random observation falling within each class is estimated.

Method b.   In this case the choice of k is more arbitrary. When the number of observations, n, is large (say, over 200) one possible rule is to take k as the integer closest to

$$k' = 4[0.75(n - 1)^2]^{1/5} \qquad (8\text{-}32)$$

(see References 8-12 and 8-15). For moderate values of n a good rule is to make k as large as possible, subject to the restriction that it must

---

* This often means that cells involving extreme observations must be combined and the test will be insensitive to deviations from the assumed model in the distribution tails. In light of this problem, some writers have suggested using smaller cells than indicated above and, in some cases, correcting the calculated value of the test statistic appropriately, see Reference 8.14.

not exceed $n/5$.* The cell boundaries $x_1, x_2, \ldots, x_k$ are determined from the cumulative distribution for the assumed model (using the estimated parameters) as the values such that

$$\Pr(x \le x_1) = 1/k, \Pr(x \le x_2) = \frac{2}{k}, \ldots, \Pr(x \le x_{k-1}) = \frac{(k-1)}{k}.$$

The lower bound of the first cell and the upper bound of the last cell are the smallest and largest values that the random variable may take on. We have thus set up the cell boundaries in such a way that the probability of a random value falling within a given class is estimated to be $1/k$ for each class.

Step 3. Multiply each of the cell probabilities by the sample size n. This yields the expected number E_i of observations for each cell under the *assumed model*. For Method 2a, we obtain E_i by multiplying the probabilities obtained from (8-31) by n. For Method 2b

$$E_i = \frac{n}{k}, \qquad i = 1, 2, \ldots, k. \tag{8-33}$$

Step 4. If the data are not initially tabulated, count the number of observed values in each cell. Denote this number as M_i, where $i = 1, 2, \ldots, k$. Otherwise, determine the M_i directly.

Step 5. Compute the test statistic

$$X^2 = \sum_{i=1}^{k} \frac{(M_i - E_i)^2}{E_i}. \tag{8-34}$$

Note that for Method 2b this expression simplifies to

$$X^2 = \frac{k}{n}\left(\sum_{i=1}^{k} M_i^2\right) - n. \tag{8-35}$$

Step 6. Compare the computed value X^2 with the tabulated percentiles for a chi-square variate as given in Table IV, using $k - r - 1$ degrees of freedom, where r is the number of parameters that were estimated in Step 1. (A more complete tabulation of chi-square percentiles is given in Reference 8-16). High values of X^2 signify that the observed data contradicts the assumed model. For example, if the above calculated value X^2 exceeds the 0.95 tabulated value of chi square, the chances are less than one in twenty that the data could have emanated from the assumed distribution and the model is

* So that the expected number of observations per cell is at least 5. However, see preceding footnote.

frequently rejected as inadequate. In this case it is instructive to compare the actual with the expected frequencies to see which classes contributed most heavily to the value of X^2. This provides an indication of the nature of the deviations from the assumed model.

The chi-squared test will be used to evaluate the reasonableness of an exponential model for time to failure for the guidance systems for which data are given in Table 8-5. In this example the data are not naturally grouped, and thus the second method of setting up frequency classes is applicable.

The procedure is as follows:

Step 1.   Using the methods of Chapter 3, we previously obtained $\lambda = 0.0045$.

Step 2.   Since $n = 20$, (8-32) is not applicable. Instead, the number of classes, k, will be chosen to equal $n/5$, so that $k = 20/5 = 4$. The cumulative exponential distribution function was given by (3-20) as $F(t; \lambda) = 1 - e^{-\lambda t}$, and hence the cell boundaries are obtained by setting:

$$\Pr(x \leq x_1) = 1 - e^{-0.0045 x_1} = \frac{1}{k} = 0.25,$$

$$\Pr(x \leq x_2) = 1 - e^{-0.0045 x_2} = \frac{2}{k} = 0.50,$$

$$\Pr(x \leq x_3) = 1 - e^{-0.0045 x_3} = \frac{3}{k} = 0.75,$$

and solving for x_1, x_2, and x_3.

Thus $x_1 = 64$, $x_2 = 154$, and $x_3 = 308$. Since an exponential variate (with $\mu = 0$) varies from 0 to ∞, the lower bound of the first cell is 0 and the upper bound of the last cell is ∞. The probability of a random value falling in a cell is estimated as 0.25 for each cell.

Step 3.   The expected number of observations per cell under the assumed model is found from (8-33) to be $E_i = n/k = 5$ for $i = 1, 2, 3,$ and 4.

Step 4.   The actual number of observations M_i in the ith class is obtained directly from the original observations in Table 8-5. The resulting comparison of M_i and E_i is shown in Table 8-6.

Step 5.   Using (8-35), the test statistic is

$$X^2 = \tfrac{4}{20}(9^2 + 5^2 + 2^2 + 4^2) - 20 = 5.2.$$

Table 8-6   Comparison of Actual and Expected Cell Frequencies Assuming Exponential Distribution for Guidance-System Times to Failure

Cell	Actual Number of Observations (M_i)	Expected Number of Observations Under Assumed Model (E_i)
0 to 63.9	9	5
64.0 to 153.9	5	5
154.0 to 307.9	2	5
308.0 and more	4	5

Step 6.   Since only one parameter was estimated from the data, $r = 1$; thus the degrees of freedom of the applicable chi-square variate are $k - r - 1 = 4 - 1 - 1 = 2$. Referring to Table IV for two degrees of freedom, we obtain

$$\Pr \{\chi^2(2) > 6.0\} = 0.05$$

and

$$\Pr (\chi^2(2) > 4.6) = 0.10,$$

hence the probability of obtaining a value of X^2 as large as 5.2 under the assumed model is between 5 and 10 per cent. Thus the probability is low that the observations came from an exponential distribution. We also note from Table 8-6 that the largest deviation of the data from the proposed exponential distribution model arises in the lower tail of the distribution—the region of greatest interest in this problem.

Let us examine another problem that illustrates the situation where the data are grouped initially. In a repair shop for klystron tubes a new inventory policy is to be developed to minimize costs. One of the required inputs is the number of parts used each week; this is believed to follow a Poisson distribution. In order to evaluate the reasonableness of this model, a chi-squared test is applied to the weekly demands over a one-year period shown in the first two columns of Table 8-7.

We proceed as follows:

Step 1.   From (4-10), the estimate of the parameter of the Poisson distribution is

$$\lambda = \frac{\text{number of parts used}}{\text{number of weeks}} = \frac{62}{52} = 1.2.$$

Step 2.   The cells are naturally established as 0 parts used, 1 part used, and so on. The expected cell probabilities are obtained from a

Table 8-7   Weekly Usage for Specified Part Over a One-Year Period and Expected Usage, Assuming a Poisson Distribution

Number of Parts Used Per Week	Actual Number of Weeks (M_i)	Expected Number of Weeks Assuming Poisson Distribution Model (E_i)
0	18	15.7
1	18	18.8
2	8	11.3
3	5⎫	4.5⎫
4	2⎬ 8	1.4⎬ 6.2
5	1⎭	0.3⎭
Total	52	52.0

tabulation of the Poisson-distribution probabilities given in Reference 4-8, using $\lambda = 1.2$, as follows:

x	Probability
0	0.301
1	0.361
2	0.217
3	0.087
4	0.026
5 or more	0.007

Step 3.   Multiplying these probabilities by 52 gives the expected number E_i shown in the third column of Table 8-7. Since the expected number in the last three cells total less than five, both the actual and the expected values for these cells are combined.

Step 4.   The count, M_i, representing the original observed values, is shown in the second column of Table 8-7.

Step 5.   From (8-34) the value of the test statistic is

$$X^2 = \frac{(18 - 15.7)^2}{15.7} + \frac{(18 - 18.8)^2}{18.8} + \frac{(8 - 11.3)^2}{11.3} + \frac{(8 - 6.2)^2}{6.2} = 1.86.$$

Step 6.   By interpolating in Table IV for $4 - 1 - 1 = 2$ degrees of freedom, we find $\Pr(\chi^2(2) > 1.86)$ is approximately 0.4. Thus the observed data do not contradict the assumption of a Poisson distribution for weekly part usage.

References

8-1   M. B. Wilk, R. Gnanadesikan, and M. J. Huyett, "Probability Plots for the Gamma Distribution," *Technometrics*, **4**, 1 (1962).

8-2   J. H. K. Kao, "A Summary of Some New Techniques on Failure Analysis," *Proc. 6th Nat. Symp. Reliability Quality Control in Electron.*, pp. 190–201, 1960.

8-3   E. J. Gumbel, *Statistics of Extremes*, Columbia University Press, New York, 1958.

8-4   G. Blom, *Statistical Estimates and Transformed Beta-Variables*, John Wiley and Sons, New York, 1958.

8-5   H. Chernoff and G. J. Lieberman, "Use of Normal Probability Paper," *J. Am. Statist. Assn.*, **49**, 778 (1954).

8-6   H. L. Harter, "Expected Values of Normal Order Statistics," *Biometrika*, **48**, 151 (1961).

8-7   B. F. Kimball, "On the Choice of Plotting Positions on Probability Paper," *J. Am. Statist. Assn.*, **55**, 546 (1960).

8-8   O. L. Davies, *Statistical Methods in Research and Production*, 3rd ed., Hafner Publishing Co., New York, 1957.

8-9   W. J. Dixon and F. J. Massey, *Introduction to Statistical Analysis*, 2nd ed., McGraw-Hill Book Co., New York, 1957.

8-10 A. C. Aitken, "On Least Squares and Linear Combination of Observations," *Proc. Royal Soc. Edinburgh*, **55**, 42 (1935).

8-11 S. S. Shapiro and M. B. Wilk, "An Analysis of Variance Test for Normality (complete samples)," *Biometrika*, **52**, 591 (1965).

8-12 C. A. Williams, "On the Choice of the Number and Width of Classes for the Chi-square Test of Goodness of Fit," *Jour. Am. Stat. Assn.*, **45**, 77 (1950).

8-13 D. J. Bartholomew, "Testing for Departure from the Exponential Distribution," *Biometrika*, **44**, 253 (1957).

8-14 W. G. Cochran, "The χ^2 Test of Goodness of Fit," *Ann. Math. Statist.*, **23**, 315 (1952).

8-15 H. B. Mann and A. Wald, "On the Choice of the Number of Intervals in the Application of the χ^2 Test," *Ann. Math. Statist.*, **13**, 306 (1942).

8-16 H. L. Harter, *New Tables of the Incomplete Gamma-Function Ratio and of Percentage Points of the Chi-square and Beta Distributions*, Aerospace Research Laboratory, U.S. Air Force, Dayton, Ohio, 1964.

8-17 S. S. Shapiro and M. B. Wilk, "Testing for Distributional Assumptions—Exponential and Uniform Distributions," unpublished manuscript.

8-18 A. E. Sarhan and B. G. Greenberg, *Contributions to Order Statistics*, John Wiley and Sons, New York, 1962.

Tables

Table I   Table of the Standard Cumulative Normal Distribution

$$F(y) = (2\pi)^{-\frac{1}{2}} \int_{-\infty}^{y} e^{-z^2/2}\, dz \qquad y = 0.00\ (0.01)\ 4.99*$$

y	·00	·01	·02	·03	·04	·05	·06	·07	·08	·09
·0	·5000	·5040	·5080	·5120	·5160	·5199	:5239	·5279	·5319	·5359
·1	·5398	·5438	·5478	·5517	·5557	·5596	·5636	·5675	·5714	·5753
·2	·5793	·5832	·5871	·5910	·5948	·5987	·6026	·6064	·6103	·6141
·3	·6179	·6217	·6255	·6293	·6331	·6368	·6406	·6443	·6480	·6517
·4	·6554	·6591	·6628	·6664	·6700	·6736	·6772	·6808	·6844	·6879
·5	·6915	·6950	·6985	·7019	·7054	·7088	·7123	·7157	·7190	·7224
·6	·7257	·7291	·7324	·7357	·7389	·7422	·7454	·7486	·7517	·7549
·7	·7580	·7611	·7642	·7673	·7703	·7734	·7764	·7794	·7823	·7852
·8	·7881	·7910	·7939	·7967	·7995	·8023	·8051	·8078	·8106	·8133
·9	·8159	·8186	·8212	·8238	·8264	·8289	·8315	·8340	·8365	·8389
1·0	·8413	·8438	·8461	·8485	·8508	·8531	·8554	·8577	·8599	·8621
1·1	·8643	·8665	·8686	·8708	·8729	·8749	·8770	·8790	·8810	·8830
1·2	·8849	·8869	·8888	·8907	·8925	·8944	·8962	·8980	·8997	·90147
1·3	·90320	·90490	·90658	·90824	·90988	·91149	·91309	·91466	·91621	·91774
1·4	·91924	·92073	·92220	·92364	·92507	·92647	·92785	·92922	·93056	·93189
1·5	·93319	·93448	·93574	·93699	·93822	·93943	·94062	·94179	·94295	·94408
1·6	·94520	·94630	·94738	·94845	·94950	·95053	·95154	·95254	·95352	·95449
1·7	·95543	·95637	·95728	·95818	·95907	·95994	·96080	·96164	·96246	·96327
1·8	·96407	·96485	·96562	·96638	·96712	·96784	·96856	·96926	·96995	·97062
1·9	·97128	·97193	·97257	·97320	·97381	·97441	·97500	·97558	·97615	·97670
2·0	·97725	·97778	·97831	·97882	·97932	·97982	·98030	·98077	·98124	·98169
2·1	·98214	·98257	·98300	·98341	·98382	·98422	·98461	·98500	·98537	·98574
2·2	·98610	·98645	·98679	·98713	·98745	·98778	·98809	·98840	·98870	·98899
2·3	·98928	·98956	·98983	$\cdot 9^2 0097$	$\cdot 9^2 0358$	$\cdot 9^2 0613$	$\cdot 9^2 0863$	$\cdot 9^2 1106$	$\cdot 9^2 1344$	$\cdot 9^2 1576$
2·4	$\cdot 9^2 1802$	$\cdot 9^2 2024$	$\cdot 9^2 2240$	$\cdot 9^2 2451$	$\cdot 9^2 2656$	$\cdot 9^2 2857$	$\cdot 9^2 3053$	$\cdot 9^2 3244$	$\cdot 9^2 3431$	$\cdot 9^2 3613$
2·5	$\cdot 9^2 3790$	$\cdot 9^2 3963$	$\cdot 9^2 4132$	$\cdot 9^2 4297$	$\cdot 9^2 4457$	$\cdot 9^2 4614$	$\cdot 9^2 4766$	$\cdot 9^2 4915$	$\cdot 9^2 5060$	$\cdot 9^2 5201$
2·6	$\cdot 9^2 5339$	$\cdot 9^2 5473$	$\cdot 9^2 5604$	$\cdot 9^2 5731$	$\cdot 9^2 5855$	$\cdot 9^2 5975$	$\cdot 9^2 6093$	$\cdot 9^2 6207$	$\cdot 9^2 6319$	$\cdot 9^2 6427$
2·7	$\cdot 9^2 6533$	$\cdot 9^2 6636$	$\cdot 9^2 6736$	$\cdot 9^2 6833$	$\cdot 9^2 6928$	$\cdot 9^2 7020$	$\cdot 9^2 7110$	$\cdot 9^2 7197$	$\cdot 9^2 7282$	$\cdot 9^2 7365$
2·8	$\cdot 9^2 7445$	$\cdot 9^2 7523$	$\cdot 9^2 7599$	$\cdot 9^2 7673$	$\cdot 9^2 7744$	$\cdot 9^2 7814$	$\cdot 9^2 7882$	$\cdot 9^2 7948$	$\cdot 9^2 8012$	$\cdot 9^2 8074$
2·9	$\cdot 9^2 8134$	$\cdot 9^2 8193$	$\cdot 9^2 8250$	$\cdot 9^2 8305$	$\cdot 9^2 8359$	$\cdot 9^2 8411$	$\cdot 9^2 8462$	$\cdot 9^2 8511$	$\cdot 9^2 8559$	$\cdot 9^2 8605$
3·0	$\cdot 9^2 8650$	$\cdot 9^2 8694$	$\cdot 9^2 8736$	$\cdot 9^2 8777$	$\cdot 9^2 8817$	$\cdot 9^2 8856$	$\cdot 9^2 8893$	$\cdot 9^2 8930$	$\cdot 9^2 8965$	$\cdot 9^2 8999$
3·1	$\cdot 9^3 0324$	$\cdot 9^3 0646$	$\cdot 9^3 0957$	$\cdot 9^3 1260$	$\cdot 9^3 1553$	$\cdot 9^3 1836$	$\cdot 9^3 2112$	$\cdot 9^3 2378$	$\cdot 9^3 2636$	$\cdot 9^3 2886$
3·2	$\cdot 9^3 3129$	$\cdot 9^3 3363$	$\cdot 9^3 3590$	$\cdot 9^3 3810$	$\cdot 9^3 4024$	$\cdot 9^3 4230$	$\cdot 9^3 4429$	$\cdot 9^3 4623$	$\cdot 9^3 4810$	$\cdot 9^3 4991$
3·3	$\cdot 9^3 5166$	$\cdot 9^3 5335$	$\cdot 9^3 5499$	$\cdot 9^3 5658$	$\cdot 9^3 5811$	$\cdot 9^3 5959$	$\cdot 9^3 6103$	$\cdot 9^3 6242$	$\cdot 9^3 6376$	$\cdot 9^3 6505$
3·4	$\cdot 9^3 6631$	$\cdot 9^3 6752$	$\cdot 9^3 6869$	$\cdot 9^3 6982$	$\cdot 9^3 7091$	$\cdot 9^3 7197$	$\cdot 9^3 7299$	$\cdot 9^3 7398$	$\cdot 9^3 7493$	$\cdot 9^3 7585$
3·5	$\cdot 9^3 7674$	$\cdot 9^3 7759$	$\cdot 9^3 7842$	$\cdot 9^3 7922$	$\cdot 9^3 7999$	$\cdot 9^3 8074$	$\cdot 9^3 8146$	$\cdot 9^3 8215$	$\cdot 9^3 8282$	$\cdot 9^3 8347$
3·6	$\cdot 9^3 8409$	$\cdot 9^3 8469$	$\cdot 9^3 8527$	$\cdot 9^3 8583$	$\cdot 9^3 8637$	$\cdot 9^3 8689$	$\cdot 9^3 8739$	$\cdot 9^3 8787$	$\cdot 9^3 8834$	$\cdot 9^3 8879$
3·7	$\cdot 9^3 8922$	$\cdot 9^3 8964$	$\cdot 9^4 0039$	$\cdot 9^4 0426$	$\cdot 9^4 0799$	$\cdot 9^4 1158$	$\cdot 9^4 1504$	$\cdot 9^4 1838$	$\cdot 9^4 2159$	$\cdot 9^4 2468$
3·8	$\cdot 9^4 2765$	$\cdot 9^4 3052$	$\cdot 9^4 3327$	$\cdot 9^4 3593$	$\cdot 9^4 3848$	$\cdot 9^4 4094$	$\cdot 9^4 4331$	$\cdot 9^4 4558$	$\cdot 9^4 4777$	$\cdot 9^4 4988$
3·9	$\cdot 9^4 5190$	$\cdot 9^4 5385$	$\cdot 9^4 5573$	$\cdot 9^4 5753$	$\cdot 9^4 5926$	$\cdot 9^4 6092$	$\cdot 9^4 6253$	$\cdot 9^4 6406$	$\cdot 9^4 6554$	$\cdot 9^4 6696$
4·0	$\cdot 9^4 6833$	$\cdot 9^4 6964$	$\cdot 9^4 7090$	$\cdot 9^4 7211$	$\cdot 9^4 7327$	$\cdot 9^4 7439$	$\cdot 9^4 7546$	$\cdot 9^4 7649$	$\cdot 9^4 7748$	$\cdot 9^4 7843$
4·1	$\cdot 9^4 7934$	$\cdot 9^4 8022$	$\cdot 9^4 8106$	$\cdot 9^4 8186$	$\cdot 9^4 8263$	$\cdot 9^4 8338$	$\cdot 9^4 8409$	$\cdot 9^4 8477$	$\cdot 9^4 8542$	$\cdot 9^4 8605$
4·2	$\cdot 9^4 8665$	$\cdot 9^4 8723$	$\cdot 9^4 8778$	$\cdot 9^4 8832$	$\cdot 9^4 8882$	$\cdot 9^4 8931$	$\cdot 9^4 8978$	$\cdot 9^5 0226$	$\cdot 9^5 0655$	$\cdot 9^5 1066$
4·3	$\cdot 9^5 1460$	$\cdot 9^5 1837$	$\cdot 9^5 2199$	$\cdot 9^5 2545$	$\cdot 9^5 2876$	$\cdot 9^5 3193$	$\cdot 9^5 3497$	$\cdot 9^5 3788$	$\cdot 9^5 4066$	$\cdot 9^5 4332$
4·4	$\cdot 9^5 4587$	$\cdot 9^5 4831$	$\cdot 9^5 5065$	$\cdot 9^5 5288$	$\cdot 9^5 5502$	$\cdot 9^5 5706$	$\cdot 9^5 5902$	$\cdot 9^5 6089$	$\cdot 9^5 6268$	$\cdot 9^5 6439$
4·5	$\cdot 9^5 6602$	$\cdot 9^5 6759$	$\cdot 9^5 6908$	$\cdot 9^5 7051$	$\cdot 9^5 7187$	$\cdot 9^5 7318$	$\cdot 9^5 7442$	$\cdot 9^5 7561$	$\cdot 9^5 7675$	$\cdot 9^5 7784$
4·6	$\cdot 9^5 7888$	$\cdot 9^5 7987$	$\cdot 9^5 8081$	$\cdot 9^5 8172$	$\cdot 9^5 8258$	$\cdot 9^5 8340$	$\cdot 9^5 8419$	$\cdot 9^5 8494$	$\cdot 9^5 8566$	$\cdot 9^5 8634$
4·7	$\cdot 9^5 8699$	$\cdot 9^5 8761$	$\cdot 9^5 8821$	$\cdot 9^5 8877$	$\cdot 9^5 8931$	$\cdot 9^5 8983$	$\cdot 9^6 0320$	$\cdot 9^6 0789$	$\cdot 9^6 1235$	$\cdot 9^6 1661$
4·8	$\cdot 9^6 2067$	$\cdot 9^6 2453$	$\cdot 9^6 2822$	$\cdot 9^6 3173$	$\cdot 9^6 3508$	$\cdot 9^6 3827$	$\cdot 9^6 4131$	$\cdot 9^6 4420$	$\cdot 9^6 4696$	$\cdot 9^6 4958$
4·9	$\cdot 9^6 5208$	$\cdot 9^6 5446$	$\cdot 9^6 5673$	$\cdot 9^6 5889$	$\cdot 9^6 6094$	$\cdot 9^6 6289$	$\cdot 9^6 6475$	$\cdot 9^6 6652$	$\cdot 9^6 6821$	$\cdot 9^6 6981$

* From A. Hald, *Statistical Tables and Formulas*, John Wiley and Sons, 1952 (Table II).

Table II   Table of the Factor $t_{CL,n-1}$ for Obtaining Two-sided Confidence Interval for the Mean*

$n-1$ \ CL	0.9	0.95	0.99
1	6.314	12.71	63.66
2	2.920	4.303	9.925
3	2.353	3.182	5.841
4	2.132	2.776	4.604
5	2.015	2.571	4.032
6	1.943	2.447	3.707
7	1.895	2.365	3.499
8	1.860	2.306	3.355
9	1.833	2.262	3.250
10	1.812	2.228	3.169
11	1.796	2.201	3.106
12	1.782	2.179	3.055
13	1.771	2.160	3.012
14	1.761	2.145	2.977
15	1.753	2.131	2.947
16	1.746	2.120	2.921
17	1.740	2.110	2.898
18	1.734	2.101	2.878
19	1.729	2.093	2.861
20	1.725	2.086	2.845
21	1.721	2.080	2.831
22	1.717	2.074	2.819
23	1.714	2.069	2.807
24	1.711	2.064	2.797
25	1.708	2.060	2.787
26	1.706	2.056	2.779
27	1.703	2.052	2.771
28	1.701	2.048	2.763
29	1.699	2.045	2.756
30	1.697	2.042	2.750
40	1.684	2.021	2.704
50	1.676	2.009	2.678
60	1.671	2.000	2.660
80	1.664	1.990	2.639
100	1.660	1.984	2.626
200	1.653	1.972	2.601
500	1.648	1.965	2.586
∞	1.645	1.960	2.576

* The greater part of this table is reproduced from Table III of R. A. Fisher and F. Yates *Statistical Tables,* Oliver and Boyd, Ltd., Edinburgh, England (1953) by permission of the authors and the publishers.

312

Table III   Table of the Factor $t'_{CL,n-1}$ for Obtaining One-sided Confidence Interval for the Mean*

$n-1$ \\ CL	0.90	0.95	0.99
1	3.078	6.314	31.82
2	1.886	2.920	6.965
3	1.638	2.353	4.541
4	1.533	2.132	3.747
5	1.476	2.015	3.365
6	1.440	1.943	3.143
7	1.415	1.895	2.998
8	1.397	1.860	2.896
9	1.383	1.833	2.821
10	1.372	1.812	2.764
11	1.363	1.796	2.718
12	1.356	1.782	2.681
13	1.350	1.771	2.650
14	1.345	1.761	2.624
15	1.341	1.753	2.602
16	1.337	1.746	2.583
17	1.333	1.740	2.567
18	1.330	1.734	2.552
19	1.328	1.729	2.539
20	1.325	1.725	2.528
21	1.323	1.721	2.518
22	1.321	1.717	2.508
23	1.319	1.714	2.500
24	1.318	1.711	2.492
25	1.316	1.708	2.485
26	1.315	1.706	2.479
27	1.314	1.703	2.473
28	1.313	1.701	2.467
29	1.311	1.699	2.462
30	1.310	1.697	2.457
40	1.303	1.684	2.423
50	1.298	1.676	2.403
60	1.296	1.671	2.390
80	1.292	1.664	2.374
100	1.290	1.660	2.365
200	1.286	1.653	2.345
500	1.283	1.648	2.334
∞	1.282	1.645	2.326

* The greater part of this table is reproduced from Table III of R. A. Fisher and F. Yates *Statistical Tables*, Oliver and Boyd Ltd., Edinburgh, England (1953) by permission of the authors and the publishers.

313

Table IV   Percentiles of the χ^2 Distribution*

Degrees of freedom (γ)	0.005	0.010	0.025	0.05	0.10	0.20	0.30	0.40
1	0.0⁴393	0.0³157	0.0³982	0.0²393	0.0158	0.0642	0.148	0.275
2	0.0100	0.0201	0.0506	0.103	0.211	0.446	0.713	1.02
3	0.0717	0.115	0.216	0.352	0.584	1.00	1.42	1.87
4	0.207	0.297	0.484	0.711	1.06	1.65	2.19	2.75
5	0.412	0.554	0.831	1.15	1.61	2.34	3.00	3.66
6	0.676	0.872	1.24	1.64	2.20	3.07	3.83	4.57
7	0.989	1.24	1.69	2.17	2.83	3.82	4.67	5.49
8	1.34	1.65	2.18	2.73	3.49	4.59	5.53	6.42
9	1.73	2.09	2.70	3.33	4.17	5.38	6.39	7.36
10	2.16	2.56	3.25	3.94	4.87	6.18	7.27	8.30
11	2.60	3.05	3.82	4.57	5.58	6.99	8.15	9.24
12	3.07	3.57	4.40	5.23	6.30	7.81	9.03	10.2
13	3.57	4.11	5.01	5.89	7.04	8.63	9.93	11.1
14	4.07	4.66	5.63	6.57	7.79	9.47	10.8	12.1
15	4.60	5.23	6.26	7.26	8.55	10.3	11.7	13.0
16	5.14	5.81	6.91	7.96	9.31	11.2	12.6	14.0
17	5.70	6.41	7.56	8.67	10.1	12.0	13.5	14.9
18	6.26	7.01	8.23	9.39	10.9	12.9	14.4	15.9
19	6.84	7.63	8.91	10.1	11.7	13.7	15.4	16.9
20	7.43	8.26	9.59	10.9	12.4	14.6	16.3	17.8
21	8.03	8.90	10.3	11.6	13.2	15.4	17.2	18.8
22	8.64	9.54	11.0	12.3	14.0	16.3	18.1	19.7
23	9.26	10.2	11.7	13.1	14.8	17.2	19.0	20.7
24	9.89	10.9	12.4	13.8	15.7	18.1	19.9	21.7
25	10.5	11.5	13.1	14.6	16.5	18.9	20.9	22.6
26	11.2	12.2	13.8	15.4	17.3	19.8	21.8	23.6
27	11.8	12.9	14.6	16.2	18.1	20.7	22.7	24.5
28	12.5	13.6	15.3	16.9	18.9	21.6	23.6	25.5
29	13.1	14.3	16.0	17.7	19.8	22.5	24.6	26.5
30	13.8	15.0	16.8	18.5	20.6	23.4	25.5	27.4
35	17.2	18.5	20.6	22.5	24.8	27.8	30.2	32.3
40	20.7	22.2	24.4	26.5	29.1	32.3	34.9	37.1
45	24.3	25.9	28.4	30.6	33.4	36.9	39.6	42.0
50	28.0	29.7	32.4	34.8	37.7	41.4	44.3	46.9
75	47.2	49.5	52.9	56.1	59.8	64.5	68.1	71.3
100	67.3	70.1	74.2	77.9	82.4	87.9	92.1	95.8

Table IV (continued)

0.50	0.60	0.70	0.80	0.90	0.95	0.975	0.990	0.995	γ
0.455	0.708	1.07	1.64	2.71	3.84	5.02	6.63	7.88	1
1.39	1.83	2.41	3.22	4.61	5.99	7.38	9.21	10.6	2
2.37	2.95	3.67	4.64	6.25	7.81	9.35	11.3	12.8	3
3.36	4.04	4.88	5.99	7.78	9.49	11.1	13.3	14.9	4
4.35	5.13	6.06	7.29	9.24	11.1	12.8	15.1	16.7	5
5.35	6.21	7.23	8.56	10.6	12.6	14.4	16.8	18.5	6
6.35	7.28	8.38	9.80	12.0	14.1	16.0	18.5	20.3	7
7.34	8.35	9.52	11.0	13.4	15.5	17.5	20.1	22.0	8
8.34	9.41	10.7	12.2	14.7	16.9	19.0	21.7	23.6	9
9.34	10.5	11.8	13.4	16.0	18.3	20.5	23.2	25.2	10
10.3	11.5	12.9	14.6	17.3	19.7	21.9	24.7	26.8	11
11.3	12.6	14.0	15.8	18.5	21.0	23.3	26.2	28.3	12
12.3	13.6	15.1	17.0	19.8	22.4	24.7	27.7	29.8	13
13.3	14.7	16.2	18.2	21.1	23.7	26.1	29.1	31.3	14
14.3	15.7	17.3	19.3	22.3	25.0	27.5	30.6	32.8	15
15.3	16.8	18.4	20.5	23.5	26.3	28.8	32.0	34.3	16
16.3	17.8	19.5	21.6	24.8	27.6	30.2	33.4	35.7	17
17.3	18.9	20.6	22.8	26.0	28.9	31.5	34.8	37.2	18
18.3	19.9	21.7	23.9	27.2	30.1	32.9	36.2	38.6	19
19.3	21.0	22.8	25.0	28.4	31.4	34.2	37.6	40.0	20
20.3	22.0	23.9	26.2	29.6	32.7	35.5	38.9	41.4	21
21.3	23.0	24.9	27.3	30.8	33.9	36.8	40.3	42.8	22
22.3	24.1	26.0	28.4	32.0	35.2	38.1	41.6	44.2	23
23.3	25.1	27.1	29.6	33.2	36.4	39.4	43.0	45.6	24
24.3	26.1	28.2	30.7	34.4	37.7	40.6	44.3	46.9	25
25.3	27.2	29.2	31.8	35.6	38.9	41.9	45.6	48.3	26
26.3	28.2	30.3	32.9	36.7	40.1	43.2	47.0	49.6	27
27.3	29.2	31.4	34.0	37.9	41.3	44.5	48.3	51.0	28
28.3	30.3	32.5	35.1	39.1	42.6	45.7	49.6	52.3	29
29.3	31.3	33.5	36.3	40.3	43.8	47.0	50.9	53.7	30
34.3	36.5	38.9	41.8	46.1	49.8	53.2	57.3	60.3	35
39.3	41.6	44.2	47.3	51.8	55.8	59.3	63.7	66.8	40
44.3	46.8	49.5	52.7	57.5	61.7	65.4	70.0	73.2	45
49.3	51.9	54.7	58.2	63.2	67.5	71.4	76.2	79.5	50
74.3	77.5	80.9	85.1	91.1	96.2	100.8	106.4	110.3	75
99.3	102.9	106.9	111.7	118.5	124.3	129.6	135.6	140.2	100

* Abridged from Table V of *Statistical Tables and Formulas* by A. Hald, John Wiley and Sons, New York, 1952.

Table V   Tables to Facilitate Fitting Johnson S_U Distribution*

Values of $-\hat{\gamma}$

b_2 \ $\sqrt{b_1}$	0·05	0·10	0·15	0·20	0·25	0·30	0·35	0·40	0·45	0·50
3·2	0·3479	0·7373	1·228	1·940	3·189	6·389				
3·3	·2328	·4834	0·7747	1·143	1·656	2·477				
3·4	·1760	·3620	·5699	0·8166	1·133	1·569	2·236	3·484		
3·5	·1421	·2905	·4528	·6384	0·8620	1·148	1·546	2·146		
3·6	0·1196	0·2435	0·3776	0·5260	0·6997	0·9115	1·187	1·565	2·139	3·157
3·7	·1035	·2102	·3238	·4487	·5907	·7586	0·9681	1·238	1·614	2·188
3·8	·0914	·1853	·2845	·3921	·5125	·6515	·8197	1·028	1·302	1·687
3·9	·0820	·1661	·2542	·3490	·4536	·5723	·7127	0·8814	1·095	1·378
4·0	·0745	·1507	·2302	·3150	·4076	·5113	·6304	·7733	0·9470	1·169
4·1	0·0684	0·1381	0·2106	0·2875	0·3707	0·4629	0·5673	0·6902	0·8363	1·018
4·2	·0633	·1276	·1943	·2647	·3404	·4234	·5165	·6243	·7503	0·9031
4·3	·0589	·1188	·1806	·2456	·3151	·3907	·4747	·5708	·6814	·8132
4·4	·0552	·1112	·1689	·2294	·2937	·3632	·4397	·5265	·6251	·7407
4·5	·0519	·1046	·1588	·2153	·2752	·3396	·4100	·4891	·5780	·6811
4·6	0·0491	0·0989	0·1499	0·2031	0·2592	0·3192	0·3844	0·4564	0·5382	0·6311
4·7	·0466	·0938	·1421	·1923	·2451	·3014	·3622	·4288	·5040	·5886
4·8	·0444	·0893	·1352	·1828	·2327	·2857	·3426	·4048	·4744	·5520
4·9	·0424	·0852	·1290	·1743	·2216	·2717	·3254	·3836	·4484	·5202
5·0	·0406	·0816	·1234	·1666	·2117	·2592	·3099	·3648	·4254	·4922
5·1	0·0390	0·0783	0·1184	0·1597	0·2027	0·2480	0·2961	0·3479	0·4050	0·4674
5·2	·0374	·0752	·1138	·1534	·1946	·2378	·2836	·3328	·3866	·4453
5·3	·0361	·0725	·1096	·1477	·1872	·2285	·2723	·3191	·3696	·4255
5·4	·0348	·0700	·1057	·1424	·1804	·2201	·2620	·3066	·3547	·4076
5·5	·0337	·0676	·1022	·1376	·1742	·2123	·2525	·2952	·3411	·3913
5·6	0·0326	0·0655	0·0989	0·1331	0·1684	0·2052	0·2438	0·2848	0·3286	0·3765
5·7	·0316	·0635	·0958	·1290	·1631	·1986	·2358	·2752	·3172	·3629
5·8	·0307	·0616	·0930	·1251	·1582	·1925	·2284	·2663	·3066	·3504
5·9	·0298	·0599	·0904	·1215	·1536	·1868	·2215	·2581	·2967	·3385
6·0	·0290	·0583	·0879	·1182	·1493	·1815	·2151	·2504	·2879	·3278
6·1	0·0283	0·0568	0·0856	0·1151	0·1453	0·1766	0·2091	0·2433	0·2794	0·3180
6·2	·0276	·0553	·0835	·1121	·1415	·1719	·2035	·2366	·2716	·3088
6·3	·0269	·0540	·0814	·1094	·1380	·1676	·1983	·2304	·2643	·3002
6·4	·0263	·0527	·0795	·1067	·1347	·1635	·1933	·2245	·2574	·2921
6·5	·0257	·0515	·0777	·1043	·1315	·1596	·1887	·2190	·2509	·2846
6·6	0·0251	0·0504	0·0760	0·1020	0·1286	0·1560	0·1843	0·2138	0·2448	0·2775
6·7	·0246	·0493	·0743	·0998	·1258	·1525	·1802	·2089	·2391	·2709
6·8	·0241	·0483	·0728	·0977	·1231	·1492	·1762	·2043	·2337	·2646
6·9	·0236	·0473	·0713	·0957	·1206	·1461	·1725	·1999	·2285	·2586
7·0	·0232	·0464	·0699	·0938	·1182	·1432	·1690	·1957	·2237	·2530
7·1	0·0227	0·0455	0·0686	0·0920	0·1159	0·1404	0·1656	0·1918	0·2190	0·2476
7·2	·0223	·0447	·0673	·0903	·1137	·1377	·1624	·1880	·2147	·2426
7·3	·0219	·0439	·0661	·0887	·1116	·1352	·1594	·1844	·2105	·2377
7·4	0215	·0431	·0650	·0871	·1096	·1327	·1565	·1810	·2065	·2331
7·5	·0212	·0424	·0639	·0856	·1077	·1304	·1537	·1777	·2027	·2287
7·6	0·0208	0·0417	0·0628	0·0842	0·1059	0·1282	0·1510	0·1746	0·1991	0·2246
7·7	·0205	·0410	·0618	·0828	·1042	·1260	·1485	·1716	·1956	·2206
7·8	·0202	·0404	·0608	·0815	·1025	·1240	·1460	·1687	·1922	·2167
7·9	·0198	·0398	·0599	·0802	·1009	·1220	·1437	·1660	·1891	·2131
8·0	·0195	·0392	·0590	·0790	·0993	·1201	·1414	·1633	·1860	·2095
8·2	0·0190	0·0380	0·0572	0·0767	0·0964	0·1165	0·1371	0·1583	0·1802	0·2029
8·4	·0185	·0370	·0557	·0745	·0937	·1132	·1332	·1537	·1749	·1968
8·6	·0180	·0360	·0542	·0725	·0912	·1101	·1295	·1494	·1699	·1912
8·8	·0175	·0351	·0528	·0707	·0888	·1073	·1261	·1454	·1653	·1859
9·0	·0171	·0342	·0515	·0689	·0866	·1046	·1229	·1417	·1610	·1810
9·2	—	—	—	—	—	—	0·1199	0·1382	0·1570	0·1764
9·4	—	—	—	—	—	—	·1171	·1349	·1532	·1721

* From N. L. Johnson, *Tables to Facilitate Fitting S_U Frequency Curves*, Biometrika, 1965, Vol. 52, pp 547–558.

316

Table V-2

Values of — $\hat{\gamma}$ (continued)

b_2 \ $\sqrt{b_1}$	0·55	0·60	0·65	0·70	0·75	0·80	0·85	0·90	0·95	1·00
3·8	2·284	3·383								
3·9	1·783	2·426								
4·0	1·469	1·906	2·621	4·104						
4·1	1·253	1·577	2·060	2·886						
4·2	1·096	1·349	1·705	2·254						
4·3	0·9748	1·182	1·460	1·860						
4·4	·8802	1·054	1·280	1·589						
4·5	·8033	0·9527	1·142	1·392						
4·6	0·7399	0·8705	1·033	1·240	1·522	1·931	2·602	4·029		
4·7	·6865	·8024	0·9434	1·121	1·353	1·676	2·167	3·038		
4·8	·6410	·7451	·8699	1·024	1·221	1·485	1·864	2·473		
4·9	·6017	·6962	·8083	0·9436	1·114	1·335	1·641	2·100		
5·0	·5675	·6539	·7550	·8761	1·025	1·215	1·469	1·832	2·407	3·538
5·1	0·5374	0·6170	0·7092	0·8154	0·9509	1·117	1·333	1·629	2·071	2·832
5·2	·5106	·5845	·6693	·7687	·8877	1·034	1·221	1·470	1·825	2·386
5·3	·4868	·5556	·6341	·7252	·8331	0·9642	1·128	1·342	1·635	2·072
5·4	·4653	·5298	·6028	·6869	·7856	·9039	1·050	1·236	1·484	1·839
5·5	·4459	·5066	·5749	·6530	·7419	·8515	0·9826	1·147	1·361	1·657
5·6	0·4283	0·4856	0·5498	0·6226	0·7067	0·8055	0·9243	1·071	1·259	1·510
5·7	·4122	·4665	·5270	·5953	·6735	·7647	·8732	1·006	1·172	1·390
5·8	·3975	·4491	·5063	·5706	·6437	·7284	·8282	0·9485	1·098	1·289
5·9	·3840	·4331	·4875	·5481	·6168	·6942	·7881	·8982	1·033	1·203
6·0	·3714	·4184	·4701	·5276	·5924	·6663	·7521	·8536	0·9765	1·129
6·1	0·3598	0·4049	0·4542	0·5088	0·5700	0·6396	0·7197	0·8138	0·9265	1·065
6·2	·3491	·3923	·4395	·4915	·5496	·6152	·6904	·7780	·8820	1·008
6·3	·3390	·3806	·4258	·4755	·5308	·5929	·6637	·7456	·8420	0·9581
6·4	·3297	·3697	·4131	·4607	·5134	·5724	·6392	·7161	·8060	·9132
6·5	·3209	·3595	·4013	·4470	·4973	·5535	·6150	·6892	·7733	·8729
6·6	0·3123	0·3500	0·3903	0·4341	0·4824	0·5359	0·5962	0·6646	0·7436	0·8364
6·7	·3046	·3410	·3799	·4221	·4684	·5197	·5770	·6419	·7164	·8033
6·8	·2973	·3326	·3702	·4109	·4554	·5045	·5592	·6209	·6914	·7730
6·9	·2904	·3247	·3611	·4004	·4433	·4904	·5427	·5951	·6683	·7453
7·0	·2839	·3172	·3524	·3905	·4318	·4772	·5273	·5835	·6470	·7198
7·1	0·2778	0·3101	0·3443	0·3812	0·4211	0·4648	0·5130	0·5666	0·6272	0·6962
7·2	·2719	·3034	·3366	·3723	·4110	·4531	·4995	·5509	·6087	·6744
7·3	·2664	·2967	·3293	·3640	·4014	·4421	·4868	·5362	·5915	·6541
7·4	·2611	·2907	·3224	·3561	·3924	·4318	·4749	·5224	·5754	·6352
7·5	·2561	·2849	·3159	·3486	·3838	·4220	·4636	·5094	·5593	·6175
7·6	0·2513	0·2795	0·3096	0·3415	0·3757	0·4127	0·4530	0·4972	0·5463	0·6010
7·7	·2467	·2742	·3037	·3347	·3680	·4039	·4429	·4857	·5328	·5855
7·8	·2423	·2692	·2980	·3283	·3607	·3956	·4334	·4747	·5203	·5709
7·9	·2381	·2645	·2926	·3221	·3537	·3876	·4244	·4644	·5084	·5571
8·0	·2341	·2599	·2871	·3163	·3470	·3801	·4158	·4546	·4971	·5442
8·1	0·2303	0·2556	0·2822	0·3106	0·3407	0·3729	0·4076	0·4452	0·4864	0·5309
8·2	·2266	·2514	·2774	·3053	·3346	·3660	·3998	·4364	·4763	·5203
8·3	·2230	·2473	·2729	·3001	·3288	·3594	·3923	·4279	·4667	·5092
8·4	·2196	·2435	·2685	·2952	·3232	·3531	·3852	·4199	·4575	·4987
8·5	·2163	·2397	·2643	·2904	·3179	·3471	·3784	·4122	·4488	·4888
8·6	0·2132	0·2362	0·2603	0·2859	0·3127	0·3413	0·3719	0·4048	0·4405	0·4793
8·7	·2101	·2327	·2564	·2812	·3078	·3358	·3657	·3978	·4325	·4702
8·8	·2072	·2294	·2526	·2770	·3031	·3305	·3597	·3910	·4248	·4616
8·9	·2044	·2262	·2490	·2730	·2985	·3253	·3539	·3845	·4175	·4533
9·0	·2016	·2231	·2455	·2691	·2941	·3204	·3484	·3783	·4105	·4454
9·2	0·1964	0·2172	0·2389	0·2617	0·2858	0·3111	0·3380	0·3666	0·3974	0·4305
9·4	·1915	·2117	·2328	·2548	·2778	·3025	·3283	·3558	·3852	·4169
9·6	—	—	—	·2483	·2706	·2944	·3193	·3457	·3739	·4042
9·8	—	—	—	·2422	·2639	·2868	·3109	·3363	·3634	·3925
10·0	—	—	—	·2365	·2575	·2798	·3030	·3275	·3537	·3816

Table V-3

Values of $-\hat{\gamma}$ (continued)

b_2 \ $\sqrt{b_1}$	1·05	1·10	1·15	1·20	1·25	1·30	1·35	1·40	1·45	1·50
5·4	2·403	3·543								
5·5	2·099	2·874								
5·6	1·871	2·451								
5·7	1·692	2·149								
5·8	1·547	1·921	2·535	3·886						
5·9	1·428	1·741	2·224	3·124						
6·0	1·327	1·596	1·990	2·654						
6·1	1·241	1·475	1·805	2·325						
6·2	1·167	1·373	1·656	2·079	2·823	5·110				
6·3	1·102	1·285	1·531	1·885	2·459	3·712				
6·4	1·044	1·210	1·427	1·729	2·192	3·054				
6·5	0·9933	1·143	1·337	1·599	1·984	2·635				
6·6	0·9477	1·085	1·259	1·490	1·817	2·335				
6·7	·9066	1·032	1·190	1·396	1·679	2·106				
6·8	·8694	0·9857	1·130	1·315	1·563	1·924	2·525	3·929		
6·9	·8356	·9435	1·076	1·243	1·464	1·775	2·259	3·213		
7·0	·8046	·9053	1·028	1·180	1·379	1·650	2·055	2·768		
7·1	0·7762	0·8705	0·9840	1·124	1·303	1·544	1·890	2·455		
7·2	·7500	·8386	·9444	1·074	1·237	1·452	1·752	2·217		
7·3	·7258	·8093	·9083	1·028	1·178	1·372	1·636	2·029		
7·4	·7034	·7823	·8753	0·9871	1·125	1·301	1·537	1·875	2·430	3·669
7·5	·6825	·7573	·8450	·9495	1·077	1·238	1·450	1·746	2·202	3·088
7·6	0·6630	0·7342	0·8170	0·9151	1·034	1·182	1·374	1·636	2·024	2·705
7·7	·6448	·7126	·7910	·8834	·9945	1·132	1·307	1·540	1·877	2·426
7·8	·6278	·6924	·7670	·8542	·9584	1·086	1·246	1·457	1·752	2·211
7·9	·6117	·6736	·7445	·8272	·9251	1·044	1·192	1·384	1·646	2·037
8·0	·5967	·6559	·7236	·8020	·8945	1·006	1·143	1·319	1·554	1·893
8·1	0·5825	0·6393	0·7040	0·7786	0·8661	0·9706	1·099	1·260	1·473	1·772
8·2	·5690	·6237	·6857	·7568	·8397	·9382	1·058	1·207	1·401	1·667
8·3	·5563	·6089	·6684	·7364	·8152	·9083	1·020	1·159	1·337	1·576
8·4	·5443	·5950	·6521	·7172	·7923	·8805	0·9860	1·115	1·279	1·496
8·5	·5328	·5818	·6368	·6991	·7709	·8546	·9542	1·075	1·227	1·425
8·6	0·5220	0·5693	0·6223	0·6822	0·7507	0·8304	0·9246	1·038	1·180	1·361
8·7	·5099	·5574	·6085	·6661	·7318	·8078	·8972	1·004	1·136	1·304
8·8	·5018	·5461	·5955	·6510	·7140	·7866	·8716	0·9729	1·096	1·252
8·9	·4924	·5354	·5831	·6366	·6972	·7667	·8477	·9436	1·060	1·204
9·0	·4834	·5251	·5714	·6230	·6813	·7480	·8252	·9163	1·026	1·161
9·1	0·4748	0·5154	0·5601	0·6101	0·6663	0·7303	0·8042	0·8908	0·9943	1·121
9·2	·4666	·5060	·5494	·5978	·6520	·7136	·7843	·8669	·9651	1·084
9·3	·4587	·4971	·5393	·5861	·6385	·6977	·7656	·8445	·9377	1·050
9·4	·4511	·4885	·5295	·5749	·6256	·6827	·7480	·8234	·9122	1·019
9·5	·4439	·4803	·5202	·5642	·6133	·6685	·7312	·8036	·8882	0·9892
9·6	0·4369	0·4724	0·5112	0·5540	0·6016	0·6549	0·7154	0·7848	0·8657	0·9616
9·7	·4302	·4648	·5027	·5443	·5904	·6420	·7003	·7671	·8445	·9359
9·8	·4237	·4576	·4945	·5349	·5797	·6297	·6860	·7503	·8245	·9117
9·9	·4175	·4506	·4866	·5260	·5695	·6180	·6724	·7343	·8056	·8889
10·0	·4115	·4438	·4790	·5174	·5597	·6067	·6594	·7192	·7877	·8675
10·2	0·4001	0·4311	0·4646	0·5012	0·5413	0·5857	0·6352	0·6910	0·7546	0·8280
10·4	·3895	·4192	·4513	·4862	·5243	·5664	·6131	·6654	·7247	·7927
10·6	·3796	·4082	·4389	·4723	·5086	·5485	·5927	·6420	·6975	·7608
10·8	·3703	·3978	·4273	·4593	·4940	·5320	·5739	·6205	·6727	·7318
11·0	·3615	·3881	·4165	·4472	·4804	·5167	·5566	·6007	·6499	·7053
11·2	0·3533	0·3789	0·4063	0·4358	0·4678	0·5025	0·5404	0·5823	0·6289	0·6811
11·4	·3455	·3703	·3968	·4252	·4559	·4891	·5254	·5653	·6095	·6588
11·6	—	—	—	—	—	—	—	·5495	·5915	·6383
11·8	—	—	—	—	—	—	—	·5347	·5748	·6192
12·0	—	—	—	—	—	—	—	·5209	·5592	·6015

Table V-4

Values of $-\hat{\gamma}$ (continued)

b_2 \ $\sqrt{b_1}$	1·55	1·60	1·65	1·70	1·75	1·80	1·85	1·90	1·95	2·00
8·0	2·459	3·813								
8·1	2·240	3·192								
8·2	2·067	2·795								
8·3	1·924	2·510								
8·4	1·803	2·291								
8·5	1·698	2·115								
8·6	1·607	1·969	2·601	4·603						
8·7	1·527	1·846	2·365	3·582						
8·8	1·456	1·740	2·181	3·061						
8·9	1·392	1·647	2·030	2·719						
9·0	1·334	1·566	1·902	2·467						
9·1	1·282	1·493	1·793	2·269						
9·2	1·234	1·428	1·697	2·108						
9·3	1·190	1·370	1·613	1·973						
9·4	1·150	1·316	1·539	1·858	2·382	3·679				
9·5	1·112	1·268	1·472	1·758	2·208	3·147				
9·6	1·078	1·223	1·412	1·670	2·062	2·793				
9·7	1·046	1·182	1·357	1·592	1·938	2·535				
9·8	1·016	1·144	1·307	1·523	1·831	2·335				
9·9	0·9881	1·109	1·261	1·460	1·738	2·172				
10·0	·9619	1·076	1·219	1·403	1·656	2·036				
10·1	0·9374	1·046	1·180	1·351	1·582	1·920				
10·2	·9142	1·017	1·144	1·304	1·516	1·819	2·310	3·475		
10·3	·8924	0·9906	1·110	1·260	1·457	1·731	2·158	3·036		
10·4	·8718	·9655	1·079	1·220	1·402	1·652	2·028	2·726		
10·5	·8523	·9419	1·050	1·183	1·353	1·582	1·917	2·495		
10·6	0·8338	0·9196	1·022	1·148	1·307	1·518	1·820	2·313		
10·7	·8163	·8985	0·9963	1·115	1·265	1·461	1·734	2·163		
10·8	·7996	·8785	·9720	1·085	1·226	1·408	1·658	2·036		
10·9	·7837	·8596	·9490	1·057	1·190	1·360	1·590	1·927		
11·0	·7686	·8416	·9274	1·030	1·156	1·316	1·528	1·832	2·331	3·612
11·1	0·7541	0·8246	0·9069	1·005	1·124	1·274	1·472	1·748	2·185	3·131
11·2	·7403	·8083	·8874	0·9811	1·095	1·236	1·420	1·673	2·058	2·804
11·3	·7272	·7928	·8689	·9587	1·067	1·201	1·373	1·605	1·950	2·565
11·4	·7145	·7780	·8513	·9375	1·041	1·168	1·329	1·544	1·855	2·377
11·5	·7024	·7638	·8346	·9174	1·016	1·137	1·289	1·489	1·771	2·224
11·6	0·6907	0·7503	0·8186	0·8983	0·9928	1·108	1·251	1·438	1·696	2·096
11·7	·6796	·7373	·8034	·8801	·9708	1·080	1·216	1·391	1·629	1·985
11·8	·6688	·7248	·7888	·8628	·9499	1·054	1·183	1·347	1·568	1·889
11·9	·6585	·7129	·7749	·8463	·9300	1·030	1·152	1·307	1·512	1·804
12·0	·6486	·7014	·7615	·8306	·9112	1·007	1·124	1·270	1·461	1·728
12·1	0·6390	0·6904	0·7487	0·8155	0·8932	0·9851	1·096	1·235	1·414	1·660
12·2	·6297	·6798	·7364	·8011	·8761	·9644	1·071	1·202	1·370	1·598
12·3	·6208	·6696	·7246	·7873	·8597	·9447	1·046	1·171	1·330	1·542
12·4	·6122	·6598	·7132	·7740	·8441	·9260	1·024	1·143	1·293	1·490
12·5	·6039	·6503	·7023	·7613	·8291	·9081	1·002	1·115	1·258	1·443
12·6	0·5959	0·6411	0·6918	0·7491	0·8148	0·8910	0·9811	1·090	1·225	1·399
12·7	·5881	·6323	·6816	·7374	·8011	·8747	·9614	1·066	1·194	1·358
12·8	·5806	·6237	·6719	·7261	·7879	·8592	·9427	1·043	1·165	1·320
12·9	·5733	·6154	·6624	·7152	·7752	·8442	·9248	1·021	1·138	1·284
13·0	·5662	·6074	·6533	·7047	·7630	·8299	·9078	1·000	1·112	1·251
13·2	—	—	—	—	0·7400	0·8030	0·8758	0·9614	1·064	1·190
13·4	—	—	—	—	·7187	·7781	·8465	·9263	1·021	1·136
13·6	—	—	—	—	·6988	·7551	·8195	·8941	0·9822	1·088
13·8	—	—	—	—	·6802	·7336	·7945	·8646	·9466	1·045
14·0	—	—	—	—	·6628	·7136	·7712	·8373	·9141	1·005
14·2	—	—	—	—	0·6464	0·6949	0·7496	0·8121	0·8842	0·9690
14·4	—	—	—	—	·6311	·6774	·7295	·7886	·8566	·9359
14·6	—	—	—	—	·6166	·6609	·7106	·7668	·8310	·9055
14·8	—	—	—	—	·6029	·6454	·6929	·7464	·8072	·8774
15·0	—	—	—	—	·5900	·6308	·6763	·7273	·7851	·8514

Table V-5

Values of $\hat{\eta}$

$\sqrt{b_1}$ / b_2	0·05	0·10	0·15	0·20	0·25	0·30	0·35	0·40	0·45	0·50
3·2	4·671	4·787	5·004	5·369	5·992	7·204				
3·3	3·866	3·927	4·036	4·208	4·469	4·875				
3·4	3·396	3·435	3·503	3·607	3·759	3·979	4·300	4·813		
3·5	3·081	3·108	3·156	3·227	3·328	3·467	3·663	3·943		
3·6	2·852	2·872	2·908	2·960	3·033	3·132	3·266	3·448	3·705	4·087
3·7	2·676	2·692	2·719	2·760	2·816	2·890	2·989	3·120	3·295	3·540
3·8	2·535	2·548	2·571	2·604	2·648	2·707	2·783	2·882	3·011	3·184
3·9	2·420	2·431	2·450	2·477	2·513	2·561	2·623	2·701	2·801	2·931
4·0	2·324	2·333	2·349	2·372	2·402	2·442	2·492	2·557	2·637	2·739
4·1	2·242	2·250	2·264	2·283	2·309	2·343	2·385	2·439	2·505	2·588
4·2	2·171	2·178	2·190	2·207	2·229	2·258	2·295	2·340	2·396	2·465
4·3	2·109	2·115	2·126	2·141	2·160	2·186	2·217	2·256	2·304	2·363
4·4	2·054	2·060	2·069	2·082	2·100	2·122	2·150	2·184	2·226	2·276
4·5	2·005	2·010	2·018	2·030	2·046	2·066	2·090	2·121	2·157	2·202
4·6	1·961	1·966	1·973	1·984	1·998	2·016	2·038	2·065	2·097	2·136
4·7	1·921	1·925	1·932	1·942	1·955	1·971	1·991	2·015	2·044	2·079
4·8	1·885	1·889	1·895	1·904	1·916	1·930	1·948	1·970	1·997	2·028
4·9	1·852	1·855	1·861	1·869	1·880	1·893	1·910	1·930	1·954	1·982
5·0	1·822	1·825	1·830	1·837	1·847	1·860	1·875	1·893	1·915	1·941
5·1	1·793	1·796	1·801	1·808	1·817	1·829	1·843	1·859	1·880	1·903
5·2	1·767	1·770	1·775	1·781	1·790	1·800	1·813	1·829	1·847	1·869
5·3	1·743	1·746	1·750	1·756	1·764	1·774	1·786	1·800	1·817	1·837
5·4	1·721	1·723	1·727	1·732	1·740	1·749	1·760	1·774	1·789	1·808
5·5	1·699	1·702	1·705	1·711	1·718	1·726	1·737	1·749	1·764	1·781
5·6	1·680	1·682	1·685	1·690	1·697	1·705	1·715	1·726	1·740	1·756
5·7	1·661	1·663	1·666	1·671	1·677	1·685	1·694	1·705	1·718	1·733
5·8	1·643	1·645	1·648	1·653	1·658	1·666	1·674	1·685	1·697	1·711
5·9	1·627	1·628	1·631	1·636	1·641	1·648	1·656	1·666	1·677	1·691
6·0	1·611	1·613	1·615	1·619	1·625	1·631	1·639	1·648	1·659	1·672
6·1	1·596	1·598	1·600	1·604	1·609	1·615	1·623	1·631	1·642	1·653
6·2	1·582	1·583	1·586	1·590	1·594	1·600	1·607	1·615	1·625	1·636
6·3	1·568	1·570	1·572	1·576	1·580	1·586	1·593	1·600	1·610	1·620
6·4	1·556	1·557	1·559	1·563	1·567	1·572	1·579	1·586	1·595	1·605
6·5	1·543	1·545	1·547	1·550	1·554	1·559	1·565	1·573	1·581	1·591
6·6	1·532	1·533	1·535	1·538	1·542	1·547	1·553	1·560	1·568	1·577
6·7	1·520	1·522	1·524	1·527	1·530	1·535	1·541	1·547	1·555	1·564
6·8	1·510	1·511	1·513	1·516	1·519	1·524	1·529	1·535	1·543	1·551
6·9	1·499	1·501	1·502	1·505	1·509	1·513	1·518	1·524	1·531	1·539
7·0	1·490	1·491	1·491	1·495	1·498	1·502	1·507	1·513	1·520	1·528
7·1	1·480	1·481	1·483	1·485	1·489	1·492	1·497	1·503	1·509	1·517
7·2	1·471	1·472	1·474	1·476	1·479	1·483	1·487	1·493	1·499	1·506
7·3	1·462	1·463	1·465	1·467	1·470	1·474	1·478	1·483	1·489	1·496
7·4	1·454	1·455	1·456	1·458	1·461	1·465	1·469	1·474	1·480	1·487
7·5	1·445	1·446	1·448	1·450	1·453	1·456	1·460	1·465	1·471	1·477
7·6	1·438	1·438	1·440	1·442	1·445	1·448	1·452	1·457	1·462	1·468
7·7	1·430	1·431	1·432	1·434	1·437	1·440	1·444	1·448	1·454	1·460
7·8	1·423	1·423	1·425	1·427	1·429	1·432	1·436	1·440	1·445	1·451
7·9	1·415	1·416	1·418	1·419	1·422	1·425	1·428	1·433	1·438	1·443
8·0	1·408	1·409	1·411	1·412	1·415	1·418	1·421	1·425	1·430	1·435
8·2	1·395	1·396	1·397	1·399	1·401	1·404	1·407	1·411	1·416	1·421
8·4	1·383	1·383	1·385	1·386	1·388	1·391	1·394	1·398	1·402	1·407
8·6	1·371	1·372	1·373	1·374	1·376	1·379	1·382	1·385	1·389	1·394
8·8	1·360	1·361	1·362	1·363	1·365	1·367	1·370	1·373	1·377	1·381
9·0	1·349	1·350	1·351	1·352	1·354	1·356	1·359	1·362	1·366	1·370
9·2	—	—	—	—	—	—	1·349	1·352	1·355	1·359
9·4	—	—	—	—	—	—	1·339	1·342	1·345	1·348

320

Table V-6

Values of $\hat{\eta}$ (continued)

$\sqrt{b_1}$ / b_2	0·55	0·60	0·65	0·70	0·75	0·80	0·85	0·90	0·95	1·00
3·8	3·424	3·776								
3·9	3·105	3·346								
4·0	2·872	3·049	3·294	3·659						
4·1	2·694	2·830	3·013	3·269						
4·2	2·552	2·662	2·804	2·996						
4·3	2·436	2·526	2·641	2·791						
4·4	2·338	2·414	2·510	2·631						
4·5	2·255	2·320	2·401	2·502						
4·6	2·183	2·240	2·309	2·395	2·503	2·641	2·828	3·093		
4·7	2·120	2·170	2·231	2·304	2·395	2·511	2·662	2·868		
4·8	2·065	2·109	2·162	2·226	2·305	2·403	2·529	2·694		
4·9	2·015	2·055	2·100	2·159	2·227	2·312	2·418	2·555		
5·0	1·971	2·007	2·049	2·099	2·160	2·234	2·325	2·441	2·592	2·799
5·1	1·931	1·963	2·001	2·045	2·100	2·165	2·245	2·344	2·472	2·641
5·2	1·894	1·924	1·958	1·999	2·048	2·105	2·176	2·262	2·371	2·512
5·3	1·860	1·888	1·919	1·957	2·000	2·052	2·115	2·191	2·285	2·406
5·4	1·830	1·855	1·884	1·918	1·958	2·005	2·061	2·128	2·211	2·315
5·5	1·801	1·824	1·851	1·883	1·918	1·962	2·012	2·073	2·146	2·237
5·6	1·775	1·796	1·821	1·850	1·884	1·923	1·969	2·023	2·089	2·170
5·7	1·750	1·770	1·794	1·820	1·851	1·887	1·929	1·979	2·038	2·110
5·8	1·728	1·746	1·768	1·793	1·821	1·855	1·893	1·939	1·992	2·057
5·9	1·706	1·724	1·744	1·767	1·794	1·824	1·860	1·902	1·951	2·009
6·0	1·686	1·703	1·722	1·743	1·768	1·797	1·830	1·868	1·913	1·967
6·1	1·667	1·683	1·701	1·721	1·744	1·771	1·802	1·837	1·879	1·928
6·2	1·649	1·664	1·681	1·700	1·722	1·747	1·776	1·809	1·847	1·892
6·3	1·633	1·647	1·663	1·681	1·701	1·725	1·752	1·782	1·818	1·860
6·4	1·617	1·630	1·645	1·662	1·682	1·704	1·729	1·758	1·791	1·830
6·5	1·602	1·614	1·629	1·645	1·663	1·684	1·707	1·735	1·766	1·802
6·6	1·587	1·599	1·613	1·628	1·646	1·666	1·688	1·713	1·742	1·776
6·7	1·574	1·585	1·598	1·613	1·629	1·648	1·669	1·693	1·721	1·752
6·8	1·561	1·572	1·584	1·598	1·614	1·632	1·652	1·674	1·700	1·730
6·9	1·548	1·559	1·571	1·584	1·599	1·616	1·635	1·656	1·681	1·708
7·0	1·537	1·547	1·558	1·571	1·585	1·601	1·619	1·639	1·663	1·689
7·1	1·525	1·535	1·546	1·558	1·572	1·587	1·604	1·623	1·645	1·670
7·2	1·514	1·524	1·534	1·546	1·559	1·573	1·590	1·608	1·629	1·653
7·3	1·504	1·513	1·523	1·534	1·547	1·561	1·576	1·594	1·614	1·636
7·4	1·494	1·503	1·512	1·523	1·535	1·548	1·563	1·580	1·599	1·620
7·5	1·484	1·493	1·502	1·512	1·524	1·537	1·551	1·567	1·585	1·605
7·6	1·475	1·483	1·492	1·502	1·513	1·525	1·539	1·555	1·572	1·591
7·7	1·466	1·474	1·483	1·492	1·503	1·515	1·528	1·543	1·559	1·578
7·8	1·458	1·465	1·473	1·483	1·493	1·504	1·517	1·531	1·547	1·565
7·9	1·450	1·457	1·465	1·474	1·483	1·494	1·507	1·520	1·536	1·552
8·0	1·442	1·448	1·456	1·465	1·474	1·485	1·497	1·510	1·524	1·541
8·1	1·434	1·440	1·448	1·456	1·466	1·476	1·487	1·500	1·514	1·529
8·2	1·426	1·433	1·440	1·448	1·457	1·467	1·478	1·490	1·504	1·519
8·3	1·419	1·425	1·432	1·440	1·449	1·458	1·469	1·481	1·494	1·508
8·4	1·412	1·418	1·425	1·433	1·441	1·450	1·460	1·472	1·484	1·498
8·5	1·405	1·411	1·418	1·425	1·433	1·442	1·452	1·463	1·475	1·489
8·6	1·399	1·405	1·411	1·418	1·426	1·435	1·444	1·455	1·467	1·479
8·7	1·392	1·398	1·404	1·411	1·419	1·427	1·437	1·447	1·458	1·471
8·8	1·386	1·392	1·398	1·404	1·412	1·420	1·429	1·439	1·450	1·462
8·9	1·380	1·386	1·391	1·398	1·405	1·413	1·422	1·431	1·442	1·454
9·0	1·374	1·380	1·385	1·392	1·399	1·406	1·415	1·424	1·434	1·446
9·2	1·363	1·368	1·373	1·379	1·386	1·393	1·401	1·410	1·420	1·431
9·4	1·353	1·357	1·362	1·368	1·374	1·381	1·389	1·397	1·406	1·416
9·6	—	—	—	1·357	1·363	1·370	1·377	1·385	1·394	1·403
9·8	—	—	—	1·347	1·353	1·359	1·366	1·373	1·381	1·390
10·0	—	—	—	1·337	1·343	1·349	1·355	1·362	1·370	1·379

Table V-7

Values of $\hat{\eta}$ (continued)

$\sqrt{b_1}$ / b_2	1·05	1·10	1·15	1·20	1·25	1·30	1·35	1·40	1·45	1·50
5·4	2·450	2·632								
5·5	2·353	2·505								
5·6	2·270	2·400								
5·7	2·199	2·311								
5·8	2·136	2·234	2·362	2·530						
5·9	2·080	2·168	2·278	2·423						
6·0	2·031	2·109	2·206	2·331						
6·1	1·986	2·056	2·143	2·253						
6·2	1·945	2·009	2·087	2·184	2·309	2·476				
6·3	1·908	1·966	2·037	2·124	2·234	2·378				
6·4	1·875	1·928	1·992	2·070	2·168	2·294				
6·5	1·843	1·893	1·951	2·022	2·109	2·221				
6·6	1·815	1·860	1·914	1·978	2·057	2·156				
6·7	1·788	1·830	1·880	1·939	2·011	2·100				
6·8	1·763	1·803	1·849	1·903	1·969	2·049	2·151	2·281		
6·9	1·740	1·777	1·820	1·870	1·930	2·003	2·094	2·210		
7·0	1·719	1·753	1·793	1·840	1·895	1·962	2·044	2·148		
7·1	1·698	1·731	1·768	1·811	1·863	1·924	1·999	2·093		
7·2	1·679	1·710	1·745	1·785	1·833	1·890	1·958	2·043		
7·3	1·661	1·690	1·723	1·761	1·806	1·858	1·921	1·998		
7·4	1·644	1·671	1·703	1·738	1·780	1·829	1·887	1·958	2·046	2·157
7·5	1·628	1·654	1·683	1·717	1·756	1·802	1·856	1·921	2·001	2·102
7·6	1·613	1·637	1·665	1·697	1·734	1·776	1·827	1·887	1·960	2·051
7·7	1·598	1·622	1·648	1·678	1·713	1·753	1·800	1·856	1·923	2·006
7·8	1·584	1·607	1·632	1·660	1·693	1·731	1·775	1·827	1·889	1·965
7·9	1·571	1·593	1·616	1·644	1·675	1·710	1·751	1·800	1·858	1·928
8·0	1·559	1·579	1·602	1·628	1·657	1·691	1·730	1·775	1·829	1·894
8·1	1·547	1·566	1·588	1·613	1·640	1·672	1·709	1·752	1·802	1·862
8·2	1·535	1·554	1·575	1·598	1·625	1·655	1·690	1·730	1·777	1·833
8·3	1·524	1·542	1·562	1·585	1·610	1·639	1·671	1·709	1·754	1·806
8·4	1·514	1·531	1·550	1·571	1·596	1·623	1·654	1·690	1·732	1·781
8·5	1·504	1·520	1·538	1·559	1·582	1·608	1·638	1·672	1·711	1·758
8·6	1·494	1·510	1·527	1·547	1·569	1·594	1·623	1·655	1·692	1·736
8·7	1·484	1·500	1·517	1·536	1·557	1·581	1·608	1·639	1·674	1·715
8·8	1·475	1·490	1·507	1·525	1·545	1·568	1·594	1·623	1·657	1·695
8·9	1·467	1·481	1·497	1·514	1·534	1·556	1·580	1·608	1·640	1·677
9·0	1·458	1·472	1·487	1·504	1·523	1·544	1·568	1·594	1·625	1·660
9·1	1·450	1·463	1·478	1·495	1·513	1·533	1·556	1·581	1·610	1·643
9·2	1·442	1·455	1·469	1·485	1·503	1·522	1·544	1·568	1·596	1·628
9·3	1·435	1·447	1·461	1·476	1·493	1·512	1·533	1·556	1·583	1·613
9·4	1·427	1·440	1·453	1·468	1·484	1·502	1·522	1·545	1·570	1·599
9·5	1·420	1·432	1·445	1·459	1·475	1·492	1·512	1·534	1·558	1·586
9·6	1·413	1·425	1·437	1·451	1·466	1·483	1·502	1·523	1·546	1·573
9·7	1·407	1·418	1·430	1·443	1·458	1·474	1·492	1·513	1·535	1·560
9·8	1·400	1·411	1·423	1·436	1·450	1·466	1·483	1·503	1·524	1·549
9·9	1·394	1·404	1·416	1·428	1·442	1·458	1·474	1·493	1·514	1·538
10·0	1·388	1·398	1·409	1·421	1·435	1·450	1·466	1·484	1·504	1·527
10·1	1·382	1·392	1·403	1·414	1·428	1·442	1·458	1·475	1·495	1·516
10·2	1·376	1·386	1·396	1·408	1·420	1·434	1·450	1·467	1·485	1·506
10·3	1·371	1·380	1·390	1·401	1·414	1·427	1·442	1·458	1·477	1·497
10·4	1·365	1·374	1·384	1·395	1·407	1·420	1·435	1·450	1·468	1·488
10·5	1·360	1·369	1·378	1·389	1·401	1·413	1·427	1·443	1·460	1·479
10·6	1·355	1·363	1·373	1·383	1·394	1·407	1·420	1·435	1·452	1·470
10·7	1·349	1·358	1·367	1·377	1·388	1·400	1·414	1·428	1·444	1·462
10·8	1·345	1·353	1·362	1·372	1·382	1·394	1·407	1·421	1·437	1·454
10·9	1·340	1·348	1·357	1·366	1·377	1·388	1·401	1·414	1·429	1·446
11·0	1·335	1·343	1·352	1·361	1·371	1·382	1·394	1·408	1·422	1·439
11·2	1·326	1·334	1·342	1·351	1·360	1·371	1·383	1·395	1·409	1·424
11·4	1·318	1·325	1·332	1·341	1·350	1·360	1·371	1·383	1·396	1·411
11·6	—	—	—	—	—	—	—	1·372	1·384	1·398
11·8	—	—	—	—	—	—	—	1·361	1·373	1·386
12·0	—	—	—	—	—	—	—	1·351	1·363	1·375

Table VI-2

α = 0.025

(Note that for positive skewness, i.e., $\mu_3 > 0$, the deviates in this table are negative.)

β_2 \ β_1	0·00	0·01	0·03	0·05	0·10	0·15	0·20	0·30	0·40	0·50	0·60	0·70	0·80	0·90	1·00
1·8	1·65	—	—	—	—	—	—	—	—	—	—	—	—	—	—
2·0	1·76	1·68	1·62	1·56	—	—	—	—	—	—	—	—	—	—	—
2·2	1·83	1·76	1·71	1·66	1·57	1·49	1·41	—	—	—	—	—	—	—	—
2·4	1·88	1·82	1·77	1·73	1·65	1·58	1·51	1·39	—	—	—	—	—	—	—
2·6	1·92	1·86	1·82	1·78	1·71	1·64	1·58	1·47	1·37	—	—	—	—	—	—
2·8	1·94	1·89	1·85	1·82	1·76	1·70	1·65	1·55	1·45	1·35	—	—	—	—	—
3·0	1·96	1·91	1·87	1·84	1·79	1·74	1·69	1·60	1·52	1·42	1·33	—	—	—	—
3·2	1·97	1·93	1·89	1·86	1·81	1·77	1·72	1·65	1·57	1·49	1·40	1·32	1·24	—	—
3·4	1·98	1·94	1·90	1·88	1·83	1·79	1·75	1·68	1·61	1·54	1·46	1·39	1·31	1·23	—
3·6	1·99	1·95	1·91	1·89	1·85	1·81	1·77	1·71	1·65	1·58	1·51	1·44	1·38	1·30	1·23
3·8	1·99	1·95	1·92	1·90	1·86	1·82	1·79	1·73	1·67	1·62	1·56	1·49	1·43	1·36	1·29
4·0	1·99	1·96	1·93	1·91	1·87	1·84	1·81	1·75	1·70	1·64	1·59	1·53	1·47	1·41	1·35
4·2	2·00	1·96	1·93	1·91	1·88	1·84	1·82	1·76	1·72	1·67	1·62	1·56	1·51	1·45	1·40
4·4	2·00	1·96	1·94	1·92	1·88	1·85	1·83	1·78	1·73	1·69	1·64	1·59	1·54	1·49	1·44
4·6	2·00	1·96	1·94	1·92	1·89	1·86	1·83	1·79	1·75	1·70	1·66	1·62	1·57	1·52	1·47
4·8	2·00	1·97	1·94	1·93	1·89	1·87	1·84	1·80	1·76	1·72	1·68	1·64	1·59	1·55	1·50
5·0	2·00	1·97	1·94	1·93	1·90	1·87	1·85	1·81	1·77	1·73	1·69	1·65	1·61	1·57	1·53

α = 0.975

β_2 \ β_1	0·00	0·01	0·03	0·05	0·10	0·15	0·20	0·30	0·40	0·50	0·60	0·70	0·80	0·90	1·00
1·8	1·65	—	—	—	—	—	—	—	—	—	—	—	—	—	—
2·0	1·76	1·82	1·86	1·89	—	—	—	—	—	—	—	—	—	—	—
2·2	1·83	1·89	1·93	1·96	2·00	2·04	2·06	—	—	—	—	—	—	—	—
2·4	1·88	1·94	1·98	2·01	2·05	2·08	2·11	2·15	—	—	—	—	—	—	—
2·6	1·92	1·97	2·01	2·03	2·08	2·11	2·14	2·18	2·22	—	—	—	—	—	—
2·8	1·94	1·99	2·03	2·05	2·09	2·13	2·15	2·20	2·24	2·27	—	—	—	—	—
3·0	1·96	2·01	2·04	2·06	2·10	2·13	2·16	2·21	2·25	2·28	2·32	—	—	—	—
3·2	1·97	2·02	2·05	2·07	2·11	2·14	2·16	2·21	2·25	2·29	2·32	2·35	2·38	—	—
3·4	1·98	2·02	2·05	2·07	2·11	2·14	2·16	2·21	2·25	2·28	2·32	2·35	2·38	2·41	—
3·6	1·99	2·02	2·05	2·07	2·11	2·14	2·16	2·20	2·24	2·28	2·31	2·34	2·37	2·41	2·44
3·8	1·99	2·03	2·05	2·07	2·11	2·13	2·16	2·20	2·24	2·27	2·30	2·33	2·36	2·40	2·43
4·0	1·99	2·03	2·05	2·07	2·11	2·13	2·15	2·19	2·23	2·26	2·29	2·32	2·35	2·38	2·41
4·2	2·00	2·03	2·05	2·07	2·10	2·13	2·15	2·19	2·22	2·25	2·28	2·31	2·34	2·37	2·40
4·4	2·00	2·03	2·05	2·07	2·10	2·13	2·15	2·18	2·22	2·25	2·28	2·31	2·33	2·36	2·39
4·6	2·00	2·03	2·05	2·07	2·10	2·12	2·14	2·18	2·21	2·24	2·27	2·30	2·32	2·35	2·38
4·8	2·00	2·03	2·05	2·07	2·10	2·12	2·14	2·17	2·21	2·23	2·26	2·29	2·31	2·34	2·36
5·0	2·00	2·03	2·05	2·07	2·09	2·12	2·14	2·17	2·20	2·23	2·25	2·28	2·30	2·33	2·35

Table VI-3

$\alpha = 0.01$

(Note that for positive skewness, i.e., $\mu_3 > 0$, the deviates in this table are negative.)

$\beta_2 \backslash \beta_1$	0·00	0·01	0·03	0·05	0·10	0·15	0·20	0·30	0·40	0·50	0·60	0·70	0·80	0·90	1·00
1·8	1·70	—	—	—	—	—	—	—	—	—	—	—	—	—	—
2·0	1·87	1·77	1·69	1·62	—	—	—	—	—	—	—	—	—	—	—
2·2	2·01	1·91	1·83	1·76	1·64	1·55	1·45	—	—	—	—	—	—	—	—
2·4	2·12	2·03	1·95	1·89	1·77	1·68	1·59	1·43	—	—	—	—	—	—	—
2·6	2·21	2·12	2·05	1·99	1·88	1·79	1·70	1·55	1·41	—	—	—	—	—	—
2·8	2·27	2·19	2·13	2·08	1·98	1·89	1·81	1·66	1·52	1·39	—	—	—	—	—
3·0	2·33	2·25	2·19	2·14	2·05	1·97	1·90	1·76	1·62	1·50	1·38	—	—	—	—
3·2	2·37	2·29	2·24	2·19	2·11	2·03	1·96	1·84	1·71	1·59	1·48	1·37	1·26	—	—
3·4	2·40	2·33	2·28	2·24	2·16	2·09	2·02	1·90	1·79	1·68	1·57	1·46	1·36	1·26	—
3·6	2·43	2·36	2·31	2·27	2·20	2·13	2·07	1·96	1·86	1·76	1·65	1·55	1·45	1·35	1·26
3·8	2·45	2·39	2·34	2·30	2·23	2·17	2·11	2·01	1·91	1·82	1·72	1·62	1·53	1·43	1·34
4·0	2·47	2·41	2·36	2·33	2·26	2·20	2·15	2·05	1·96	1·87	1·78	1·69	1·60	1·51	1·42
4·2	2·49	2·43	2·38	2·35	2·28	2·23	2·18	2·09	2·00	1·92	1·83	1·75	1·66	1·58	1·49
4·4	2·50	2·44	2·40	2·37	2·31	2·25	2·21	2·12	2·04	1·96	1·88	1·80	1·72	1·64	1·56
4·6	2·51	2·46	2·42	2·38	2·32	2·27	2·23	2·15	2·07	2·00	1·92	1·84	1·77	1·70	1·62
4·8	2·52	2·47	2·43	2·40	2·34	2·29	2·25	2·17	2·10	2·03	1·96	1·88	1·81	1·74	1·67
5·0	2·53	2·48	2·44	2·41	2·36	2·31	2·27	2·19	2·12	2·06	1·99	1·92	1·85	1·79	1·72

$\alpha = 0.99$

$\beta_2 \backslash \beta_1$	0·00	0·01	0·03	0·05	0·10	0·15	0·20	0·30	0·40	0·50	0·60	0·70	0·80	0·90	1·00
1·8	1·70	—	—	—	—	—	—	—	—	—	—	—	—	—	—
2·0	1·87	1·95	2·00	2·03	—	—	—	—	—	—	—	—	—	—	—
2·2	2·01	2·10	2·15	2·18	2·22	2·24	2·25	—	—	—	—	—	—	—	—
2·4	2·12	2·20	2·25	2·28	2·33	2·36	2·38	2·40	—	—	—	—	—	—	—
2·6	2·21	2·28	2·33	2·36	2·42	2·45	2·48	2·51	2·52	—	—	—	—	—	—
2·8	2·27	2·34	2·39	2·43	2·48	2·52	2·55	2·59	2·61	2·63	—	—	—	—	—
3·0	2·33	2·40	2·44	2·48	2·53	2·56	2·59	2·64	2·68	2·70	2·71	—	—	—	—
3·2	2·37	2·44	2·48	2·51	2·56	2·60	2·63	2·68	2·72	2·75	2·77	2·79	2·80	—	—
3·4	2·40	2·47	2·51	2·54	2·59	2·63	2·66	2·71	2·75	2·79	2·82	2·84	2·86	2·87	—
3·6	2·43	2·49	2·53	2·56	2·61	2·65	2·68	2·74	2·78	2·81	2·85	2·87	2·90	2·91	2·93
3·8	2·45	2·51	2·55	2·58	2·63	2·67	2·70	2·75	2·80	2·83	2·87	2·90	2·92	2·95	2·97
4·0	2·47	2·53	2·57	2·60	2·65	2·68	2·71	2·77	2·81	2·85	2·88	2·91	2·94	2·97	2·99
4·2	2·49	2·54	2·58	2·61	2·66	2·69	2·73	2·78	2·82	2·86	2·89	2·92	2·95	2·98	3·01
4·4	2·50	2·56	2·59	2·62	2·67	2·70	2·73	2·78	2·83	2·86	2·90	2·93	2·96	2·99	3·02
4·6	2·51	2·57	2·60	2·63	2·68	2·71	2·74	2·79	2·83	2·87	2·90	2·94	2·97	3·00	3·03
4·8	2·52	2·58	2·61	2·64	2·68	2·72	2·75	2·80	2·84	2·87	2·91	2·94	2·97	3·00	3·03
5·0	2·53	2·58	2·62	2·64	2·69	2·72	2·75	2·80	2·84	2·88	2·91	2·95	2·97	3·00	3·03

Table VI-4

$\alpha = 0.005$

(Note that for positive skewness, i.e., $\mu_3 > 0$, the deviates in this table are negative.)

β_2 \ β_1	0·00	0·01	0·03	0·05	0·10	0·15	0·20	0·30	0·40	0·50	0·60	0·70	0·80	0·90	1·00
1·8	1·71	—	—	—	—	—	—	—	—	—	—	—	—	—	—
2·0	1·92	1·80	1·71	1·64	—	—	—	—	—	—	—	—	—	—	—
2·2	2·10	1·99	1·89	1·82	1·68	1·56	1·46	—	—	—	—	—	—	—	—
2·4	2·26	2·14	2·04	1·97	1·83	1·71	1·62	1·44	—	—	—	—	—	—	—
2·6	2·38	2·27	2·18	2·12	1·98	1·87	1·77	1·58	1·42	—	—	—	—	—	—
2·8	2·49	2·38	2·30	2·23	2·10	1·99	1·89	1·71	1·55	1·41	—	—	—	—	—
3·0	2·58	2·48	2·39	2·33	2·21	2·11	2·01	1·84	1·68	1·53	1·40	—	—	—	—
3·2	2·65	2·55	2·48	2·42	2·30	2·20	2·11	1·95	1·79	1·65	1·51	1·39	1·27	—	—
3·4	2·71	2·61	2·54	2·48	2·38	2·28	2·20	2·04	1·90	1·76	1·62	1·50	1·38	1·27	—
3·6	2·76	2·67	2·60	2·54	2·44	2·35	2·27	2·13	1·99	1·85	1·72	1·60	1·48	1·37	1·27
3·8	2·80	2·71	2·65	2·60	2·50	2·41	2·34	2·20	2·07	1·94	1·82	1·70	1·58	1·47	1·37
4·0	2·83	2·75	2·69	2·64	2·54	2·47	2·39	2·26	2·14	2·02	1·90	1·78	1·67	1·56	1·45
4·2	2·87	2·79	2·72	2·68	2·59	2·51	2·44	2·32	2·20	2·09	1·97	1·86	1·75	1·65	1·54
4·4	2·90	2·82	2·76	2·71	2·62	2·55	2·49	2·37	2·25	2·15	2·04	1·93	1·83	1·73	1·62
4·6	2·92	2·85	2·79	2·74	2·66	2·59	2·52	2·41	2·30	2·20	2·10	2·00	1·90	1·80	1·70
4·8	2·94	2·87	2·81	2·77	2·69	2·62	2·56	2·45	2·35	2·25	2·15	2·05	1·96	1·87	1·77
5·0	2·96	2·89	2·83	2·79	2·71	2·65	2·59	2·48	2·39	2·29	2·20	2·11	2·01	1·92	1·84

$\alpha = 0.995$

β_2 \ β_1	0·00	0·01	0·03	0·05	0·10	0·15	0·20	0·30	0·40	0·50	0·60	0·70	0·80	0·90	1·00
1·8	1·71	—	—	—	—	—	—	—	—	—	—	—	—	—	—
2·0	1·92	2·01	2·06	2·09	—	—	—	—	—	—	—	—	—	—	—
2·2	2·10	2·19	2·24	2·27	2·31	2·33	2·35	—	—	—	—	—	—	—	—
2·4	2·26	2·35	2·41	2·44	2·49	2·52	2·53	2·53	—	—	—	—	—	—	—
2·6	2·38	2·48	2·54	2·57	2·63	2·66	2·68	2·70	2·69	—	—	—	—	—	—
2·8	2·49	2·58	2·64	2·68	2·73	2·77	2·80	2·83	2·84	2·83	—	—	—	—	—
3·0	2·58	2·66	2·72	2·76	2·82	2·86	2·89	2·93	2·95	2·96	2·95	—	—	—	—
3·2	2·65	2·73	2·79	2·83	2·89	2·93	2·96	3·01	3·04	3·06	3·07	3·06	3·04	—	—
3·4	2·71	2·79	2·85	2·88	2·95	2·99	3·02	3·07	3·11	3·13	3·15	3·16	3·15	3·14	—
3·6	2·76	2·84	2·89	2·93	2·99	3·03	3·07	3·12	3·16	3·19	3·22	3·23	3·24	3·24	3·23
3·8	2·80	2·88	2·93	2·97	3·03	3·07	3·1L	3·16	3·20	3·24	3·27	3·29	3·30	3·31	3·32
4·0	2·83	2·91	2·96	3·00	3·06	3·10	3·14	3·20	3·24	3·28	3·31	3·34	3·36	3·37	3·38
4·2	2·87	2·94	2·99	3·03	3·09	3·13	3·17	3·22	3·27	3·31	3·34	3·37	3·40	3·42	3·43
4·4	2·90	2·97	3·02	3·05	3·11	3·15	3·19	3·25	3·29	3·33	3·37	3·40	3·42	3·45	3·47
4·6	2·92	2·99	3·04	3·07	3·13	3·17	3·21	3·27	3·31	3·36	3·39	3·42	3·44	3·47	3·50
4·8	2·94	3·01	3·06	3·09	3·15	3·19	3·23	3·28	3·33	3·37	3·41	3·44	3·47	3·49	3·52
5·0	2·96	3·03	3·07	3·11	3·16	3·21	3·24	3·30	3·35	3·39	3·43	3·46	3·49	3·52	3·54

Table VII   Table of Random Values ($\times 10^5$) from Uniform Distribution Over $(0,1)$*

10097	32533	76520	13586	34673	54876	80959	09117	39292	74945
37542	04805	64894	74296	24805	24037	20636	10402	00822	91665
08422	68953	19645	09303	23209	02560	15953	34764	35080	33606
99019	02529	09376	70715	38311	31165	88676	74397	04436	27659
12807	99970	80157	36147	64032	36653	98951	16877	12171	76833
66065	74717	34072	76850	36697	36170	65813	39885	11199	29170
31060	10805	45571	82406	35303	42614	86799	07439	23403	09732
85269	77602	02051	65692	68665	74818	73053	85247	18623	88579
63573	32135	05325	47048	90553	57548	28468	28709	83491	25624
73796	45753	03529	64778	35808	34282	60935	20344	35273	88435
98520	17767	14905	68607	22109	40558	60970	93433	50500	73998
11805	05431	39808	27732	50725	68248	29405	24201	52775	67851
83452	99634	06288	98083	13746	70078	18475	40610	68711	77817
88685	40200	86507	58401	36766	67951	90364	76493	29609	11062
99594	67348	87517	64969	91826	08928	93785	61368	23478	34113
65481	17674	17468	50950	58047	76974	73039	57186	40218	16544
80124	35635	17727	08015	45318	22374	21115	78253	14385	53763
74350	99817	77402	77214	43236	00210	45521	64237	96286	02655
69916	26803	66252	29148	36936	87203	76621	13990	94400	56418
09893	20505	14225	68514	46427	56788	96297	78822	54382	14598
91499	14523	68479	27686	46162	83554	94750	89923	37089	20048
80336	94598	26940	36858	70297	34135	53140	33340	42050	82341
44104	81949	85157	47954	32979	26575	57600	40881	22222	06413
12550	73742	11100	02040	12860	74697	96644	89439	28707	25815
63606	49329	16505	34484	40219	52563	43651	77082	07207	31790
61196	90446	26457	47774	51924	33729	65394	59593	42582	60527
15474	45266	95270	79953	59367	83848	82396	10118	33211	59466
94557	28573	67897	54387	54622	44431	91190	42592	92927	45973
42481	16213	97344	08721	16868	48767	03071	12059	25701	46670
23523	78317	73208	89837	68935	91416	26252	29663	05522	82562
04493	52494	75246	33824	45862	51025	61962	79335	65337	12472
00549	97654	64051	88159	96119	63896	54692	82391	23287	29529
35963	15307	26898	09354	33351	35462	77974	50024	90103	39333
59808	08391	45427	26842	83609	49700	13021	24892	78565	20106
46058	85236	01390	92286	77281	44077	93910	83647	70617	42941
32179	00597	87379	25241	05567	07007	86743	17157	85394	11838
69234	61406	20117	45204	15956	60000	18743	92423	97118	96338
19565	41430	01758	75379	40419	21585	66674	36806	84962	85207
45155	14938	19476	07246	43667	94543	59047	90033	20826	69541
94864	31994	36168	10851	34888	81553	01540	35456	05014	51176
98086	24826	45240	28404	44999	08896	39094	73407	35441	31880
33185	16232	41941	50949	89435	48581	88695	41994	37548	73043
80951	00406	96382	70774	20151	23387	25016	25298	94624	61171
79752	49140	71961	28296	69861	02591	74852	20539	00387	59579
18633	32537	98145	06571	31010	24674	05455	61427	77938	91936
74029	43902	77557	32270	97790	17119	52527	58021	80814	51748
54178	45611	80993	37143	05335	12969	56127	19255	36040	90324
11664	49883	52079	84827	59381	71539	09973	33440	88461	23356
48324	77928	31249	64710	02295	36870	32307	57546	15020	09994
69074	94138	87637	91976	35584	04401	10518	21615	01848	76938

* From the RAND Corporation, *A Million Random Digits with* 100,000 *Normal Deviates*, 1955, The Free Press, Macmillan.

Table VIII Table of Random Values from Standard Normal Distributions*

1.276–	1.218–	0.453–	0.350–	0.723	0.676	1.099–	0.314–	0.394–	0.633–
0.318–	0.799–	1.664–	1.391	0.382	0.733	0.653	0.219	0.681–	1.129
1.377–	1.257–	0.495	0.139–	0.854–	0.428	1.322–	0.315–	0.732–	1.348–
2.334	0.337–	1.955–	0.636–	1.318–	0.433–	0.545	0.428	0.297–	0.276
1.136–	0.642	3.436	1.667–	0.847	1.173–	0.355–	0.035	0.359	0.930
0.414	0.011–	0.666	1.132–	0.410–	1.077–	0.734	1.484	0.340–	0.789
0.494–	0.364	1.237–	0.044–	0.111–	0.210–	0.931	0.616	0.377–	0.433–
1.048	0.037	0.759	0.609	2.043–	0.290–	0.404	0.543–	0.486	0.869
0.347	2.816	0.464–	0.632–	1.614–	0.372	0.074–	0.916–	1.314	0.038–
0.637	0.563	0.107–	0.131	1.808–	1.126–	0.379	0.610	0.364–	2.626–
2.176	0.393	0.924–	1.911	1.040–	1.168–	0.485	0.076	0.769–	1.607
1.185–	0.944–	1.604–	0.185	0.258–	0.300–	0.591–	0.545–	0.018	0.485–
0.972	1.170	2.682	2.813	1.531–	0.490–	2.071	1.444	1.092–	0.478
1.210	0.294	0.248–	0.719	1.103	1.090	0.212	1.185–	0.338–	1.134–
2.647	0.777	0.450	2.247	1.151	1.676–	0.384	1.133	1.393	0.814
0.398	0.318	0.928–	2.416	0.936–	1.036	0.024	0.560–	0.203	0.871–
0.846	0.699–	0.368–	0.344	0.926–	0.797–	1.404–	1.472–	0.118–	1.456
0.654	0.955–	2.907	1.688	0.752	0.434–	0.746	0.149	0.170–	0.479–
0.522	0.231	0.619–	0.265–	0.419	0.558	0.549–	0.192	0.334–	1.373
1.288–	0.539–	0.824–	0.244	1.070–	0.010	0.482	0.469–	0.090–	1.171
1.372	1.769	1.057–	1.646	0.481	0.600–	0.592–	0.610	0.096–	1.375–
0.854	0.535–	1.607	0.428	0.615–	0.331	0.336–	1.152–	0.533	0.833–
0.148–	1.144–	0.913	0.684	1.043	0.554	0.051–	0.944–	0.440–	0.212–
1.148–	1.056–	0.635	0.328–	1.221–	0.118	2.045–	1.977–	1.133–	0.338
0.348	0.970	0.017–	1.217	0.974–	1.291–	0.399–	1.209–	0.248–	0.480
0.284	0.458	1.307	1.625–	0.629–	0.504–	0.056–	0.131–	0.048	1.879
1.016–	0.360	0.119–	2.331	1.672	1.053–	0.840	0.246–	0.237	1.312–
1.603	0.952–	0.566–	1.600	0.465	1.951	0.110	0.251	0.116	0.957–
0.190–	1.479	0.986–	1.249	1.934	0.070	1.358–	1.246–	0.959–	1.297–
0.722–	0.925	0.783	0.402–	0.619	1.826	1.272	0.945–	0.494	0.050
1.696–	1.879	0.063	0.132	0.682	0.544	0.417–	0.666–	0.104–	0.253–
2.543–	1.333–	1.987	0.668	0.360	1.927	1.183	1.211	1.765	0.035
0.359–	0.193	1.023–	0.222–	0.616–	0.060–	1.319–	0.785	0.430–	0.298–
0.248	0.088–	1.379–	0.295	0.115–	0.621–	0.618–	0.209	0.979	0.906
0.099–	1.376–	1.047	0.872–	2.200–	1.384–	1.425	0.812–	0.748	1.093–
0.463–	1.281–	2.514–	0.675	1.145	1.083	0.667–	0.223–	1.592–	1.278–
0.503	1.434	0.290	0.397	0.837–	0.973–	0.120–	1.594–	0.996–	1.244–
0.857–	0.371–	0.216–	0.148	2.106–	1.453–	0.686	0.075–	0.243–	0.170–
0.122–	1.107	1.039–	0.636–	0.860–	0.895–	1.458–	0.539–	0.159–	0.420–
1.632	0.586	0.468–	0.386–	0.354–	0.203	1.234–	2.381	0.388–	0.063–
2.072	1.445–	0.680–	0.224	0.120–	1.753	0.571–	1.223	0.126–	0.034
0.435–	0.375–	0.985–	0.585–	0.203–	0.556–	0.024	0.126	1.250	0.615–
0.876	1.227–	2.647–	0.745–	1.797	1.231–	0.547	0.634–	0.836–	0.719–
0.833	1.289	0.022–	0.431–	0.582	0.766	0.574–	1.153–	0.520	1.018–
0.891–	0.332	0.453–	1.127–	2.085	0.722–	1.508–	0.489	0.496–	0.025–
0.644	0.233–	0.153–	1.098	0.757	0.039–	0.460–	0.393	2.012	1.356
0.105	0.171–	0.110–	1.145–	0.878	0.909–	0.328–	1.021	1.613–	1.560
1.192–	1.770	0.003–	0.369	0.052	0.647	1.029	1.526	0.237	1.328–
0.042–	0.553	0.770	0.324	0.489–	0.367–	0.378	0.601	1.996–	0.738–
0.498	1.072	1.567	0.302	1.157	0.720–	1.403	0.698	0.370–	0.551–

* From the RAND Corporation, *A Million Random Digits with* 100,000 *Normal Deviates*, 1955, The Free Press, Macmillan.

Table IX   Table of Coefficients $\{a_{n-i+1}\}$ Used in W Test for Normality, for $n = 3(1)50$

i＼n	3	4	5	6	7	8	9	10	11	12	13	14	15	16	17	18
1	0.7071	0.6872	0.6646	0.6431	0.6233	0.6052	0.5888	0.5739	0.5601	0.5475	0.5359	0.5251	0.5150	0.5056	0.4968	0.4886
2		0.1677	0.2413	0.2806	0.3031	0.3164	0.3244	0.3291	0.3315	0.3325	0.3325	0.3318	0.3306	0.3290	0.3273	0.3253
3				0.0875	0.1401	0.1743	0.1976	0.2141	0.2260	0.2347	0.2412	0.2460	0.2495	0.2521	0.2540	0.2553
4						0.0561	0.0947	0.1224	0.1429	0.1586	0.1707	0.1802	0.1878	0.1939	0.1988	0.2027
5								0.0399	0.0695	0.0922	0.1099	0.1240	0.1353	0.1447	0.1524	0.1587
6										0.0303	0.0539	0.0727	0.0880	0.1005	0.1109	0.1197
7												0.0240	0.0433	0.0593	0.0725	0.0837
8														0.0196	0.0359	0.0496
9																0.0163

i＼n	19	20	21	22	23	24	25	26	27	28	29	30	31	32	33	34
1	0.4808	0.4734	0.4643	0.4590	0.4542	0.4493	0.4450	0.4407	0.4366	0.4328	0.4291	0.4254	0.4220	0.4188	0.4156	0.4127
2	0.3232	0.3211	0.3185	0.3156	0.3126	0.3098	0.3069	0.3043	0.3018	0.2992	0.2968	0.2944	0.2921	0.2898	0.2876	0.2854
3	0.2561	0.2565	0.2578	0.2571	0.2563	0.2554	0.2543	0.2533	0.2522	0.2510	0.2499	0.2487	0.2475	0.2463	0.2451	0.2439
4	0.2059	0.2085	0.2119	0.2131	0.2139	0.2145	0.2148	0.2151	0.2152	0.2151	0.2150	0.2148	0.2145	0.2141	0.2137	0.2132
5	0.1641	0.1686	0.1736	0.1764	0.1787	0.1807	0.1822	0.1836	0.1848	0.1857	0.1864	0.1870	0.1874	0.1878	0.1880	0.1882
6	0.1271	0.1334	0.1399	0.1443	0.1480	0.1512	0.1539	0.1563	0.1584	0.1601	0.1616	0.1630	0.1641	0.1651	0.1660	0.1667
7	0.0932	0.1013	0.1092	0.1150	0.1201	0.1245	0.1283	0.1316	0.1346	0.1372	0.1395	0.1415	0.1433	0.1449	0.1463	0.1475
8	0.0612	0.0711	0.0804	0.0878	0.0941	0.0997	0.1046	0.1089	0.1128	0.1162	0.1192	0.1219	0.1243	0.1265	0.1284	0.1301
9	0.0303	0.0422	0.0530	0.0618	0.0696	0.0764	0.0823	0.0876	0.0923	0.0965	0.1002	0.1036	0.1066	0.1093	0.1118	0.1140
10		0.0140	0.0263	0.0368	0.0459	0.0539	0.0610	0.0672	0.0728	0.0778	0.0822	0.0862	0.0899	0.0931	0.0961	0.0988
11				0.0122	0.0228	0.0321	0.0403	0.0476	0.0540	0.0598	0.0650	0.0697	0.0739	0.0777	0.0812	0.0844
12						0.0107	0.0200	0.0284	0.0358	0.0424	0.0483	0.0537	0.0585	0.0629	0.0669	0.0706
13								0.0094	0.0178	0.0253	0.0320	0.0381	0.0435	0.0485	0.0530	0.0572
14										0.0084	0.0159	0.0227	0.0289	0.0344	0.0395	0.0441
15												0.0076	0.0144	0.0206	0.0262	0.0314
16														0.0068	0.0131	0.0187
17																0.0062

Table IX (continued)

i \ n	35	36	37	38	39	40	41	42	43	44	45	46	47	48	49	50
1	0.4096	0.4068	0.4040	0.4015	0.3989	0.3964	0.3940	0.3917	0.3894	0.3872	0.3850	0.3830	0.3808	0.3789	0.3770	0.3751
2	0.2834	0.2813	0.2794	0.2774	0.2755	0.2737	0.2719	0.2701	0.2684	0.2667	0.2651	0.2635	0.2620	0.2604	0.2589	0.2574
3	0.2427	0.2415	0.2403	0.2391	0.2380	0.2368	0.2357	0.2345	0.2334	0.2323	0.2313	0.2302	0.2291	0.2281	0.2271	0.2260
4	0.2127	0.2121	0.2116	0.2110	0.2104	0.2098	0.2091	0.2085	0.2078	0.2072	0.2065	0.2058	0.2052	0.2045	0.2038	0.2032
5	0.1883	0.1883	0.1883	0.1881	0.1880	0.1878	0.1876	0.1874	0.1871	0.1868	0.1865	0.1862	0.1859	0.1855	0.1851	0.1847
6	0.1673	0.1678	0.1683	0.1686	0.1689	0.1691	0.1693	0.1694	0.1695	0.1695	0.1695	0.1695	0.1695	0.1693	0.1692	0.1691
7	0.1487	0.1496	0.1505	0.1513	0.1520	0.1526	0.1531	0.1535	0.1539	0.1542	0.1545	0.1548	0.1550	0.1551	0.1553	0.1554
8	0.1317	0.1331	0.1344	0.1356	0.1366	0.1376	0.1384	0.1392	0.1398	0.1405	0.1410	0.1415	0.1420	0.1423	0.1427	0.1430
9	0.1160	0.1179	0.1196	0.1211	0.1225	0.1237	0.1249	0.1259	0.1269	0.1278	0.1286	0.1293	0.1300	0.1306	0.1312	0.1317
10	0.1013	0.1036	0.1056	0.1075	0.1092	0.1108	0.1123	0.1136	0.1149	0.1160	0.1170	0.1180	0.1189	0.1197	0.1205	0.1212
11	0.0873	0.0900	0.0924	0.0947	0.0967	0.0986	0.1004	0.1020	0.1035	0.1049	0.1062	0.1073	0.1085	0.1095	0.1105	0.1113
12	0.0739	0.0770	0.0798	0.0824	0.0848	0.0870	0.0891	0.0909	0.0927	0.0943	0.0959	0.0972	0.0986	0.0998	0.1010	0.1020
13	0.0610	0.0645	0.0677	0.0706	0.0733	0.0759	0.0782	0.0804	0.0824	0.0842	0.0860	0.0876	0.0892	0.0906	0.0919	0.0932
14	0.0484	0.0523	0.0559	0.0592	0.0622	0.0651	0.0677	0.0701	0.0724	0.0745	0.0765	0.0783	0.0801	0.0817	0.0832	0.0846
15	0.0361	0.0404	0.0444	0.0481	0.0515	0.0546	0.0575	0.0602	0.0628	0.0651	0.0673	0.0694	0.0713	0.0731	0.0748	0.0764
16	0.0239	0.0287	0.0331	0.0372	0.0409	0.0444	0.0476	0.0506	0.0534	0.0560	0.0584	0.0607	0.0628	0.0648	0.0667	0.0685
17	0.0119	0.0172	0.0220	0.0264	0.0305	0.0343	0.0379	0.0411	0.0442	0.0471	0.0497	0.0522	0.0546	0.0568	0.0588	0.0608
18		0.0057	0.0110	0.0158	0.0203	0.0244	0.0283	0.0318	0.0352	0.0383	0.0412	0.0439	0.0465	0.0489	0.0511	0.0532
19				0.0053	0.0101	0.0146	0.0188	0.0227	0.0263	0.0296	0.0328	0.0357	0.0385	0.0411	0.0436	0.0459
20						0.0049	0.0094	0.0136	0.0175	0.0211	0.0245	0.0277	0.0307	0.0335	0.0361	0.0386
21								0.0045	0.0087	0.0126	0.0163	0.0197	0.0229	0.0259	0.0288	0.0314
22										0.0042	0.0081	0.0118	0.0153	0.0185	0.0215	0.0244
23												0.0039	0.0076	0.0111	0.0143	0.0174
24														0.0037	0.0071	0.0104
25																0.0035

Table X   Percentage Points of W Test for Normality for n = 3(1)50

n	1	2	5	10	50
3	0.753	0.756	0.767	0.789	0.959
4	0.687	0.707	0.748	0.792	0.935
5	0.686	0.715	0.762	0.806	0.927
6	0.713	0.743	0.788	0.826	0.927
7	0.730	0.760	0.803	0.838	0.928
8	0.749	0.778	0.818	0.851	0.932
9	0.764	0.791	0.829	0.859	0.935
10	0.781	0.806	0.842	0.869	0.938
11	0.792	0.817	0.850	0.876	0.940
12	0.805	0.828	0.859	0.883	0.943
13	0.814	0.837	0.866	0.889	0.945
14	0.825	0.846	0.874	0.895	0.947
15	0.835	0.855	0.881	0.901	0.950
16	0.844	0.863	0.887	0.906	0.952
17	0.851	0.869	0.892	0.910	0.954
18	0.858	0.874	0.897	0.914	0.956
19	0.863	0.879	0.901	0.917	0.957
20	0.868	0.884	0.905	0.920	0.959
21	0.873	0.888	0.908	0.923	0.960
22	0.878	0.892	0.911	0.926	0.961
23	0.881	0.895	0.914	0.928	0.962
24	0.884	0.898	0.916	0.930	0.963
25	0.888	0.901	0.918	0.931	0.964
26	0.891	0.904	0.920	0.933	0.965
27	0.894	0.906	0.923	0.935	0.965
28	0.896	0.908	0.924	0.936	0.966
29	0.898	0.910	0.926	0.937	0.966
30	0.900	0.912	0.927	0.939	0.967
31	0.902	0.914	0.929	0.940,	0.967
32	0.904	0.915	0.930	0.941	0.968
33	0.906	0.917	0.931	0.942	0.968
34	0.908	0.919	0.933	0.943	0.969
35	0.910	0.920	0.934	0.944	0.969
36	0.912	0.922	0.935	0.945	0.970
37	0.914	0.924	0.936	0.946	0.970
38	0.916	0.925	0.938	0.947	0.971
39	0.917	0.927	0.939	0.948	0.971
40	0.919	0.928	0.940	0.949	0.972
41	0.920	0.929	0.941	0.950	0.972
42	0.922	0.930	0.942	0.951	0.972
43	0.923	0.932	0.943	0.951	0.973
44	0.924	0.933	0.944	0.952	0.973
45	0.926	0.934	0.945	0.953	0.973
46	0.927	0.935	0.945	0.953	0.974
47	0.928	0.936	0.946	0.954	0.974
48	0.929	0.937	0.947	0.954	0.974
49	0.929	0.937	0.947	0.955	0.974
50	0.930	0.938	0.947	0.955	0.974

Table XI   *Constants Used in Obtaining Probability of Calculated W in Test for Normality*

n	γ	η	ϵ	n	γ	η	ϵ
3	−0.625	0.386	0.7500	27	−5.905	1.905	0.1980
4	−1.107	0.714	0.6297	28	−5.988	1.919	0.1943
5	−1.530	0.935	0.5521	29	−6.074	1.934	0.1907
6	−2.010	1.138	0.4963	30	−6.160	1.949	0.1872
7	−2.356	1.245	0.4533	31	−6.248	1.965	0.1840
8	−2.696	1.333	0.4186	32	−6.324	1.976	0.1811
9	−2.968	1.400	0.3900	33	−6.402	1.988	0.1781
10	−3.262	1.471	0.3660	34	−6.480	2.000	0.1755
11	−3.485	1.515	0.3451	35	−6.559	2.012	0.1727
12	−3.731	1.571	0.3270	36	−6.640	2.024	0.1702
13	−3.936	1.613	0.3111	37	−6.721	2.037	0.1677
14	−4.155	1.655	0.2969	38	−6.803	2.049	0.1656
15	−4.373	1.695	0.2842	39	−6.887	2.062	0.1633
16	−4.567	1.724	0.2727	40	−6.961	2.075	0.1612
17	−4.713	1.739	0.2622	41	−7.035	2.088	0.1591
18	−4.885	1.770	0.2528	42	−7.111	2.101	0.1572
19	−5.018	1.786	0.2440	43	−7.188	2.114	0.1552
20	−5.153	1.802	0.2359	44	−7.266	2.128	0.1534
21	−5.291	1.818	0.2264	45	−7.345	2.141	0.1516
22	−5.413	1.835	0.2207	46	−7.414	2.155	0.1499
23	−5.508	1.848	0.2157	47	−7.484	2.169	0.1482
24	−5.605	1.862	0.2106	48	−7.555	2.183	0.1466
25	−5.704	1.876	0.2063	49	−7.615	2.198	0.1451
26	−5.803	1.890	0.2020	50	−7.677	2.212	0.1436

Table XII   Percentage Points for WE_0 Test

| | 95% Range | | 90% Range | |
| | Lower | Upper | Lower | Upper |
n	Point	Point	Point	Point
7	0.025	0.260	0.033	0.225
8	0.025	0.230	0.032	0.200
9	0.025	0.205	0.031	0.177
10	0.025	0.184	0.030	0.159
11	0.025	0.166	0.030	0.145
12	0.025	0.153	0.029	0.134
13	0.025	0.140	0.028	0.124
14	0.024	0.128	0.027	0.115
15	0.024	0.119	0.026	0.106
16	0.023	0.113	0.025	0.098
17	0.023	0.107	0.024	0.093
18	0.022	0.101	0.024	0.087
19	0.022	0.096	0.023	0.083
20	0.021	0.090	0.023	0.077
21	0.020	0.085	0.022	0.074
22	0.020	0.080	0.022	0.069
23	0.019	0.075	0.021	0.065
24	0.019	0.069	0.021	0.062
25	0.018	0.065	0.020	0.058
26	0.018	0.062	0.020	0.056
27	0.017	0.058	0.020	0.054
28	0.017	0.056	0.019	0.052
29	0.016	0.054	0.019	0.050
30	0.016	0.053	0.019	0.048
31	0.016	0.051	0.018	0.047
32	0.015	0.050	0.018	0.045
33	0.015	0.048	0.018	0.044
34	0.014	0.046	0.017	0.043
35	0.014	0.045	0.017	0.041

Table XIII   Percentage Points for WE Test

	95% Range		90% Range	
n	Lower Point	Upper Point	Lower Point	Upper Point
7	0.062	0.404	0.071	0.358
8	0.054	0.342	0.062	0.301
9	0.050	0.301	0.058	0.261
10	0.049	0.261	0.056	0.231
11	0.046	0.234	0.052	0.208
12	0.044	0.215	0.050	0.191
13	0.040	0.195	0.046	0.173
14	0.038	0.178	0.043	0.159
15	0.036	0.163	0.040	0.145
16	0.034	0.150	0.038	0.134
17	0.030	0.135	0.034	0.120
18	0.028	0.123	0.031	0.109
19	0.026	0.114	0.029	0.102
20	0.025	0.106	0.028	0.095
21	0.024	0.101	0.027	0.091
22	0.023	0.094	0.026	0.084
23	0.022	0.087	0.025	0.078
24	0.021	0.082	0.024	0.074
25	0.021	0.078	0.023	0.070
26	0.020	0.073	0.022	0.066
27	0.020	0.070	0.022	0.063
28	0.019	0.067	0.021	0.061
29	0.019	0.064	0.021	0.058
30	0.018	0.060	0.020	0.054
31	0.017	0.057	0.019	0.052
32	0.017	0.055	0.019	0.050
33	0.017	0.053	0.018	0.048
34	0.017	0.051	0.018	0.047
35	0.016	0.049	0.018	0.045

Categorized Bibliography

As indicated initially, we have made no attempt to discuss all areas of probability and statistics of interest to engineers; for example, little or nothing has been said about statistical inference, the planning of engineering experiments, and queueing theory. Fortunately, these subjects are well covered in numerous texts, and for this reason a rather extensive bibliography is given below. It is divided into the following categories:

General Applications—Elementary Level
General Applications—Intermediate Level
General Applications—Advanced Level
General Theory—Elementary Level
General Theory—Intermediate Level
General Theory—Advanced Level
Handbooks and Manuals
Programmed (Self-Teaching) Texts
Design of Experiments
Probability, Random Processes, and Queueing Theory
Reliability Methods
Statistical Decision Theory
Statistical Quality Control
Other Specialized Applications
General Statistical Tables
Miscellaneous

The compilation is limited to books directed at least in part, at engineers and scientists, books of main concern to workers in psychology, economics, business administration, and other social sciences have been omitted. Also, with the exception of "General Theory—Advanced Level," books that are primarily of interest to mathematicians and statisticians are not included.

In assigning books to these categories, we naturally encountered borderline cases that required arbitrary decisions. For example, should a book on statistical methods, written for quality control applications, be categorized under General Applications or under Statistical Quality Control? How should we classify a book that deals principally with general applications but also has some chapters on experimental design? (In both cases we decided on the General Applications category.)

The books in the first six categories require special explanation. These have two things in common: they presuppose no previous background in probability and statistics and they are general in the nature of their subject material, in contrast to subsequent specific categories. We have classified a book as "applied" if the main emphasis is on applications in spite of the fact that underlying theoretical concepts are also discussed. A book is designated as "theoretical" if the main purpose is to provide an appreciation of theoretical concepts in spite of the fact that applications are sometimes included (needless to say, we would regard our own book as applied). Level of presentation refers to the general sophistication, mathematical and otherwise, expected of the reader. In the applied category "elementary" level generally (but not always) implies a knowledge of high school mathematics and college algebra, "intermediate" level implies elementary calculus (we regard our book as intermediate), and "advanced" level requires more advanced mathematical or analytic maturity. In the theoretical category more mathematics is generally required than in the corresponding applications category. Note that by level we do *not* mean the amount of subject material covered. A book may cover a great deal of material in an elementary fashion or only very basic concepts in an advanced manner. Some idea of the extent of the material covered may be gathered from the title of the book.

The books included are those sufficiently well known to us to be categorized. The list is not exhaustive and the inclusion or omission of a book should not be taken as a reflection of its merits. (For a synopsis of reviews of many texts published before 1960 see the book by Buckland and Fox listed under "Miscellaneous.")

The categorized bibliography is followed by a listing of the main statistical and related journals.

GENERAL APPLICATIONS—ELEMENTARY LEVEL

Brownlee, Kenneth A., *Industrial Experimentation*, illus, 3rd ed., Chemical Publishing Co., Tudor, New York, 1952.

Clark, Charles E., *Introduction to Statistics*, Wiley, New York, 1953.

Dixon, Wilfred J., and F. J. Massey Jr., *Introduction to Statistical Analysis*, 2nd ed. McGraw-Hill, New York, 1957.

Freund, John, *Modern Elementary Statistics*, 2nd ed., Prentice-Hall, Englewood Cliffs, N.J., 1960.

Fryer, H. C., *Concepts and Methods of Experimental Statistics*, Allyn and Bacon, Boston, 1966.

Fryer, H. C., *Elements of Statistics*, Wiley, New York, 1954.

Hoel, Paul G., *Elementary Statistics*, Wiley, New York, 1960.

Huntsberger, David V., *Elements of Statistical Inference*, Allyn and Bacon, Boston, 1961.

Leeming, J. J., *Statistical Methods for Engineers*, illus, Blackie, London, 1963.

Moroney, M. J., *Facts from Figures*, (Pelican A236) Penguin, Baltimore, 1956.

Mosteller, Frederick, Robert E. K. Rourke, and George B. Thomas Jr., *Probability with Statistical Applications* Addison-Wesley, Reading, Mass., 1961.

Parrott, Lyman G., *Probability and Experimental Errors in Science*, Wiley, New York, 1961.

Quenouille, M. H., *Rapid Statistical Calculations*, Hafner, New York, 1960.

Volk, W., *Applied Statistics for Engineers*, McGraw-Hill, New York, 1958.

Wallis, W. A., and H. V. Roberts, *Statistics: A New Approach*, Free Press, New York, 1956.

Wortham, A. W., and T. E. Smith, *Practical Statistics in Experiment Design*, Dallas Publishing House, Dallas, 1959.

Young, Hugh D., *Statistical Treatment of Experimental Data*, McGraw-Hill, New York, 1962.

GENERAL APPLICATIONS—INTERMEDIATE LEVEL

Bennett, Carl A., and N. L. Franklin, *Statistical Analysis in Chemistry and the Chemical Industry*, Wiley, New York, 1954.

Bowker, Albert H., and Gerald J. Lieberman, *Engineering Statistics*, Prentice-Hall, Englewood Cliffs, N.J., 1959.

Davies, Owen L., ed., *Statistical Methods in Research and Production*, 3rd ed. Hafner, New York, 1957.

Fry, Thornton C., *Probability and Its Engineering Uses*, 2nd ed., Van Nostrand, Princeton, N.J., 1965.

Goulden, C. H., *Methods of Statistical Analysis*, 2nd ed., Wiley, New York, 1952.

Johnson, Norman L., and F. C. Leone, *Statistics and Experimental Design in Engineering and the Physical Sciences*, 2 vols., Wiley, New York, 1964.

Lindgren, Bernard W., and G. W. McElrath, *Introduction to Probability and Statistics*, illus, Macmillan, New York, 1959.

Mandel, John, *The Statistical Analysis of Experimental Data*, Wiley, New York, 1964.

Miller, Irwin, and J. E. Freund, *Probability and Statistics for Engineers*, illus, Prentice-Hall, Englewood Cliffs, N.J., 1965.

Nalimov, V. V., *The Application of Mathematical Statistics to Chemical Analysis*, Addison-Wesley, Reading, Mass., 1962.

Ostle, Bernard, *Statistics in Research*, 2nd ed., Iowa State Univ. Press, Ames, 1963.

Paradine, Charles G., and B. H. Rivett, *Statistical Methods for Technologists*, illus, Van Nostrand, Princeton, N.J., 1960.

Snedecor, George W., *Statistical Methods*, 5th ed., Iowa State Univ. Press, Ames, 1956.

Wilks, Samuel S., *Elementary Statistical Analysis*, Princeton Univ. Press, Princeton, N.J., 1948.

Wine, Russell Lowell, *Statistics for Scientists and Engineers*, Prentice-Hall, Englewood Cliffs, N.J., 1964.

GENERAL APPLICATIONS—ADVANCED LEVEL

Brownlee, Kenneth A., *Statistical Theory and Methodology in Science and Engineering*, 2nd ed., Wiley, New York, 1965.

Ehrenfeld, Sylvain, and Sebastian Littauer, *Introduction to Statistical Method*, McGraw-Hill, New York, 1964.

Guttmann, Irwin, and S. S. Wilks, *Introductory Engineering Statistics*, Wiley, New York, 1965.

Hald, A., *Statistical Theory with Engineering Applications*, Wiley, New York, 1952.

GENERAL THEORY—ELEMENTARY LEVEL

Brunk, H. D., *Introduction to Mathematical Statistics*, illus, 2nd ed., Blaisdell, Waltham Mass., 1965.

Cramer, H., *Elements of Probability Theory*, Wiley, New York, 1955.

David, F. N., *Probability Theory for Statistical Methods*, Cambridge Univ. Press, England, 1949.

Fraser, Donald, *Statistics, An Introduction*, Wiley, New York, 1958.

Freund, John E., *Mathematical Statistics*, illus, Prentice-Hall, Englewood Cliffs, N.J., 1962.

Goldberg, Samuel, *Probability, An Introduction*, Prentice-Hall, Englewood Cliffs, N.J., 1960.

Hodges, J. L., Jr., and E. L. Lehmann, *Basic Concepts of Probability and Statistics*, Holden-Day, San Francisco, 1964.

Hoel, Paul G., *Introduction to Mathematical Statistics*, 3rd ed., Wiley, New York, 1962.

Kurtz, Thomas, *Basic Statistics*, Prentice-Hall, Englewood Cliffs, N.J., 1963.

Lindgren, Bernard W., *Statistical Theory*, Macmillan, New York, 1962.

Munroe, Marshall E., *Theory of Probability*, McGraw-Hill, New York, 1951.

Neyman, Jerzy, *First Course in Probability and· Statistics*, illus, Holt, Rinehart, and Winston, New York, 1950.

Wadsworth, George P., and Joseph H. Bryan, *Introduction to Probability and Random Variables*, McGraw-Hill, New York, 1960.

Weatherburn, C. E., *First Course in Mathematical Statistics*, Cambridge Univ. Press, England, 1949.

Wolf, Frank L., *Elements of Probability and Statistics*, McGraw-Hill, New York, 1962.

GENERAL THEORY—INTERMEDIATE LEVEL

Alexander, Howard W., *Elements of Mathematical Statistics*, Wiley, New York, 1961.

Anderson, Richard L., and T. A. Bancroft, *Statistical Theory in Research*, illus, McGraw-Hill, New York, 1952.

Birnbaum, Zygmunt, W., *Introduction to Probability and Mathematical Statistics*, illus, Harper and Row, New York, 1962.

Fisz, M., *Probability Theory and Mathematical Statistics*, 3rd ed., Wiley, New York, 1963.

Freeman, H. A., *Introduction to Statistical Inference*, Addison-Wesley, Reading, Mass., 1963.

Hamilton, W. C., *Statistics in Physical Science*, Ronald, Oxford, 1964.

Harris, Bernard, *Theory of Probability*, Addison-Wesley, Reading, Mass., 1966.

Hogg, Robert V., and A. T. Craig, *Introduction to Mathematical Statistics*, illus, 2nd ed., Macmillan, New York, 1965.

Kenney, John F., and E. S. Keeping, *Mathematics of Statistics*, pt. 1, 3rd ed., pt 2, 2nd ed., Van Nostrand, Princeton, N.J., 1954.

Meyer, P. L., *Introductory Probability and Statistical Applications*, Addison-Wesley, Reading, Mass., 1965.

Mood, Alexander M., and F. A. Graybill, *Introduction to the Theory of Statistics*, 2nd ed., McGraw-Hill, New York, 1963.

Pfeiffer, Paul, *Concepts of Probability Theory*, McGraw-Hill, New York, 1965.

Thorp, Edward O., *Elementary Probability*, Wiley, New York, 1966.

Tucker, Howard G., *Introduction to Probability and Mathematical Statistics*, Academic Press, New York, 1962.

GENERAL THEORY—ADVANCED LEVEL

Aitken, A. C., *Statistical Mathematics*, Wiley Interscience, New York, 1952.

Cramer, H., *Mathematical Methods of Statistics*, Princeton Univ. Press, Princeton, N.J., 1946.

Kendall, Maurice G., and A. Stuart, *Advanced Theory of Statistics*, vol. 1: *Distribution Theory*, rev. ed., 1958; vol. 2: *Statistical Inference and Statistical Relationship*, rev. ed. 1961; vol. 3: *Planning and Analysis and Time Series*, in preparation, Hafner, New York.

Wilks, S. S., *Mathematical Statistics*, 2nd ed., Wiley, New York, 1962.

HANDBOOKS AND MANUALS

Bauer, Edward L., *A Statistical Manual for Chemists*, Academic Press, New York, 1960.

Bowker, Albert H. and Gerald J. Lieberman, *Handbook of Industrial Statistics*, Prentice-Hall, Englewood Cliffs, N.J., 1955.

Burington, Richard, and D. C. May, *Handbook of Probability and Statistics, with Tables* McGraw-Hill, New York, 1953.

Crow, E. L., F. A. David, and M. W. Maxfield, *Statistics Manual with Examples Taken From Ordnance Development*, Dover, New York, 1960.

Freund, John E., Paul E. Livermore, and Irwin Miller, *Manual of Experimental Statistics*, Prentice-Hall, Englewood Cliffs, N.J., 1960.

Natrella, Mary Gibbons, *Experimental Statistics*, Nat. Bur. Std. (*U.S.*), *Handbook*, **91**, U.S. Government Printing Office, 1961.

PROGRAMMED (SELF-TEACHING) TEXTS

Dixon, John R., *A Programmed Introduction to Probability*, Wiley, New York, 1964.

Introductory Statistics. (Secondary Mathematics) vol. 1: *Descriptive Statistics;* vol. 2: *Statistical Inference*, Watts, New York, 1964.

McCollough, Celeste, and Loche VanAtta, *Statistical Concepts; A Program for Self-Instruction*, McGraw-Hill, New York, 1963.

DESIGN OF EXPERIMENTS

Chew, Victor, ed., *Experimental Designs in Industry*, Wiley, New York, 1958.
Cochran, W. G., and G. M. Cox, *Experimental Designs*, 2nd ed., Wiley, New York, 1957.
Cox, David R., *Planning of Experiments*, illus, Wiley, New York, 1958.
Davies, Owen L., ed., *Design and Analysis of Industrial Experiments*, 2nd ed., Hafner, New York, 1956.
Federer, Walter T., *Experimental Design: Theory and Application*, illus, Macmillan, New York, 1955.
Fisher, Ronald A., *Design of Experiments*, 7th ed., Hafner, New York, 1960.
Hicks, Charles R., *Fundamental Concepts in the Design of Experiments*, Holt, Rinehart and Winston, New York, 1964.
Kempthorne, Oscar, *Design and Analysis of Experiments*, Wiley, New York, 1952.
Quenouille, Maurice H., *Design and Analysis of Experiment*, Hafner, New York, 1953.

PROBABILITY, RANDOM PROCESSES AND QUEUEING THEORY

Bailey, Norman, *Elements of Stochastic Processes with Applications to the Natural Sciences*, Wiley, New York, 1964.
Cox, David R., *Renewal Theory*, Wiley, New York, 1962.
Cox, David R., and W. L. Smith, *Queues*, Wiley, New York, 1961.
Feller, William, *Introduction to Probability Theory and Its Applications*, vol. 1, 2nd ed., 1957; vol. 2, 1965; Wiley, New York.
Kemeny, J. G., and J. L. Snell, *Finite Markov Chains*, Van Nostrand, Princeton, N.J., 1959.
Morse, Philip M., *Queues, Inventories and Maintenance*, Wiley, New York, 1958.
Papoulis, Athanias, *Probability, Random Variables and Stochastic Processes*, McGraw-Hill, New York, 1965.
Parzen, Emanuel, *Modern Probability Theory and Its Applications*, illus, Wiley, New York, 1960.
Parzen, Emanuel, *Stochastic Processes*, illus, Holden-Day, San Francisco, 1962.
Saaty, Thomas L., *Elements of Queueing Theory with Applications*, illus, McGraw-Hill, New York, 1961.

RELIABILITY METHODS

A.R.I.N.C. Research Corporation, *Reliability Engineering*, Prentice-Hall, Englewood Cliffs, N.J., 1964.
Barlow, Richard E., and F. Proschan, *Mathematical Theory of Reliability*, illus, Wiley, New York, 1965.
Bazovsky, Igor, *Reliability Theory and Practice*, illus, Prentice-Hall, Englewood Cliffs, N.J., 1961.
Buckland, William R., *Statistical Assessment of the Life Characteristic*, a bibliographical account, Hafner, New York, 1964.

Calabro, S. R., *Reliability Principles and Practices*, McGraw-Hill, New York, 1962.

Haviland, Robert P., *Engineering Reliability and Long Life Design*, illus, Van Nostrand, Princeton, N.J., 1964.

Landers, Richard R., *Reliability and Product Assurance*, illus, Prentice-Hall, Englewood Cliffs, N.J., 1963.

Lloyd, David K., and Myron Lipow, *Reliability: Management Methods and Mathematics*, illus, Prentice-Hall, Englewood Cliffs, N.J., 1962.

Pieruschka, Erich, *Principles of Reliability*, illus, Prentice-Hall, Englewood Cliffs, N.J., 1963.

Roberts, Norman, *Mathematical Methods in Reliability Engineering*, illus, McGraw-Hill, New York, 1964.

Sandler, Gerald, *System Reliability Engineering*, illus, Prentice-Hall, Englewood Cliffs, N.J., 1963.

Zelen, Marvin, Ed., *Statistical Theory of Reliability*, illus, Univ. of Wisconsin Press, Madison, 1963.

STATISTICAL DECISION THEORY

Bross, Irwin D., *Design for Decision*, Macmillan, New York, 1953.

Chernoff, Herman, and Lincoln Moses, *Elementary Decision Theory*, illus, Wiley, New York, 1959.

Schlaifer, Robert, *Introduction to Statistics for Business Decisions*, McGraw-Hill, New York, 1961.

Schlaifer, Robert, *Probability and Statistics for Business Decisions*, McGraw-Hill, New York, 1959.

Weiss, Lionel, *Statistical Decision Theory*, McGraw-Hill, New York, 1961.

STATISTICAL QUALITY CONTROL

Burr, Irving, W., *Engineering Statistics and Quality Control*, McGraw-Hill, New York, 1953.

Cowden, Dudley J., *Statistical Methods in Quality Control*, Prentice-Hall, Englewood Cliffs, N.J., 1957.

Duncan, Acheson J., *Quality Control and Industrial Statistics*, 3rd ed., Irwin, Homewood, Ill., 1965.

Enrick, Norbert L., *Quality Control*, 5th ed., Industrial Press, New York, 1966.

Grant, Eugene L., *Statistical Quality Control*, 3rd ed., McGraw-Hill, New York, 1964.

Hansen, Bertrand, *Quality Control*, Prentice-Hall, Englewood Cliffs, N.J., 1963.

Schrock, Edward M., *Quality Control and Statistical Methods*, 2nd ed., Reinhold, New York, 1950.

Tippett, L. H. C., *Technological Application of Statistics*, Wiley, New York, 1950.

OTHER SPECIALIZED APPLICATIONS

Acton, Forman S., *Analysis of Straight-Line Data*, Wiley, New York, 1959.

Aitchison, John, and A. C. Brown, *Lognormal Distributions*, Cambridge Univ. Press, New York, 1957.

David, H. A., *The Method of Paired Comparisons*, Hafner, New York, 1963.

Draper, Norman, and Harry Smith, *Applied Regression Analysis*, Wiley, New York, 1966.

Ezekiel, M., and K. A. Fox, *Methods of Correlation and Regression Analysis*, 3rd ed., Wiley, New York, 1959.

Finney, D. J., *Probit Analysis*, rev. ed., Cambridge Univ. Press, New York, 1963.

Fisher, Ronald A., *Statistical Methods for Research Workers*, 13th ed., Prentice-Hall, Englewood Cliffs, N.J., 1958.

Guenther, William, C., *Analysis of Variance*, illus, Prentice-Hall, Englewood Cliffs, N.J., 1963.

Gumbel, E. J., *Statistics of Extremes*, Columbia Univ. Press, New York, 1958.

Kendall, Maurice G., *Course in Multivariate Analysis*, Hafner, New York, 1957.

Mace, Arthur E., *Sample Size Determination*, Reinhold, New York, 1964.

Maxwell, Albert E., *Analyzing Qualitative Data*, Wiley, New York, 1961.

Siegel, S., *Nonparametric Statistics for the Behavioral Sciences*, McGraw-Hill, New York, 1956.

Walsh, John E., *Handbook of Nonparametric Statistics*, vol. 1, 1962; vol. 2, 1965, Van Nostrand, Princeton, N.J.

Wetherill, G. Barrie, *Sequential Methods in Statistics*, Wiley, New York, 1966.

Williams, E. J., *Regression Analysis*, illus, Wiley, New York, 1959.

Youden, W. J., *Statistical Methods for Chemists*, Wiley, New York, 1951.

GENERAL STATISTICAL TABLES

Arkin, Herbert and Raymond Colton, *Tables for Statisticians*, illus, 2nd ed., (College Outline Series), Barnes and Noble, New York, 1963.

Beyer, William H., *Handbook of Tables for Probability and Statistics*, The Chemical Rubber Company, Cleveland, 1966.

Fisher, Ronald A., and Frank Yates, *Statistical Tables for Biological, Agricultural and Medical Research*, 6th ed., Hafner, New York, 1964.

Greenwood, J. Arthur, and H. O. Hartley, *Guide to Tables in Mathematical Statistics*, illus, Princeton Univ. Press, Princeton, N.J., 1962.

Hald, A., *Statistical Tables and Formulas*, Wiley, New York, 1952.

Owen, D., *Handbook of Statistical Tables*, Addison-Wesley, Reading, Mass., 1962.

Pearson, Egon S., and H. A. Hartley, Eds., *Biometrika Tables for Statisticians*, vol. 1, Cambridge Univ. Press, England, 1954.

MISCELLANEOUS

Buckland, W. R., and R. Fox, *Bibliography of Basic Texts and Monographs on Statistical Methods*, Hafner, New York, 1963.

Huff, Darrell, and Irving Geis, *How to Lie with Statistics*, Norton, New York, 1954.

Kendall, Maurice, and W. R. Buckland, *Dictionary of Statistical Terms*, 2nd ed., Hafner, New York, 1960.

Kendall, M. G., and A. L. Doig, *Bibliography of Statistical Literature*, vol. 1, 1950–1958; vol. 2, 1940–1949; vol. 3, in preparation, Hafner, New York.

Mosteller, Frederick, *Fifty Challenging Problems in Probability*, Addison-Wesley, Reading, Mass., 1965.

Savage, I. Richard, *Bibliography of Nonparametric Statistics*, Harvard Univ. Press, Cambridge, Mass., 1962.

JOURNALS IN STATISTICS AND CLOSELY RELATED FIELDS

Annals of Mathematical Statistics (published by the Institute of Mathematical Statistics)

Applied Statistics (published by the Royal Statistical Society)

The Australian Journal of Statistics (Department of Mathematical Statistics, University of Sydney, Sydney, N.S.W. Australia)

Biometrics (journal of the Biometric Society of the American Statistical Association)

Biometrika (issued by the Biometrika Office, University College, London)

Industrial Quality Control (published by the American Society for Quality Control)

Journal of the American Statistical Association (published by the American Statistical Association)

Journal of the Royal Statistical Society, Series B, Methodological (published by the Royal Statistical Society)

Management Science (published by the Institute of Management Science)

Operations Research (published by the Operations Research Society of America)

Sankhya (the Indian journal of statistics)

Statistical Theory and Method Abstracts (published by International Statistical Institute, The Hague, Netherlands)

The Statistician (published by Institute of Statisticians, London, England)

Technometrics (a journal of statistics for the physical, chemical and engineering sciences, published by the American Society for Quality Control and the American Statistical Association)

Theory of Probability and Its Applications (an English translation of the Russian journal *Teoriya Veroyatnostei i ee Primencniya*, prepared and published by the Society for Industrial and Applied Mathematicians)

Index

α_3, 45
α_4, 46
Approximating distributions,
    195-224
Arithmetic mean, 35
Auxiliary variables, 183
Average, 35

$\sqrt{b_1}$, 48
b_2, 48
$\sqrt{\beta_1}$, 45
    use in selecting distribution,
        196-198, 202, 203, 220,
        221
β_2, 46
    use in selecting distribution,
        196-198, 202, 203, 220,
        221
Bathtub curve, 104
Bayesian methods, 23, 84, 94
Bayes' Theorem, 20-23
Bernoulli trials, 138
Beta distribution, 91-97
    applications, 94
    definition, 91
    estimation of parameters, 95
    generalized form, 96, 179
    generation of random values,
        243, 259
    plot, 92, 93
    probability plots, 292
    region in β_1-β_2 plane, 196,
        197

Beta distribution,
    relation to binomial distribu-
        tion, 162
    summary, 126-128, 133
    tables, 91
Bias, 47
Binomial distribution, 138-151
    applications, 138, 139, 141, 144
    confidence interval for param-
        eter, 146-148
    definition, 139
    effect of population size, 148-150
    estimation of parameter, 146-148
    generalization to $\underline{k}$ outcomes,
        150, 151
    generation of random values,
        243, 259
    moments, 144, 170, 171
    normal distribution approxima-
        tion, 144-146
    plots, 140
    Poisson distribution approxima-
        tion, 159
    relation to beta distribution, 162
    relation to hypergeometric
        distribution, 152
    summary, 163-166
    tables of cumulative values,
        141-143, 145
Bivariate cumulative distribution,
    52-58
Bivariate normal distribution,
    78-83
    applications, 80, 81

347

Bivariate normal distribution,
    moments, 79
    plot, 79
    tabulations, 80, 81
Bivariate probability density
    function, 52-58
Bivariate probability function,
    52
Bivariate random variable,
    51-65
Burn-in time, 103

Cauchy distribution, 101-103,
    118
    plot, 102
    summary, 130-132, 134
Censored sample, 89, 261, 285,
    286
Central limit theorem, 72, 186,
    226-228
Central moments, 42
Central values, 36-40
    comparison, 38
    estimated from data, 38-40
    expected value, 35, 36, 38,
        39
    mean, 35, 36, 38, 39
    median, 36-40
    mode, 38-40
Chi-square distribution, 81 (fn),
    90, 107 (fn), 191
    generation of random values,
        242, 259
    probability plot, 284-286
    relation to gamma distribution,
        90
    table of percentiles, 314, 315
Chi-squared test, 302-307
Coefficient of correlation, 63,
    64, 80
Complement of set, 8
Computer generation of random
    variables, 240, 241

Conditional distribution, 60-62
Conditional failure function, 103
Conditional probability, 18-23
Conditional probability density,
    60-62
Conditional probability function,
    60-62
Confidence bound, 77
Confidence interval, 75
    definition, 75
    for mean time-to-failure, 107
    for normal distribution
        parameter μ, 75, 76
    for parameter of binomial
        distribution, 146-148
    for parameter of Poisson
        distribution, 158
Confidence level, 75
Continuous distributions, 68-137
Convolution, 194
Cornish-Fisher expansion, 198
Correlated variables in generating
    system moments, 235,
    255-257
Correlation, 63, 64, 80
Covariance, 63, 80
Cumulative distribution function,
    for continuous random
        variable, 29-32
    for discrete random variable,
        27-29

Decile, 50
Degrees of freedom, 90, 304
Delta method, 229
Density function, see Probability
    density function
Discrete distributions, 138-174
Discrete sample space, 25
Dispersion, measure of, 43
Distribution, 33
Distributional tests, see Tests for
    distributional assumptions

Distribution function, see Cumulative distribution function

Edgeworth series, 198
Element, 7
Empirical distributions, 195-224
Empirical frequency distribution, 34
Empirical sampling, 236
Empty set, 7
Erlangian distribution, 90
Error propagation, see Generation of system moments
Event, 12
Expected value, 35, 36
  of a function of random variable, 40-42, 62
  of multivariate random variable, 62
  operational rules, 41, 42, 62, 63
  of order statistics, 292-294
  of system performance, 229-231
Exponential distribution, 31, 36-38, 40, 41, 43, 45-47, 49, 90, 91, 104-108
  applications, 90
  confidence interval for parameter, 107, 108
  estimation of parameter, 91, 106, 107, 285, 286
  generation of random values, 242, 258
  hazard function, 104, 105
  maximum value, 112
  point in β_1-β_2 plane, 196
  plot, 84
  probability plot, 284-286
  relation to Poisson distribution, 159
  random values plotted on normal probability paper, 273-282

Exponential distribution,
  relation to gamma distribution, 90
  summary 122-124, 133
  test of assumption, 284-286, 298-301, 305, 306
  as time-to-failure model, 105-108
Exponential-type distributions, 112
Extreme value distributions, 111-118
  applications, 112, 116
  definition, 111-113, 116, 117
  estimation of parameters, 290-292
  exact (non-asymptotic) results, 117, 118
  hazard function, 113, 114
  plot, 114
  probability plots, 290-292
  summary, 130-132, 134
  tables, 115
  types, 111, 118

Failure rate, 105
Folded normal distribution, 78
Force of mortality, 103
Fractiles, 49
Frequency distribution, 34
Function of random variable, 34

Gamma distribution, 83-91, 118-120, 192
  applications, 83, 84
  curve in β_1-β_2 plane, 196
  definition, 83
  estimation of parameters, 87-89, 285, 286
  generalized form, 89, 90, 179
  generation of random values, 242, 259
  hazard function, 119, 120
  maximum value, 112, 116
  minimum value, 116
  normal distribution approximation, 86, 87

Gamma distribution,
  plot, 84, 85
  probability plot, 284-286
  relation to Poisson distribu-
    tion, 162
  summary, 122-124, 133
  tables, 85
  as time to failure model,
    118-120
Gamma function, 83
Gaussian distribution, see
  Normal distribution
Generalized least squares, 294
Generation of system moments,
    228, 236, 252-257
  comparison with other methods,
    245-247
  correlated variables, 235,
    255-257
  higher moments of system
    performance, 232, 233
  mean system performance,
    229, 230
  review of method, 236
  variance of system
    performance, 231, 232
Geometric distribution, 152-154
  plot, 167
  summary, 163, 167-169
GPSS, 251
Gram-Charlier series, 198
Gumbel, E. J., 112
Gumbel extreme value distribution, see Extreme value
  distributions

Half-life, 37
Half normal distribution, 77, 78,
    172-174
Hazard function, 103-105
Histogram, 34
Hypergeometric distribution,
    151, 152
  relation to binomial distri-
    bution, 152

Hypergeometric distribution,
  plot, 152
  summary, 163-166

Identity set, 7
Incomplete beta function, 91
Incomplete gamma function, 85
Independence of random variables,
    59-63, 80
Independent events, 13, 14
Infant mortality, 103
Intensity function, 103
Interdecile range, 50
Intersection of sets, 8

Jacobian, 178, 183
Job shop simulation, 249
Johnson, N. L., 198
Johnson distributions, 198-220
  estimation of parameters,
    202-220
  general forms, 198-201
  generation of random values,
    242, 259
  S_B distribution, 200
    both end points known, 213-
      215
    neither end point known, 217
    one end point known, 215, 216
  S_L distribution, 199, 203-212
    range of variation known,
      207, 208
    range of variation unknown,
      208-212
  S_U distribution, 218-220
    tables to facilitate fit, 316-323
  selection of family, 202, 203
  use in representing system
    performance, 233, 234
Joint cumulative distribution, see
  Joint distribution function
Joint distribution function, 52-58
  continuous random variables,
    54-58

Joint distribution function,
  discrete random variables, 52
Joint probability, 14, 15
Joint probability density function,
  52-58
Joint probability function, 52-58

Kurtosis, 46, 47

Largest element distribution, see
  Extreme value distributions
Least squares estimates, 294
Life test models, 103-120
Linear transformations, 178
Location parameter, 68, 179
Lognormal distribution, 98-100;
  see also Johnson S_L
    distribution
  applications, 99, 100
  estimation of parameters, 283,
    284
  geneation of random values,
    242, 259
  hazard function, 119, 120
  maximum value, 112
  plot, 98
  point in β_1-β_2 plane, 196
  probability plot, 282-284
  relation to normal distri-
    bution, 179
  summary, 126-128, 134
  test of assumption, 282-284,
    295-298, 301, 302
  as time-to-failure model, 118-
    120

Marginal distribution, 58, 59
Marginal probability density
  function, 58, 59
Marginal probability function,
  58, 59
Matching moments, 87, 95, 218
Matching percentiles, 208-215
Maximum likelihood, 87, 95

Maximum value distribution, see
  Extreme value distribution
Mean, 35, 36, 38, 39
Mean system performance, 229-231
Mean time to failure, 107
Median, 36-40
Minimum value distribution, see
  Extreme value distributions
Mode, 38-40
Moment generating function, 43 (fn)
Moments of a distribution, 42-49
  generation for systems, 228-236,
    252-257
  about mean, 42-49
  multivariate, 62
  about zero, 42
Monte Carlo simulation, 236-251
  comparison with other methods,
    245-247
  error bands, 241-245
  general languages, 251
  generation of random values,
    240, 241, 257-259
  miscellaneous uses, 247-251
  sample size, 241-245
  use in reliability estimation,
    247-249
  use in waiting-line problems, 249
  use with Johnson or Pearson
    distribution fits, 240
Multinomial distribution, 150, 151,
  163, 164-166
Multivariate random variable,
  51-65
Mutually exclusive events, 15, 16
Mutually exclusive sets, 10

Negative binomial distribution,
  154, 158, 159, 163, 167-169
Negative exponential distribution,
  see Exponential distribution
Normal distribution, 45-47, 69-83
  bivariate normal distribution,
    78-83

Normal distribution,
  confidence interval for μ,
    75, 76
  definition, 69
  estimation of parameters,
    74, 75, 281, 282
  folded normal distribution, 78
  general applicability, 72-74
  generation of random values,
    73, 240
  half-normal distribution, 77,
    78
  hazard function, 104, 105
  maximum value, 112
  minimum value, 112
  moments, 69
  multivariate normal distribu-
    tion, 78-83
  plot, 70
  point in β_1-β_2 plane, 196
  probability plot, 261-282
  ratio of two normal variates,
    101
  standardized, 71, 178
  summary, 122-124, 133
  sum of normally distributed
    variates, 186
  table of cumulative values, 311
  table of random values, 329
  test of assumption, 261-282,
    295-298
  as time to failure model, 105,
    119
  tolerance interval, 77, 94, 95
  trivariate normal distribution,
    82, 189
  truncated, 74
  use with central limit theorem,
    226-228
Null set, 7

Order statistics, 292-294

Parabolic distribution, 97

Parabolic distribution,
  plot, 93
Parameter, 33, 34
Pascal distribution, 154, 163,
  167-169
Peakedness, 46-49
  estimate of, 47-49
  measure of, 46
Pearson distributions, 220-223
  estimation of percentiles, 222
  general definition, 220
  table of percentiles, 324-327
  use in representing system
    performance, 233-235
Percentage point, 50
Percentiles, 50, 51
  estimated from probability
    plot, 279
PERT, 94
Poisson distribution, 154-162
  adequacy of model, 158
  applications, 155, 158, 159
  approximation to binomial
    distribution, 159, 174
  confidence interval for parame-
    ter, 158
  definition, 155
  derivation, 172, 173
  estimation of parameters, 158
  generation of random values,
    243, 259
  moments, 158, 173, 174
  plot, 155
  relation to exponential distribu-
    tion, 159
  relation to gamma distribution,
    162
  summary, 163, 167-169
  tables, 156
  test of assumption, 306, 307
Probability, 5-7, 14-23
  classical interpretation, 5, 6
  conditional, 18-23
  definitions, 5-7

Probability,
  frequency interpretation, 6
  laws, 14-18, 19
  posterior, 21
  prior, 21
  as the ratio of size of sets, 12
  set theory concepts, 12, 13
  subjective interpretation,
    6, 23
Probability density function,
  31-33
Probability function, 26-29
Probability plotting, 260-294
  beta distribution plots, 292
  chi-square distribution plots,
    284-286
  estimating line by least
    squares, 294
  evaluation of plots, 263-276
  exponential distribution plots,
    284-286
  extreme value distribution
    plots, 290-292
  fundamentals, 292-294
  gamma distribution plots,
    284-286
  lognormal distribution plots,
    282-284
  normal distribution plots,
    261-282
  operational procedure,
    261-263
  plotting positions, 262, 263
  random variations, 263-282
  uniform distribution plots,
    292
  use for estimating distribu-
    tion parameters, 281, 283,
    285, 287-289, 290-292
  use for estimating distribu-
    tion percentiles, 279
  use for evaluating distribu-
    tional assumptions,
    261-276

Probability plotting,
  use with censored samples,
    261, 285, 286
  Weibull distribution plots,
    287-289
Propagation of errors, see
  Generation of system moments
Pseudo random variates, 240

Quantile, 50

Random sample, 34
Random values, generation of,
  240, 241, 257-259
Random variables, 23-34
  continuous, 26, 68-137
  definition, 23-26
  discrete, 25, 26, 138-174
Range, 50
Raw moments, 42
Rayleigh distribution, 100, 101,
  109, 190
  plot, 101
  summary, 130-132, 134
Rectangular distribution, see
  Uniform distribution
Reference set, 7, 23
Reliability simulation, 247-249
Right triangular distribution, 97
  plot, 93

Sample point, 12
Sample space, 12, 19
Sampling with replacement, 149
Scale parameter, 68, 179
Semi-triangular distribution, 97
Set, 7
Set theory concepts, complement
  operation, 8
  definition of special sets, 7
  identities, 10
  intersection operation, 8
  relation to probability, 12, 13
  set operations, 7, 8

Set theory concepts,
  size of sets, 10, 11
  union operation, 7
Shape parameter, 68
Shapiro, S. S., 295
SIMSCRIPT, 251
Size of set, 10, 11
Skewness, 45
Smallest element distribution,
  see Extreme value
    distributions
Standard deviation, 43-45, 47-49
Statistical tolerance interval,
  77, 94, 95
Statistics, general discussion, 2
Student's distribution, see
  t distribution
Subset, 7
Summary of continuous distri-
  butions, 120-134
Summary of discrete distri-
  butions, 162-169
Symmetry, 45-49
  estimate of, 47-49
  measure of, 45
Synthetic sampling, 236
System performance estimation,
  225-259

Taylor series expansion,
  228-236
Tchebychev's Inequality, 45
t distribution, 75 (fn), 196
  tables of selected values,
    312, 313
Test statistic, 294
Tests for distributional assumptions, 260-308
  chi-squared test, 302-307
  general discussion, 260, 294,
    295
  probability plots, 260-294
  W tests, 295-302
Theory of errors, 72

Tolerance interval, 77, 94, 95
Transformation of variables,
  175-194
  discrete random variables,
    176, 177
  several continuous random
    variables, 182-186
  single continuous random
    variable, 177-182
  table of transformations, 193
  use of non-independent auxiliary
    variables, 191, 192
Trivariate normal distribution,
  82, 189
Truncated distribution, 74 (fn),
  89 (fn)

Uniform distribution, 46, 55-58,
  96, 97
  generation of random values,
    240
  hazard function, 104, 105
  probability plot, 292
  point in β_1-β_2 plane, 196
  random values plotted on
    normal probability paper,
    268-272
  summary, 126-128, 134
  table of random values, 328
  as time to failure model, 105
  use in generating normal
    variates, 73
Uniform probability transformation, 257
Union of sets, 7

Variance, 43-45, 47-49
  of a linear function, 66, 67
  operational rules, 66, 67
  of system performance, 231,
    232
Variate, see Random variables
Venn diagram, 8

W tests, 294-302
  for exponentiality, 298-301
  general comments, 294, 295
  for lognormality, 295-298,
    301, 302
  for normality, 295-298
  table of coefficients for
    normality test, 330, 331
  table of constants to obtain
    probability of calculated W,
    333
  tables of percentiles for
    exponentiality tests, 334,
    335
  tables of percentiles for
    normality test, 332
WE test, see W test for
    exponentiality

WE$_0$ test, see W test for
    exponentiality
Wear-out failures, 103
Weibull distribution, 108-111
  applications, 109
  definition, 108
  estimate of parameters,
    111, 287-289
  as extreme value distribu-
    tion, 111, 116
  generation of random
    values, 243, 259
  hazard function, 108
  plot, 110
  probability plot, 290-292
  summary, 130-132, 134
Wilk, M.B., 295

Zero set, 7